MONEY IN THE BANK

MONEY IN THE BANK

THE KATHERINE KIERLAND HERBERGER COLLECTION

CORINE WEGENER & KARAL ANN MARLING

The Minneapolis Institute of Arts
Distributed by the University of Minnesota Press

First edition

2400 Third Avenue South
Minneapolis, MN 55404
www.artsmia.org

Distributed by the University of Minnesota Press
111 Third Avenue South, Suite 290
Minneapolis, MN 55401-2520
www.upress.umn.edu

Editor: Phil Freshman, St. Louis Park, Minnesota
Designer: Deborah Littlejohn, Two, Minneapolis
Indexer: Enid L. Zafran, Lewes, Delaware
Photographer: Robert Fogt, Minneapolis
Cover photograph: Daniel Dennehy, The Minneapolis Institute of Arts
Publishing and production management: Jim Bindas, Book Productions LLC, Minnetonka, Minnesota
Printer: Friesens, Canada

This book was typeset in Fedra Serif A, designed by Peter Bilak in 2003, and Klavika, designed by Eric Olson in 2004.

Printed in Canada

This book was made possible by the Katherine Kierland Herberger Fund and by the generosity of the Herberger family.

Library of Congress Cataloguing-in-Publication Data

Minneapolis Institute of Arts.
Money in the bank : the Katherine Kierland Herberger collection / Corine Wegener and Karal Ann Marling. – 1st ed.
p. cm.
Includes bibliographical references and index.
ISBN 0-8166-4903-0 (pb : alk. paper)
1. Coin banks–Private collections–Minnesota–Minneapolis–Catalogues. 2. Herberger, Katherine Kierland, 1912–2003–Art collections–Catalogues. 3. Coin banks–Minnesota–Minneapolis–Catalogues. 4. Minneapolis Institute of Arts–Catalogues. I. Wegener, Corine A. II. Marling, Karal Ann. III. Title.
NK4698.M56 2006
688.7'2–dc22
2005035591

Front cover:
Safety Locomotive, c. 1887
Iron, pigment

Back cover (clockwise from right):
Clown, Harlequin, and Columbine, c. 1906
Iron, pigment

Girl Skipping Rope, c. 1890
Iron, pigment

Shoot the Chute, c. 1906
Iron, pigment

Professor Pug Frog's Great Bicycle Feat, c. 1892
Iron, pigment

CONTENTS

Foreword

Mechanical banks made their debut at The Minneapolis Institute of Arts in 1998, when Trustee Mary Ingebrand-Pohlad lent several examples for display in the Bell Family Decorative Arts Court during that year's *Holiday Traditions* exhibition. They had been in the collection of the old Farmers and Mechanics Savings Bank of Minneapolis (owned by the Pohlad family), which, around the turn of the twentieth century, had handed out mechanical banks as customer premiums. As Karal Ann Marling mentions in her insightful essay for this catalogue, bank presidents were among the first Americans who collected toy banks seriously, during the 1920s.

The year 1998 also saw the debut of the museum's Family Center, part of a large-scale expansion program undertaken by then-Director Evan Maurer and Board of Trustees Chair Bob Ulrich. Included in the Family Center is gallery space where curators and educators can mount displays of works from the permanent collection aimed at very young museum visitors. Ulrich was impressed by the enthusiastic responses to the Family Center by children and parents alike.

While living in Scottsdale, Arizona, Ulrich had gotten to know Gary Herberger and his wife, Jeanne, and, through them, Gary's mother, Katherine—whom everyone called Kax. He knew she had assembled one of the nation's foremost collections of toy banks and that she had begun thinking about finding a permanent museum home for it. Thinking about the Family Center and about the deep Minnesota roots of Kax and her late husband, G. Robert Herberger (both had grown up in this state, and were wed and began raising their children here), Ulrich saw an opportunity to bring these elements together.

In the winter of 2001, he arranged for Maurer, newly appointed Board Chair Beverly Grossman, and James Ford Bell Curator Christopher Monkhouse to visit the Herberger collection in Scottsdale. Their enthusiastic response, and their subsequent proposal to feature the banks in a specially designated gallery adjacent to the Family Center, kept the door open for further discussion.

By 2002 Mrs. Herberger had decided that her collection of 277 mechanical and 812 still banks should come to the Minneapolis Institute of Arts. In March 2003 she invited Monkhouse to return to Scottsdale with Assistant Curator Corine Wegener to learn more about the collection. Three tape-recorded sessions with Mrs. Herberger proved to be both invaluable and timely, as she died the next month.

When I arrived at the museum, in the autumn of 2005, the Katherine Kierland Herberger Gallery had been open for two years. Selections from the collection had already appeared in the architecturally themed show *Buildings to Bank On* and in *Banks with Bite*, in which animal banks ruled the roost. Fortunately, given the nearly eleven hundred objects in the collection, there are more than enough varieties in type, form, and media to inspire exhibition themes for years to come. Thanks to Mrs. Herberger's collecting acumen and the great generosity of her family, these banks can inspire museum visitors in our day and well into the future.

William M. Griswold
Director and President,
The Minneapolis Institute of Arts

Acknowledgments

The mammoth project of cataloguing the Katherine Kierland Herberger Collection for publication could not have been undertaken without the enthusiastic and sustained involvement of a great many people. First, I must express heartfelt thanks to the Herberger family. I was fortunate enough to meet and interview Katherine Herberger in her home shortly before her death. Despite her grave illness, her knowledge of and passion for her collection shone through. The generosity of her son Gary and his wife, Jeanne, and their dedication to Mrs. Herberger's memory made this project possible in the first place. They were thoughtful hosts during a very difficult time for the family and displayed remarkable patience when I was suddenly called to military duty in Iraq in April 2003 and remained there for nine months — postponing publication of this catalogue. Thanks also go to Gary's brother, Judd Herberger, for offering me his memories of growing up with all those toy banks around the house.

I thank Evan Maurer, Director Emeritus, The Minneapolis Institute of Arts, and Christopher Monkhouse, James Ford Bell Curator of Architecture, Design, Decorative Arts, Craft, and Sculpture, for seeing the potential of acquiring the Herberger Collection and for supporting the catalogue project, especially during my long overseas absence.

Robert Fogt exhibited both great stamina and professionalism in photographing nearly eleven hundred still and mechanical banks in the Herberger home and here at the museum. Although he was on a tight schedule, Bob managed to capture the subtle qualities that make each bank special. I thank intern Karen Spillman for helping me organize the vast quantity of images. Thanks also go to Devin Matticks, Fine Art Packer, for traveling to Arizona to assist Bob Fogt during my time away and for making sure each bank arrived safely — and exquisitely packed — in Minneapolis.

Registrars process every object that enters a museum for acquisition and exhibition — and the Minneapolis Institute of Arts has the best in the profession. I thank Leslie Ory Lewellen, Assistant Registrar for Acquisitions, for her patience, perseverance, and attention to detail in registering the multitude of objects in the Herberger Collection. Gratitude is also due to her assistants: Shilpa Rele, Registration Intern; and Virginia Lang and Diane Williams, Registration Volunteers. Also, I am lastingly grateful to Ken Krenz, Assistant Registrar for Storage, who found space for the many Herberger toy banks in the museum's already cramped storage areas, knows exactly where each bank is located, and can retrieve it on a moment's notice.

Special gratitude goes to my curatorial colleagues Jason Busch, Jennifer Carlquist, Jennifer Komar Olivarez, David Ryan, and again Christopher Monkhouse for supporting me both while I was in Iraq and when I returned to resume this vast project. Jennifer Carlquist and Christopher organized the first exhibition in the Herberger Gallery, *Buildings to Bank On*, early in 2004.

Russ Harrington, of Russ Harrington Antique Toys in Baltimore, contributed invaluable research assistance to enhance and solidify the captions in this catalogue; however, any factual errors are mine alone. I am grateful to Max N. Berry for recommending Russ to me. The archival materials, newsletters, and Web sites of the Mechanical Bank Collectors of America and the Still Bank Collectors Club of America also proved to be indispensable as I gathered information about the banks.

I thank Anne-Marie Wagener, Director of External Affairs, and Jim Bindas, Book Productions LLC, for all their hard work in coordinating production of this catalogue. Thanks also go to Laura DeBiaso, Administrator of Curatorial Affairs, for her deft handling of publication contracts and finances. I am deeply grateful to editor Phil Freshman for his positive attitude and meticulous work on the manuscript and page proofs and to designer Deborah Littlejohn for successfully tackling the complex task of unifying the illustrations and copious text for a huge variety of objects and, in the process, creating a beautiful book. Thanks are also due to Charles Walbridge, Digital Imaging Specialist, for his calm expertise in preparing more than a thousand digital images for the printer, and to Dan Dennehy, Chief Photographer, for shooting such a splendid cover image.

My husband, Paul, read the seemingly endless series of drafts of my essay and was always there for me.

Finally, I express appreciation to University of Minnesota Professor Karal Ann Marling, my coauthor and mentor, for her contagious enthusiasm and for bringing to this book her singularly fascinating perspective on American popular culture.

Corine Wegener
Assistant Curator, Architecture, Design, Decorative Arts, Craft, and Sculpture
The Minneapolis Institute of Arts

Money in the Bank: The Katherine Kierland Herberger Collection

Corine Wegener

Save a penny yesterday
Another save today
Tomorrow save another
To keep the wolf away
– Inscription on *The Wise Pig* still bank, c. 1929

Katherine Herberger's spontaneous purchase of a mechanical toy bank as a birthday present for her young son nearly sixty years ago was the genesis of an astonishingly diverse collection of both mechanical and still banks, assembled over five decades, that ultimately numbered nearly eleven hundred items. Encompassing objects that are variously ingenious, entertaining, quizzical, and just plain rare, the collection is today considered one of the most important of its kind amassed in the twentieth century.

Katherine Kierland Herberger and Her Family's Legacy

Katherine Kierland was born in 1912 in the northern Minnesota town of Mahnomen. Her family moved to Alexandria, Minnesota, several years later. Her parents, Dr. and Mrs. Peter Ernest Kierland, were well-known residents of the area, where her father practiced medicine. Katherine's brother, Robert, became a physician, practicing at the prestigious Mayo Clinic in Rochester. Her sister, Edith, grew up to become the renowned golfing champion Edith Kierland Lowry. As a young girl, Katherine acquired the nickname Kax, after a favorite relative, but also to distinguish her from the several other Katherines at her school; it would stick with her for the rest of her life.

Kax majored in studio art at the University of Minnesota, becoming an accomplished sculptor and developing a lifelong devotion to the arts. She married G. Robert (Bob) Herberger in Alexandria, Minnesota, in 1934

Bob Herberger had learned retailing by working with his father, George, who owned a general store in Osakis, Minnesota. Bob's first venture was the purchase of a failing dry goods store in St. Cloud, which he transformed into a successful business. In 1927 he founded Herberger's Department Store there; its specialty was to offer products he felt would appeal specifically to local homemakers. Under his able management the operation flourished, and in 1943 Herberger's was incorporated. By 1972 it had grown from its single St. Cloud location into an eleven-store interstate chain. Ultimately, there were forty Herberger's stores, stretching from Wisconsin to Montana.

Bob Herberger's success drew national notice, and numerous retailers sought his advice. One of these, the Chicago-based catalog merchandiser Butler Brothers, Inc., which also owned the national Ben Franklin retail-store chain, went a step further. Faltering in the tough U.S. economy that immediately followed World War II, Butler Brothers asked Herberger to take over as president, running its day-to-day operations. Confident in his department-store management team and ready for a new challenge, he accepted the offer and moved his family to Winnetka, Illinois, in 1947.

Over the years, the Herbergers had regularly vacationed in Arizona. Although by the end of the 1940s he was chairman of both the Butler Brothers and Herberger's corporations, Bob was also becoming increasingly involved in Arizona real estate development. So in 1949 the family relocated again, this time to Scottsdale, which was then a quiet, unincorporated town on the outskirts of Phoenix.

Bob and Kax became leaders in the Phoenix-area arts community. In addition to Mrs. Herberger's collecting of toy banks, they jointly acquired paintings, sculpture, and other fine art (fig. 3). Over the years they lent vigorous support to civic and cultural institutions that included, among others, the Salvation Army, the Phoenix Symphony, the Phoenix Art Museum, the Scottsdale Artists School, and the Arizona State University Foundation. One of the couple's crowning achievements was the establishment in 1989 of the Herberger Theater Center, Phoenix's premier performing arts venue.

Often referred to as the unofficial "First Lady of Arizona," Mrs. Herberger served on the boards of numerous cultural organizations. In 1999 she founded Artswork: The Kax Herberger Center for Children and the Arts at Arizona State University; its focus is on art education. Her long-standing support of the university's arts programs led it to name its college of fine arts in her honor in 2000.

Portrait of a Collection

Katherine Herberger began collecting mechanical toy banks some years prior to acquiring her first still banks. She made these early purchases well before an active market existed for mechanical banks, a time when examples that today sell for thousands of dollars apiece went for a tenth as much. As a result, she obtained numerous rare examples — created by highly skilled designers and manufacturers — that are thought to be among the finest achievements in this specialized medium. Bob Herberger was initially skeptical about the "high" prices his wife

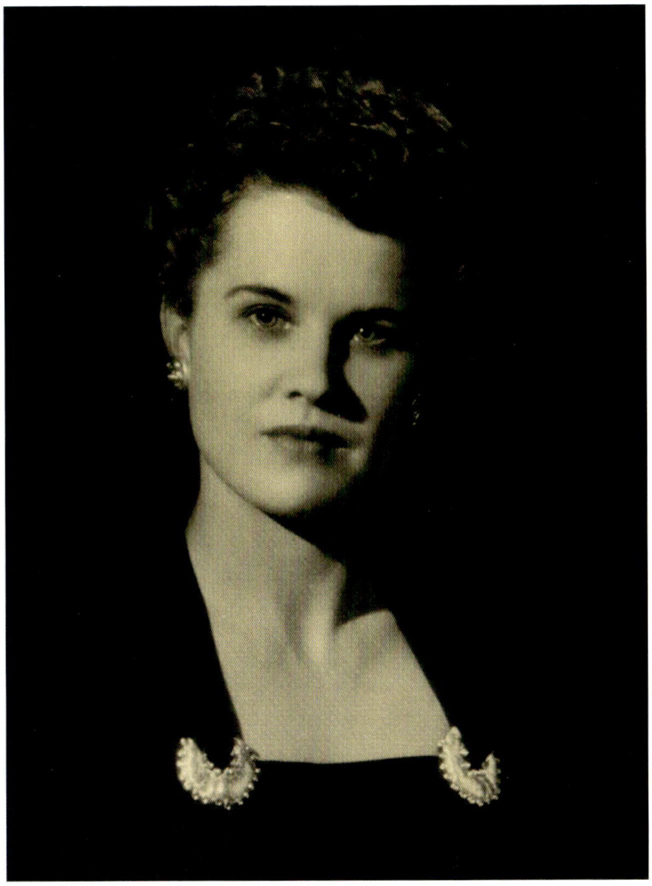

FIG. 1: Katherine Kierland Herberger, 1942

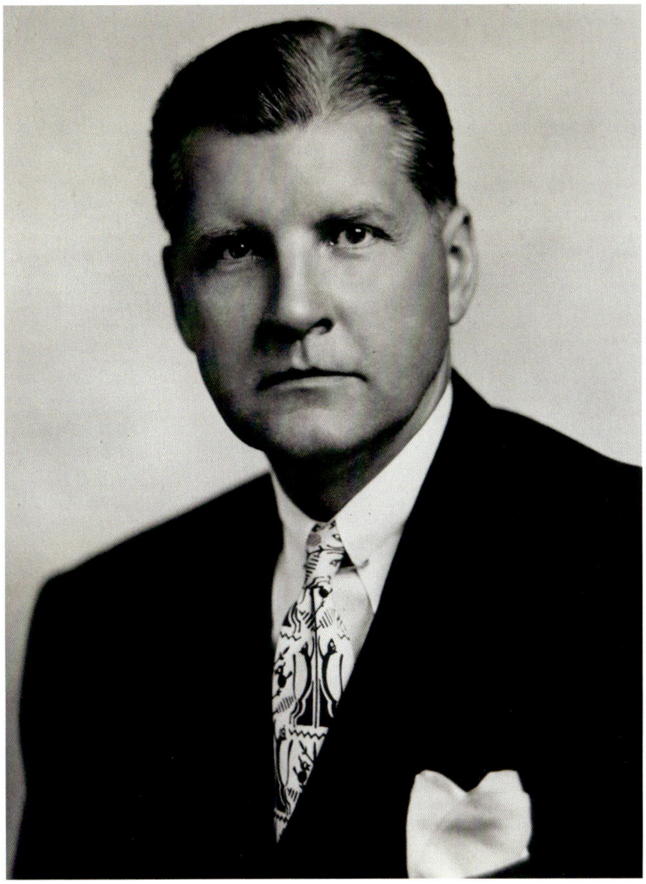

FIG. 2: G. Robert Herberger, 1948

paid for some of the banks. But later, as their values continued to climb, he would commend her business acumen.

Mechanical toy banks were predominantly made of cast iron, though tin, brass, and wood were also occasionally used. The first American cast-iron model was *Hall's Excelsior*, patented in December 1869 by its designer, John D. Hall, and mass-produced by the J. & E. Stevens Company of Cromwell, Connecticut. Fashioned to resemble a bank building, it boasts a monkey "cashier," seated at a desk, that rises up out of the roof when a string is pulled (fig. 4 and p. 36). The weight of a coin placed on the desk makes the monkey drop back down. J. & E. Stevens, which operated from 1843 until the 1950s, eventually became the most prolific manufacturer of cast-iron mechanical banks in the United States, where the vast majority of them were produced. The English also developed a taste for these objects, creating cast-iron banks that were largely based on American designs. In addition, a small number of tin banks were created and manufactured in Germany during the late nineteenth and early twentieth centuries.

The American cast-iron mechanical bank had its heyday from about 1875 to just after 1900, but production of many models lasted well into the 1930s. The cost of iron had begun increasing around the turn of the twentieth century, and the manufacture of all cast-iron toys, including mechanical banks, became correspondingly less profitable. Iron-toy production ceased almost entirely during World War II due to the military's enormous demand for the metal.

Most mechanical bank designs were produced in the thousands or even tens of thousands, but their typically fragile nature and the fact that they normally received hard use by enthusiastic children led them to become relatively rare. Still banks fared somewhat better, partly due to their hardier designs and lack of moving parts.

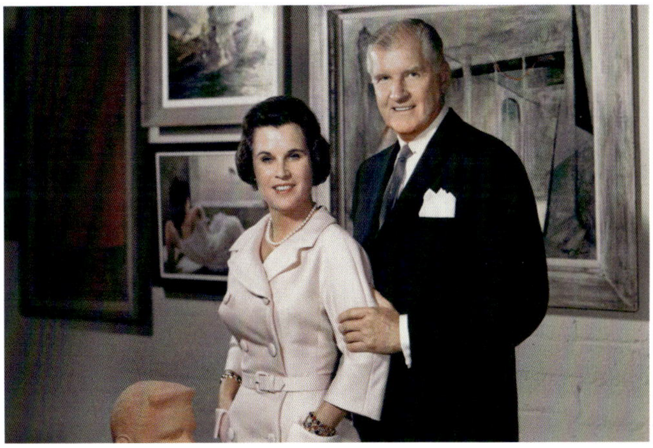

FIG. 3: Kax and Bob Herberger in their Scottsdale home, 1964

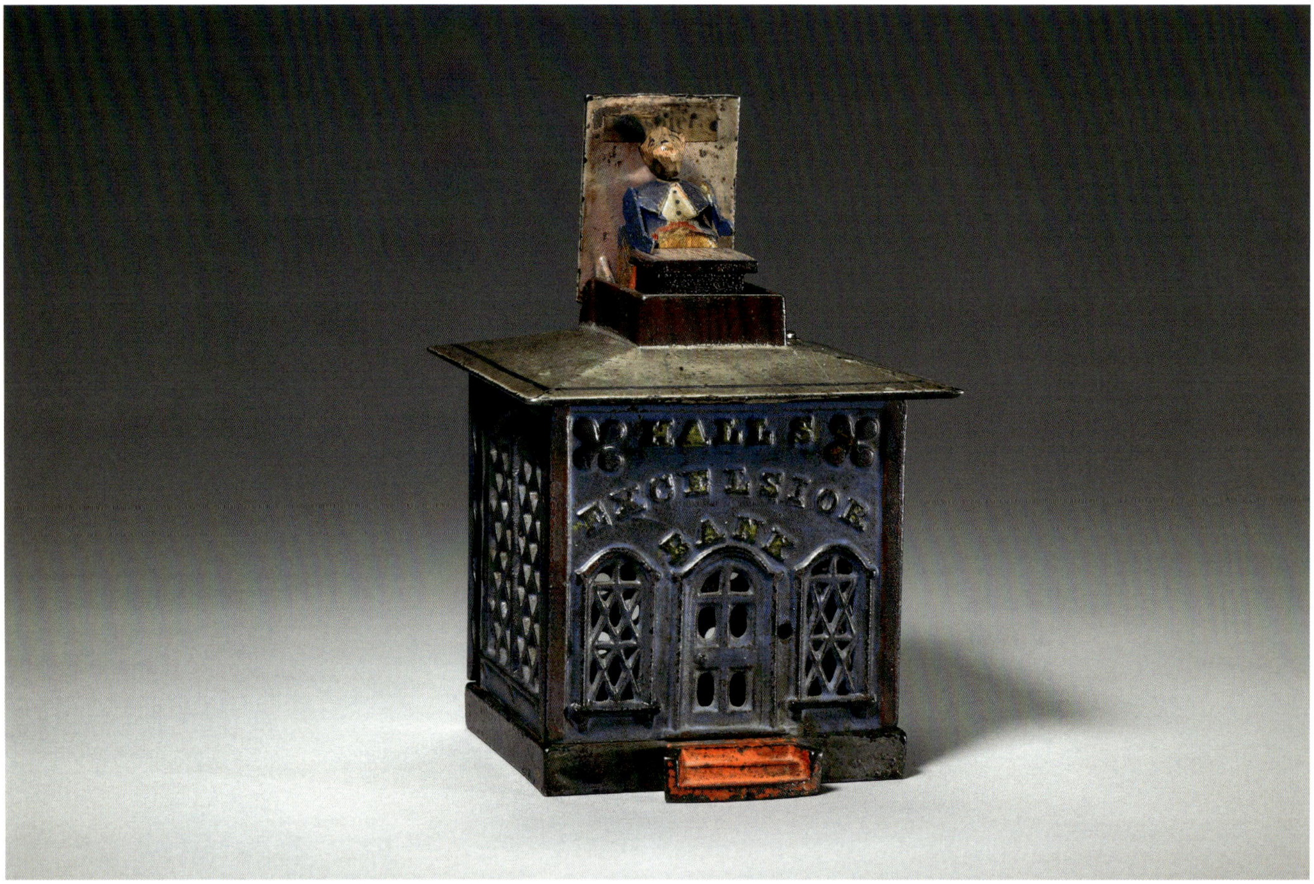

FIG. 4: *Hall's Excelsior* (or *Cashier Bank*), 1869. Iron, pigment, 5 ¼ x 4 x 4 ⅛ in.

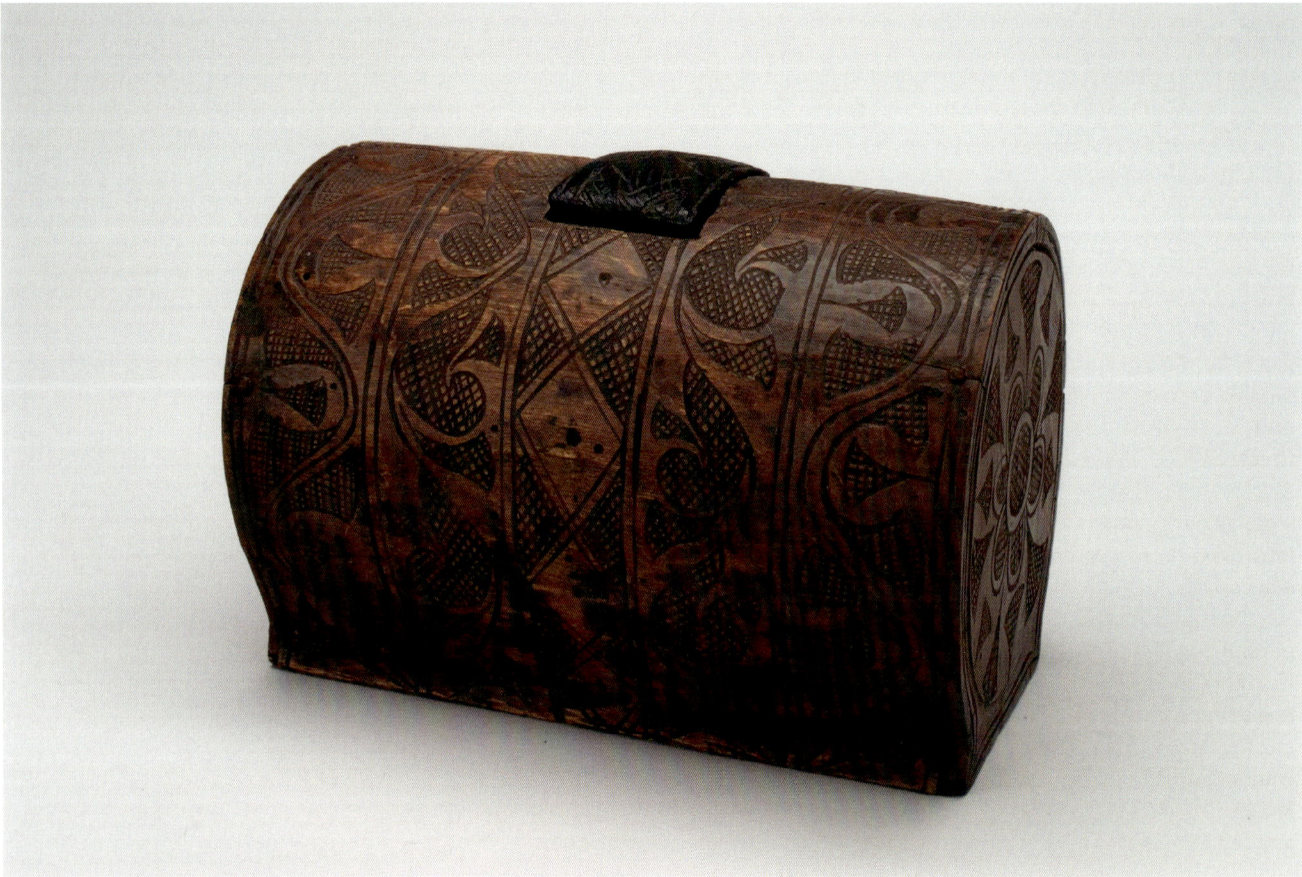

FIG. 5: Moravian box, c. 1756. Wood, 3 ¾ x 5 ¾ x 3 ½ in.

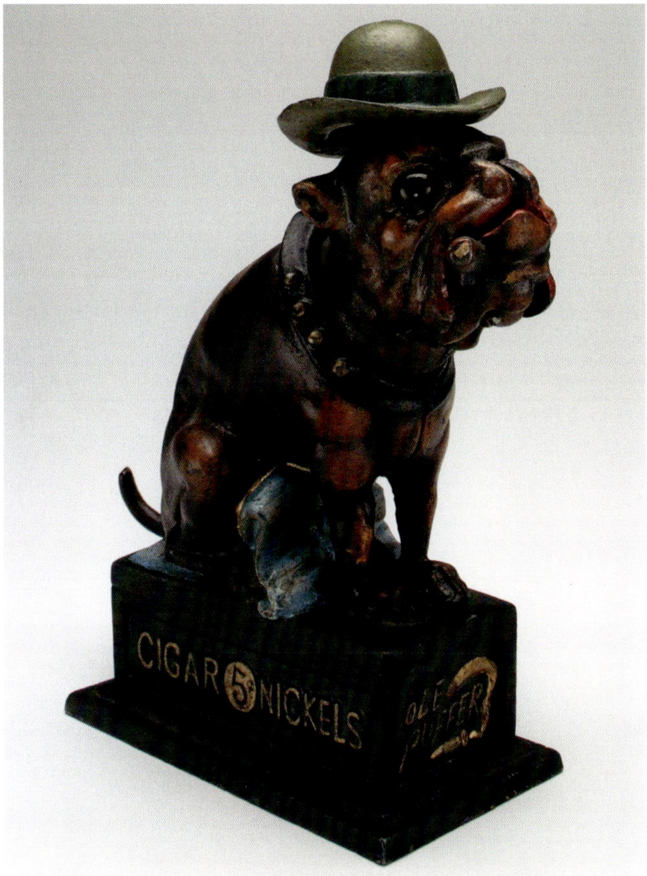

Fig. 6: *Ole Puffer*, c. 1998. Iron, pigment, glass, 8 ½ x 8 ⅜ x 3 ⅛ in.

Due to these various factors, by the mid-twentieth century mechanical and still banks alike were much-sought-after collectors' items.

The Katherine Kierland Herberger Collection spans more than two centuries. The earliest piece is a carved-wood Moravian still bank from Adamstown, Pennsylvania, dating to about 1756 (fig. 5 and p. 172). One of the most recent, *Ole Puffer* (fig. 6 and p. 85), is a late-1990s reproduction of the *Bull Dog* mechanical bank, first produced by the J. & E. Stevens Company in 1880 (p. 40).

Mechanical banks appealed to Mrs. Herberger not only for their clever apparatuses that encouraged children to save but also for their sculptural and artistic qualities. Moreover, they reflected her abiding interest in history, since each one provided a snapshot of the social, economic, and political climate of its time. The several examples discussed below were among her favorites.

Darktown Battery was the first toy bank Kax Herberger purchased, and though she would go on to acquire a great many more, it remained her very favorite (fig. 7 and p. 53). She bought it in a Winnetka, Illinois, antique shop as a gift for her son Gary's tenth birthday in 1948. When he went off to college, he returned it to her to add to the collection. In 1971 she bought Gary another *Darktown Battery* as a replacement.

Also known as *Baseball Bank*, *Darktown Battery* was designed and patented by James H. Bowen of Philadelphia about 1888 and manufactured by J. & E. Stevens. Bowen was one of the nation's most skilled designers of mechanical toy banks, producing them first in his own workshop and then becoming chief designer for the Stevens firm.

Mechanically, *Darktown Battery* is among the most complex banks in the collection, and it is one of just a few containing three figures with a range of body movements; another is *Elephant and Three Clowns on Tub* (c. 1882, p. 45), which Bowen also designed. To operate the bank, one cocks the pitcher's arm back into position, an action that also lowers his head. After placing a coin between the pitcher's thumb and fingers, one presses the lever near the tree stump. The pitcher throws the coin toward the batter as he raises his head. Simultaneously, the batter raises his bat and turns his head from right to left, as if following the coin's movement. The catcher's head moves forward as his hand tries to snag the coin, which drops into a hole at his feet, in the base of the bank.

Beginning in the mid-nineteenth century, a number of American and European mechanical and still banks featured racial and ethnic caricatures, particularly of blacks. *Darktown Battery* is a product of the years when African Americans were playing on military, college, and company baseball teams. Several players, such as Bud Fowler and Moses Fleetwood Walker, made their way onto professional teams alongside white players; the Jim Crow laws of the early 1900s forced them out. In response they started their own teams, playing all comers and, in the 1920s and 1930s, forming the Negro Leagues. This historic backdrop, as well as the complex mechanism, skillful modeling, and vivid colors of *Darktown Battery*, have made it one of the most popular and collectible of all American mechanical toy banks.

For some years, Mrs. Herberger acquired mechanical banks casually, picking up the occasional item on visits to antique shops during her travels. She made many of these early purchases at M. S. Rau Antiques in New Orleans on springtime trips there, including banks well known to collectors, such as *Creedmoor* (c. 1877, p. 37), *Humpty Dumpty* (c. 1882, pp. 26, 45), *Speaking Dog* (c. 1885, p. 52), and *Bad Accident* (c. 1888, p. 53) — each for less than $200.

She did not begin collecting mechanical banks in earnest until the 1960s, spurred in part by the forces of supply and demand. Because only about three hundred models of mechanical banks were ever produced worldwide — mostly in America — and often in small quantities, by the late 1960s the supply of them on the antiques market was dwindling. In order to continue building her collection, Mrs. Herberger began relying on her contacts in the Mechanical Bank Collectors of America (MBCA). Established in 1958, this rather exclusive club enabled members to buy, sell, and trade with one another. In fact, it was through the MBCA in the 1960s and 1970s that she

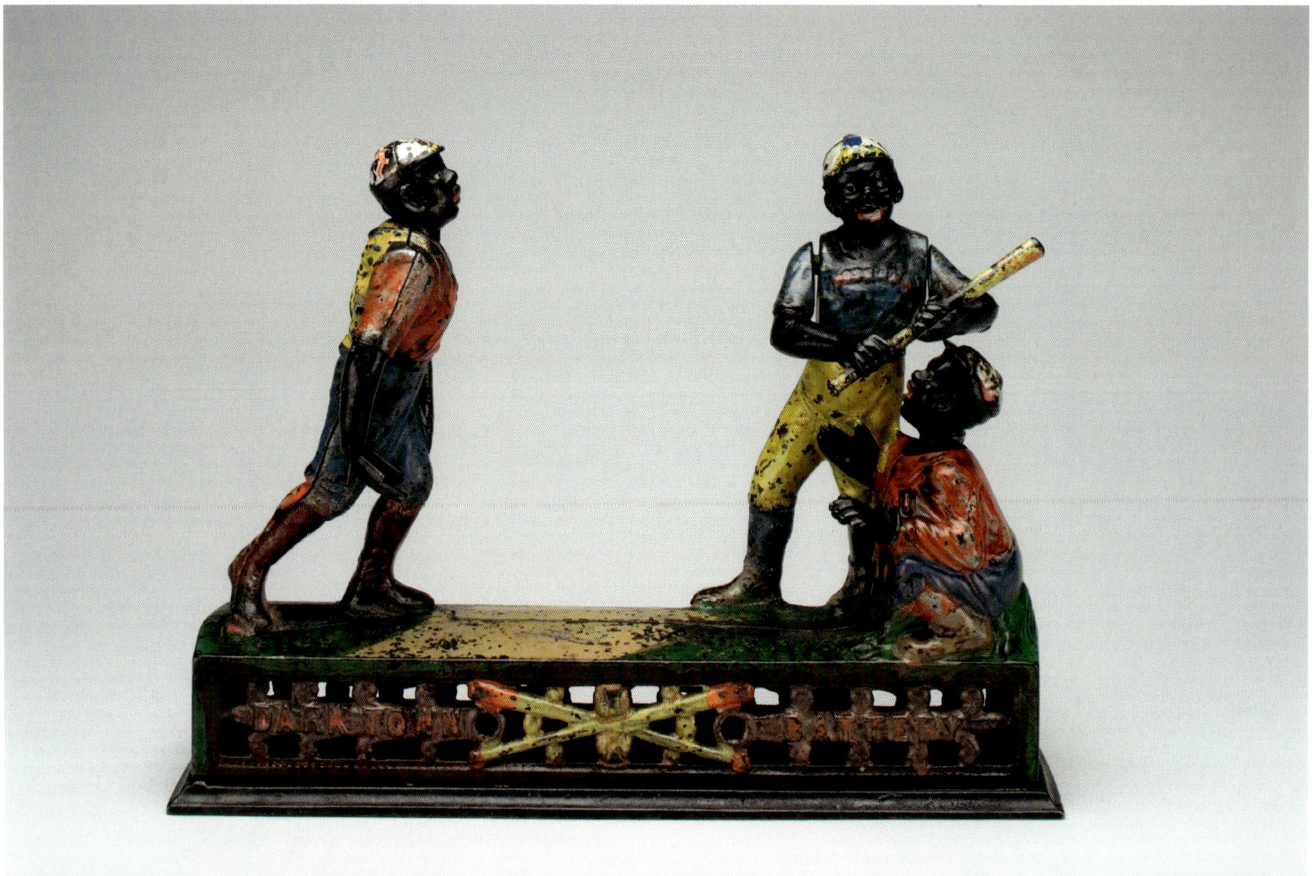

FIG. 7: *Darktown Battery* (or *Baseball Bank*), c. 1888. Iron, pigment, 7 ½ x 10 ⅞ x 2 ¹¹⁄₁₆ in.

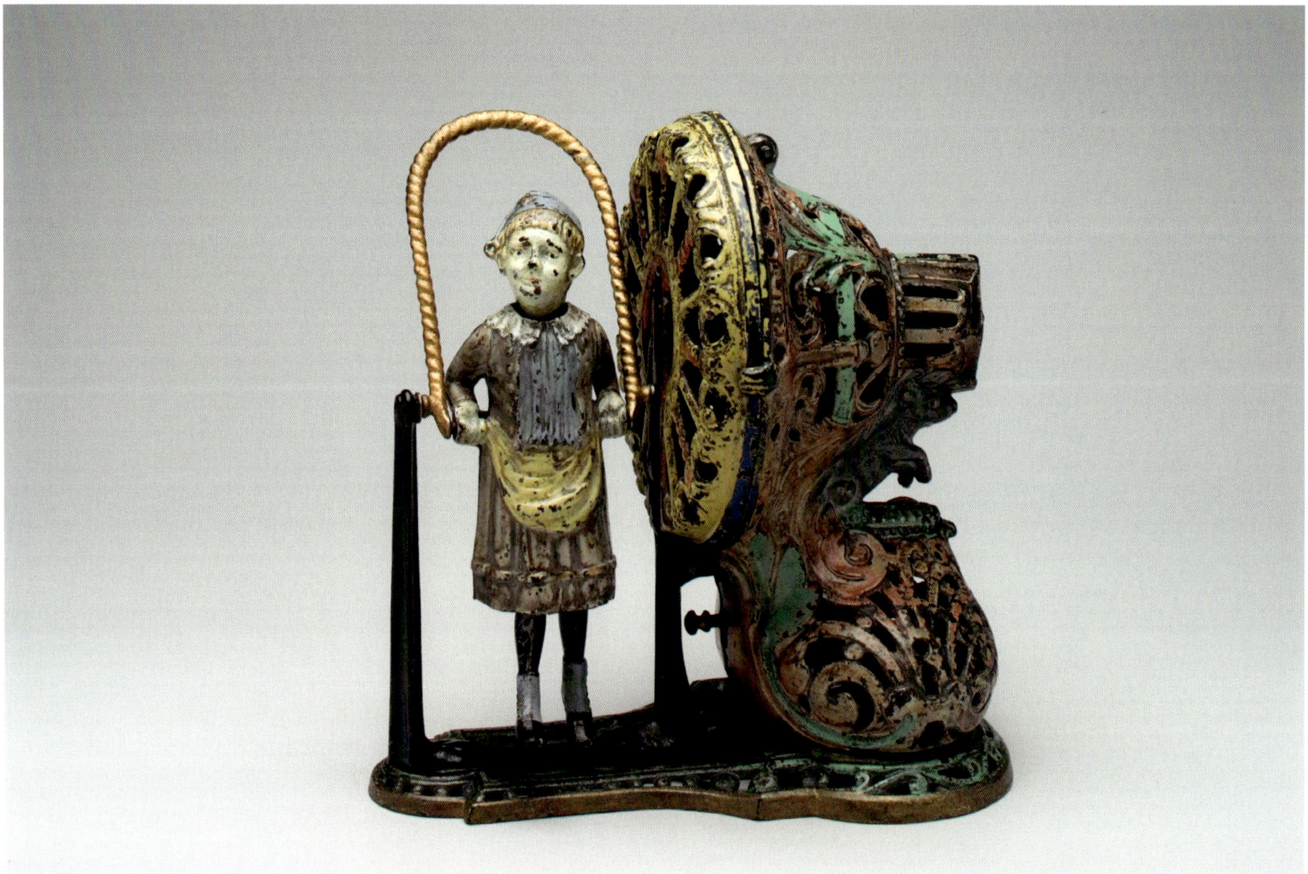

FIG. 8: *Girl Skipping Rope*, c. 1890. Iron, pigment, 7 ¾ x 8 ³⁄₁₆ x 5 ⅜ in.

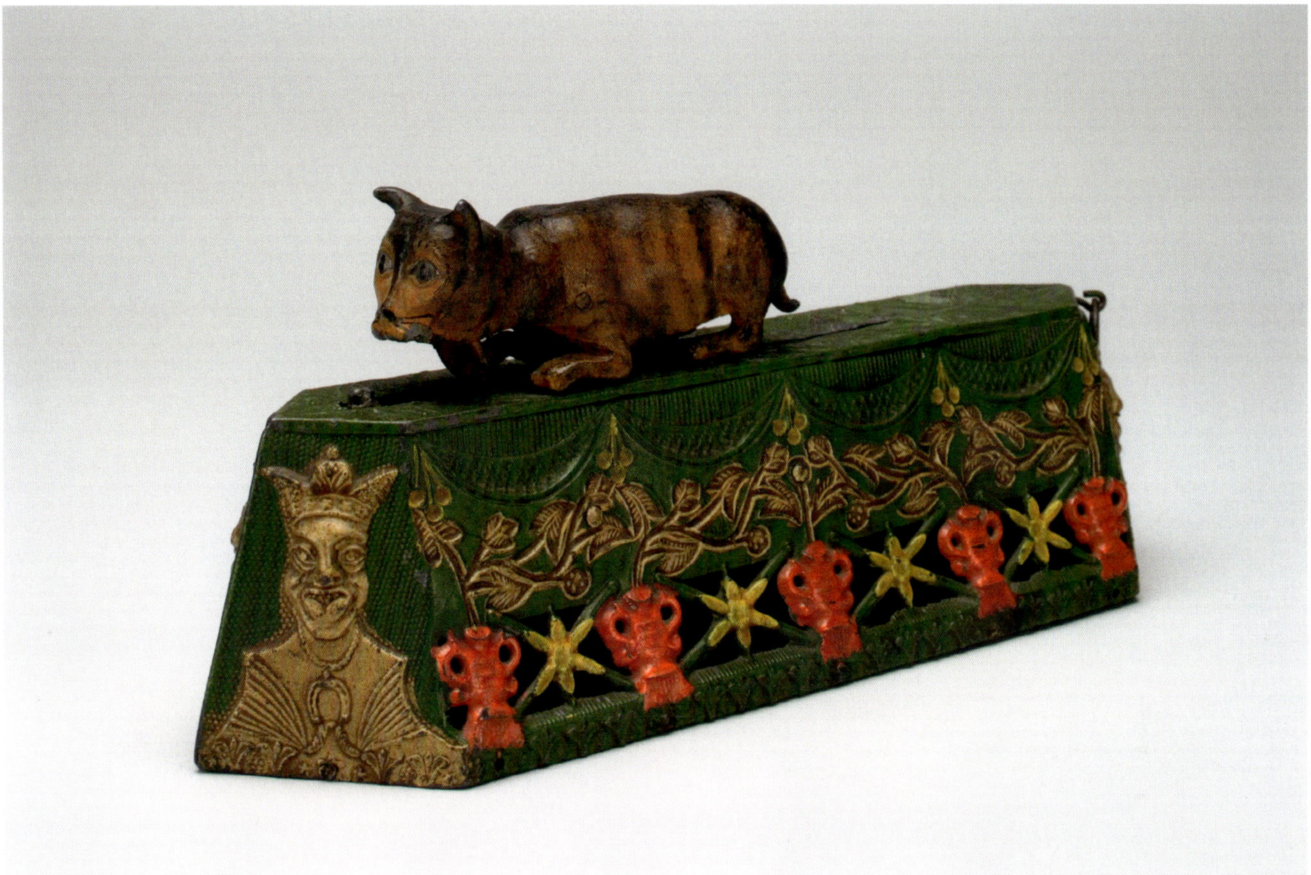

FIG. 9: *Springing Cat*, c. 1882. Lead alloy, wood, pigment, 3 ¾ x 9 ⅛ x 2 ⅝ in

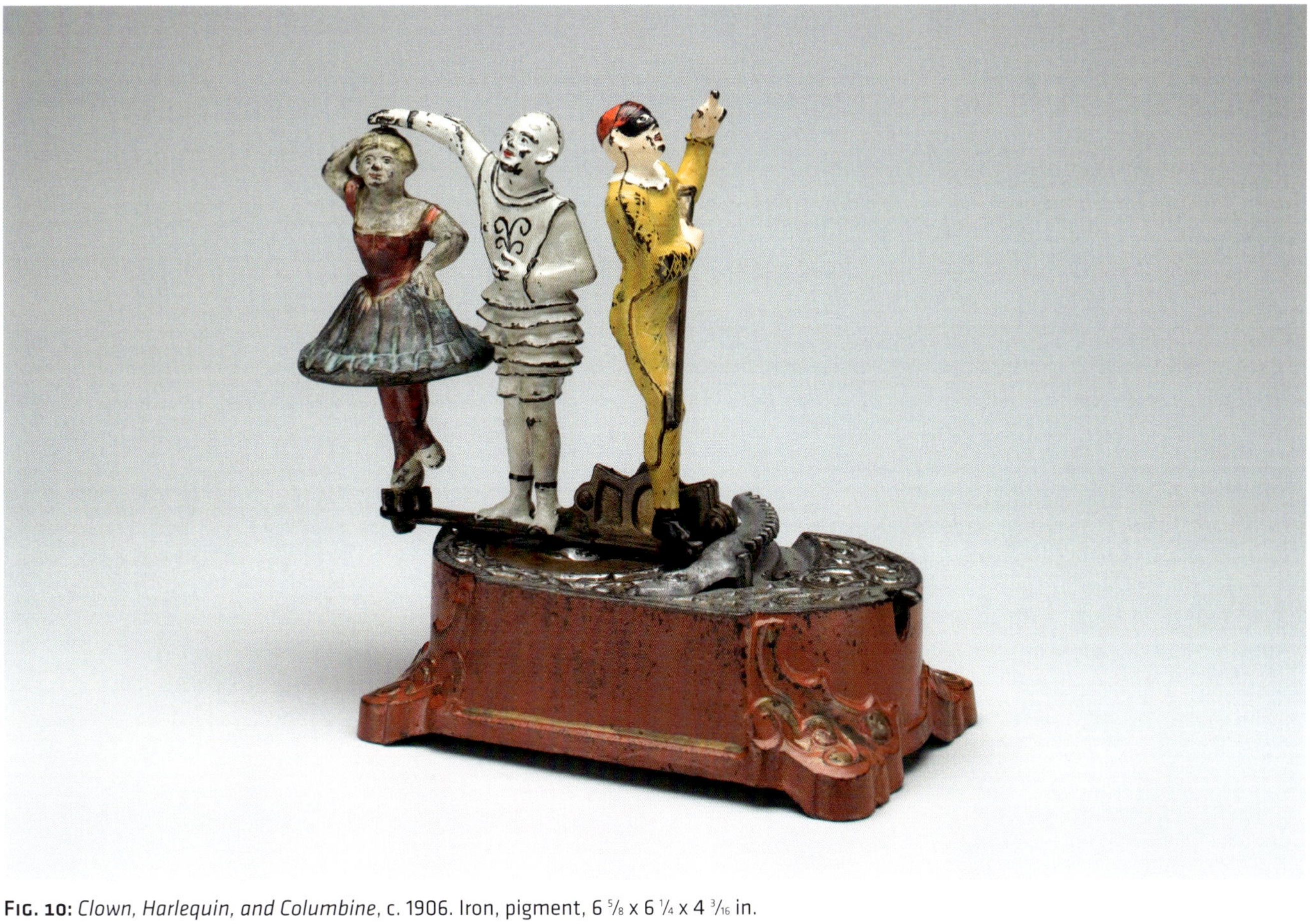

FIG. 10: *Clown, Harlequin, and Columbine*, c. 1906. Iron, pigment, 6 ⅝ x 6 ¼ x 4 3/16 in.

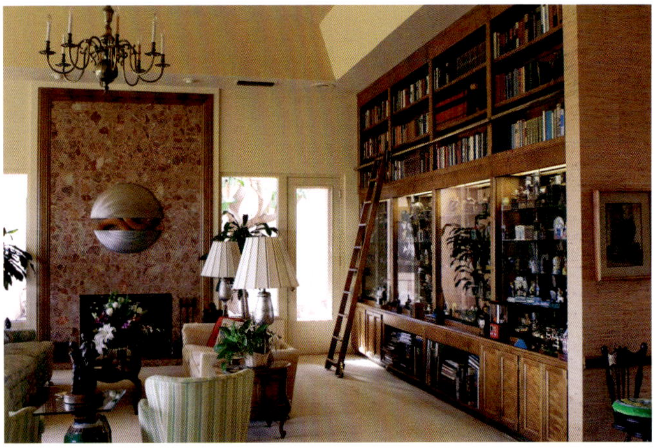

Fig. 11: Most of the mechanical banks in the collection were on view in the living room of the Herbergers' Paradise Valley, Arizona, home.

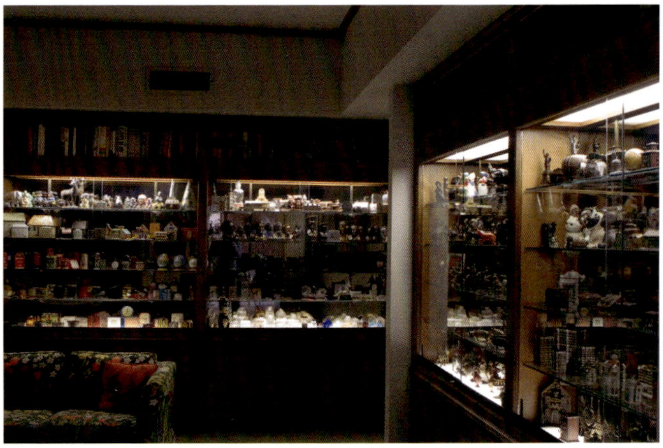

Fig. 12: Custom-built display cases in the family room and hallways housed most of the still banks in Mrs. Herberger's collection.

acquired most of her mechanical banks, buying from and trading with such notable collectors and dealers as Oliver Clark, Al Davidson, Robert McCumber, and Hubert Whiting. Through them she was able to obtain banks disbursed from great collections, such as those of Bernard Berenholtz, Walter P. Chrysler, and Edward Richards, who had all been MBCA founding members.

It was also in the 1960s, perhaps due to the shortage of mechanical banks on the market, that Katherine Herberger began acquiring still banks, becoming an active member of the Still Bank Collectors Club of America. By 1972, when a profile of her appeared in *Scrapbook*, the MBCA's newsletter, her collection numbered just over one hundred mechanicals and more than three hundred still banks. The latter grouping spanned a wide variety of subject matter, ranging from animals to architecture to characters (including cartoon, police, and Indian figures), and media that included iron, wood, glass, ceramic, tin, lead, silver, and brass. As well, she took care to gather examples in each size and color available.

Yet even though she ultimately owned many more still banks than mechanical ones, Kax Herberger considered herself a mechanical bank collector first and foremost. Among those she most cherished was *Girl Skipping Rope*, from about 1890 (fig. 8 and p. 56), another James H. Bowen design manufactured by J. & E. Stevens. Several qualities make this a must-have piece for serious collectors. It is prized for being one of the few mechanical banks ever made that appealed directly to girls; most were aimed at both genders. It is also relatively rare because its intricate design made it a difficult object to cast. Finally, *Girl Skipping Rope* is especially valued because its mechanical action is unique.

To set *Girl Skipping Rope* in motion, one inserts a coin vertically between the paws of the waiting squirrel and winds the mechanism with a large key. Pressing a lever engages a heavy flywheel, causing the squirrel to drop the coin into the base of the bank and the girl to skip rope up to several dozen times. As she goes up and down, her head turns from side to side and her legs rotate naturalistically.

Another of Mrs. Herberger's most treasured banks was *Springing Cat*, which Charles A. Bailey designed and manufactured in his Cobalt, Connecticut, workshop around 1882 (fig. 9 and p. 48). (Bailey would go on to become a lead designer for the J. & E. Stevens Company.) This bank is unusual in that it is one of the few mechanicals ever produced that was not made of cast iron but rather of a lead alloy with a wooden base.

To operate the bank, one places a coin in the slot in the base and then pulls the spring-loaded cat back into a locked position. When the lever is pressed, a small gray mouse appears from inside the base, pushing the coin into the slot. The cat leaps at the mouse, but it disappears back from where it came. Several decorative features distinguish this bank from all others ever made. Asian-looking figures appear at either end of the base, linked along the sides by a band of alternating red lanterns and stylized flowers — all evoking a sense of the exotic. This bank is quite rare, with only about a dozen examples known to exist.

Yet probably the rarest and most and sought-after bank Katherine Herberger acquired is *Clown, Harlequin, and Columbine*, manufactured by J. & E. Stevens beginning in 1906 (fig. 10 and p. 65). Although the design was patented in 1877 by an otherwise unknown person named J. Blanc, most collectors attribute it to James H. Bowen because of the similarity between its characters' movements and the movements of those in his *Calamity* bank, patented in 1905 and also produced by J. & E. Stevens — a piece not included in the Herberger collection. After locking the spring-loaded figures into place, the operator places a coin in the slot between the harlequin and clown and then presses the lever. The columbine (or dancer) springs free and spins around while the harlequin and clown exchange places, and the coin drops into the base. Today, there are fewer than a dozen examples of this piece in private collections.

Mrs. Herberger's collection attracted local interest and was highlighted in several local exhibitions over the

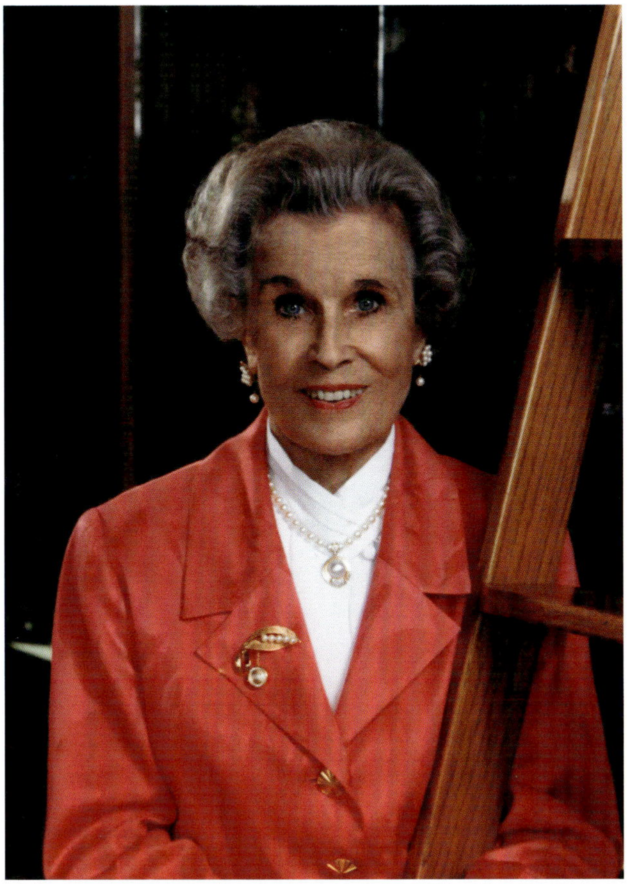

Fig. 13: Kax Herberger in her Paradise Valley home, 1997. Several of the cases exhibiting her collection are visible behind her.

years. In 1975 the Phoenix Art Museum featured 107 of the mechanical banks in a show focused on the collection that was mounted by the museum's Collectors' Study Group. Two years later, the group included three of her Santa Claus banks in a Christmas exhibition at the museum. In 1981 the Arizona Bank Galleria in Phoenix showcased 105 objects in *Mechanical Banks, 1869–1976*, another exhibition centered on her collection. Accompanying the show was a handout, written by Kax Herberger, summarizing the history, design, and increasingly collectable nature of mechanical banks. Finally, the Matthews Center at Arizona State University, Tempe, borrowed several of her banks for inclusion in an exhibition of advertising memorabilia.

By 1987 Mrs. Herberger had acquired more than a thousand banks. When the couple built a new home in Paradise Valley, Arizona, that year, she had a number of museum-quality cases installed to display the collection. She gave her guests tours, providing them with pennies to work selected mechanical banks (figs. 11, 12).

Katherine Herberger's comprehensive approach to toy-bank collecting set her apart from many of her peers, who tended to acquire either mechanical or still pieces but not both. She cast her net widely, bringing together examples from the United States and abroad that ranged from the mid-eighteenth to the late twentieth centuries. Although she bought numerous banks from major dealers, she also took delight in under-appreciated examples that she acquired from modest antique and secondhand dealers and as gifts from family members and friends. And while she clearly had her favorites, she asserted in an interview just before her death that she did not consider any of the pieces she owned to be "frivolous," meaning that she found value in them all.

The extraordinary range of the collection made it ideally suited for inclusion in an art museum with an encyclopedic mission. In 2002, three years after Bob's death, Kax Herberger and her children decided to donate the collection to The Minneapolis Institute of Arts; 277 mechanical and 812 still banks came to the museum as a bequest shortly after her death in April 2003, along with a generous endowment for their care and exhibition. The Katherine Kierland Herberger Gallery, situated on the ground floor between the Family Center and the children's classrooms, was established for thematic exhibitions to be on view for about a year apiece. The first one, *Buildings to Bank On*, a selection of more than a hundred architecture-related examples, went on view in January 2004. Following this was *Banks with Bite*, an installation of animal-themed pieces.

Katherine Kierland Herberger's munificent gift ensures that future generations of museum visitors will have an opportunity to see toy banks that, in many instances, exist only in private collections and allow them to share in her enthusiasm for these intriguing artifacts, which offer telling glimpses of the social, political, and commercial tenors of their times.

American "Argyrothecology,"* or The Art and Commerce of the Penny Bank

Karal Ann Marling

* ar-gy-ro-the-co-logy *n* (c. 2005) 1: collecting money boxes such as those found in churches or dispensing machines; 2: the collection and study of toy banks

It began quietly enough, the great penny bank craze of the last century. Here, a slotted pottery pig from Scotland. There, a grimacing human face made in Bennington, Vermont. The antique shops of New England were full of them. Or a rarer item, an elaborate cast-iron mechanism (often broken) — a toy, really — an automaton that put on a little show before snatching one's coin away. In October 1926, a brief notice in *Antiques* magazine made mention of such banks as potential collectors' items.[1] And the hunt was on.

In later years, everybody claimed to have been the very first to "discover" banks in the 1920s. A prominent collector of the 1930s and 1940s told of stumbling upon a little iron man who slipped pennies into his vest pocket during a long-ago vacation trip — and recognizing the *Tammany Bank* (also known as *Little Fat Man* or *Boss Tweed*, patented on December 23, 1873, fig. 1 and p. 37) as a beloved plaything of his childhood years.[2] A Pittsburgh aficionado recalled having started his own collection after seeing three mechanical banks on display somewhere in New York City in 1929.[3] Others remembered old banks emerging from the dusty attics of ancestral homes in the 1920s, as a rising generation inherited the household treasures of their parents. But questions remained. Why collect old banks? What did they mean? When and where and why were they made in the first place?

Most members of the founding cadre of avid collectors were bankers by profession. And there is a fine irony in the fact that bankers became the primary custodians of the nation's penny banks at the very moment when, in the aftermath of the Crash of 1929, bank failures were calling the solvency and trustworthiness of their insti-tutions into serious question. Frank Capra's classic Christmas movie, *It's a Wonderful Life* (1946), hinges on a potentially catastrophic "run" on Jimmy Stewart's small-town bank, with angry Depression-era depositors clamoring for their money. American history is rife with good reasons to keep one's cash under the mattress — or to spend it as quickly as possible. Between 1890 and 1908, according to one authority, there were no fewer than six major financial "panics" and fifteen minor ones, all of which eroded public confidence in brick-and-mortar banks.[4]

In the nineteenth century, when agriculture was a dominant force in the economy, skeptical farmers were apt to save by putting surplus funds into land and improvements instead of banks. In the cities, working-men were paid in cash — and coin. Banks established to service their small accounts failed with predictable frequency because the average deposit was so small.[5] In such a climate, the penny bank on the mantelpiece was a fine alternative to the granite-columned edifice on Main Street, with its scrolled and gilded safe and florid banker, haunted by dime-novel tales of daring daylight robberies.

On the other hand, while commercial banks remained a risky proposition until reform legislation during the New Deal period mitigated the chances of outright collapse, mutual-savings banks, descended from British building societies of the eighteenth century, fared better. Small institutions designed to help ordinary people own their homes, building-and-loan-style banks (the first was founded in 1831 in Frankfort, Pennsylvania) maintained an impeccable record of safety, even during the turbulent years of the Great Depression.[6] These banks, primarily located in New England and the East, helped make thrift a venerable Puritan virtue on a par with godliness. Horatio Alger, Louisa May Alcott, Ben Franklin: their maxims about saving one's pennies (so the dollars would take care of themselves!) were cited by earnest bankers as the commandments of a new gospel of thrift.

Penny banks first appeared in America in 1793, along with the first large copper pennies. Those who mistrusted paper currency (with good reason) saved their "hard" money in vessels of pottery, glass, and tin. "Pinchpenny" became a synonym for a typical Yankee, who was said to "squeeze the eagle" on a coin "until it screamed." Round, capacious, and quick to eat up whatever was offered, the pig made an ideal penny bank. In the 1890s *China Pig*, with a slit in its back, sold for a dime.[7] Some purists believe that the piggy bank came about because the orange clay once used to make inexpensive jars for coins was known in olden days as "pygg."[8] But it is just as likely that plump pigs and pennies went together like thrift and future success. In the Victorian era, pink pigs were holiday symbols of good health, luck, and prosperity in the year ahead—the fat of the land! So why not a nice pig for a bank? In time, the classic pottery piggy was joined by cast-iron pigs of all description, including a pig lolling in a high chair, a self-described "Lucky Pig," and one from which Otto von Bismarck himself popped up when the penny was placed in the slot (p. 49).

Most bank pigs, however, neither kicked up their feet in imitation of the "learned pigs" that appeared in circuses and sideshows, nor did they spew forth political

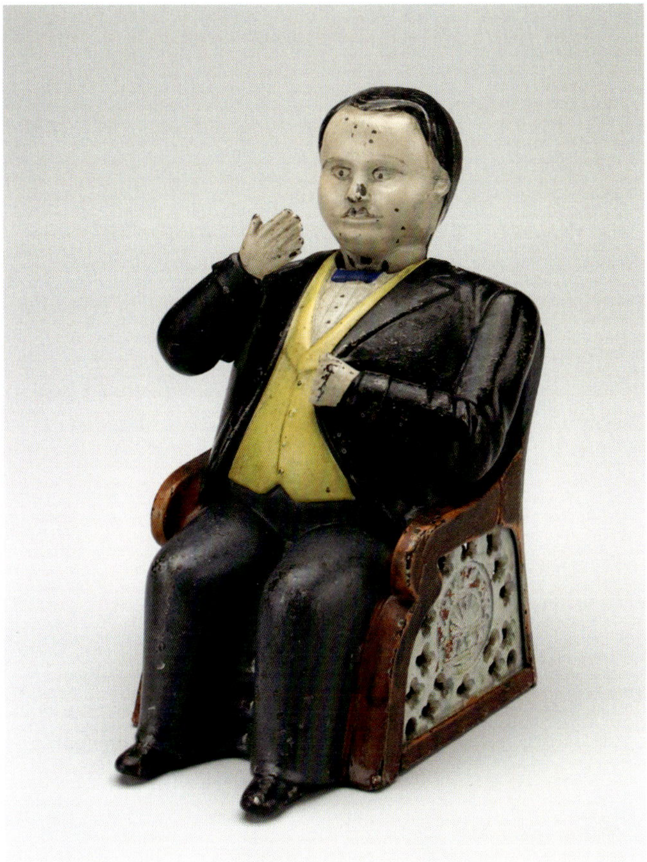

Fig. 1: *Tammany Bank* (or *Little Fat Man*), c. 1873. Iron, pigment, 5 3/4 x 3 1/2 x 4 3/8 in.

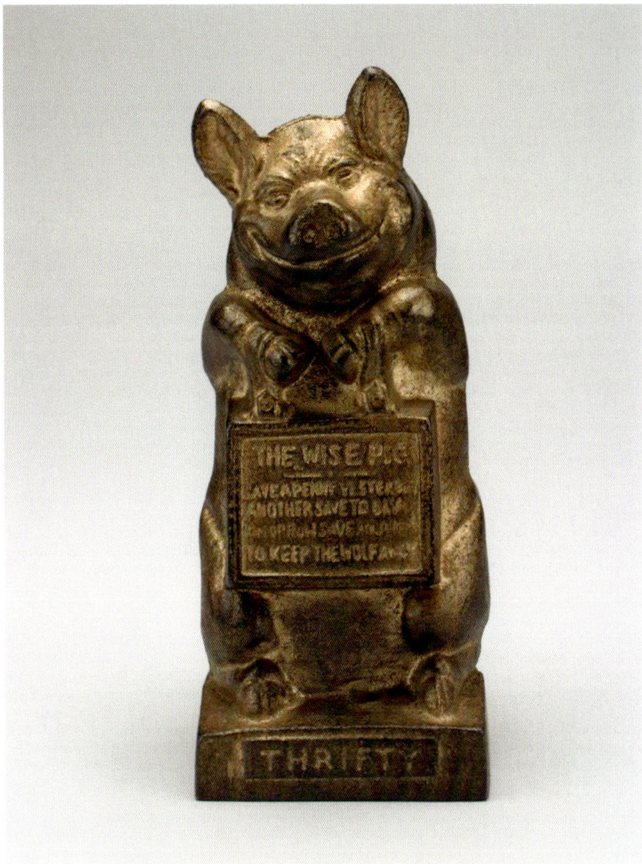

Fig. 2: *The Wise Pig*, c. 1929. Lead, pigment, 6 3/16 x 2 13/16 x 2 7/8 in.

figures.[9] *The Wise Pig* (c. 1929, fig. 2 and p. 160), a still or "dumb" bank made of lead, merely carried a little sign that exhorted the owner to save, pig-wise, in order "To keep the wolf away."[10] The oldest bank in the possession of Arthur E. Corby, a Manhattan dentist who emerged as one of few leading collectors of the 1930s not well versed in current interest rates, was a Roman money box made of clay; it was shaped like a leather trunk and surmounted by the likeness of a pig labeled "Felix" (or Lucky).[11] Among the most desirable of the mechanical or moving banks on Corby's shelves was the *Shamrock*, more often known as *Paddy* or *Murphy and the Pig*. An expert who devised a kind of ranking of mechanical banks for *Hobbies* magazine in the 1960s gave *Shamrock* a low grade because it had been manufactured in such large numbers that it was no special rarity. Patented in Philadelphia in 1882 by James H. Bowen and made by the J. & E. Stevens Company of Cromwell, Connecticut, it was, in other words, a wildly popular bank in its day. An ingenious variation on the traditional piggy bank, the *Paddy* model consisted of a caricatured Irishman in a green jacket (a clay pipe and a shamrock in his hatband completed the ethnic identification), clutching a pig to his bosom. The coin was placed on the tip of the pig's snout. When the control lever was engaged, the pig's leg moved upward and kicked the penny toward Paddy, who opened his mouth, caught it on his tongue, and swallowed the money down in a single gulp.

A persistent legend in the annals of bankdom holds that *Paddy and the Pig* (c. 1882, fig. 3 and p. 48), which had been created in reaction to the successive waves of Irish immigration that spilled over the East Coast from the 1840s through the 1880s and 1890s, was abruptly taken out of production because it was deemed derogatory by members of a Hibernian protective society. Although the tale was repeated endlessly, the Irish did not kill off the pig. The complex internal mechanism of the device may have been one factor in its demise—another, the waning novelty of the stereotypical Irish comedian.[12] But artifacts like this one, grounded in popular culture, fads, prejudice, and mechanics, had a special appeal to the nominally conservative bankers who built the first great American collections of penny banks. However inaccurate or fanciful, the stories attached to the banks conjured up in the minds of those who owned them visions of simpler times, before respectable Americans of Irish extraction might reasonably object to the sight of one of their own kinsmen locked in a fervid embrace with a pig.

Why did successful bankers take up this particular hobby? For one thing, saving money was a rebuke to those

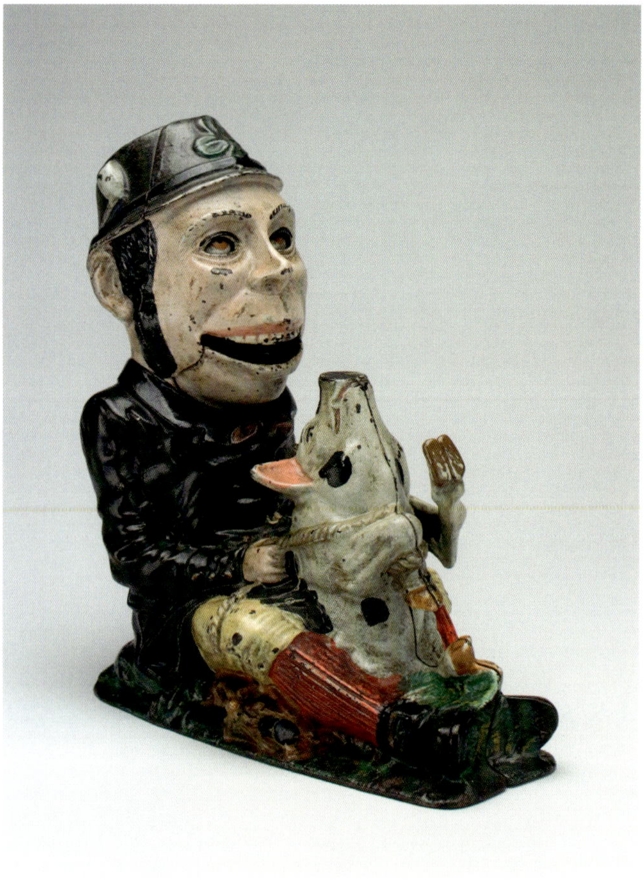

Fig. 3: *Paddy and the Pig*, c. 1882. Iron, pigment, glass, 8 ½ x 7 3/16 x 3 5/16 in.

who spent funds they didn't have, on easy-credit terms. And repeatedly, bankers asserted that the lesson of thrift reinforced by their own penny-saving days had shaped their destiny. Boys who put pennies in toy banks (and heeded the relevant passages in *Poor Richard's Almanack*) grew up to become the stalwart men who ran America's *real* banks and steered them through the perilous fiscal waters of hard times. Like most collectors, hard-nosed bankers, too, were sentimental souls at bottom who clung to memories of the joys of youth.[13] They waxed nostalgic about indulgent old uncles dropping pennies into their banks, about their delight at watching the animated tricks performed by cast-iron whales and frogs and baseball players whenever a coin was produced.

Men who worked with pens and telephones were also apt to be boundless in their admiration for the nimble-fingered craftsmen of the past who had devised the springs and levers inside the old banks. And the moving figures, they insisted, were important inducements for children to learn the value of saving money. That, at least, was the ultimate justification many otherwise blameless bank officers in stiff collars used to justify the thrill of the hunt for rare and increasingly expensive specimens. Toy banks were repositories of virtue as well as pocket change!

In discussing their shared hobby, the banker-collectors of the 1930s were quick to invoke the good old days and the parents who once inculcated the habit of thrift into their offspring with birthday or Christmas banks. If the device entertained the child in the process of teaching a useful lesson, so much the better. But the point of toy banks of all descriptions was to nurture the practice of saving money regularly. Andrew Emerine, president of the First National Bank of Fostoria, Ohio, and one of the premier early collectors, published pamphlets throughout the 1930s and 1940s full of pictures of his treasures on display in his place of business. According to one of these pamphlets, both kinds of banks — real ones and toys — "have stood the test of time."[14] But the toy banks had the advantage of instructing children in responsible fiscal practices in the most painless way possible. Thus, like many of his peers, Emerine was besotted with cast-iron banks that did something clever when used — and thereby rewarded a good boy or girl for saving a penny.[15]

Over the course of a long career in banking, Emerine would write articles about his hobby, seek out the old patent papers and sales catalogs that dated choice items more precisely, and inspire others to exhibit their banks in the cause of encouraging thrift. During World War II, for instance, when the federal government attempted to regulate inflationary spending and fund the costs of combat with U.S. Savings Bonds, displays of trick penny banks became important devices for selling bonds and stamps. A vice-president of the Mercantile-Commerce Bank and Trust of St. Louis allowed his private collection of banks to be shown in the lobby to help promote the Sixth War Loan Drive in 1944.[16] On her popular radio show, *The Women's Page of the Air*, Adelaide Hawley (the onetime radio voice of Betty Crocker) interviewed Arthur Corby for a nationwide "Promotion of Thrift" campaign in the summer of 1942. He provided vivid descriptions of how several of his banks worked — including *The Dentist*, in which, during the course of an extraction, the doctor's one-cent fee flies into an old-time gasbag of anesthetic. But the best bank in his collection, said Corby, was a simple little wooden spice box into which a boy in 1780 had carved his initials and a coin slot. That lad grew up to be the founder of the famous Mott Iron Works, Corby revealed. The moral of the story? "Many American fortunes [and] industries got their start because some little boy had a bank into which he dropped his pennies."[17]

Corby and Emerine were joined in the hunt for mechanical banks during the 1930s by a host of others: Elmer Rand Jacobs of the Seaman's Bank for Savings in New York; Wilmont R. Evans of the Boston Five Cent Savings Bank; William F. Ferguson of New York's Bank for Savings; a smattering of doctors and dentists (whose income remained relatively constant, even during the Depression); and no less a figure than Walter P. Chrysler, the industrialist/automaker whose large collection had

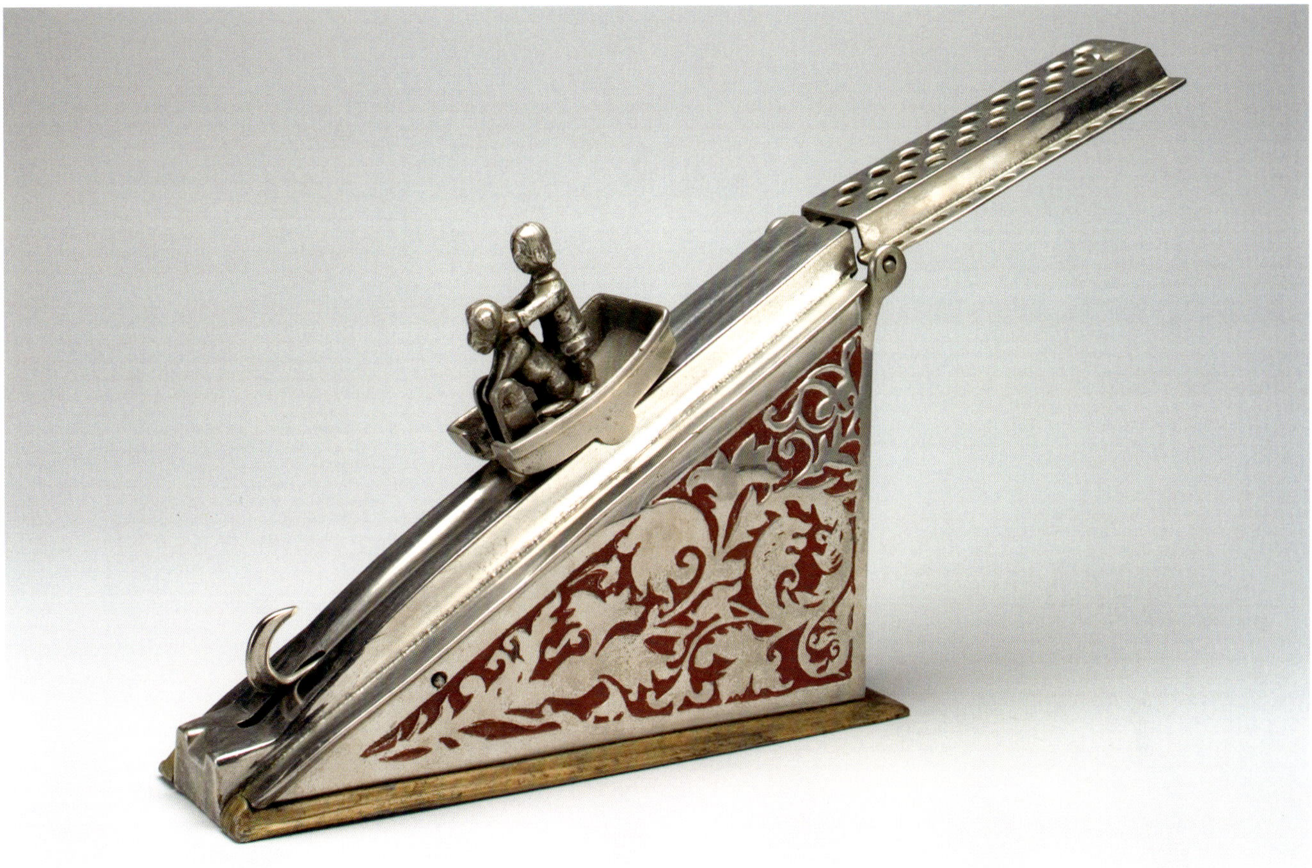

FIG. 4: *Shoot the Chute*, c. 1906. Iron, pigment, 6 5/16 x 9 11/16 x 2 11/16 in.

pride of place in his new office on the fifty-sixth floor of the Chrysler Building in Manhattan when it opened in 1930.[18] Chrysler's conversion to the cause gave bank-hunting instant cachet. A poem by the dealer and collector Norman Sherwood, published in a hobby magazine in 1938, has Chrysler describing his banks as "a sort of symbol in the 'Game of Life.'"[19] But he took the game seriously. In a glass case in the public observatory atop his building only two items were to be seen: the chest of homemade tools with which he had forged his career and the choicest of the toy banks that delighted him in retirement.[20]

Like Henry Ford, whose banks seem to have been incidental items in his massive collection of Americana, Chrysler loved the old machines displaced by the new ones he had helped invent.[21] The clunky, cast-iron devices that were also banks (and three-dimensional, moving cartoons) harkened back to a not-so-long-ago past, when men such as Ford and Chrysler tinkered with bicycles, clockworks, locomotives, and horseless carriages — the great mechanical advances of the nineteenth century. In a peculiar way, then, banks became yardsticks of progress for the titans of industry. A bank with a little girl skipping an iron rope at the touch of a lever (pp. 12, 56) measured just how far technology had leaped into the new age of the Model T and the Chrysler Airflow. More than anything else, mechanical banks affirmed a man's personal gains. They chronicled the change from the moment the boy dropped a penny into a bank in order to watch the rabbit's ears twitch to the moment when the man he had become was named president of some mighty bastion of industry or high finance.

"Man" is a fairly accurate description of the average first-generation collector, too. There were exceptions. A Mrs. May Bliss Dickinson Kimball of Boston operated a museum of old banks, briefly, in the late 1930s in a historic inn in Amherst, Massachusetts.[22] A Mrs. George Thompson, who wrote several articles on the lure of bank collecting, loaned her mechanicals for exhibition purposes to the Union Dime Savings Bank of New York and several other trust institutions in 1937.[23] Ina Bellows's 1940 book, *Old Mechanical Banks*, is a landmark in the field.[24] But as collectors gradually became "stars" in the firmament of devotees, women were rarely numbered among the ten or twelve "significant" figures jockeying for position in the pages of newspaper columns and magazines devoted to antiquing and other leisure-time pursuits. In such venues, the typical collector was generally pictured as a man of affairs. If not a banker, then a doctor or a company president.[25] Or a millionaire, bent on getting a prize

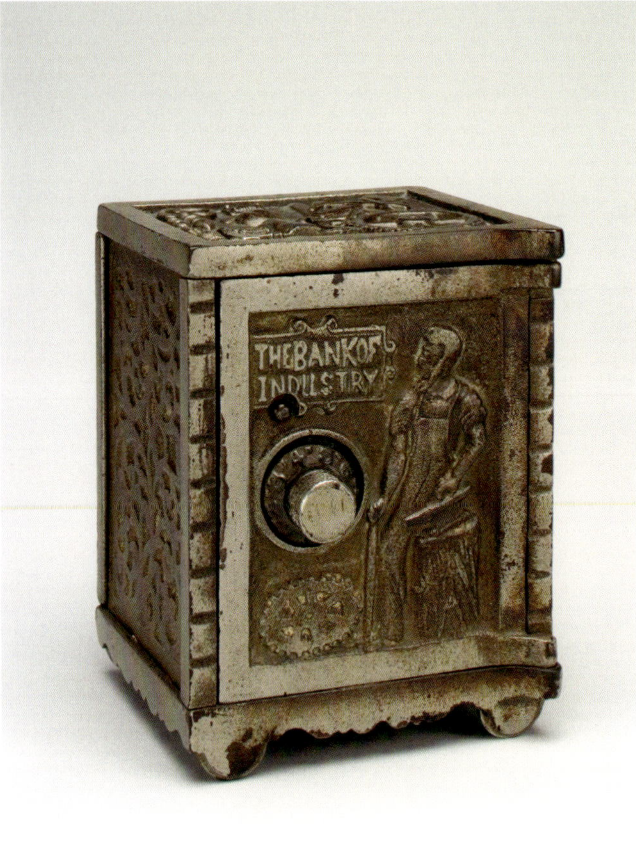

Fig. 5: *Bank of Industry*, c. 1904. Iron, 5 3/8 x 4 1/4 x 3 15/16 in.

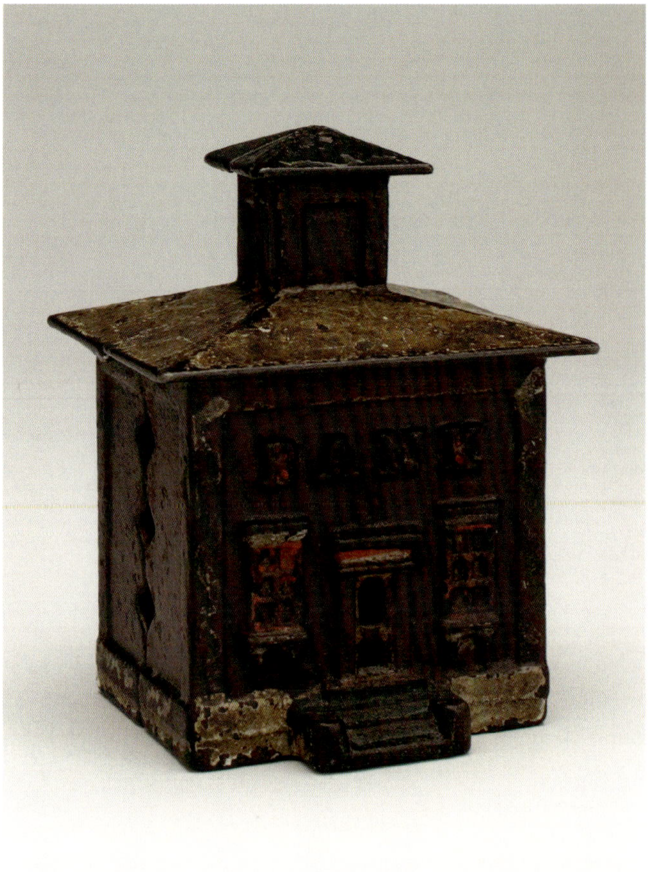

Fig. 6: *Cupola Bank*, 1869. Iron, pigment, 3 3/8 x 2 9/16 x 2 1/2 in.

specimen at any cost. Since expensive banks in the years before the post–World War II boom in prices still went for $25, the hobby seems inexpensive to modern eyes. But the joy of being rich and a collector was the chance to wrest an unobtainable treasure from the grasp of a fellow hunter. Like warfare or football, bank collecting in the early days could be a very rough affair indeed.

The stakes rose considerably with the dispersal of several high-profile collections. Walter Chrysler's thousand banks went on the block in 1955 with an elaborate illustrated catalog and stratospheric prices. *A Clown, Harlequin, and Columbine* manufactured around 1906 (pp. 13, 65) went for $2,000, while another mechanical of that date — *Shoot the Chute* (fig. 4 and p. 65), showing Buster Brown of comic-strip fame and his stalwart dog, Tige, on a Coney Island ride — commanded $1,200.[26] The elders of the "bankiana" community snapped up the rarest and priciest items on the first day of the sale, latecomers complained.[27] And thereafter, the days of the $25 bank were numbered. A decade later, the sale was still a source of griping, especially among collectors of do-a-stunt banks. "Walter [Chrysler] drove the price of penny banks sky high and it's never come down since," lamented an airline executive who owned eight hundred of them (plus what he claimed was the world's largest doll collection).[28] Ironically, however, as prices rose, more and more newcomers entered the field, buoyed up by postwar prosperity: a detective, a machinist, and a government clerk all developed noteworthy collections thanks to dogged persistence and a willingness to search in attics too dusty for the moneyed elite.

In 1952, after almost thirty years at the helm of his Ohio bank (including a hair-raising encounter with John Dillinger), Andrew Emerine retired. A few years later, he held a special showing of his toy bank collection, bemoaning once again the sharp rise in prices after the Chrysler sale. The exhibition was mounted to announce that the Emerine collection had been willed to his granddaughters, with the understanding that it would remain on display in its usual place "as long as the First National Bank building is intact."[29] But such was not to be. Even before Emerine's death in 1967, the collection — including one of the few intact examples of the rare *Freedman* bank — was sold to Edwin Mosler, Jr., head of the Mosler Safe Company, who promptly became a key figure in the close-knit world of mechanical and still bank enthusiasts.[30] Within that world, the names of daring collectors such as Mosler took on mythical dimensions. What they had and how they had gotten it became marks of genuine distinction. Thus the correspondence whereby Emerine had obtained the *Freedman* bank from a Mexican dealer in 1939

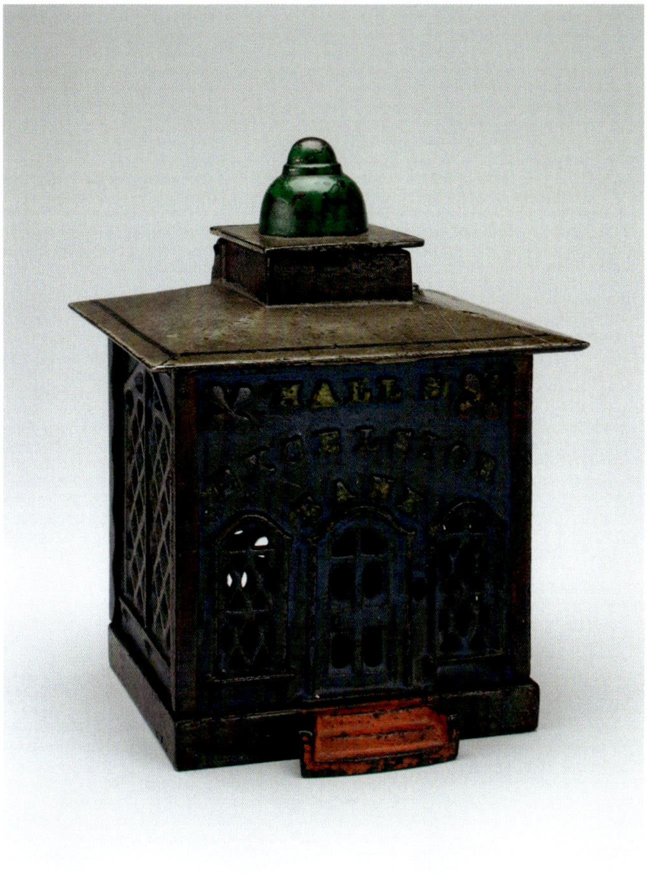

FIG. 7: *Hall's Excelsior* (or *Cashier Bank*), 1869. Iron, pigment, 5 ¼ x 4 x 4 ⅛ in.

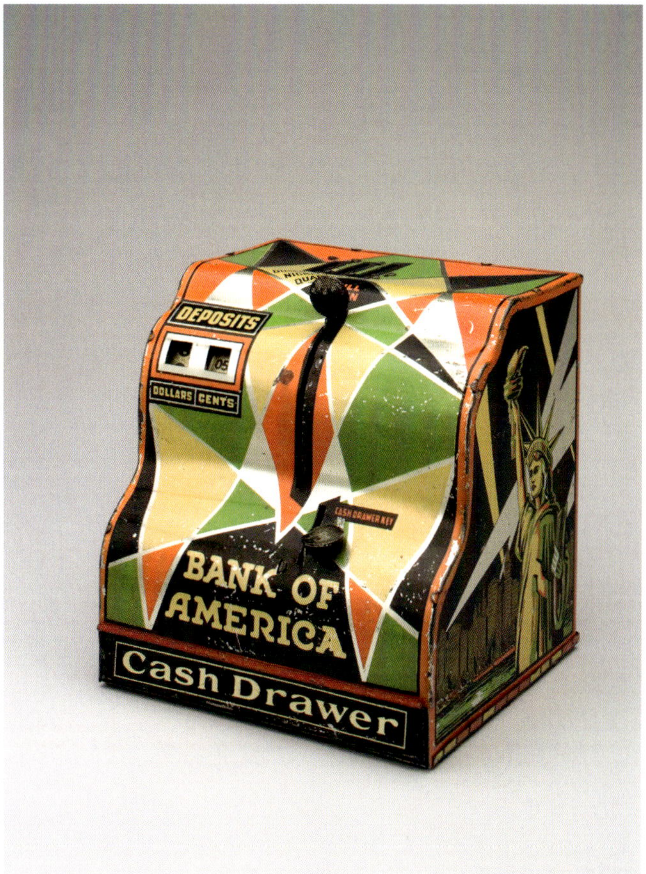

FIG. 8: *Bank of America Cash Drawer* (registering), c. 1920. Tin, pigment, 4 ⅝ x 4 ½ x 4 ⅛ in.

for $8 plus postage and duty was reprinted time and time again, the *Iliad* and *Odyssey* of bank lovers everywhere.[31]

Ed Mosler's interest in toy banks, unlike that of many of his peers, had been kindled by still banks — fashioned to resemble the massive safes that his family firm manufactured. Old-fashioned safes were so impressive, in fact, with their shiny hardware and baroque decorations, that they were often situated out in the lobby, where bank customers could marvel at the devices provided expressly to keep their deposits secure. In the banking business, appearances counted — especially classicism for the street facade and lots of curlicues for the safe indoors. The Stevens Company and its late-nineteenth-century competitors all made miniature cast-iron safes in a variety of sizes for home use. Some had working combination mechanisms. Most did not; the iconography sufficed. But all of them were beautifully decorated with images of Roman goddesses, heroic workers, and sonorous names: *Bank of Columbia*, *Bank of Industry* (fig. 5 and p. 101), or simply *Safe*, in bold Spencerian script with appended flourishes.[32]

In fact, the most common of all cast-iron banks, whether still or mechanical, was a likeness of a bank (or some portion thereof). According to a leading student of the subject, the first iron "architectural" bank ever made in the United States — by the Dover Stamping Company of Boston — was the *Cupola Bank* of 1869 (fig. 6 and p. 89), a neat little structure in the Greek Revival mode with the word BANK inscribed in block letters right above the front door. It was cast in two halves, with the money slot in the back, just below the canted roofline. A set of decorative holes afforded a tantalizing glimpse of the riches inside. To extract the money, however, the owner needed to undo a very long screw, which literally broke the poor bank in two.[33]

Such banks seem to have been produced by iron-casting firms that geared up during the Civil War and thereafter turned to the manufacture of all kinds of metal articles for peacetime use: hooks, chains, hinges, and most important, toys such as the wagons, miniature stoves, and sewing machines that began flooding the market in quantity around 1865.[34] Yet as early as the 1840s, Henry David Thoreau, visiting a backwoods town north of Bangor, Maine, expressed his bafflement at a store full of toy "dogs to bark, and cats to mew" in a place "where natives there hardly are yet."[35] Centered in Connecticut and surrounding Eastern states, the burgeoning mechanical-toy business laid the foundations for the golden age of action banks in the 1880s and 1890s. The first cast-iron mechanical bank ever made was a toy Bank-bank, or an image of a grown-up financial institution, known as *Hall's Excelsior* (fig. 7 and pp. 10, 36).[36] The idea for the bank (a "toy safe," as it's described in the original documents) was patented in 1869 by John D. Hall, a Yankee tinkerer from Massachusetts, and manufactured thereafter at the J. & E. Stevens plant in a picturesque valley in Connecticut called Frog Hollow.[37] Stevens rapidly became the General Motors of the toy bank industry.

The full title of the premier mechanical—Hall's/ Excelsior/ Bank—appears on the facade of a small building, slightly more ornate in detail than the *Cupola Bank*. The depositor pulls a doorbell to the right of the entrance. This gesture pops open the top of the cupola to reveal a tiny wooden monkey (sometimes a man) sitting at a teller's desk who receives the coin and drops it back inside to make the deposit.[38] There are countless variations on the theme of the Bank-bank: buildings of all shapes and sizes, tellers and clerks holding tiny trays for pennies, banks with and without monkey attendants. *The Tall Teller* (or *Bank Teller*, 1876), another Stevens Company product, is one of many such banks operated by gravity. A mustachioed bank officer standing at the ready in his fancy iron cage takes the deposit in his extended left hand. The weight of the coin lowers his arm into the innards of the mechanism, and he nods politely to acknowledge another successful transaction.[39]

Registering banks, which counted up the value of the coins deposited, were further byproducts of the conceit linking the miniature with the original. Sold under the rubric of "educational toys" in the Sears, Roebuck catalogs, registering banks were still popular in the 1920s, when the parents who bought them were avidly watching their own investments multiply (fig. 8 and p. 137). The Sears models of that time were priced from $.87 to $2.79, depending on how many denominations of coin they could tote up accurately.[40] Banking houses themselves also distributed "commercials," or still banks shaped like the headquarters building, some of which required a teller's key to open them on the premises. The savings-and-loan industry encouraged deposits by giving away banks in the form of satchels, purses, barrels, or little dream homes that reminded savers of what their accumulated capital could someday buy.[41] Finally, savings "clubs," already popular in the early 1890s, when putting aside money for a trip to the World's Columbian Exposition in Chicago accounted for a sharp rise in deposits (fig. 9 and p. 96), often issued toy banks devoted exclusively to hoarding nickels and dimes in anticipation of Christmas giving, tax bills, or even the cost of a winter's supply of coal.[42]

When journalists and collectors waxed poetic over old banks, however, it was rarely the little safes or the miniature bank tellers they had in mind. What they loved were the mechanicals: the movement, the bright colors, the bold shapes, the jokes and stories they told. For every old banker who shed a tear over a timeworn toy bank and the "Boy Blue" who had once cherished it, there were a dozen others fascinated by what they did, how they worked, and the crude, unconscious beauty of their forms. Banks were precious bits of nineteenth-century Americana. Not quite art, maybe, but something close to it, like Currier and Ives lithographs or Rogers Groups of sculpture.[43]

In 1948, when Katherine (Kax) Herberger spotted her first cast-iron bank in the window of a Winnetka, Illinois, antique shop, it was *Darktown Battery* (or *Baseball Bank*, c. 1888, pp. 12, 53) that caught her eye.[44] Dressed in colorful reds, blues, and yellows, a pitcher and a catcher conspire to throw out a rival batter wearing the exuberantly striped uniform of the "Possums." The coin serves as the baseball. Tension mounts when the press of a lever (disguised as a tree stump) engages the pitcher, who sends the penny rocketing toward home plate. The batter turns, swings, and misses. The ball/coin scoots into the catcher's pads and disappears. Strike one! It's over in an instant, in a blur of primary hues set off against the pinks and greens of the base, with its pattern of plumes, crossed bats, and balls.[45] Surely a bank like that was more than a mere bank, more than a toy! It was almost a work of art.

The same formal qualities and dramatic action that made *Darktown Battery* so appealing to Kax Herberger made banks such as *I Always Did 'Spise a Mule* great favorites among collectors, too. The title, couched in stage-"darky" dialect, is the supposed reaction of an African-American youngster to being bucked abruptly off the back of a mule, carrying the owner's coin with it. (This bank exists in two versions. In one, produced around 1879, the victim is dressed as a jockey [p. 40]. In the other, from about 1897, the boy is seated on a bench [fig. 10 and p. 61].) *'Spise a Mule* is only the best known of a large class of mechanical joke banks in which the humor generally comes at the expense of a person of color. For instance, the *Bad Accident* bank (c. 1888, p. 53) dumps the black driver of a mule cart onto a country road. The oddly named *Initiating Bank, First Degree*, made in New Britain, Connecticut (c. 1880, fig. 11 and p. 41), shows a black man being butted by a goat. "Mammy" of *Mammy and Child* (c. 1884, p. 49) rolls her eyes and feeds her sick child a penny instead of a dose of medicine. Stereotypes such as these reflect the low status of the former slave in the decades following the Civil War; much of the intended fun comes through violence visited upon the person of a hapless black (also known as a "Jolly Nigger" in the titles of many best-selling banks).

While banks such as the bucolic *Milking Cow* (c. 1888, fig. 12 and p. 53) mistreat white boys classified as bumpkins—the cow kicks over the bucket, the boy topples over backward, and the money disappears into the body of Old Bossie—the racist content of the large number of African-American images is impossible to deny. But what is noteworthy from a historical perspective is the manifest indifference of collectors and experts alike to the topical content of their banks. In addition to an attitude of casual contempt toward African Americans, a whole host of

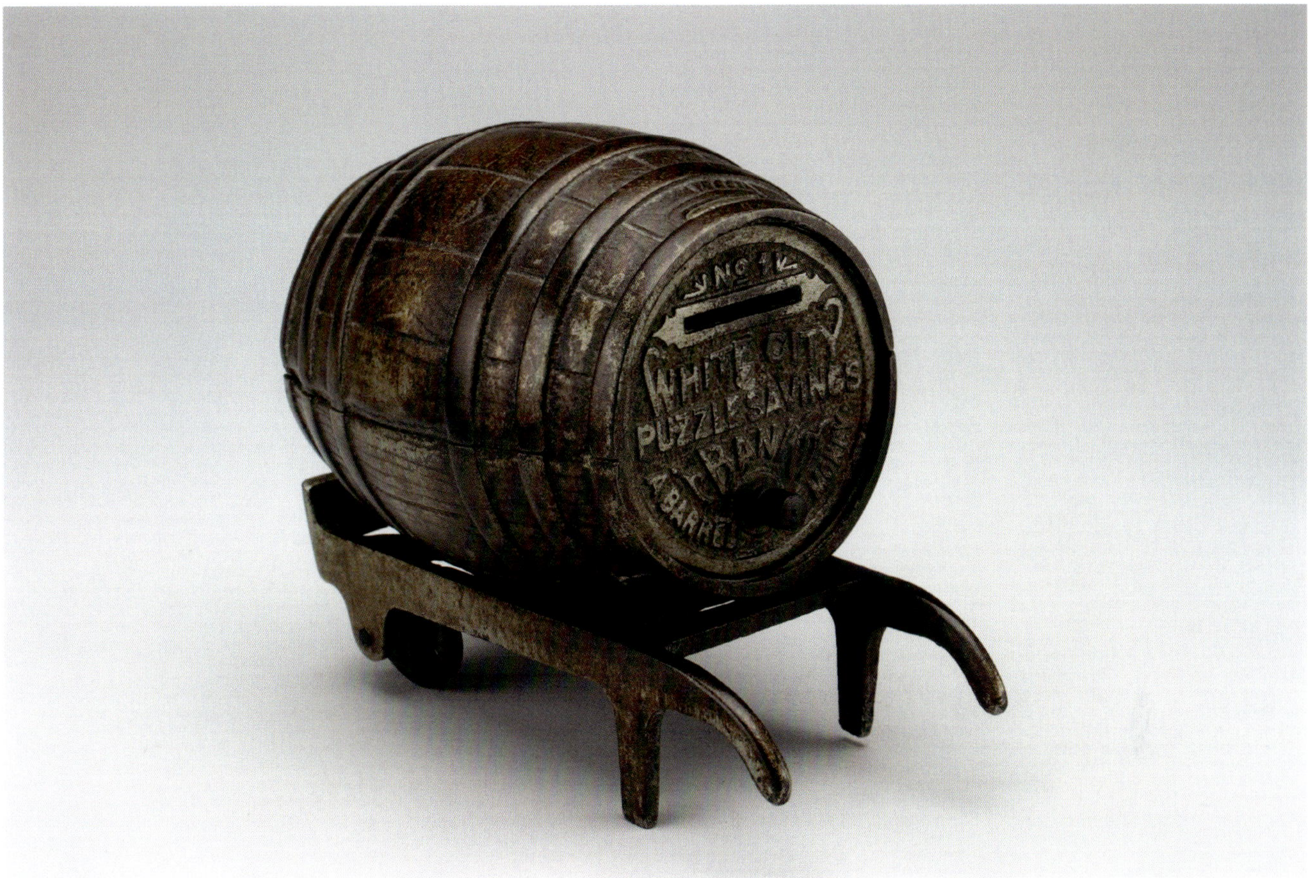

Fig. 9: *White City Barrel, No. 1, on Cart*, 1894. Iron, pigment, 5 x 3 ⁷⁄₈ x 3 ¼ in.

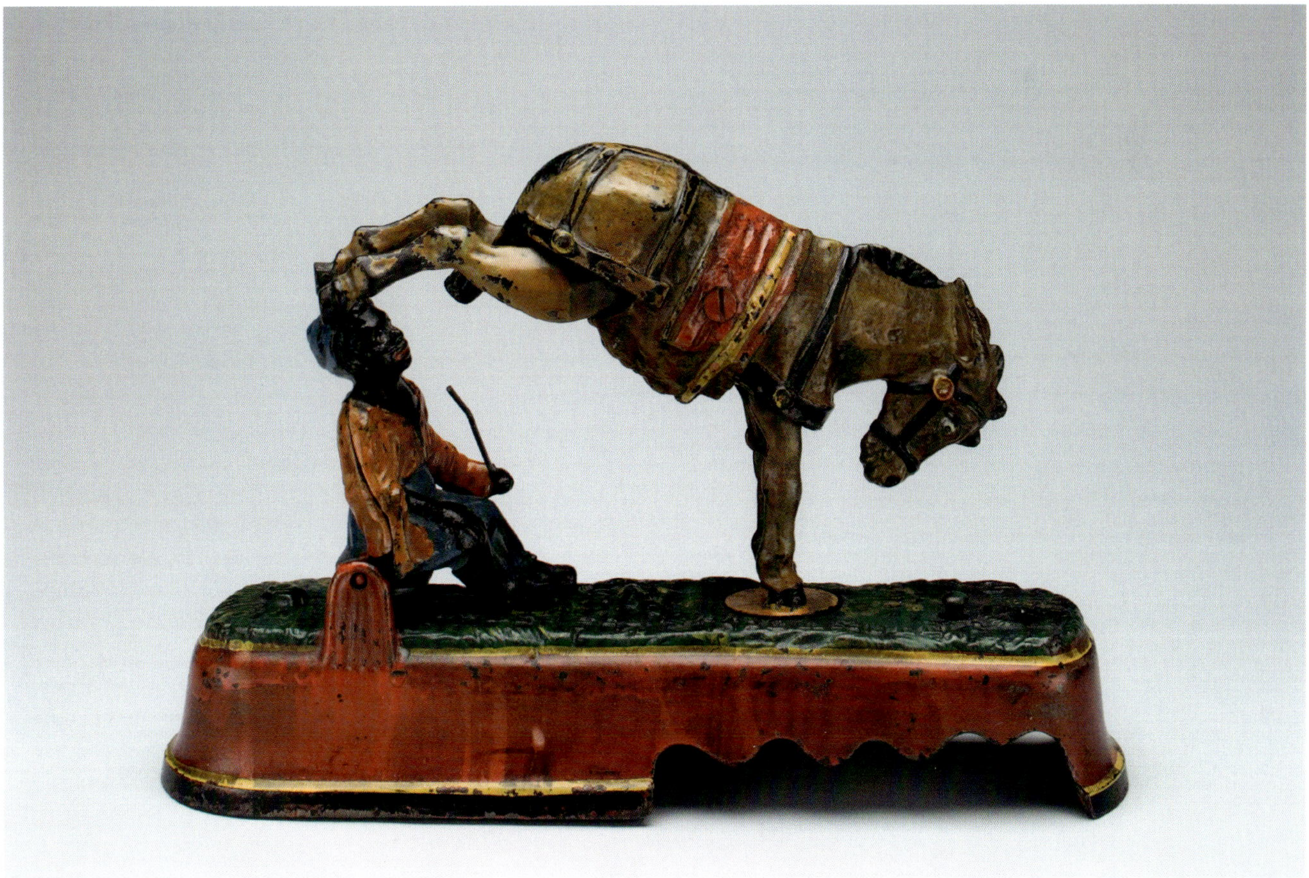

Fig. 10: *I Always Did 'Spise a Mule, Boy Seated on Bench*, c. 1897. Iron, pigment, 5 ¾ x 10 ⅛ x 2 ¹⁵⁄₁₆ in.

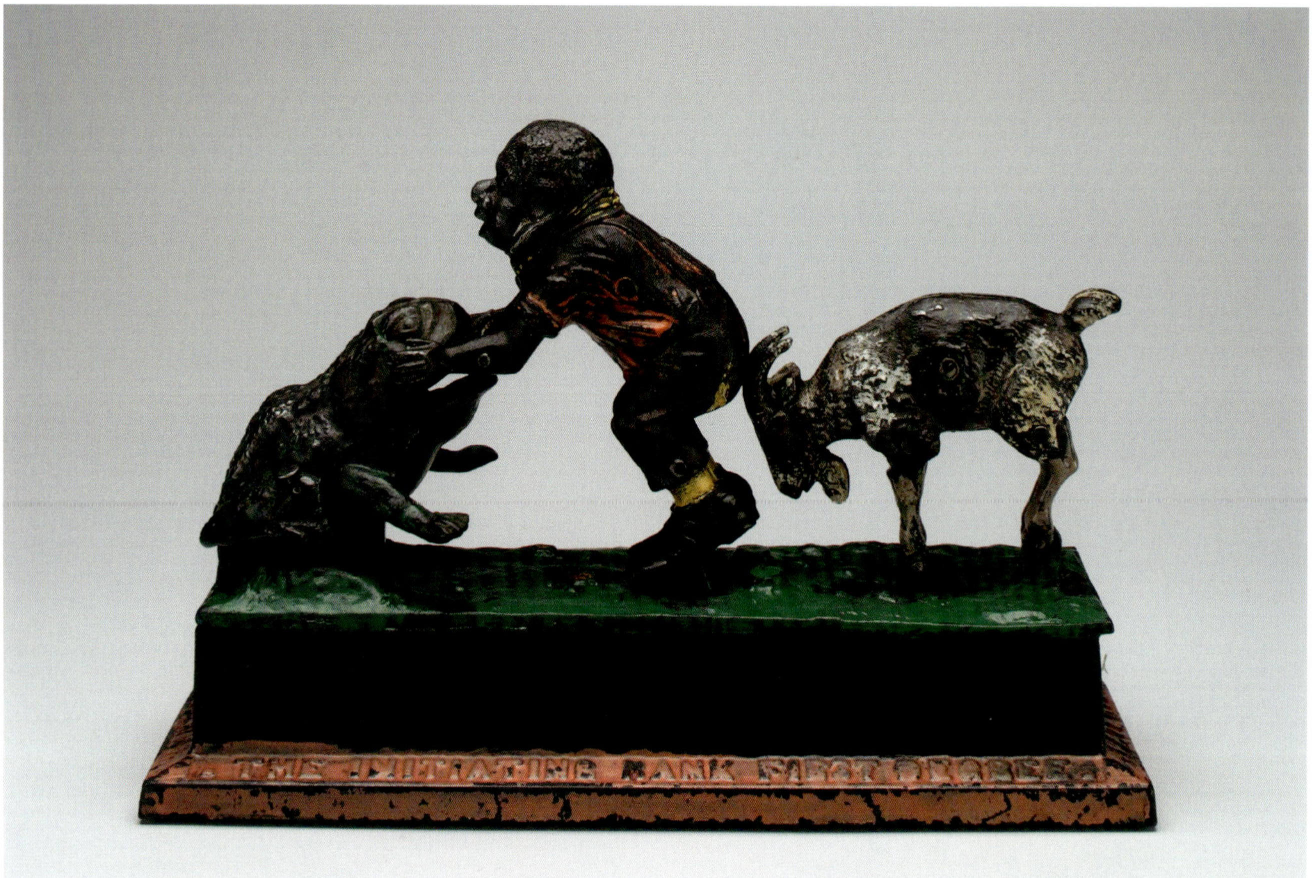

FIG. 11: *Initiating Bank, First Degree*, c. 1880. Iron, pigment, 6 ½ x 10 ⅜ x 3 5/16 in.

minorities — the Irish, the Chinese, and rural people in general — came in for a drubbing by the mechanical bank industry in the late nineteenth century. There was, it appears, a particularly Eastern, urban, nativist, middle-class sensibility at work in the choice of the themes designed to appeal to the mass market of potential buyers.

The two distinct types of black characters deployed on banks were stock figures in the national repertory of non-white, non-urban, non-Eastern "others." One was the mule-tending, chicken-snatching Uncle Remus, a farm laborer in a straw hat, while the other was the slickest of city slickers, dressed to the nines in fancy collars and ties. Both came directly from the world of popular entertainment. They were, on the one hand, the quasi-mythical "Southern Negroes" of Joel Chandler Harris and Thomas Nelson Page and, on the other, the comic Jim Crow and Zip Coon of the minstrel and the blackface circuits.[46] As late as 1929, when the craze for collecting mechanical banks began in earnest, the Sears, Roebuck catalog featured a "very funny action toy." When the key was wound, "the scared looking negro shuffle[d] along with a chicken dangling in his hand and a dog hanging on the seat of his pants."[47]

The collectors' curious disinterest in what the banks depict and why extends to other examples, to which no hint of racism attaches. Take *Professor Pug Frog's Great Bicycle Feat* (the title is molded on the base), from about 1892 (fig. 13 and p. 60): large, complex, and painted in lovely, clear primary colors — a prize in any collection. Pictured on the cover of a J. & E. Stevens catalog of the early 1890s, this bank is a puzzling artifact. At one end is a clown in a slashed tunic of European appearance, clutching a large perforated container. At the other is a stout woman, identified by the words "Mother Goose Circus" painted in black letters on the book immediately in front of her. In the middle is a high-wheeled bicycle, ridden by a strange beast with a doglike head: the presumptive Pug Frog. In any case, through a complex sequence of winding cranks, pressing levers, and coin positioning (*not*, for proper operation, in the animal's mouth, although it fits nicely there), the action commences. The Pug Frog rides in a circle, the penny plops into the basket, and Mother Goose falls over on her back clutching her book — and wagging her tiny cast-iron tongue furiously (singing?).

A bank that ought to have been odd enough to intrigue the most hardened collector, this one is clearly based on arcane entertainment conventions of the late nineteenth century, when "Perfesser" was the honorific applied to anyone prepared to dazzle a paying audience.[48] And Mother Goose was no stranger to the circus ring, either: in 1885 the Barnum and Bailey Circus adopted

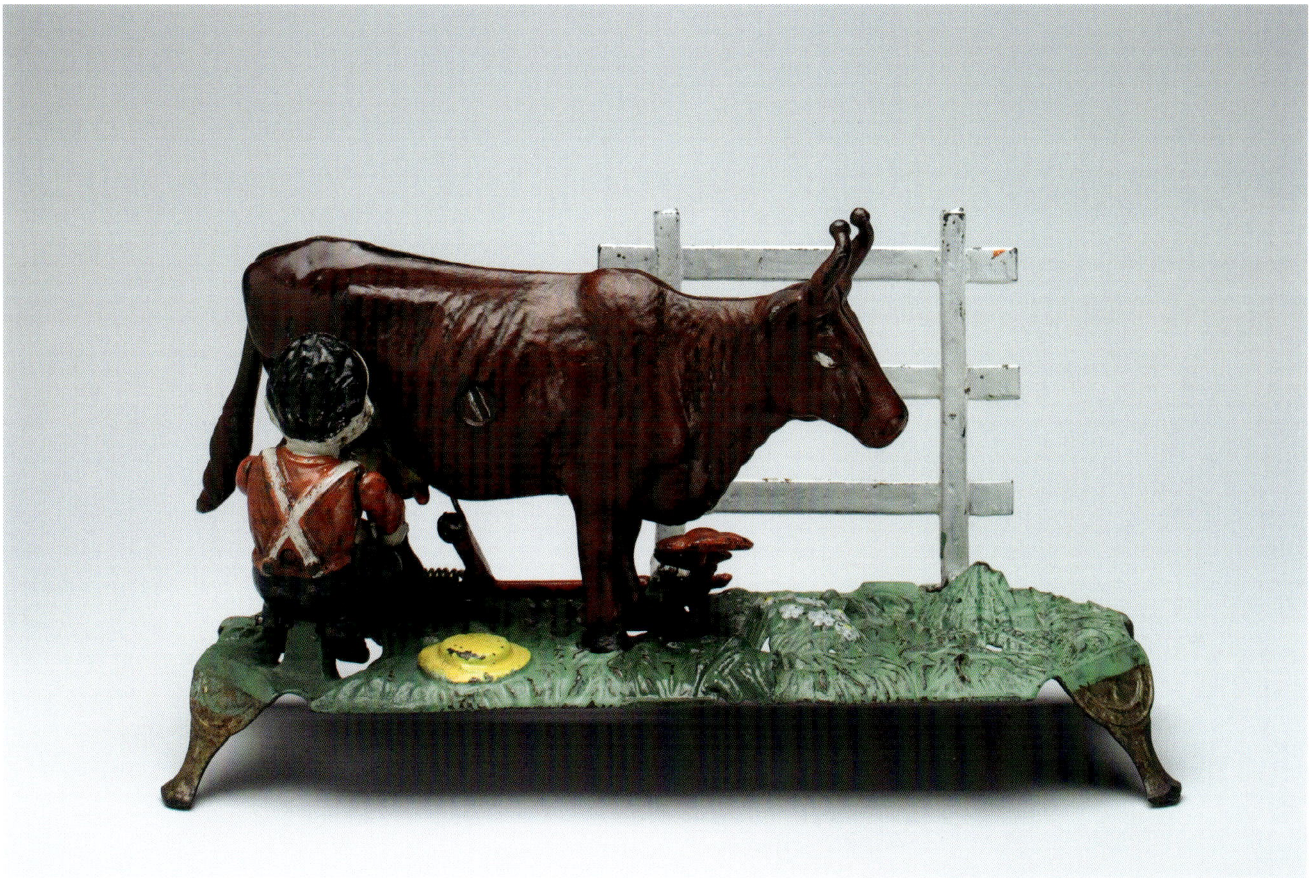

Fig. 12: *Milking Cow*, c. 1888. Iron, pigment, 5 3/8 x 9 3/4 x 3 1/16 in.

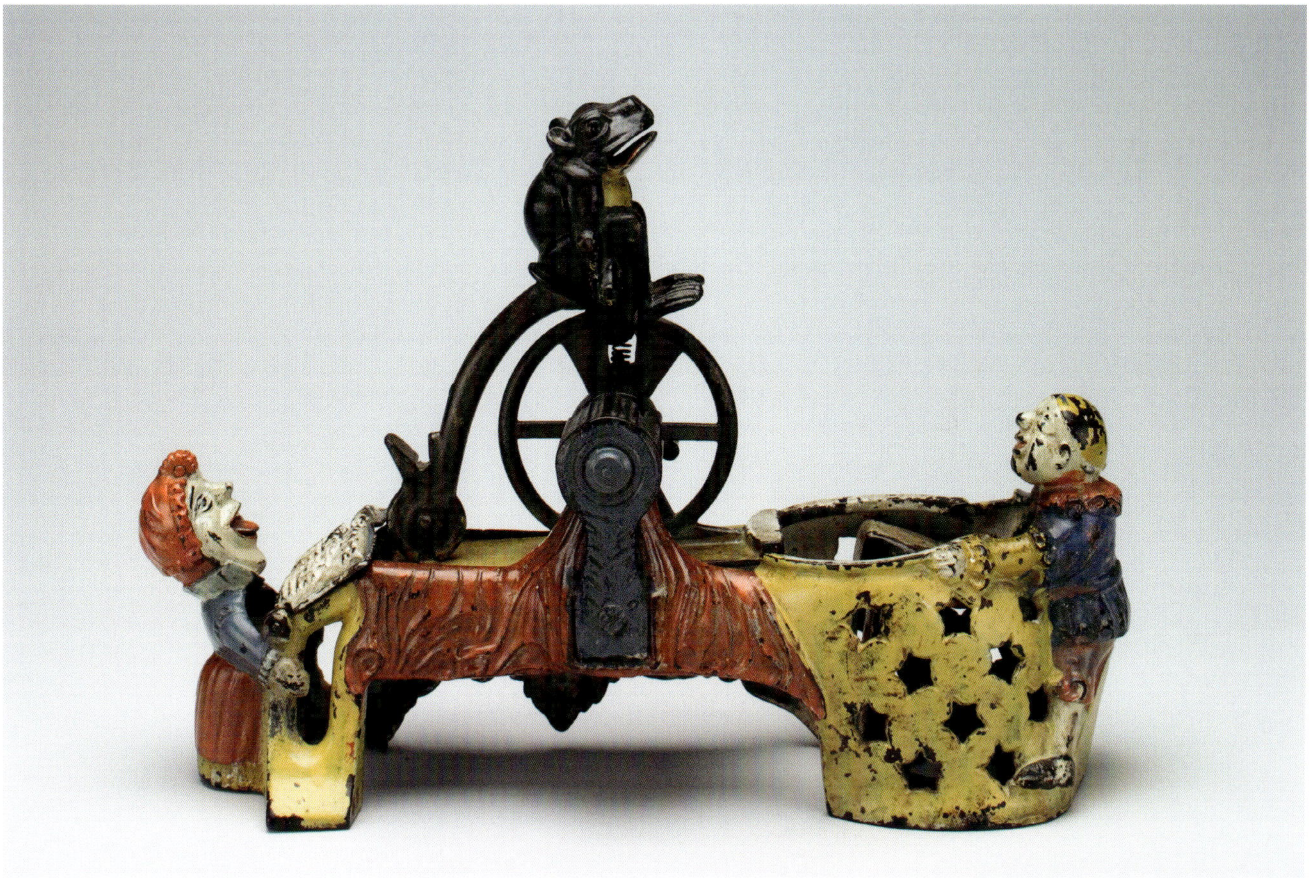

Fig. 13: *Professor Pug Frog's Great Bicycle Feat*, c. 1892. Iron, pigment, 7 3/4 x 10 3/16 x 3 3/16 in.

a nursery rhyme theme for its big parade, with the good lady directing the action from a horse-drawn float of her own.[49] As for the Pug Frog, if such a creature existed, he was surely a medicine-show wonderment, a fairy tale, a freak—or a humbug in the noble tradition of P. T. Barnum.[50]

It is hard to overestimate the popularity of the traveling circus in the heyday of the cast-iron bank, or the scope of its influence on the imagery of items ranging from cartoons, textiles, household items, and posters to toys and banks. Clowns, trick ponies, elephants, trained dogs, acrobats, and the lovely dancing columbine of the commedia del'arte were ubiquitous motifs. At the same time, the origins of these characters seem to have been of little concern to the collecting community, even in cases where the title of a bank is virtually meaningless without some broader cultural context. A whiteface clown bank that gulps down coins went by the title *Humpty Dumpty* for generations, even though it is clearly not the fantastic egg of the children's verse (fig. 14 and p. 45). Only in the 1950s did a bank collector who also went in for carved cigar-store figures notice the similarity between two of his treasures. Both of them, it emerged, were likenesses of the great nineteenth-century circus clown George Lafayette Fox, who performed under the name Humpty Dumpty.[51]

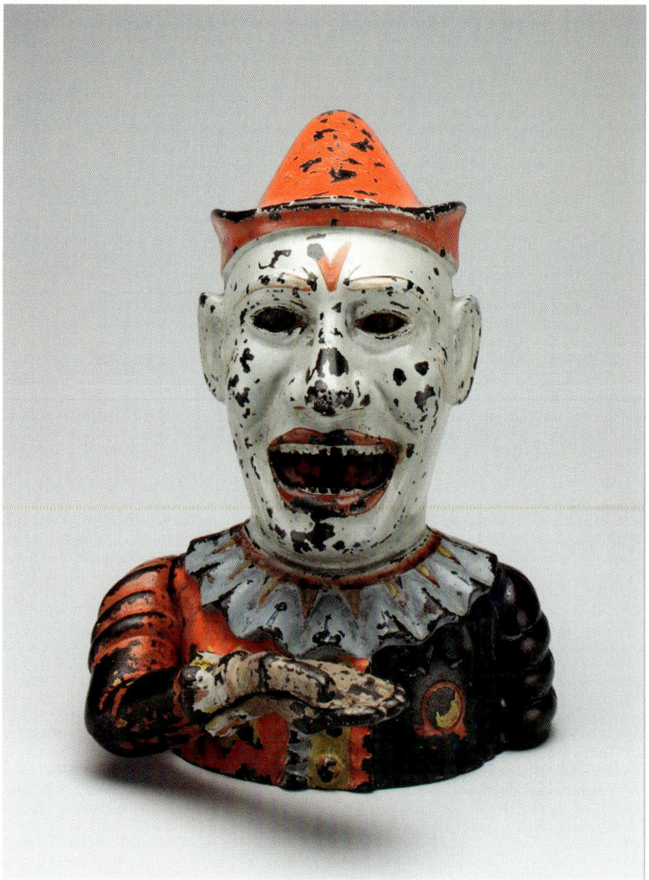

Fig. 14: *Humpty Dumpty*, c. 1882. Iron, pigment, 8 x 5 ½ x 5 ½ in.

The iconography of American penny banks remains a fertile field for inquiry. Their status as fine examples of Yankee craftsmanship, works of art, and even folk art (despite having been mass produced by mechanical means) was dramatically affirmed in the 1930s by the Index of American Design. Founded at the very end of 1935, the Index was one of many innovative New Deal projects aimed at preserving the usable skills of unemployed artists while also adding to the aesthetic wealth of the nation.[52] Unlike earlier programs for mural painters, writers, and musicians, the Index arose from a serious interest in collecting and preserving folk art that had gathered strength in the 1920s, alongside the hobbyists' fascination with banks. Spearheaded by key leaders in the visual arts—New York dealer Edith Halpert, curator Holger Cahill, collector Abby Aldrich Rockefeller, and sculptor Elie Nadelman—the folk art movement was both a response to the challenge of European modernism and a discovery that the formal elements of American vernacular products of the past prefigured the design features of contemporary abstract art. Nadelman's wood sculpture of the 1920s, with its crisp outlines, simple volumetric shapes, and forceful colors, bears more than a passing resemblance to the best of the multi-figured mechanical banks, for example.[53] And banks loomed large on the list of significant examples of American design chosen for reproduction by the Index.

The biographies of most of the artists who worked for the Index of American Design are sketchy. Often they were commercial artists; with the return of prosperity in the 1940s, they disappeared back into the ranks of the gainfully employed. While they were on the federal payroll, their creativity was also severely curtailed. Index plates were prepared using techniques perfected by archaeologists. Watercolor renderings of assigned models were most satisfactory to officials when they were most accurate and objective, without any mark of the maker's individuality. But it is clear that these government workers, like the thousands of viewers who have flocked to touring exhibits of Index plates in the years since, were captivated by the banks, both dumb and moving. *Teddy [Roosevelt] and the Bear* (fig. 15 and p. 68). *Frog on Round Base* (p. 36). *Speaking Dog* (p. 52). *Punch and Judy* (p. 49). *Uncle Sam* (p. 52). *Darktown Battery*. *Humpty Dumpty*. *Bank of Industry*. Safes. Animals. Houses. *Excelsior*. *Tammany*. Virtually all the banks that fascinated the collectors of the 1920s and 1930s appealed as well to the administrators of the 1930s and 1940s who chose the subject matter for the Index artists. As a consequence of the Index's work, preserved at the National Gallery of Art, there is no longer any doubt that banks are important works of vernacular sculpture that showcase America's long native traditions of mechanical ingenuity and commercial acumen.

In *The House of the Seven Gables* (1851), one of the early masterpieces of American literature, Nathaniel Hawthorne

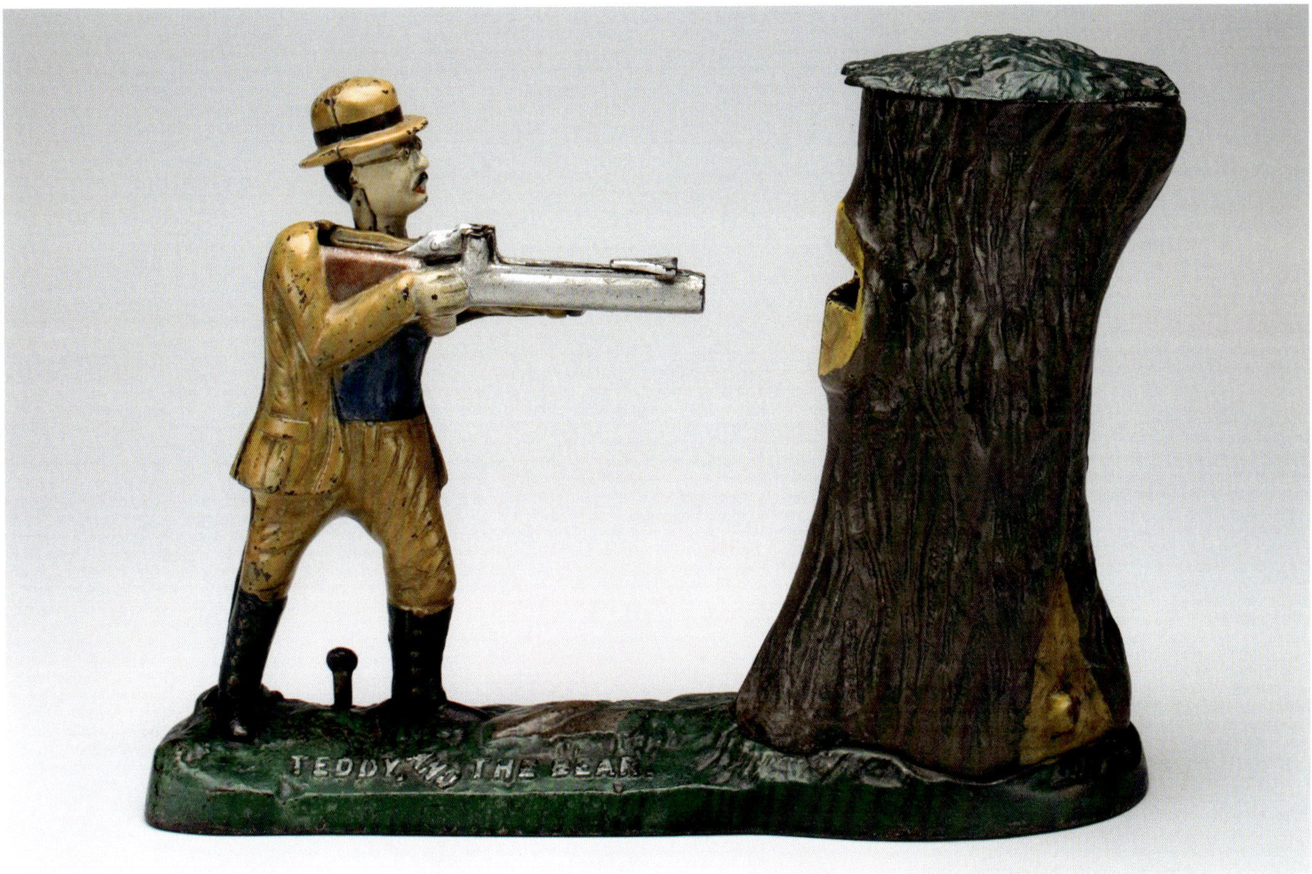

FIG. 15: *Teddy and the Bear*, c. 1907. Iron, pigment. 7 ¼ x 10 ³⁄₁₆ x 3 in.

offered an extended, meticulously detailed description of a street organ — a kind of crank-operated peepshow run for pennies by an Italian boy.[54] As he turned the handle, little paper figures appeared in his glass box. A milkmaid milked her cow. A miser counted out his gold. A lady swished her fan. A soldier raised his sword. Or the kind of subject matter apt to be found on later mechanical banks. (There are patent submissions for Italian organ-grinder banks from 1883 and 1891.) All of these devices — the fifty-cent iron banks, the automatons, the hurdy-gurdy machines — responded to America's rage for movement, for doing, for going, for avoiding stasis at any cost. And for magic: touch a lever, turn a crank, and presto (the name of several banks), something amazing always happens!

If bank collecting was a hobby for financial wizards in the early days, by the 1940s and 1950s the base of interest had widened dramatically. A club organized in Rhode Island among regional owners of toy banks of recognized value evolved in 1958 into the Mechanical Bank Collectors of America. The Still Bank Collectors Club of America followed in 1966. These organizations served to stabilize the market, identify major collections, and create the beginnings of a sketchy artifactual history. At the same time, the general public began taking an interest in banks for their decorative and nostalgic value. For example, A&P coffee used color photos of "antique bank collections" in its ads to suggest the savings offered by the use of its product. As the copy read, "You can bank on superb flavor in every cupful."[55] Southern Comfort (pp. 77, 80), Sears, *Liberty* magazine, at least one commercial bank, and the Book of Knowledge encyclopedia (p. 80) all offered inexpensive replicas (which have risen incrementally into the six-figure range between 1960 and the present). Some bank lovers even experimented with making brand-new old banks, using time-honored methods.[56] Enthusiasm was widespread enough to prompt an article in *American Home* in 1963 showing the homemaker how to display a collection of banks, patent papers, and similar memorabilia in the most effective way.[57]

But banks have even greater relevance in the twenty-first century as genuine historical documents revealing the values and preoccupations of an earlier day. Despite the distasteful racial biases and crude humor of some favorite examples, there are also banks clearly designed to set children on the path of virtues other than thrift. Among the prettiest of these preaching examples is *Tree Bank* (or *Boy Robbing Bird's Nest*, fig. 16 and p. 65), pictured in a 1906 Stevens Company catalog. Appealing for its wealth of natural detail, including vines, flowers, and berries, all painted in true-to-life colors, the bank depicts a lad

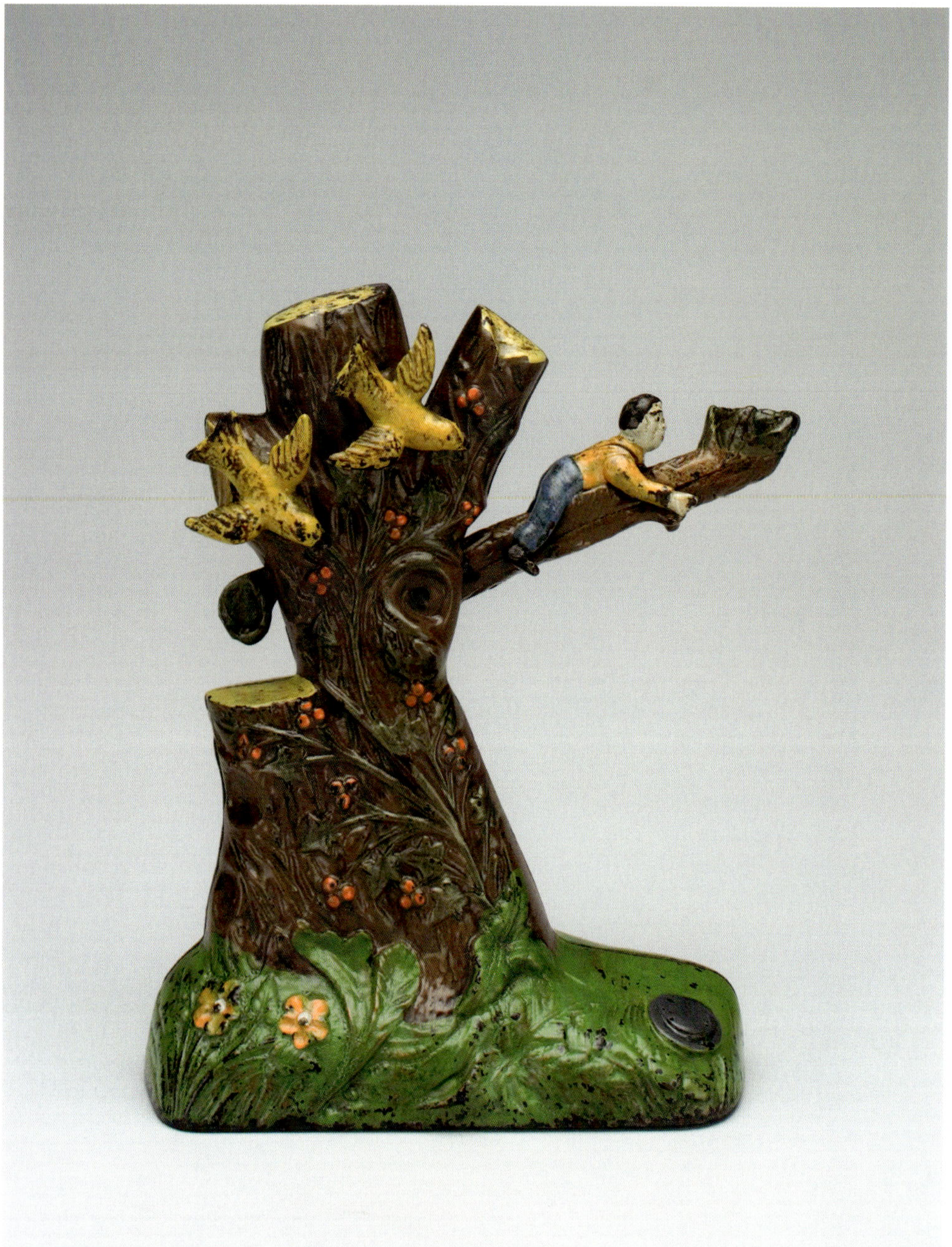

Fig. 16: *Boy Robbing Bird's Nest*, c. 1906. Iron, pigment, 7 ¼ x 6 x 3 3/16 in.

stretched out on a tree limb, trying to steal three tiny bird's eggs from a nest as the anxious avian parents hover nearby. To prove that stealing and cruelty to animals are very wrong indeed, operation of the bank causes the limb to snap and the little thief to plummet downward.

This is the kind of moralizing anecdote that dominates the pages of nineteenth-century American schoolbooks. The tale-in-verse of Mary and her lamb, a mainstay of the *McGuffey Readers*, was a lesson in kindness to God's creatures. The vignette of the boy and the eggs — the naughty-boy version of Mary — seems to have been a universal favorite, known in French and English retellings and often featured in Sunday-school papers.[58] Henry Ford, whose museum of American stuff in Dearborn, Michigan, housed banks along with the prodigious number of other items he collected, was a champion of the *McGuffey Readers* and sponsored new editions in the hope of reviving their ethical and moral influence on American youth. *Tree Bank*, then, is a reminder of that pervasive strain in nineteenth-century American thought and of the longing for the old certainties expressed in the collecting vogue of the pre–World War II years.[59]

Afghanistan (fig. 17 and p. 49), on the other hand, reminds us of how little has changed since this small bank, manufactured around 1885, alluded to the bloody news of the day. It shows the "Irak" Gate of the walled city of Herat in that nation's northwest quadrant, where the Second Anglo-Afghani War had recently been raging. An armed struggle between Great Britain and the Russian czar in which a secure overland route to England's Indian empire was at stake, hostilities around this twenty-five-hundred-year-old trading center dragged on intermittently from the 1840s until World War I. For Americans, the conflict yielded up heroic newspaper images of dashing British officers in khakis and pith helmets facing fierce, bearded Cossacks. The bank describes their struggle in terms of a heraldic British lion flanking one side of the gate and a Russian bear on the other.[60] Manufactured today — in plastic, of course — the same bank would be just as timely, although designers might be hard pressed to decide what heraldic symbol ought to appear opposite the American eagle.

Like other banks grounded in current affairs — the Spanish-American War, the conquest of the North Pole, the rise of the Anti-Monopolist Party in 1884 — *Afghanistan* suggests that the bank trade relied as heavily on what might be called novelties, or the iconography of the day's news and passing fancies, as it did on timeless parables. And that the banks of the period from 1870 to 1929 (the date of the last patent granted on a cast-iron mechanical) appealed to a broad spectrum of the buying public on widely assorted grounds. The early collectors, drawing on their own memories, tended to see banks in one primary dimension — as ideal children's Christmas presents, educating the young by reinforcing good behavior. Some banks put on a show. Some mimicked important grown-up activities. Some even gave the saver a piece of candy. But it seems likely that adults bought banks for their own use, too, largely on the basis of topicality or humor. Banks in this category were, or could be, transient objects of interest: cheap, engaging, but ultimately destined for the attic.

Modern banks made of china and plastic and rubber, while in no way as serious in content as *Afghanistan*, tend to be transitory in theme, too. Famous cartoon characters, advertising logos, tourist landmarks, and comic-book heroes dominate the inventory of banks manufactured since the 1960s.[61] Today's indulgent parent is likely to wrap up a Miss Piggy or a Batman bank (fig. 18 and p. 200) on Christmas Eve; the easy-to-remove rubber stoppers show that thrift is not the moral of this story. And scholars of the future will be left to ponder the deeper meanings of banks shaped like Mickey Mouse or something called the Pillsbury Doughboy. Meanwhile, it is a continual delight to marvel at the variousness, the high spirits, the color, and the canny sense of the moment demonstrated by these potent little specimens of American popular art.

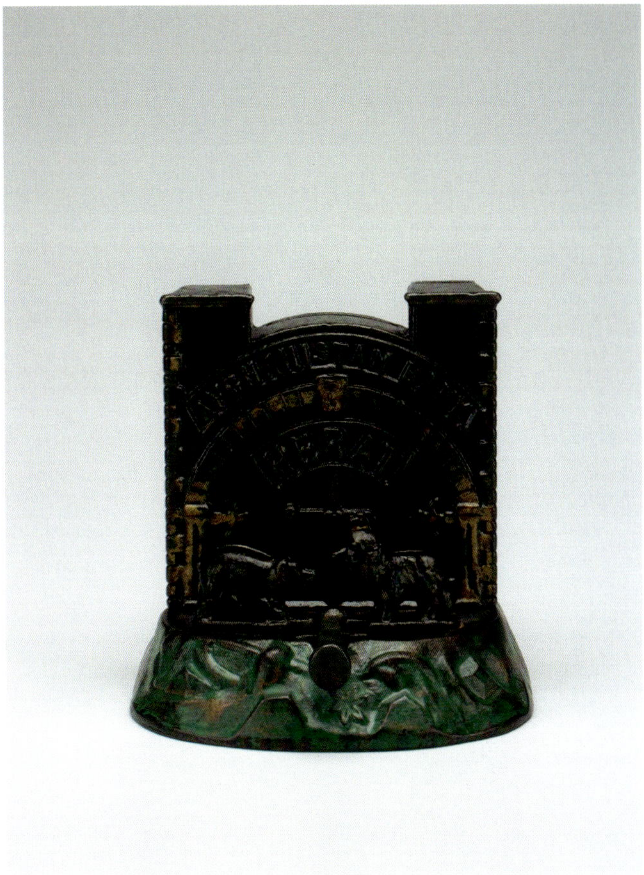

Fig. 17: *Afghanistan*, c. 1885. Iron, pigment, 3 1/2 x 3 7/16 x 3 1/8 in.

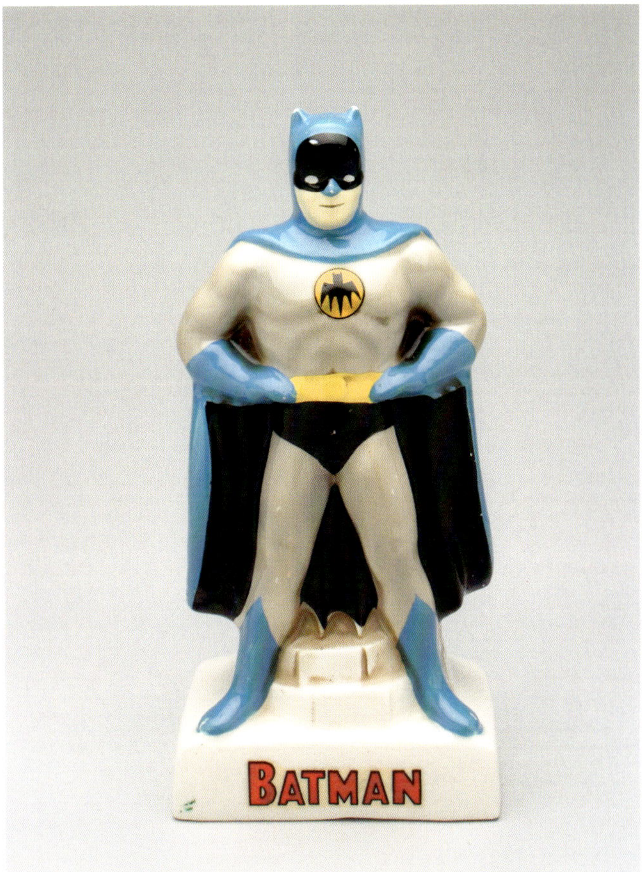

Fig. 18: *Batman*, c. 1950s – 60s. Ceramic, 6 15/16 x 3 3/8 x 2 5/16 in.

Notes

1. The most complete bibliography of articles on banks appears on the Mechanical Bank Collectors of America (MBCA) Web site, www.mechanicalbanks.org. The Scrapbook heading on this site reproduces the relevant literature in full, although the original page numbers for the periodicals are not listed. Given the rarity of that specialized literature in conventional libraries, it seems more useful to refer to the Web site material exactly as it is cited there.

   See, for example, MBCA Scrapbook, Norman Sherwood, "The Rarest Bank?" *Vocations* (February 1938), for a discussion of the 1926 *Antiques* notice, which was about the Moskowitz Collection. David Moskowitz is subsequently credited with having the first substantial mechanical bank collection in the United States, although he (and his banks) had dropped from sight by the time the craze peaked in the 1930s; see MBCA Scrapbook, Richard M. Lederer, Jr., "The Mechanical Banker, Part V," *Collectors Roundup* (March 1947). The Scrapbook is hereafter cited as MBCA.

2. Elmer Rand Jacobs's story is recounted in MBCA, "When Thrift Was Fun," *New York Visitor* (October 1943). The Jacobs Collection was displayed at the Seaman's Bank for Savings in New York City. J. Hall of Watertown, Massachusetts, patented the mechanism for the *Tammany Bank*; see MBCA, H. Blair Hull, "The First Five Years of Patented Toy Banks," *Antiques* (March 1941), fig. 9. Hall, who was obsessed with banks that disposed of coins with a gravity-operated mechanism, took out many similar patents as well.

3. For the H. W. Griffith Collection of two hundred mechanical banks, see "Toy Banks Make It Fun to Save," *Pittsburgh Press*, December 16, 1945.

4. Elmus Wicker, *Banking Panics of the Gilded Age* (New York: Cambridge University Press, 2000), xii.

5. Howard Bodenhorn, *A History of Banking in Antebellum America* (New York: Cambridge University Press, 2000), 7.

6. Franklin Ornstein, *Savings Banking: An Industry in Change* (Reston, Va.: Reston Publishing, 1985), 6, 154.

7. MBCA, Ruth and Larry Freeman, *Cavalcade of Toys*, Chapter 9 (1942).

8. "History of the Piggy Bank," www.piggybankworld.com.

9. For performing pigs of the nineteenth century, see Ricky Jay, *Learned Pigs and Fireproof Women* (New York: Warner Books, 1986), 9–27.

10. "Savings Official Loses Money in Banks," *New York Sun*, April 17, 1946.

11. Arthur E. Corby, "Penny Banks Show Makers' Odd Fancies," *New York Sun*, August 31, 1931.

12. MBCA, Ruth Lee Webb," Mechanical Banks, Old and New," *American Collector* (September 1938).

13. Werner Muensterberger, *Collecting: An Unruly Passion* (New York: Harcourt Brace, 1994), 14–24, offers a psychological explanation for the collecting itch, linked to the child's use of toys to assuage feelings of abandonment and loneliness. He cites the critic and theorist Walter Benjamin: "Like the dedicated collector, the child absorbed with his toys 'dreams his way not only into a remote or bygone world, but at the same time into a better one.'"

    See also Philipp Blom, *To Have and to Hold: An Intimate History of Collectors and Collecting* (Woodstock, N.Y.: Overlook Press, 2003), 206–7, who argues that the accumulation of artifacts structures life and keeps chaos at bay. Susan Stewart, *On Longing: Narratives of the Miniature, the Gigantic, the Souvenir, the Collection* (Durham, N.C.: Duke University Press, 1993), 162, calls the collector's ordered place a "homemade universe."

14. MBCA, pamphlet, First National Bank of Fostoria, Ohio, c. 1939.

15. See MBCA, "The Bulletin Board," *House and Garden* (June 1939), with photos of mechanical banks in the collection of the First National Bank of Boston. The article argues that these banks taught thrift by making saving into a delightful game.

16. Reulah Schact, "Rare Collection of Old, Mechanical Banks to Be Displayed during 6th War Loan Drive," *St. Louis Globe Democrat*, November 26, 1944.

17. MBCA, "On the Air," *New Bulletin* (Savings Banks Association of New York) 22 (August 21, 1942).

18. Mark Haber, "Mechanical Penny Banks," *Hartford Banker* (December 1937): 5; and MBCA, "Walter's Banks," *New Yorker* (1938).

19. MBCA, Norman Sherwood, "The Walter P. Chrysler Collection of Old Mechanical Penny Banks," *Avocations* (December 1938). A piece of bumper-sticker theology attributes a similar quote to the late billionaire collector Malcolm Forbes: "The one who dies with the most toys wins!"

20. Walter P. Chrysler, with Boyden Sparkes, *The Life of an American Workman* (New York: Dodd, Mead, 1937), 37, 208. Although he kept his office, Chrysler retired in 1935 and spent his time collecting banks, fishing, and working on his autobiography.

21. Curator Donna Braden of the Henry Ford Museum, in a letter to the author (July 19, 2005), discusses the provenance of the Ford banks, most of which the automaker did not collect personally, although maxims about thrift, plucked from the *McGuffey Readers* and similar sources, were part of his working vocabulary.

22. William Gebmain Dooley, "Penny Bank Collectors," *New York Times*, May 9, 1937.

23. MBCA, Mrs. George Thompson, "Children's Banks of Other Days," *Savings Banker* (January 1937).

24. The complete text of this rare book is available on the MBCA Web site.

25. MBCA, narrative ad for Norman Sherwood's New Jersey shop, "All This Talk about Banks Is So . . . Confusing," *Hobbies* (September 1935).

26. *The Chrysler Collection of Mechanical and Still Banks* (New York: David Hollander, 1955), unpaginated.

27. "Collectors Stage Run on Toy Banks," *New York Times*, April 9, 1955.

28. "Old Penny Banks Pay off in Gold," *Hobby Digest* (July 1967): 4.

29. MBCA, unidentified newspaper clipping, Connie Barton, "Fostoria Ex-Banker Spends 35 Years Collecting Banks," October 31, 1958.

30. Harry Stoneberger, "Andrew Emerine, 94, Claimed Early Today," [Fostoria, Ohio] *Review Times*, July 3, 1967; and MBCA, F. H. Griffith, "20th-Century Savings Bank," *Hobbies* (January 1973).

31. MBCA, unsigned, untitled article, *Mechanical Banker* (April 1983). This is the official journal of the Mechanical Bank Collectors of America. The same issue announced that Emerine's *Freedman*, which had been sold to Mosler, had recently become the property of Stephan A. Steckbeck, one of the magazine's editors.

32. Andy and Susan Moore, *The Penny Bank Book: Collecting Still Banks* (Atglen, Pa.: Schiffer Publishing, 2000), 19; and Don Duer, *Penny Banks around the World* (Atglen, Pa.: Schiffer Publishing, 1997), 9.

33. Don Duer, *A Penny Saved: Still and Mechanical Banks* (Atglen, Pa.: Schiffer Publishing, 1993), 7. Duer co-curated a 1983 exhibition of architecture-themed banks at the Cooper-Hewitt Museum in New York City; reviewed by the *New York Times*, the show proved to be a milestone in the scholarly appreciation of banks. See Rita

Reif, "Penny Banks as Miniature Buildings," *New York Times*, August 7, 1983.

34. Harvey Green, *The Light of the Home: An Intimate View of the Lives of Women in Victorian America* (New York: Pantheon, 1983), 48 – 51.

35. Karal Ann Marling, *Merry Christmas!: Celebrating America's Greatest Holiday* (Cambridge, Mass.: Harvard University Press, 2000), 297 – 99.

36. MBCA, Louis H. Hertz, "Mechanical Toy Banks," 1947, typescript.

37. Hall apparently sold or assigned his patents to Stevens. In any case, *Excelsior* was being made in Connecticut before 1871.

38. MBCA, John D. Meyer and Larry Freeman, "Old Penny Banks" (1952) on the action of *Hall's Excelsior*.

39. MBCA, F. H. Griffith, "Bank Teller Bank," *Hobbies* (February 1953).

40. Joseph J. Schroeder, Jr., ed., *1923 Sears, Roebuck Catalogue* (Northfield, Ill.: Digest Books, 1973), 495.

41. MBCA, "Old Coin Banks Now Collector's Item," *Burroughs Clearing House* (October 1938).

42. Helen J. Lang, "Old Style Mechanical Coin Banks Again Are Popular," *Boston Evening Transcript*, January 8, 1938; and MBCA, Frederic Seabranch, "The 'Acorns' from Which Our National Thrift Has Grown," *Building-Loan Journal* (June 1939).

43. MBCA, Walter A. Dyer, "'A Penny Saved . . . ' Quaint Curios of a 19th-Century Childhood," *House and Garden* (July 1930).

44. MBCA, Katherine Robertson, "Fascinating Slice of Early Americana," *Phoenix* (January 1972). See also the essay by Corine Wegner in the present book, p. 11.

45. MBCA, F. H. Griffith, "Darktown Battery Bank," *Hobbies* (June 1965).

46. Robert Toll, *Blacking Up* (New York: Oxford University Press, 1988), 36ff. A widely circulated quiz for schoolchildren during Black History Month in 2005, "Toys Ain't Us," identified a number of racist banks but did not comment on the origins of their pictorial conventions. For printed nineteenth-century advertising caricatures of minstrel-show stars virtually identical to the black figures on the banks, see David Carlyon, *Dan Rice* (New York: Public Affairs, 2001), 52. Rice himself wore a short, striped tunic for his circus act almost identical to that of Professor Pug Frog's clown.

47. Pamela B. Nelson, "Toys as History: Ethnic Images and Cultural Change," unpaginated; www.ferris.edu/news/jim crow/links.toys.

48. On "Perfessers," see David Armstrong and Elizabeth Metzger Armstrong, *The Great American Medicine Show* (New York: Prentice Hall, 1991), 175 – 84.

49. Tom Ogden, *Two Hundred Years of the American Circus* (New York: Facts on File, 1973), 156.

50. There are several varieties of puglike frogs, that is, frogs with the features of pug dogs, but none of bicycle-riding size. For "humbuggery," see Bluford Adams, *E Pluribus Barnum: The Great Showman and the Making of U.S. Popular Culture* (Minneapolis: University of Minnesota Press, 1997), 91, and Janet M. Davis, *The Great Circus Age* (Chapel Hill: University of North Carolina Press, 2002), 223.

51. The mystery and the solution (once in the 1950s and again in 1975) are revealed in an unsigned, untitled note in the April 1981 issue of the MBCA's *Mechanical Banker*.

52. Erwin O. Christensen, *The Index of American Design* (Washington, D.C.: National Gallery of Art, 1950), xii – xiii.

53. Erika Doss, "American Folk Art's 'Distinctive Character'," in *Drawing on America's Past: Folk Art, Modernism, and the Index of American Design* (Washington, D.C.: National Gallery of Art, 2002), 68.

54. This passage from Hawthorne's novel is discussed in Patricia Sawyer Lord and Daniel J. Foley, *The Folk Arts and Crafts of New England* (Radnor, Pa.: Chilton Books, 1975), 248

55. The 1949 A&P ad, which can be found in the MBCA files, ran in many magazines of the period. F. A. O. Schwartz, the New York City toy emporium, carried "antique" cast-iron banks for many years.

56. *Liberty's Uncle Sam*, for example, was issued in 1974 and sold for $19.95, delivered. The *Southern Comfort* bank of 1953 (p. 80), offered first to legitimate collectors upon receipt of requests on letterhead, was a shooting bank (a *Creedmore* type), with a Confederate soldier firing on a liquor bottle. By the early 1950s, quantities of replicas (and fake versions of the bank) were in wide circulation.

57. MBCA, "You Can Enjoy the Fascinating Fun of Old-Time Penny Banks," *American Home* (November 1961). The photograph in the article pictures an *Excelsior*, a *Speaking Dog*, an *Uncle Sam*, and a large cast-iron still bank in the form of a pig.

58. According to Karen Nelson Hoyle, director of the Children's Literature Research Collection at the Elmer L. Andersen Library, University of Minnesota, an 1853 collection of children's stories included "The Little Robbers" by the French academic Guizot. A second tale, "The Brigand's Son" (1846), was published in a collection entitled *Moral Tales* in 1852; both contained versions of the egg-stealing tale. Such volumes of ethical instruction were ubiquitous. See, for example, Joseph Alden's *Choice Stories* for the Young (n.d.), which includes "The Young Robber." *The Webster's Speller* ("Old Blue Back") of 1857 featured strong injunctions against stealing and an illustration of "The Country Maid and Her Milk Pail," which seems to be the model for another popular bank, in which the cow kicks a boy and the pail spills.

59. On Ford and the readers, see Harvey C. Minnich, *Old Favorites from the McGuffey Readers* (New York: American Book, 1936), compiled at the height of the revival with Ford, Hamlin Garland, and John Studebaker listed among the associate editors.

60. Until 1910 or so, products such as Liebig's famous meat extract came in packages adorned with exotic scenes of Western military figures in the bazaars of Afghanistan.

61. See Vickie Stulb, *Modern Banks* (Gas City, Ind.: L-W Book Sales, 1997).

THE KATHERINE KIERLAND HERBERGER COLLECTION

Catalogue of the Herberger Collection

SCOPE

The following catalogue includes objects in two main categories, Mechanical Banks and Still Banks. The latter are subcategorized Iron, Tin, Other Metals, Wood and Other Organic Media, Ceramic, Glass, and Plastic; items are included in a given subcategory according to the primary material used.

ORDER

Historical records for many banks in the collection are spotty, inconclusive, or even nonexistent. Nonetheless, every effort has been made to ascertain specific data for each object; several sample captions appear at right.

Individual entries are organized by a bank's known title or, where untitled, by its type (e.g., Safe) or with a simple identification (e.g., Drum); designer (with life or active dates where known); manufacturer/maker and place of manufacture (where known); date (whether exact or approximate); materials employed; dimensions (height by width by depth); and Minneapolis Institute of Arts accession number.

Catalogue illustrations are organized within a chronological framework and, within that, alphabetically and by accession-number order. Captions appear on the reverse of the pages on which banks are illustrated (e.g., *Elephant and Three Clowns on Tub* is illustrated on page 45, and its caption is on page 46). Banks that could not be dated precisely are grouped by approximate year (e.g., c. 1870), decade, or general period, depending on the information available.

Examples:

Elephant and Three Clowns on Tub, c. 1882
James H. Bowen, American (active c. 1877–1906), designer
J. & E. Stevens Company, Cromwell, Connecticut (1843–1950s), manufacturer
Iron, pigment
5 11/16 x 5 11/16 x 3 11/16 in.
2003.236.4a,b

Toy block, 20th century
Hong Kong
Metal, silver plate
2 15/16 x 2 7/8 x 2 7/8 in.
2003.236.832

MECHANICAL BANKS

Horse Race, Flanged Base, c. 1871
John D. Hall, American, designer
J. & E. Stevens Company, Cromwell, Connecticut (1843 – 1950s), manufacturer
Iron, tin, pigment, thread
5 1/2 x 6 1/2 x 6 1/4 in.
2003.236.1

Hall's Excelsior
(or *Cashier Bank*), 1869
John D. Hall, American, designer
J. & E. Stevens Company, Cromwell, Connecticut (1843 – 1950s), manufacturer
Iron, pigment
5 1/4 x 4 x 4 1/8 in.
2003.236.931

Jolly Nigger, c. 1872
Peter Adams and Charles G. Shepard, American, designers
Shepard Hardware Company, Buffalo, New York (1866 – 92), manufacturer
Iron, pigment
6 3/4 x 4 7/8 x 4 7/8 in.
2003.236.712

Bear and Tree Stump, c. 1870 – 80
H. L. Judd Manufacturing Company, Wallingford, Connecticut (c. 1830 – 1960s), manufacturer
Iron, pigment
5 x 2 7/8 x 1 5/8 in.
2003.236.11

Horse Race, Straight Base, c. 1871
John D. Hall, American, designer
J. & E. Stevens Company, Cromwell, Connecticut (1843 – 1950s), manufacturer
Iron, metal, pigment, thread
4 3/4 x 5 5/8 x 5 5/8 in.
2003.236.113

Home Bank, with Dormer Windows, 1872
Doras A. Stiles, American, designer
J. & E. Stevens Company, Cromwell, Connecticut (1843 – 1950s), manufacturer
Iron, pigment
5 1/4 x 4 3/8 x 4 7/8 in.
2003.236.930

Home Bank, No Dormer Windows, 1872
Doras A. Stiles, American, designer
J. & E. Stevens Company, Cromwell, Connecticut (1843 – 1950s), manufacturer
Iron, pigment
5 1/4 x 4 3/8 x 4 7/8 in.
2003.236.937

Frog on Round Base, c. 1872
Russell Frisbie, American, designer
J. & E. Stevens Company, Cromwell, Connecticut (1843 – 1950s), manufacturer
Iron, lead, pigment
4 x 4 7/16 x 4 7/16 in.
2003.236.313

Magic Bank, 1873
Henry W. Prouty, American, designer
J. & E. Stevens Company, Cromwell, Connecticut (1843 – 1950s), manufacturer
Iron, pigment
5 1/4 x 4 1/4 x 5 1/4 in.
2003.236.928

MECHANICAL BANKS

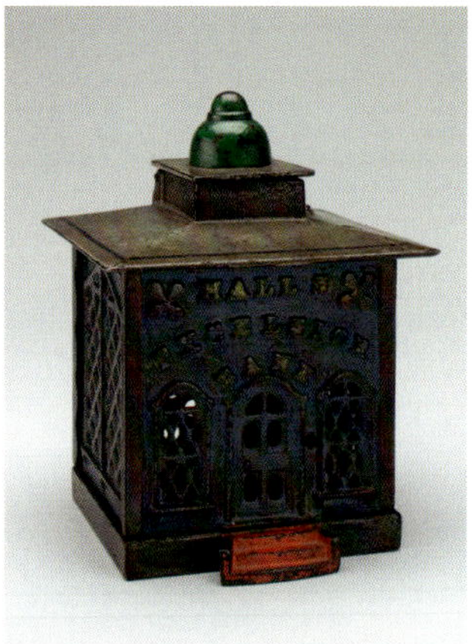

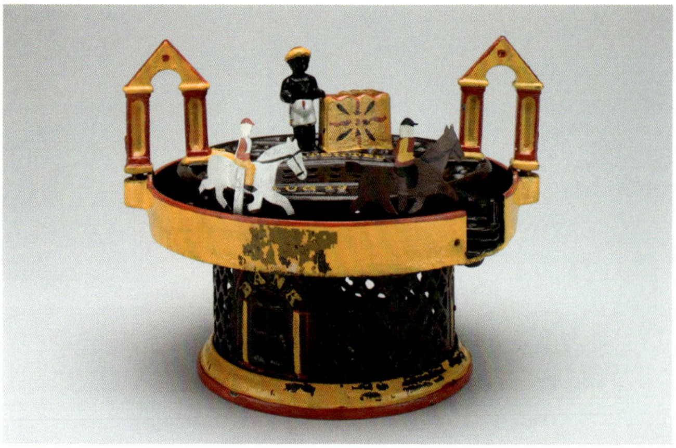

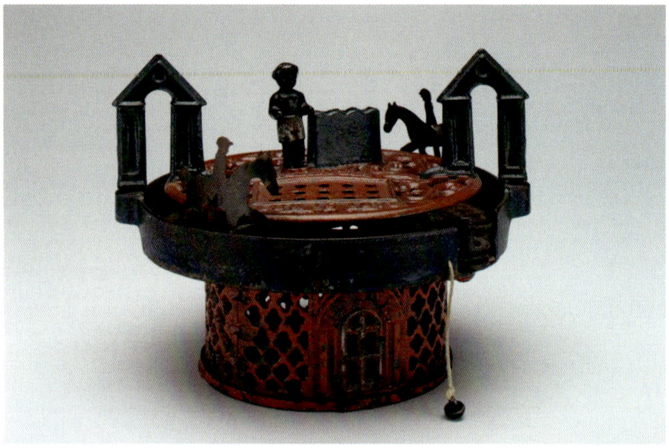

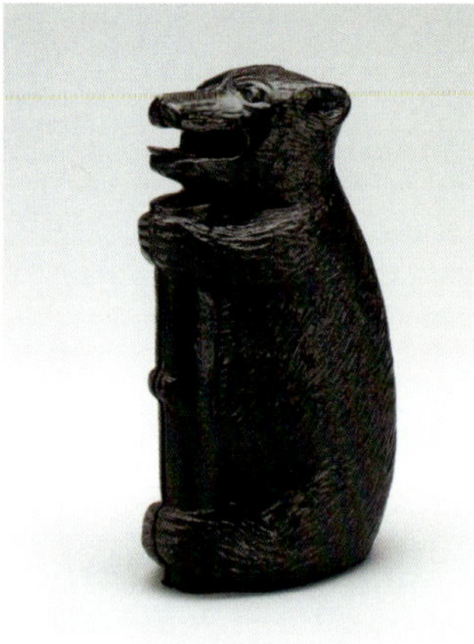

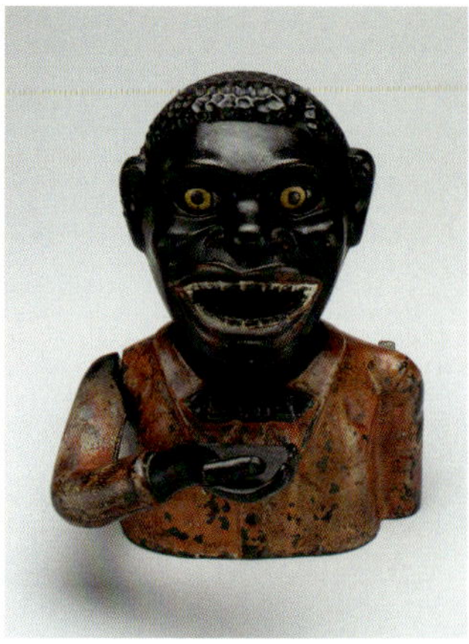

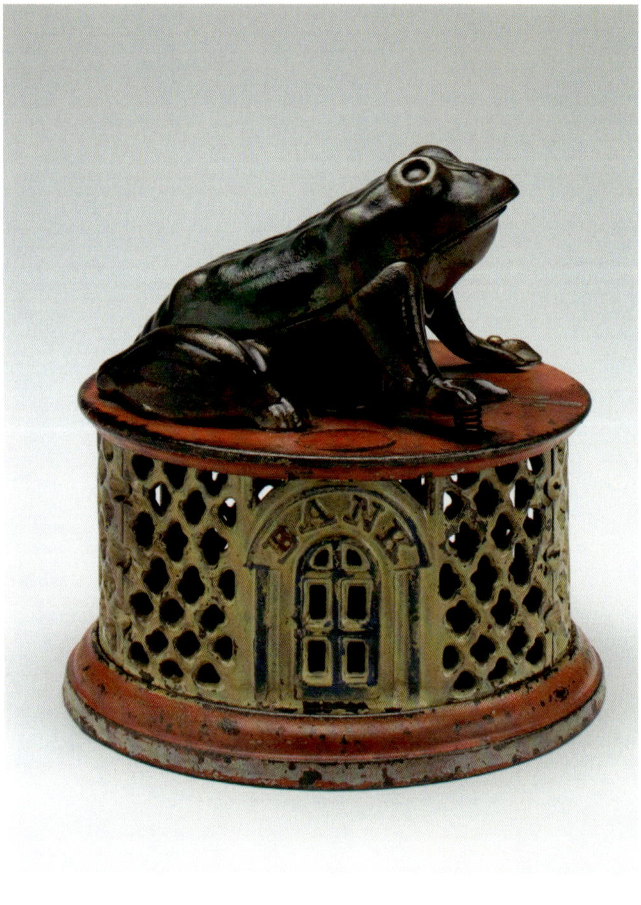

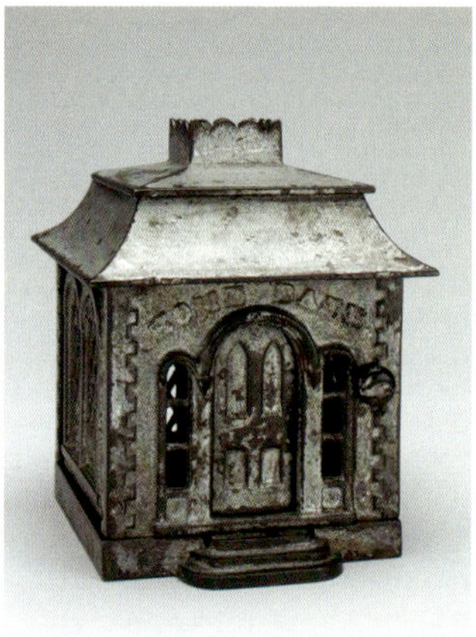

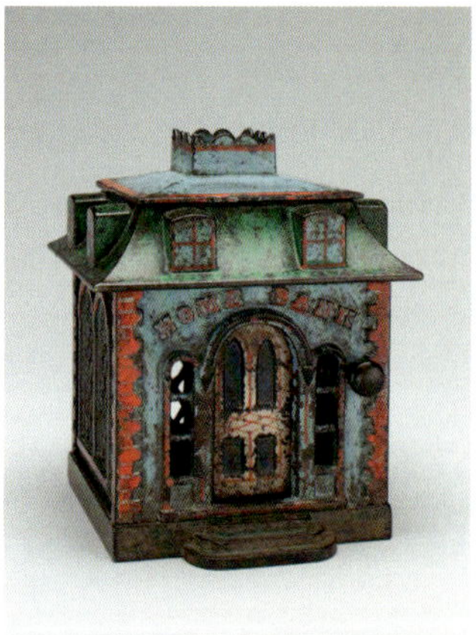

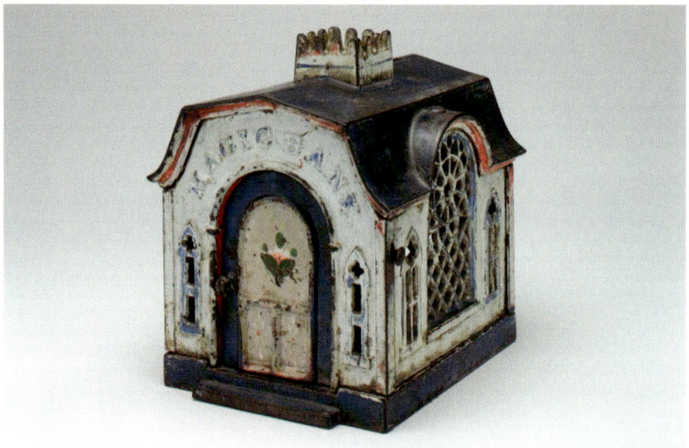

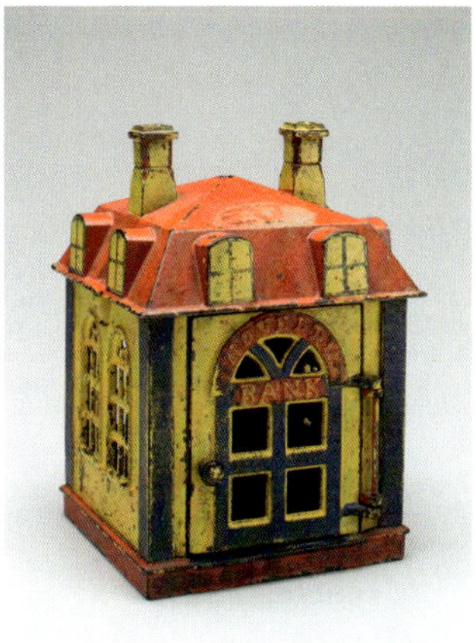
BANK

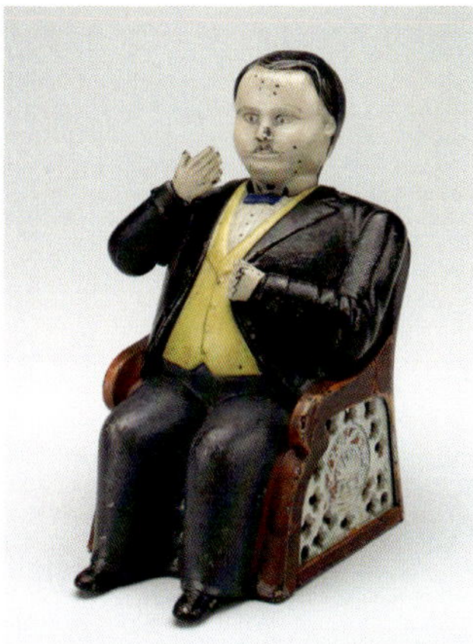

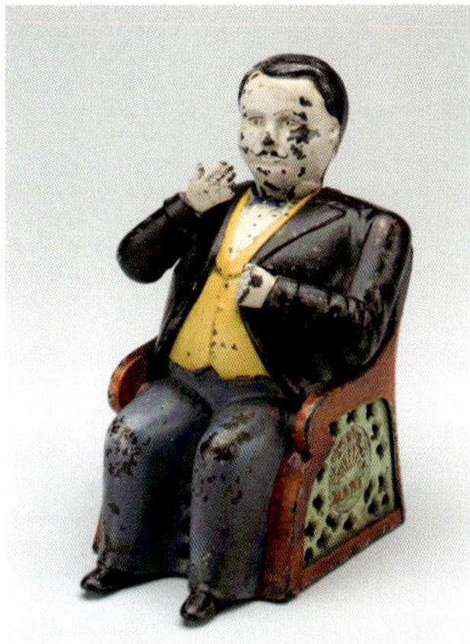

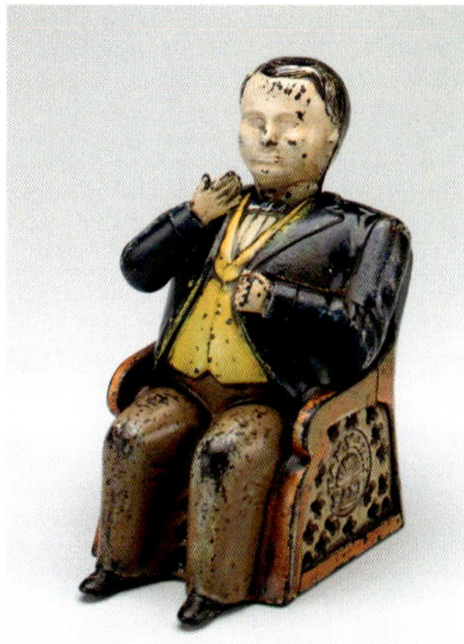

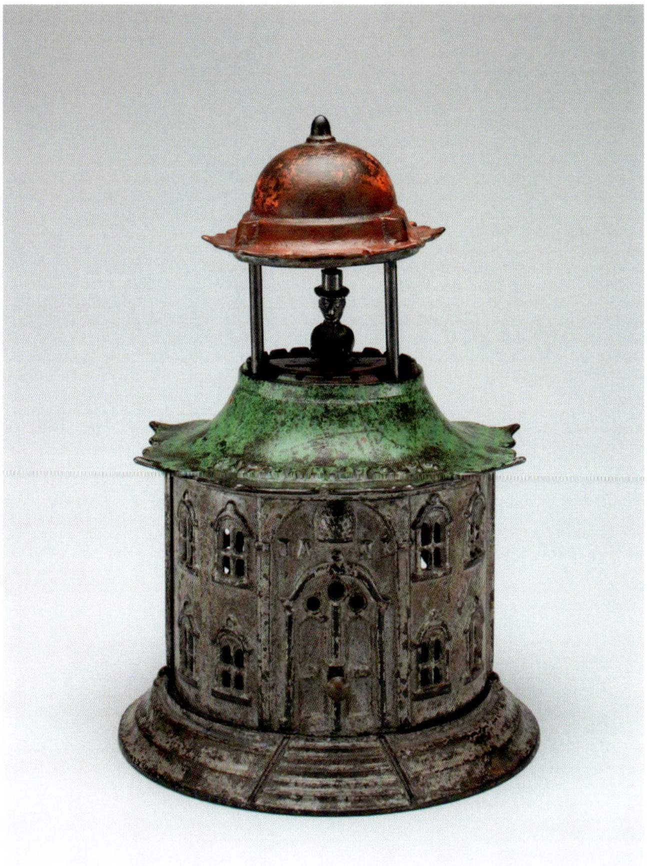

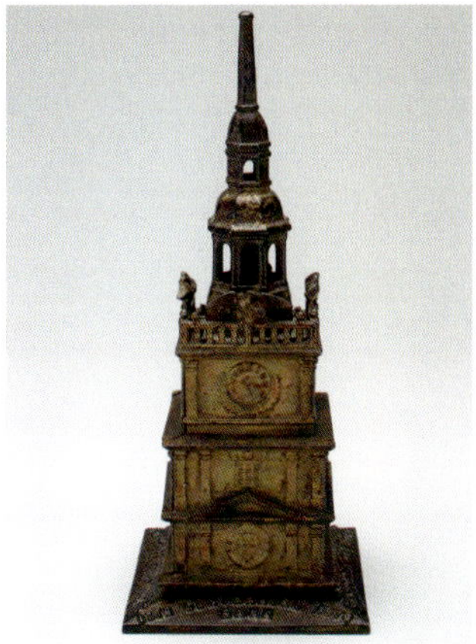

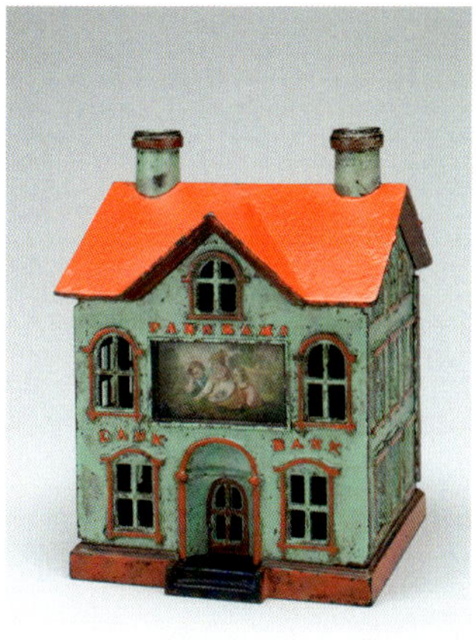

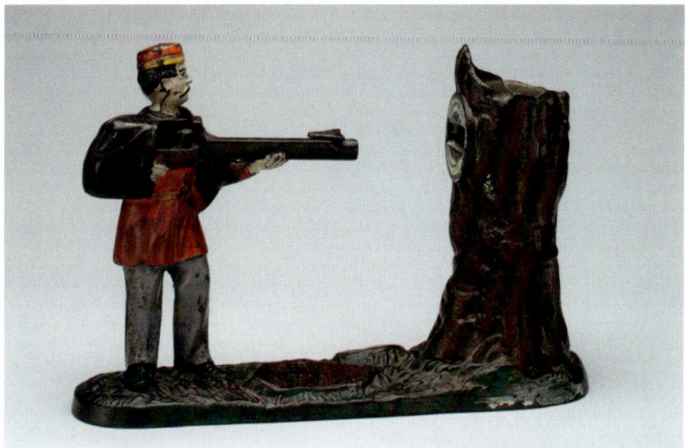

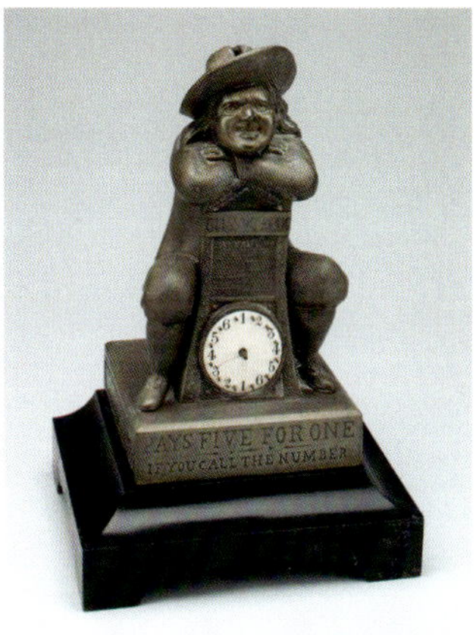
PAYS FIVE FOR ONE
IF YOU CALL THE NUMBER

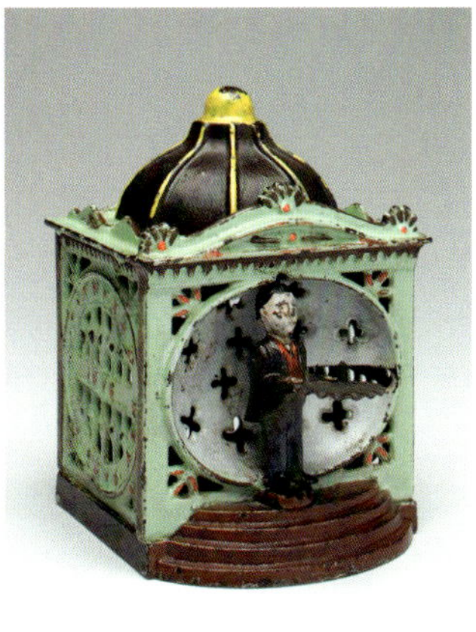

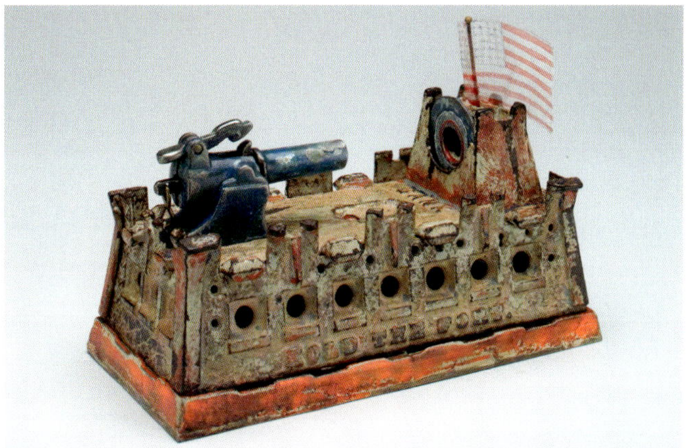

Tammany Bank
(or *Little Fat Man*), c. 1873
"Tammany Bank" appears on left side of chair; "Hall's Patd" appears on right side.
John D. Hall, American, designer
J. & E. Stevens Company, Cromwell, Connecticut (1843–1950s), manufacturer
Iron, pigment
5 3/4 x 3 1/2 x 4 3/8 in.
2003.236.335

Tammany Bank
(or *Little Fat Man*), c. 1873
"Tammany Bank" appears on both sides of chair; sliding trap includes patent mark.
John D. Hall, American, designer
J. & E. Stevens Company, Cromwell, Connecticut (1843–1950s), manufacturer
Iron, pigment
5 3/4 x 3 1/2 x 4 3/8 in.
2003.236.334

Tammany Bank
(or *Little Fat Man*), c. 1873
"Tammany Bank" appears on both sides of chair; sliding trap does not include patent mark.
John D. Hall, American, designer
J. & E. Stevens Company, Cromwell, Connecticut (1843–1950s), manufacturer
Iron, pigment
5 3/4 x 3 1/2 x 4 3/8 in.
2003.236.333

Novelty Bank, 1872
Charles C. Johnson, American, designer
J. & E. Stevens Company, Cromwell, Connecticut (1843–1950s), manufacturer
Iron, pigment
6 1/2 x 4 1/2 x 4 1/2 in.
2003.236.927

Panorama Bank, c. 1876
J. Butler, American, designer
J. & E. Stevens Company, Cromwell, Connecticut (1843–1950s), manufacturer
Iron, pigment, glass
6 1/2 x 4 5/8 x 4 5/8 in.
2003.236.82

Independence Hall Tower (semi-mechanical), 1875
Enterprise Manufacturing Company, Philadelphia (1875–88), manufacturer
Iron, pigment
9 1/2 x 3 15/16 x 3 15/16 in.
2003.236.365

Cupola, c. 1874
Deidrich Diekmann, American, designer
J. & E. Stevens Company, Cromwell, Connecticut (1843–1950s), manufacturer
Iron, pigment
8 1/8 x 5 7/8 x 5 7/8 in.
2003.236.104

Creedmoor, c. 1877
James H. Bowen, American (active c. 1877–1906), designer
J. & E. Stevens Company, Cromwell, Connecticut (1843–1950s), manufacturer
Iron, pigment
6 3/4 x 10 3/16 x 2 11/16 in.
2003.236.74

Hold the Fort, 7 Holes, c. 1877
Samuel Clark, American, designer
Iron, pigment, cloth
5 x 7 1/4 x 3 7/16 in.
2003.236.54a,b

Hall's Liliput Bank, with Tray, c. 1877
John D. Hall, American, designer
J. & E. Stevens Company, Cromwell, Connecticut (1843–1950s), manufacturer
Iron, pigment
4 5/16 x 3 x 3 3/8 in.
2003.236.32

Guessing Bank, Man's Figure, c. 1877
Edward J. McLoughlin, American, designer
Iron, pigment, enamel
9 7/8 x 6 1/16 x 5 5/16 in.
2003.236.100

Gem Bank (or *Watchdog of the Treasury*), c. 1878
H. L. Judd Manufacturing Company, Wallingford, Connecticut (c. 1830 – 1960s), manufacturer
Iron, pigment
$3\frac{1}{4}$ x $5\frac{1}{2}$ x $2\frac{1}{4}$ in.
2003.236.22

New Bank, c. 1877
Anthony Smith, American, designer
J. & E. Stevens Company, Cromwell, Connecticut (1843 – 1950s), manufacturer
Iron, pigment
$5\frac{3}{4}$ x $4\frac{1}{2}$ x $4\frac{1}{2}$ in.
2003.236.929

Patronize the Blind Man and His Dog, c. 1878
William H. Lotz, American, designer
J. & E. Stevens Company, Cromwell, Connecticut (1843 – 1950s), manufacturer
Iron, pigment
$5\frac{1}{8}$ x $6\frac{13}{16}$ x $2\frac{1}{16}$ in.
2003.236.139

Circus Ticket Collector, c. 1879
H. L. Judd Manufacturing Company, Wallingford, Connecticut (c. 1830 – 1960s), manufacturer
Iron, pigment
5 1/4 x 3 3/16 x 2 3/8 in.
2003.236.900

Pelican, Man Thumbing Nose, c. 1878
John Gerard, American, designer
J. & E. Stevens Company, Cromwell, Connecticut (1843 – 1950s), manufacturer
Iron, pigment
$8\frac{3}{16}$ x $4\frac{11}{16}$ x $5\frac{5}{16}$ in.
2003.236.129

Pelican, Arab in Beak, c. 1878
John Gerard, American, designer
J. & E. Stevens Company, Cromwell, Connecticut (1843 – 1950s), manufacturer
Iron, pigment
8 3/16 x 4 11/16 x 5 5/16 in.
2003.236.128

Bird on Roof, c. 1878
Elisha Stevens, American, designer
J. & E. Stevens Company, Cromwell, Connecticut (1843 – 1950s), manufacturer
Iron, pigment
$5\frac{15}{16}$ x $4\frac{3}{16}$ x $3\frac{5}{16}$ in.
2003.236.16

Bull Dog Bank, c. 1880
James H. Bowen, American (active c. 1877 – 1906), designer
J. & E. Stevens Company, Cromwell, Connecticut (1843 – 1950s), manufacturer
Iron, pigment, glass
$7\frac{9}{16}$ x $5\frac{5}{8}$ x $3\frac{1}{16}$ in.
2003.236.136a,b

Atlas Bank, c. 1880
Attributed to North Brothers, Philadelphia, manufacturer
Iron, pigment, paper, wood
$8\frac{1}{4}$ x $5\frac{3}{4}$ x 4 in.
2003.236.59

"I Always Did 'Spise a Mule," Jockey, c. 1879
James H. Bowen, American (active c. 1877 – 1906), designer
J. & E. Stevens Company, Cromwell, Connecticut (1843 – 1950s), manufacturer
Iron, pigment
$8\frac{1}{4}$ x $10\frac{1}{4}$ x $3\frac{13}{16}$ in.
2003.236.24

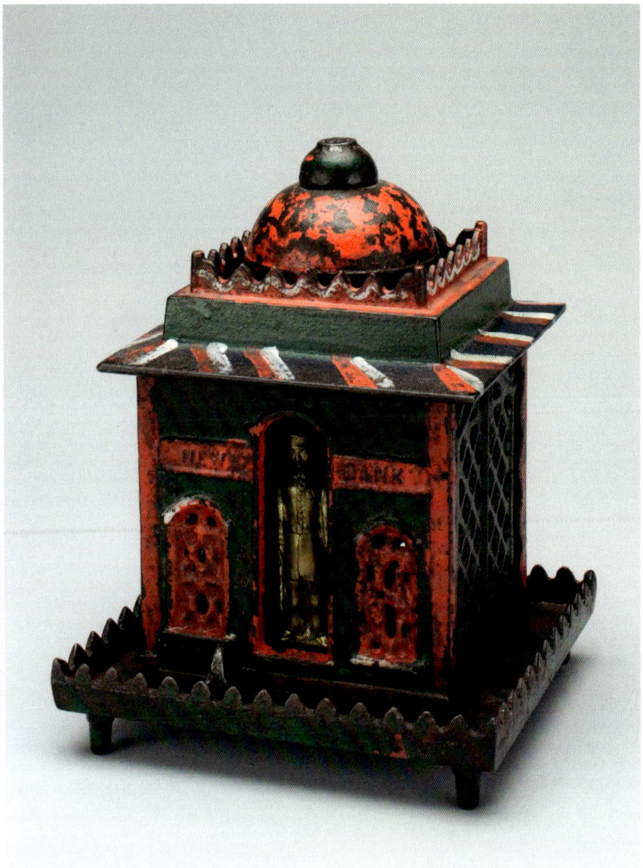
NEW
BANK

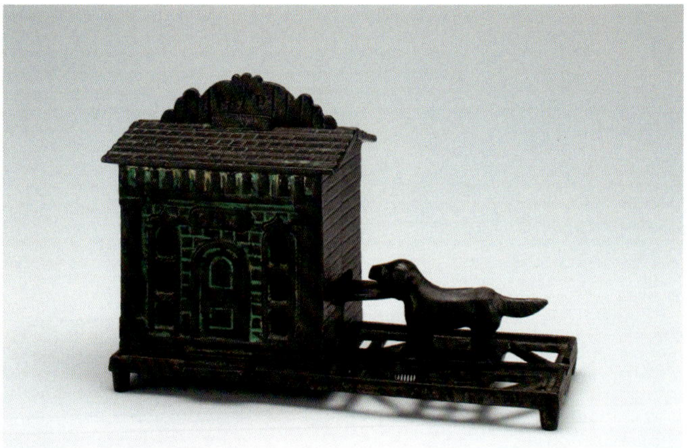

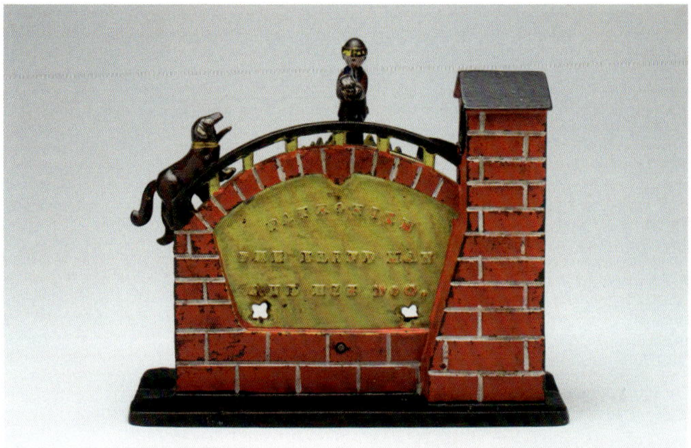

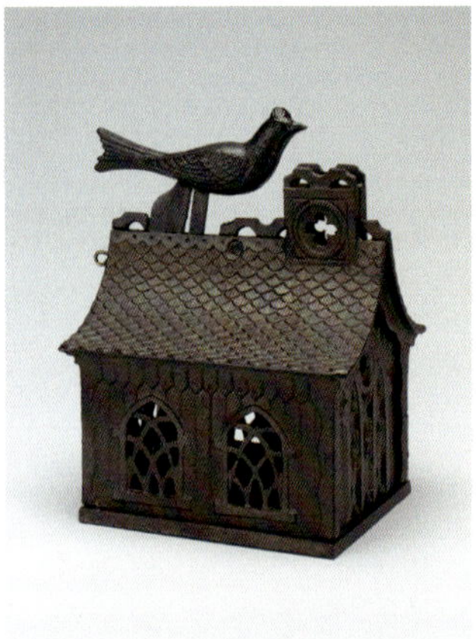

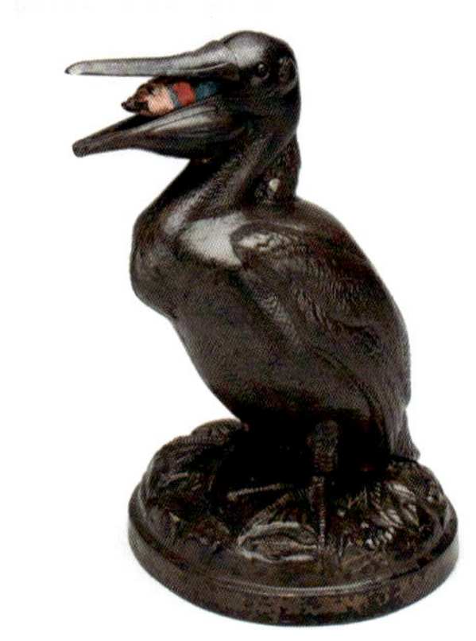

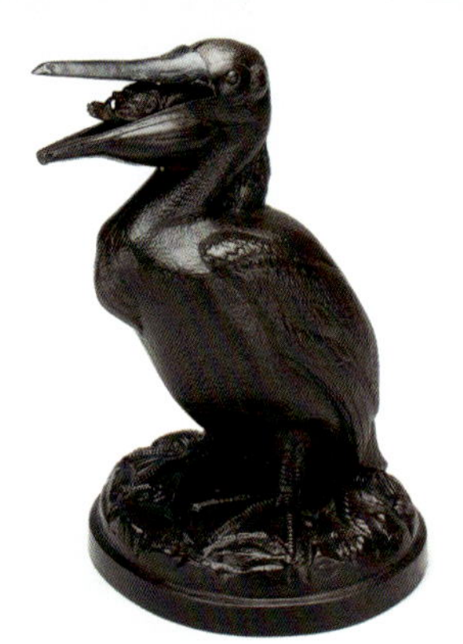

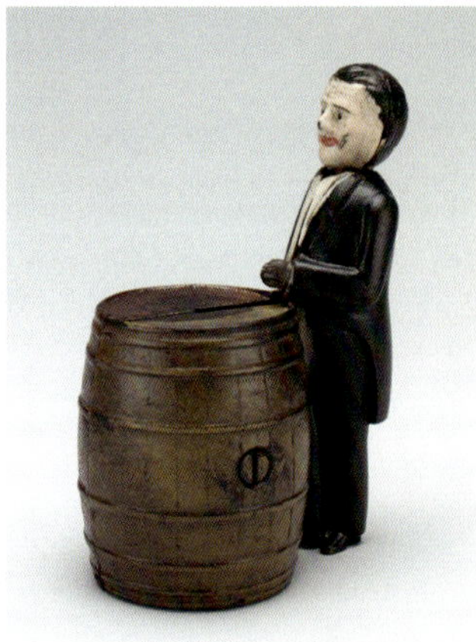

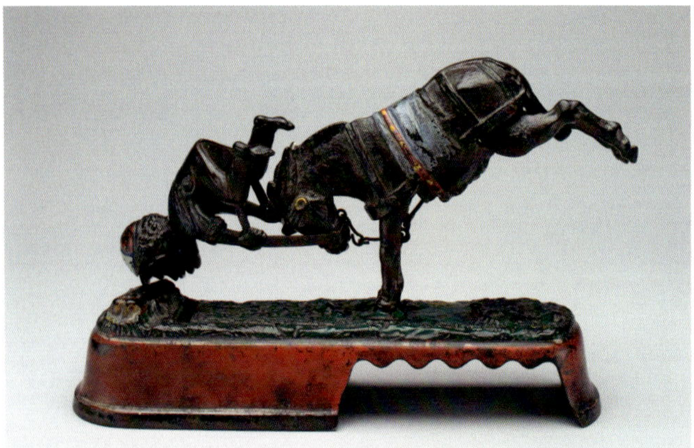

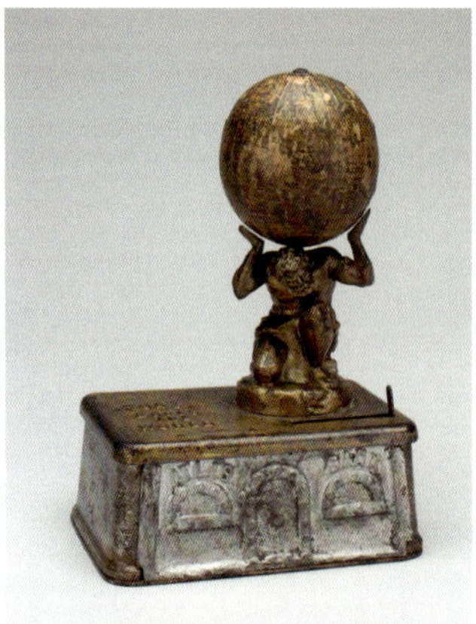

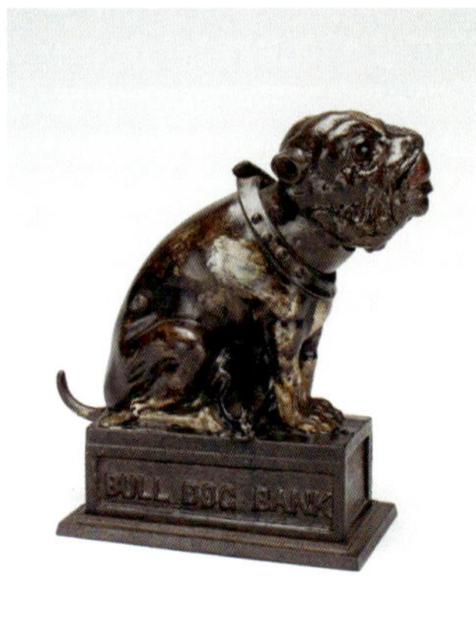
BULL DOG BANK

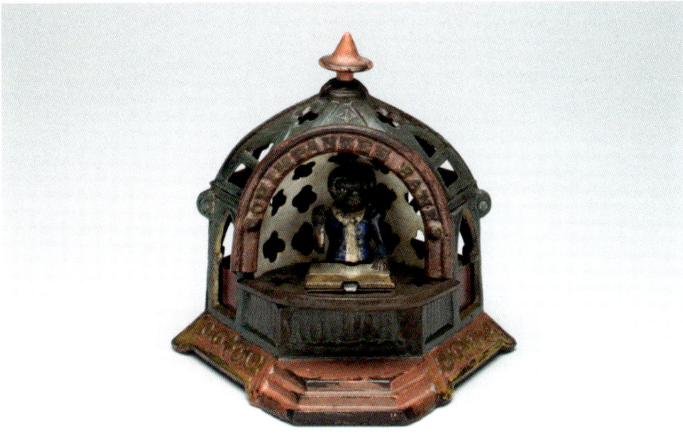
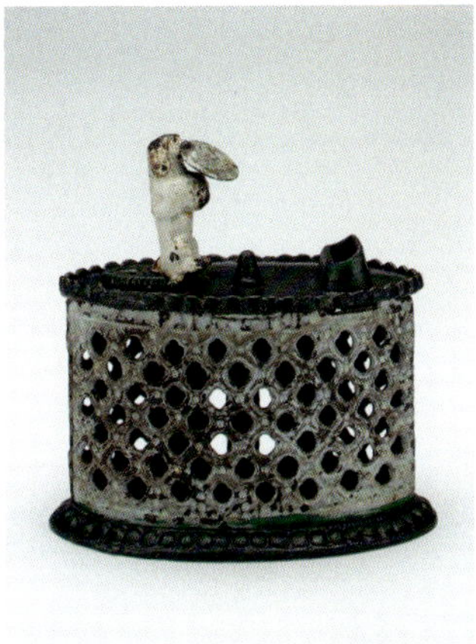
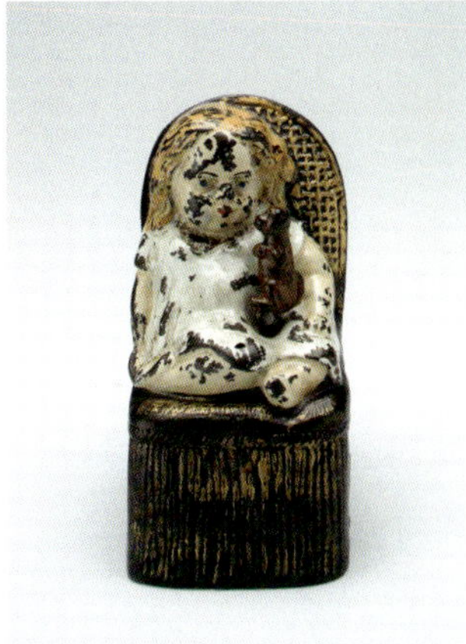
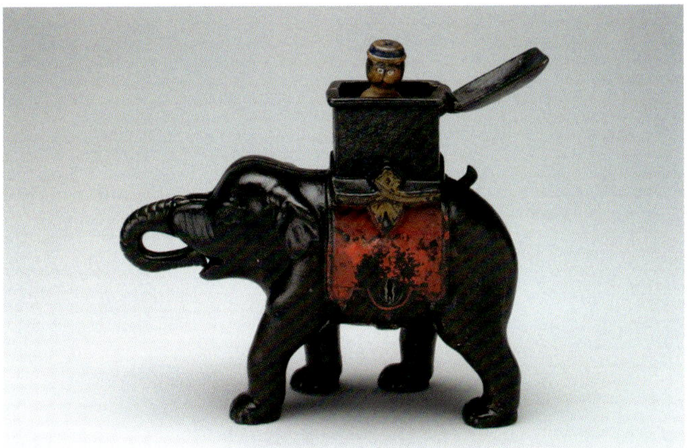
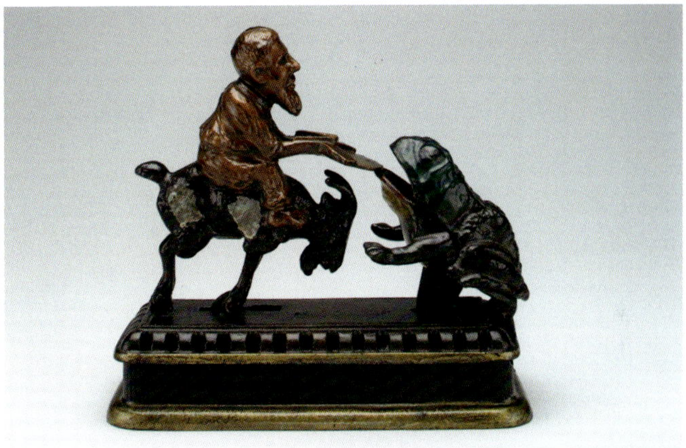
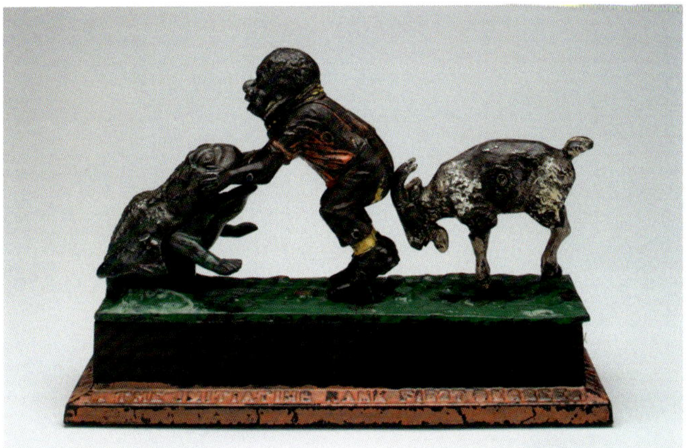
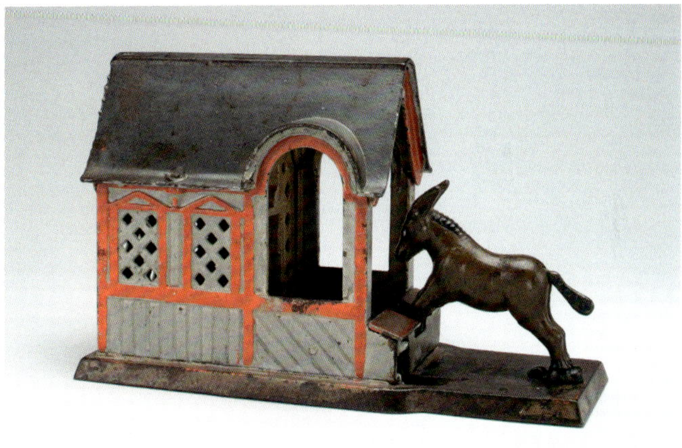
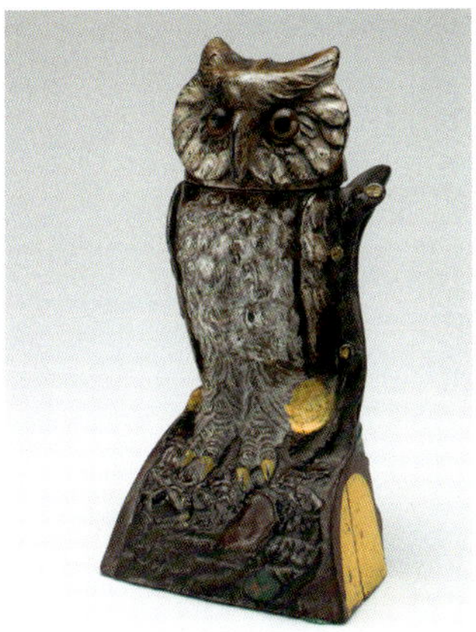
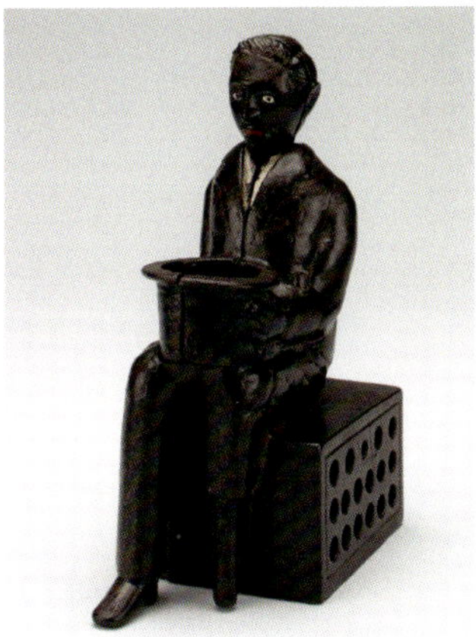
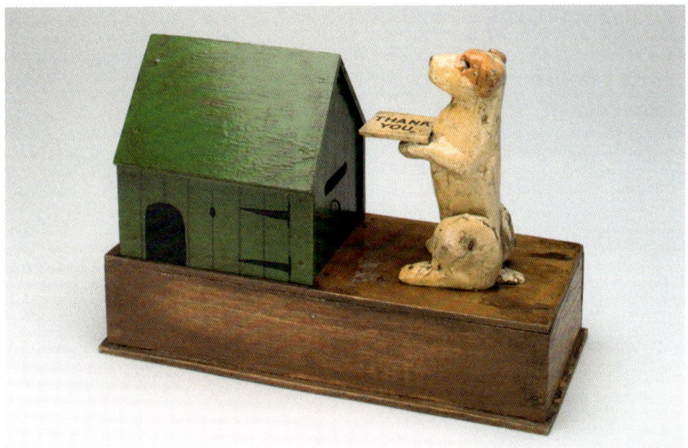

Girl in Victorian Chair, c. 1880
W. S. Reed Toy Company, Leominster, Massachusetts (1875 – 97), or J. & E. Stevens Company, Cromwell, Connecticut (1843 – 1950s), manufacturer
Iron, pigment
4 x 2 1/16 x 2 3/16 in.
2003.236.21

Dog Tray Bank, c. 1880
Louis Kyser and Alfred C. Rex, American, designers
Kyser & Rex Company, Philadelphia (c. 1879 – 98), manufacturer
Iron, pigment
4 1/4 x 4 5/16 x 2 7/16 in.
2003.236.35

Chimpanzee Bank, c. 1880
Louis Kyser and Alfred C. Rex, American, designers
Kyser & Rex Company, Philadelphia (c. 1879 – 98), manufacturer
Iron, pigment
5 3/8 x 6 x 5 7/8 in.
2003.236.897

Goat, Frog, and Old Man (or *Initiating Bank, Second Degree*), c. 1880
George Eddy, American, designer
Mechanical Novelty Works, New Britain, Connecticut (1870s – 90s), manufacturer
Iron, pigment
6 3/4 x 7 5/8 x 3 1/16 in.
2003.236.110

Elephant Howdah, Man Pops Out, c. 1880
Enterprise Manufacturing Company, Philadelphia (1875 – 88), manufacturer
Iron, pigment, wood, fabric
5 15/16 x 6 11/16 x 2 1/2 in.
2003.236.279

Mule Entering Barn (or *Malicious Donkey*), c. 1880
Edward L. Morris, American, designer
J. & E. Stevens Company, Cromwell, Connecticut (1843 – 1950s), manufacturer
Wood, paper, pigment
5 1/4 x 8 5/8 x 3 3/8 in.
2003.236.819

Initiating Bank, First Degree, c. 1880
George Eddy, American, designer
Mechanical Novelty Works, New Britain, Connecticut (1870s – 90s), manufacturer
Iron, pigment
6 1/2 x 10 3/8 x 3 5/16 in.
2003.236.25

Thank You Dog Tray, c. 1880
R. R. Thompson, Ltd., Surrey, England, manufacturer
Wood, pigment
6 9/16 x 10 1/8 x 4 1/4 in.
2003.236.604

Peg-Leg Beggar, c. 1880
H. L. Judd Manufacturing Company, Wallingford, Connecticut (c. 1830 – 1960s), manufacturer
Iron, pigment
5 x 2 1/16 x 3 5/8 in.
2003.236.31

Owl, Turns Head, c. 1880
James H. Bowen, American (active c. 1877 – 1906), designer
J. & E. Stevens Company, Cromwell, Connecticut (1843 – 1950s), manufacturer
Iron, pigment, glass
7 3/4 x 3 7/8 x 3 1/16 in.
2003.236.238a,b

Mosque, c. 1880s
H. L. Judd Manufacturing Company, Wallingford, Connecticut (c. 1830 – 1960s), manufacturer
Iron, pigment
8 7/8 x 6 1/4 x 6 1/4 in
2003.236.687

Light of Asia, c. 1880s
Attributed to J. & E. Stevens Company, Cromwell, Connecticut (1843 – 1950s), or Kyser & Rex Company, Philadelphia (c. 1879 – 98), manufacturer
Iron, pigment
3 5/8 x 3 3/8 x 1 3/4 in.
2003.236.103

United States Bank, c. 1880
J. & E. Stevens Company, Cromwell, Connecticut (1843 – 1950s), manufacturer
Metal, pigment, leather, paper
6 1/4 x 4 3/16 x 3 5/8 in.
2003.236.690a,b

Rooster, c. 1880 – 90
Attributed to Kyser & Rex Company, Philadelphia (c. 1879 – 98), manufacturer
Iron, pigment
6 x 3 1/2 x 2 5/16 in.
2003.236.143

Weeden's Plantation Saving Bank, c. 1880s
Weeden Manufacturing Company, New Bedford, Massachusetts (est. 1882), manufacturer
Tin, pigment, wood, paper
5 1/2 x 3 7/8 x 3 5/8 in.
2003.236.846

Octagonal Fort (or *Fort Sumter*), c. 1880s
Attributed to Edward Brueninghausen, American, designer
Iron, pigment
4 3/16 x 11 3/16 x 2 7/8 in.
2003.236.53a,b

Organ Bank, Miniature, c. 1881
Louis Kyser and Alfred C. Rex, American, designers
Kyser & Rex Company, Philadelphia (c. 1879 – 98), manufacturer
Iron, pigment
3 5/8 x 3 1/4 x 2 1/4 in.
2003.236.33

Volunteer Bank, c. 1880s – 90s
Attributed to John Harper & Company, Ltd., Willenhall, England (1790 – 1980s), manufacturer
Iron, brass, pigment
6 1/2 x 10 x 2 11/16 in.
2003.236.76

Stollwerck, Hand Shadows (vending), c. 1880 – 90s
Stollwerck Chocolate, Cologne, Germany (est. 19th century), manufacturer
Tin, pigment, glass
6 7/16 x 3 x 2 1/2 in.
2003.236.337

Hindu, c. 1882
Louis Kyser and Alfred C. Rex, American, designers
Kyser & Rex Company, Philadelphia (c. 1879 – 98), manufacturer
Iron, pigment
6 x 4 3/16 x 3 5/8 in.
2003.236.898

Squirrel and Tree Stump, c. 1881
Robert E. Turnbull, American, designer
Mechanical Novelty Works, New Britain, Connecticut (1870s – 90s), manufacturer
Iron, pigment
4 1/2 x 6 3/4 x 4 in.
2003.236.142

Organ Bank, Monkey, c. 1881
Louis Kyser and Alfred C. Rex, American, designers
Kyser & Rex Company, Philadelphia (c. 1879 – 98), manufacturer
Iron, pigment
5 1/16 x 4 x 3 in.
2003.236.34

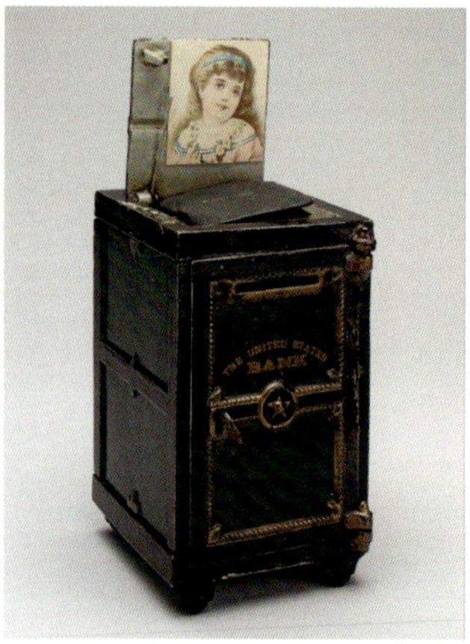

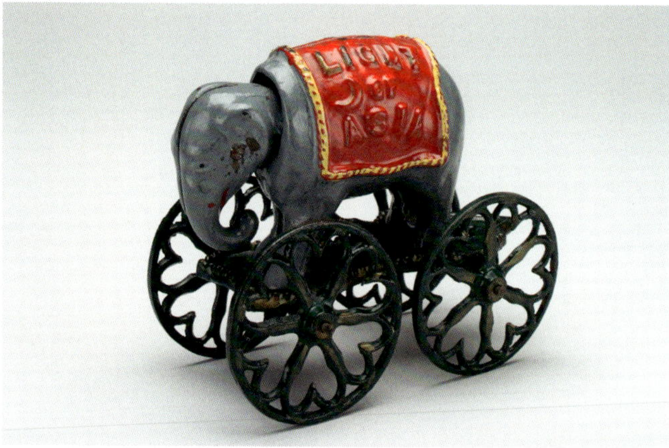

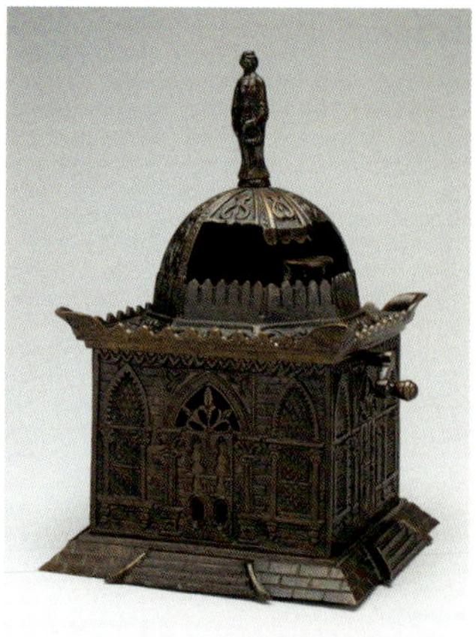

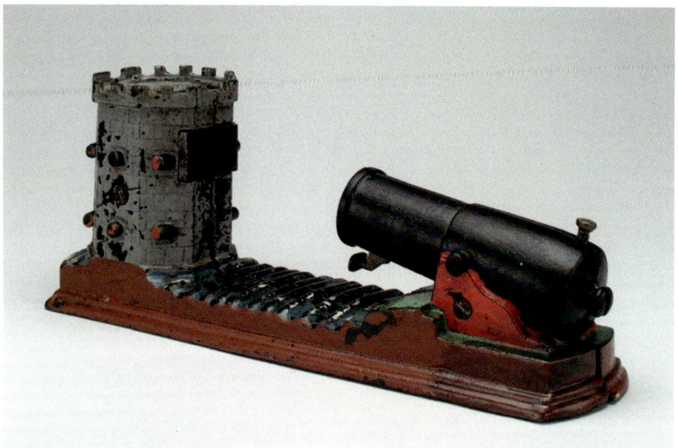

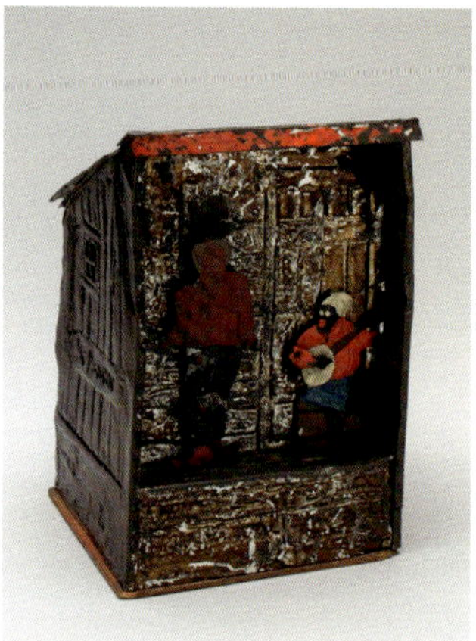

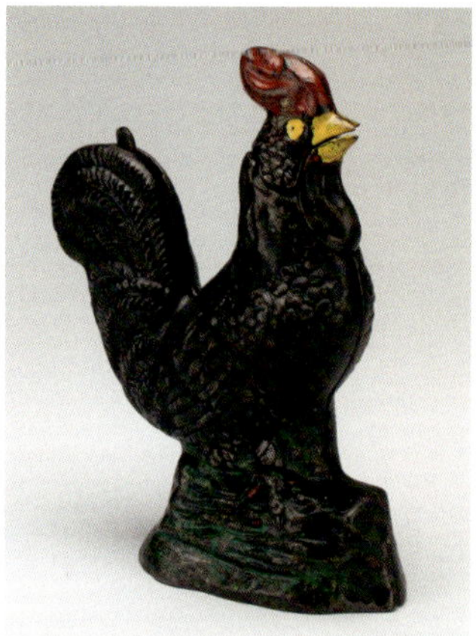

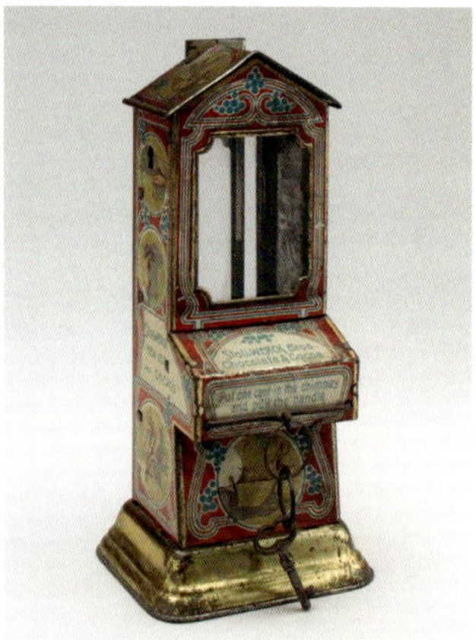

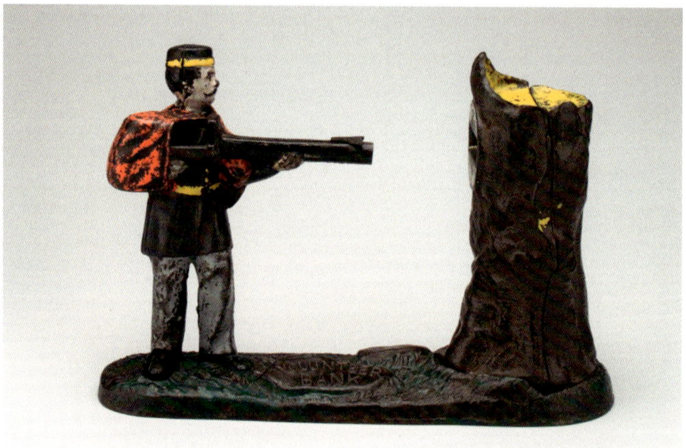

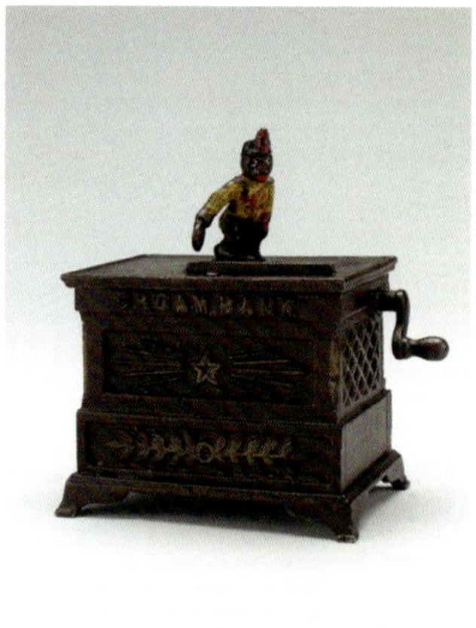

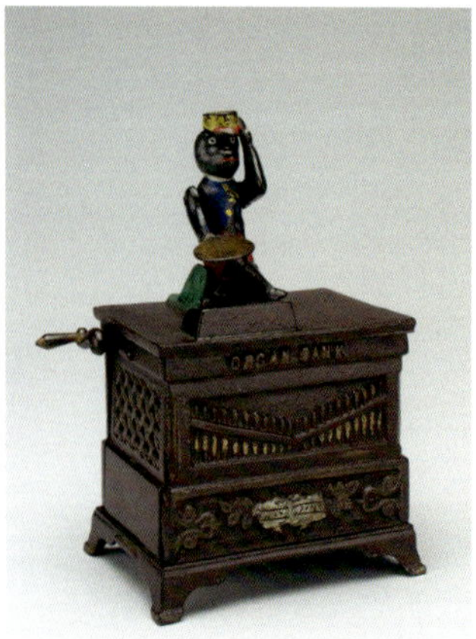
ORGAN BANK

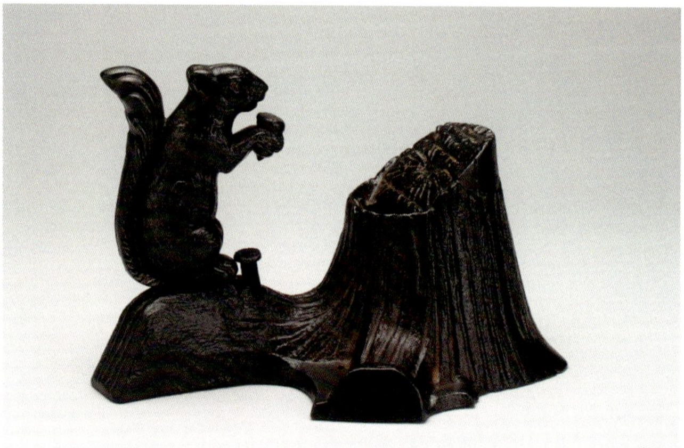

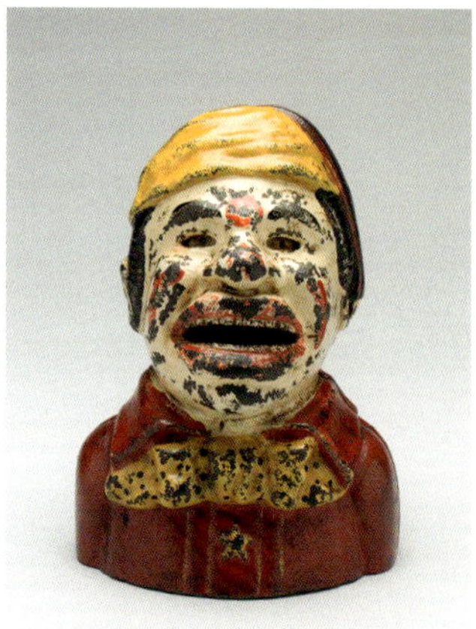

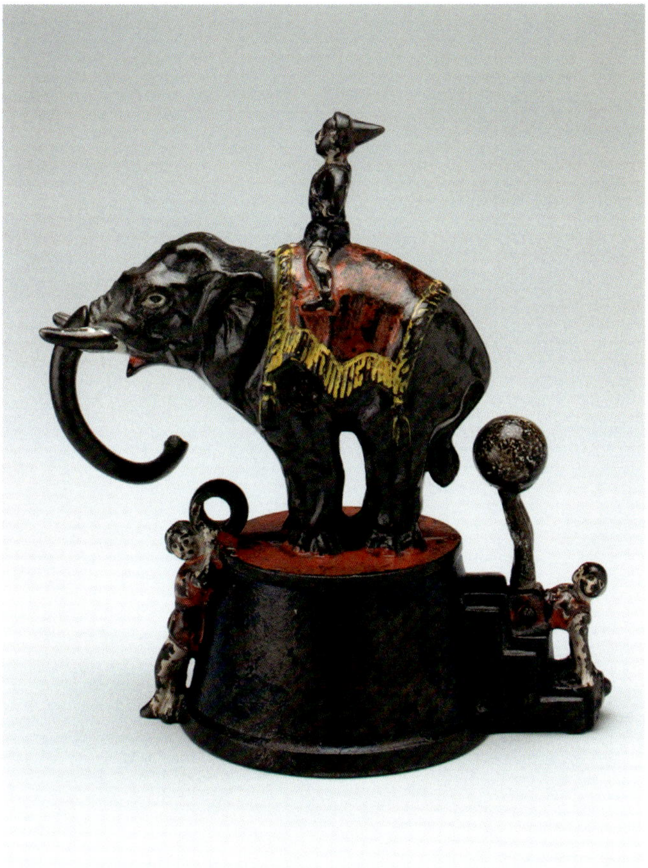

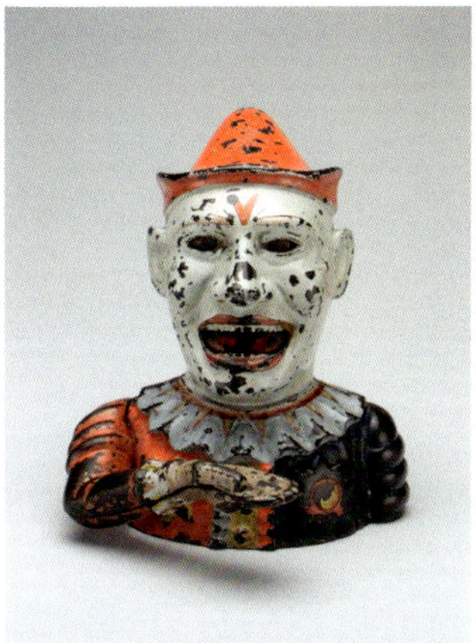

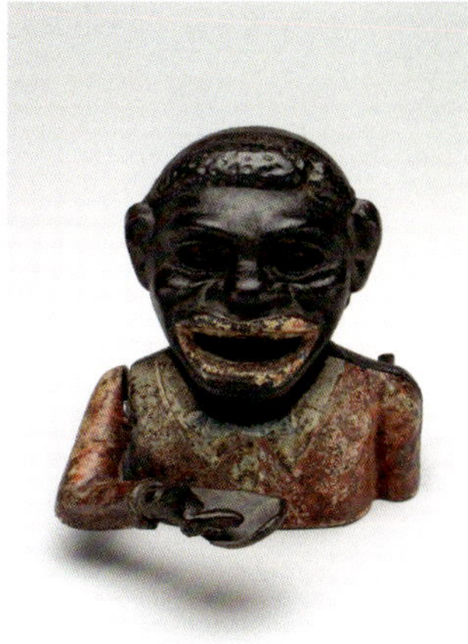

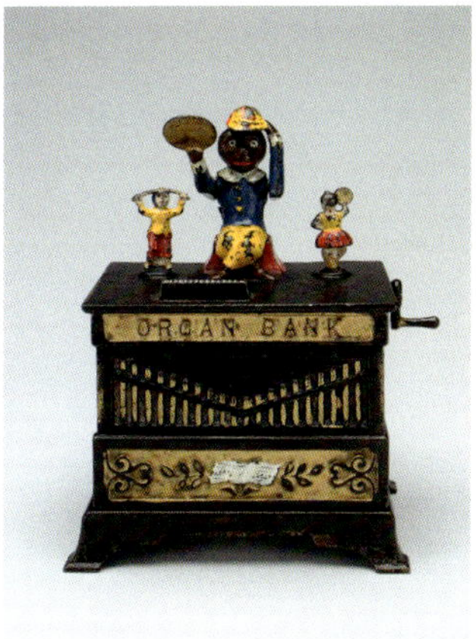
ORGAN BANK

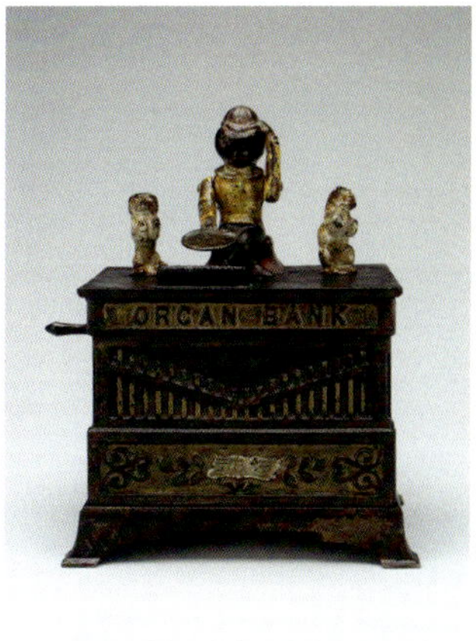
ORGAN BANK

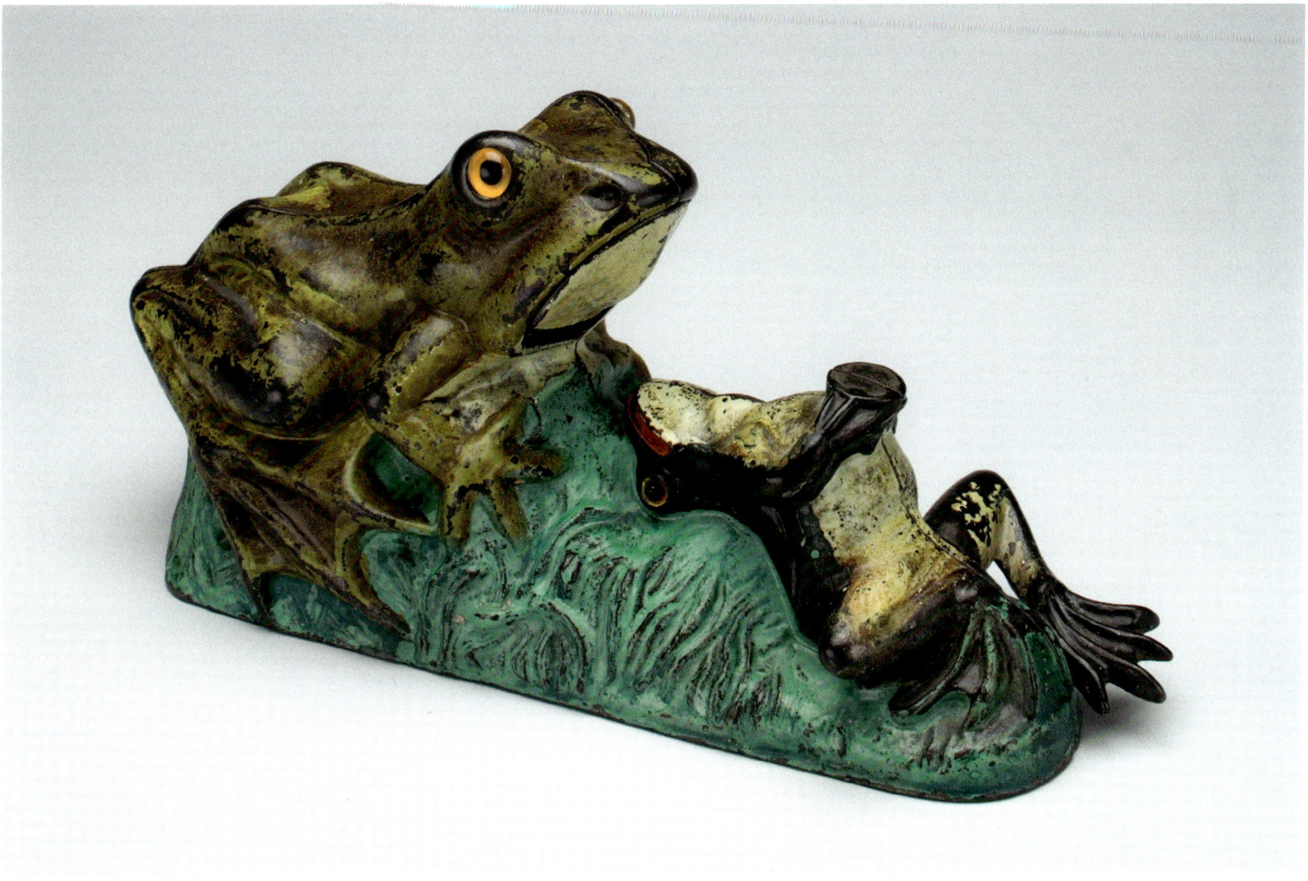

Jolly Nigger, c. 1882
Peter Adams and Charles G. Shepard, American, designers
Shepard Hardware Company, Buffalo, New York (1866 – 92), manufacturer
Iron, pigment
$6\frac{1}{4} \times 4\frac{3}{4} \times 5\frac{1}{4}$ in.
2003.236.703

Humpty Dumpty, c. 1882
Peter Adams and Charles G. Shepard, American, designers
Shepard Hardware Company, Buffalo, New York (1866 – 92), manufacturer
Iron, pigment
$8 \times 5\frac{1}{2} \times 5\frac{1}{2}$ in.
2003.236.348

Elephant and Three Clowns on Tub, c. 1882
James H. Bowen, American (active c. 1877 – 1906), designer
J. & E. Stevens Company, Cromwell, Connecticut (1843 – 1950s), manufacturer
Iron, pigment
$5\frac{11}{16} \times 5\frac{11}{16} \times 3\frac{11}{16}$ in.
2003.236.4a,b

Organ Bank, Cat and Dog, c. 1882
Louis Kyser and Alfred C. Rex, American, designers
Kyser & Rex Company, Philadelphia (c. 1879 – 98), manufacturer
Iron, pigment
$7\frac{1}{4} \times 5\frac{3}{8} \times 4$ in.
2003.236.37

Organ Bank, Boy and Girl, c. 1882
Louis Kyser and Alfred C. Rex, American, designers
Kyser & Rex Company, Philadelphia (c. 1879 – 98), manufacturer
Iron, pigment
$7\frac{1}{4} \times 5\frac{3}{8} \times 4$ in.
2003.236.36

Frog Bank (or *Two Frogs*), c. 1882
James H. Bowen, American (active c. 1877 – 1906), designer
J. & E. Stevens Company, Cromwell, Connecticut (1843 – 1950s), manufacturer
Iron, pigment, glass
$4\frac{1}{4} \times 8\frac{1}{2} \times 2$ in.
2003.236.310

Uncle Tom, with Star, No Lapels, c. 1882
Louis Kyser and Alfred C. Rex, American, designers
Kyser & Rex Company, Philadelphia (c. 1879 – 98), manufacturer
Iron, pigment
5 1/2 x 4 1/8 x 3 in.
2003.236.701

Uncle Tom, with Star, Lapels, c. 1882
Louis Kyser and Alfred C. Rex, American, designers
Kyser & Rex Company, Philadelphia (c. 1879 – 98), manufacturer
Iron, pigment
5 5/8 x 4 1/16 x 3 1/8 in.
2003.236.702

Organ Grinder and Performing Bear, c. 1882
Louis Kyser and Alfred C. Rex, American, designers
Kyser & Rex Company, Philadelphia (c. 1879 – 98), manufacturer
Iron, pigment
6 5/16 x 6 5/16 x 4 3/4 in.
2003.236.109

Springing Cat, c. 1882
Charles A. Bailey, American (1848 – 1926), designer
Charles A. Bailey, Cobalt, Connecticut, manufacturer
Lead alloy, wood, pigment,
3 3/4 x 9 1/8 x 2 5/8 in.
2003.236.229a,b

Reclining Chinaman, c. 1882
James H. Bowen, American (active c. 1877 – 1906), designer
J. & E. Stevens Company, Cromwell, Connecticut (1843 – 1950s), manufacturer
Iron, pigment
4 1/2 x 8 3/8 x 2 1/2 in.
2003.236.93a,b

Acrobat, c. 1883
Edward L. Morris, American, designer
J. & E. Stevens Company, Cromwell, Connecticut (1843 – 1950s), manufacturer
Iron, pigment
5 x 7 5/16 x 3 7/8 in.
2003.236.60a,b

Paddy and the Pig, c. 1882
James H. Bowen, American (active c. 1877 – 1906), designer
J. & E. Stevens Company, Cromwell, Connecticut (1843 – 1950s), manufacturer
Iron, pigment, glass
8 1/2 x 7 3/16 x 3 5/16 in.
2003.236.140a,b

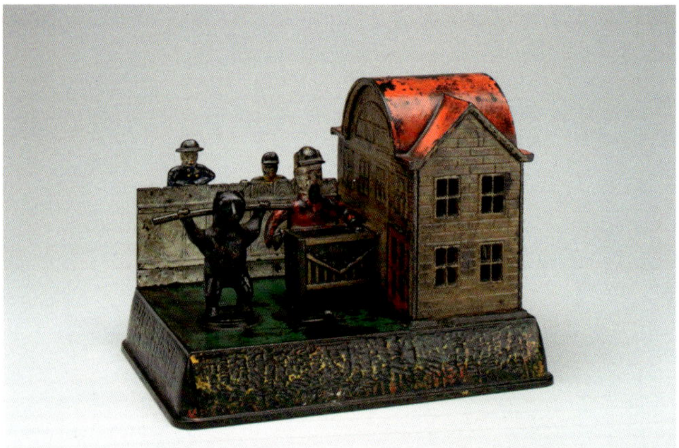

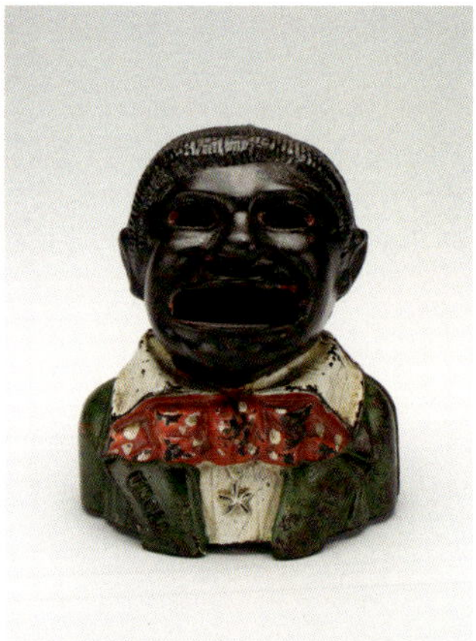

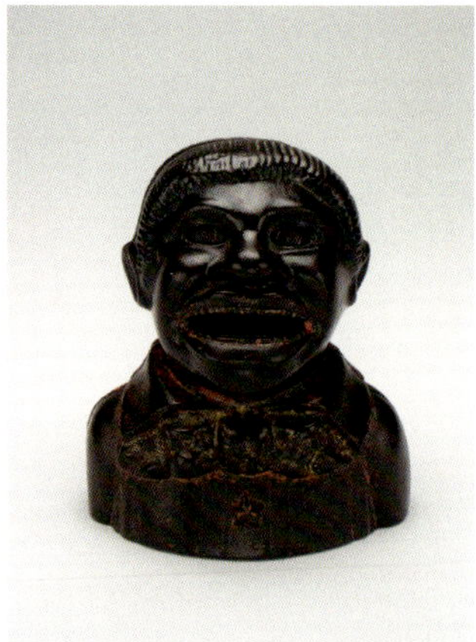

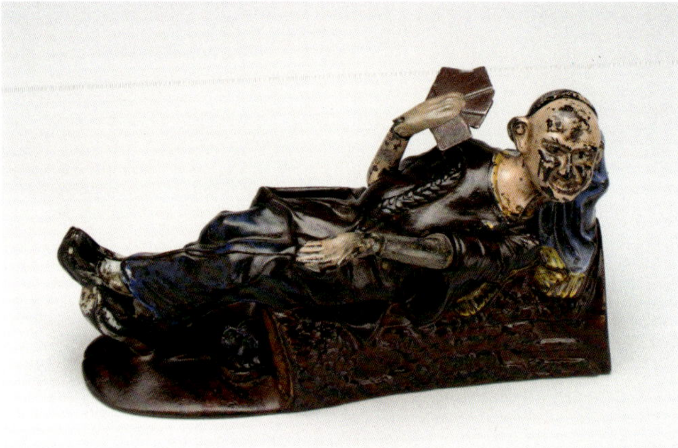

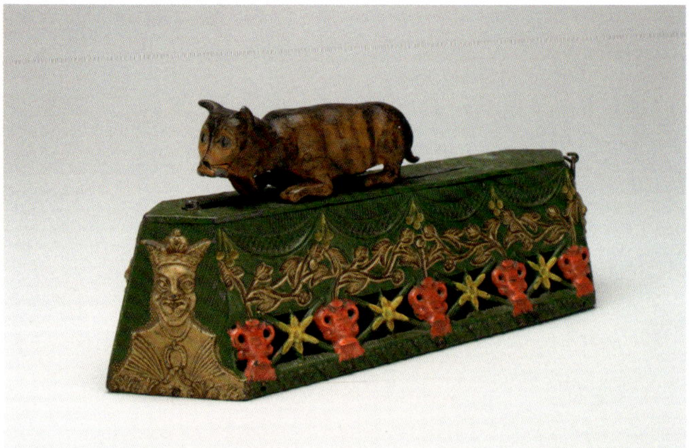

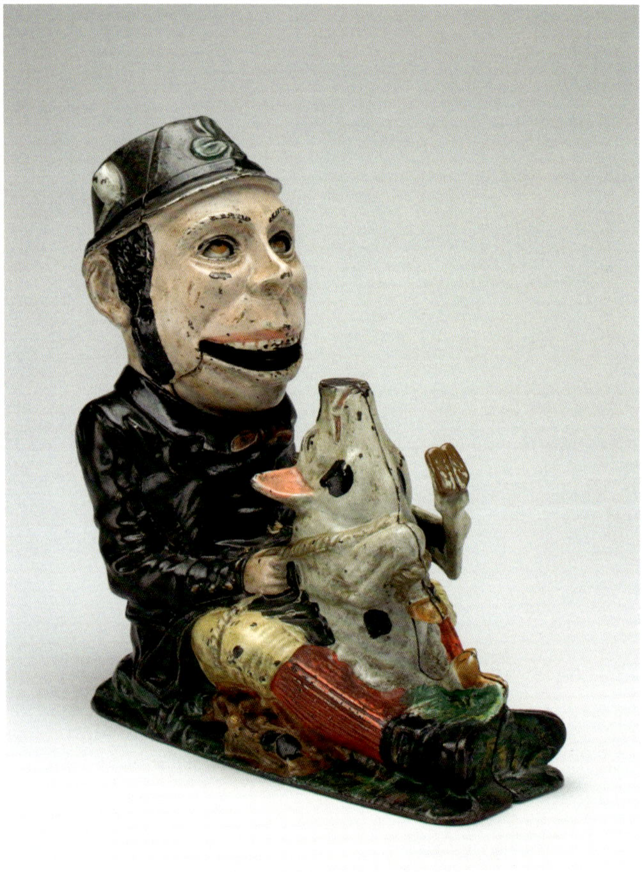

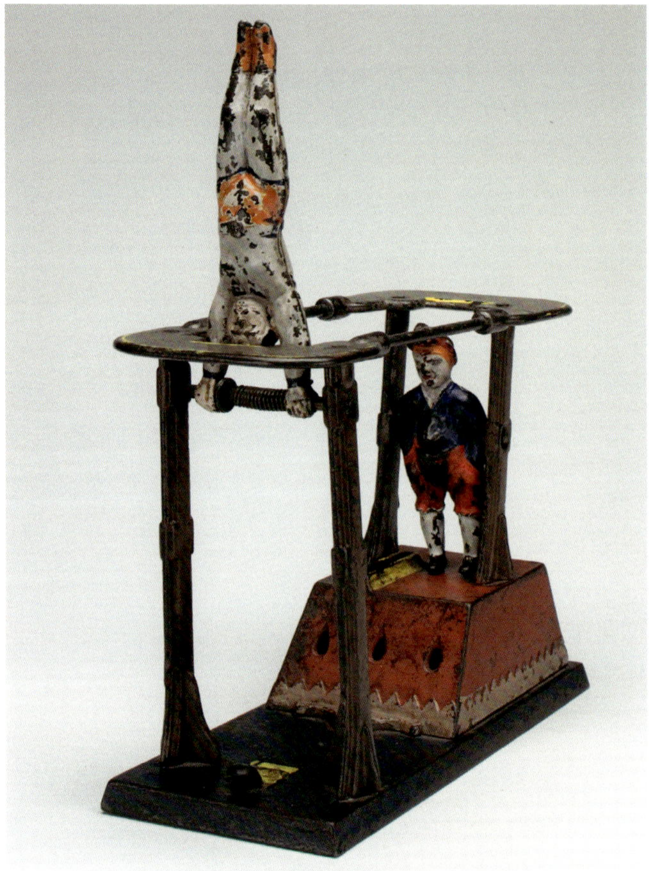

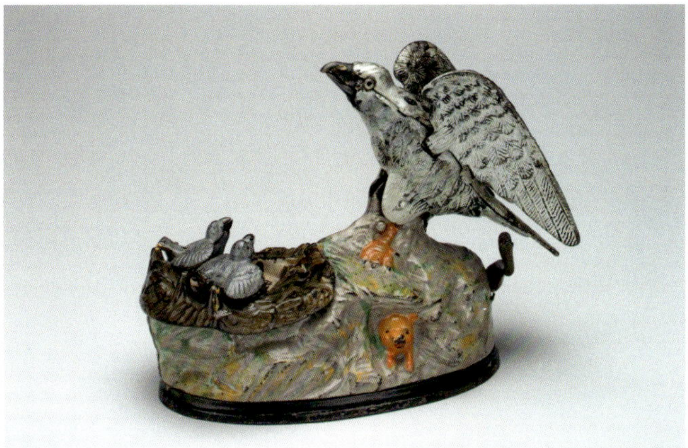

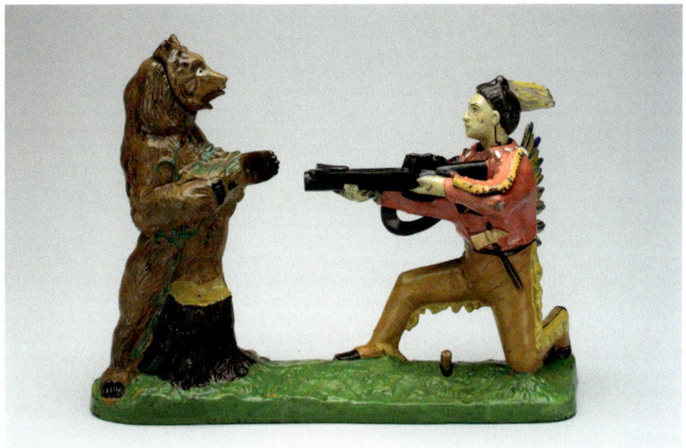

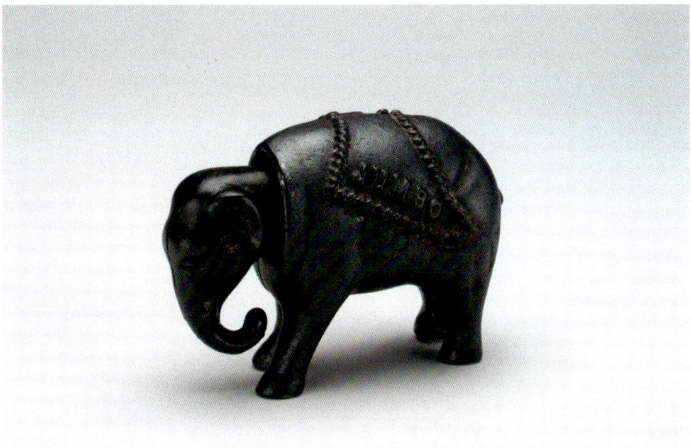

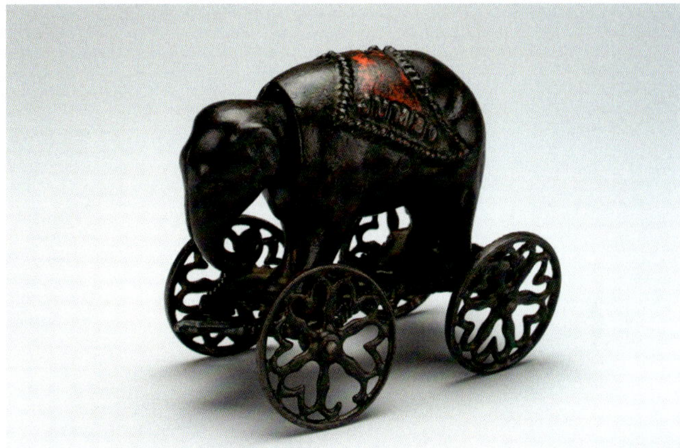

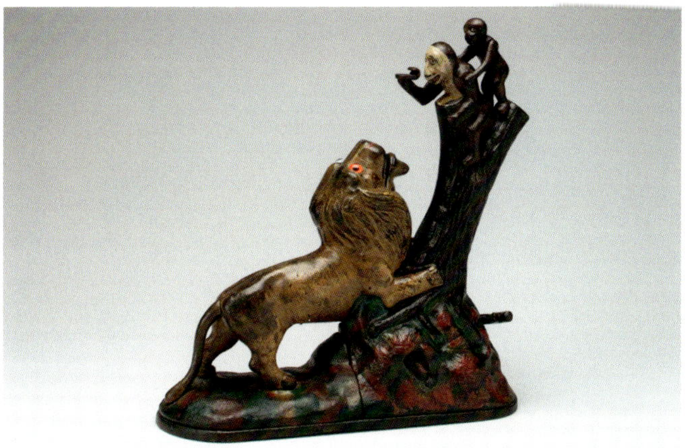

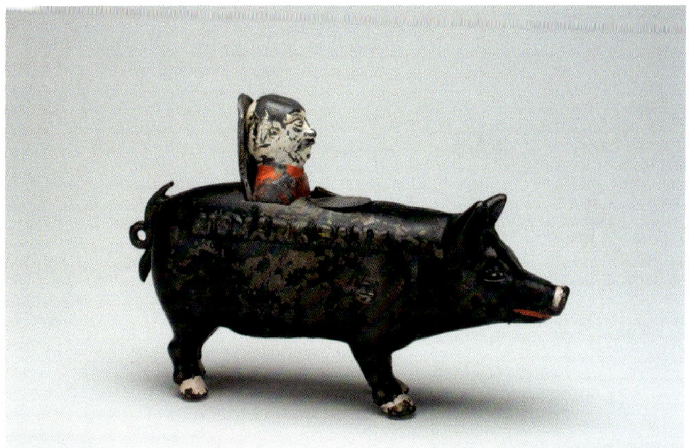

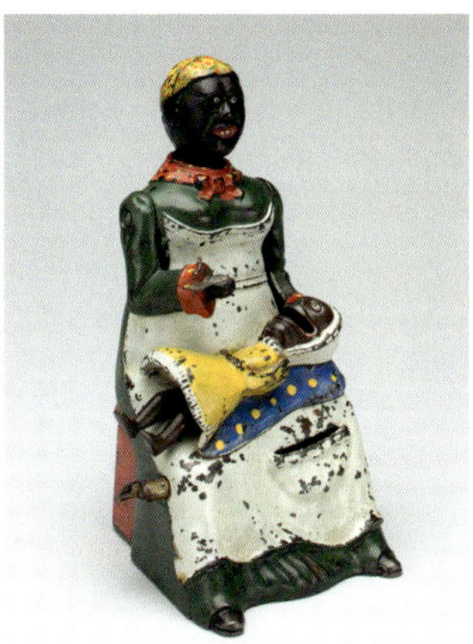

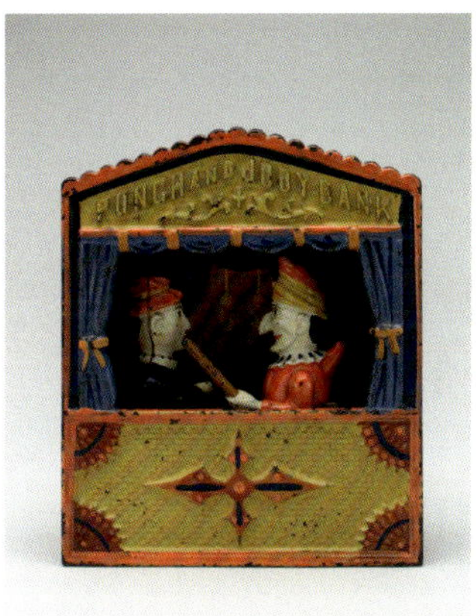
PUNCH AND JUDY BANK

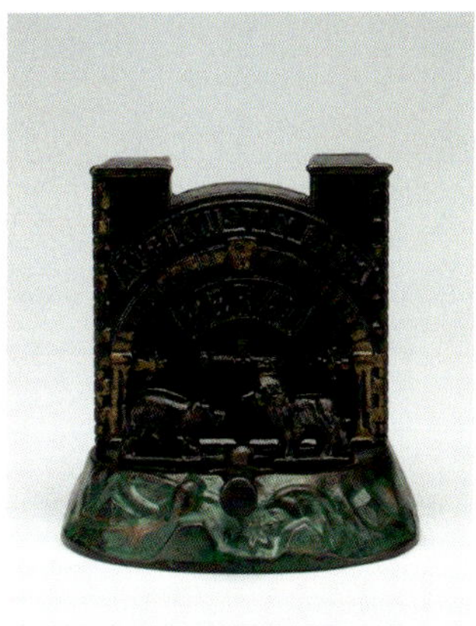

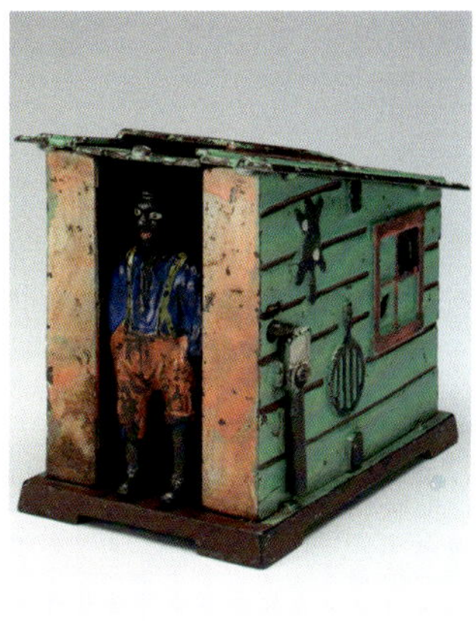

Indian Shooting Bear, c. 1883
J. & E. Stevens Company, Cromwell, Connecticut (1843 – 1950s), manufacturer
Iron, pigment
7 9/16 x 10 7/16 x 2 5/8 in.
2003.236.40a,b

Eagle and Eaglets (or *American Eagle*), c. 1883
Charles M. Henn, American, designer
J. & E. Stevens Company, Cromwell, Connecticut (1843 – 1950s), manufacturer
Iron, pigment
5 1/4 x 6 3/4 x 4 in.
2003.236.72a,b

Jumbo on Wheels, Small, c. 1883
J. & E. Stevens Company, Cromwell, Connecticut (1843 – 1950s), or Kyser & Rex Company, Philadelphia (c. 1879 – 98), manufacturer
Iron, pigment
3 7/16 x 4 3/8 x 2 in.
2003.236.102

Jumbo (base and wheels missing), c. 1883
J. & E. Stevens Company, Cromwell, Connecticut (1843 – 1950s), or Kyser & Rex Company, Philadelphia (c. 1879 – 98), manufacturer
Iron, pigment
4 x 2 5/8 x 1 5/8 in.
2003.236.88

Bismark [sic] *Bank*, c. 1883 – 84
Charles A. Bailey, American (1848 – 1926), designer
J. & E. Stevens Company, Cromwell, Connecticut (1843 – 1950s), manufacturer
Iron, lead, tin, pigment
5 1/4 x 7 1/2 x 2 1/2 in.
2003.236.23

Lion and Two Monkeys, c. 1883
Louis Kyser and Alfred C. Rex, American, designers
Kyser & Rex Company, Philadelphia (c. 1879 – 98), manufacturer
Iron, brass, pigment
9 1/4 x 9 1/16 x 3 1/2 in.
2003.236.81

Cabin Bank, c. 1885
Edward L. Morris, American, designer
J. & E. Stevens Company, Cromwell, Connecticut (1843 – 1950s), manufacturer
Tin, pigment
3 5/8 x 4 3/16 x 2 7/8 in.
2003.236.15a,b

Afghanistan, c. 1885
Kyser & Rex Company, Philadelphia (c. 1879 – 98), or Mechanical Novelty Works, New Britain, Connecticut (1870s – 90s), manufacturer
Iron, pigment
3 1/2 x 3 7/16 x 3 1/8 in.
2003.236.57

Punch and Judy, c. 1884
Peter Adams and Charles G. Shepard, American, designers
Shepard Hardware Company, Buffalo, New York (1866 – 92), manufacturer
Iron, pigment
7 7/16 x 6 3/16 x 3 3/4 in.
2003.236.138

Mammy and Child, c. 1884
Alfred C. Rex, American, designer
Kyser & Rex Company, Philadelphia (c. 1879 – 98), manufacturer
Iron, pigment
7 1/2 x 3 13/16 x 4 1/4 in.
2003.236.883

Snap It (eight-sided building), c. 1885 – 90
H. L. Judd Manufacturing Company, Wallingford, Connecticut, (c. 1830 – 1960s), manufacturer
Iron, pigment
4 x 3 x 3 in.
2003.236.121

Speaking Dog, c. 1885
Peter Adams and Charles G. Shepard, American, designers
J. & E. Stevens Company, Cromwell, Connecticut (1843 – 1950s), manufacturer
Iron, pigment
7 x 7 1/4 x 3 in.
2003.236.47

Picture Gallery, c. 1885
Attributed to Peter Adams and Charles G. Shepard, American, designers
Shepard Hardware Company, Buffalo, New York (1866 – 92), manufacturer
Iron, pigment
8 1/4 x 5 7/8 x 2 7/8 in.
2003.236.144

Wimbledon Bank, c. 1885
John Harper & Company, Ltd., Willenhall, England (1790 – 1980s), manufacturer
Iron, brass, pigment
5 3/8 x 12 3/16 x 2 15/16 in.
2003.236.823

Trick Pony, c. 1885
Juleus Mueller, American, designer
Shepard Hardware Company, Buffalo, New York (1866 – 92), manufacturer
Iron, pigment
7 1/2 x 7 1/8 x 2 1/2 in.
2003.236.39

Stump Speaker, c. 1886
Peter Adams and Charles G. Shepard, American, designers
Shepard Hardware Company, Buffalo, New York (1866 – 92), manufacturer
Iron, pigment
9 7/8 x 5 x 3 15/16 in.
2003.236.677

Monkey and Cocoanut, c. 1886
James H. Bowen, American (active c. 1877 – 1906), designer
J. & E. Stevens Company, Cromwell, Connecticut (1843 – 1950s), manufacturer
Iron, pigment
8 3/8 x 3 1/8 x 5 1/8 in.
2003.236.880

Boys Stealing Watermelons, c. 1885 – 95
Attributed to Kyser & Rex Company, Philadelphia (c. 1879 – 98), manufacturer
Iron, pigment
5 7/8 x 6 5/8 x 1 3/16 in.
2003.236.70

Uncle Sam, c. 1886
Peter Adams and Charles G. Shepard, American, designers
Shepard Hardware Company, Buffalo, New York (1866 – 92), manufacturer
Iron, pigment
11 x 5 15/16 x 3 7/8 in.
2003.236.65

Toad on Stump, c. 1886
J. & E. Stevens Company, Cromwell, Connecticut (1843 – 1950s), manufacturer
Iron, pigment
3 x 4 x 3 11/16 in.
2003.236.106

Tabby Bank, c. 1886
Iron, pigment
4 1/4 x 2 1/2 x 2 1/2 in.
2003.236.52

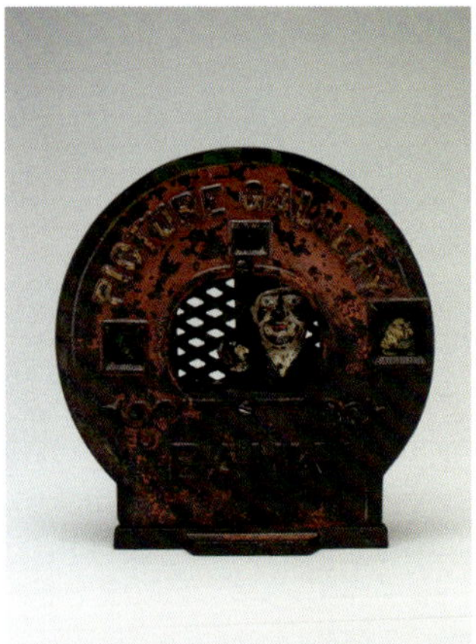

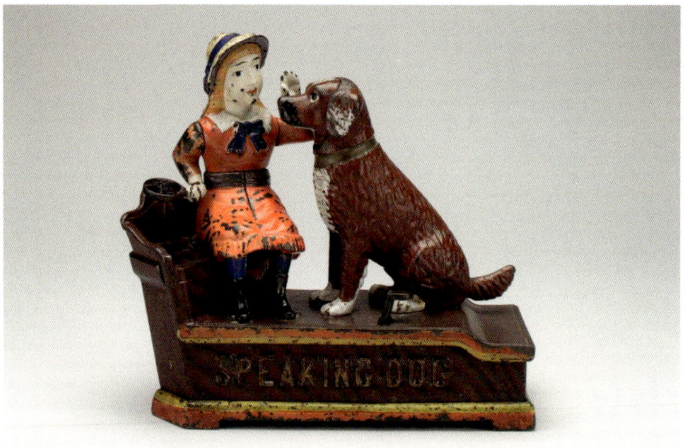
SPEAKING DOG

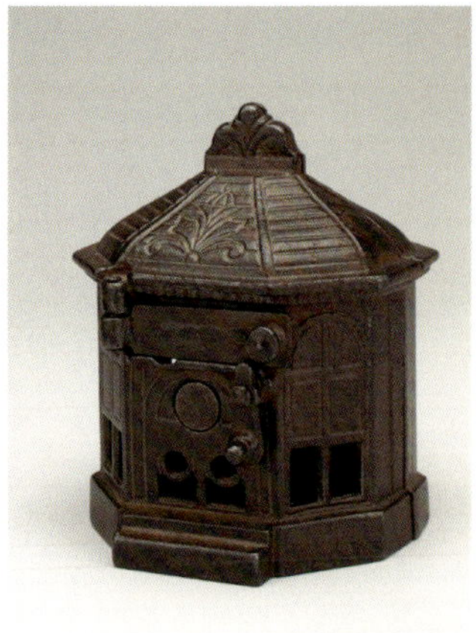

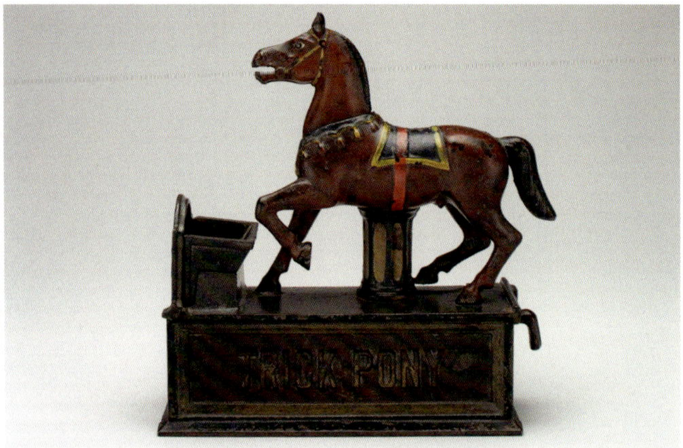
TRICK PONY

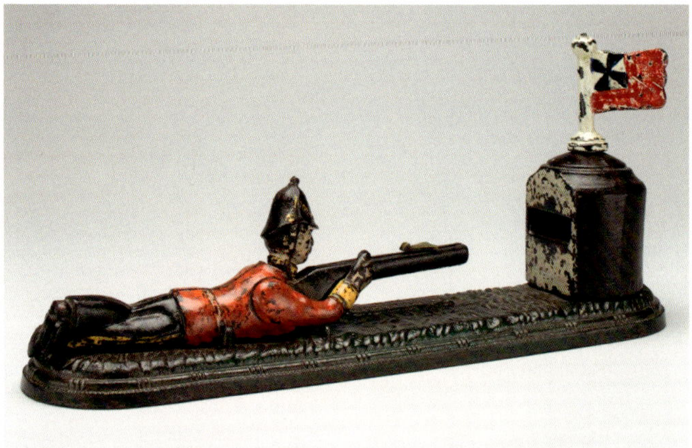

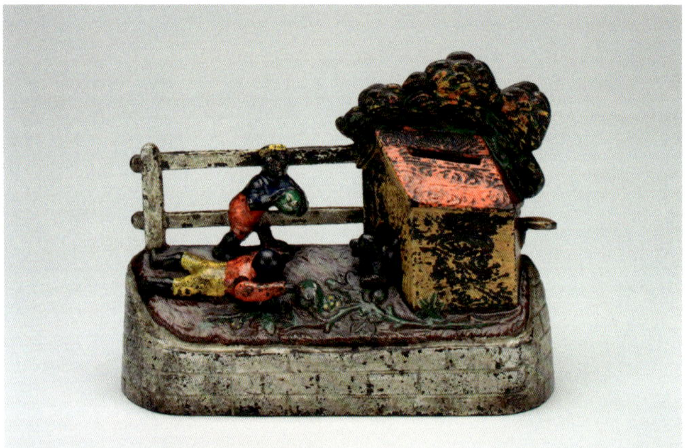

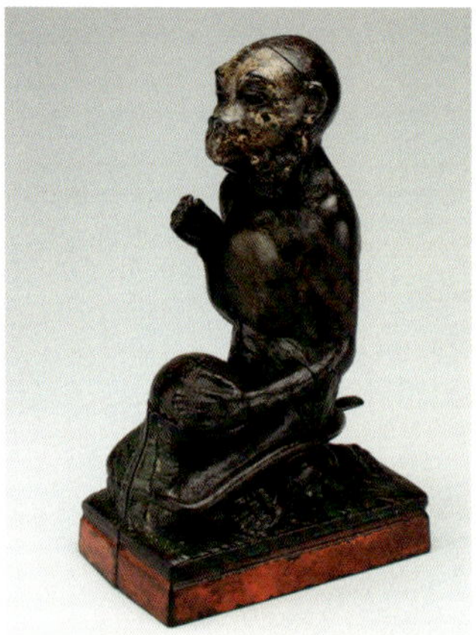

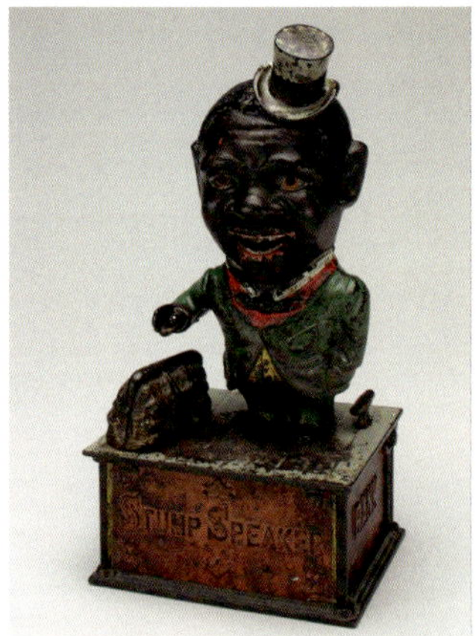
STUMP SPEAKER

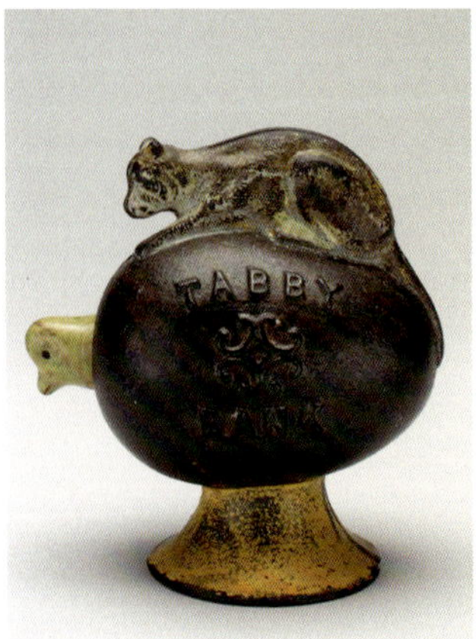
TABBY

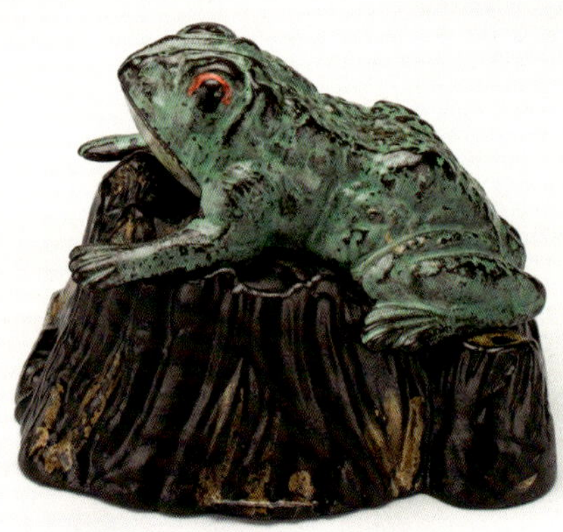

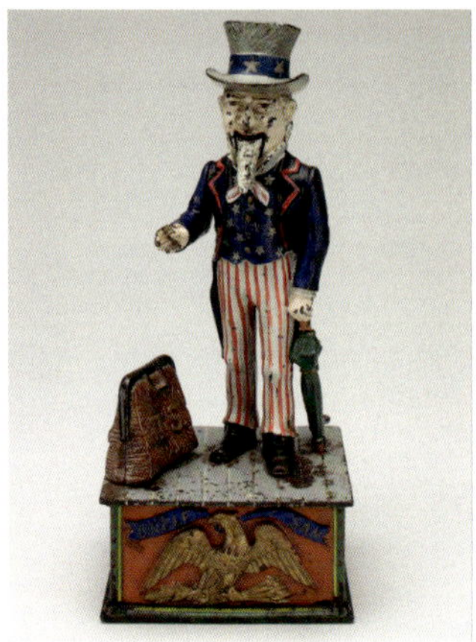

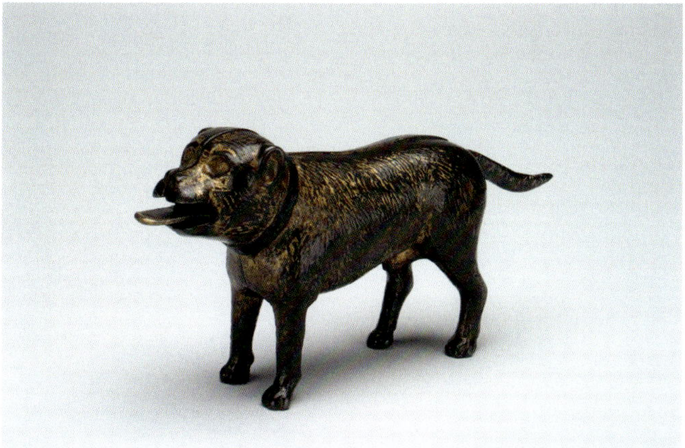

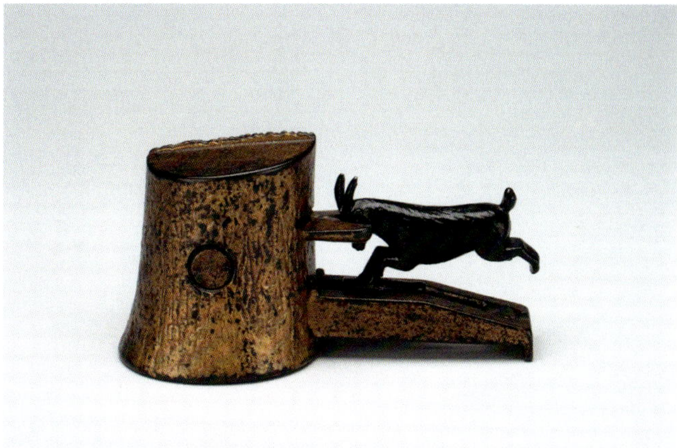

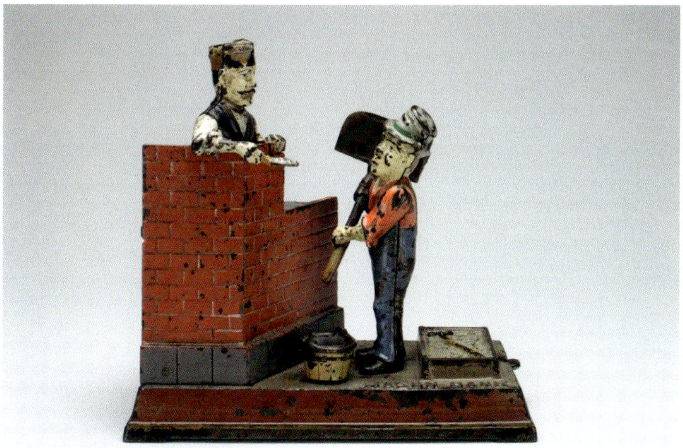

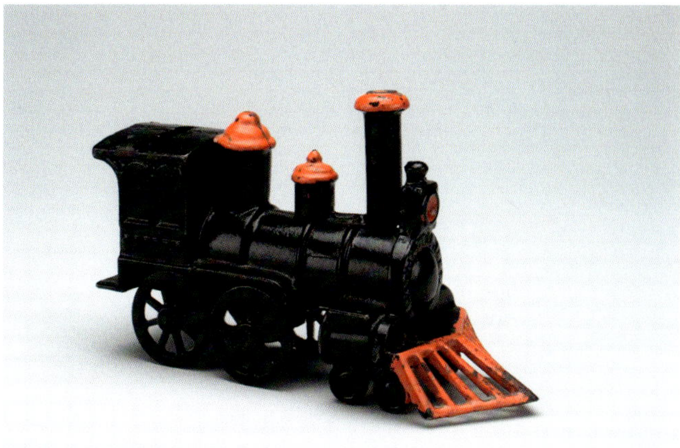

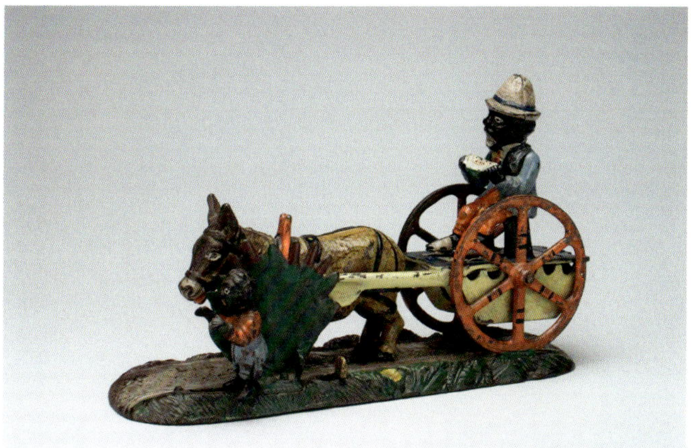

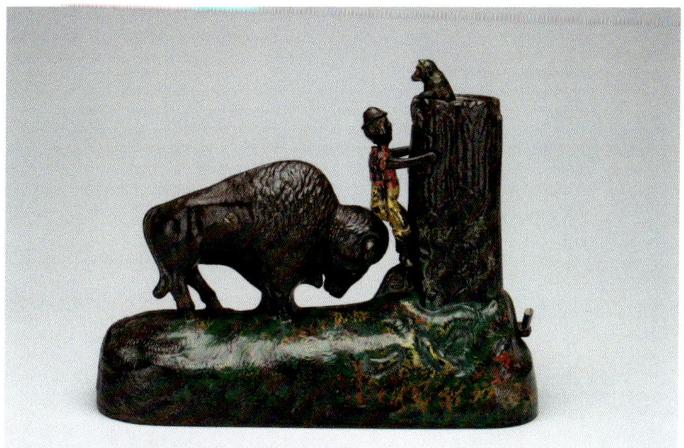

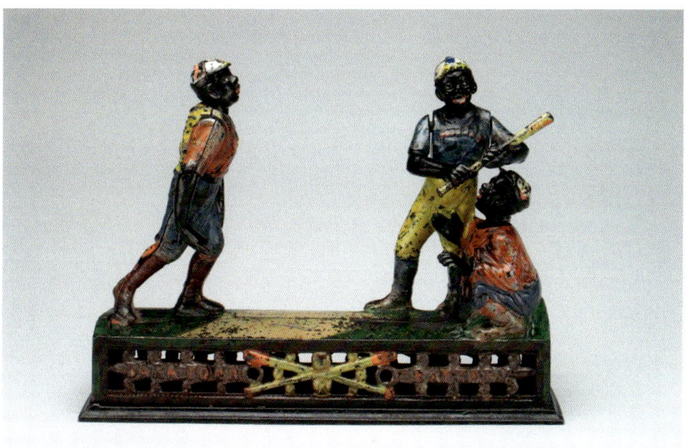

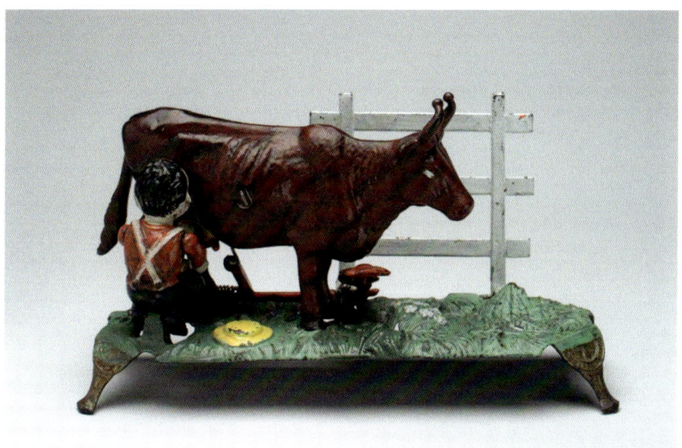

Butting Goat, Tree Stump, c. 1887
H. L. Judd Manufacturing Company, Wallingford, Connecticut (c. 1830 – 1960s), manufacturer
Iron, pigment
2 7/16 x 4 3/4 x 2 7/16 in.
2003.236.18

Bull Dog, Standing, Coin on Tongue, c. 1887
H. L. Judd Manufacturing Company, Wallingford, Connecticut (c. 1830 – 1960s), manufacturer
Iron, pigment
3 1/2 x 6 11/16 x 2 9/16 in.
2003.236.19

Safety Locomotive, c. 1887
Edward J. Colby, American, designer
Iron, pigment
3 9/16 x 5 11/16 x 2 3/8 in.
2003.236.30

Mason Bank, c. 1887
Peter Adams and Charles G. Shepard, American, designers
Shepard Hardware Company, Buffalo, New York (1866 – 92), manufacturer
Iron, pigment
7 15/16 x 7 7/16 x 3 15/16 in.
2003.236.111

Butting Buffalo, c. 1888
Alfred C. Rex, American, designer
Kyser & Rex Company, Philadelphia (c. 1879 – 98), manufacturer
Iron, pigment
5 7/8 x 7 7/8 x 2 9/16 in.
2003.236.98

Bad Accident, c. 1888
Attributed to Charles A. Bailey, American (1848 – 1926), designer
J. & E. Stevens Company, Cromwell, Connecticut (1843 – 1950s), manufacturer
Iron, pigment
5 9/16 x 10 1/4 x 3 7/16 in.
2003.236.13a,b

Milking Cow, c. 1888
Attributed to Charles A. Bailey, American (1848 – 1926), designer
J. & E. Stevens Company, Cromwell, Connecticut (1843 – 1950s), manufacturer
Iron, pigment
5 3/8 x 9 3/4 x 3 1/16 in.
2003.236.97

Darktown Battery (or *Baseball Bank*), c. 1888
James H. Bowen, American (active c. 1877 – 1906), designer
J. & E. Stevens Company, Cromwell, Connecticut (1843 – 1950s), manufacturer
Iron, pigment
7 1/2 x 10 7/8 x 2 11/16 in.
2003.236.3

Santa Claus, c. 1889
Peter Adams and Charles G. Shepard, American, designers
Shepard Hardware Company, Buffalo, New York (1866 – 92), manufacturer
Iron, pigment
5 3/4 x 4 1/8 x 3 1/8 in.
2003.236.133

Santa Claus, c. 1889
Peter Adams and Charles G. Shepard, American, designers
Shepard Hardware Company, Buffalo, New York (1866 – 92), manufacturer
Iron, pigment
5 3/4 x 4 1/8 x 3 1/8 in.
2003.236.132

Boy on Trapeze, c. 1888
J. Barton Smith Company, Philadelphia, manufacturer
Iron, pigment
10 1/2 x 5 x 5 in.
2003.236.73a,b

Zoo Bank, c. 1890s
Kyser & Rex Company, Philadelphia (c. 1879 – 98), manufacturer
Iron, pigment
4 x 4 3/16 x 1 1/2 in.
2003.236.42a,b

Clown on Globe, c. 1890
James H. Bowen, American (active c. 1877 – 1906), designer
J. & E. Stevens Company, Cromwell, Connecticut (1843 – 1950s), manufacturer
Iron, pigment
9 1/8 x 5 1/16 x 5 1/16 in.
2003.236.802

Jolly Nigger Bank, Butterfly Tie, c. 1890s – 1920s
John Harper & Company, Ltd., Willenhall, England (1790 – 1980s), manufacturer
Iron, pigment
6 3/4 x 5 x 5 1/4 in.
2003.236.710

Jolly Nigger Bank, Butterfly Tie, c. 1890s – 1920s
John Harper & Company, Ltd., Willenhall, England (1790 – 1980s), manufacturer
Iron, pigment
6 1/2 x 5 1/2 x 5 1/2 in.
2003.236.705

Girl Skipping Rope, c. 1890
James H. Bowen, American (active c. 1877 – 1906), designer
J. & E. Stevens Company, Cromwell, Connecticut (1843 – 1950s), manufacturer
Iron, pigment
7 3/4 x 8 3/16 x 5 3/8 in.
2003.236.99a,b

Cat and Mouse, Cat Balancing, c. 1891
James H. Bowen, American (active c. 1877 – 1906), designer
J. & E. Stevens Company, Cromwell, Connecticut (1843 – 1950s), manufacturer
Iron, pigment
12 x 5 3/8 x 3 9/16 in.
2003.236.17a,b

Jolly Nigger Bank, Small, High Hat, c. 1890s – 1920s
Probably John Harper & Company, Ltd., Willenhall, England (1790 – 1980s), manufacturer
Iron, pigment
6 7/16 x 4 11/16 x 5 1/2 in.
2003.236.612

Jolly Nigger Bank, High Hat, c. 1890s – 1920s
John Harper & Company, Ltd., Willenhall, England (1790 – 1980s), manufacturer
Iron, pigment
7 7/8 x 5 3/8 x 6 3/4 in.
2003.236.614

Jolly Nigger Bank, High Hat, c. 1890s – 1920s
John Harper & Company, Ltd., Willenhall, England (1790 – 1980s), manufacturer
Iron, pigment
7 1/2 x 5 1/8 x 6 7/8 in.
2003.236.613

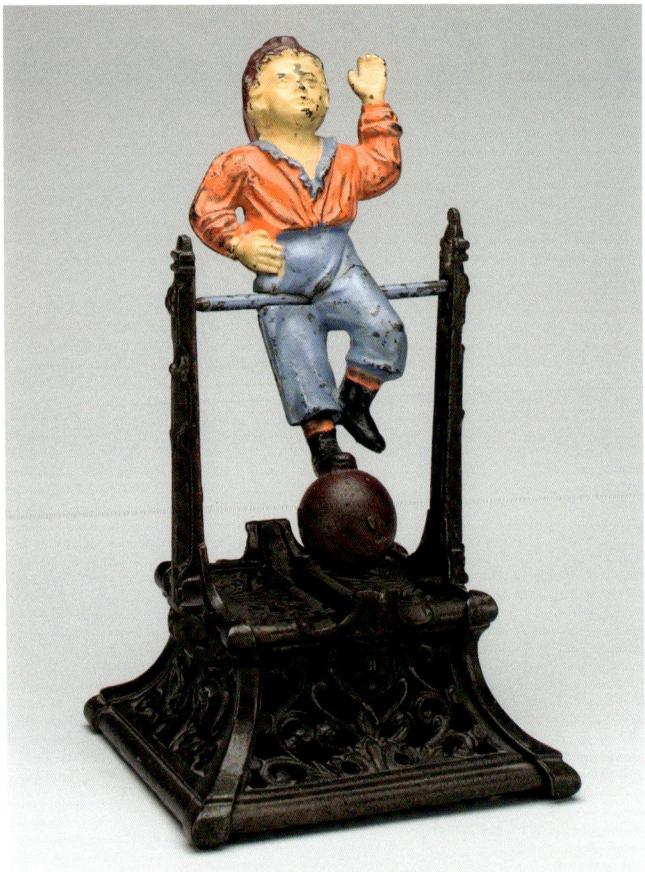

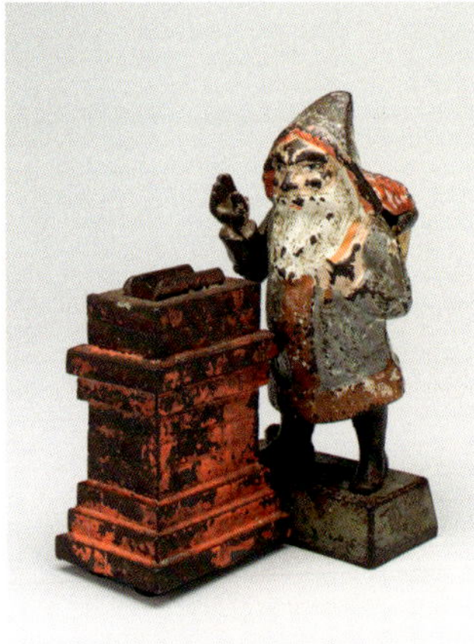

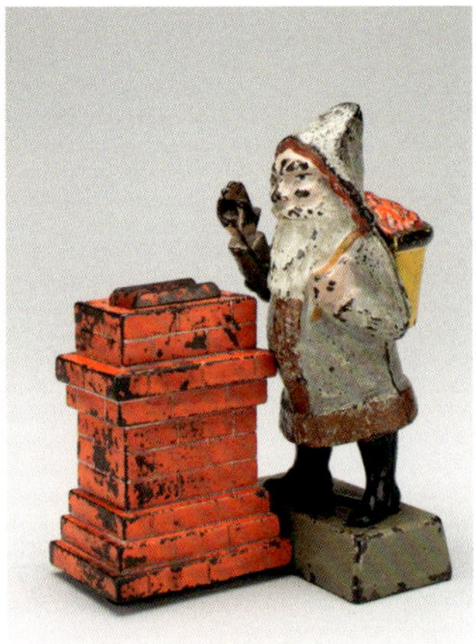

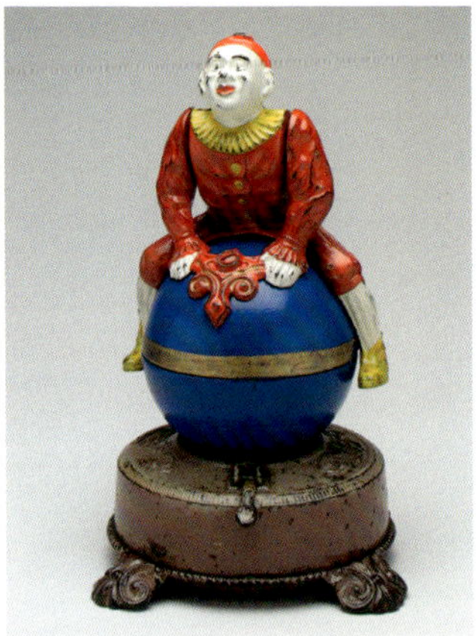

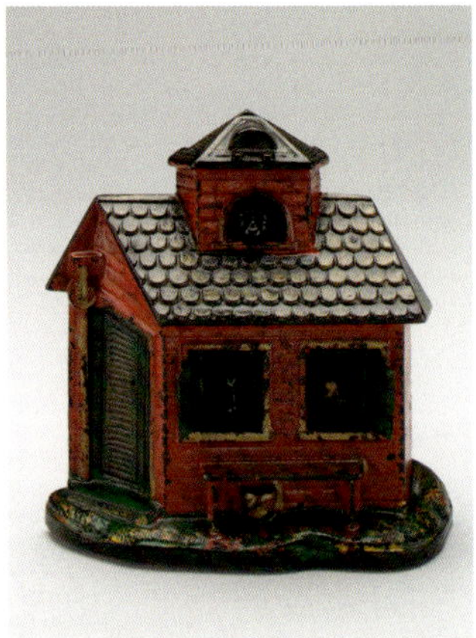

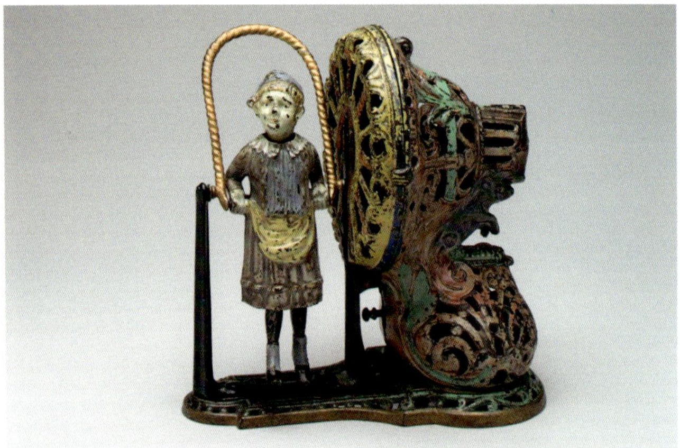

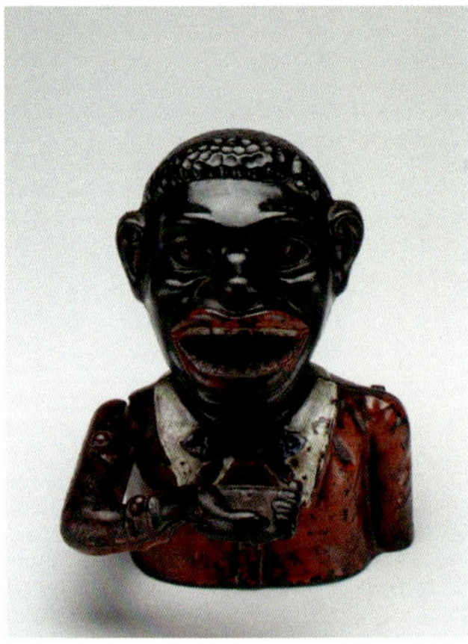

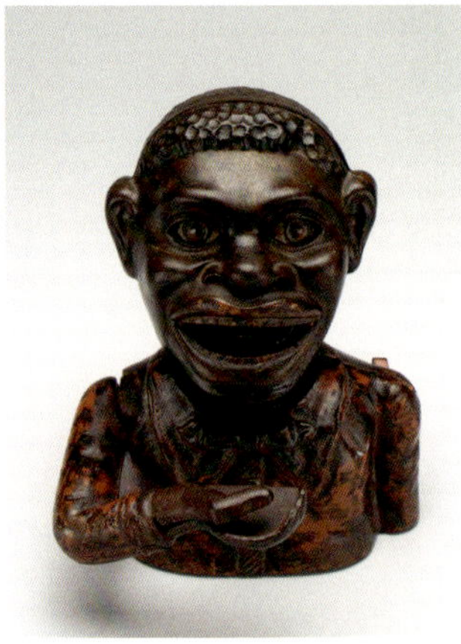

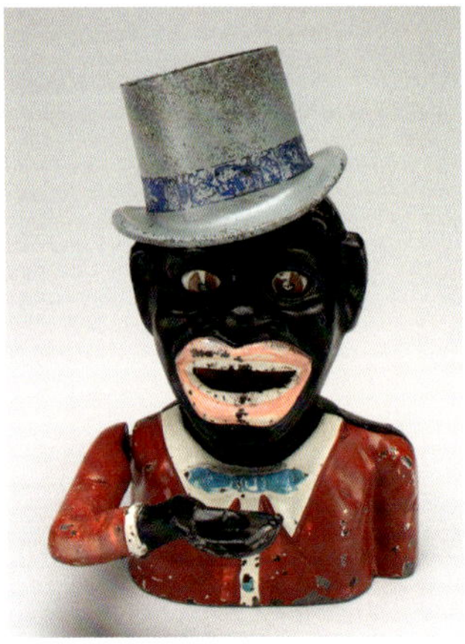

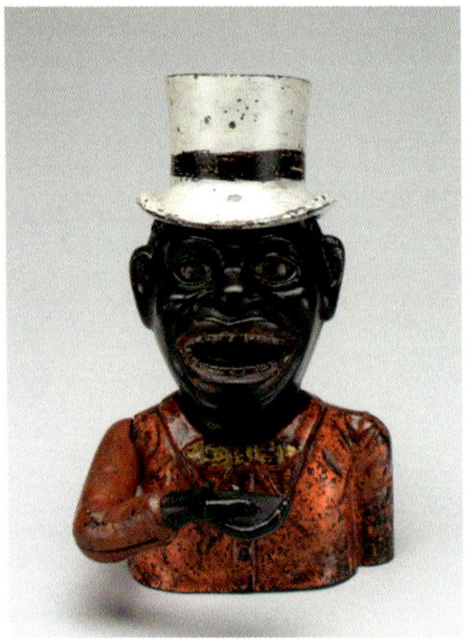

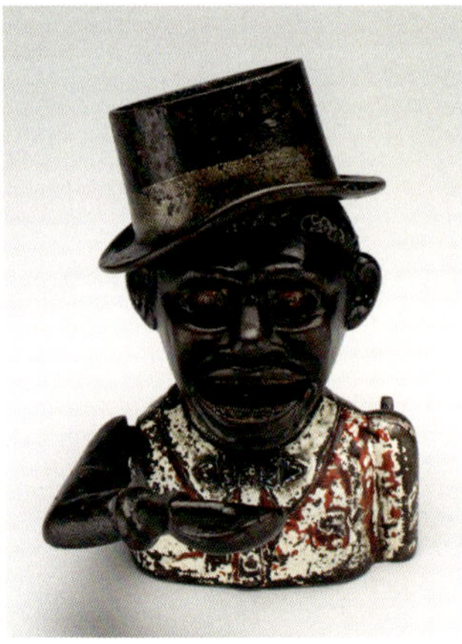

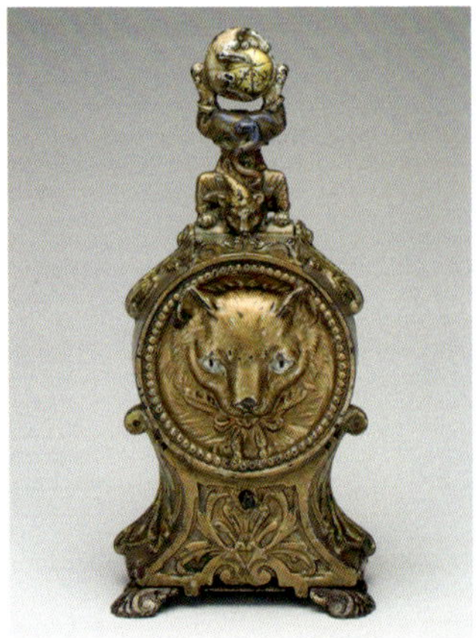

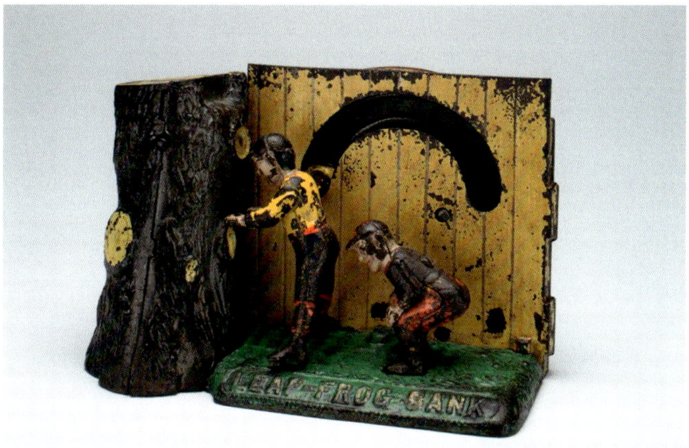
LEAP-FROG-BANK

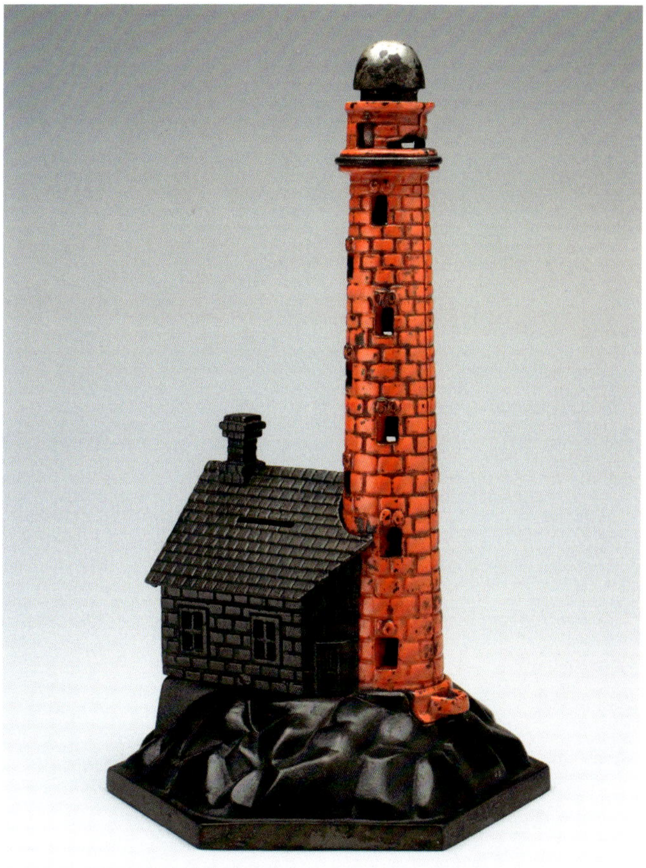

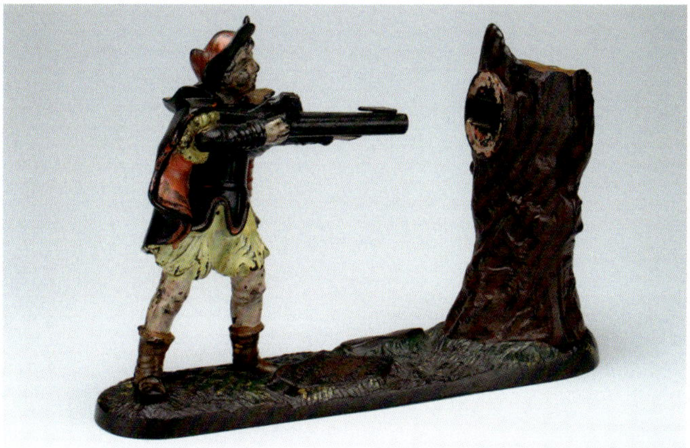

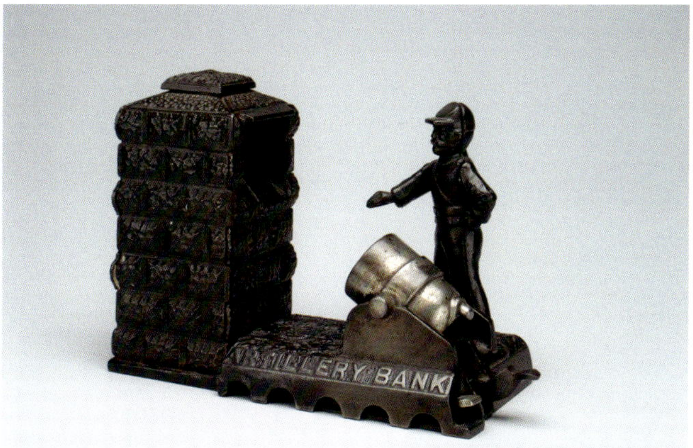

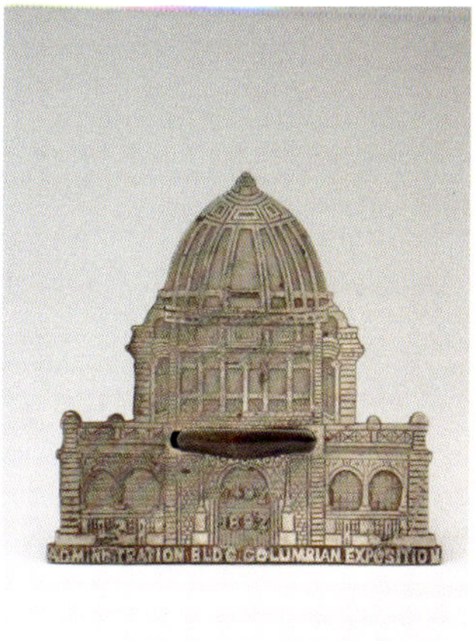
COLUMBIAN EXPOSITION

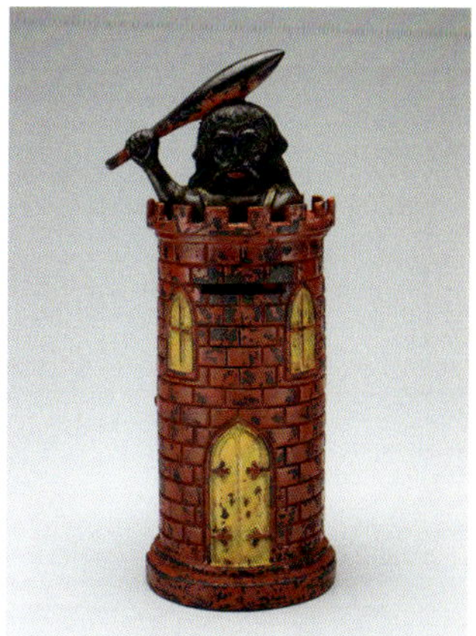

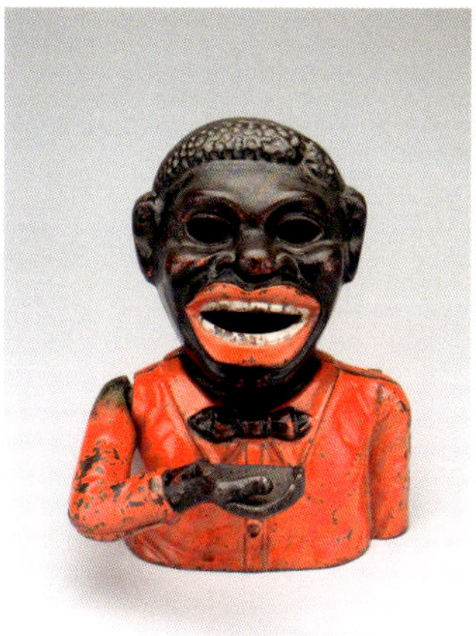

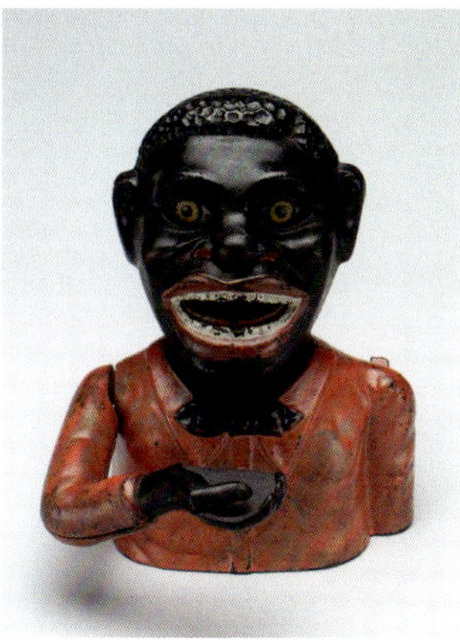

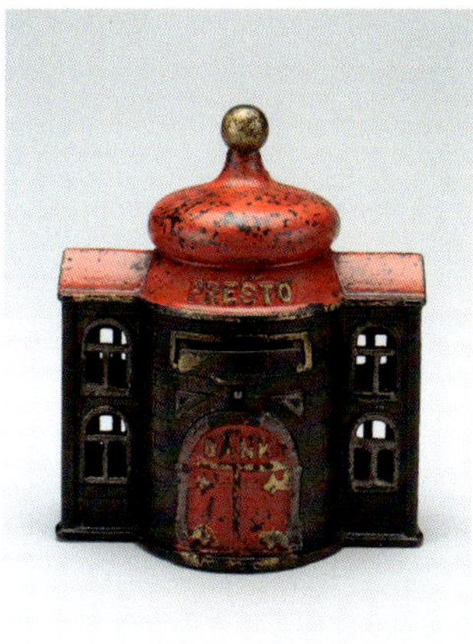

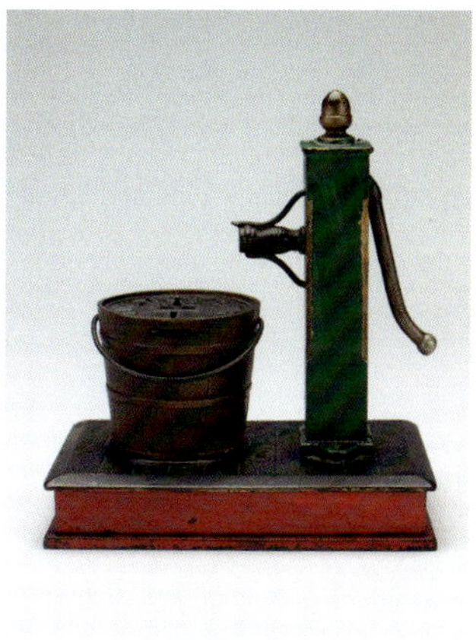

Lighthouse Bank, c. 1891
Iron, pigment
10 7/16 x 6 3/8 x 6 3/8 in.
2003.236.69a,b

Leap Frog Bank, c. 1891
Peter Adams and Charles G. Shepard, American, designers
Shepard Hardware Company, Buffalo, New York (1866 – 92), manufacturer
Iron, pigment
5 x 7 9/16 x 3 3/8 in.
2003.236.108

New Creedmoor, c. 1891
James H. Bowen, American (active c. 1877 – 1906), designer
Based on Bowen's *Creedmoor*, c. 1877, manufactured by J. & E. Stevens Company
J. & E. Stevens Company, Cromwell, Connecticut (1843 – 1950s), manufacturer
Iron, pigment
6 3/4 x 10 3/16 x 2 11/16 in.
2003.236.56a,b

Giant in Tower, c. 1892
John Harper & Company, Ltd., Willenhall, England (1790 – 1980s), manufacturer
Iron, pigment
9 1/4 x 3 3/8 x 3 3/8 in.
2003.236.64

Columbian Magic Savings Bank, c. 1892
In Production Company, New York, manufacturer
Iron, pigment
5 x 5 1/4 x 2 11/16 in.
2003.236.38a,b

Artillery Bank, Rectangular Trap, c. 1892
Peter Adams and Charles G. Shepard, American, designers
Shepard Hardware Company, Buffalo, New York (1866 – 92), manufacturer
Iron, pigment
6 7/8 x 7 7/8 x 3 3/4 in.
2003.236.62

Pump and Bucket (registering), c. 1892
Iron, pigment, glass
6 5/16 x 5 11/16 x 3 9/16 in.
2003.236.131

Presto Bank, c. 1892
Kyser & Rex Company, Philadelphia (c. 1879 – 98), or Kenton Hardware Manufacturing Company, Kenton, Ohio (1890 – 1950), manufacturer
Iron, pigment
4 3/16 x 3 13/16 x 2 1/2 in.
2003.236.90

Jolly Nigger Bank, c. 1892
Peter Adams and Charles G. Shepard, American, designers
J. & E. Stevens Company, Cromwell, Connecticut (1843 – 1950s), manufacturer
Iron, pigment
7 x 4 7/8 x 5 1/2 in.
2003.236.709

Jolly Nigger Bank, c. 1892
Peter Adams and Charles G. Shepard, American, designers
J. & E. Stevens Company, Cromwell, Connecticut (1843 – 1950s), manufacturer
Iron, pigment
6 1/4 x 4 13/16 x 4 1/4 in.
2003.236.616

Perfection Registering Bank, c. 1893
Charles A. Bailey, American (1848 – 1926), designer
J. & E. Stevens Company, Cromwell, Connecticut (1843 – 1950s), manufacturer
Iron, pigment, paper
4 1/4 x 6 1/16 x 2 3/4 in.
2003.236.239

Professor Pug Frog's Great Bicycle Feat, c. 1892
Attributed to Charles A. Bailey, American (1848 – 1926)
J. & E. Stevens Company, Cromwell, Connecticut (1843 – 1950s), manufacturer
Iron, pigment
7 3/4 x 10 3/16 x 3 3/16 in.
2003.236.95

Dog on Turntable, c. 1895
H. L. Judd Manufacturing Company, Wallingford, Connecticut (c. 1830 – 1960s), manufacturer
Iron, pigment
5 x 3 3/8 x 5 3/8 in.
2003.236.314

World's Fair Bank (or *Columbus Bank*), c. 1893
Charles A. Bailey, American (1848 – 1926), designer
J. & E. Stevens Company, Cromwell, Connecticut (1843 – 1950s), manufacturer
Iron, pigment
6 1/4 x 8 5/16 x 3 3/16 in.
2003.236.48

Bank of Education and Economy, c. 1895
James S. Barcus, American, designer
Proctor-Raymond Company, Buffalo, New York, manufacturer
Iron, nickel plate, paper, glass
4 5/8 x 3 1/16 x 3 1/16 in.
2003.236.6a,b

Pig in High Chair, c. 1897
Peter Adams, American, designer
J. & E. Stevens Company, Cromwell, Connecticut (1843 – 1950s), manufacturer
Brass, nickel plate
5 1/2 x 2 3/16 x 3 3/8 in.
2003.236.814

Trick Dog, Six-Part Base, c. 1894 – 1925
Daniel Cooke, American, designer
Hubley Manufacturing Company, Lancaster, Pennsylvania (est. 1894), manufacturer
Iron, pigment
7 3/8 x 8 3/4 x 2 15/16 in.
2003.236.28

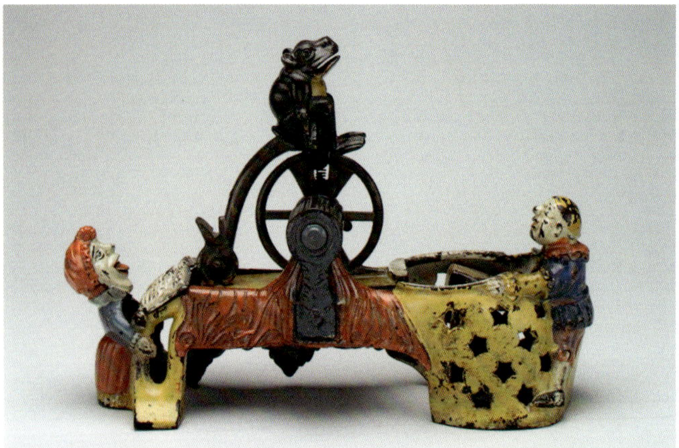

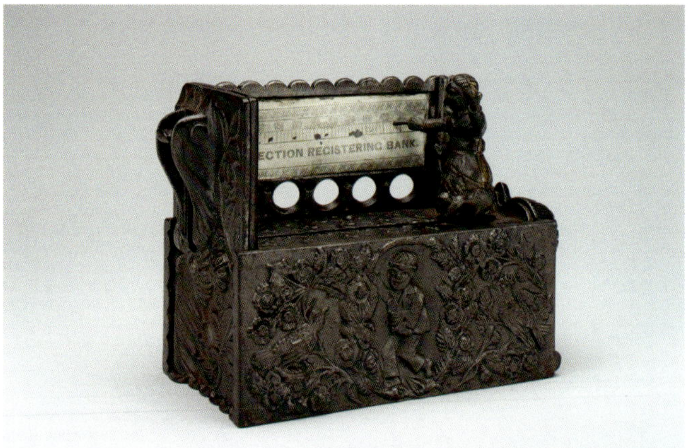

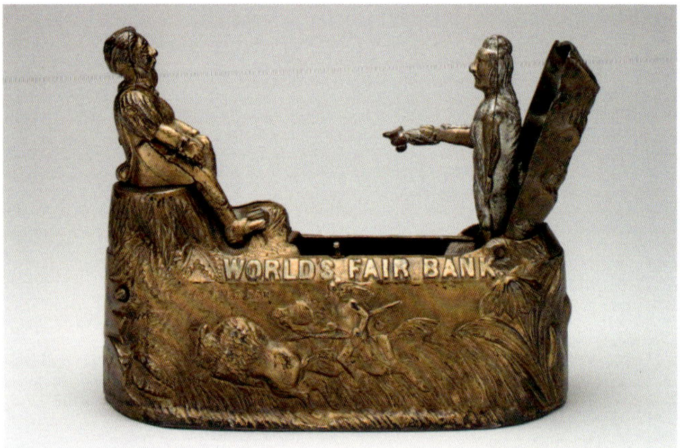
WORLD'S FAIR BANK

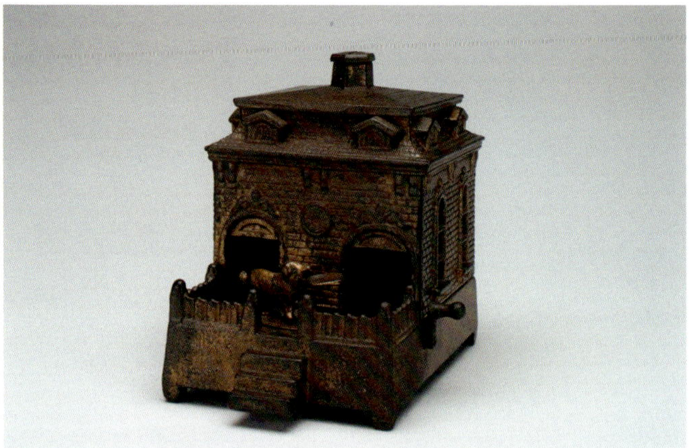

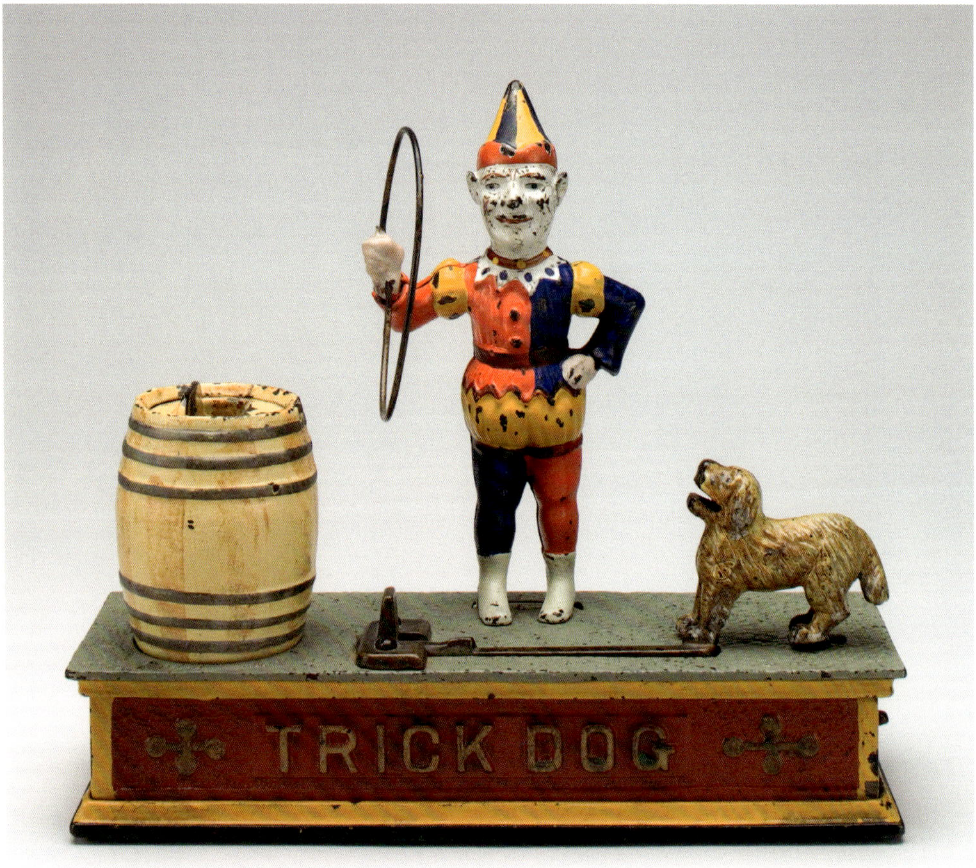
TRICK DOG

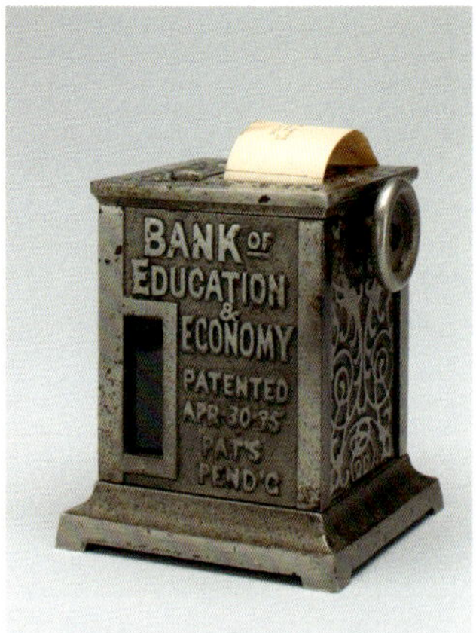
BANK OF
EDUCATION
&
ECONOMY
PATENTED
APR-30-95
PAT'S
PEND-G

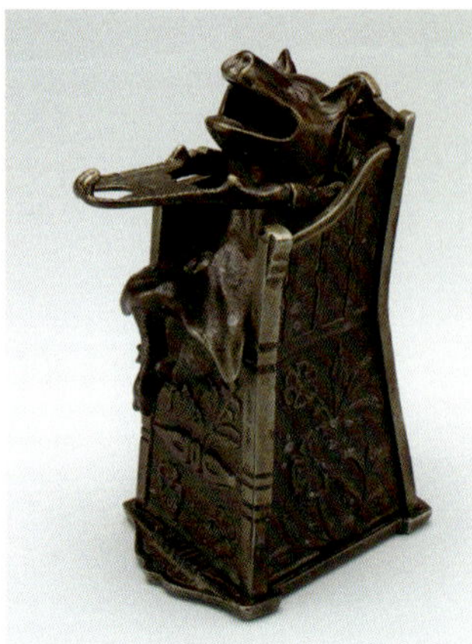

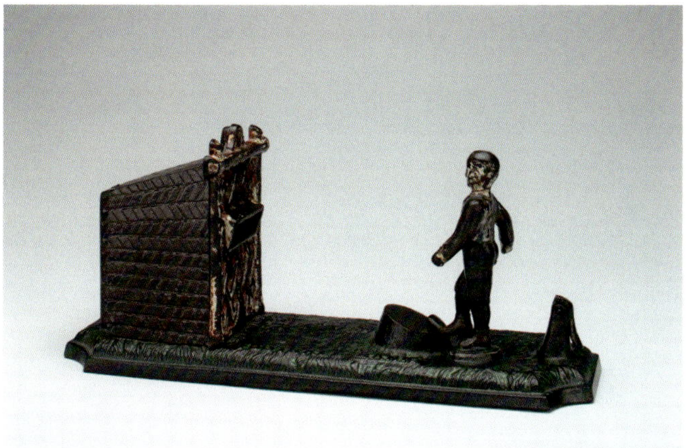

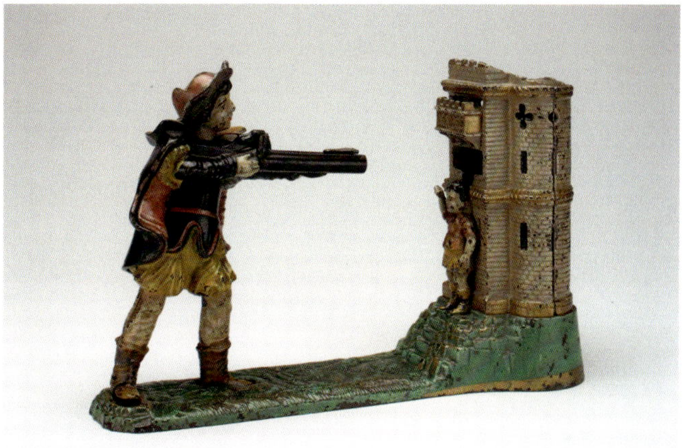

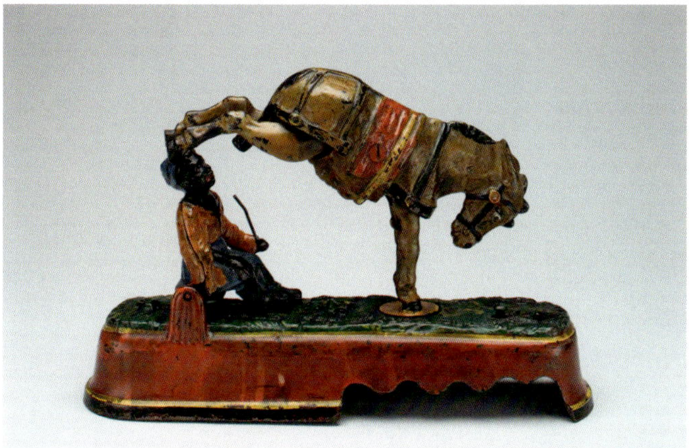

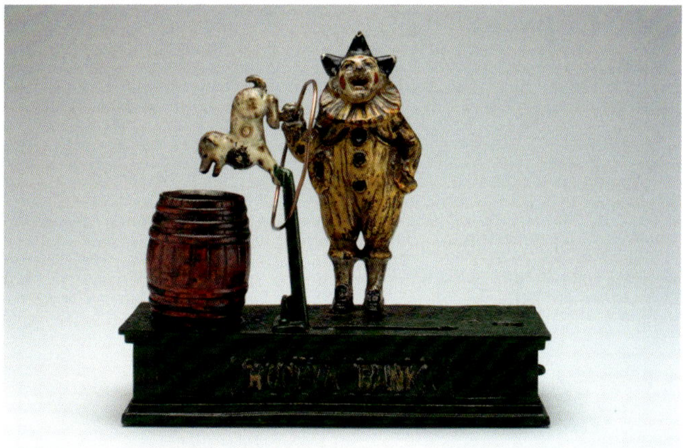

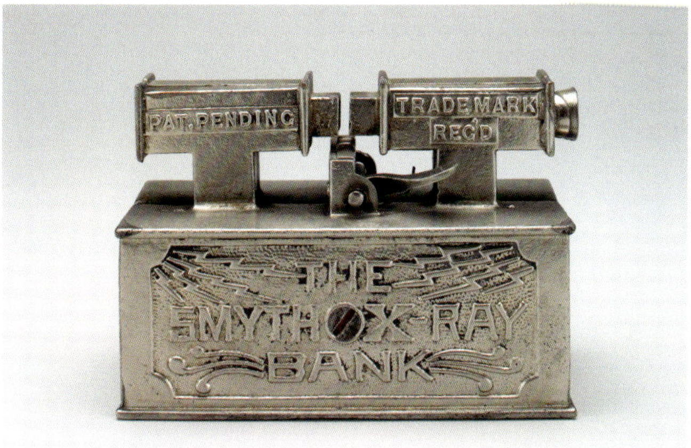
PAT. PENDING
TRADE MARK
REG'D
THE
SMYTH X-RAY
BANK

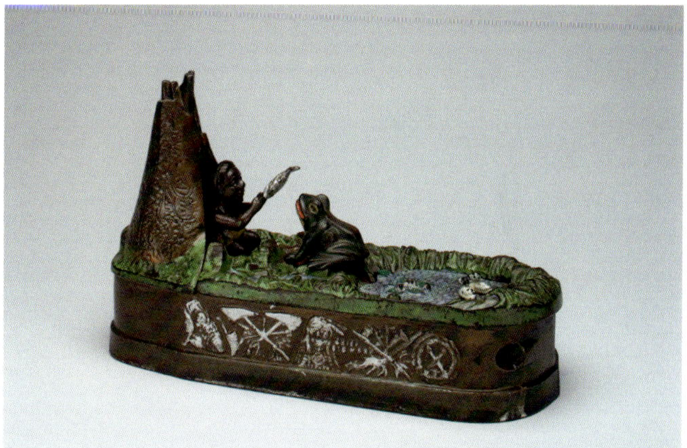

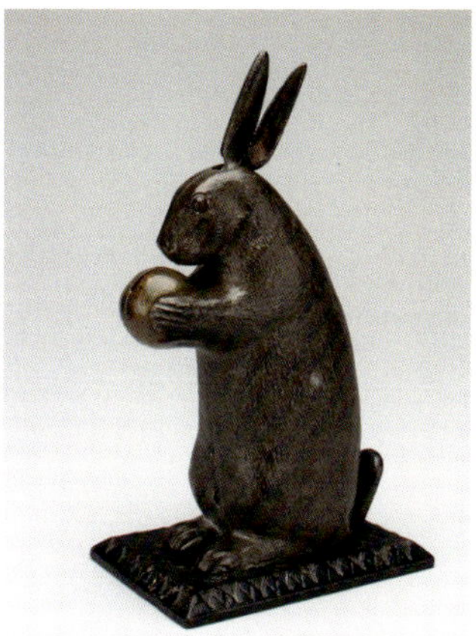

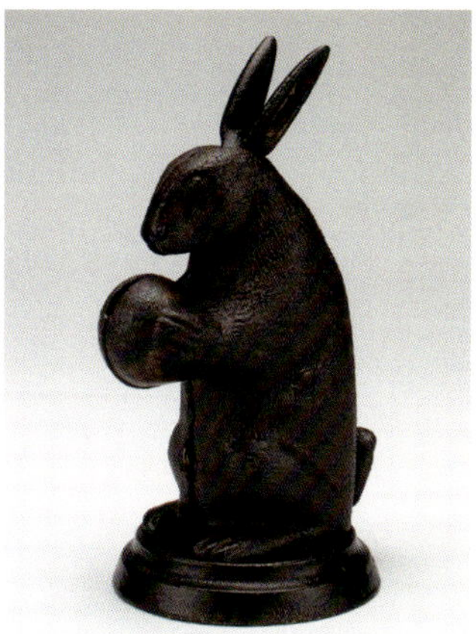

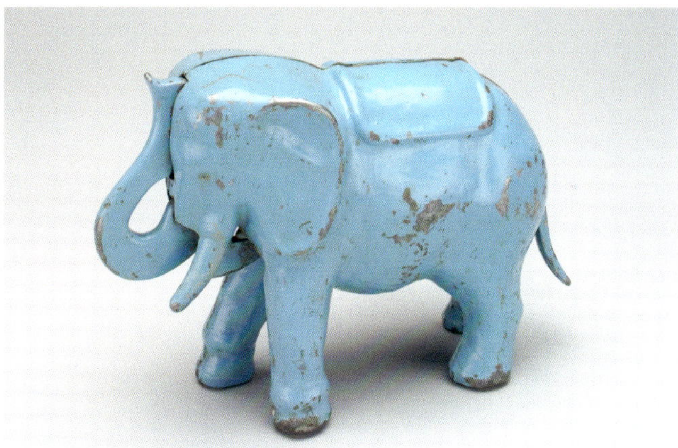

William Tell, c. 1896
Russell Frisbie, American, designer
J. & E. Stevens Company, Cromwell, Connecticut (1843 – 1950s), manufacturer
Iron, pigment
6 5/8 x 10 9/16 x 3 11/16 in.
2003.236.55a,b

Football Bank, c. 1895
John Harper & Company, Ltd., Willenhall, England (1790 – 1980s), manufacturer
Iron, pigment
4 3/8 x 10 1/4 x 3 3/8 in.
2003.236.80

Hoop-La Bank, c. 1897 – 1920s
John Harper & Company, Ltd., Willenhall, England (1790 – 1980s), manufacturer
Iron, pigment
7 3/8 x 8 3/8 x 2 11/16 in.
2003.236.27a,b

I Always Did 'Spise a Mule, Boy Seated on Bench, c. 1897
James H. Bowen, American (active c. 1877 – 1906), designer
J. & E. Stevens Company, Cromwell, Connecticut (1843 – 1950s), manufacturer
Iron, pigment
5 3/4 x 10 1/8 x 2 15/16 in.
2003.236.114

Chief Big Moon, c. 1899
Charles A. Bailey, American (1848 – 1926), designer
J. & E. Stevens Company, Cromwell, Connecticut (1843 – 1950s), manufacturer
Iron, pigment
6 1/8 x 10 x 4 in.
2003.236.5a,b

Smyth X-ray Bank, c. 1898
Charles Smyth, American
Henry C. Hart Manufacturing Company, Detroit, manufacturer
Iron, pigment
3 1/2 x 5 1/4 x 2 1/2 in.
2003.236.137

Elephant, c. 1900
Aluminum, pigment
4 7/8 x 2 5/8 x 7 1/4 in.
2003.236.411

Rabbit Standing, Small, late 19th century
Henry S. Lockwood, American, designer
Lockwood Manufacturing Company, South Norwalk, Connecticut, manufacturer
Iron, pigment
6 x 2 3/4 x 2 3/4 in.
2003.236.117

Rabbit Standing, Large, late 19th century
Henry S. Lockwood, American, designer
Lockwood Manufacturing Company, South Norwalk, Connecticut, manufacturer
Iron, pigment
8 x 4 5/16 x 3 1/16 in.
2003.236.118

Elephant with Howdah, Locked, c. 1900
Charles F. Olm, Sr., and John Thalheim, American, designers
Gurney Refrigerator Company, Fond du Lac, Wisconsin, manufacturer
Iron, pigment
7 1/4 x 7 x 2 5/8 in.
2003.236.408

Elephant, c. 1900
Brass
4 3/4 x 8 x 2 1/4 in.
2003.236.280

Bear Standing, Slot in Chest, c. 1900
Kenton Hardware Manufacturing Company, Kenton, Ohio (1890 – 1950), manufacturer
Iron, pigment
6 9/16 x 3 x 2 13/16 in.
2003.236.10a,b

Captain Kidd (converted semi-mechanical), c. 1901
Iron, pigment
5 5/8 x 4 1/8 x 2 1/8 in.
2003.236.852

Old Tip, c. 1900
England
Tin, pigment
5 9/16 x 8 1/16 x 2 13/16 in.
2003.236.295a,b

Jolly Nigger, String Tie, Round Eyes, c. 1900
Probably England
Aluminum, pigment
6 1/8 x 4 7/8 x 4 3/4 in.
2003.236.708

Two Towers, c. 1900
Wood, pigment, metal
5 3/4 x 6 3/8 x 3 3/4 in.
2003.236.331

Piano (converted still bank), c. 1900
E. M. Roche Novelty Company, Newark, New Jersey, manufacturer
Iron, nickel plate
7 1/4 x 11 7/8 x 2 3/4 in.
2003.236.45

Magician, c. 1901
William C. Bull, American, designer
J. & E. Stevens Company, Cromwell, Connecticut (1843 – 1950s), manufacturer
Iron, pigment
8 1/16 x 7 x 3 13/16 in.
2003.236.71a,b

Fortune Teller Savings Bank, c. 1901
Aaron Kaufman, American, designer
Baumgarten & Company, Baltimore, manufacturer
Iron, paper
6 3/4 x 4 3/4 x 4 15/16 in.
2003.236.554

Artillery Bank, Round Trap, c. 1900 – 1932
Peter Adams and Charles G. Shepard, American, designers
Based on Adams and Shepard's *Artillery Bank, Rectangular Trap*, c. 1892, manufactured by Shepard Hardware Company, Buffalo, New York (1866 – 92)
J. & E. Stevens Company, Cromwell, Connecticut (1843 – 1950s), manufacturer
Iron, pigment
6 7/8 x 7 7/8 x 3 3/4 in.
2003.236.63a,b

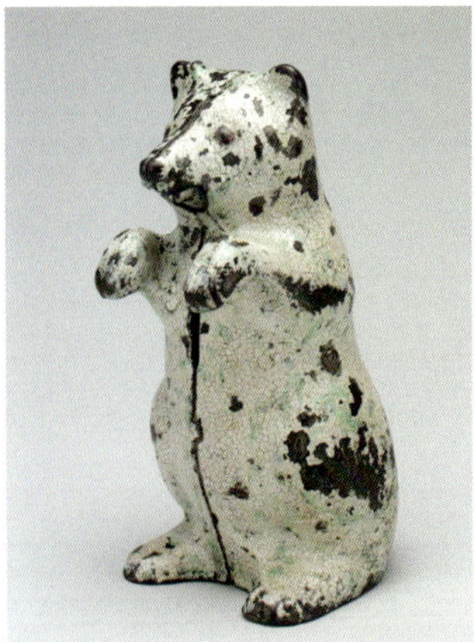

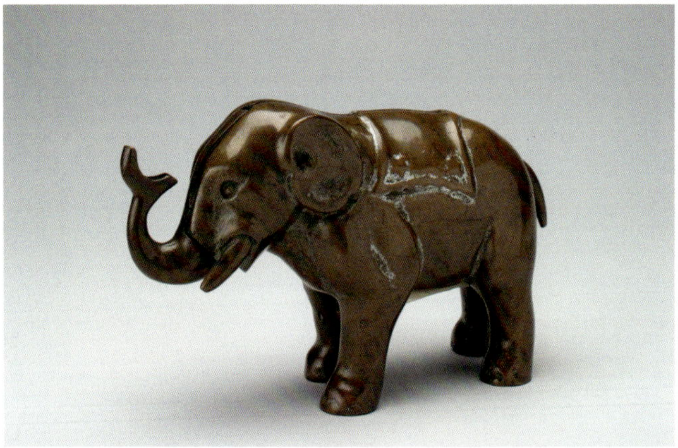

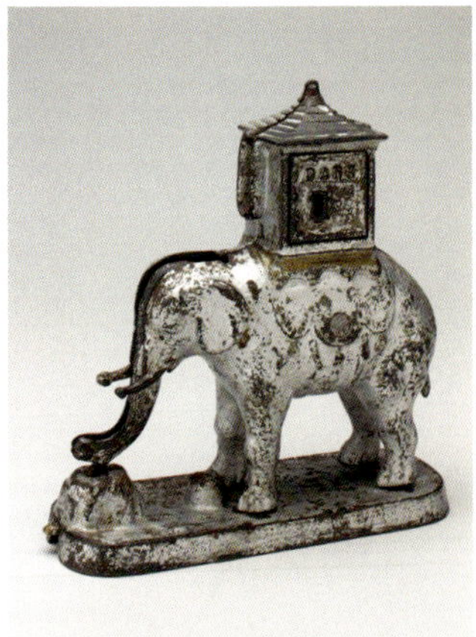

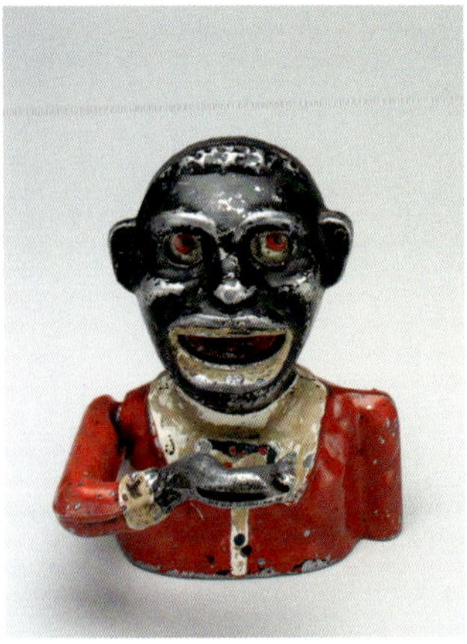

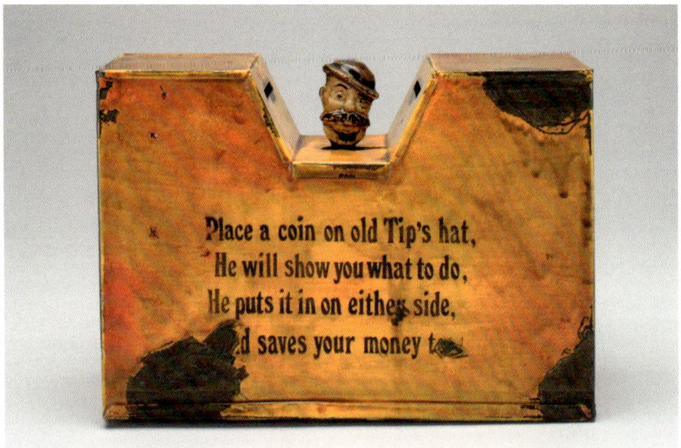
Place a coin on old Tip's hat,
He will show you what to do,
He puts it in on either side,

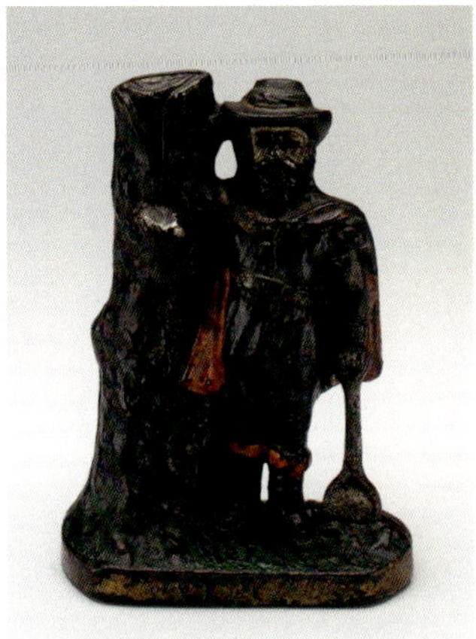

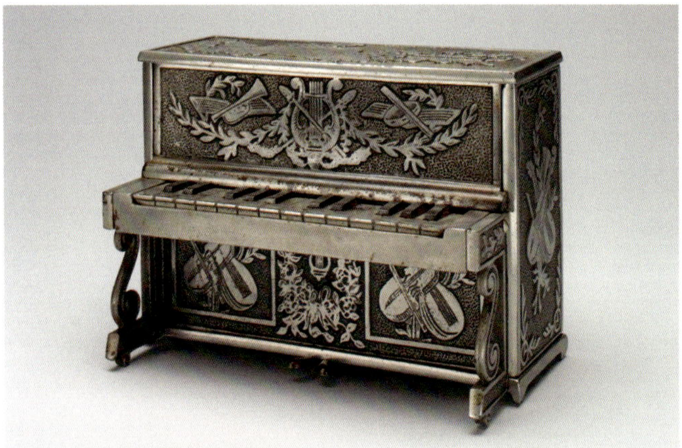

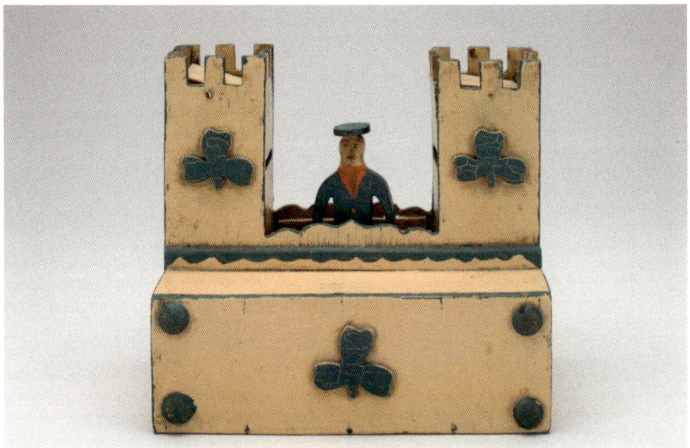

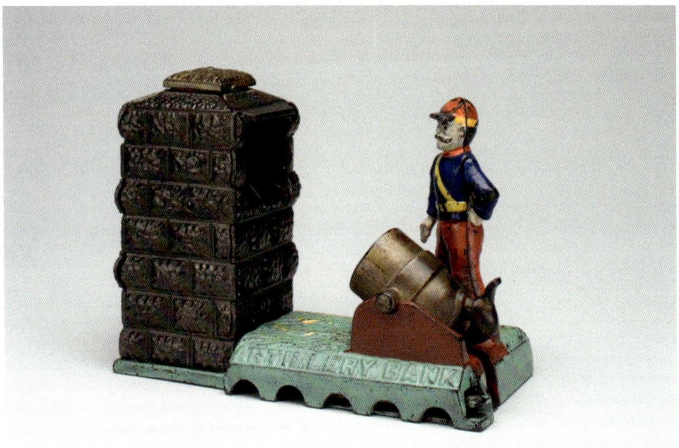
ARTILLERY BANK

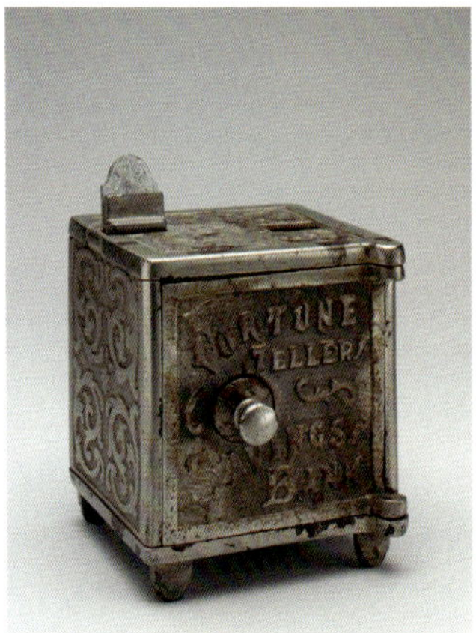

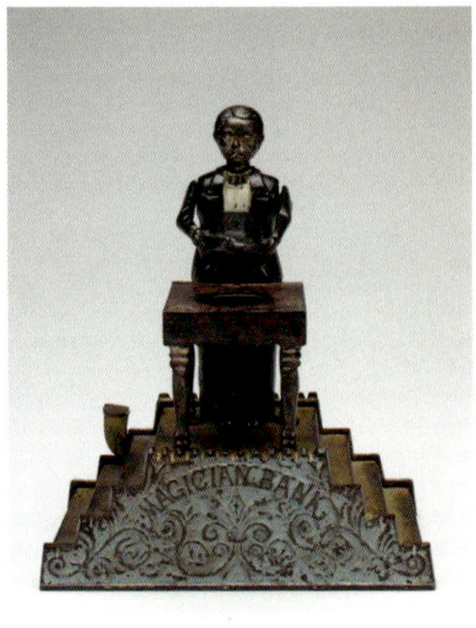
MAGICIAN BANK

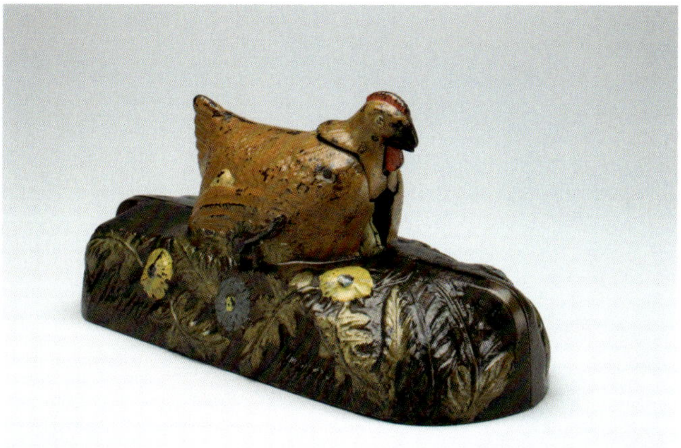

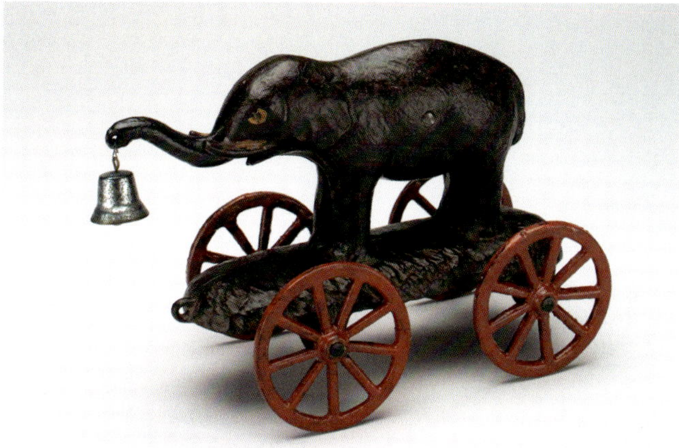

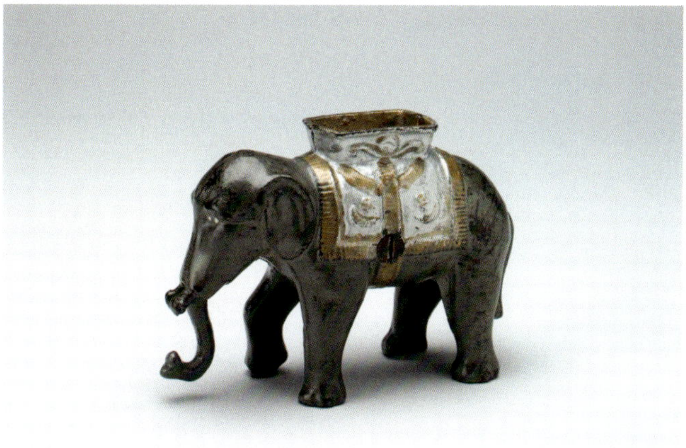

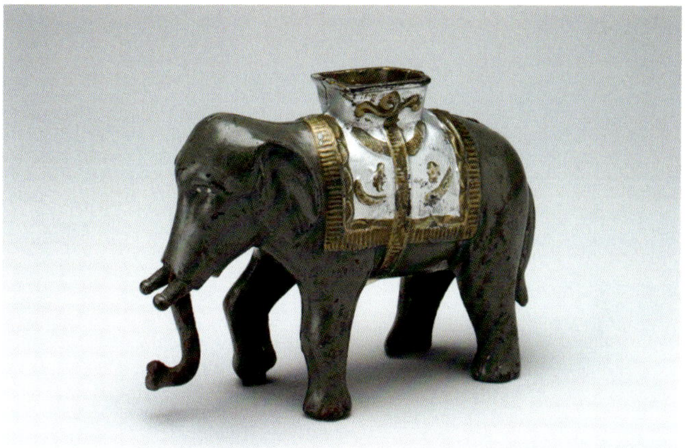

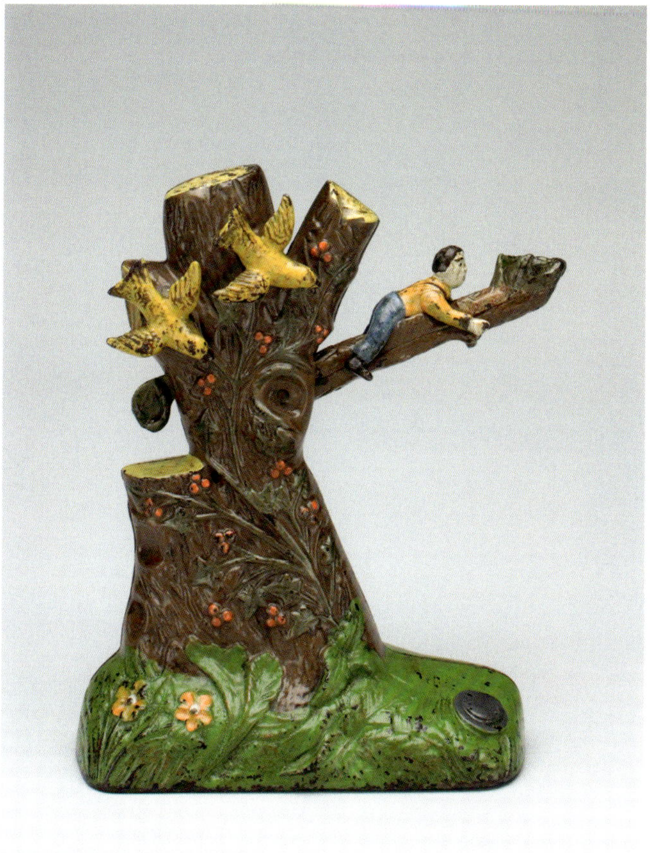

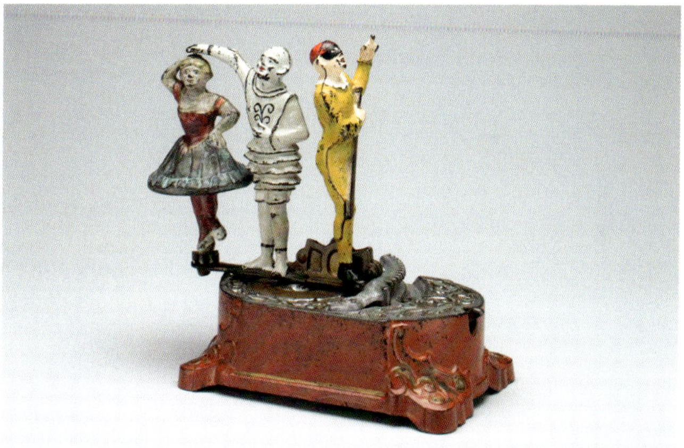

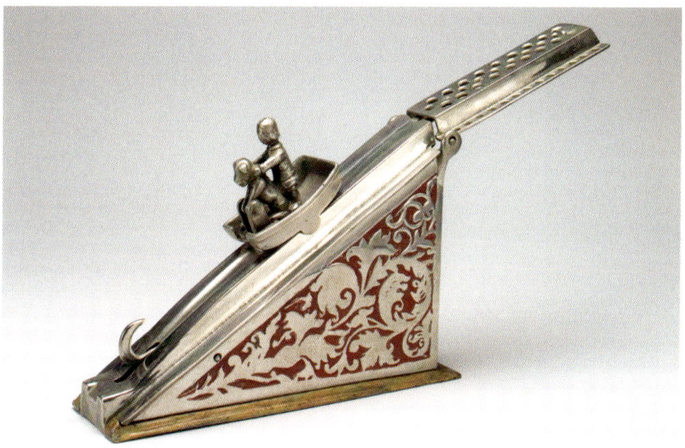

Elephant on Wheels (converted bell toy), c. 1905
Iron, pigment
4 1/2 x 5 1/4 x 1 3/4 in.
2003.236.51

Hen and Chick, c. 1901
Charles A. Bailey, American (1848 – 1926), designer
J. & E. Stevens Company, Cromwell, Connecticut (1843 – 1950s), manufacturer
Iron, pigment
4 1/2 x 9 7/8 x 3 7/8 in.
2003.236.46a,b

Elephant Moves Trunk, Large, c. 1905 – 34
A. C. Williams Company, Ravenna, Ohio (est. 1886), manufacturer
Iron, pigment
4 3/4 x 6 3/4 x 2 5/16 in.
2003.236.294

Elephant Moves Trunk, Small, c. 1905 – 20s
A. C. Williams Company, Ravenna, Ohio (est. 1886), manufacturer
Iron, pigment
3 1/2 x 5 1/8 x 1 7/8 in.
2003.236.293

Clown, Harlequin, and Columbine, c. 1906
Attributed to James H. Bowen, American (active c. 1877 – 1906), designer
J. & E. Stevens Company, Cromwell, Connecticut (1843 – 1950s), manufacturer
Iron, pigment
6 5/8 x 6 1/4 x 4 3/16 in.
2003.236.105

Boy Robbing Bird's Nest, c. 1906
Charles A. Bailey, American (1848 – 1926), designer
J. & E. Stevens Company, Cromwell, Connecticut (1843 – 1950s), manufacturer
Iron, pigment
7 1/4 x 6 x 3 3/16 in.
2003.236.75a,b

Shoot the Chute, c. 1906
Charles A. Bailey, American (1848 – 1926), designer
J. & E. Stevens Company, Cromwell, Connecticut (1843 – 1950s), manufacturer
Iron, pigment
6 5/16 x 9 11/16 x 2 11/16 in.
2003.236.101a,b

Cross-Legged Minstrel, c. 1909
J. Levy Company, London, manufacturer
Tin, pigment
7 x 2 5/8 x 3 1/8 in.
2003.236.882

Monkey with Tray (or *Monkey, Automatic*), c. 1908
Maienthau & Wolff, Nuremberg, Germany, manufacturer
Tin, pigment
6 1/4 x 3 3/4 x 2 7/8 in.
2003.236.77a,b

Teddy and the Bear, c. 1907
Charles A. Bailey, American (1848 – 1926), designer
J. & E. Stevens Company, Cromwell, Connecticut (1843 – 1950s), manufacturer
Iron, pigment
7 1/4 x 10 3/16 x 3 in.
2003.236.84

Thrifty Tom (windup), c. 1910
The Ferdinand Straus Corporation, New York, manufacturer
Tin, pigment
10 1/4 x 4 5/8 x 3 3/16 in.
2003.236.14a,b

Home Bank, Morrison's, c. 1910
William Morrison, Baltimore, manufacturer
Tin, pigment
6 x 5 x 5 7/8 in.
2003.236.899

Pistol, c. 1909
James Hall Bevington, American, designer
Richard Elliott Company, Chicago, manufacturer
Tin, pigment
3 3/8 x 5 11/16 x 7/16 in.
2003.236.92

Dinah, Short Sleeves, c. 1911
John Harper & Company, Ltd., Willenhall, England (1790 – 1980s), manufacturer
Iron, pigment
6 1/2 x 5 1/4 x 4 1/8 in.
2003.236.609

Dinah, Long Sleeves, c. 1911
John Harper & Company, Ltd., Willenhall, England (1790 – 1980s), manufacturer
Iron, pigment
6 3/8 x 5 3/16 x 4 1/16 in.
2003.236.610

Snake and Frog in Pond, c. 1910 – 20
German
Tin, pigment
3 5/8 x 5 1/4 x 2 9/16 in.
2003.236.112

Bill E. Grin, c. 1915
J. W. Schmitt, American, designer
J. & E. Stevens Company, Cromwell, Connecticut (1843 – 1950s), manufacturer
Iron, pigment
4 3/8 x 3 3/8 x 2 3/8 in.
2003.236.9a,b

Dinah, c. 1911 – 20s
Probably England
Aluminum, pigment
6 3/4 x 4 x 4 1/8 in.
2003.236.349

Lion Hunter, c. 1911
Charles A. Bailey, American (1848 – 1926), designer
J. & E. Stevens Company, Cromwell, Connecticut (1843 – 1950s), manufacturer
Iron, pigment
7 1/4 x 11 7/8 x 2 3/4 in.
2003.236.44

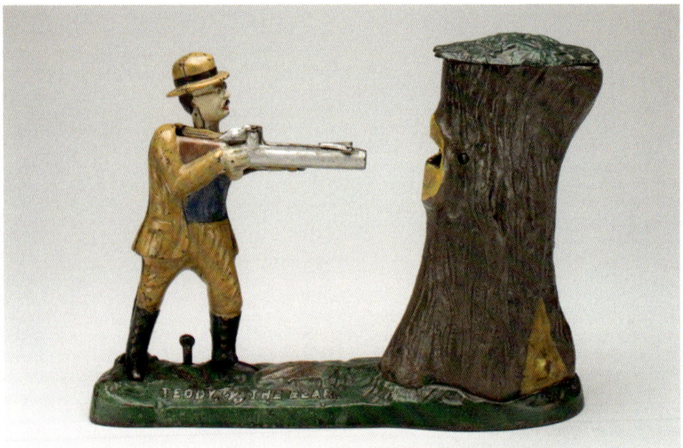

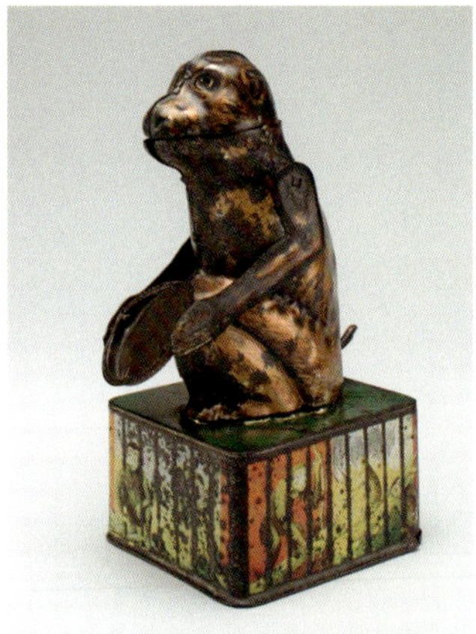

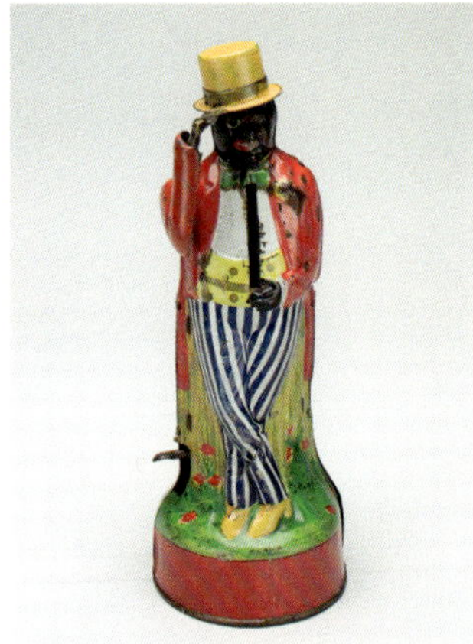

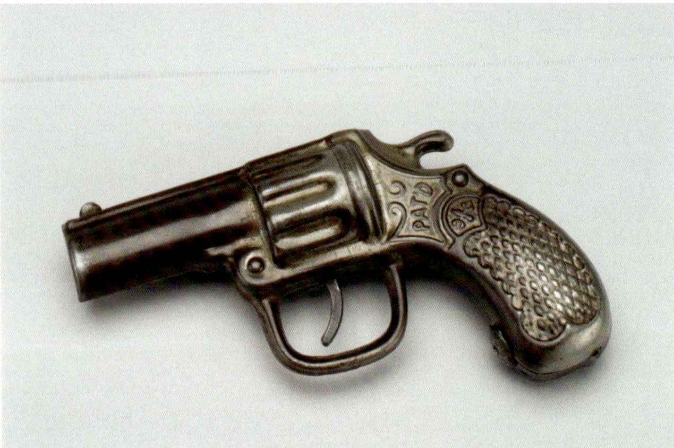

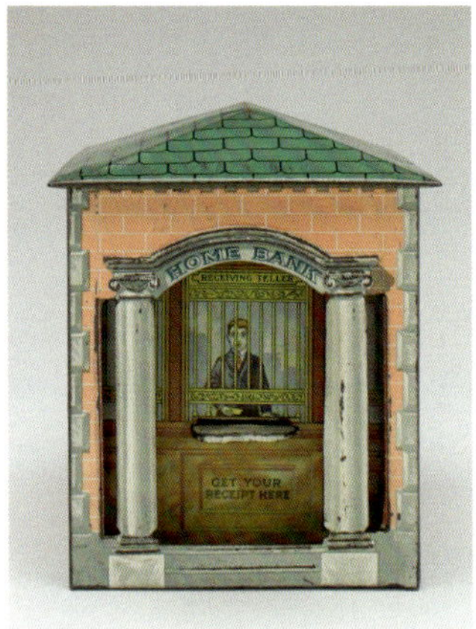
HOME BANK
GET YOUR
RECEIPT HERE

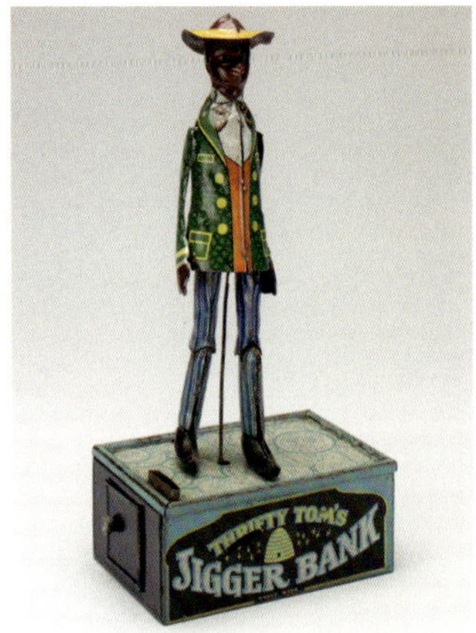
THRIFTY TOM'S
JIGGER BANK

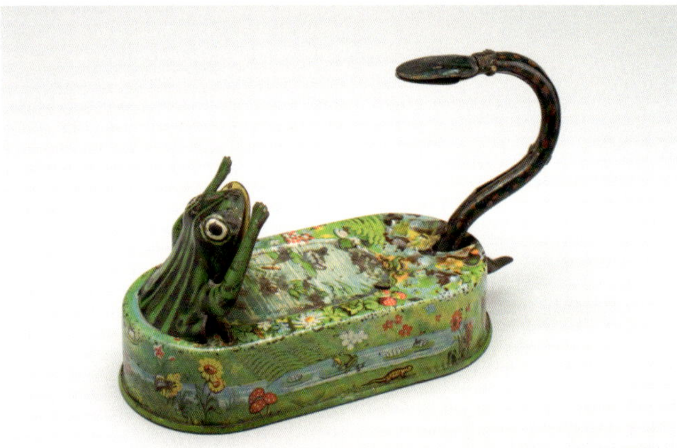

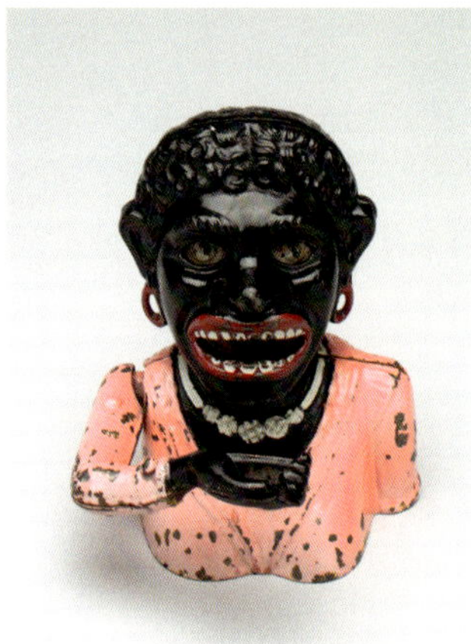

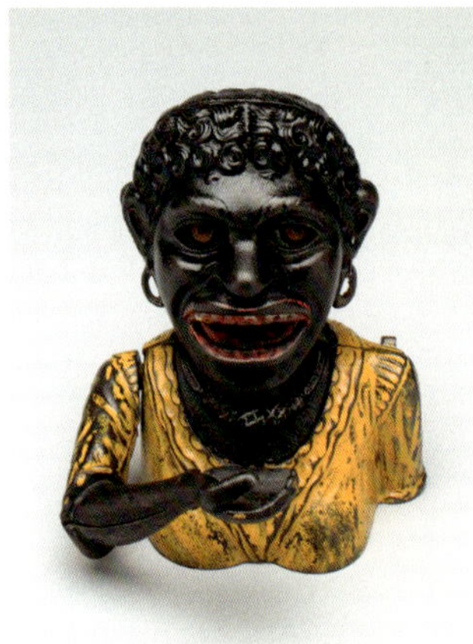

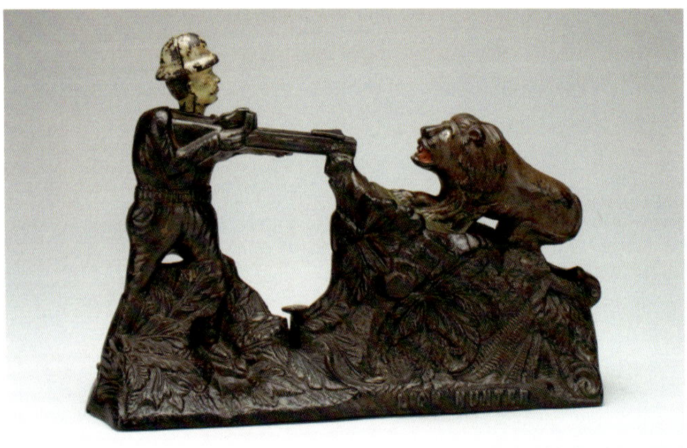

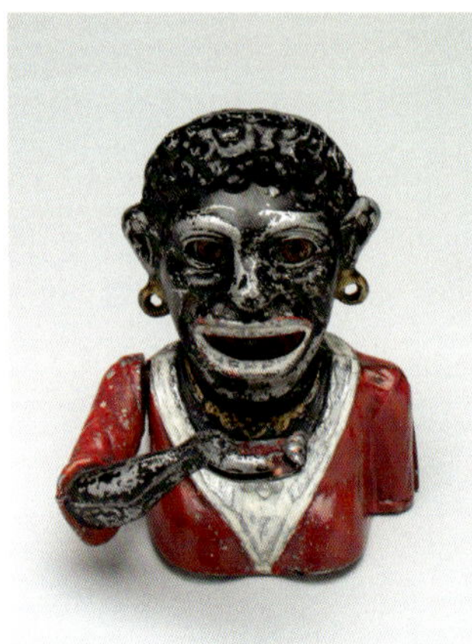

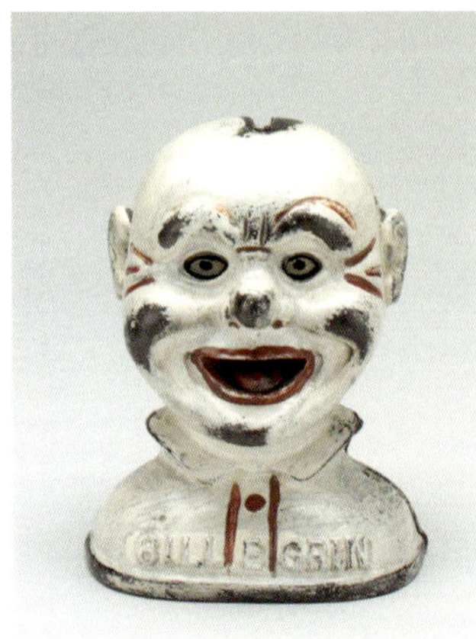

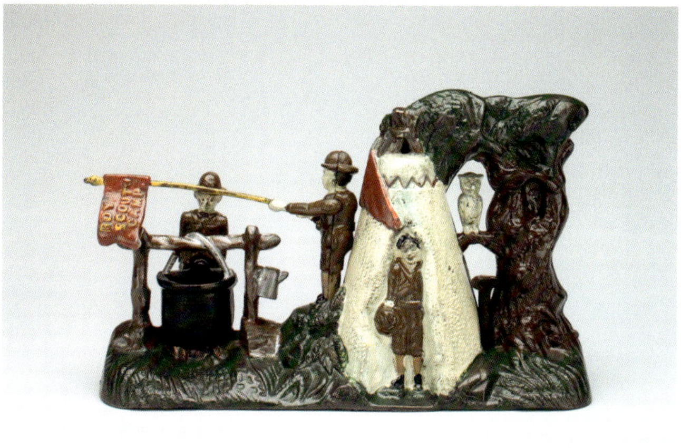

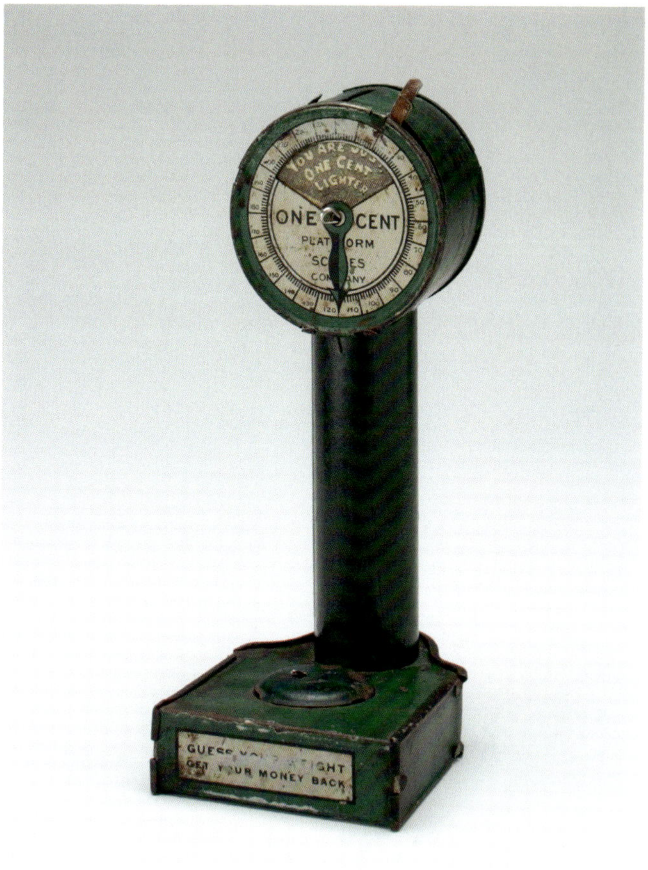
ONE CENT
MONEY BACK

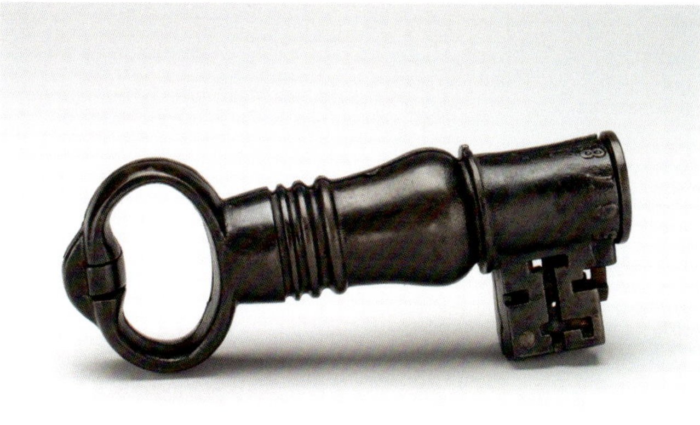

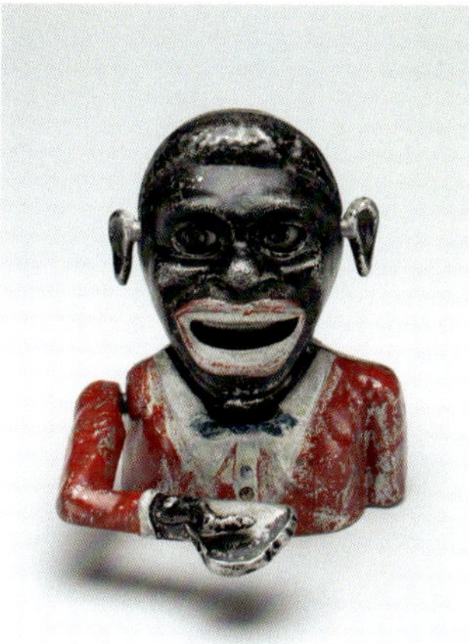

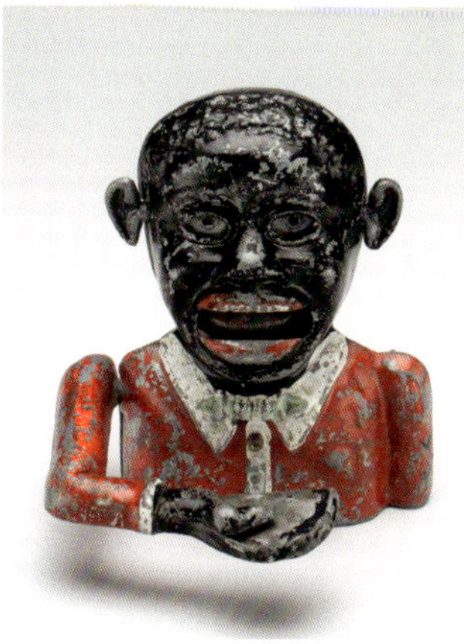

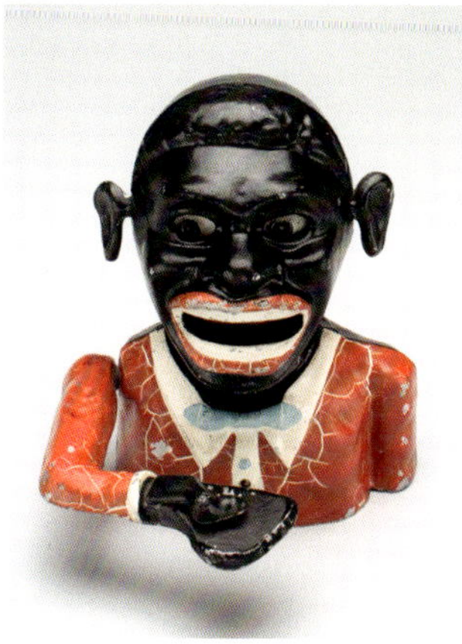

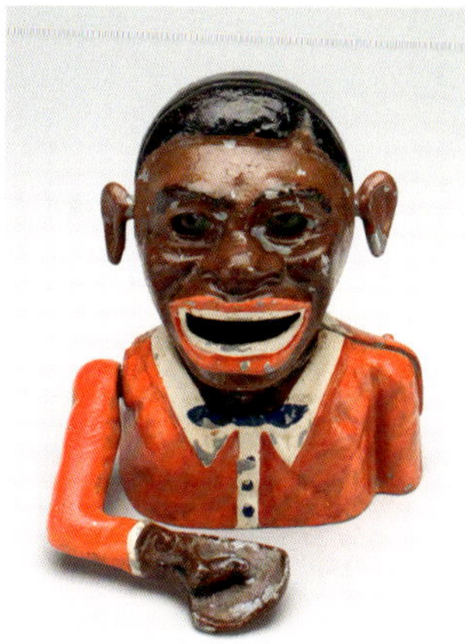

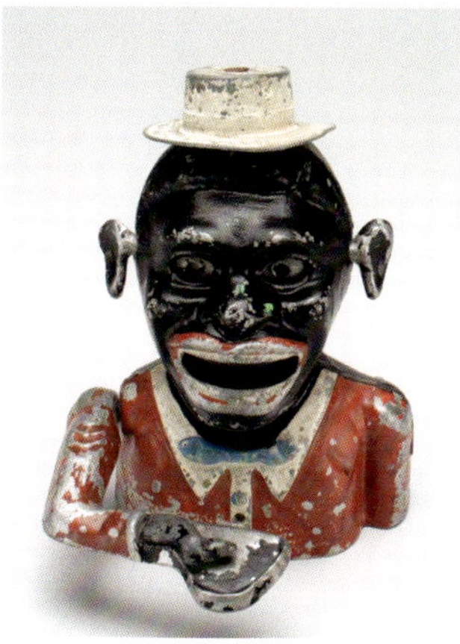

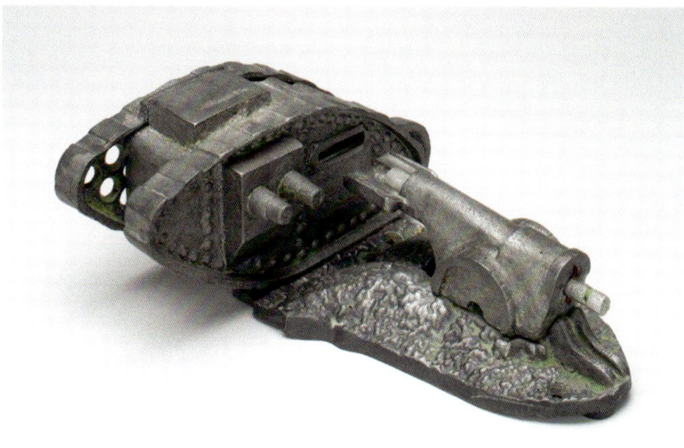

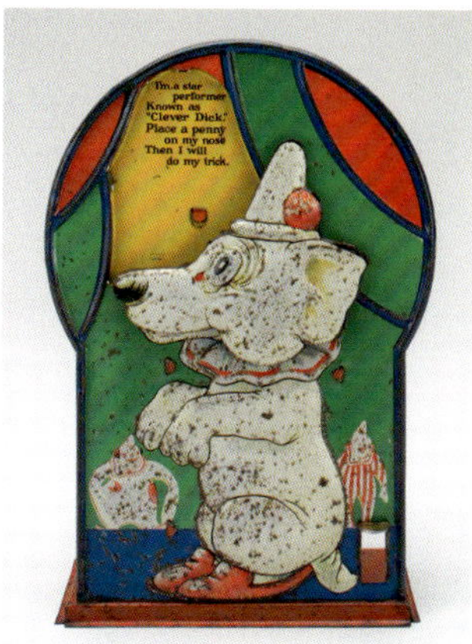
I'm a star performer Known as "Clever Dick." Place a penny on my nose Then I will do my trick.

Fun-Producing Savings Bank, c. 1918
Silver-Mirror Company, Inc., Chicago (1914 – 43), manufacturer
Tin, pigment
5 5/16 x 2 13/16 x 2 1/16 in.
2003.236.107

Boy Scout Camp, c. 1912 – 17
Charles A. Bailey, American (1848 – 1926), designer
J. & E. Stevens Company, Cromwell, Connecticut (1843 – 1950s), manufacturer
Iron, pigment
5 3/4 x 10 x 3 5/8 in.
2003.236.61a,b

Key, Golden Gate (semi-mechanical), c. 1915
W. J. Somerville, American, designer
Iron, pigment
5 7/8 x 2 1/4 x 1 1/16 in.
2003.236.89

Jolly Nigger, Moves Ears, Starkie Patent, c. 1920
Robert Eastwood Starkie, English, designer
Starkie, Burnley, England, manufacturer
Aluminum, pigment (repainted)
6 x 4 3/4 x 5 in.
2003.236.711

Jolly Nigger, Moves Ears, Starkie Patent, c. 1920
Robert Eastwood Starkie, English, designer
Starkie, Burnley, England, manufacturer
Aluminum, pigment
6 1/4 x 4 3/4 x 5 1/4 in.
2003.236.700

Jolly Nigger, Moves Ears, Starkie Patent, c. 1920
Robert Eastwood Starkie, English, designer
Starkie, Burnley, England, manufacturer
Aluminum, pigment
5 1/16 x 4 13/16 x 4 1/4 in.
2003.236.615

Jolly Nigger, Moves Ears, Starkie Patent, c. 1920
Robert Eastwood Starkie, English, designer
Starkie, Burnley, England, manufacturer
Aluminum, pigment
6 1/4 x 4 3/4 x 5 1/4 in.
2003.236.345

Clever Dick, c. 1920s
Germany
Tin, pigment
6 15/16 x 4 7/8 x 2 1/8 in.
2003.236.296

Tank and Cannon, c. 1920
Nellie Starkie and Robert Eastwood Starkie, English, designers
Starkie, Burnley, England, manufacturer
Aluminum, pigment
4 1/2 x 9 1/2 x 8 in.
2003.236.601

Jolly Nigger, Moves Ears, Starkie Patent (hat added), c. 1920
Robert Eastwood Starkie, English, designer
Starkie, Burnley, England, manufacturer
Aluminum, pigment
7 x 4 3/4 x 5 1/4 in.
2003.236.346

Kick Inn, c. 1920s
Melville E. Stoltz, American, designer
Wilder Manufacturing Company, St. Louis, manufacturer
Wood, pigment, paper, metal, leather
6 1/2 x 4 1/16 x 9 1/2 in.
2003.236.342a,b

Jolly Nigger Bank, High Hat, c. 1920s
Probably John Harper & Company, Ltd., Willenhall, England (1790 – 1980s), manufacturer
Iron, pigment
6 x 4 1/16 x 4 7/16 in.
2003.236.611

Dapper Dan, c. 1920s
Louis Marx & Company, New York (1919 – 79), manufacturer
Tin, pigment
10 3/4 x 4 3/4 x 3 3/16 in.
2003.236.58

Calumet Bank, Cardboard, c. 1924
Edward E. Barnes, American, designer
Tin, cardboard, pigment
6 3/4 x 2 3/8 x 2 3/8 in.
2003.236.2a,b

Little Miss Muffet, c. 1920s – 30s
Tin, pigment
4 1/8 x 4 x 2 1/4 in.
2003.236.434

Frog on Rock, c. 1920s – 30s
M. Elizabeth Cook, American, designer
Kilgore Manufacturing Company, Westerville, Ohio (1920s – 30s), manufacturer
Iron, pigment
2 11/16 x 3 x 2 5/8 in.
2003.236.20

Trick Dog, Solid Base, c. 1925 – 42
Hubley Manufacturing Company, Lancaster, Pennsylvania (est. 1894), manufacturer
Iron, pigment
6 1/2 x 8 9/16 x 3 in.
2003.236.29

Monkey Bank, c. 1925 – 40s
Hubley Manufacturing Company, Lancaster, Pennsylvania (est. 1894), manufacturer
Iron, pigment
7 7/8 x 8 7/8 x 3 1/16 in.
2003.236.26

Minstrel, c. 1928
Saalheimer & Strauss, Germany (1928 – 36), manufacturer
Tin, pigment
6 7/8 x 3 9/16 x 2 1/8 in.
2003.236.67

Owl, Slot in Head, c. 1926
M. Elizabeth Cook, American, designer
Kilgore Manufacturing Company, Westerville, Ohio (1920s – 30s), manufacturer
Iron, pigment
5 3/4 x 2 1/4 x 1 13/16 in.
2003.236.49a,b

Owl, Slot in Book, c. 1926
M. Elizabeth Cook, American, designer
Kilgore Manufacturing Company, Westerville, Ohio (1920s – 30s), manufacturer
Iron, pigment
5 3/4 x 2 1/4 x 1 13/16 in.
2003.236.50a,b

Little Joe Bank, c. 1924 – 32
John Harper & Company, Ltd., Willenhall, England (1790 – 1980s), manufacturer
Iron, pigment
5 3/8 x 4 x 4 1/2 in.
2003.236.706

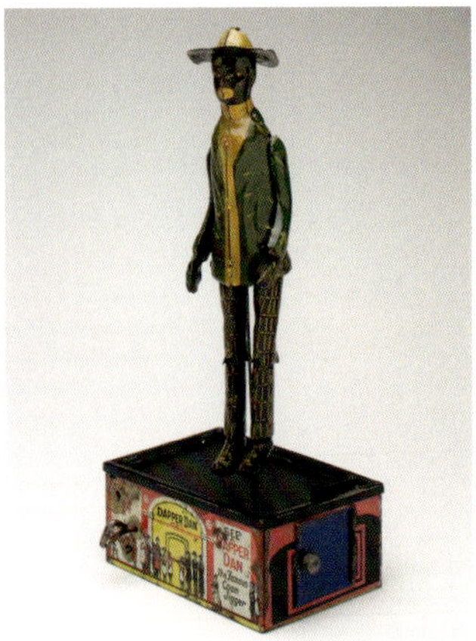

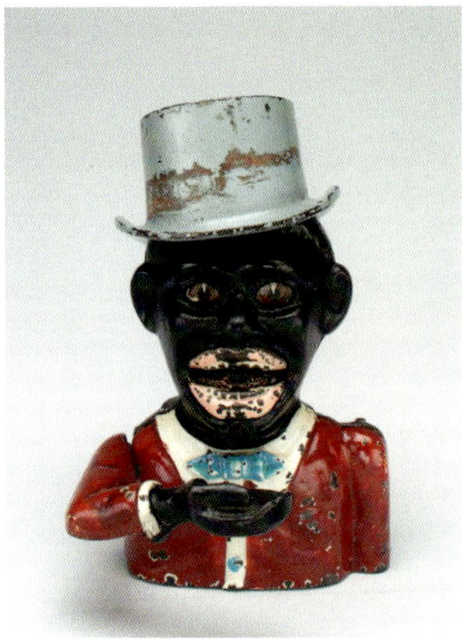

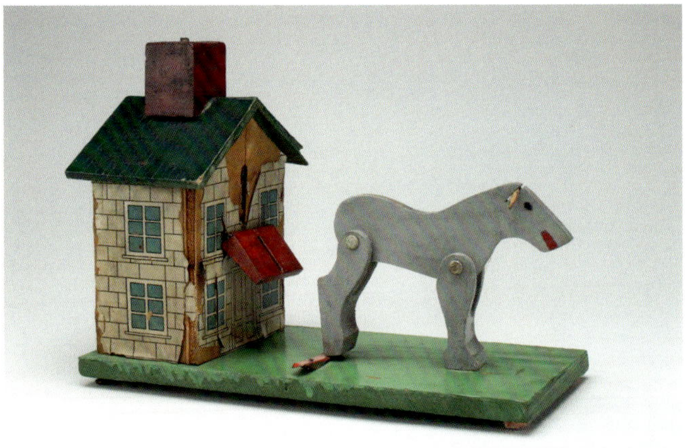

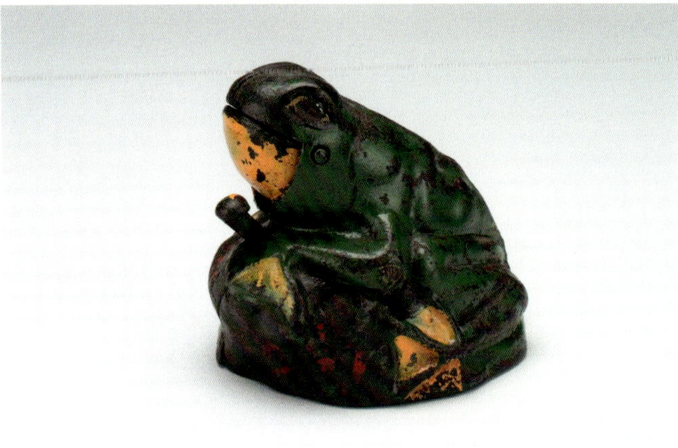

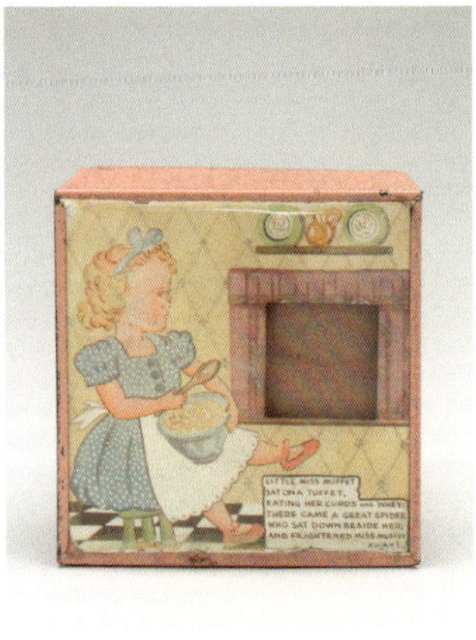

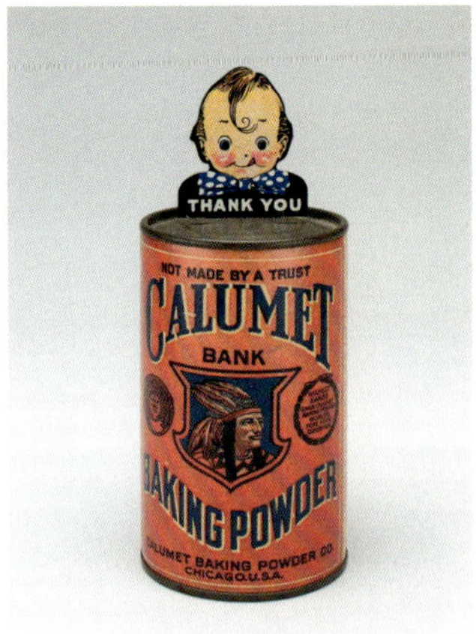
THANK YOU
NOT MADE BY A TRUST
CALUMET
BANK
BAKING POWDER
CALUMET BAKING POWDER CO.
CHICAGO, U.S.A.

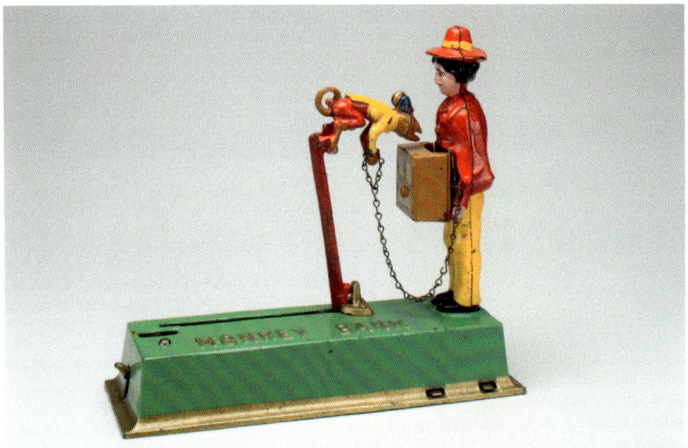
MONKEY BANK

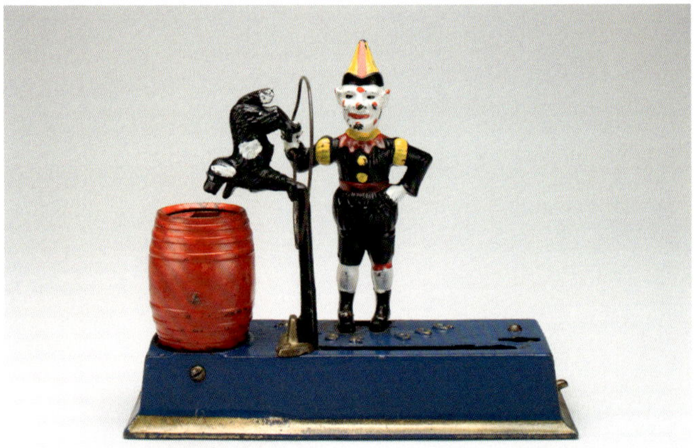

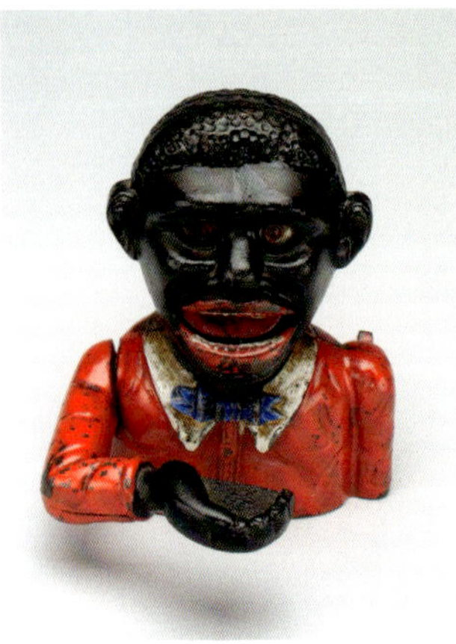

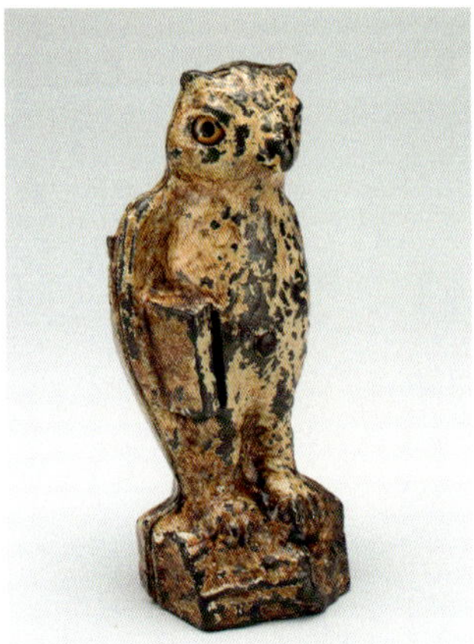

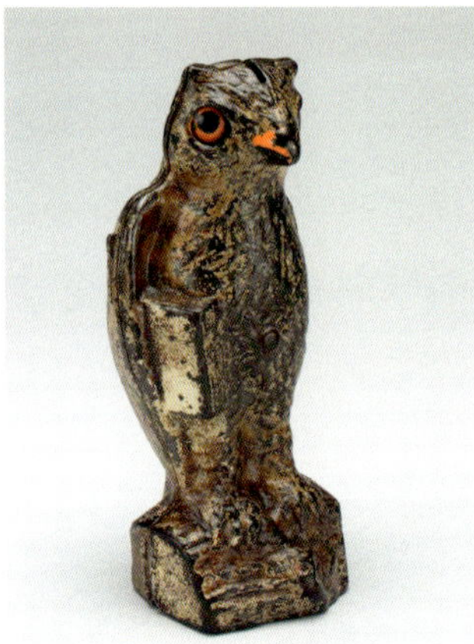

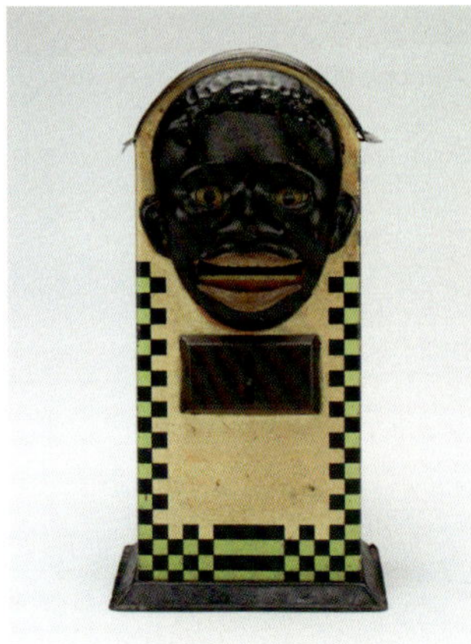

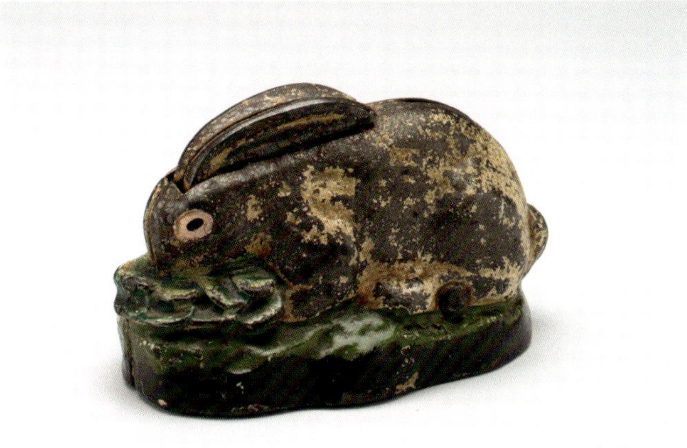

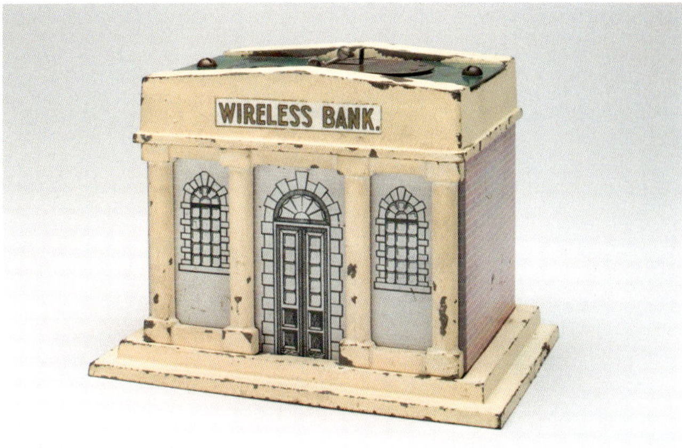
WIRELESS BANK.

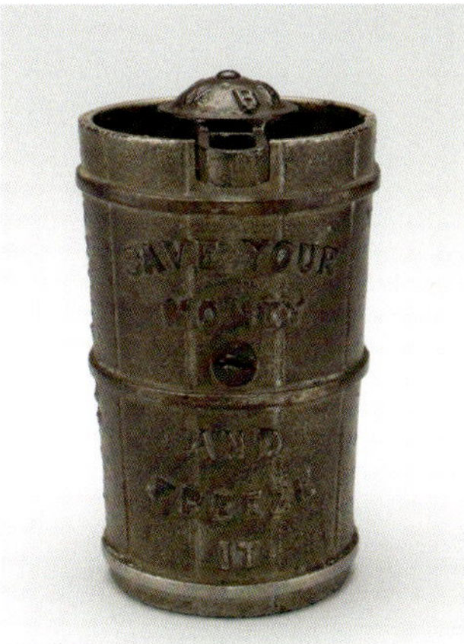
SAVE YOUR

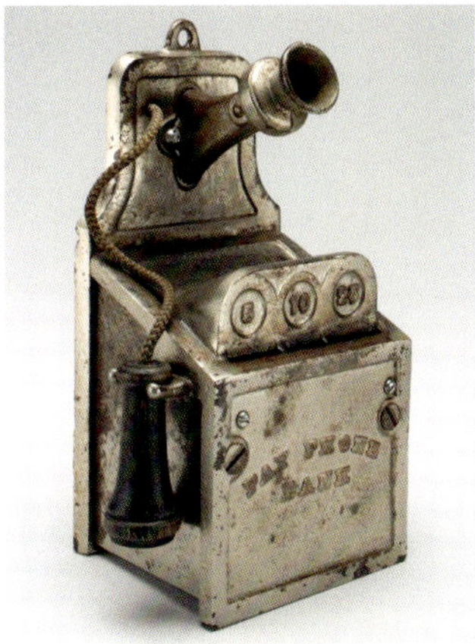

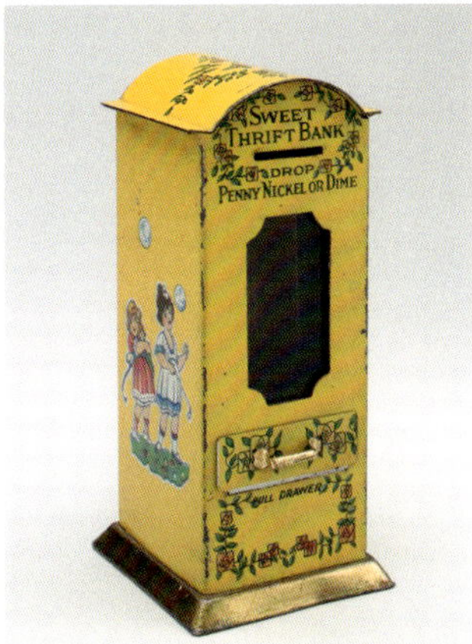
SWEET THRIFT BANK
DROP PENNY NICKEL OR DIME

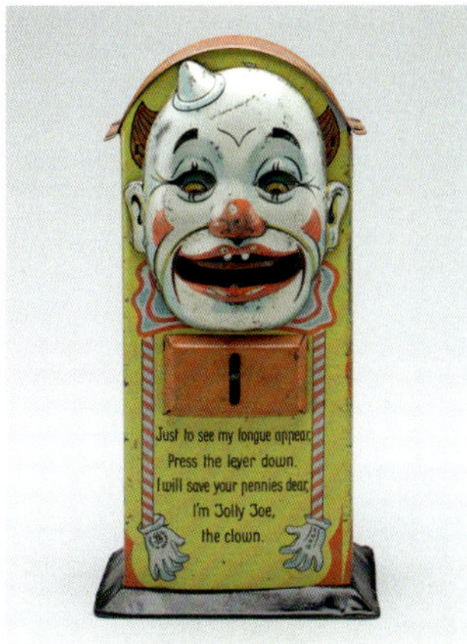
Just to see my tongue appear,
Press the lever down.
I will save your pennies dear,
I'm Jolly Joe,
the clown.

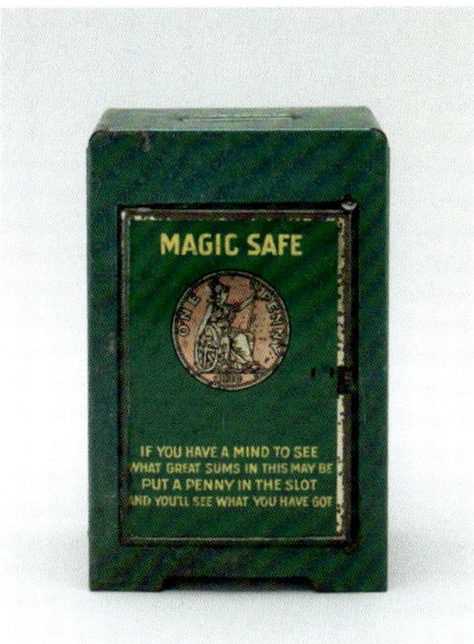
MAGIC SAFE
IF YOU HAVE A MIND TO SEE
WHAT GREAT SUMS IN THIS MAY BE
PUT A PENNY IN THE SLOT
AND YOU'LL SEE WHAT YOU HAVE GOT

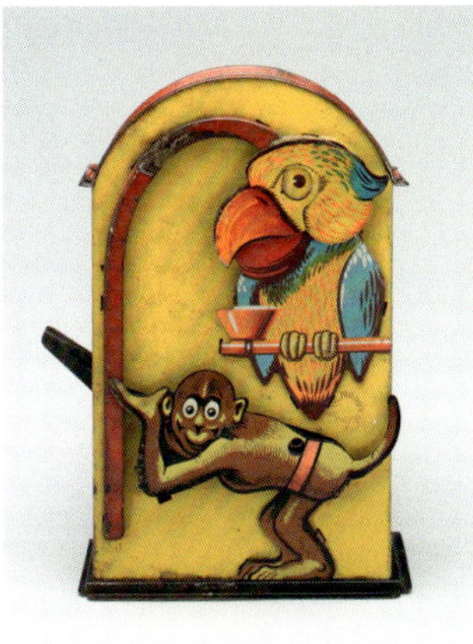

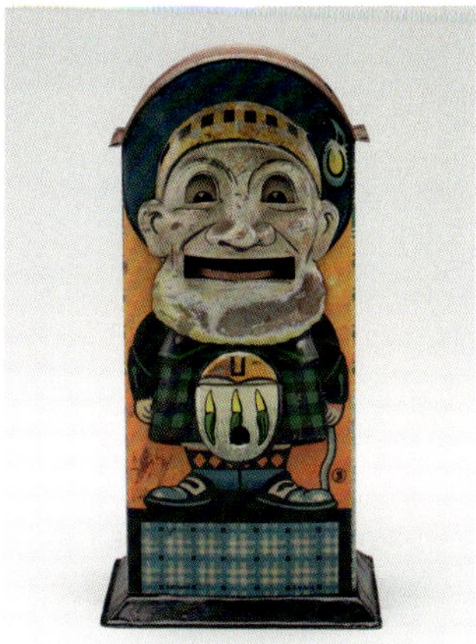

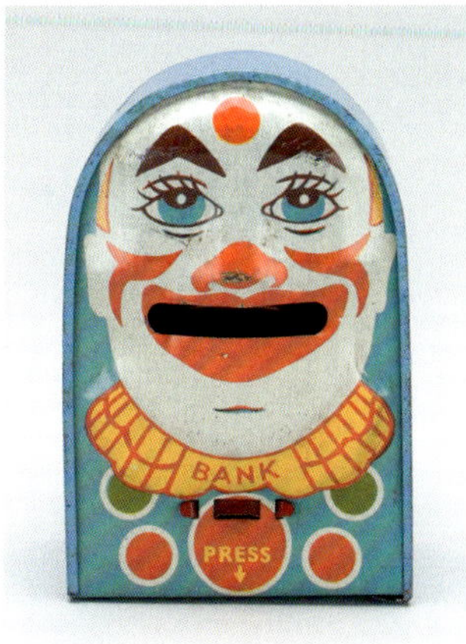
BANK
PRESS

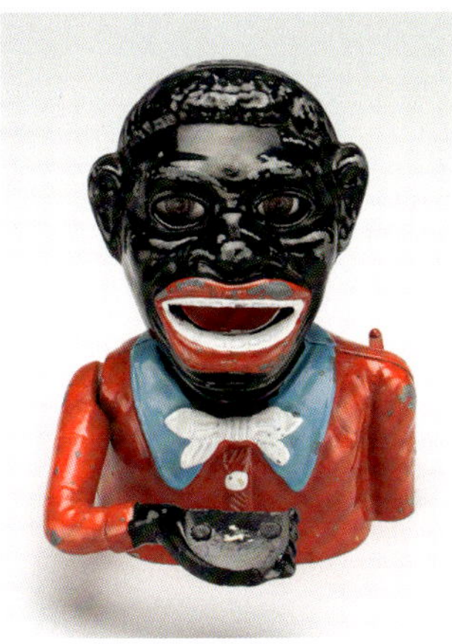

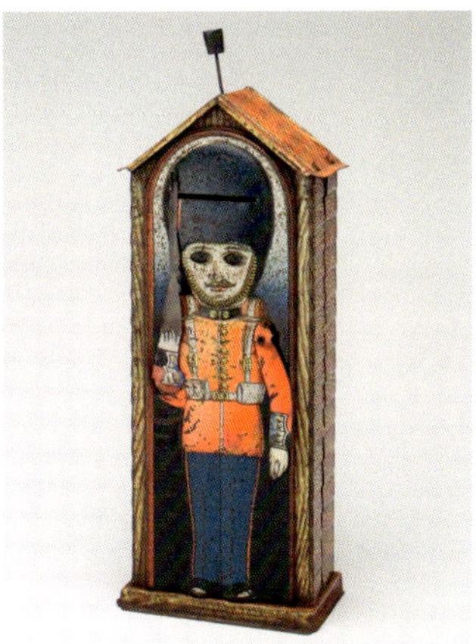

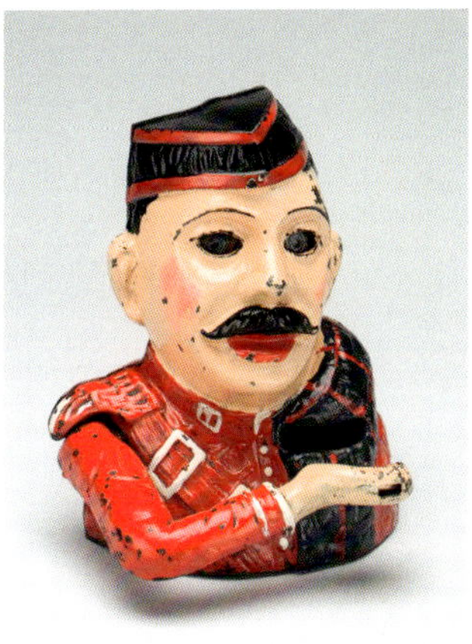

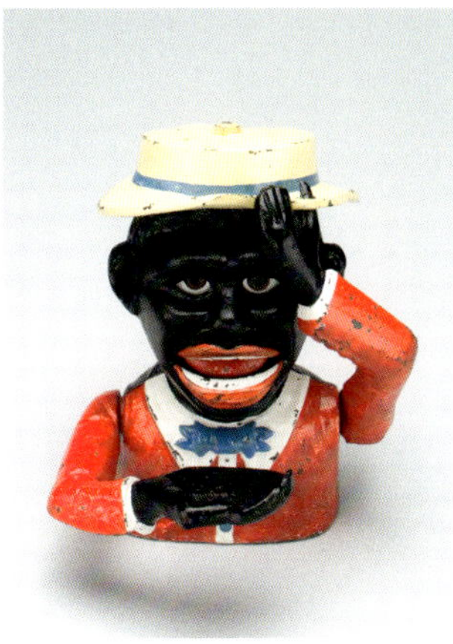

Wireless Bank, c. 1926
Christian Berger, American, designer
John Hugo Manufacturing Company, New Haven, Connecticut, manufacturer
Iron, tin, wood, pigment
4 15/16 x 6 11/16 x 4 1/2 in.
2003.236.297

Rabbit in Cabbage, c. 1926
M. Elizabeth Cook, American, designer
Kilgore Manufacturing Company, Westerville, Ohio (1920s – 30s), manufacturer
Iron, pigment
2 1/2 x 4 1/8 x 2 3/8 in.
2003.236.91

Jolly Joe Clown Bank, c. 1929 – 33
Saalheimer & Strauss, Germany (1928 – 36), manufacturer
Tin, pigment
6 7/8 x 3 9/16 x 2 1/8 in.
2003.236.66

Sweet Thrift (vending), c. 1928
Isidor Sanford Kronowit, American, designer
Beverly Novelty Corporation, New York, manufacturer
Tin, glass, pigment
6 x 3 x 2 3/4 in.
2003.235.600

Pay Phone, c. 1928
Russell A. Frisbie, designer
J. & E. Stevens Company, Cromwell, Connecticut (1843 – 1950s), manufacturer
Iron, metal, pigment, wood, string
7 3/16 x 3 5/8 x 2 7/8 in.
2003.236.817

North Pole Bank, Ice Cream Freezer, c. 1928
Grey Iron Casting Company, Mount Joy, Pennsylvania (1881 – 1969), manufacturer
Iron, pigment
4 5/16 x 2 9/16 x 2 9/16 in.
2003.236.135

Clown, Arched Top, c. 1930s
Great Britain
Tin, pigment
4 3/16 x 2 13/16 x 1 1/2 in.
2003.236.86

Scotchman, c. 1930 – 36
Saalheimer & Strauss, Germany (c. 1928 – 36), manufacturer
Tin, pigment
6 13/16 x 3 9/16 x 2 1/16 in.
2003.236.78

Monkey and Parrot, c. 1930 – 36
Attributed to Saalheimer & Strauss, Germany (c. 1928 – 36), manufacturer
Tin, pigment
6 x 4 x 1 3/4 in.
2003.236.79

Magic Safe, c. 1930
Germany
Tin, pigment
4 13/16 x 3 3/16 x 1 3/4 in.
2003.236.96

Little Moe, c. 1931
Chamberlin & Hill, Ltd., Walsall, England, manufacturer
Iron, pigment
6 x 4 1/2 x 4 1/4 in.
2003.236.347

Kiltie Bank, c. 1931
John Harper & Company, Ltd., Willenhall, England (1790 – 1980s), manufacturer
Iron, pigment
6 5/8 x 5 1/2 x 4 3/4 in.
2003.236.879

Sentry, c. 1930s
Saalheimer & Strauss, Germany (c. 1928 – 36), manufacturer
Tin, pigment
8 7/16 x 3 1/8 x 2 13/16 in.
2003.236.68

Greedy Nigger Boy, c. 1930s
H. C. Urlwin, Christchurch, New Zealand, manufacturer
Iron, pigment
6 1/4 x 4 1/2 x 5 1/4 in.
2003.236.704

Joe Socko Novelty Bank, c. 1937
Straits Corporation, Detroit, manufacturer
Tin, pigment
4 9/16 x 3 1/2 x 2 1/4 in.
2003.236.7a,b

Popeye Knockout Bank, c. 1935
Straits Corporation, Detroit, manufacturer
Tin, pigment
4 9/16 x 3 1/2 x 2 1/4 in.
2003.236.8a,b

Elephant with Howdah, Pull Tail, c. 1934
Hubley Manufacturing Company, Lancaster, Pennsylvania (est. 1894), manufacturer
Iron, pigment
5 1/2 x 7 3/16 x 2 3/4 in.
2003.236.274

Atomic, c. 1940s
Duro Pattern and Mold Company, Detroit, manufacturer
Aluminum
3 3/4 x 2 3/4 x 8 1/2 in.
2003.236.430

Jolly Nigger Bank, Small, c. 1940
Iron, pigment
5 1/4 x 3 7/8 x 4 in.
2003.236.707

Clown, Chein, c. late 1930s
J. Chein & Company, New York (1903 – 92), manufacturer
Tin, pigment
5 1/8 x 2 5/8 x 2 1/2 in.
2003.236.851

Uncle Wiggley, c. 1949
J. Chein & Company, New York (1903 – 92), manufacturer
Tin, pigment
5 x 2 9/16 x 2 9/16 in.
2003.236.116a,b

Monkey Tips Hat, c. 1945
J. Chein & Company, New York (1903 – 92), manufacturer
Tin, pigment
4 15/16 x 2 1/2 x 2 1/2 in.
2003.236.115a,b

Elf House (vending), c. 1945
England
Tin, pigment
5 3/4 x 3 1/4 x 2 1/4 in.
2003.236.384

Elephant, c. 1940s – 50s
J. Chein & Company, New York (1903 – 92), manufacturer
Tin, pigment
4 15/16 x 2 1/2 x 5 in.
2003.236.847

Bird, Mushroom, and Squirrel, c. 1950s
Lorenz Bolz Zirndorf, Nuremberg, Germany, manufacturer
Tin, pigment
5 1/8 x 3 3/16 x 3 7/8 in.
2003.236.438

Archie Andrews, c. 1950s
England
Iron, pigment
4 5/8 x 4 1/4 x 3 7/8 in.
2003.236.843

The Sportsman, c. 1950
Duro Mold and Manufacturing, Inc., Detroit, manufacturer
Zinc alloy, pigment
4 13/16 x 8 1/2 x 2 7/16 in.
2003.236.607

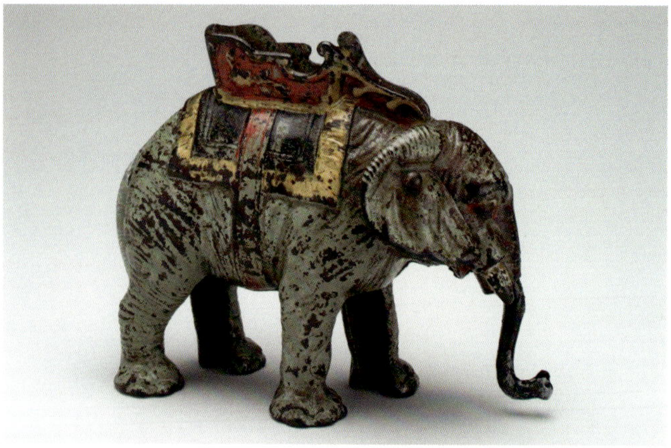

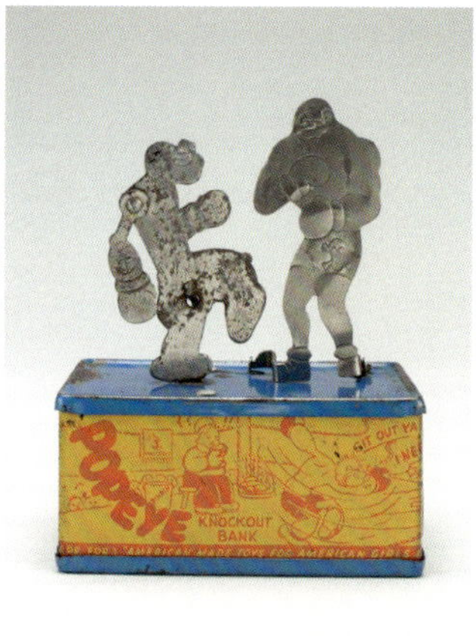
POPEYE
KNOCKOUT BANK

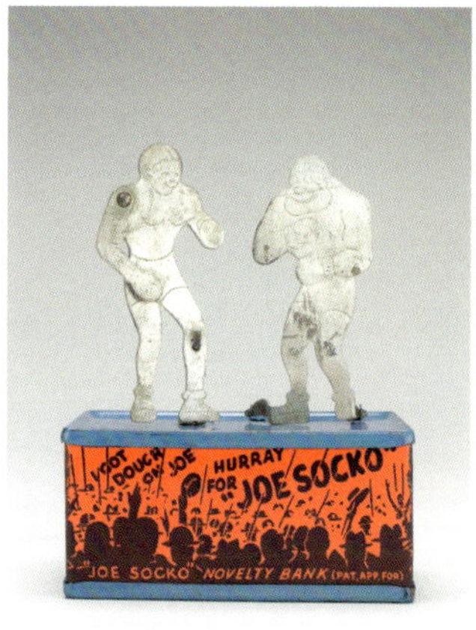
HURRAY FOR JOE SOCKO
JOE SOCKO NOVELTY BANK (PAT. APP. FOR)

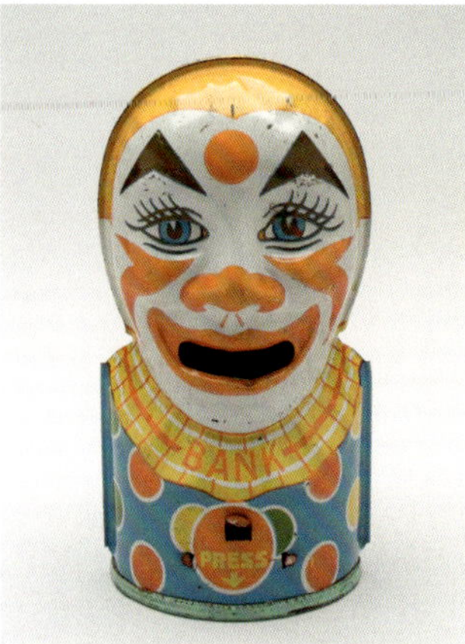
BANK
PRESS

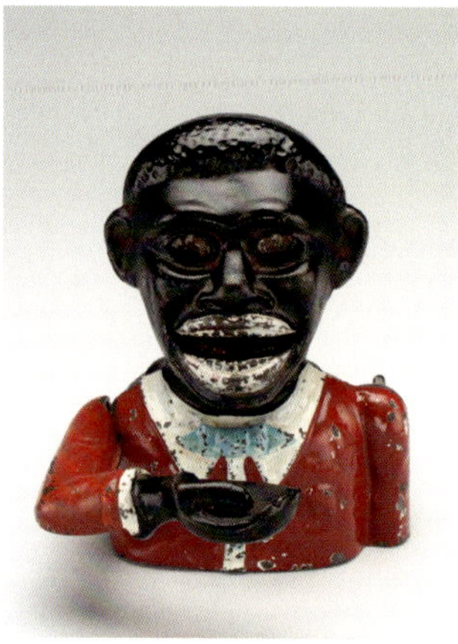

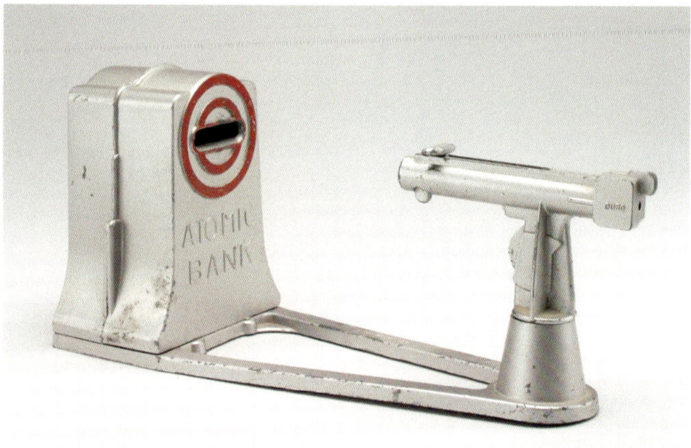
ATOMIC BANK

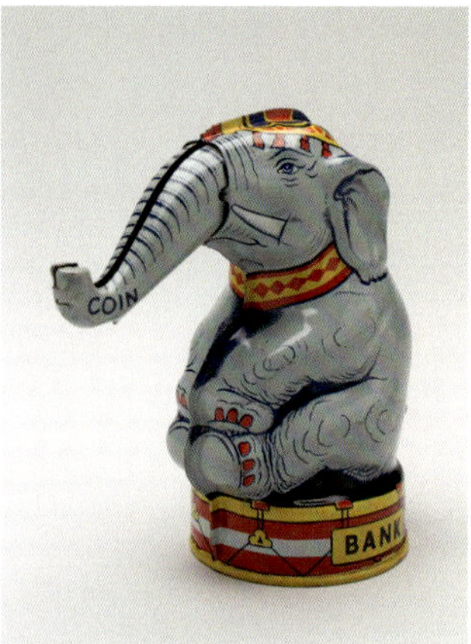
COIN
BANK

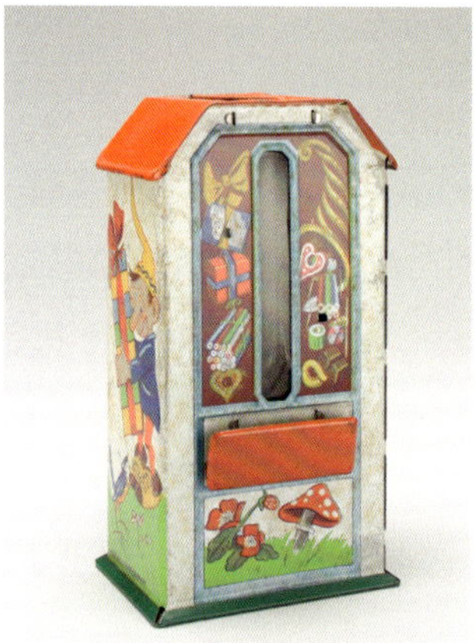

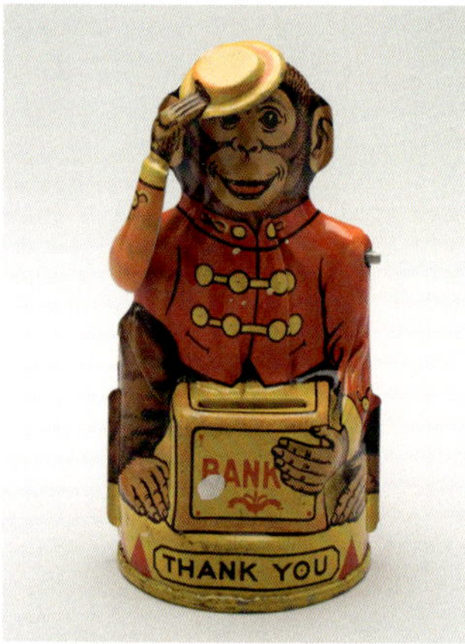
BANK
THANK YOU

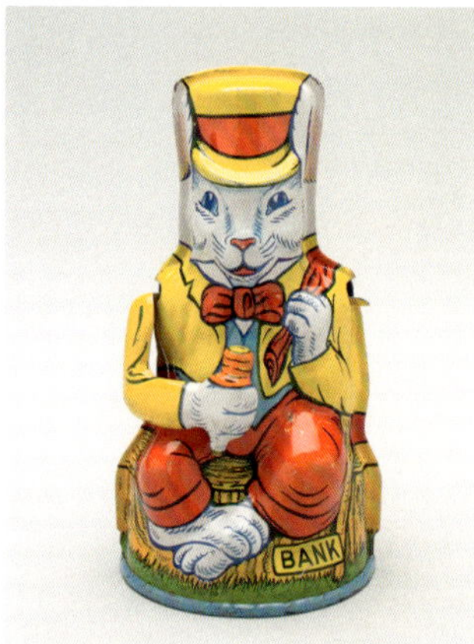
BANK

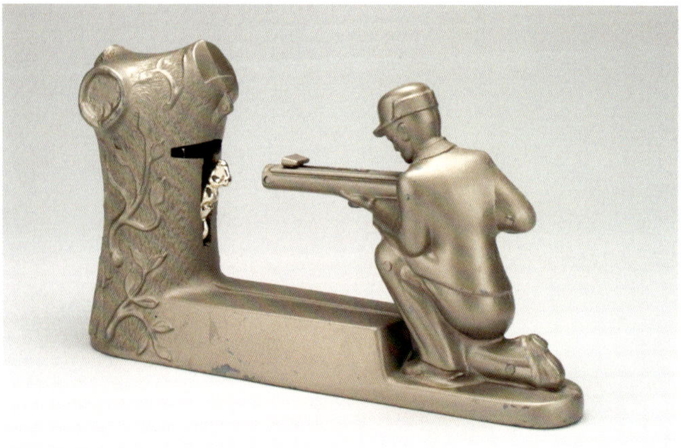

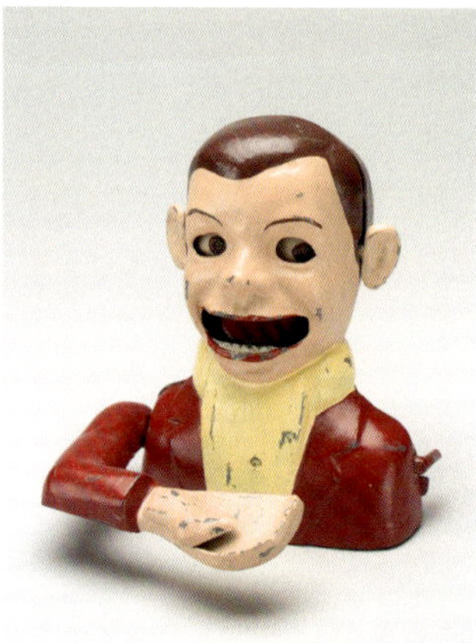

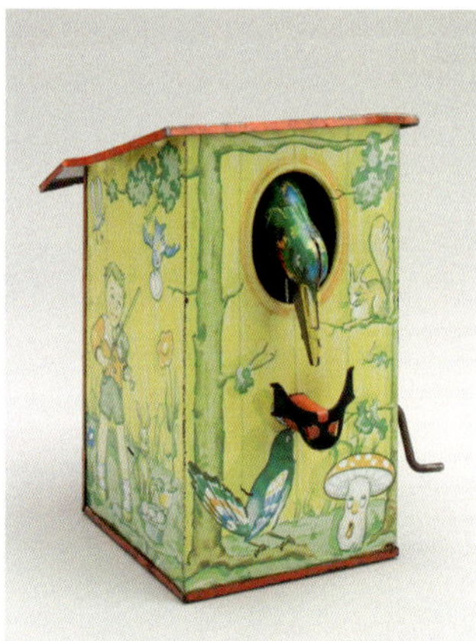

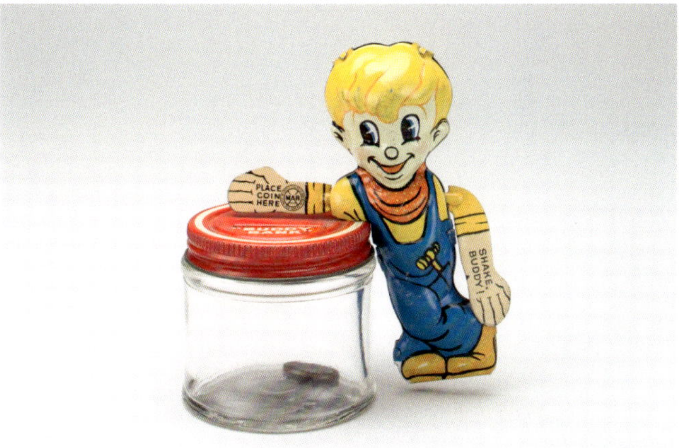
SHAKE, BUDDY!

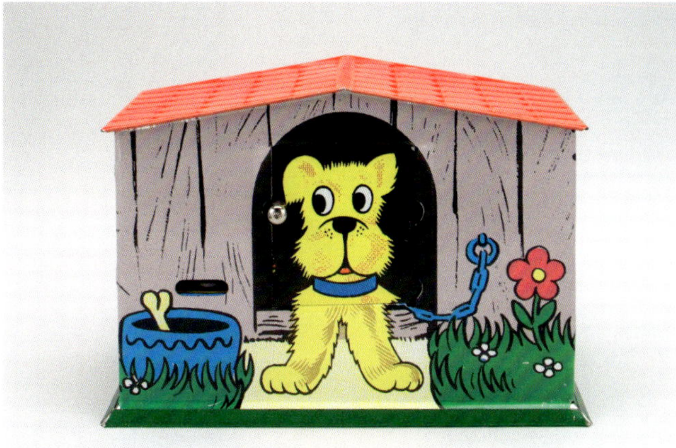

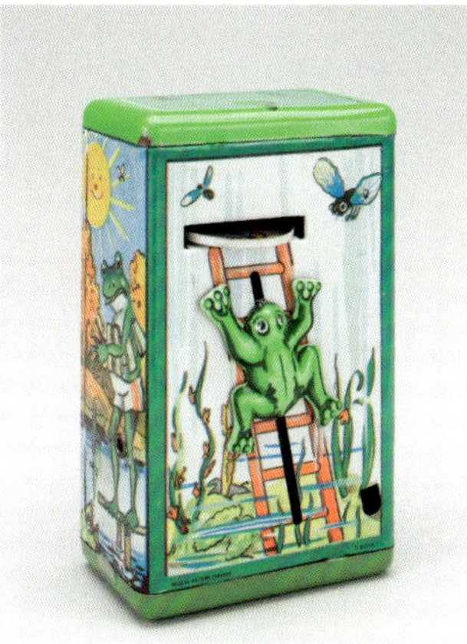

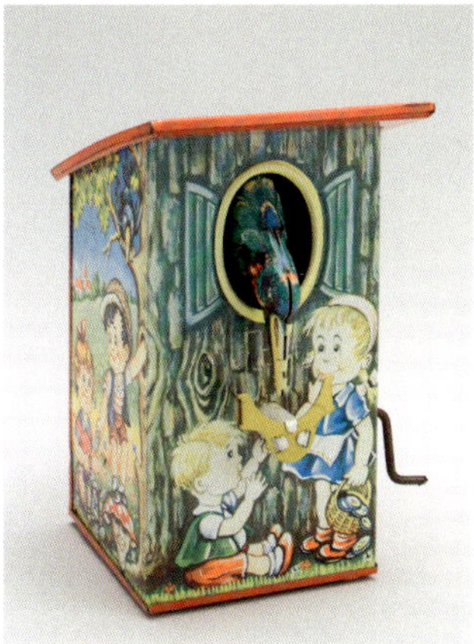

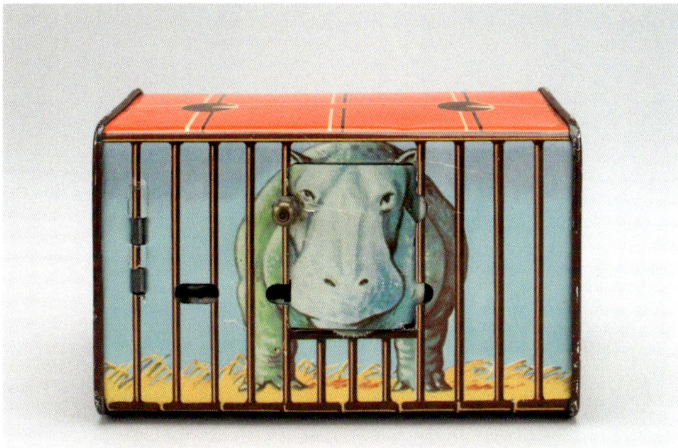

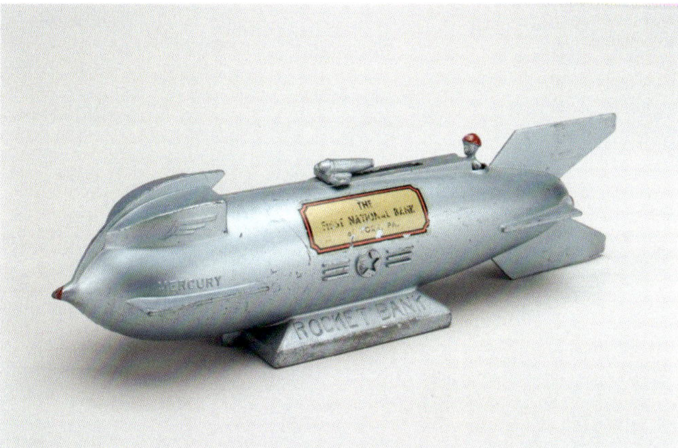
MERCURY
ROCKET BANK

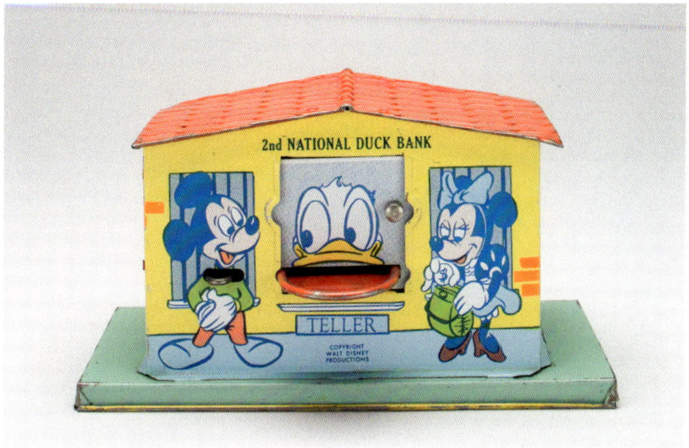
2nd NATIONAL DUCK BANK
TELLER
COPYRIGHT WALT DISNEY PRODUCTIONS

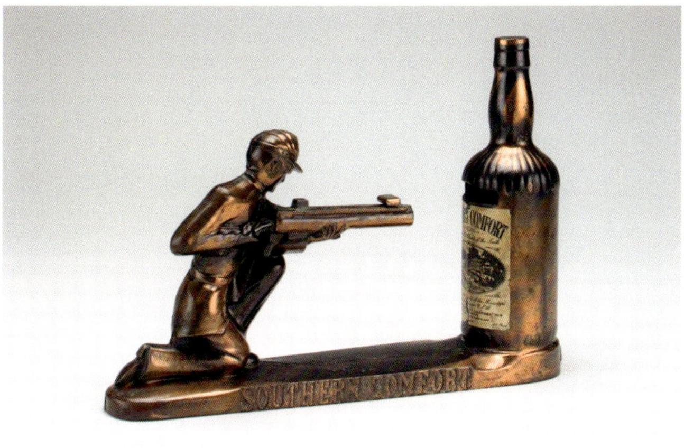

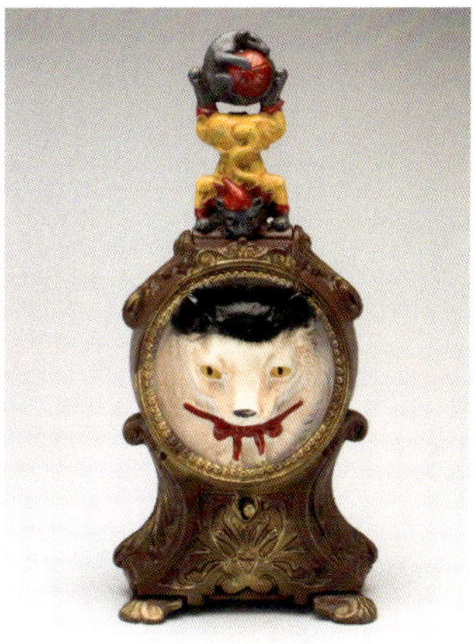

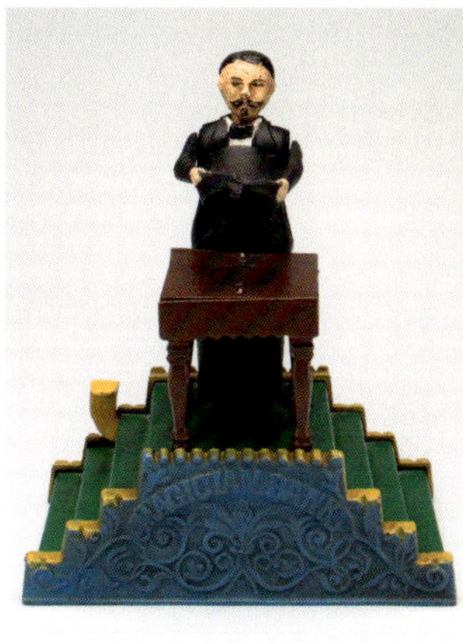

Doghouse, c. 1950s
Metal, pigment
3 1/4 x 5 1/8 x 2 1/4 in.
2003.236.436

Buddy Bank, c. 1950s
Louis Marx & Company, New York (1919 – 79), manufacturer
Tin, pigment, glass
4 x 2 3/8 x 2 3/8 in.
2003.236.94a,b

Money-Eating Hippopotamus, c. 1950s
Tin, pigment
3 x 5 x 3 In.
2003.236.433

Little Girl with Boy Sitting, c. 1950s
Lorenz Bolz Zirndorf, Nuremberg, Germany, manufacturer
Tin, pigment
5 3/16 x 2 3/4 x 2 7/8 in.
2003.236.344

Frogs at Play, c. 1950s
West Germany
Metal, pigment
5 1/8 x 3 1/8 x 2 1/4 in.
2003.236.439

Second National Duck Bank, c. 1950s
J. Chein & Company, New York (1903 – 92), manufacturer
Metal, pigment
3 1/2 x 6 1/2 x 3 in.
2003.236.845

Rocket Bank, c. 1950s
Duro Mold and Manufacturing, Inc., Detroit, manufacturer
Zinc alloy, pigments
2 1/4 x 8 1/16 x 1 3/4 in.
2003.236.750

Magician (reproduction), c. 1950s – 60s
Based on c. 1901 design by William C. Bull, American, and manufactured by J. & E. Stevens Company, Cromwell, Connecticut (1843 – 1950s), from the Book of Knowledge Collection, Grolier, Inc.
John Wright, Wrightsville, Pennsylvania (est. 1880), manufacturer
Iron, pigment
7 15/16 x 6 5/8 x 3 13/16 in.
2003.236.881

Cat and Mouse, Cat Balancing (reproduction), c. 1950s – 60s
Based on c. 1891 design by James H. Bowen, American (active c. 1877 – 1906), and manufactured by J. & E. Stevens Company, Cromwell, Connecticut (1843 – 1950s), from the Book of Knowledge Collection, Grolier, Inc.
John Wright, Wrightsville, Pennsylvania (est. 1880), manufacturer
Iron, pigment
11 1/8 x 5 1/4 x 3 3/4 in.
2003.236.803

Southern Comfort (copper color), c. 1950s
Duro Mold and Manufacturing, Inc., Detroit, manufacturer
Zinc alloy, pigment
6 x 8 9/16 x 1 7/8 in.
2003.236.608

Milking Cow (reproduction), c. 1950s – 60s
Based on c. 1888 design attributed to Charles A. Bailey, American (1848 – 1926), and manufactured by J. & E. Stevens Company, Cromwell, Connecticut (1843 – 1950s), from the Book of Knowledge Collection, Grolier, Inc.
John Wright, Wrightsville, Pennsylvania (est. 1880), manufacturer
Iron, pigment
5 5/16 x 9 5/8 x 3 3/8 in.
2003.236.308

Jonah and the Whale (reproduction, replaced boat), c. 1950s – 60s
Based on c. 1890 design by Peter Adams, American, and manufactured by Shepard Hardware Company, Buffalo, New York (1866 – 92), from the Book of Knowledge Collection, Grolier, Inc.
John Wright, Wrightsville, Pennsylvania (est. 1880), manufacturer
Iron, pigment
5 x 10 1/16 x 3 9/16 in.
2003.236.602

Strato Bank, c. 1950s – 60s
Duro Mold and Manufacturing, Inc., Detroit, manufacturer
Zinc alloy, pigments
3 3/8 x 8 5/16 x 2 13/16 in.
2003.236.753

Strato Bank, c. 1950s – 60s
Duro Mold and Manufacturing, Inc., Detroit, manufacturer
Zinc alloy, pigments
3 3/8 x 8 5/16 x 2 13/16 in.
2003.236.752

Wild West Bank, c. 1950s – 60s
Duro Pattern and Mold Company, Detroit, manufacturer
Aluminum
3 1/2 x 2 11/16 x 7 7/8 in.
2003.236.431

Trick Pony (reproduction), c. 1950s – 60s
Based on c. 1885 design by Peter Adams and Charles G. Shepard, American, and manufactured by Shepard Hardware Company, Buffalo, New York (1866 – 92), from the Book of Knowledge Collection, Grolier, Inc.
John Wright, Wrightsville, Pennsylvania (est. 1880), manufacturer
Iron, pigment
8 x 7 1/16 x 2 1/2 in.
2003.236.877

Astro Bank, c. 1957
Astro Manufacturing, East Detroit, Michigan, manufacturer
Zinc alloy, pigments, plastic
13 1/8 x 3 7/8 x 3 7/8 in.
2003.236.751a,b

Flying Saucer Bank, 1956
Duro Mold and Manufacturing Inc., Detroit, manufacturer
Zinc alloy, pigment
4 1/8 x 5 1/8 x 5 7/16 in.
2003.236.754

Southern Comfort (silver color), 1953
Duro Mold and Manufacturing, Inc., Detroit, manufacturer
Zinc alloy, paper
6 1/16 x 8 9/16 x 1 7/8 in.
2003.236.442a,b

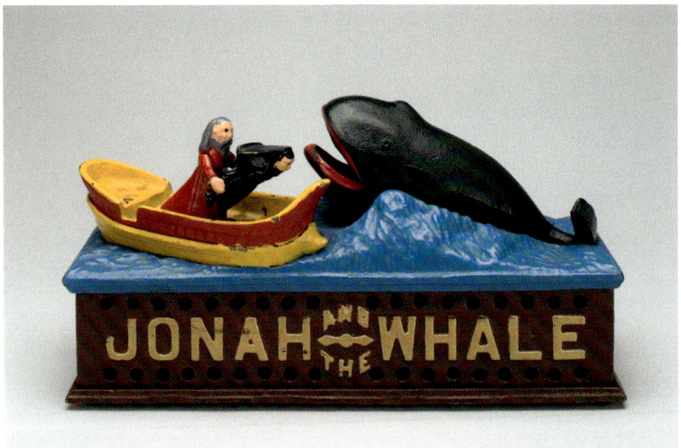
JONAH AND THE WHALE

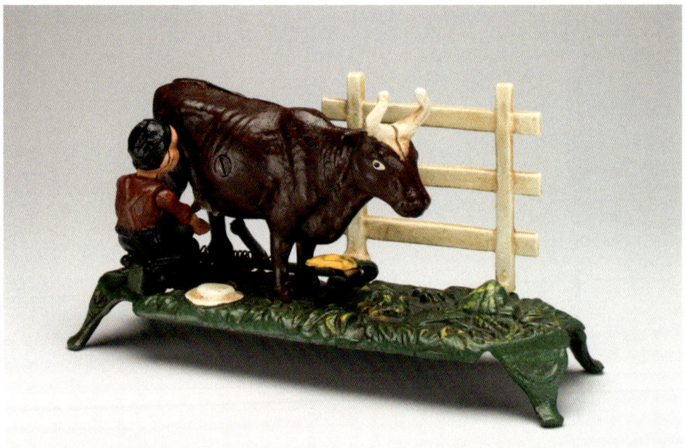

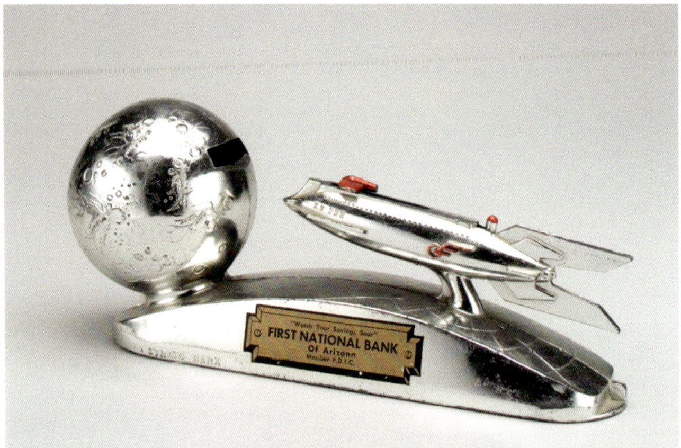
FIRST NATIONAL BANK
Of Arizona

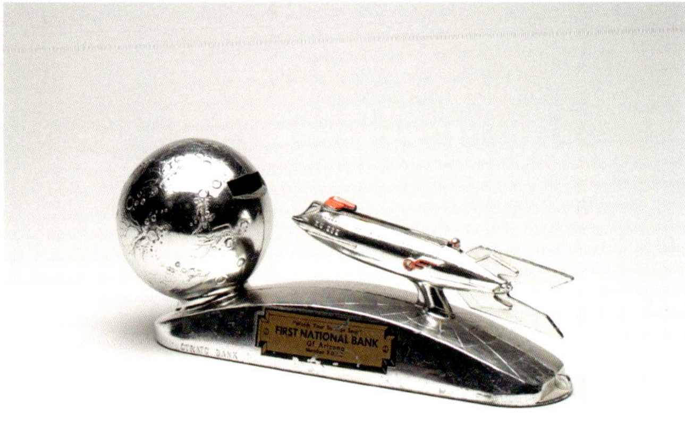
FIRST NATIONAL BANK
Of Arizona

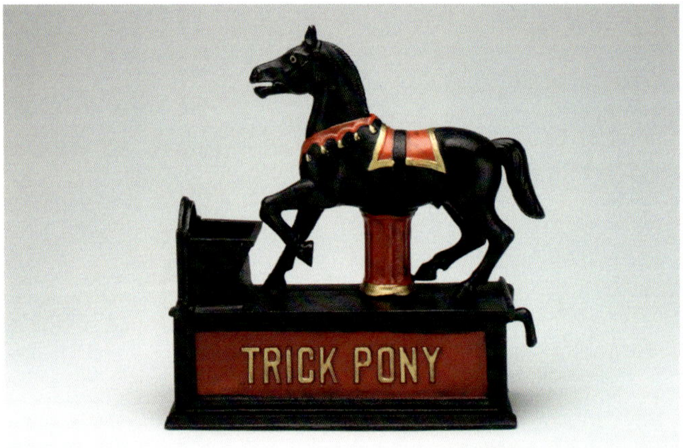
TRICK PONY

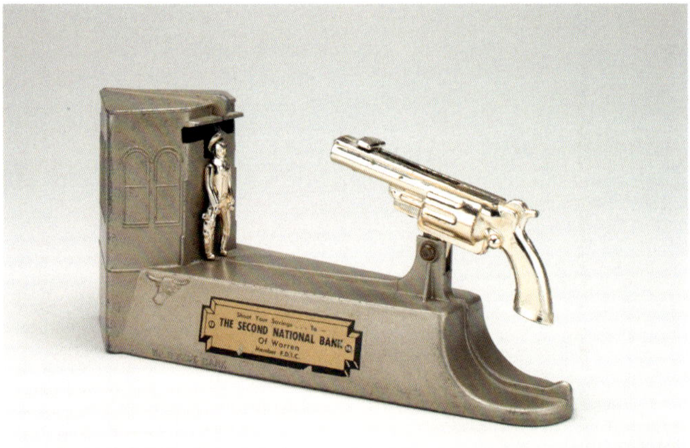
THE SECOND NATIONAL BANK
Of Warren

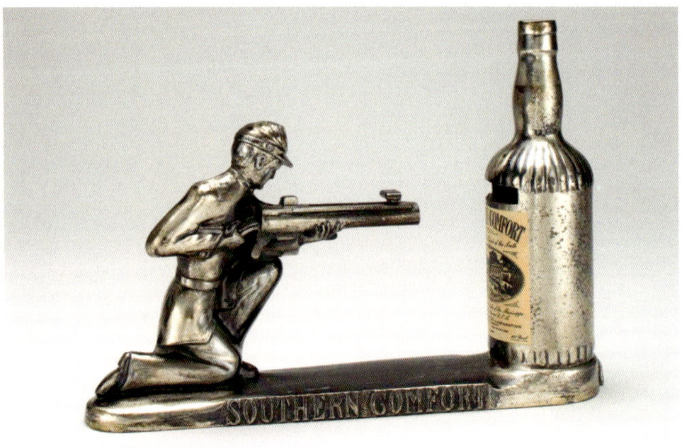
SOUTHERN COMFORT

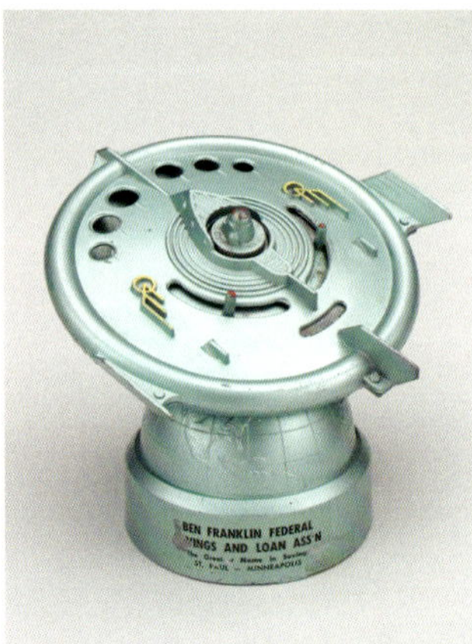
BEN FRANKLIN FEDERAL

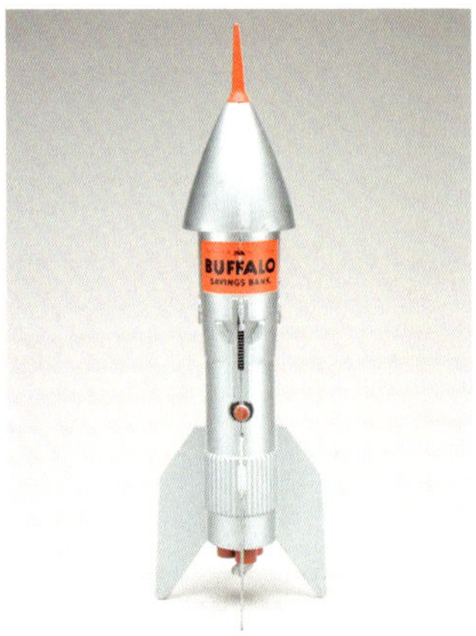
BUFFALO
SAVINGS BANK

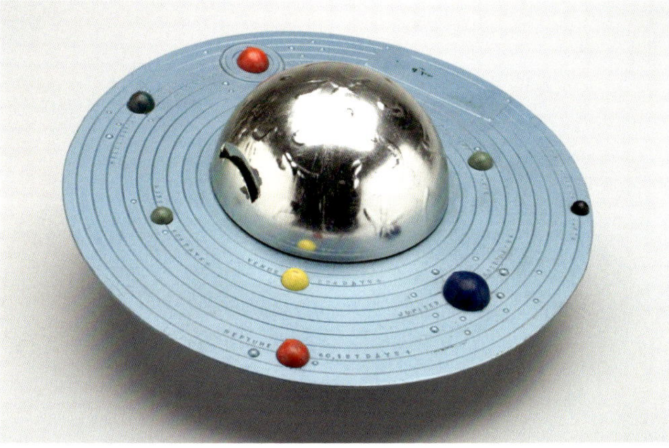

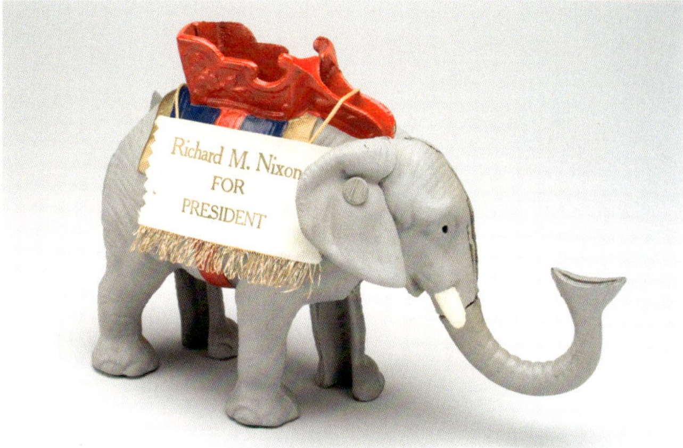
Richard M. Nixon
FOR
PRESIDENT

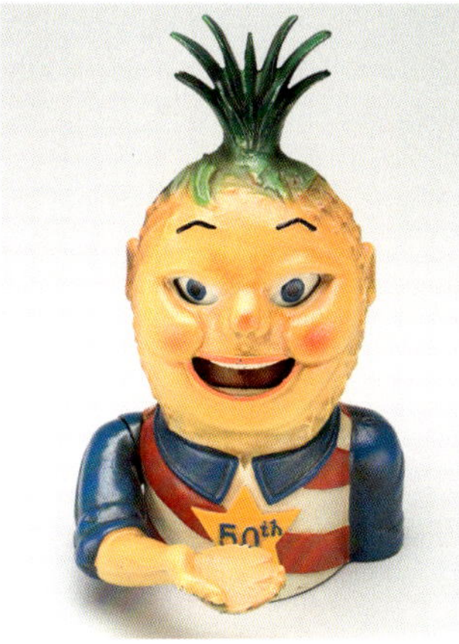
50th

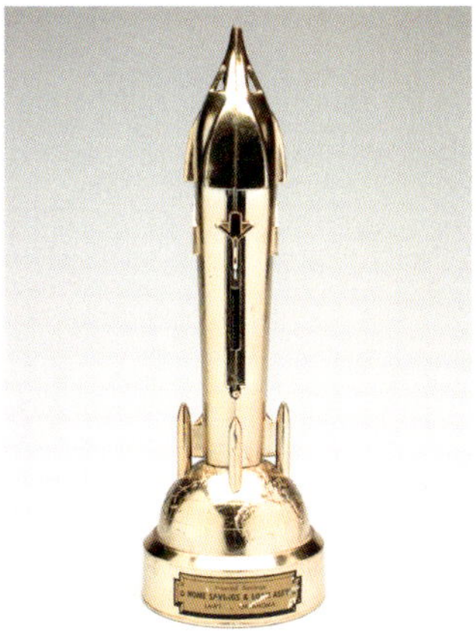

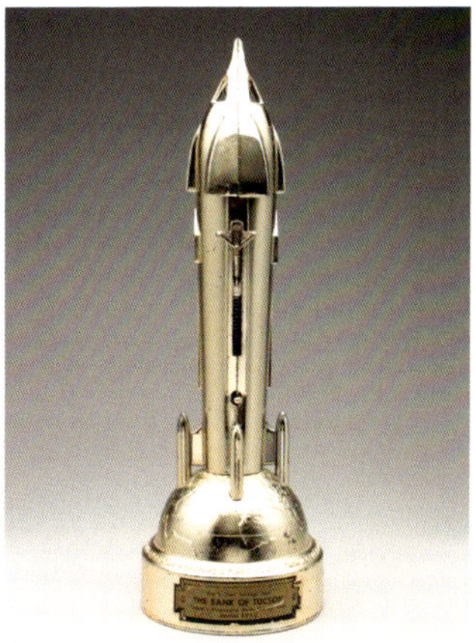

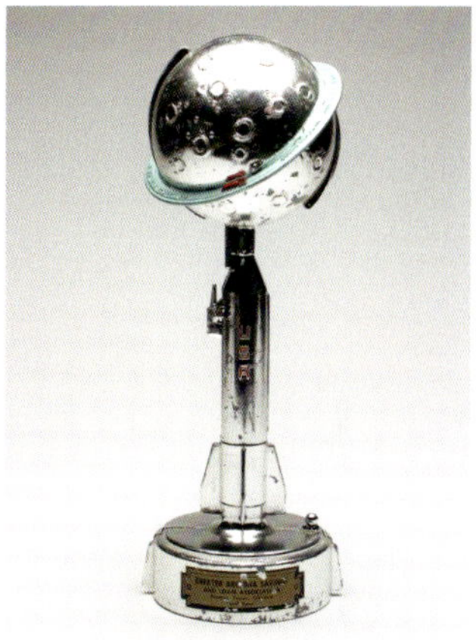

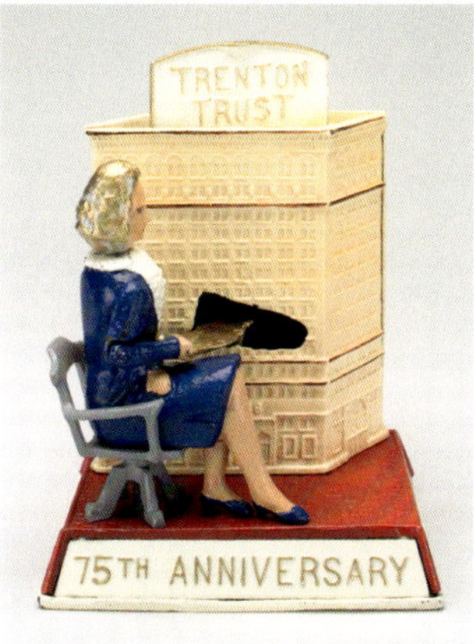
TRENTON
TRUST
75TH ANNIVERSARY

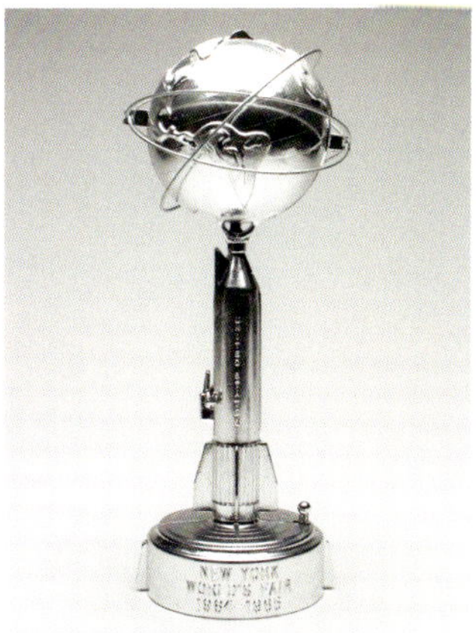
NEW YORK

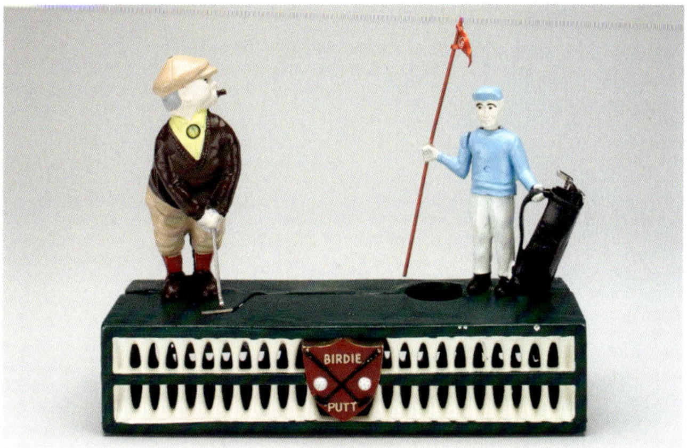
BIRDIE
PUTT

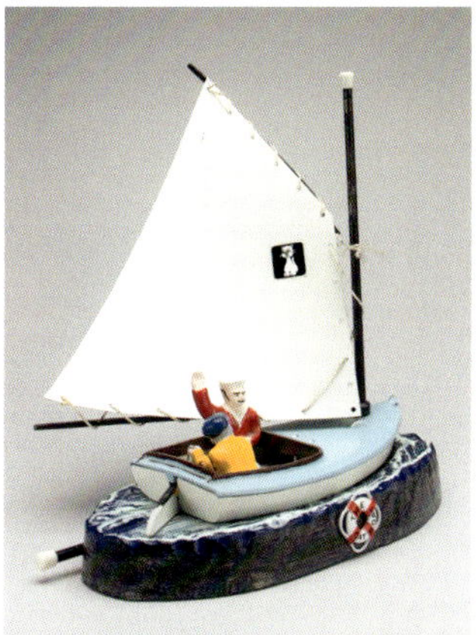

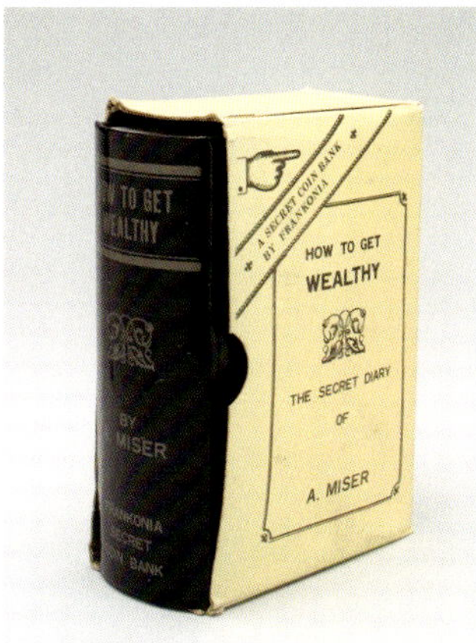
HOW TO GET
WEALTHY
THE SECRET DIARY
OF
A. MISER

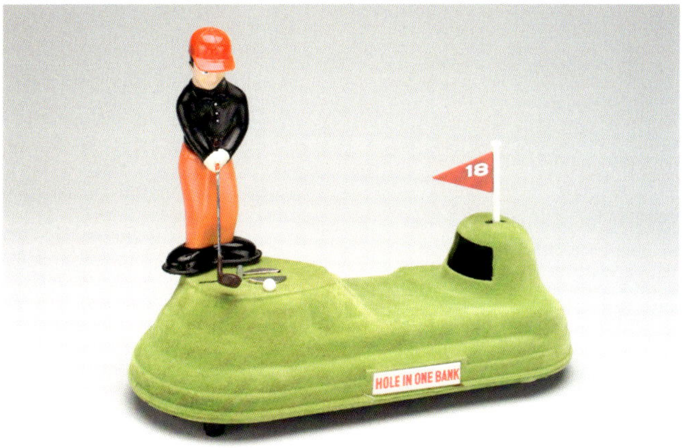
18
HOLE IN ONE BANK

Elephant with Howdah, Pull Tail (reproduction), c. 1960
Based on c. 1934 design by Hubley Manufacturing Company, Lancaster, Pennsylvania (est. 1894)
Iron, pigment, ribbon, cord, textile
5 1/2 x 8 3/4 x 2 7/8 in.
2003.236.502a,b

Spinaround Plan-It Coin Bank, 1959
Astro Manufacturing, East Detroit, Michigan, manufacturer
Zinc alloy, pigment, plastic
4 1/8 x 9 1/16 x 9 1/16 in.
2003.236.755

Destination Moon Bank, c. 1962
Duro Mold and Manufacturing, Inc., Detroit, manufacturer
Zinc alloy, chrome, pigment
10 3/4 x 4 5/16 x 4 5/16 in.
2003.236.759

Satellite, c. 1960s
Duro Mold and Manufacturing, Inc., Detroit, manufacturer
Zinc alloy, pigment
10 9/16 x 3 1/2 x 3 1/2 in.
2003.236.757

Satellite, c. 1960s
Duro Mold and Manufacturing, Inc., Detroit, manufacturer
Zinc alloy, pigment
10 5/8 x 3 1/2 x 3 1/2 in.
2003.236.756

Penny Pineapple Bank, 1960
Thomas M. Imswiler, American, designer
Iron, pigment
8 11/16 x 5 5/16 x 5 9/16 in.
2003.236.298

Birdie Putt, 1967
Littlestown Hardware & Foundry, Littlestown, Pennsylvania (1916 – present), manufacturer
Iron, pigment
6 7/8 x 8 3/4 x 3 1/4 in.
2003.236.41a,b

New York World's Fair Bank, c. 1964
RMS SALES Corporation, East Orange, New Jersey, manufacturer
Zinc alloy, chrome, plastic, pigment
10 5/8 x 4 3/16 x 4 3/16 in.
2003.236.758

Mary Roebling, Trenton Trust, 1963
Anthony Greenwood and J. E. Brubaker, American, designers
Grey Iron Casting Company, Mount Joy, Pennsylvania (1881 – 1969), manufacturer
Iron, pigment
8 x 6 1/16 x 4 7/8 in.
2003.236.367

Hole in One Bank, c. 1969
Plastic, pigment
6 13/16 x 8 3/4 x 3 13/16 in.
2003.236.505

How to Get Wealthy (book), c. 1968
Frankonia Products, Inc., Japan, manufacturer
Paper, metal, pigment, string, plastic
2 1/8 x 3 5/8 x 5 3/8 in.
2003.236.739

The Cat Boat, c. 1968
Littlestown Hardware & Foundry, Littlestown, Pennsylvania (1916 – present), manufacturer
Iron, nylon string, enamel paint
12 x 10 3/4 x 5 3/8 in.
2003.236.399

Dog Kennel, c. 1970
Germany
Metal, pigment
1 ¾ x 2 ⅝ x 1 ⅜ in.
2003.236.432

Bank Closed, c. 1970
Germany
Metal, pigment
3 ¼ x 5 ⅛ x 2 ¾ in.
2003.236.435

Strike, 1970
Littlestown Hardware & Foundry, Littlestown, Pennsylvania (1916 – present), manufacturer
Iron, pigment, paper
6 ¾ x 11 13/16 x 2 9/16 in.
2003.236.272a,b

Fisherman, c. 1970
Littlestown Hardware & Foundry, Littlestown, Pennsylvania (1916 – present), manufacturer
Iron, pigment, plastic
6 x 12 5/16 x 2 15/16 in.
2003.236.87a,b

Black Box, c. 1972
Poynter Products, Inc., Cincinnati, manufacturer
Plastic, metal
3 3/16 x 2 ¾ x 3 15/16 in.
2003.236.459

Taxes Taxes, c. 1970s
Japan
Tin, plastic, flocking
6 ¾ x 8 ⅞ x 3 ⅞ in.
2003.236.398

St. Nicholas, c. 1975
Reynolds Toys, Falls Church, Virginia (est. 1964), manufacturer
Iron, pigment
9 ⅝ x 3 15/16 x 3 ⅞ in.
2003.236.605

Mary and the Lamb, 1974
Reynolds Toys, Falls Church, Virginia (est. 1964), manufacturer
Iron, pigment
4 ¾ x 6 ⅞ x 2 ⅞ in.
2003.236.307

Uncle Sam, U.S. Savings Bonds Campaign (reproduction), 1970
Based on c. 1886 design by Peter Adams and Charles G. Shepard, American, and manufactured by Shepard Hardware Company, Buffalo, New York (1866 – 92)
Sears, Minneapolis (est. 1883) and Chicago (since 1887), manufacturer
Iron, pigment
10 x 4 ⅝ x 3 ¾ in.
2003.236.807

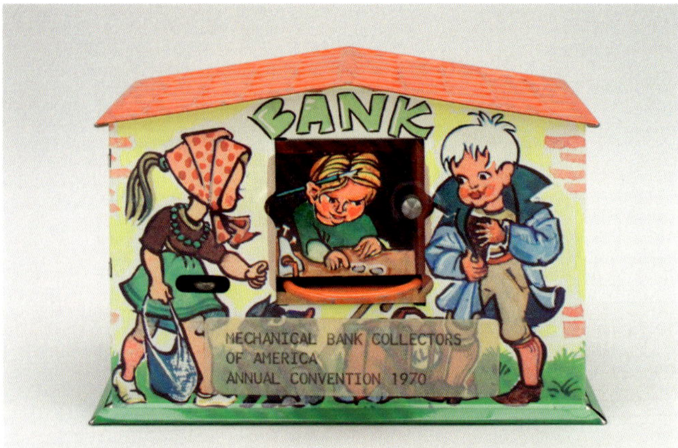
BANK
MECHANICAL BANK COLLECTORS
OF AMERICA
ANNUAL CONVENTION 1970

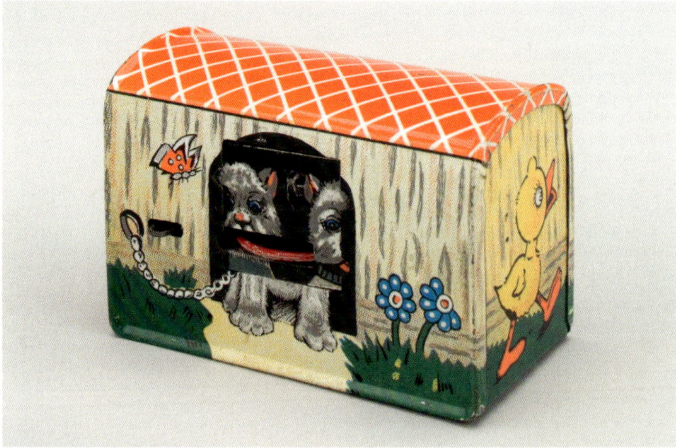

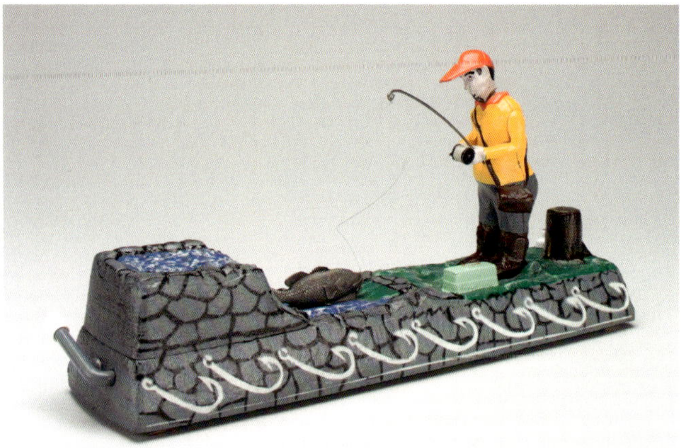

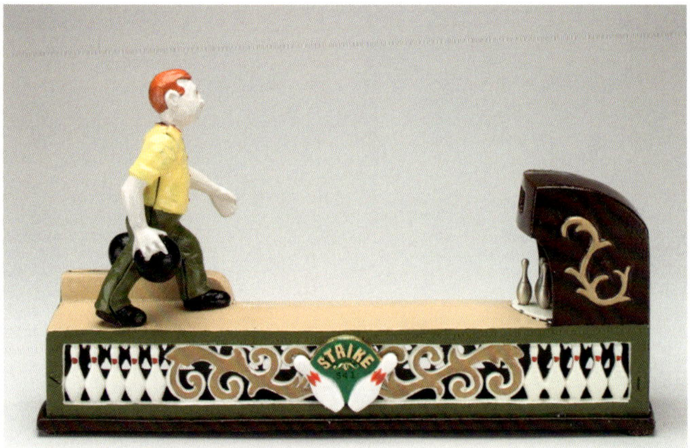
STRIKE

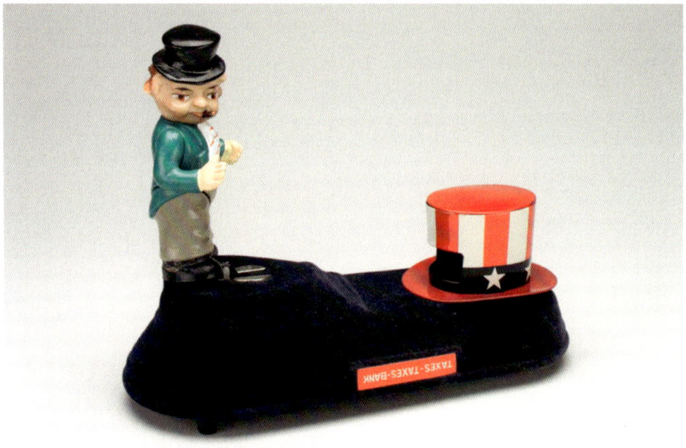
TAXES-TAXES-BANK

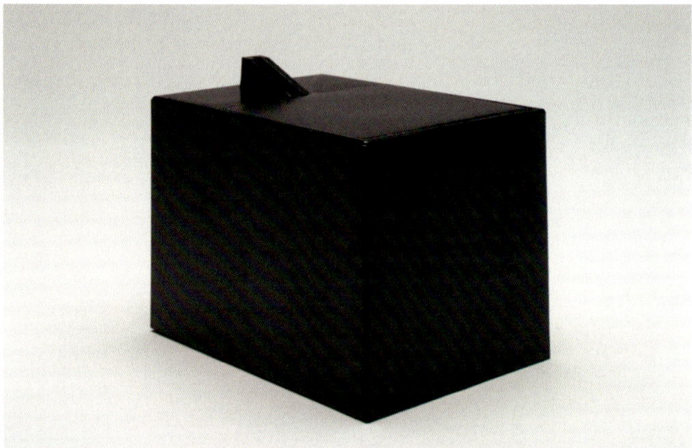

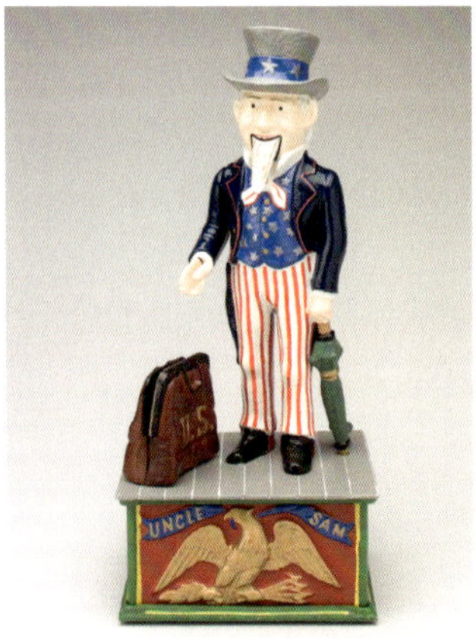
U.S.
UNCLE SAM

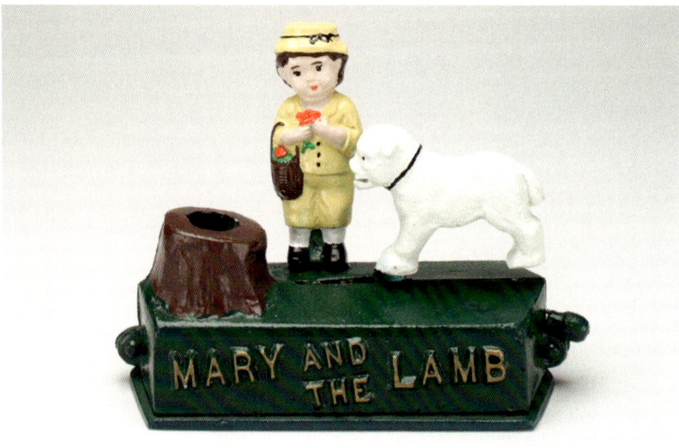
MARY AND THE LAMB

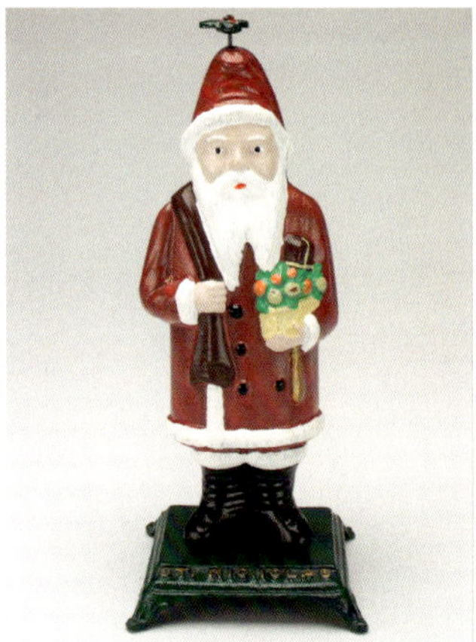

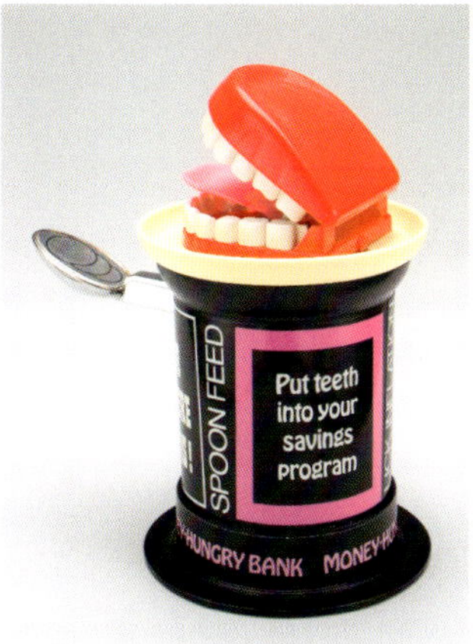
SPOON FEED
Put teeth
into your
savings
program
HUNGRY BANK

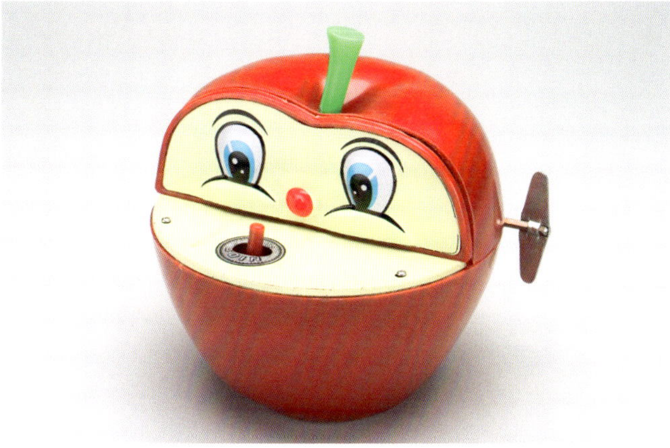

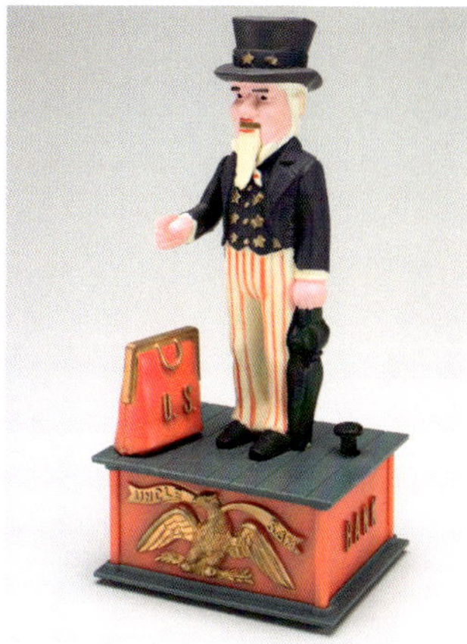

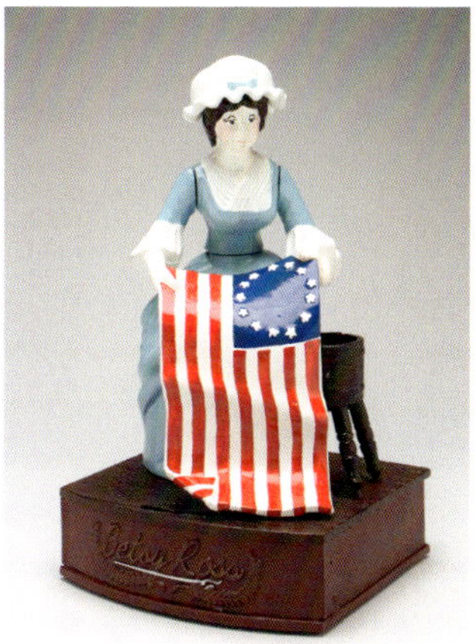

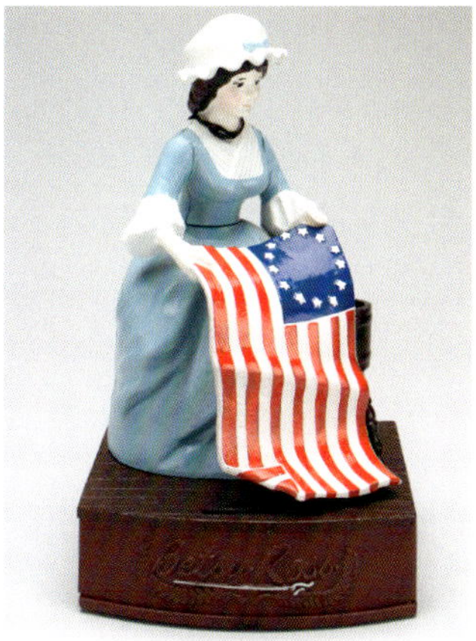

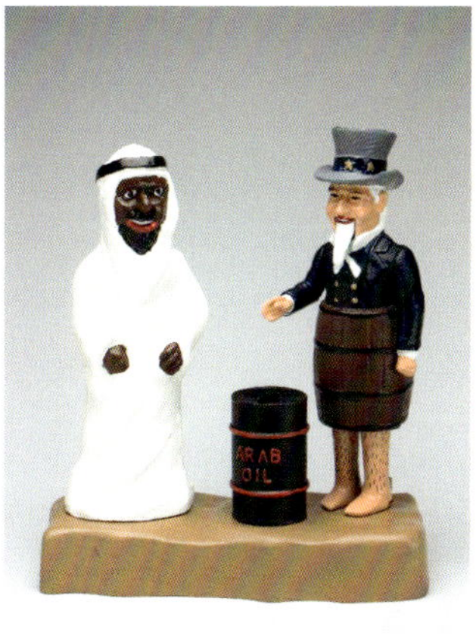
ARAB
OIL

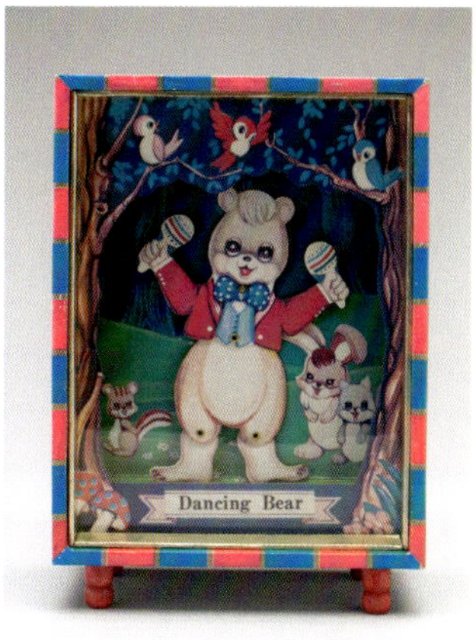
Dancing Bear

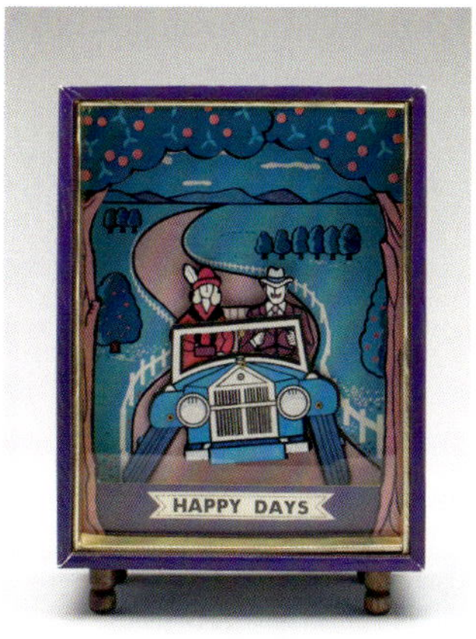
HAPPY DAYS

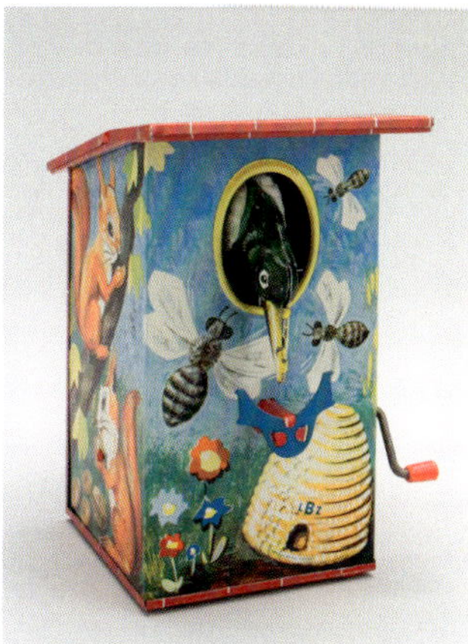

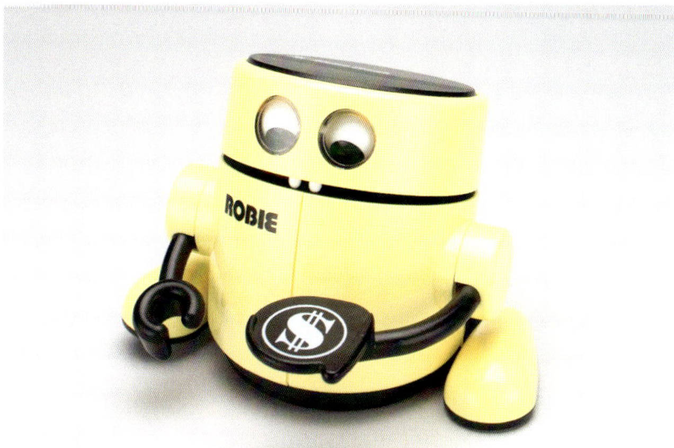
ROBIE

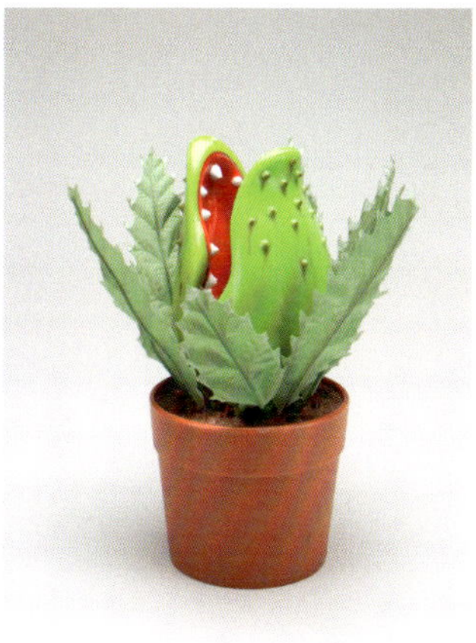

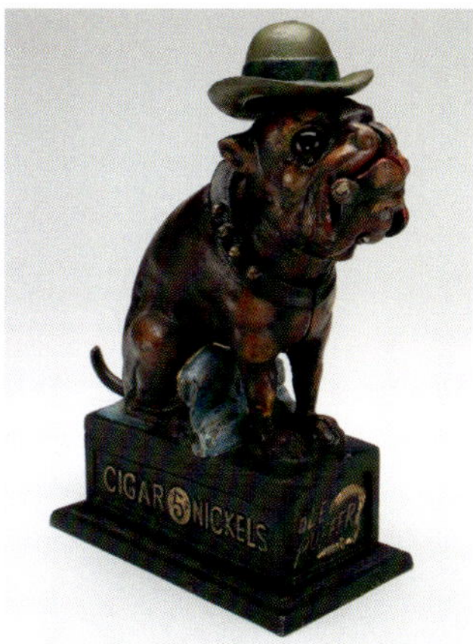
CIGAR 5 NICKELS

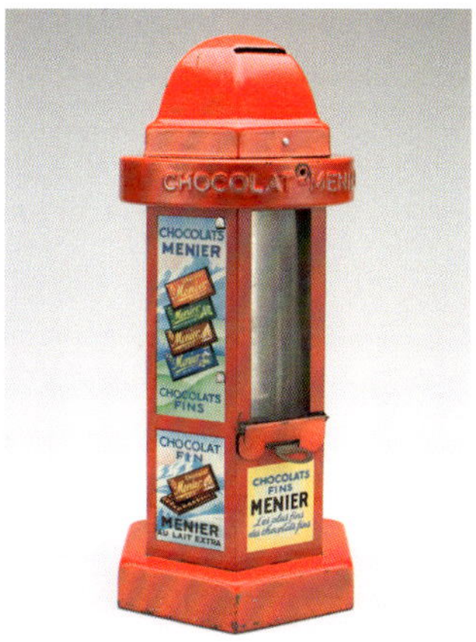
MENIER

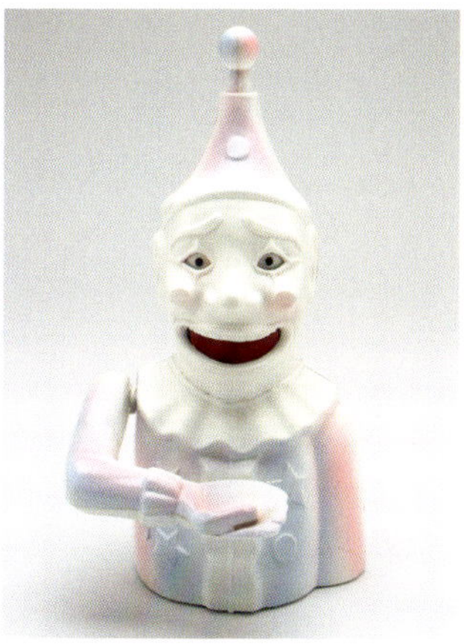

Uncle Sam, c. 1976
Hong Kong
Plastic
9 x 4 1/4 x 3 3/8 in.
2003.236.397

Apple and Worm, c. 1976
Yone, Japan, manufacturer
Plastic, tin
5 x 5 1/8 x 4 3/4 in.
2003.236.552a,b

Money-Hungry Bank, 1975
Poynter Products, Inc.,
Cincinnati, manufacturer
Plastic, metal
6 x 6 1/2 x 4 3/16 in.
2003.236.396a,b

Dancing Bear (music box),
c. 1979
Otagiri, Japan, manufacturer
Cardboard, paper, metal, rubber
7 3/4 x 5 3/8 x 3 1/4 in.
2003.236.646

Uncle Sam and Arab with Oil Drum, 1976
John Wright, Wrightsville,
Pennsylvania (est. 1880),
manufacturer
Iron, pigment
10 3/4 x 9 3/4 x 4 3/16 in.
2003.236.809

Betsy Ross Bicentennial Bank, 1976
Al Davidson, American
(1936–1992), designer
Iron, aluminum pigment
10 1/2 x 6 3/8 x 5 11/16 in.
2003.236.805

Betsy Ross Bicentennial Bank, 1976
Al Davidson, American
(1936–1992), designer
Iron, aluminum, pigment
11 1/8 x 6 3/16 x 5 11/16 in.
2003.236.644

Robie the Robot, c. 1980s
China
Plastic
4 1/4 x 5 7/8 x 5 in.
2003.236.395

Beehive and Bees, c. 1980s
Lorenz Bolz Zirndorf,
Nuremberg, Germany,
manufacturer
Tin, pigment
5 1/4 x 3 3/16 x 4 in.
2003.236.437

Happy Days (music box), c. 1979
Otagiri, Japan, manufacturer
Cardboard, paper, metal
7 11/16 x 5 1/2 x 3 1/16 in.
2003.236.647

Clown, 20th century
Plastic, pigment
8 x 4 3/8 x 3 7/8 in.
2003.236.501

"Chocolats Menier" (vending),
20th century
Paris
Metal, pigment, plastic
10 1/8 x 5 1/4 x 5 1/4 in.
2003.236.737

Ole Puffer, c. 1998
Based on c. 1880 design of
Bull Dog Bank by James H.
Bowen, American (active c.
1877–1906), and manufactured
by J. & E. Stevens Company,
Cromwell, Connecticut
(1843–1950s)
Xonex International, Inc.,
Cleveland, manufacturer
Iron, pigment, glass
8 1/2 x 8 3/8 x 3 1/8 in.
2003.236.801

Little Shop of Horrors, Audrey II, c. 1985
Poynter Products, Inc.,
Cincinnati, manufacturer
Plastic, metal, pigment
7 5/16 x 3 1/2 x 3 1/2 in.
2003.236.448

Dog and Cat, 20th century
Japan
Wood, pigment
6 1/4 x 4 3/16 x 2 1/2 in.
2003.236.428

Crane Bank, 20th century
China
Plastic, metal
12 9/16 x 7 7/8 x 4 3/8 in.
2003.236.429a – p

Coffin Bank, 20th century
Yone, Japan, manufacturer
Metal, pigment, fabric, plastic
1 3/4 x 6 3/8 x 2 5/8 in.
2003.236.469

The One That Got Away, 20th century
China
Metal, pigment, rubber
6 7/8 x 7 1/4 x 4 in.
2003.236.606

Elephant, 20th century
Ru Gar Enterprises Company, Long Beach, California, manufacturer
Aluminum, pigment
4 3/8 x 8 15/16 x 2 3/8 in.
2003.236.503

Robot Machine Bank,
20th century
Everlast Toys, Hong Kong,
manufacturer
Plastic, paper, pigment
4 1/2 x 4 1/2 x 4 3/4 in.
2003.236.740

Piggy Bank, 20th century
Japan
Metal, pigment, rubber
3 1/4 x 4 3/4 x 2 7/8 in.
2003.236.525

Love Bank, 20th century
YAP, Hong Kong, manufacturer
Plastic, pigment
6 1/4 x 4 1/4 x 3 3/8 in.
2003.236.506

Victorian House (music box),
20th century
Otagiri, Japan, manufacturer
Cardboard, colored paper, metal
7 1/8 x 3 3/8 x 4 in.
2003.236.648

Tico Tico (music box),
20th century
Reuge, Switzerland,
manufacturer
Wood, pigment, metal, plastic
6 x 4 9/16 x 2 15/16 in.
2003.236.649

Thrifty Tower, 20th century
England
Wood, pigment
8 1/4 x 8 7/8 x 5 1/4 in.
2003.236.514

Saluting Sailor, 20th century
Germany
Tin, pigment
6 3/4 x 4 1/8 x 2 in.
2003.236.854

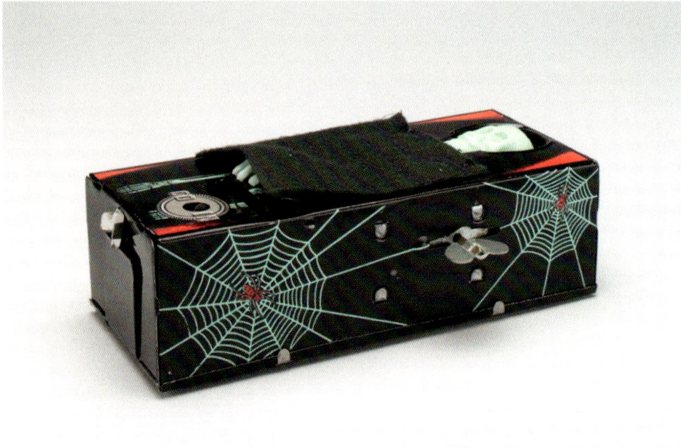

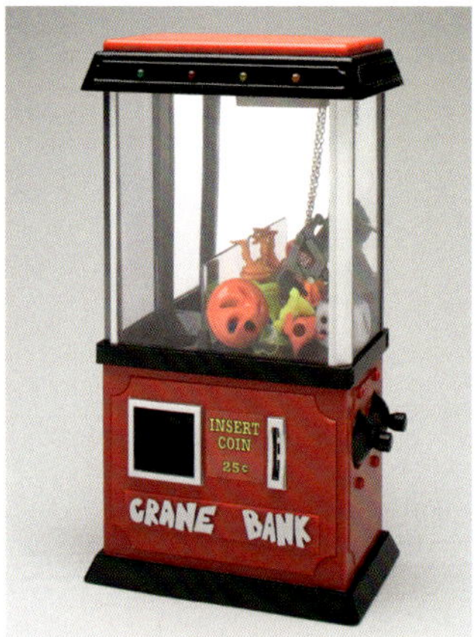
INSERT
COIN
25¢
CRANE BANK

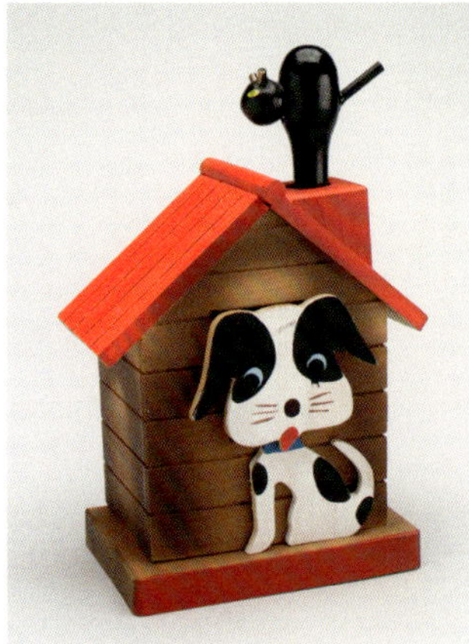

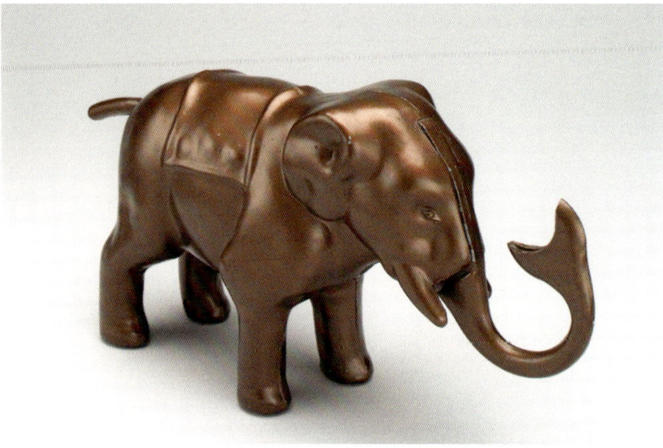

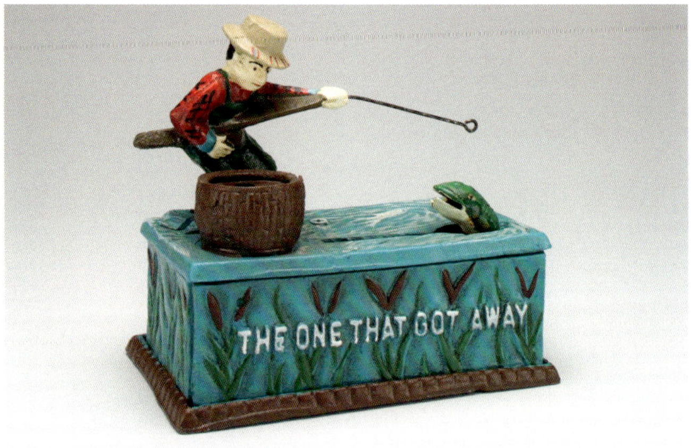
THE ONE THAT GOT AWAY

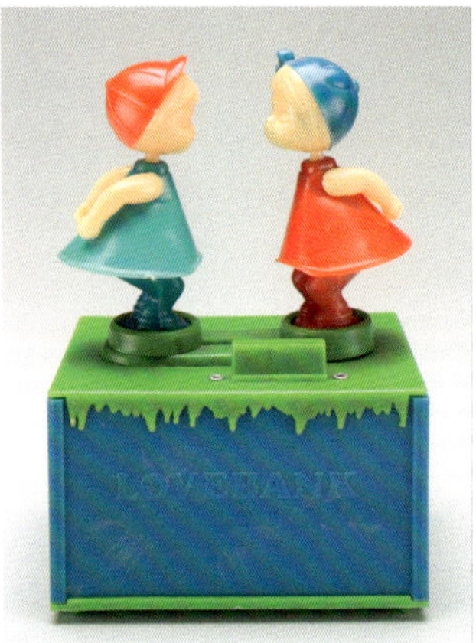
LOVEBANK

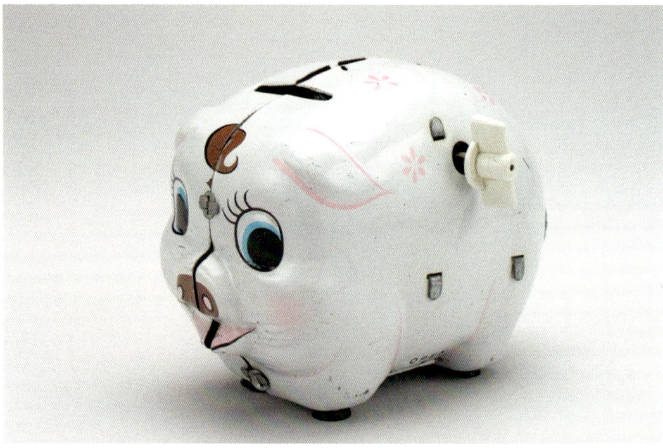

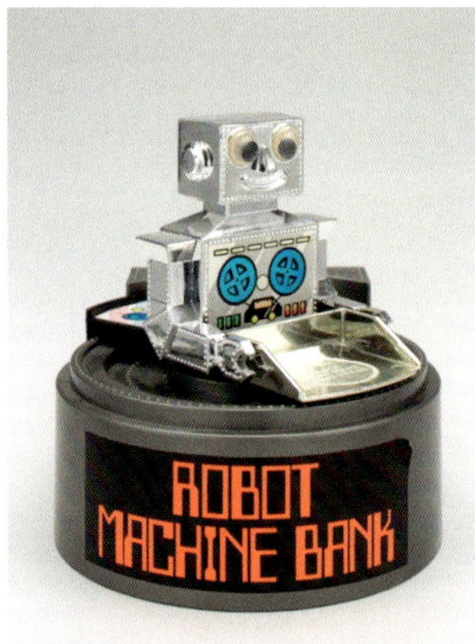
ROBOT
MACHINE BANK

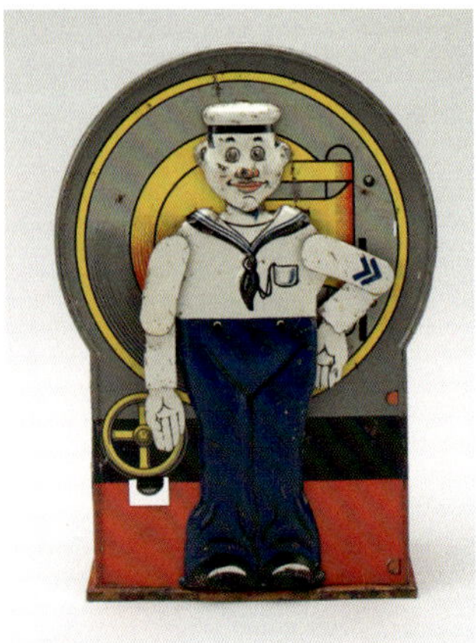

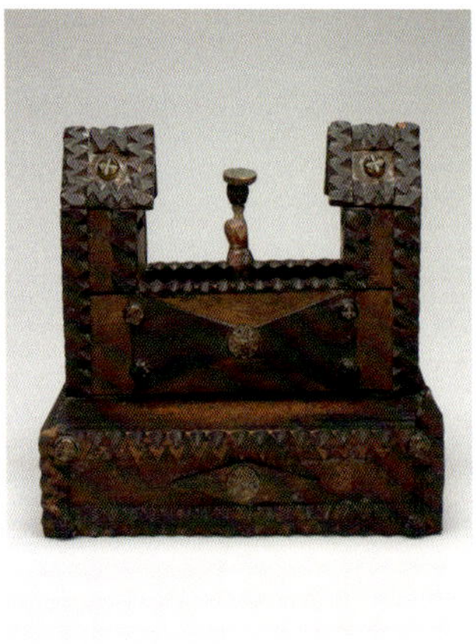

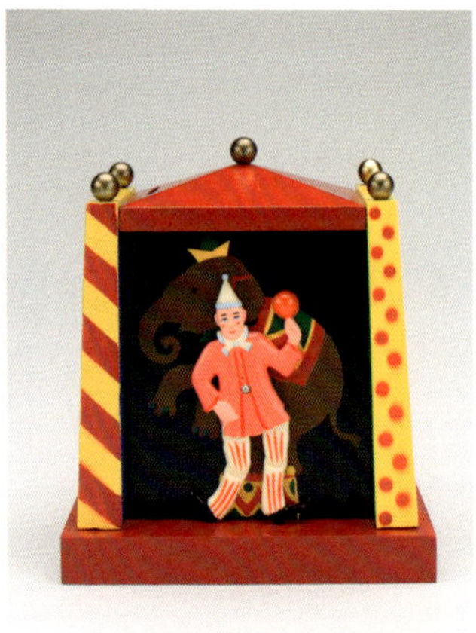

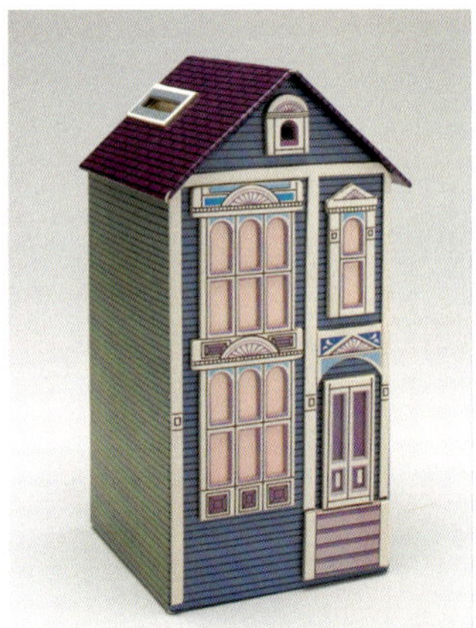

STILL BANKS: Iron

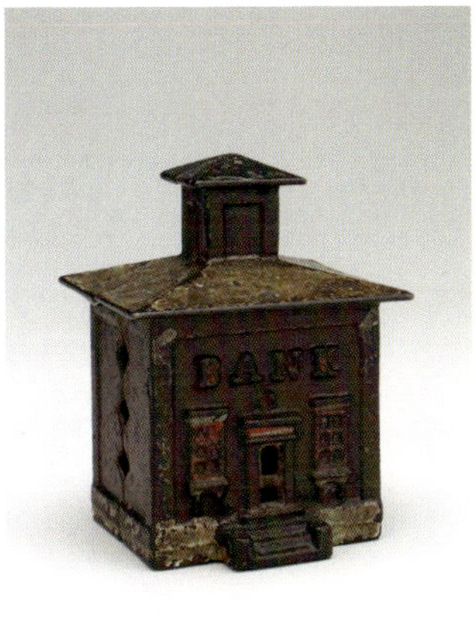

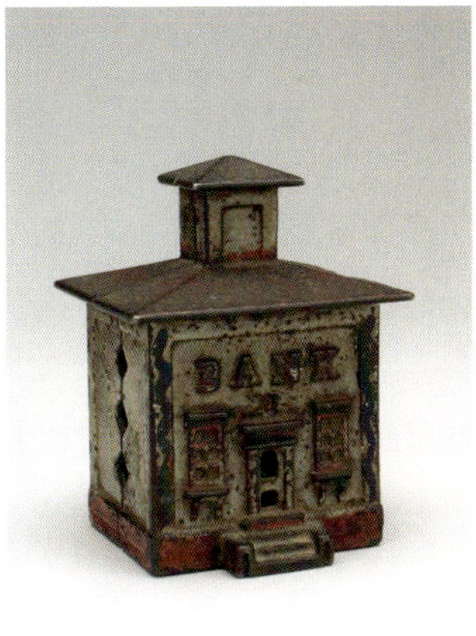

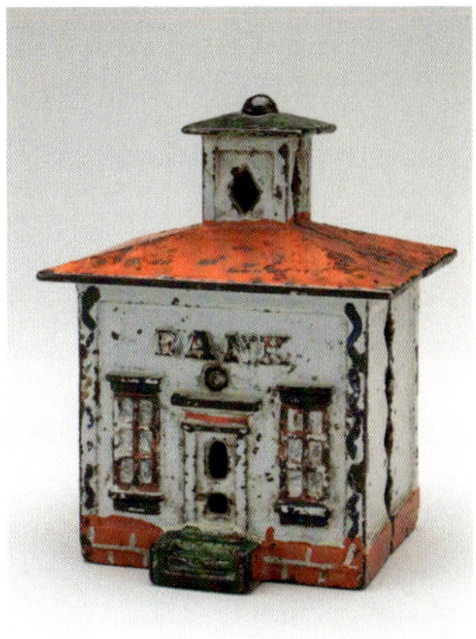

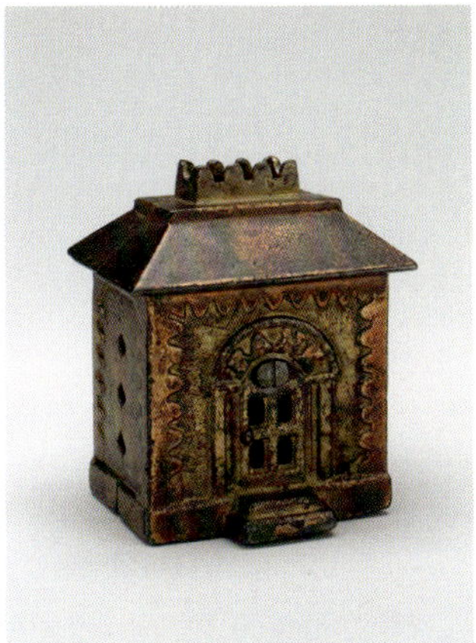
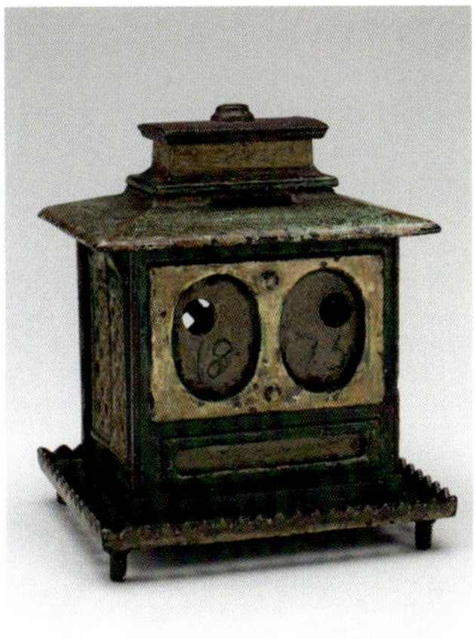
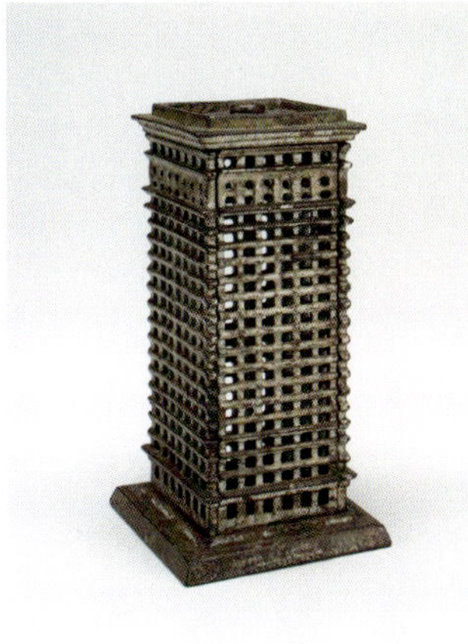
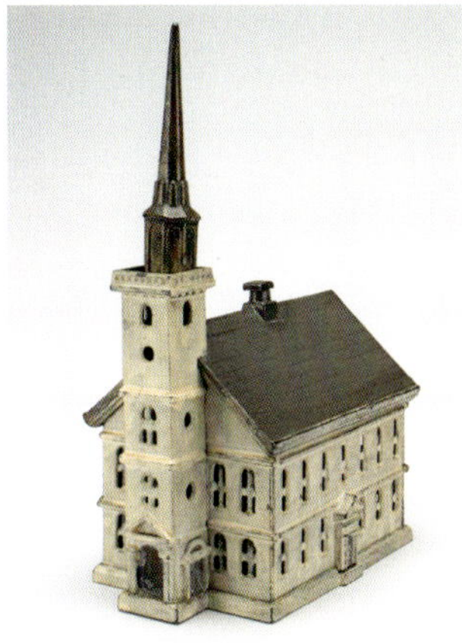
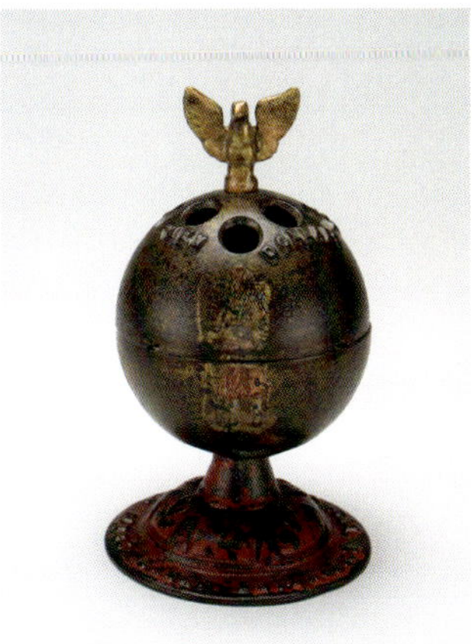
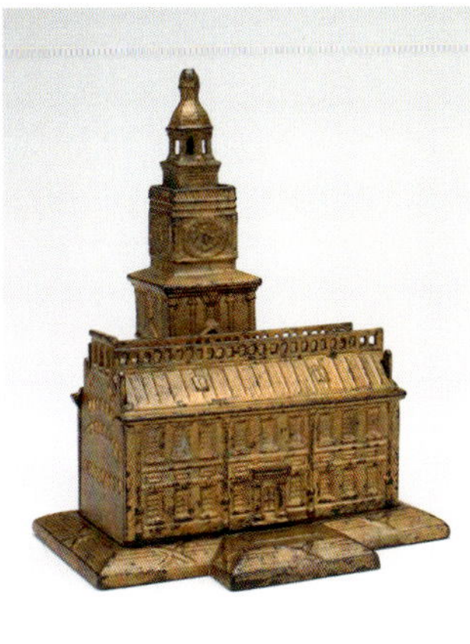
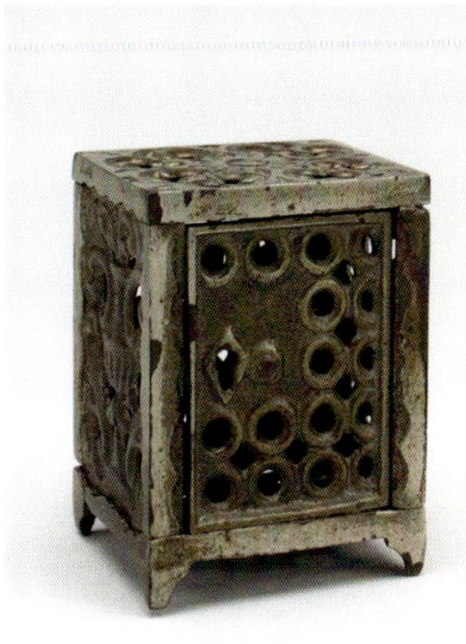
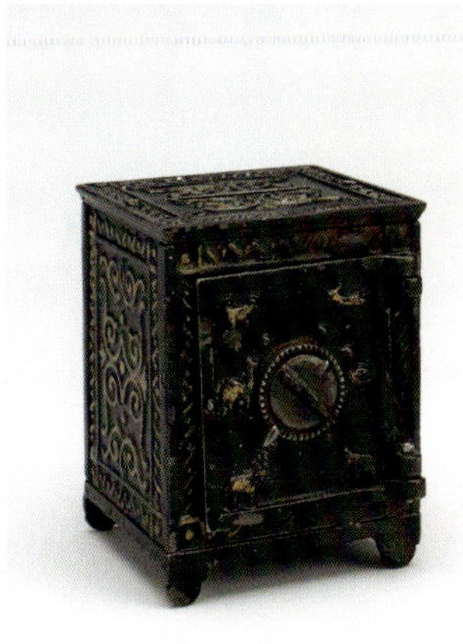
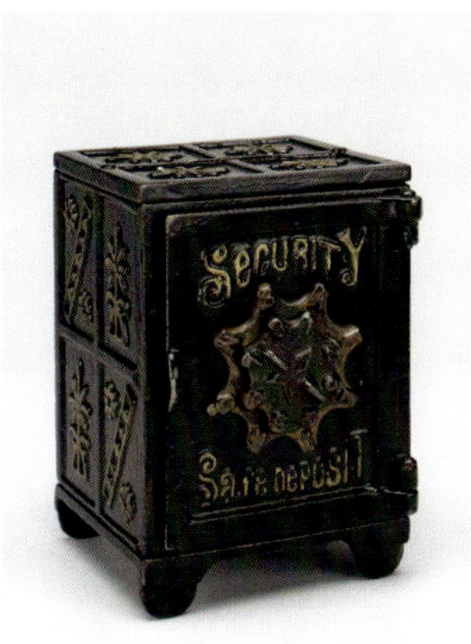

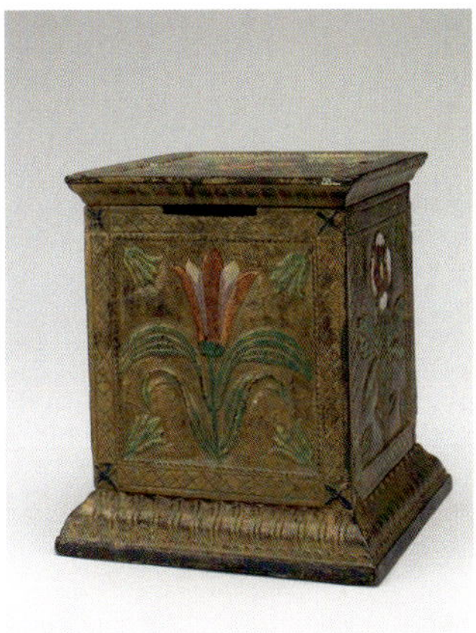
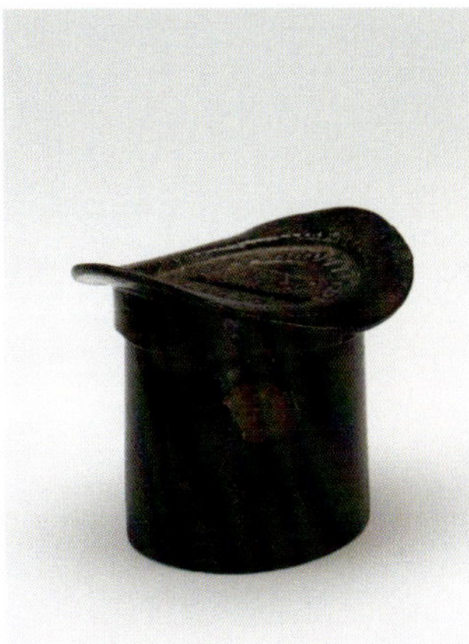
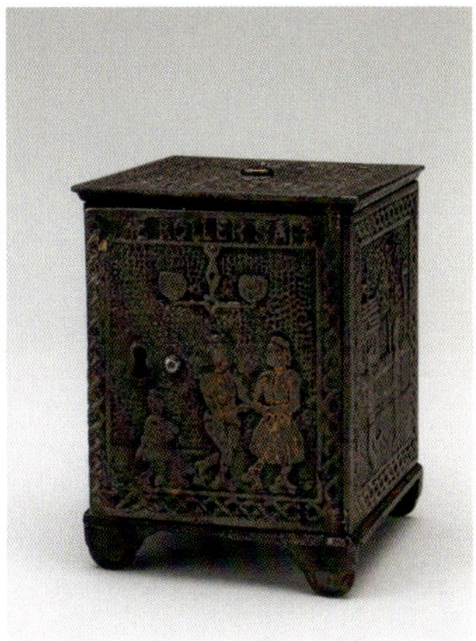

STILL BANKS: Iron

Cupola Bank, 1872
J. & E. Stevens Company, Cromwell, Connecticut (1843–1950s), manufacturer
Iron, pigment
4 5/16 x 3 3/8 x 2 3/4 in.
2003.236.775

Cupola Bank, 1872
J. & E. Stevens Company, Cromwell, Connecticut (1843–1950s), manufacturer
Iron, pigment
3 1/8 x 2 5/8 x 2 3/16 in.
2003.236.661

Cupola Bank, 1869
Dover Stamping Company, Boston (1833–present), manufacturer
Iron, pigment
3 3/8 x 2 9/16 x 2 1/2 in.
2003.236.778

Old South Church, 1874
United States
Iron, pigment
9 1/4 x 4 x 6 3/8
2003.236.685

High Rise, 1874
Kenton Hardware Manufacturing Company, Kenton, Ohio (1890–1950), manufacturer
6 1/2 x 2 7/8 x 2 7/8 in.
Iron, pigment
2003.236.923

Moody and Sankey (portraits missing), c. 1874
Smith & Egge, Bridgeport, Connecticut (est. 1874), manufacturer
Iron, pigment
5 x 4 1/8 x 3 3/8 in.
2003.236.654

Crown Bank, c. 1873–1928
J. & E. Stevens Company, Cromwell, Connecticut (1843–1950s), or Grey Iron Casting Company, Mount Joy, Pennsylvania (1881–1969), manufacturer
Iron, pigment
3 1/2 x 3 1/8 x 2 1/2 in.
2003.236.403

Security Safe Deposit, c. 1881
Kyser & Rex Company, Philadelphia (c. 1879–98), manufacturer
Iron, pigment
3 1/8 x 2 3/8 x 2 3/8 in.
2003.236.413

Safe, 1879–98
Kyser & Rex Company, Philadelphia (c. 1879–98), manufacturer
Iron
3 3/8 x 2 1/2 x 2 1/4 in.
2003.236.368

Independence Hall, 1875
Enterprise Manufacturing Company, Philadelphia (1875–88), manufacturer
Iron, pigment
10 x 9 3/8 x 8 in.
2003.236.686

Globe Bank, c. 1875
Enterprise Manufacturing Company, Philadelphia (1875–88), manufacturer
Iron, pigment, paper
5 1/2 x 3 3/8 x 3 3/8 in.
2003.236.371

Roller Safe, c. 1882
Kyser & Rex Company, Philadelphia (c. 1879–98), manufacturer
Iron, pigment
3 5/8 x 2 3/4 x 2 13/16 in.
2003.236.783

Lincoln High Hat, "*Pass around the Hat*," c. 1882
United States
Iron, pigment
2 1/4 x 2 7/16 x 2 15/16 in.
2003.236.944

Floral Safe (or *National Safe*), c. 1882
Kyser & Rex Company, Philadelphia (c. 1879–98), manufacturer
Iron, pigment
4 5/8 x 4 1/4 x 4 1/4 in.
2003.236.776

Security Safe Deposit, c. 1881
Kyser & Rex Company, Philadelphia (c. 1879–98), manufacturer
Iron, pigment
3 7/8 x 2 13/16 x 2 3/4 in.
2003.236.766

Apple, 1882
Kyser & Rex Company, Philadelphia (c. 1879 – 98), manufacturer
Iron, pigment
4 $\frac{5}{8}$ x 4 $\frac{1}{8}$ x 5 $\frac{3}{16}$ in.
2003.236.949

Young America, c. 1882
Kyser & Rex Company, Philadelphia (c. 1879 – 98), manufacturer
Iron, pigment
4 $\frac{7}{16}$ x 3 $\frac{1}{8}$ x 3 $\frac{1}{4}$ in.
2003.236.784

Sport Safe, c. 1882
Kyser & Rex Company, Philadelphia (c. 1879 – 98), manufacturer
Iron, pigment
3 $\frac{1}{16}$ x 2 $\frac{1}{4}$ x 2 $\frac{1}{4}$ in.
2003.236.153

Fidelity Trust Sampler Safe, c. 1885
Henry C. Hart Manufacturing Company, Detroit, manufacturer
Iron, pigment
8 $\frac{3}{4}$ x 6 $\frac{3}{16}$ x 3 $\frac{3}{8}$ in.
2003.236.191a,b

Multiplying Bank, 1883
Possibly J. & E. Stevens Company, Cromwell, Connecticut (1843 – 1950s), manufacturer
Iron, pigment, glass
6 $\frac{1}{2}$ x 5 $\frac{1}{8}$ x 5 $\frac{1}{8}$ in.
2003.236.83a,b

Japanese Safe, 1882
Kyser & Rex Company, Philadelphia (c. 1879 – 98), manufacturer
Iron, pigment
4 $\frac{11}{16}$ x 5 $\frac{7}{16}$ x 4 $\frac{3}{4}$ in.
2003.236.595

Arabian Safe, 1882
Kyser & Rex Company, Philadelphia (c. 1879 – 98), manufacturer
Iron
4 $\frac{1}{4}$ x 4 $\frac{5}{8}$ x 4 $\frac{3}{16}$ in.
2003.236.594

Middy, 1887
United States
Iron, pigment
5 $\frac{5}{8}$ x 2 $\frac{1}{2}$ x 2 $\frac{1}{8}$ in.
2003.236.638

American Trust and Safe Deposit, c. 1887
United States
Iron
6 x 6 $\frac{3}{8}$ x 3 $\frac{5}{8}$ in.
2003.236.466

Log Cabin, c. 1885
United States
Iron, pigment
2 $\frac{5}{8}$ x 3 $\frac{7}{16}$ x 2 $\frac{3}{4}$ in.
2003.236.659

Phoenix Dime Register Trunk, c. 1890
Piaget, United States, manufacturer
Iron, paper, glass
3 $\frac{3}{4}$ x 4 $\frac{1}{2}$ x 2 $\frac{3}{4}$ in.
2003.236.662

Pug Dog, Seated, 1889
Kyser & Rex Company, Philadelphia (c. 1879 – 98), manufacturer
Iron, pigment
3 $\frac{11}{16}$ x 3 $\frac{1}{8}$ x 1 $\frac{11}{16}$ in.
2003.236.980

Security Safe Deposit, c. 1889
Kyser & Rex Company, Philadelphia (c. 1879 – 98), manufacturer
Iron, pigment
4 $\frac{3}{16}$ x 2 $\frac{15}{16}$ x 3 $\frac{1}{4}$ in.
2003.236.414

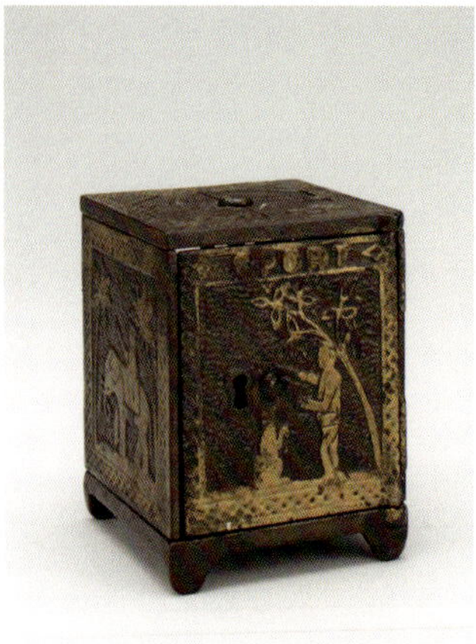

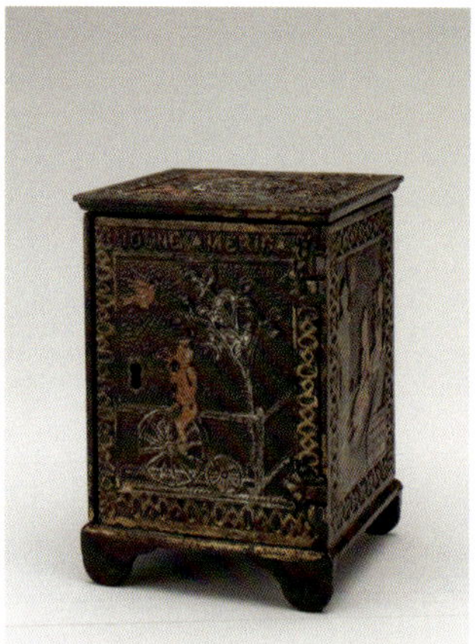

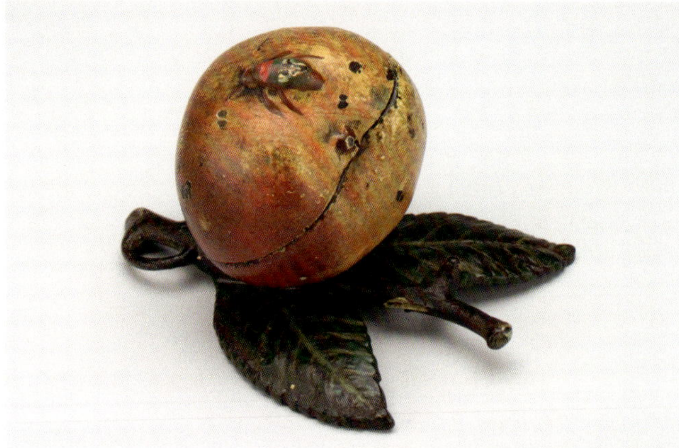

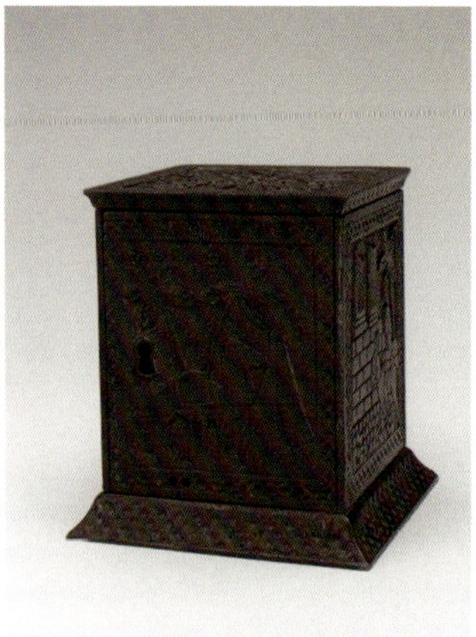

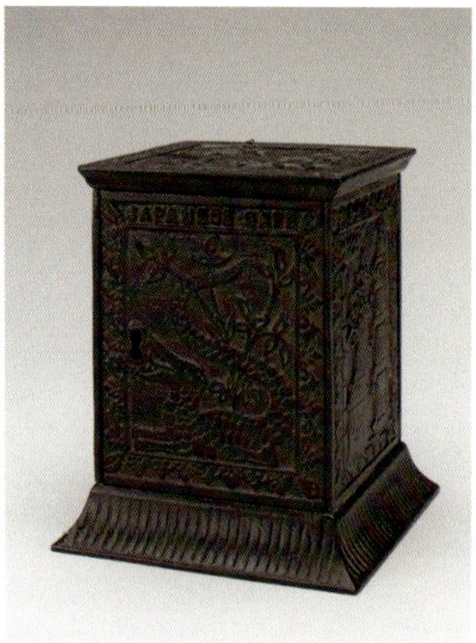

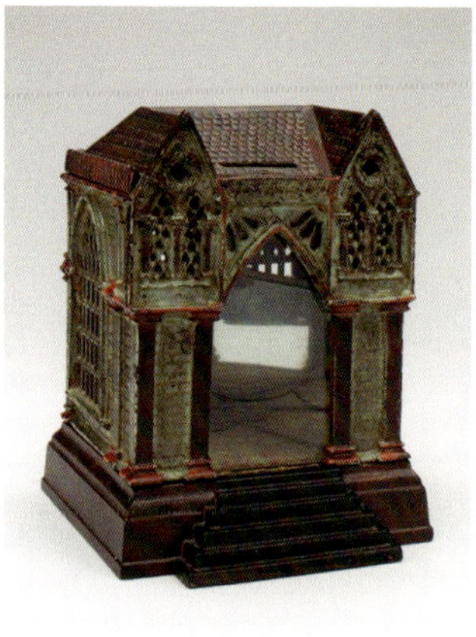

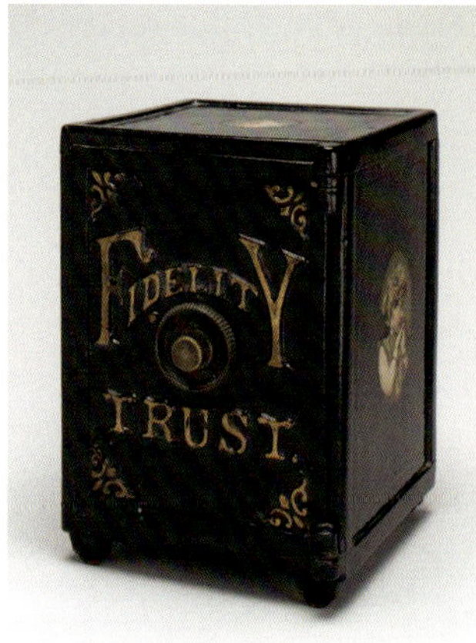
FIDELITY
TRUST

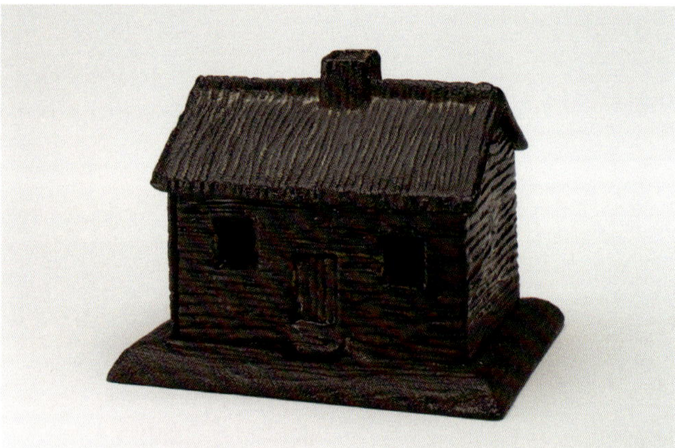

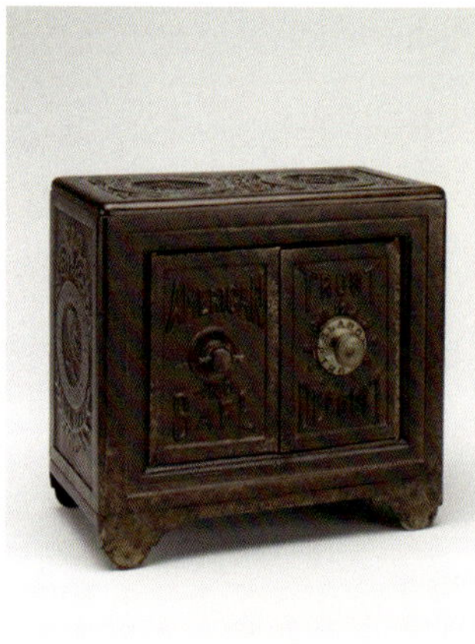

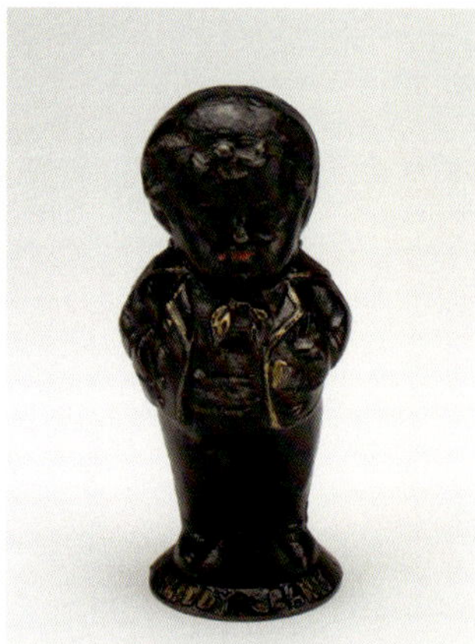

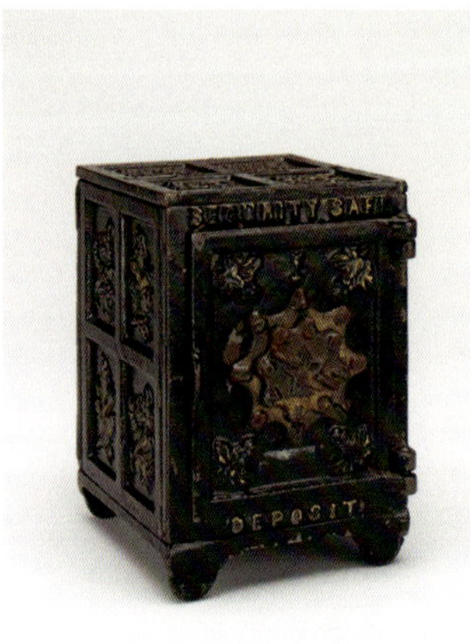
DEPOSIT

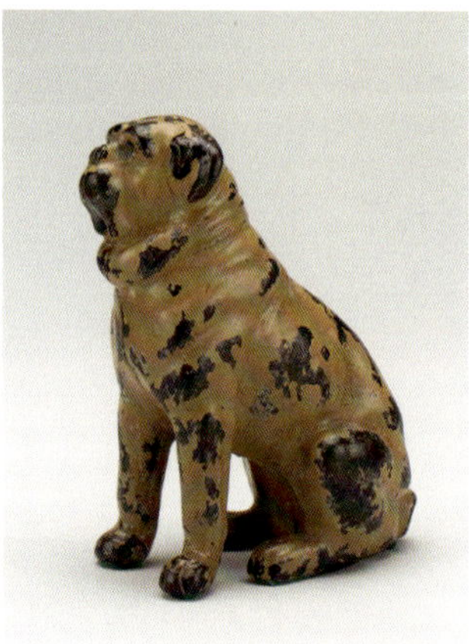

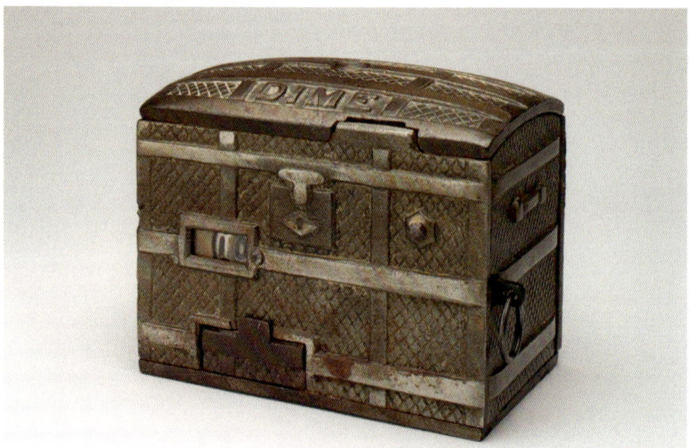
DIME

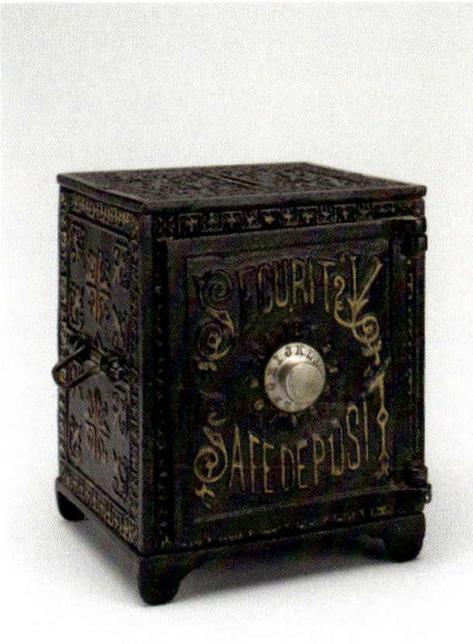
SAFE DEPOSIT

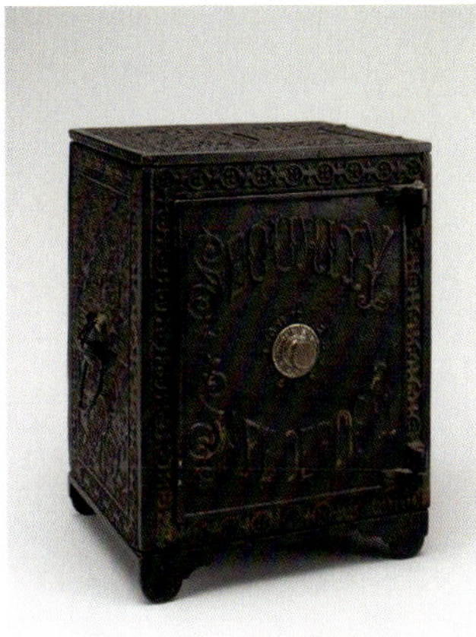

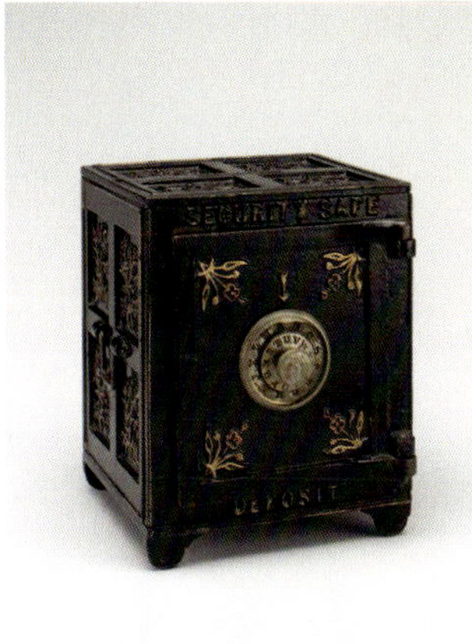
SECURITY SAFE
DEPOSIT

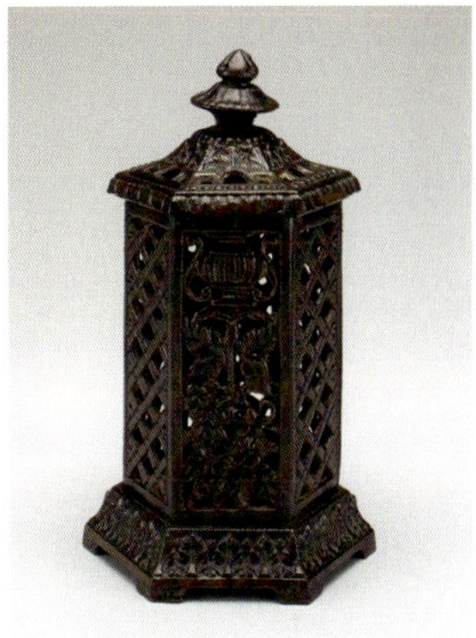

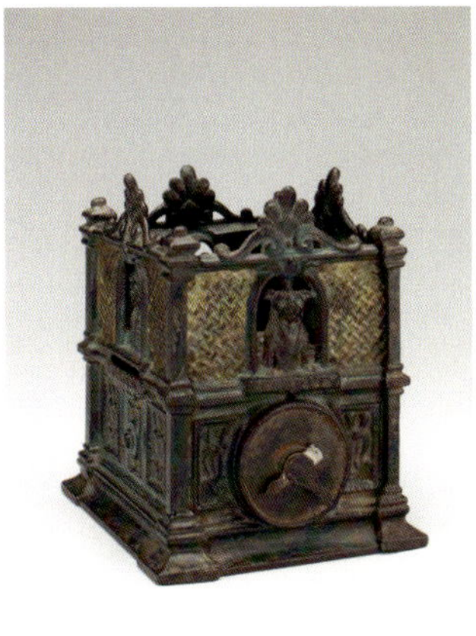

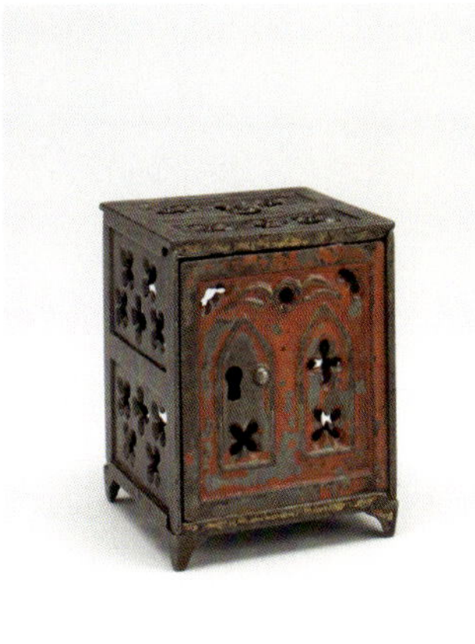

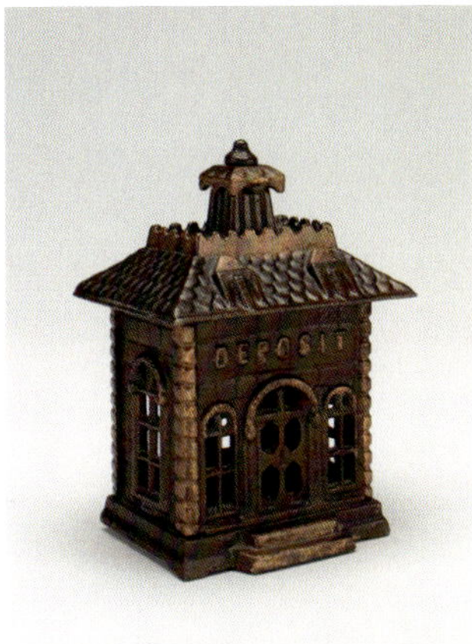
DEPOSIT

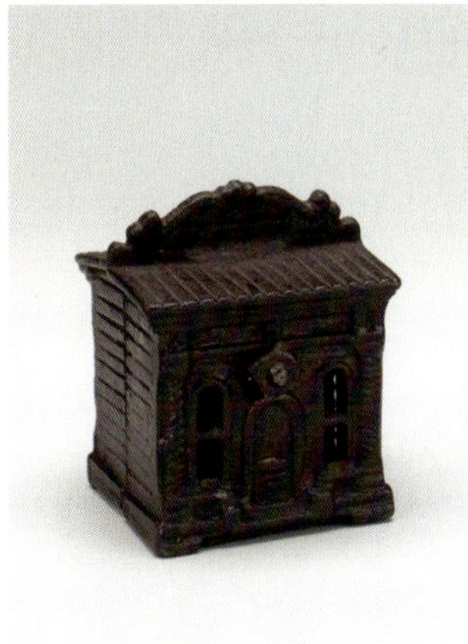

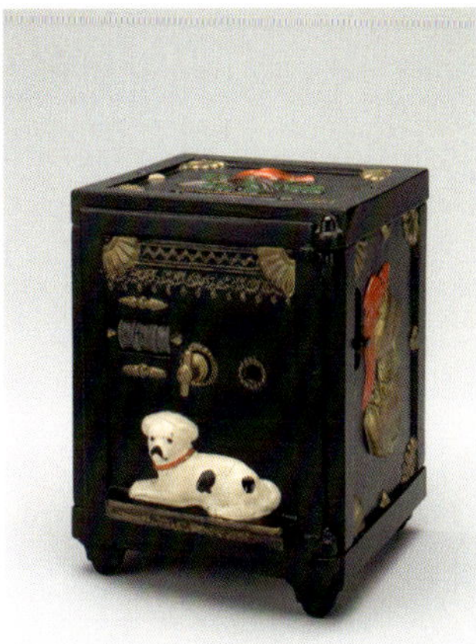

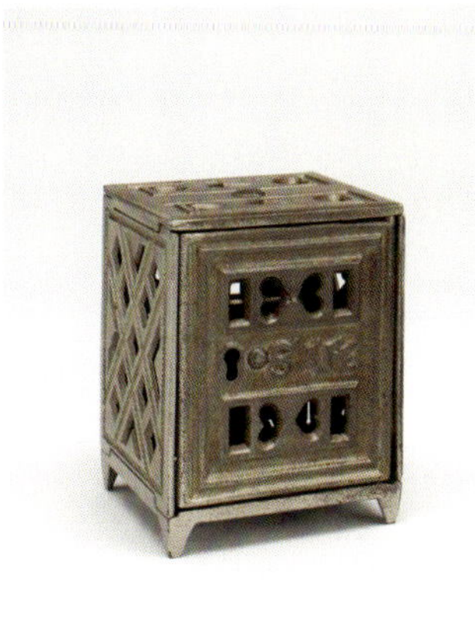

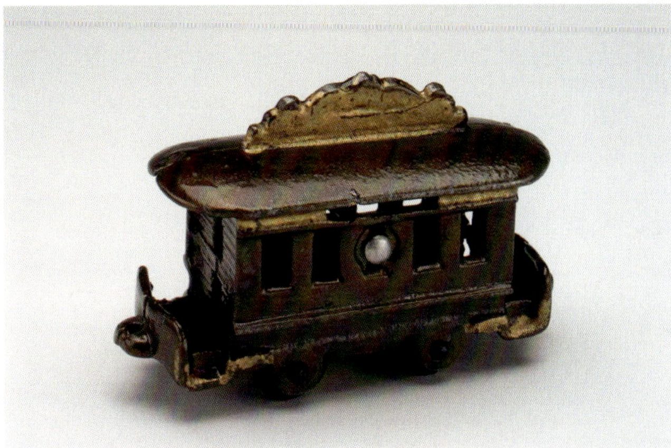

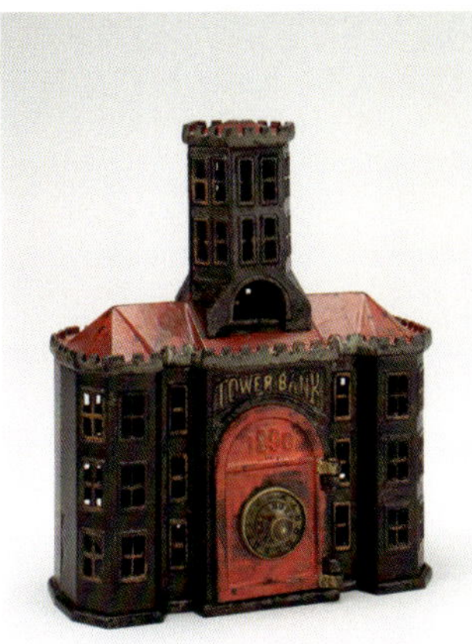
TOWER BANK

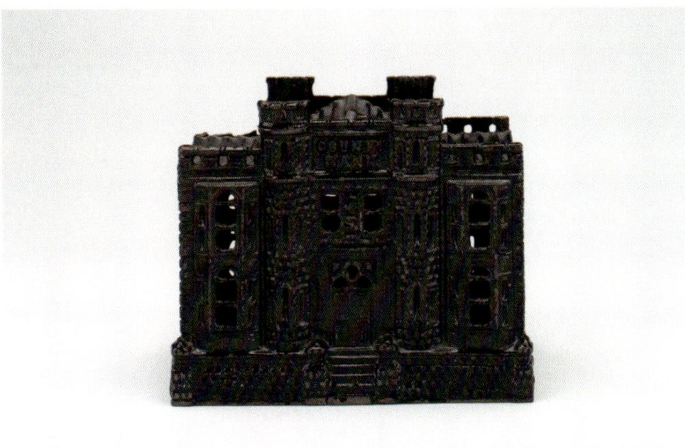

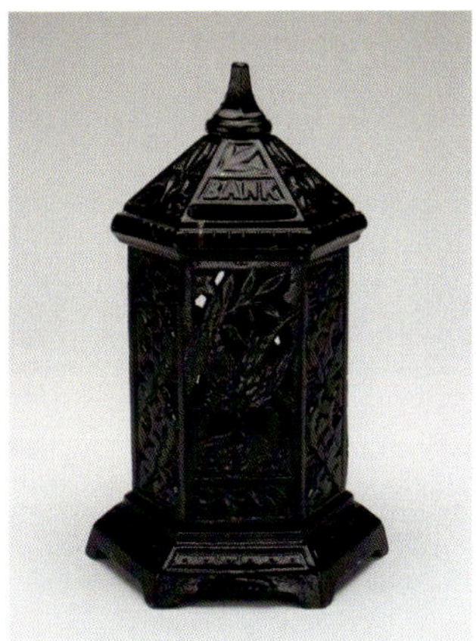
BANK

Space Heater, Flowers, c. 1890
England
Iron, pigment
6 1/2 x 3 7/8 x 3 7/8 in.
2003.236.966

Security Safe Deposit, c. 1890
Iron, wood, pigment
6 x 5 1/8 x 4 13/16 in.
2003.236.765

Security Safe Deposit, c. 1890
Iron, wood, pigment
8 3/16 x 7 1/8 x 6 5/8 in.
2003.236.764

Security Safe Deposit, c. 1890
Iron, pigment
5 7/16 x 4 3/8 x 4 5/8 in.
2003.236.763

1876 Bank, c. 1890s
A. C. Williams Company,
Ravenna, Ohio (est. 1886),
manufacturer
Iron
2 3/4 x 2 1/8 x 1 3/4 in.
2003.236.149

Deposit, c. 1890s
Grey Iron Casting Company,
Mount Joy, Pennsylvania
(1881 – 1969), manufacturer
Iron, pigment
4 1/2 x 3 x 2 3/8 in.
2003.236.240

Church Window, c. 1890s
Shimer Toy Company,
Bethlehem, Pennsylvania
(c. 1899 – 1915), manufacturer
Iron, pigment
3 x 2 3/16 x 2 1/4 in.
2003.236.932

Fidelity Trust Vault with Little Lord Fauntleroy, 1890
J. Barton Smith Company,
Philadelphia, manufacturer
Iron, pigment
5 x 4 1/2 x 4 in.
2003.236.302

Streetcar, 1891
Columbia Grey Iron Company, Columbia, Pennsylvania, manufacturer
Iron, pigment
2 7/8 x 4 1/2 x 1 1/8 in.
2003.236.971

Safe, c. 1891
J. & E. Stevens Company,
Cromwell, Connecticut
(1843 – 1950s), manufacturer
Iron
3 1/8 x 2 1/2 x 2 1/4 in.
2003.236.828

Watchdog, c. 1890s
J. & E. Stevens Company,
Cromwell, Connecticut
(1843 – 1950s), manufacturer
Iron, pigment
5 13/16 x 4 7/16 x 4 in.
2003.236.815

Space Heater, Bird, c. 1892
Chamberlin & Hill, Ltd., Walsall,
England, manufacturer
Iron, pigment
6 1/2 x 4 1/16 x 4 1/16 in.
2003.236.967

County Bank, c. 1892
John Harper & Company, Ltd., Willenhall, England (1790 – 1980s),
manufacturer
Iron, pigment
4 3/16 x 5 1/8 x 2 5/8 in.
2003.236.127

Tower Bank (safe), 1890 – 98
Kyser & Rex Company,
Philadelphia (c. 1879 – 98),
manufacturer
Iron, pigment
6 7/8 x 5 7/8 x 2 1/2 in.
2003.236.681

White City Trick Bank (or *Puzzle Bank*), c. 1894
Nicol and Company, Chicago (est. 1893), manufacturer
Iron, pigment
3 3/4 x 2 7/8 x 2 7/8 in.
2003.236.963

White City Pail, 1893
Nicol and Company, Chicago (est. 1893), manufacturer
Iron, pigment
2 5/8 x 2 5/8 x 2 5/8 in.
2003.236.982

Columbia, 1893
Kenton Hardware Manufacturing Company, Kenton, Ohio (1890 – 1950), manufacturer
Iron, pigment
7 1/4 x 5 1/2 x 5 1/2 in.
2003.236.680

White City Puzzle Safe, No. 326, c. 1893
Nicol and Company, Chicago (est. 1893), manufacturer
Iron
4 3/16 x 2 3/4 x 2 3/4 in.
2003.236.464

Four Tower, c. 1895
Kenton Hardware Manufacturing Company, Kenton, Ohio (1890 – 1950), manufacturer
Iron, pigment
5 1/2 x 4 1/4 x 3 5/16 in.
2003.236.156

White City Barrel, No. 1, on Cart, 1894
Nicol and Company, Chicago (est. 1893), manufacturer
Iron, pigment
5 x 3 7/8 x 3 1/4 in.
2003.236.996

1876 Bank, c. 1895
H. L. Judd Manufacturing Company, Wallingford, Connecticut (c. 1830 – 1960s), manufacturer
Iron, pigment
3 1/4 x 2 5/8 x 2 3/8 in.
2003.236.151

Columbia Bank, c. 1897
Columbia Grey Iron Company, Columbia, Pennsylvania manufacturer
Iron, pigment
3 1/2 x 2 5/8 x 2 3/8 in.
2003.236.461

Roof Bank, 1896
J. & E. Stevens Company, Cromwell, Connecticut (1843 – 1950s), manufacturer
Iron, pigment
5 1/8 x 3 3/4 x 3 3/16 in.
2003.236.154

Crown Bank, 1896
J. & E. Stevens Company, Cromwell, Connecticut (1843 – 1950s), manufacturer
Iron, pigment
2 7/8 x 2 1/2 x 2 3/16 in.
2003.236.777

Safe, c. 1896
Kyser & Rex Company, Philadelphia (c. 1879 – 98), manufacturer
Iron, pigment
3 5/16 x 2 1/2 x 2 3/16 in.
2003.236.769

Key Lock Safe, No. 50, c. 1897
J. & E. Stevens Company, Cromwell, Connecticut (1843 – 1950s), manufacturer
Iron
4 1/8 x 3 1/16 x 2 5/8 in.
2003.236.394

Maine, Small, c. 1897 – 1903
Grey Iron Casting Company, Mount Joy, Pennsylvania (1881 – 1969), manufacturer
Iron, pigment
5 x 1 1/2 x 4 5/8 in.
2003.236.311

Pig with Bow, 1899
Shimer Toy Company, Bethlehem, Pennsylvania (c. 1899 – 1915), manufacturer
Iron, pigment
2 15/16 x 5 1/4 x 2 3/8 in.
2003.236.283

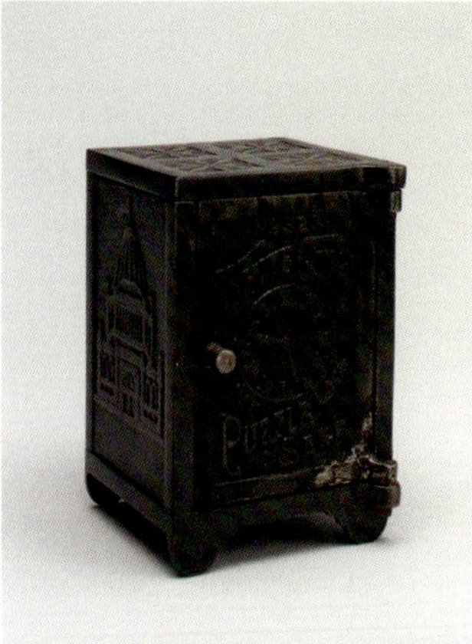
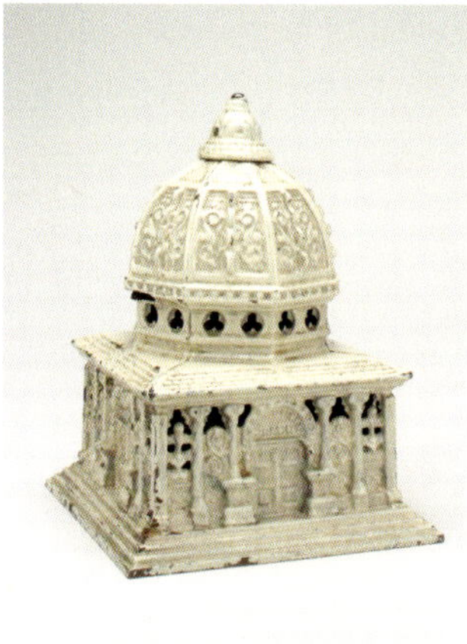
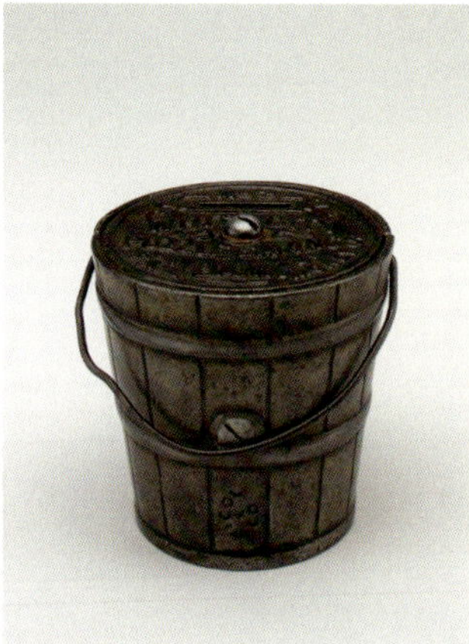
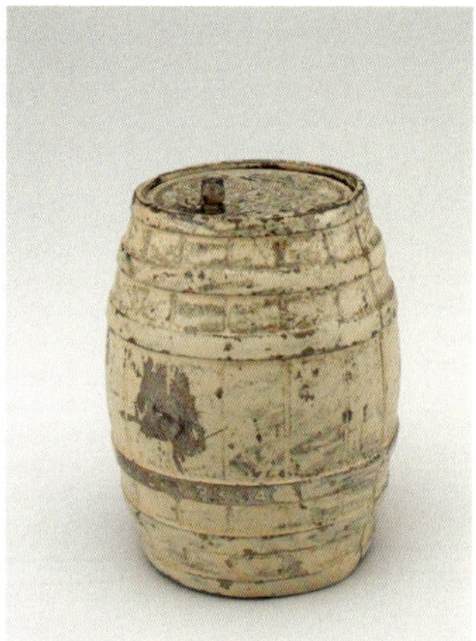
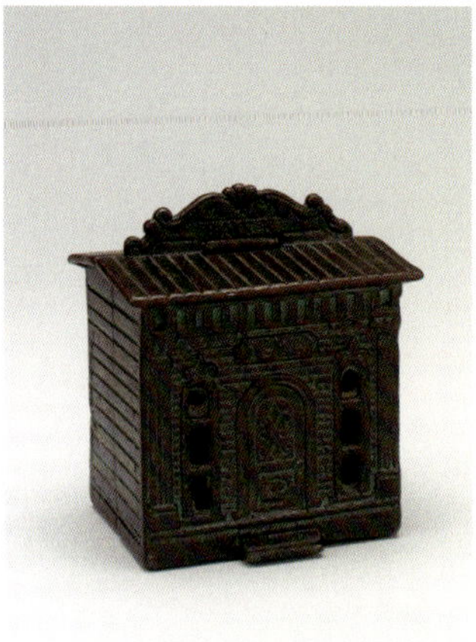
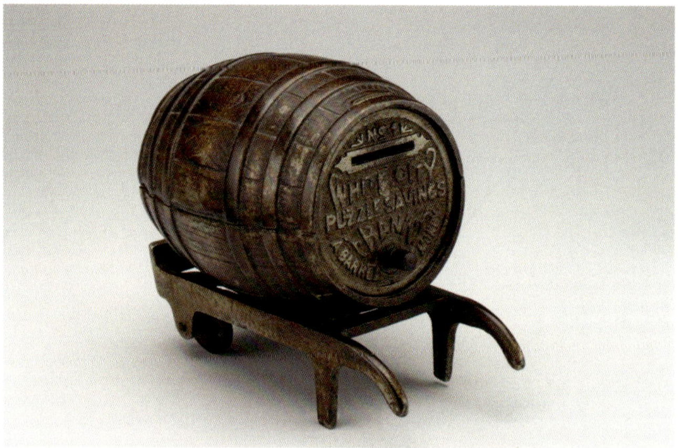
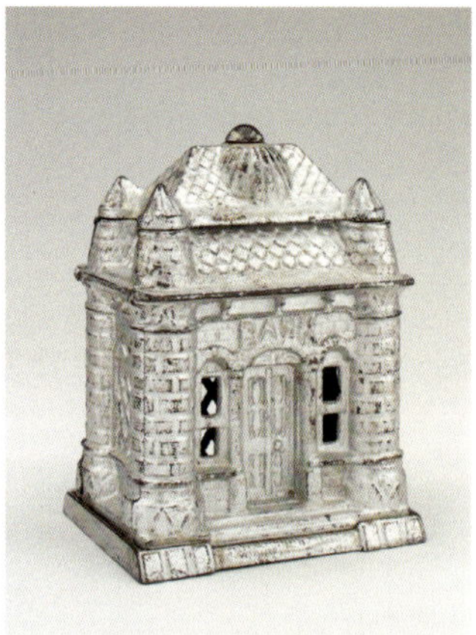
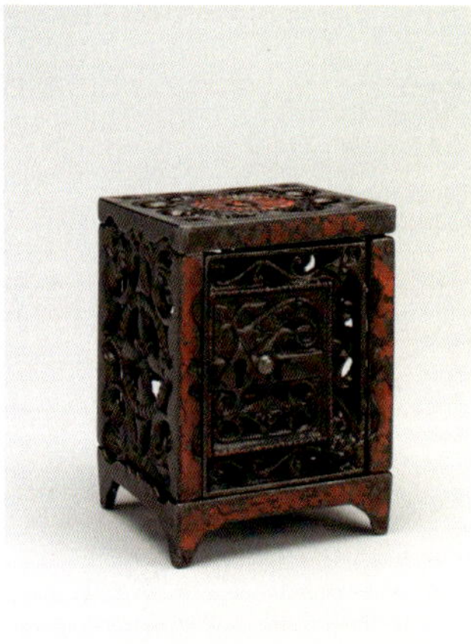
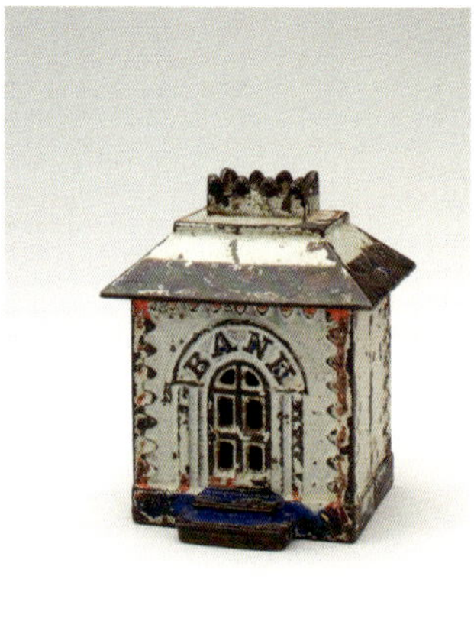
BANK
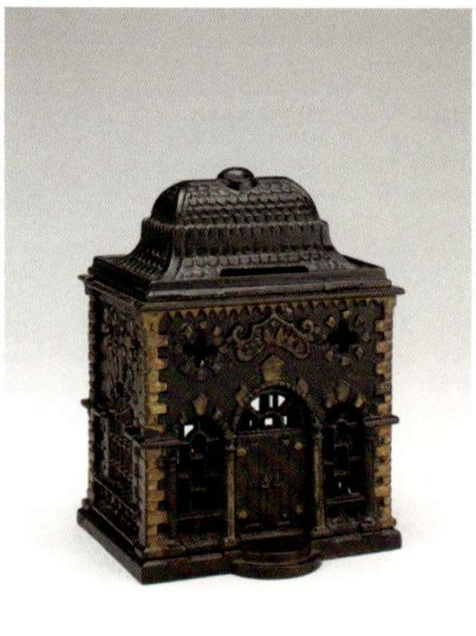
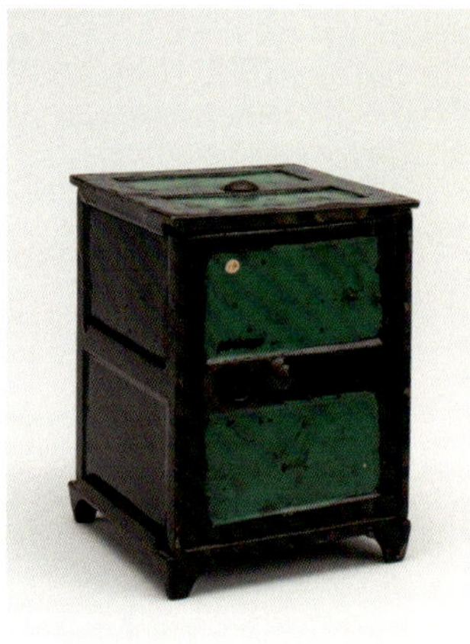
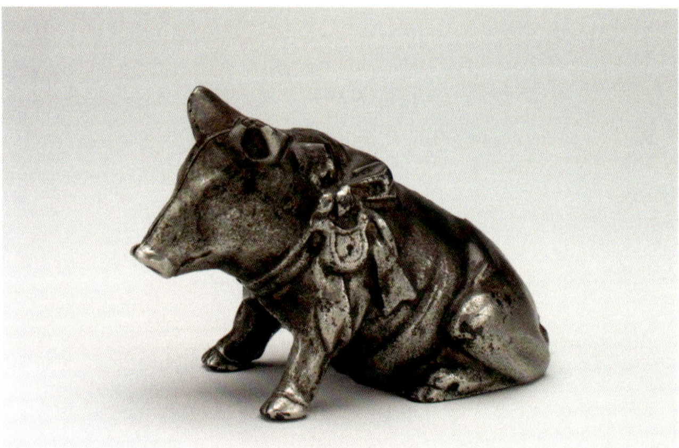
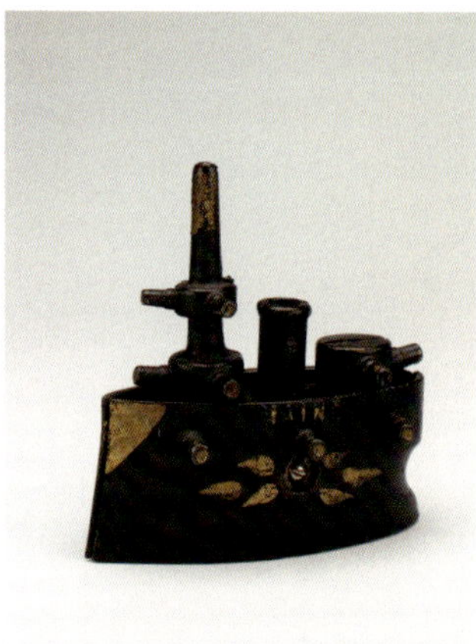
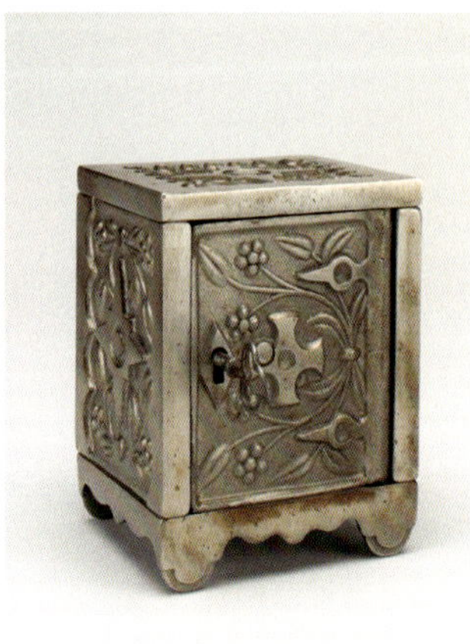

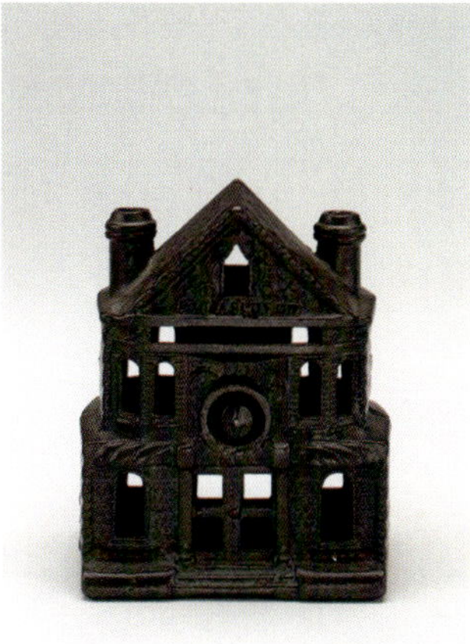

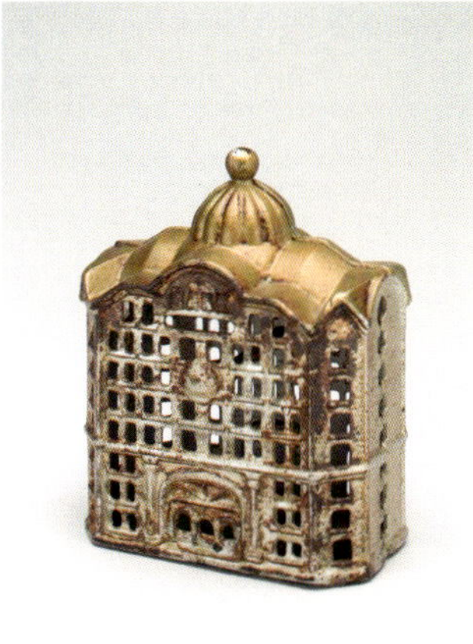

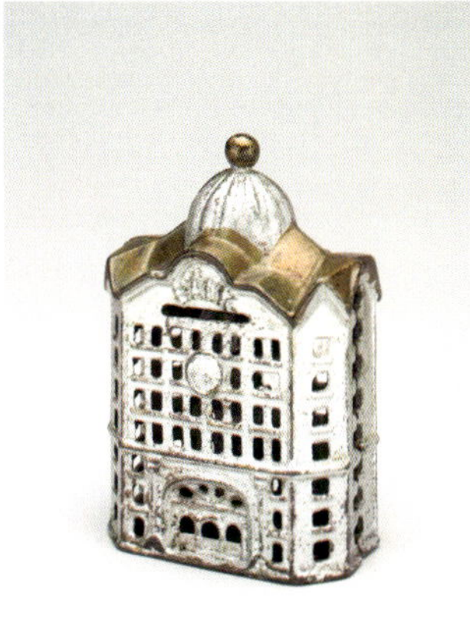

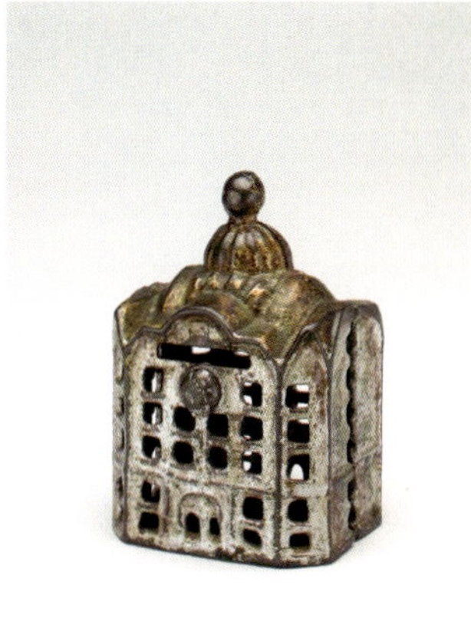

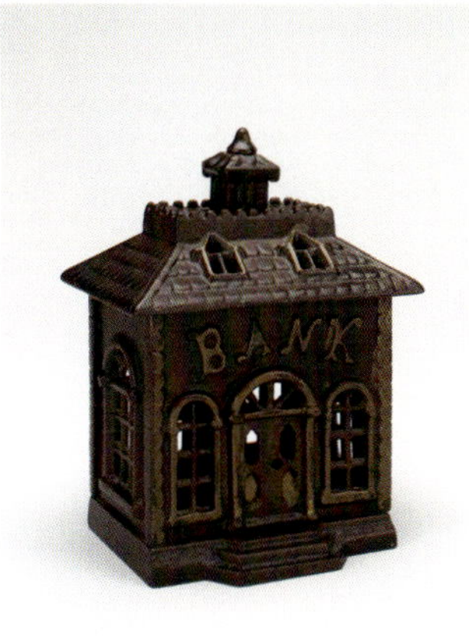
BANK

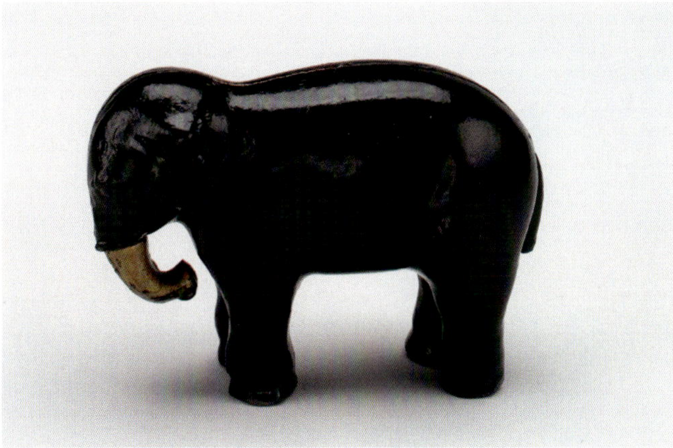

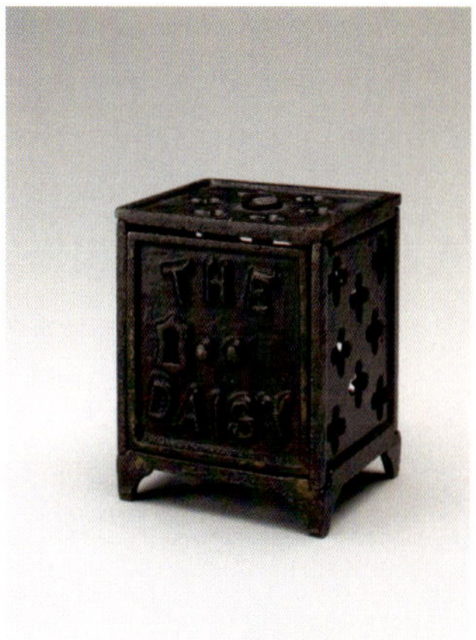

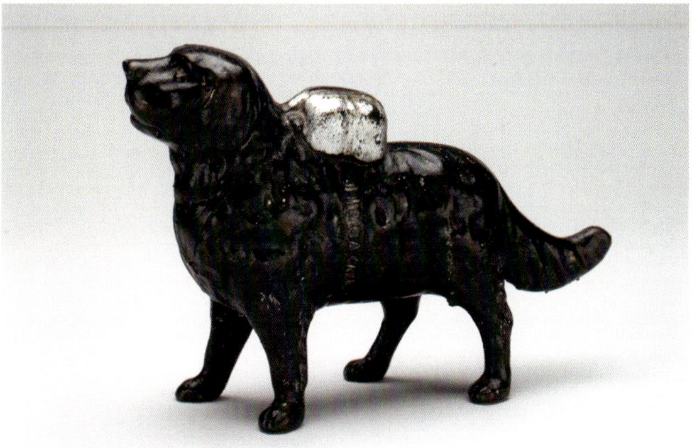

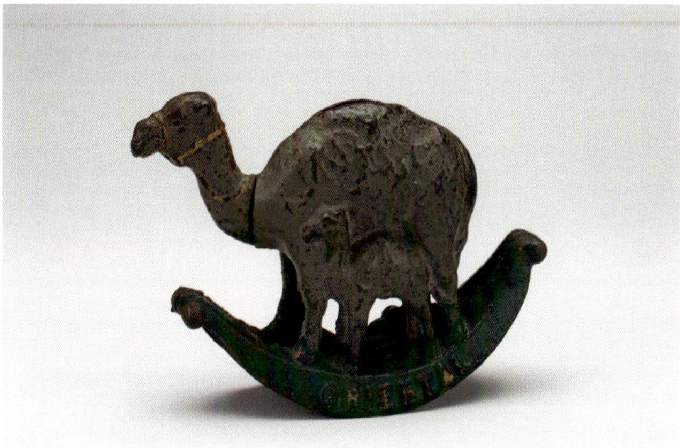

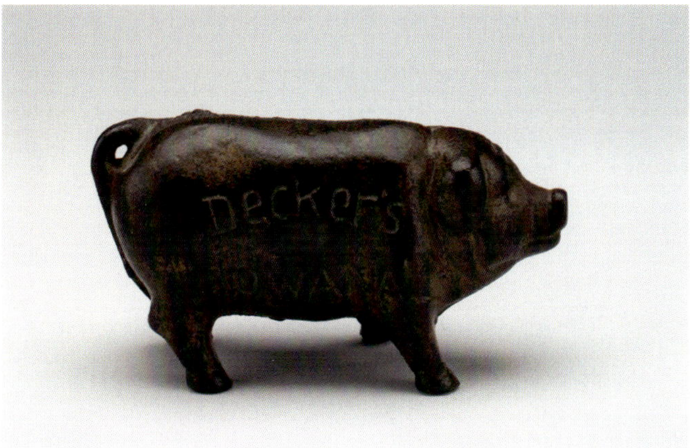
Decker's

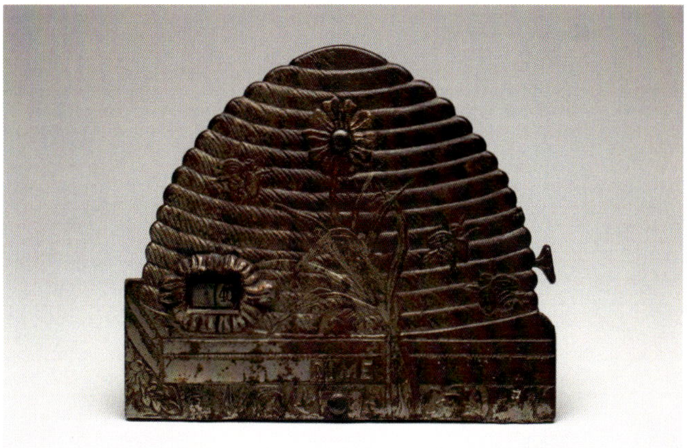

Domed Bank, Small,
c. 1899 – 1934
A. C. Williams Company,
Ravenna, Ohio (est. 1886),
manufacturer
Iron, pigment
3 1/8 x 2 1/8 x 2 in.
2003.236.233

Domed Bank, c. 1899 – 1934
A. C. Williams Company,
Ravenna, Ohio (est. 1886),
manufacturer
4 3/4 x 3 1/4 x 2 in.
Iron, pigment
2003.236.935

Domed Bank, c. 1899 – 1934
A. C. Williams Company,
Ravenna, Ohio (est. 1886),
manufacturer
4 3/4 x 4 7/8 x 2 3/8 in.
Iron, pigment
2003.236.934

Victorian House, c. 1898
J. & E. Stevens Company,
Cromwell, Connecticut
(1843 – 1950s), manufacturer
Iron, pigment
3 5/16 x 2 3/4 x 1 7/8 in.
2003.236.150

The Daisy, c. 1900
Shimer Toy Company,
Bethlehem, Pennsylvania
(c. 1899 – 1915), manufacturer
Iron
2 3/16 x 1 3/4 x 1 1/2 in.
2003.236.658

Elephant, late 19th – early 20th century
Ives Blakeslee Company, Bridgeport, Connecticut (1868 – 1930),
manufacturer
Iron, pigment
2 1/2 x 1 1/16 x 3 5/16 in.
2003.236.1004

Bank, late 19th – early 20th
century
Iron, pigment
6 x 4 5/16 x 3 3/16 in.
2003.236.227

Oriental, c. 1900
Iron, pigment
4 1/8 x 5 3/8 x 1 13/16 in.
2003.236.292

I Hear a Call (or *Water Spaniel with Pack*), c. 1900
United States
Iron, pigment
5 1/4 x 8 1/2 x 1 3/4 in.
2003.236.43

H & H Registering Beehive Savings Bank, early 20th century
Possibly England
Iron, pigment, glass
5 15/16 x 6 7/16 x 2 in.
2003.236.598

Decker's Iowana, early 20th century
United States
Iron
2 3/8 x 4 1/2 x 1 3/4 in.
2003.236.276

Round Grenade, early 20th century
England
Iron
$3 \times 3 \times 3$ in.
2003.236.141

Pickaninny Money Bank, early 20th century
England
Iron, pigment
$5\frac{1}{2} \times 4\frac{3}{8} \times 3\frac{1}{8}$ in.
2003.236.839

Moon and Stars, early 20th century
Iron, pigment
$4 \times 2\frac{11}{16} \times 2\frac{13}{16}$ in.
2003.236.463

Santa with Tree, c. 1900
Wing Manufacturing and Plating Company, Chicago (1894 – 1904), manufacturer
Iron, pigment
$6 \times 2\frac{5}{16} \times 2$ in.
2003.236.619

Young Negro, early 20th century
Iron, pigment
$4\frac{5}{8} \times 3\frac{5}{8} \times 3\frac{1}{4}$ in.
2003.236.842

Save Your Pennies, early 20th century
Kenton Hardware Manufacturing Company, Kenton, Ohio (1890 – 1950), manufacturer
Iron
$3\frac{9}{16} \times 2\frac{11}{16} \times 2\frac{5}{16}$ in.
2003.236.462

Save and Smile Money Box, early 20th century
Sydenham & McOustra, Walsall, England, manufacturer
Iron, pigment
$4\frac{1}{4} \times 4\frac{3}{16} \times 3$ in.
2003.236.841

Santa Save and Smile, Hanging, early 20th century
England
Iron, pigment
$7\frac{1}{4} \times 1\frac{3}{8} \times 2$ in.
2003.236.122

Darkey (or *Sharecropper*), 1901
A. C. Williams Company, Ravenna, Ohio (est. 1886), manufacturer
Iron, pigment
$5\frac{1}{2} \times 2\frac{7}{8} \times 1\frac{13}{16}$ in.
2003.236.629

Captain Kidd, 1901
United States
Iron, pigment
$5\frac{3}{16} \times 4\frac{1}{8} \times 2\frac{1}{4}$ in.
2003.236.634

Skyscraper, Six Posts, c. 1900 – 1909
A. C. Williams Company, Ravenna, Ohio (est. 1886), manufacturer
Iron, pigment
$6\frac{1}{2} \times 4 \times 3$
2003.236.684

Globe on Arc, c. 1900 – 1903
Grey Iron Casting Company, Mount Joy, Pennsylvania (1881 – 1969), manufacturer
Iron, pigment
$5\frac{1}{8} \times 3\frac{1}{4} \times 2\frac{1}{2}$ in.
2003.236.370

Two-Faced Black Boy (or *Negro Toy Bank*), c. 1901 – 19
A. C. Williams Company, Ravenna, Ohio (est. 1886), manufacturer
Iron, pigment
$4 \times 3\frac{1}{2} \times 3\frac{1}{16}$ in.
2003.236.850

Two-Faced Black Boy (or *Negro Toy Bank*), c. 1901 – 19
A. C. Williams Company, Ravenna, Ohio (est. 1886), manufacturer
Iron, pigment
$3 \times 2\frac{3}{4} \times 2\frac{5}{8}$ in.
2003.236.849

Skyscraper, c. 1901 – 06
A. C. Williams Company, Ravenna, Ohio (est. 1886), manufacturer
$5\frac{5}{8} \times 2\frac{5}{8} \times 2\frac{5}{8}$ in.
Iron, pigment
2003.236.936

Mary and Little Lamb, 1901
United States
Iron, pigment
$4\frac{1}{4} \times 4\frac{1}{2} \times 2\frac{1}{16}$ in.
2003.236.637

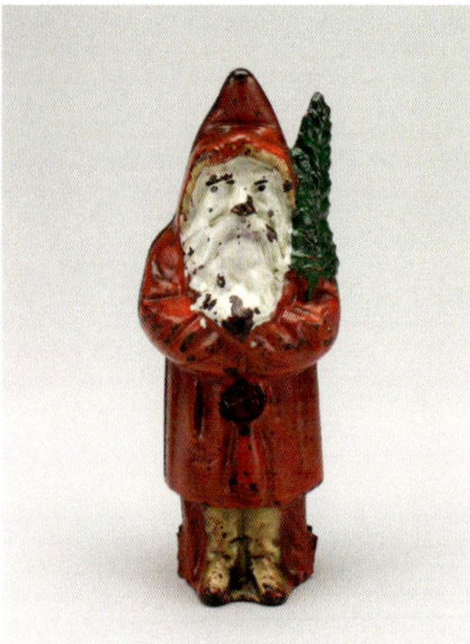
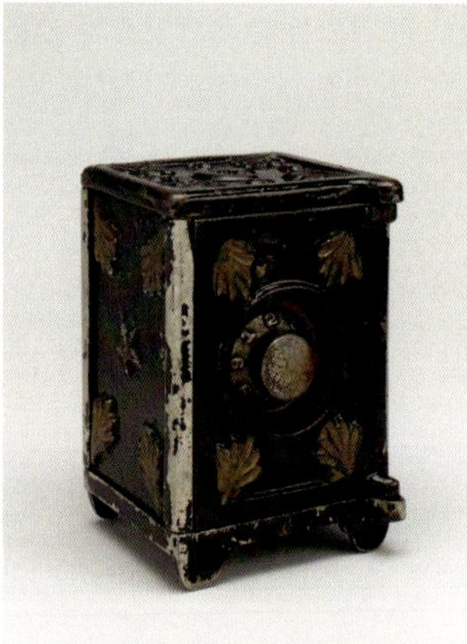
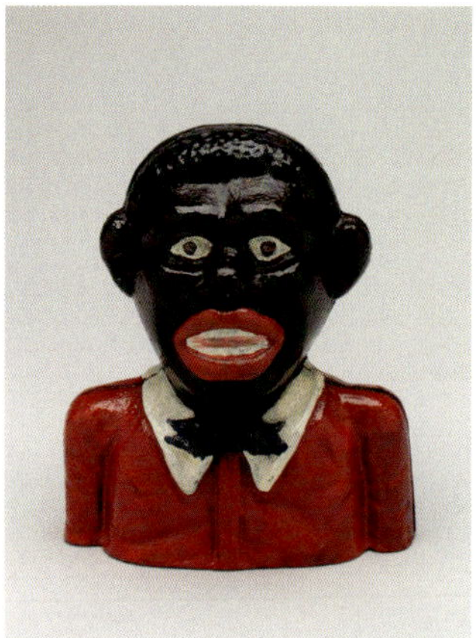
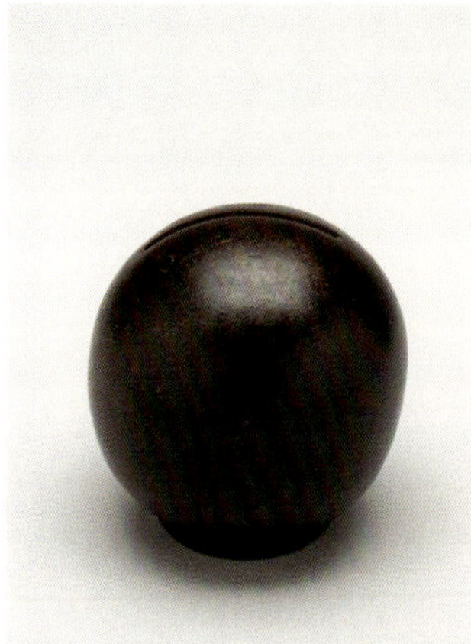
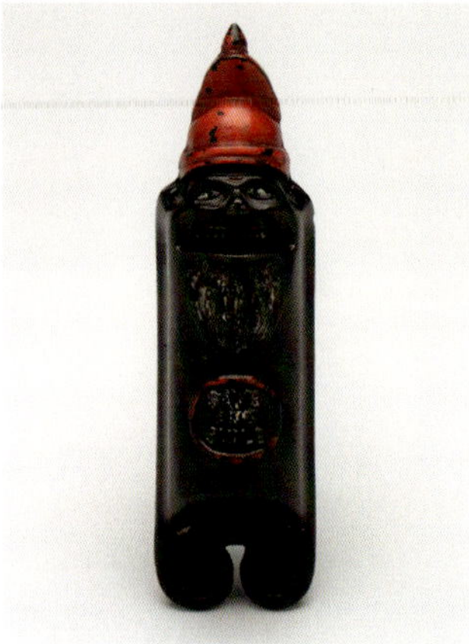
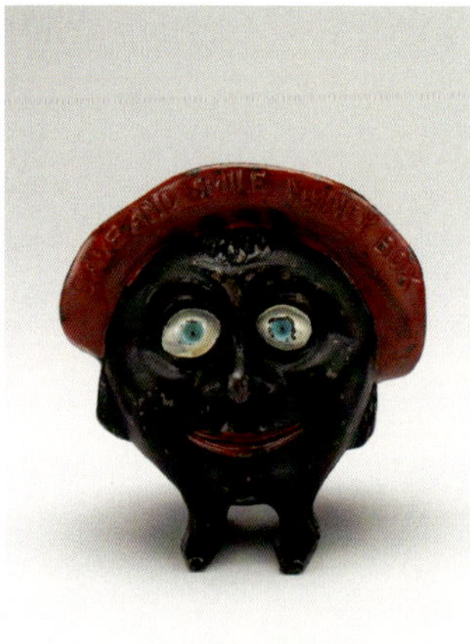
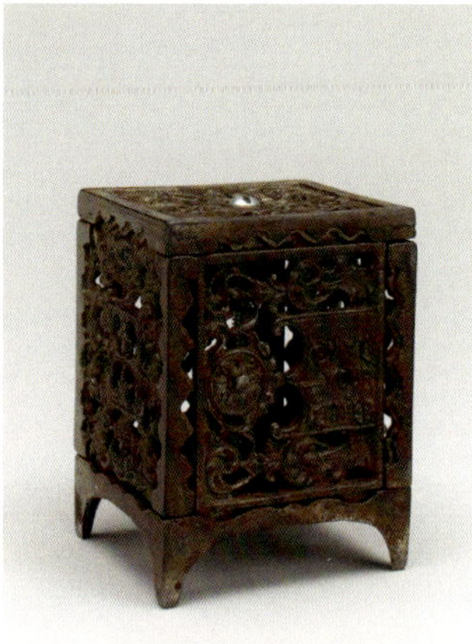
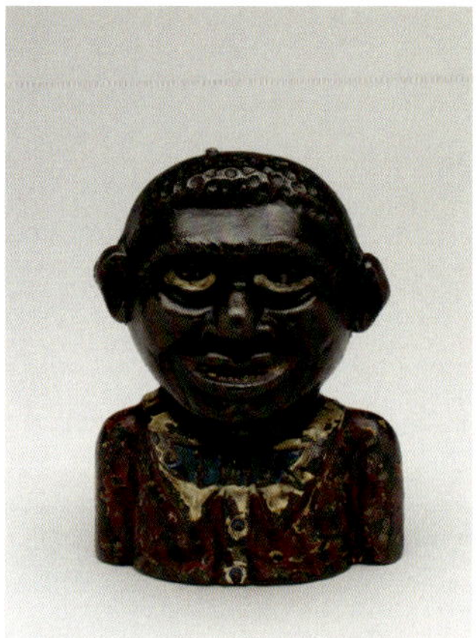
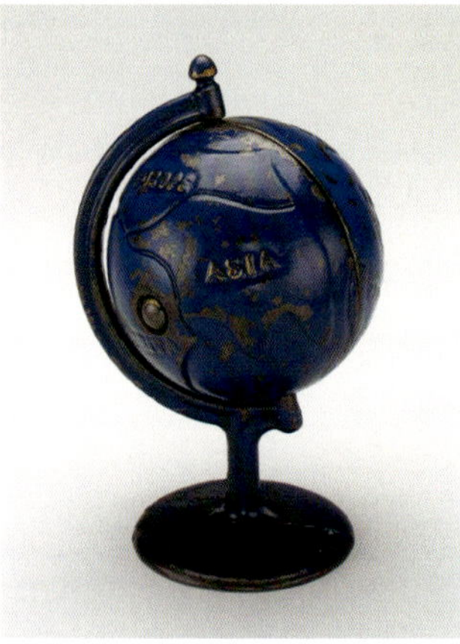
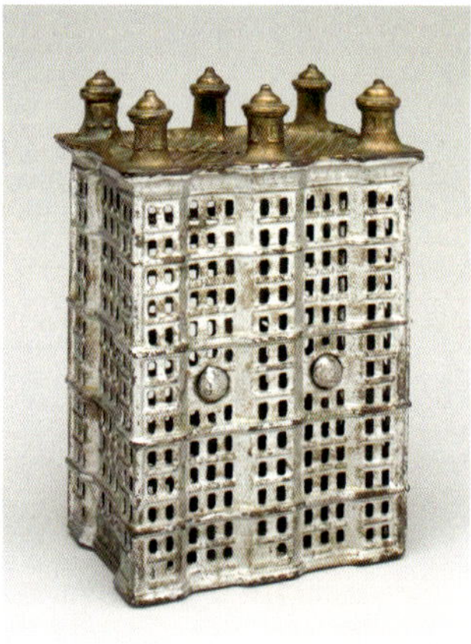
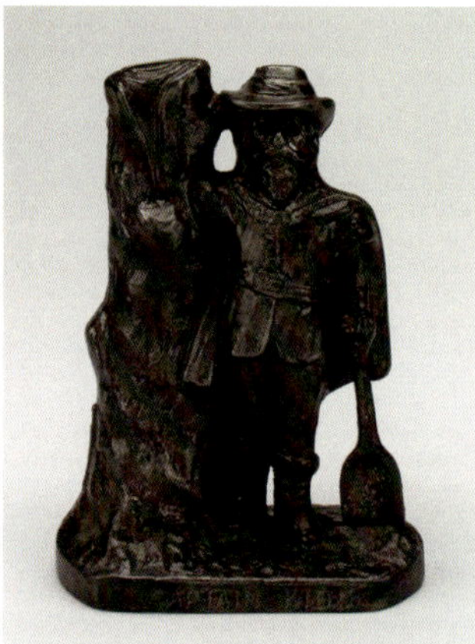
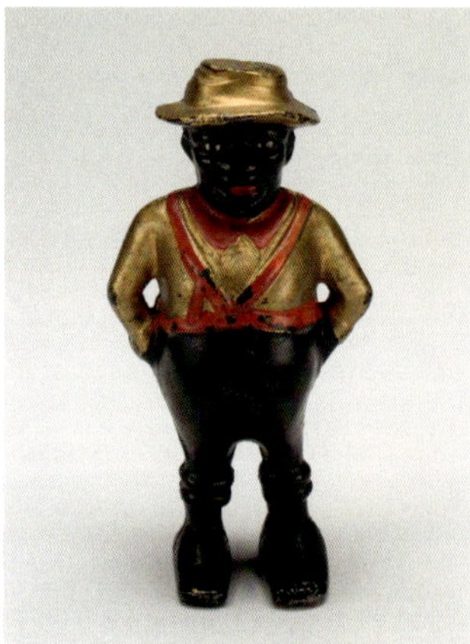
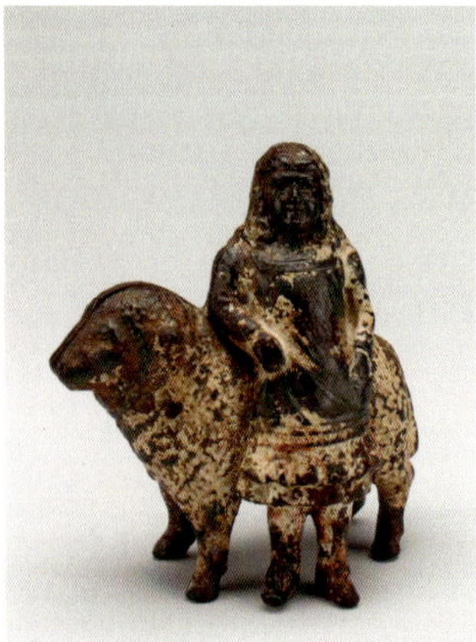
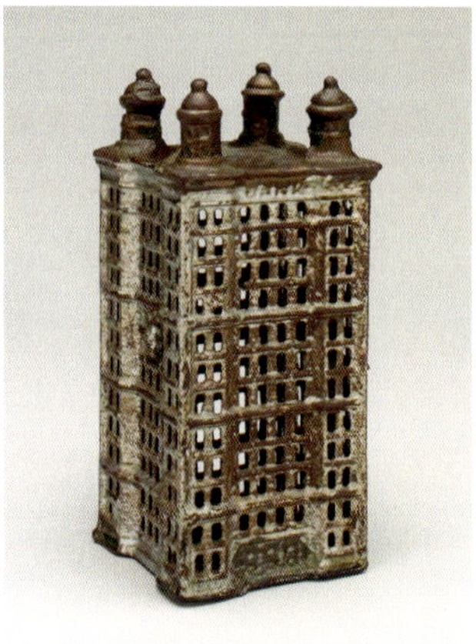
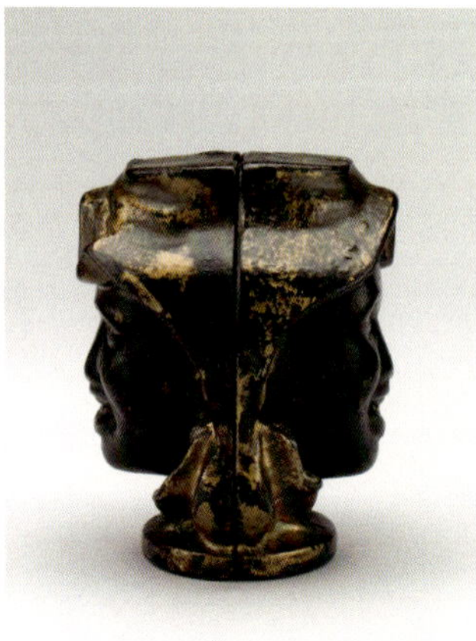
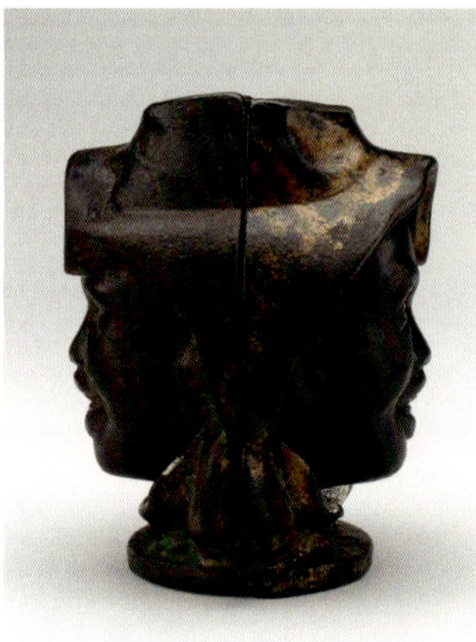

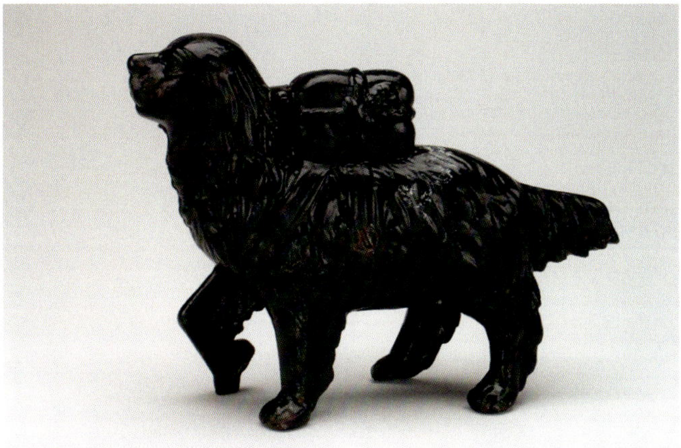
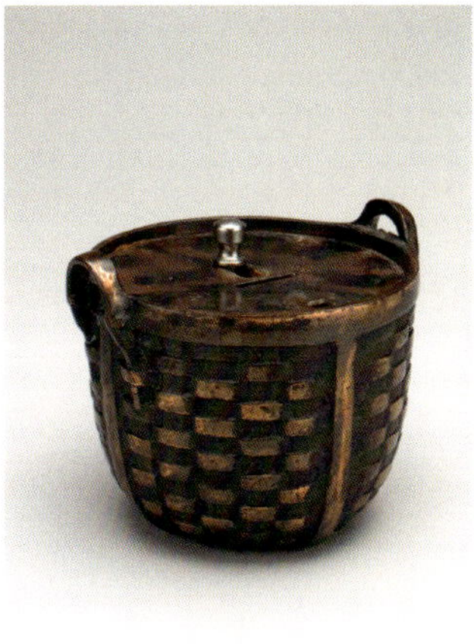
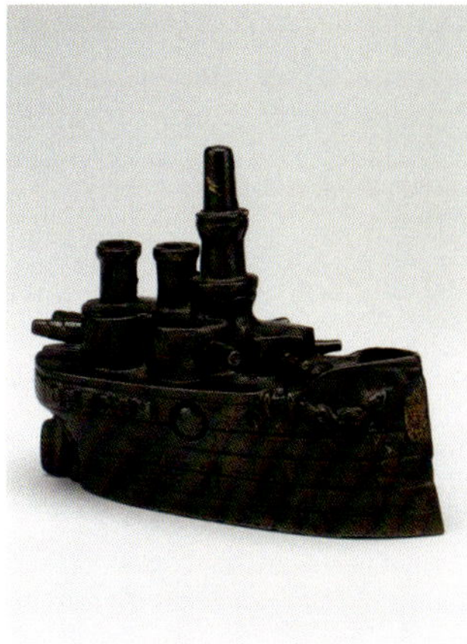
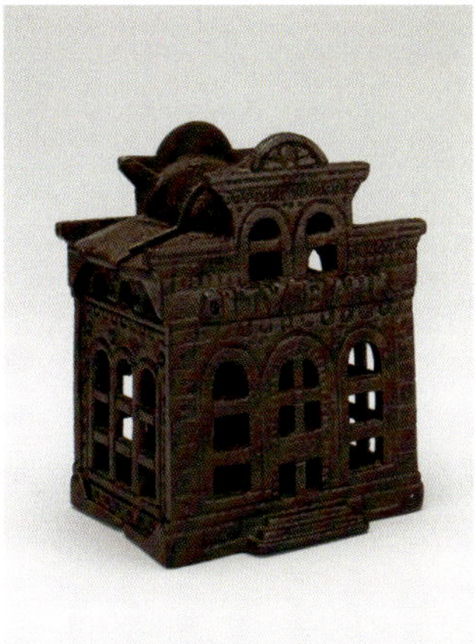
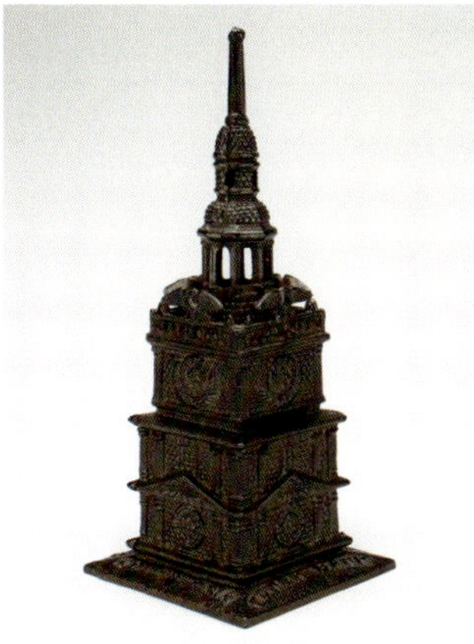
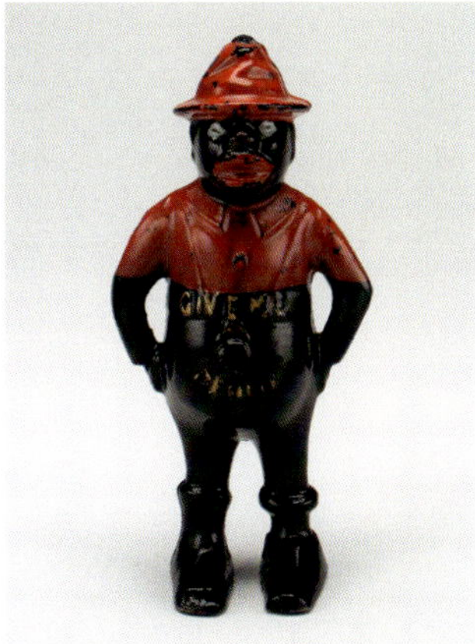
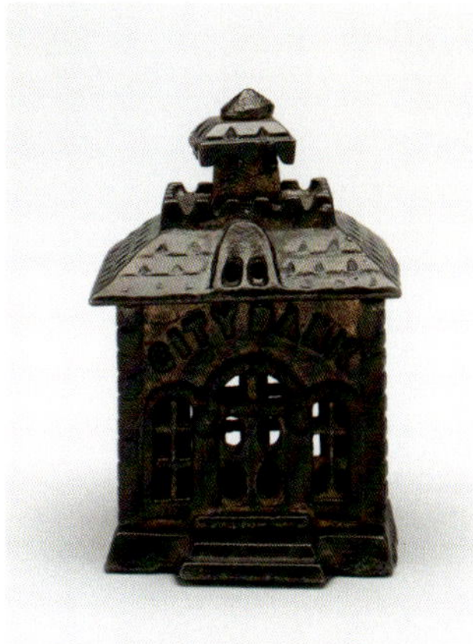
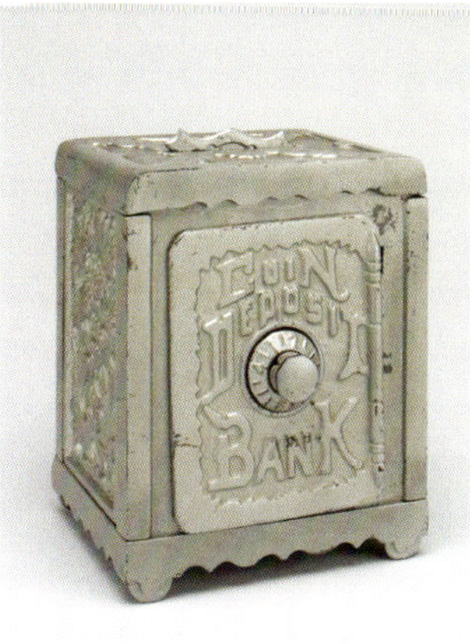
COIN
DEPOSIT
BANK
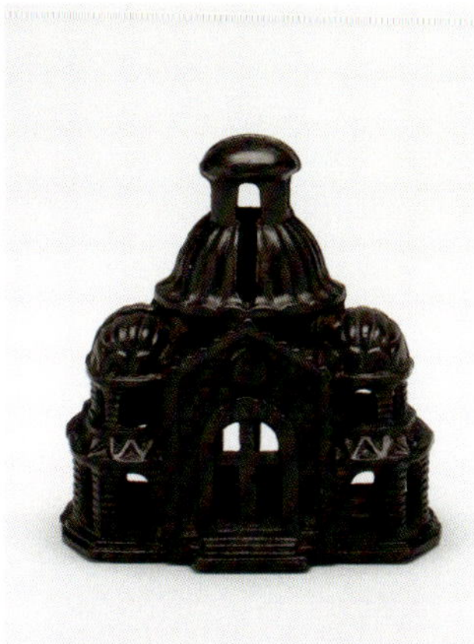
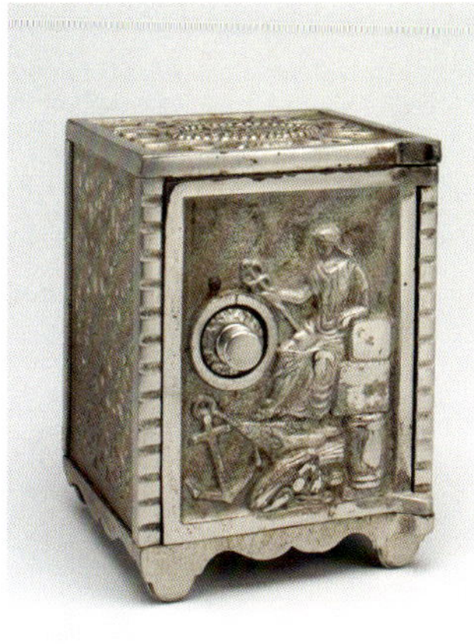
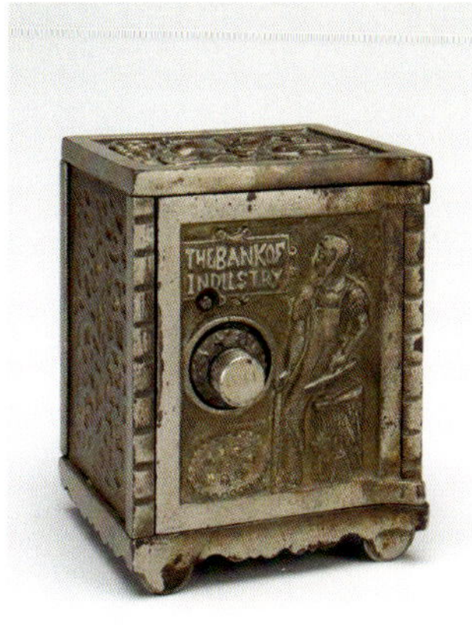
THE BANK OF
INDUSTRY
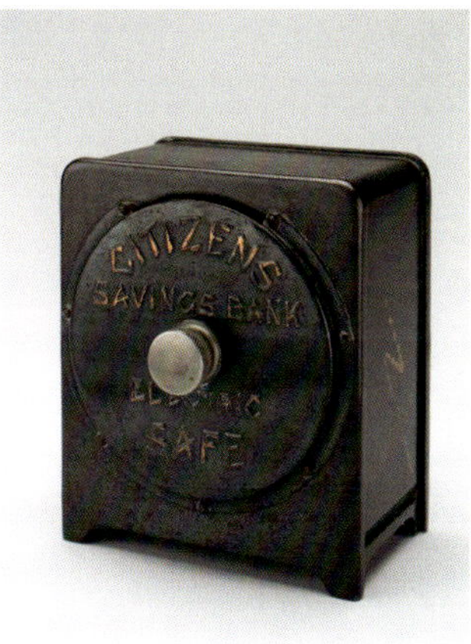
CITIZENS
SAVINGS BANK
ELECTRIC
SAFE
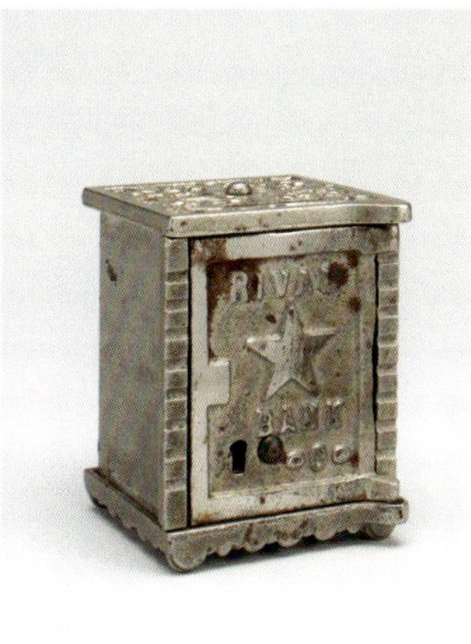
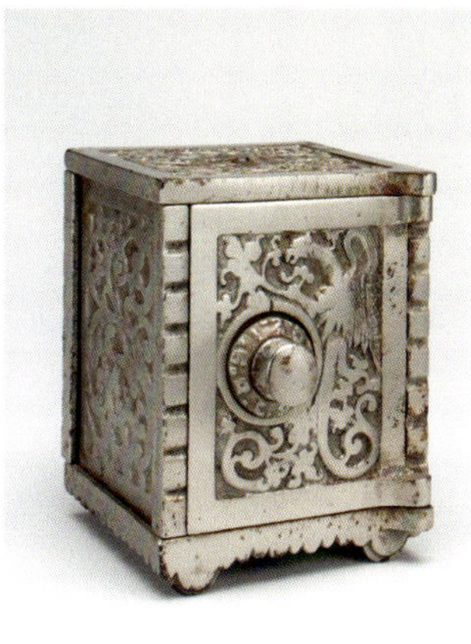
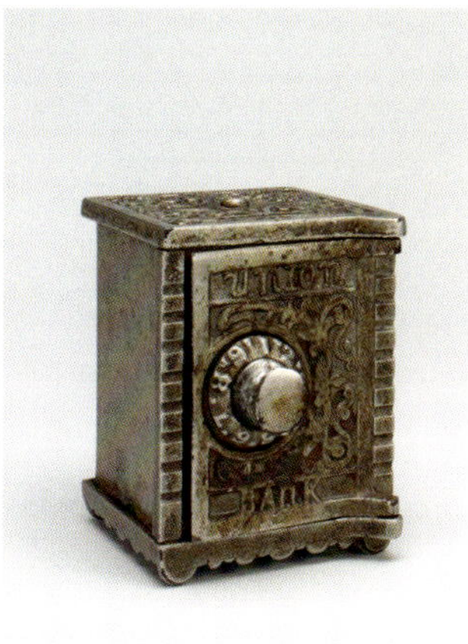

Battleship Maine, c. 1902
J. & E. Stevens Company, Cromwell, Connecticut (1843 – 1950s), manufacturer
Iron, pigment
$4 \times 4\frac{15}{16} \times 1\frac{3}{4}$ in.
2003.236.289

Basket Bank, Woven, c. 1902
Charles A. Braun, American, designer
Iron, pigment
$2\frac{3}{4} \times 3\frac{1}{2} \times 3\frac{1}{8}$ in.
2003.236.663

St. Bernard with Pack, Large, c. 1901 – mid-1930s
A. C. Williams Company, Ravenna, Ohio (est. 1886), manufacturer
Iron, pigment
$5\frac{9}{16} \times 8\frac{1}{4} \times 1\frac{5}{8}$ in.
2003.236.159

City Bank, c. 1903
Grey Iron Casting Company, Mount Joy, Pennsylvania (1881 – 1969), manufacturer
Iron, pigment
$3\frac{5}{16} \times 2\frac{1}{8} \times 1\frac{15}{16}$ in.
2003.236.126

Give Me a Penny, c. 1902 – 26
Hubley Manufacturing Company, Lancaster, Pennsylvania (est. 1894), manufacturer
Iron, pigment
$5\frac{3}{4} \times 2\frac{13}{16} \times 1\frac{5}{8}$ in.
2003.236.628

Tower Bank, c. 1902 – 11
John Harper & Company, Ltd., Willenhall, England (1790 – 1980s), manufacturer
Iron, pigment
$9\frac{1}{4} \times 4\frac{3}{4} \times 4\frac{3}{4}$ in.
2003.236.678

City Bank with Director's Room on Top, c. 1902
John Harper & Company, Ltd., Willenhall, England (1790 – 1980s), manufacturer
Iron
$4 \times 3\frac{7}{16} \times 2\frac{1}{8}$ in.
2003.236.243

Bank of Industry, c. 1904
Kenton Hardware Manufacturing Company, Kenton, Ohio (1890 – 1950), manufacturer
Iron
$5\frac{3}{8} \times 4\frac{1}{4} \times 3\frac{15}{16}$ in.
2003.236.465

Bank of Commerce, c. 1904
Kenton Hardware Manufacturing Company, Kenton, Ohio (1890 – 1950), manufacturer
Iron
$6\frac{7}{16} \times 5 \times 4\frac{3}{4}$ in.
2003.236.467

Domed Mosque, c. 1903 – 28
Grey Iron Casting Company, Mount Joy, Pennsylvania (1881 – 1969), manufacturer
Iron, pigment
$3\frac{1}{8} \times 3\frac{1}{8} \times 1\frac{15}{16}$ in.
2003.236.125

Coin Deposit Bank, c. 1903
Grey Iron Casting Company, Mount Joy, Pennsylvania (1881 – 1969), manufacturer
Iron, pigment
$6\frac{11}{16} \times 5\frac{7}{16} \times 4\frac{1}{2}$ in.
2003.236.767

Union Bank, c. 1904
Kenton Hardware Manufacturing Company Kenton, Ohio (1890 – 1950), manufacturer
Iron, nickel plate
$3\frac{1}{4} \times 2\frac{1}{2} \times 3\frac{1}{4}$ in.
2003.236.770

Saving Bank, c. 1904
Kenton Hardware Manufacturing Company, Kenton, Ohio (1890 – 1950), manufacturer
Iron
$4\frac{1}{4} \times 3\frac{5}{16} \times 3\frac{1}{4}$ in.
2003.236.417

Rival Bank, c. 1904
Kenton Hardware Manufacturing Company, Kenton, Ohio (1890 – 1950), manufacturer Iron
$3\frac{1}{4} \times 2\frac{1}{2} \times 2\frac{1}{2}$ in.
2003.236.369

Electric Safe, c. 1904
St. Louis Manufacturing Company, manufacturer
Iron, pigment
$4\frac{1}{16} \times 3\frac{7}{16} \times 2\frac{5}{8}$ in.
2003.236.844

Soldier (or *Minuteman*),
c. 1905 – 06
Hubley Manufacturing Company, Lancaster, Pennsylvania (est. 1894), manufacturer
Iron, pigment
6 3/16 x 1 3/4 x 2 9/16 in.
2003.236.632

Star Safe, c. 1905
Iron, pigment
3 1/2 x 2 1/2 x 2 7/8 in.
2003.236.821

Flatiron Building Bank, Medium, c. 1904 – 26
Kenton Hardware Manufacturing Company, Kenton, Ohio (1890 – 1950), manufacturer
Iron, pigment
5 3/4 x 4 1/2 x 3 11/16 in.
2003.236.146

Flatiron Building Bank, Large, c. 1904 – 13
Kenton Hardware Manufacturing Company, Kenton, Ohio (1890 – 1950), manufacturer
Iron, pigment
9 1/16 x 6 1/8 x 4 3/4 in.
2003.236.147

Cat Playing with Ball, c. 1905 – 19
A. C. Williams Company, Ravenna, Ohio (est. 1886), manufacturer
Iron, pigment
2 1/2 x 5 5/8 x 1 5/8 in.
2003.236.281

Turkey, Large, c. 1905 – 12
A. C. Williams Company, Ravenna, Ohio (est. 1886), manufacturer
Iron, pigment
4 1/2 x 3 5/16 x 3 13/16 in.
2003.236.952

Lion, Tail Right, c. 1905 – 31
A. C. Williams Company, Ravenna, Ohio (est. 1886), manufacturer
Iron, pigment
5 1/8 x 6 1/2 x 2 in.
2003.236.169

Teddy Bear, c. 1905 – 25
Arcade Manufacturing Company, Freeport, Illinois (1868 – 1946), manufacturer
Iron, pigment
2 3/4 x 3 7/8 x 1 1/2 in.
2003.236.959

Double Door, c. 1905 – 20
A. C. Williams Company, Ravenna, Ohio (est. 1886), manufacturer
Iron, pigment
5 5/16 x 4 7/8 x 3 in.
2003.236.155

Turkey, Small, c. 1905 – 35
A. C. Williams Company, Ravenna, Ohio (est. 1886), manufacturer
Iron, pigment
3 7/16 x 2 5/8 x 3 5/16 in.
2003.236.985

Presto, c. 1905 – 34
A. C. Williams Company, Ravenna, Ohio (est. 1886), manufacturer
Iron, pigment
3 1/4 x 2 3/4 x 1 3/4 in.
2003.236.124

Presto, c. 1905 – 34
A. C. Williams Company, Ravenna, Ohio (est. 1886), manufacturer
Iron, pigment
3 1/4 x 2 5/16 x 1 3/4 in.
2003.236.123

Mulligan (or *Policeman*),
c. 1905 – 32
A. C. Williams Company, Ravenna, Ohio (est. 1886), manufacturer
Iron, pigment
5 15/16 x 2 7/8 x 2 1/8 in.
2003.236.620

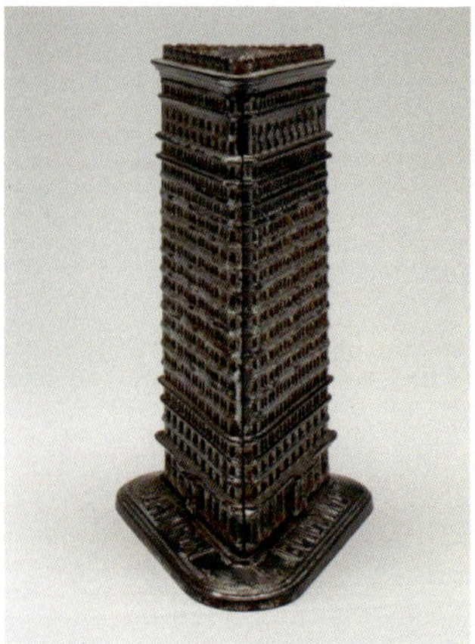
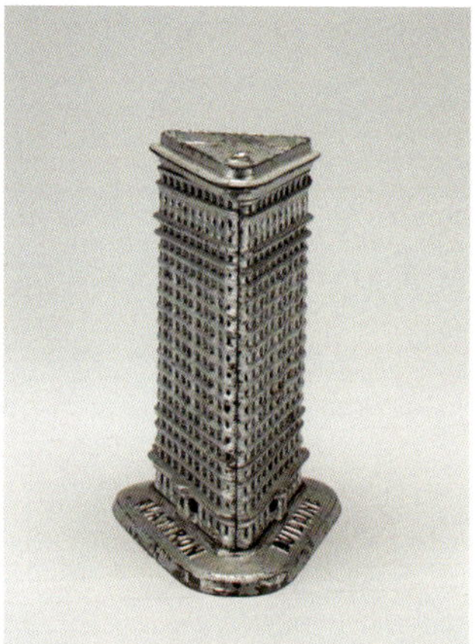
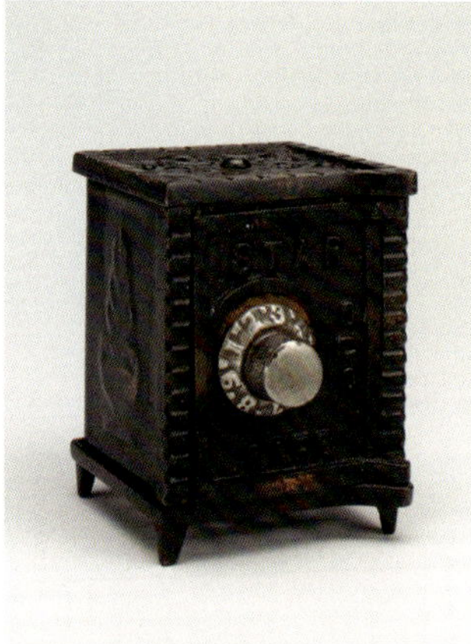
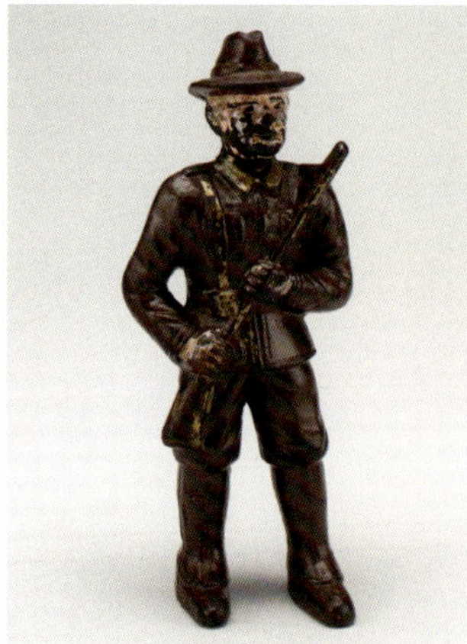
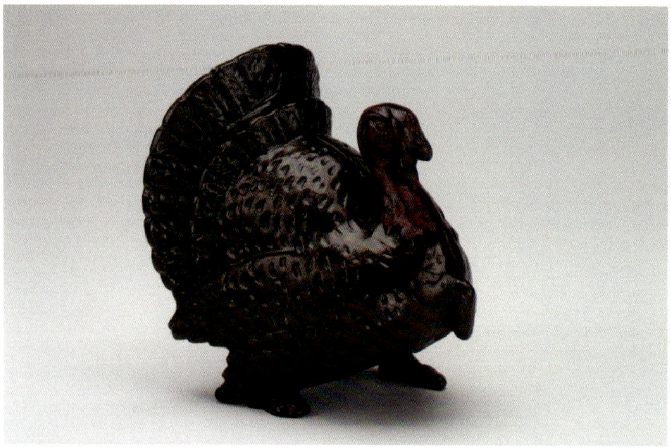
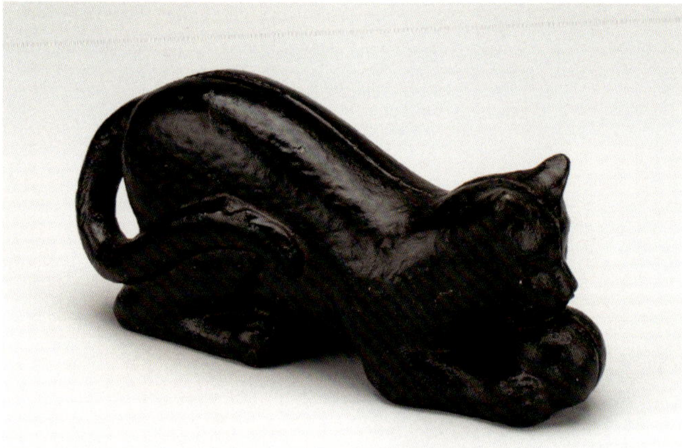
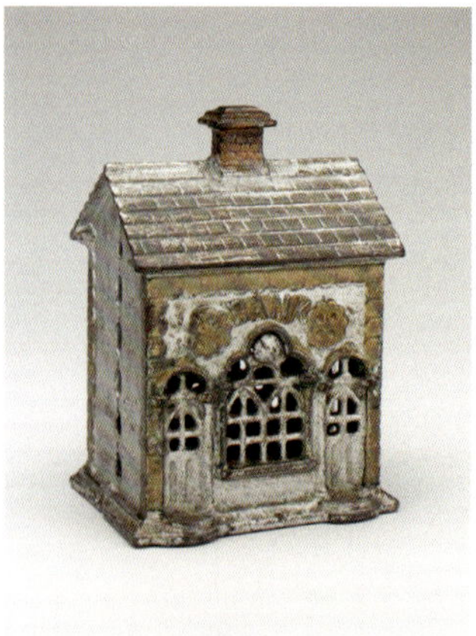
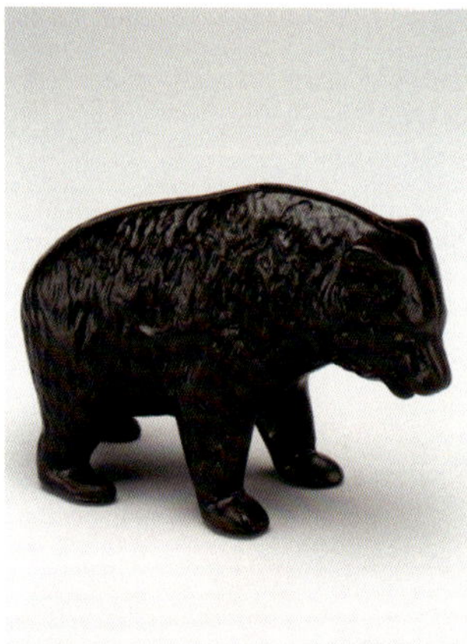
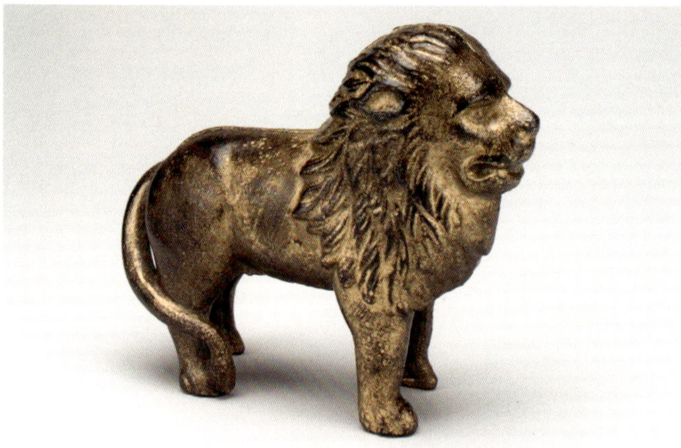
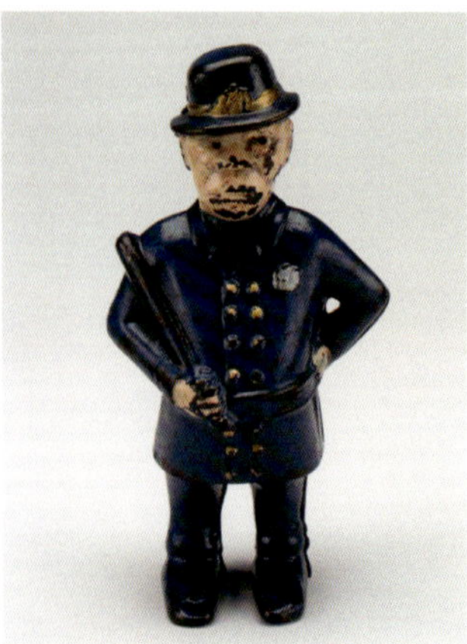
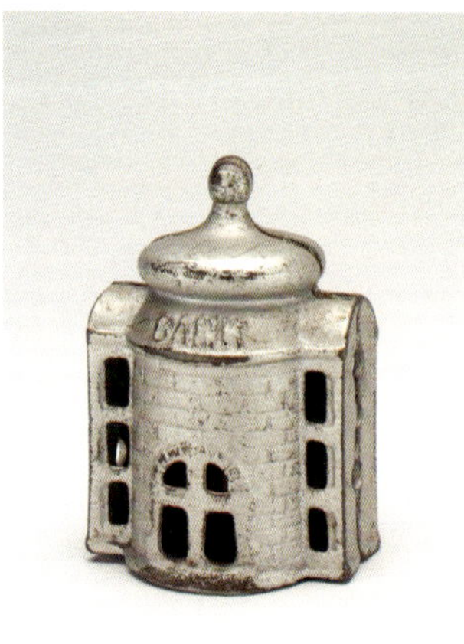
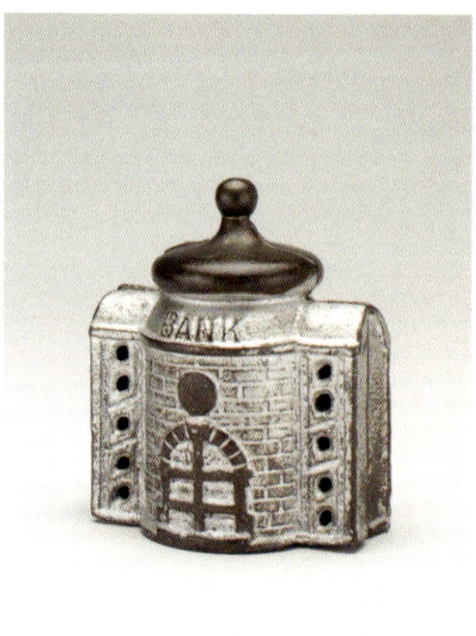
BANK
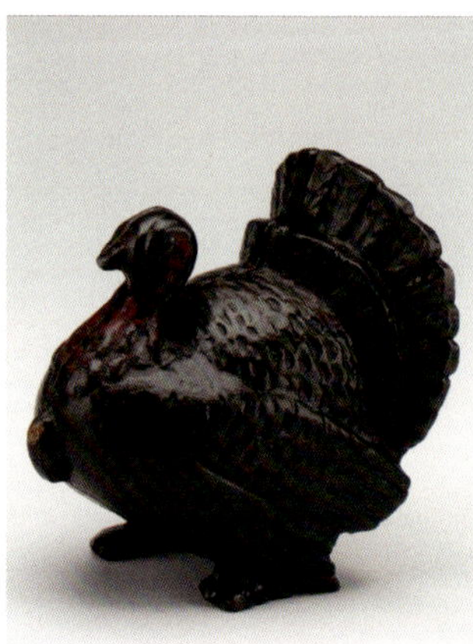

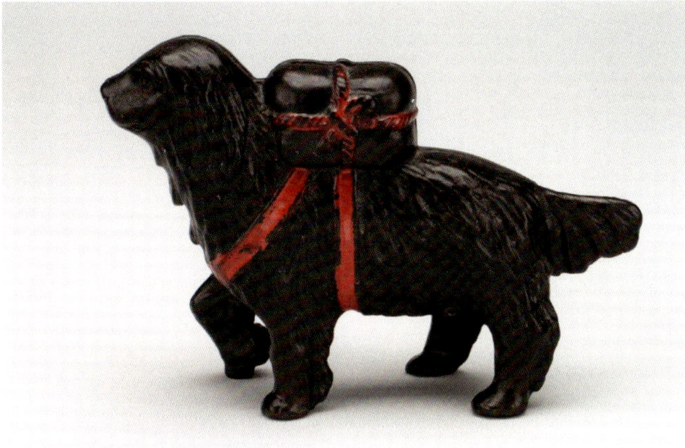

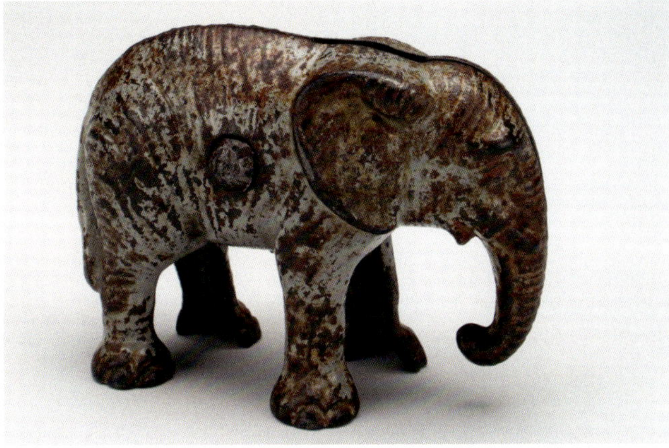

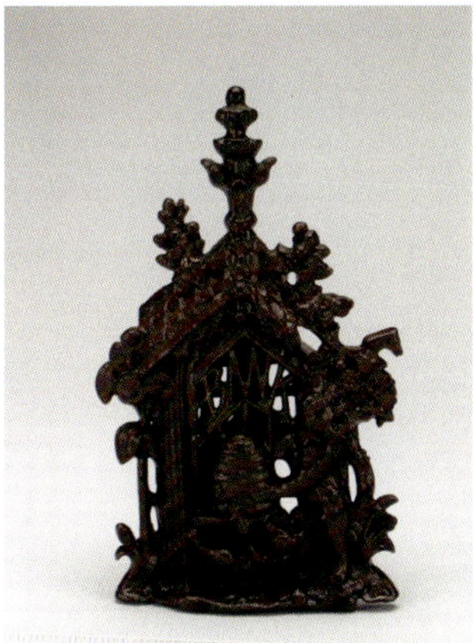

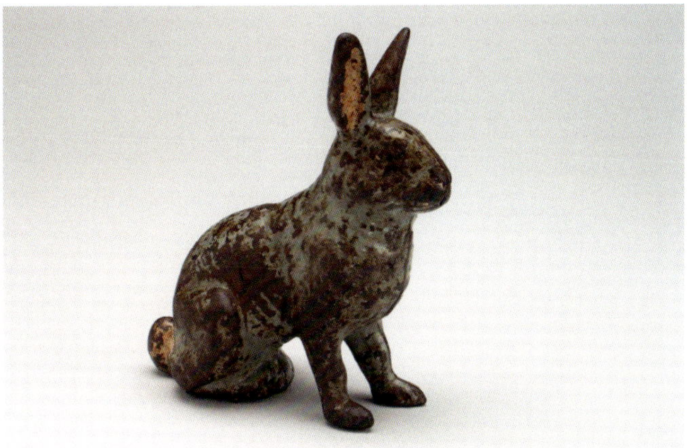

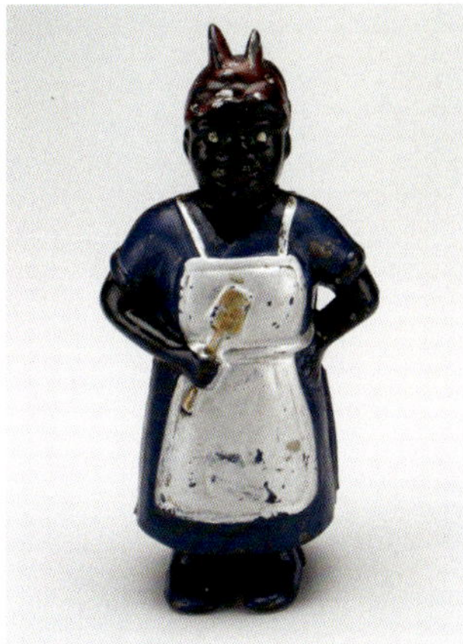

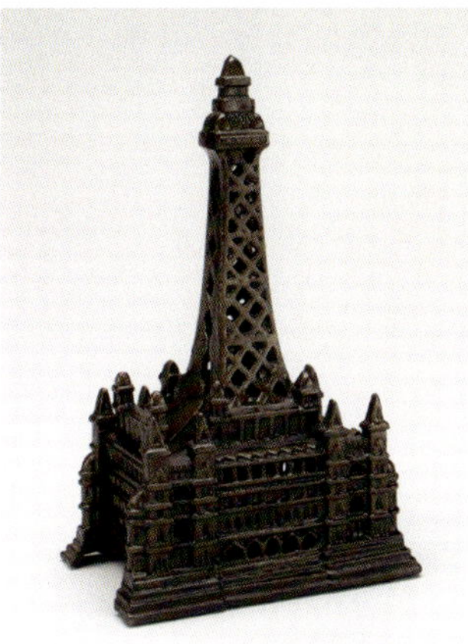

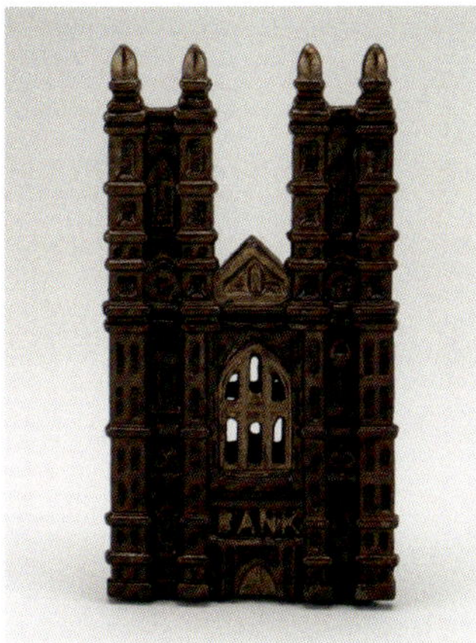
BANK

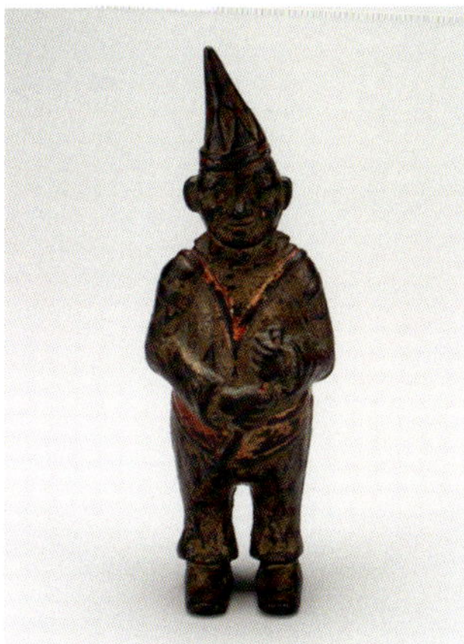

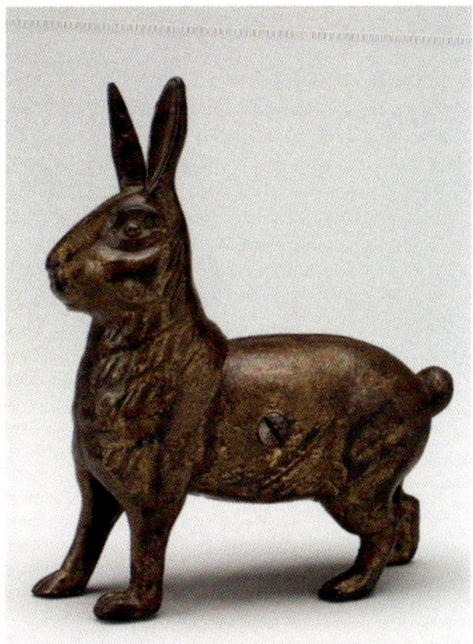

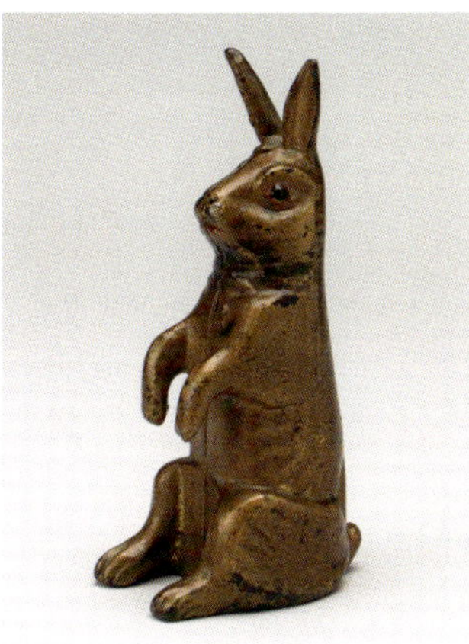

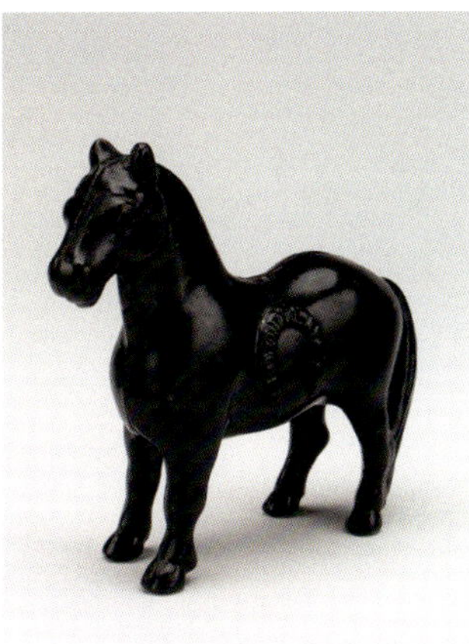

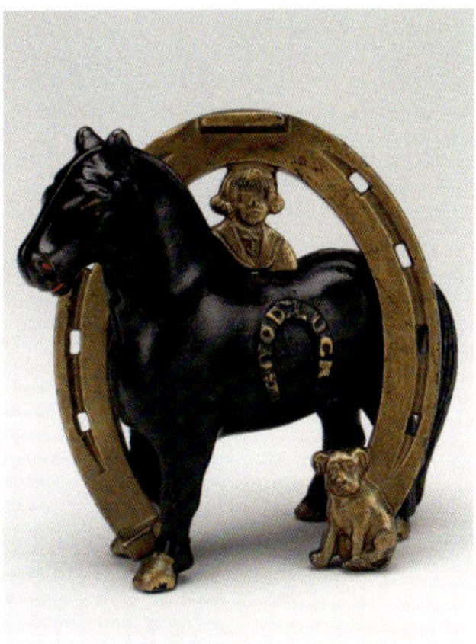

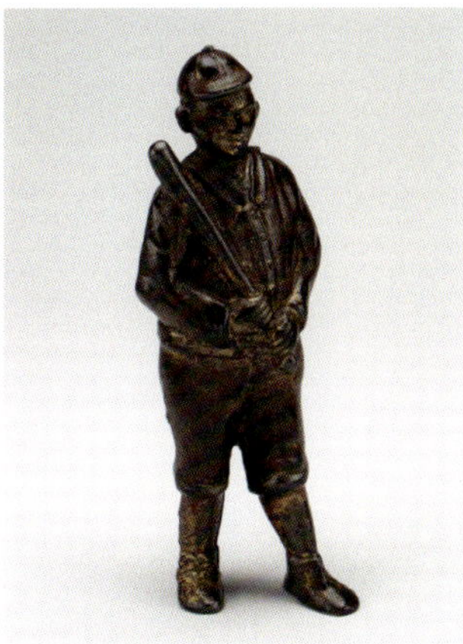

Elephant, c. 1906
Hubley Manufacturing Company, Lancaster, Pennsylvania (est. 1894), manufacturer
Iron, pigment
3 3/8 x 4 9/16 x 2 in.
2003.236.837

St. Bernard Dog with Pack, Small, c. 1905 – 30s
A. C. Williams Company, Ravenna, Ohio (est. 1886), manufacturer
Iron, pigment
3 3/4 x 5 7/8 x 1 11/16 in.
2003.236.984

Aunt Jemima, c. 1905 – 30s
A. C. Williams Company, Ravenna, Ohio (est. 1886), manufacturer
Iron, pigment
5 15/16 x 3 x 2 in.
2003.236.623

Large Seated Rabbit, c. 1906 – 20s
Hubley Manufacturing Company, Lancaster, Pennsylvania (est. 1894), manufacturer
Iron, pigment
4 11/16 x 4 5/16 x 2 1/8 in.
2003.236.164

Bear Stealing Honey, c. 1908
Sydenham & McOustra, Walsall, England, manufacturer
Iron
7 1/8 x 4 7/16 x 1 7/8 in.
2003.236.269

Rabbit Standing, c. 1908 – mid-1920s
A. C. Williams Company, Ravenna, Ohio (est. 1886), manufacturer
Iron, pigment
6 1/2 x 5 3/4 x 2 in.
2003.236.176

Clown, 1908
A. C. Williams Company, Ravenna, Ohio (est. 1886), manufacturer
Iron, pigment
6 3/8 x 1 3/8 x 1 7/8 in.
2003.236.635

Westminster Abbey, c. 1908
Sydenham & McOustra, Walsall, England, manufacturer
Iron, pigment
6 1/4 x 3 3/8 x 1 3/8 in.
2003.236.271

Blackpool Tower, c. 1908
Chamberlin & Hill, Walsall, England, manufacturer
Iron, pigment
7 3/16 x 4 1/2 x 2 7/8 in.
2003.236.507

Baseball Player, c. 1909
A. C. Williams Company, Ravenna, Ohio (est. 1886), manufacturer
Iron, pigment
5 3/4 x 2 1/4 x 2 1/16 in.
2003.236.631

Good Luck Horseshoe with Buster Brown and Tige, c. 1908 – 32
Arcade Manufacturing Company, Freeport, Illinois (1868 –1946), manufacturer
Iron, pigment
4 1/8 x 4 11/16 x 3 in.
2003.236.1003

Good Luck Horseshoe, c. 1908 – 32
Arcade Manufacturing Company, Freeport, Illinois (1868 –1946), manufacturer
Iron, pigment
4 3/16 x 5 x 1 1/8 in.
2003.236.166

Begging Rabbit, c. 1908 – 20s
A. C. Williams Company, Ravenna, Ohio (est. 1886), manufacturer
Iron, pigment
5 1/8 x 2 9/16 x 1 5/8 in.
2003.236.177

Clock Bank, c. 1910
Arcade Manufacturing Company, Freeport, Illinois (1868 – 1946), manufacturer
Iron, pigment
3 3/4 x 2 7/8 x 1 13/16 in.
2003.236.943

Goose, c. 1909 – 35
A. C. Williams Company, Ravenna, Ohio (est. 1886), manufacturer
Iron, pigment
5 x 1 15/16 x 3 in.
2003.236.954

Time Is Money, c. 1909 – 31
A. C. Williams Company, Ravenna, Ohio (est. 1886), manufacturer
Iron, pigment
3 13/16 x 3 1/16 x 1 3/4 in.
2003.236.948

Billiken, c. 1909 – 12
A. C. Williams Company, Ravenna, Ohio (est. 1886), manufacturer
Iron, pigment
4 1/8 x 2 1/4 x 2 7/16 in.
2003.236.1002

Workhorse, c. 1910
Arcade Manufacturing Company, Freeport, Illinois (1868 – 1946), manufacturer
Iron, pigment
4 1/8 x 5 x 1 3/16 in.
2003.236.165

Rumpelstiltskin, c. 1910
Probably A. C. Williams Company, Ravenna, Ohio (est. 1886), manufacturer
Iron, pigment
6 x 2 5/16 x 2 1/2 in.
2003.236.622

Prancing Horse on Pebbled Base, c. 1910
United States
Iron, pigment
7 5/8 x 6 1/2 x 2 11/16 in.
2003.236.1032

Gold Dollar, c. 1910
Arcade Manufacturing Company, Freeport, Illinois (1868 – 1946), manufacturer
Iron, steel, pigment
3 3/4 x 2 15/16 x 1 15/16 in.
2003.236.942

Begging Bear, c. 1910s
A. C. Williams Company, Ravenna, Ohio (est. 1886), manufacturer
Iron, pigment
5 3/8 x 1 7/8 x 2 3/16 in.
2003.236.961

Skyscraper, 1910
A. C. Williams Company, Ravenna, Ohio (est. 1886), manufacturer
3 5/8 x 1 7/8 x 2 in.
Iron, pigment
2003.236.933

Skyscraper, 1910
A. C. Williams Company, Ravenna, Ohio (est. 1886), manufacturer
4 1/2 x 2 1/8 x 2 1/8 in.
Iron, pigment
2003.236.925

One-Story House, 1910
J. & E. Stevens Company, Cromwell, Connecticut (1843 – 1950s), manufacturer
Iron, pigment
3 1/4 x 2 1/16 x 1 15/16 in.
2003.236.779

Sea Lion (or *Seal on Rock*), c. 1910 – 13
Arcade Manufacturing Company, Freeport, Illinois (1868 – 1946), manufacturer
Iron, pigment
3 1/2 x 4 5/16 x 2 1/8 in.
2003.236.282

Lion, Tail Right, c. 1910 – 13
Arcade Manufacturing Company, Freeport, Illinois (1868 – 1946), manufacturer
Iron, pigment
3 13/16 x 5 1/4 x 1 3/8 in.
2003.236.170

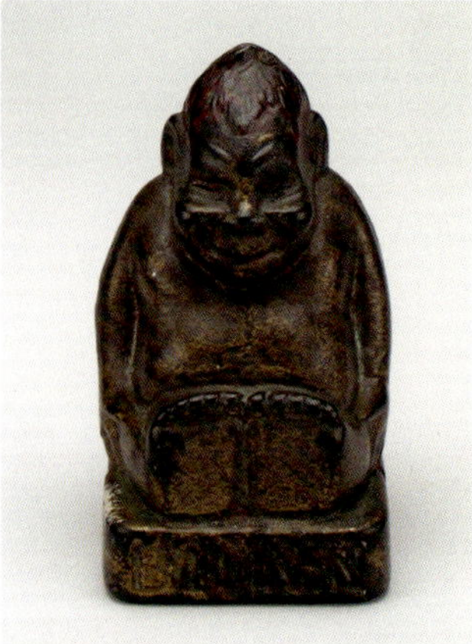

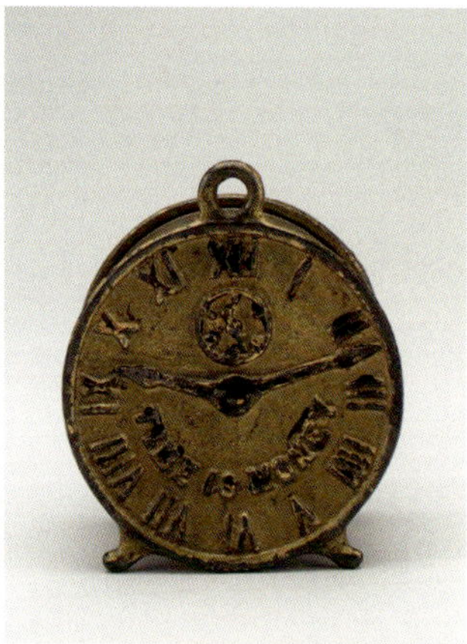
TIME IS MONEY

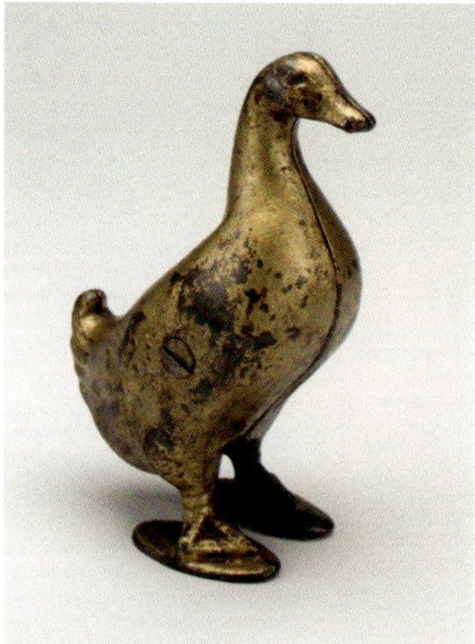

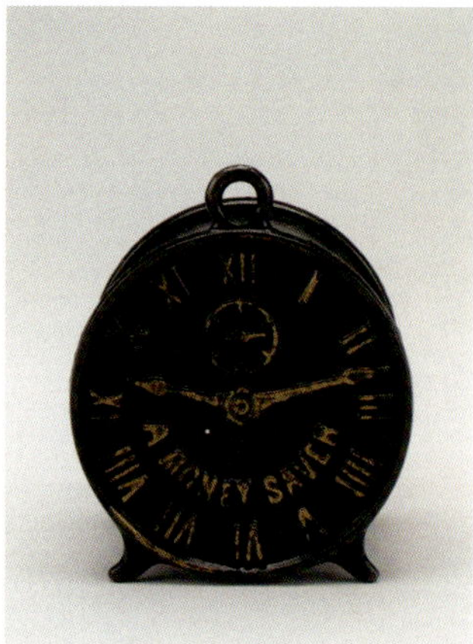
A MONEY SAVER

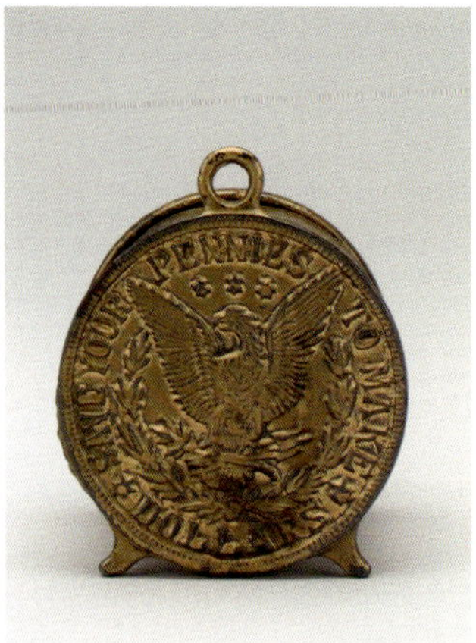

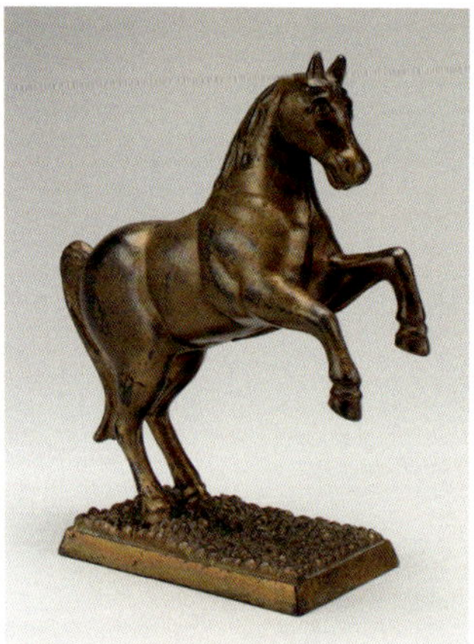

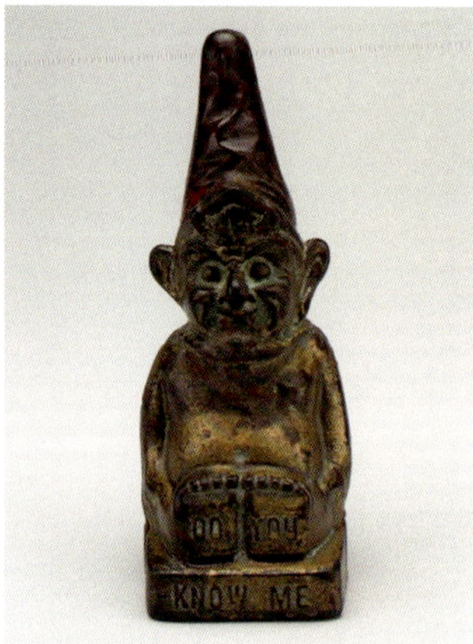
DO YOU
KNOW ME

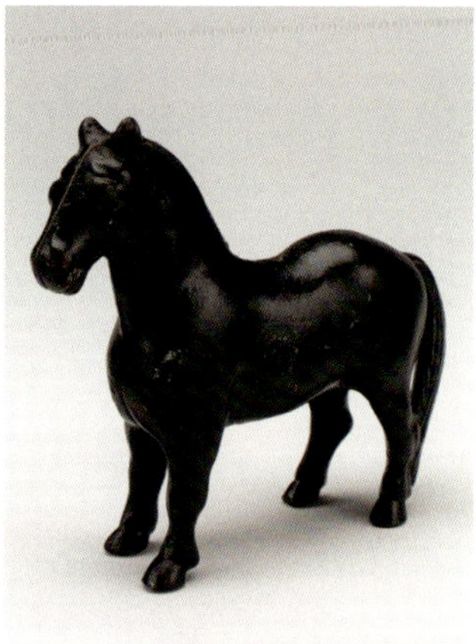

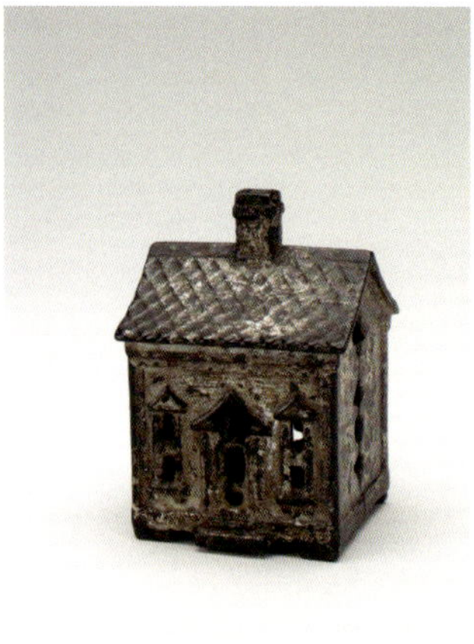

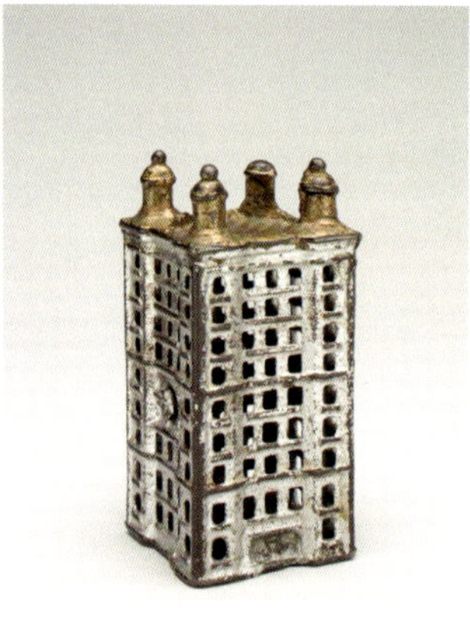

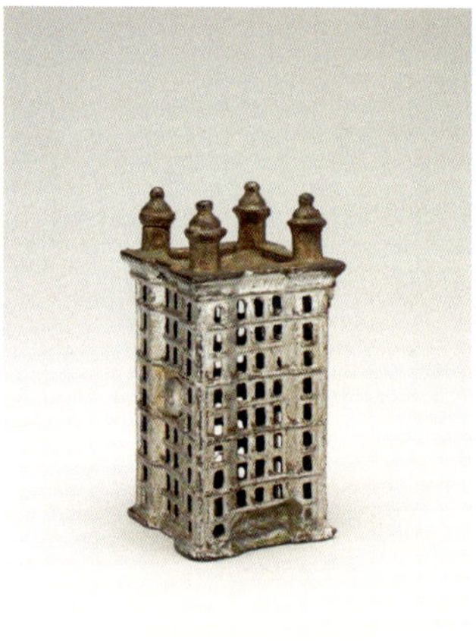

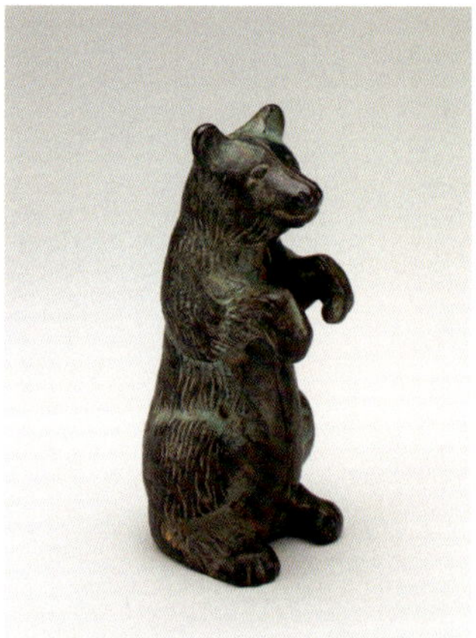

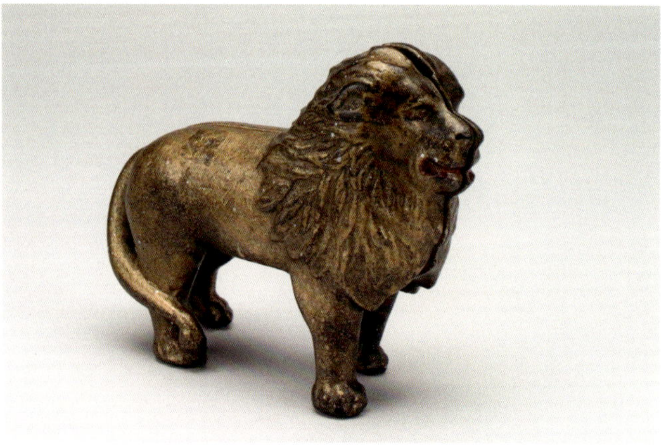

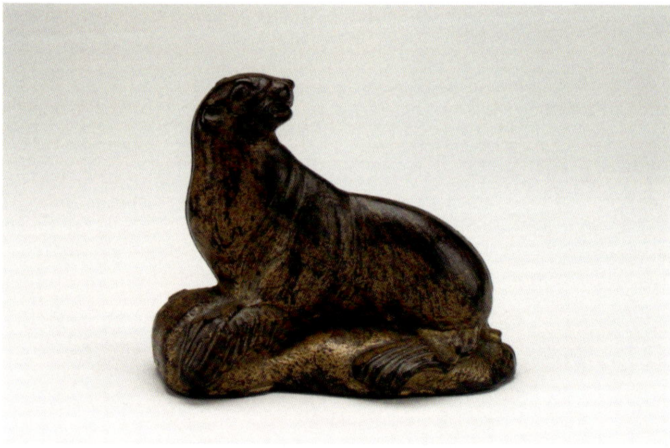

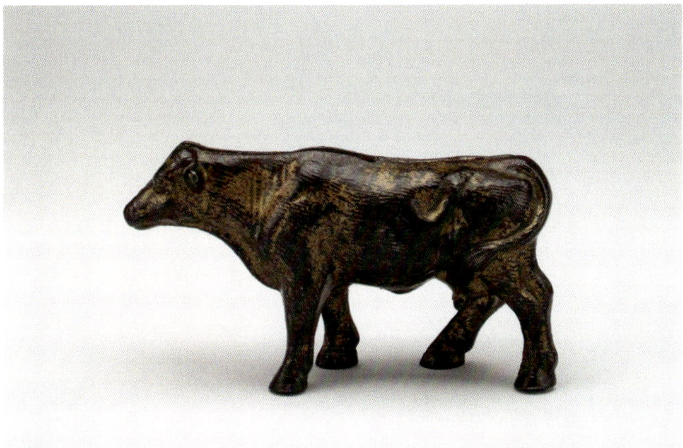
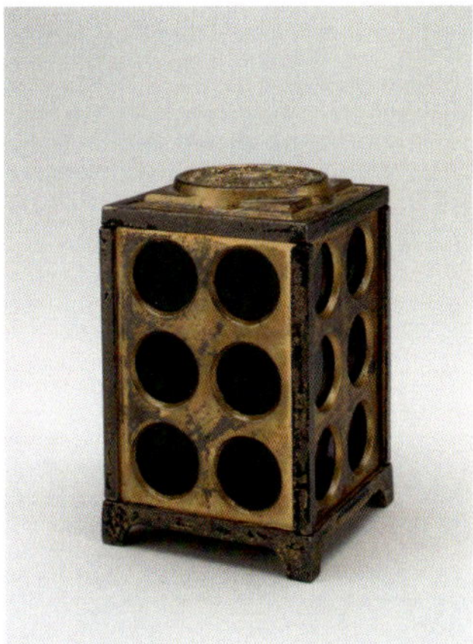
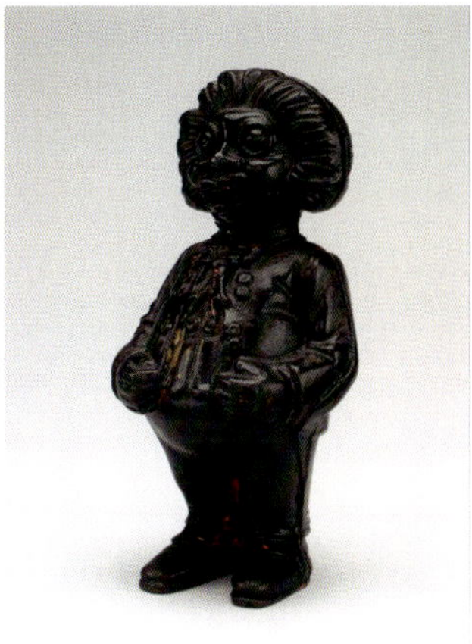
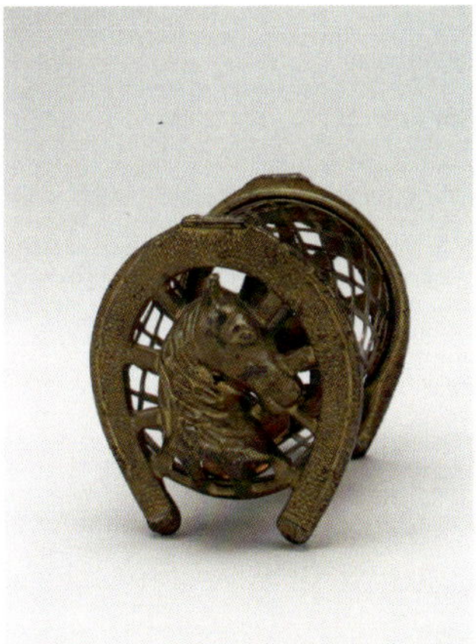
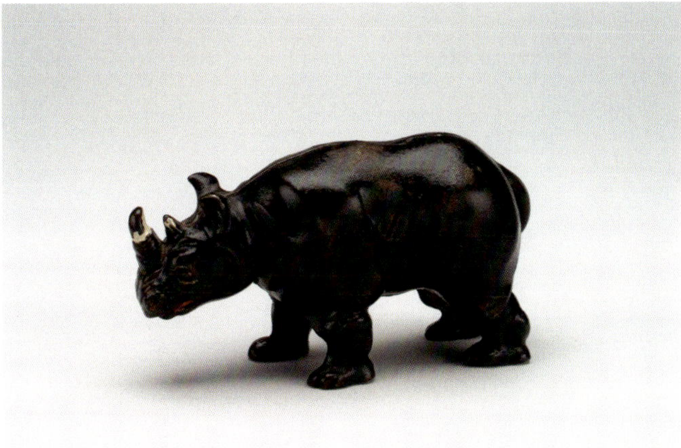
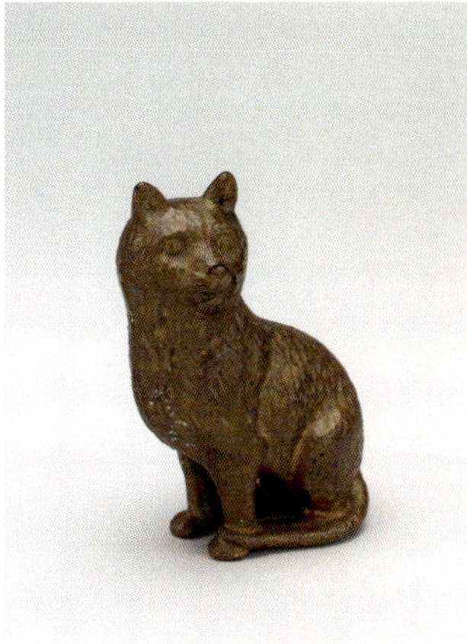
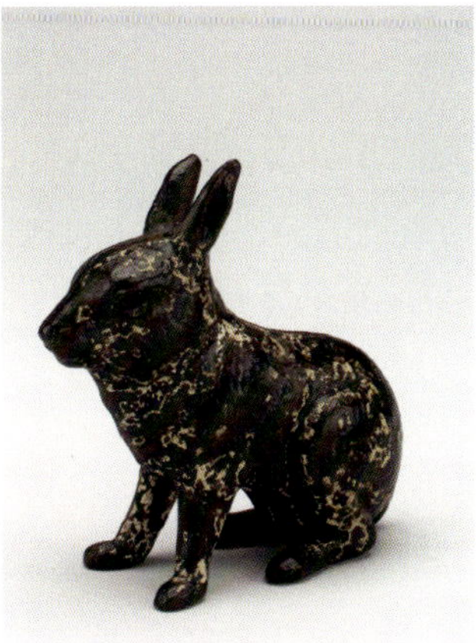
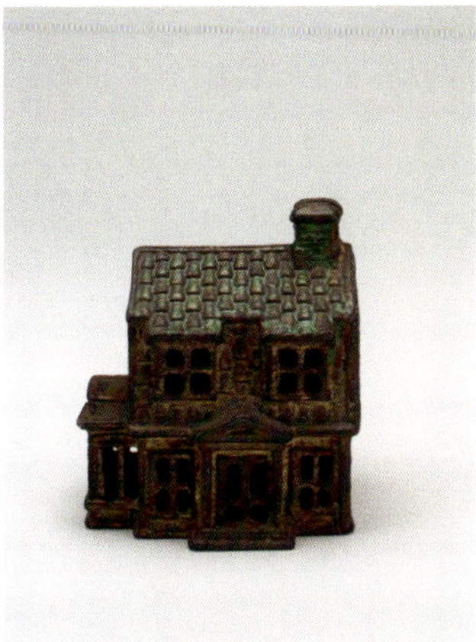
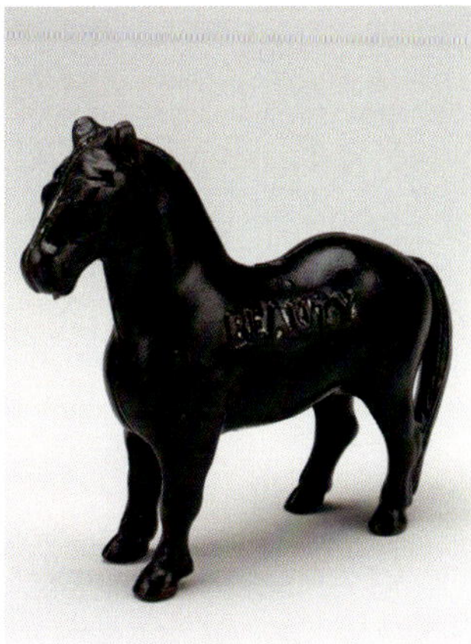
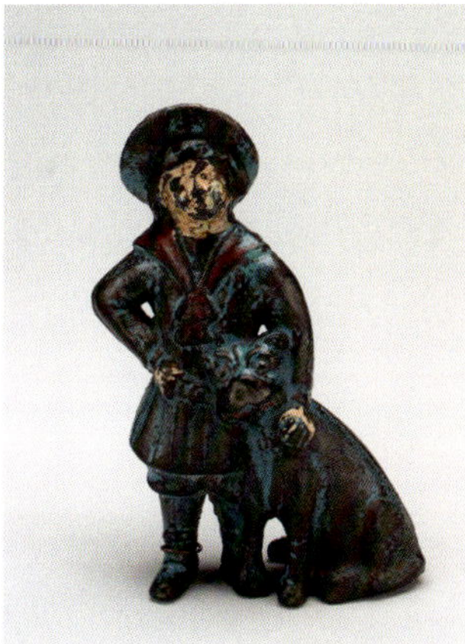
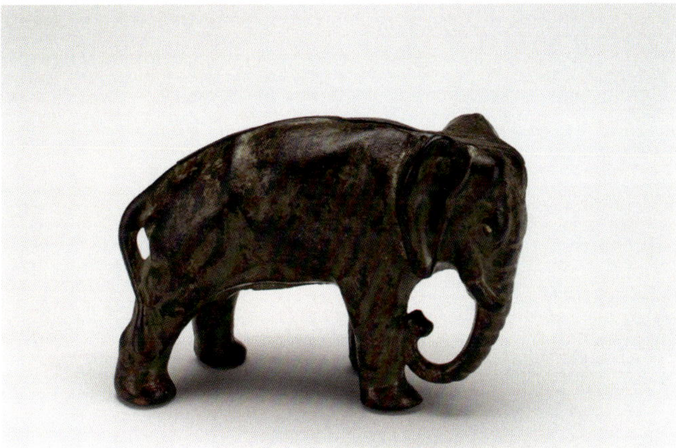
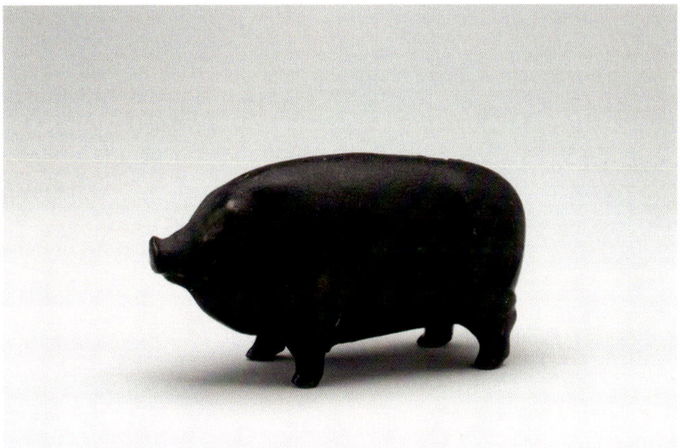

Golliwog, c. 1910 – 25
John Harper & Company, Ltd., Willenhall, England (1790 – 1980s), manufacturer
Iron, pigment
6 1/4 x 3 1/16 x 2 1/2 in.
2003.236.626

World Time Bank (paper dials missing), c. 1910 – 20
Arcade Manufacturing Company, Freeport, Illinois (1868 – 1946), manufacturer
Iron, pigment
4 1/8 x 2 5/8 x 2 5/8 in.
2003.236.1009

Cow, c. 1910 – 20
Arcade Manufacturing Company, Freeport, Illinois (1868 – 1946), manufacturer
Iron, pigment
2 11/16 x 4 11/16 x 1 1/8 in.
2003.236.989

Seated Cat with Soft Hair, c. 1910 – 29
Arcade Manufacturing Company, Freeport, Illinois (1868 – 1946), manufacturer
Iron, pigment
4 1/4 x 2 7/8 x 1 11/16 in.
2003.236.945

Rhinoceros, c. 1910 – 25
Arcade Manufacturing Company, Freeport, Illinois (1868 – 1946), manufacturer
Iron, pigment
2 3/4 x 1 13/16 x 5 in.
2003.236.273

Horseshoe with Wire Mesh, c. 1910 – 25
Arcade Manufacturing Company, Freeport, Illinois (1868 – 1946), manufacturer
Iron, pigment
3 1/2 x 3 5/16 x 2 13/16 in.
2003.236.939

Buster Brown and Tige, c. 1910 – 32
A. C. Williams Company, Ravenna, Ohio (est. 1886), manufacturer
Iron, pigment
5 1/4 x 4 5/8 x 1 9/16 in.
2003.236.621

Beauty, c. 1910 – 32
Arcade Manufacturing Company, Freeport, Illinois (1868 – 1946), manufacturer
Iron, pigment
4 1/8 x 5 x 1 3/16 in.
2003.236.162

Colonial House (or *House with Porch*), c. 1910 – 31
A. C. Williams Company, Ravenna, Ohio (est. 1886), manufacturer
Iron, pigment
3 x 2 9/16 x 2 1/8 in.
2003.236.152

Seated Rabbit, Small, c. 1910 – 20s
Arcade Manufacturing Company, Freeport, Illinois (1868 – 1946), manufacturer
Iron, pigment
3 11/16 x 3 15/16 x 1 1/2 in.
2003.236.1010

Pig, Small, c. 1910 – 32
Arcade Manufacturing Company, Freeport, Illinois (1868 – 1946), manufacturer
Iron, pigment
2 x 1 5/16 x 3 7/8 in.
2003.236.990

Elephant with Tucked Trunk, c. 1910 – 32
Arcade Manufacturing Company, Freeport, Illinois (1868 – 1946), manufacturer
Iron, pigment
2 3/4 x 3 7/8 x 1 13/16 in.
2003.236.1006

Reindeer, Large, c. 1910 – 35
A. C. Williams Company, Ravenna, Ohio (est. 1886), manufacturer
Iron, pigment
9 1/4 x 4 1/4 x 7 1/4 in.
2003.236.406

Rooster, c. 1910 – 34
Hubley Manufacturing Company, Lancaster, Pennsylvania (est. 1894), manufacturer
Iron, pigment
4 15/16 x 3 1/4 x 1 7/8 in.
2003.236.987

Colonial House (or *House with Porch*), c. 1910 – 34
A. C. Williams Company, Ravenna, Ohio (est. 1886), manufacturer
Iron, pigment
4 1/8 x 3 7/8 x 2 3/4 in.
2003.236.300

Boy Scout (or *Soldier Boy*), c. 1910 – 34
A. C. Williams Company, Ravenna, Ohio (est. 1886), manufacturer
Iron, pigment
5 15/16 x 2 3/16 x 1 13/16 in.
2003.236.630

Coronation Bank, George V, 1911
Probably Sydenham & McOustra, Walsall, England, manufacturer
Iron, pigment
6 1/2 x 4 1/2 x 1 3/4 in.
2003.236.747

Statue of Liberty, c. 1910 – 30s
A. C. Williams Company, Ravenna, Ohio (est. 1886), manufacturer
Iron, pigment
6 1/8 x 2 1/4 x 2 1/4 in.
2003.236.964

Newfoundland Dog, c. 1910 – 30s
Arcade Manufacturing Company, Freeport, Illinois (1868 – 1946), manufacturer
Iron, pigment
3 5/8 x 5 1/2 x 1 3/4 in.
2003.236.988

Be Wise, Save Money, c. 1912 – 20s
A. C. Williams Company, Ravenna, Ohio (est. 1886), manufacturer
Iron, pigment
5 x 3 13/16 x 1 15/16 in.
2003.236.969

Boxer (or *Bulldog*), c. 1912 – 28
A. C. Williams Company, Ravenna, Ohio (est. 1886), manufacturer
Iron, pigment
4 1/2 x 3 13/16 x 2 in.
2003.236.978

Large Statue of Liberty, c. 1911 – 32
Kenton Hardware Manufacturing Company, Kenton, Ohio (1890 – 1950), manufacturer
Iron, pigment
9 3/4 x 3 1/2 x 3 1/2 in.
2003.236.968

Globe Safe with Hinged Door, c. 1911 – 31
Kenton Hardware Manufacturing Company, Kenton, Ohio (1890 – 1950), manufacturer
Iron, pigment
5 1/2 x 4 1/2 x 4 3/16 in.
2003.236.130

Mutt and Jeff, c. 1912 – 31
A. C. Williams Company, Ravenna, Ohio (est. 1886), manufacturer
Iron, pigment
5 3/8 x 3 3/4 x 1 15/16 in.
2003.236.625

Steamboat, c. 1912 – 20s
A. C. Williams Company, Ravenna, Ohio (est. 1886), manufacturer
Iron, pigment
2 1/2 x 7 5/8 x 1 3/8 in.
2003.236.309

Songbird on Stump (or *Bird Toy Bank*), c. 1912 – 20s
A. C. Williams Company, Ravenna, Ohio (est. 1886), manufacturer
Iron, pigment
4 15/16 x 3 3/4 x 1 7/8 in.
2003.236.960

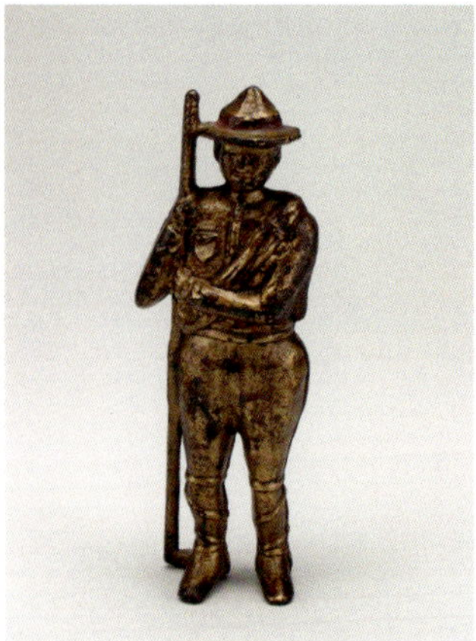

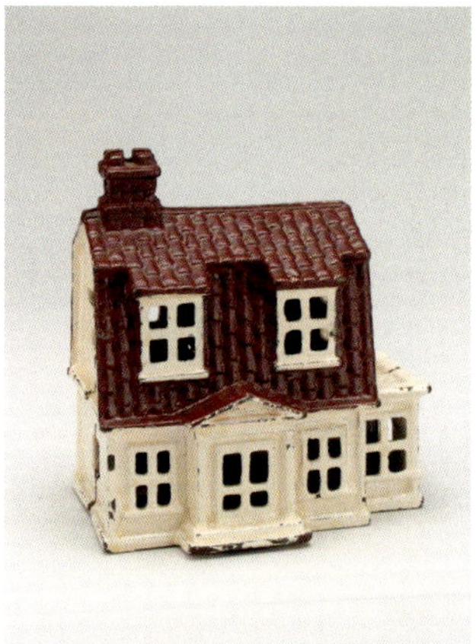

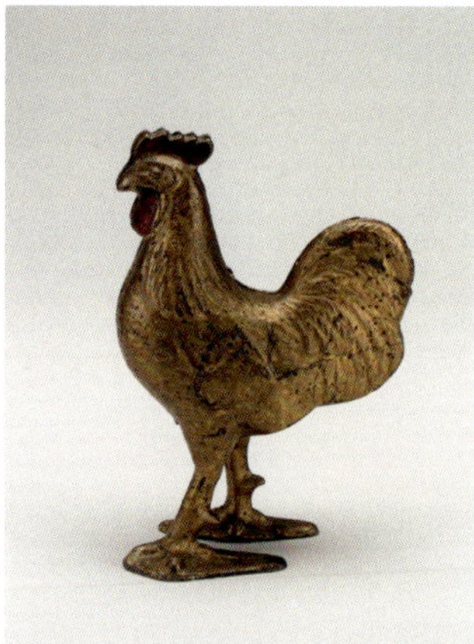

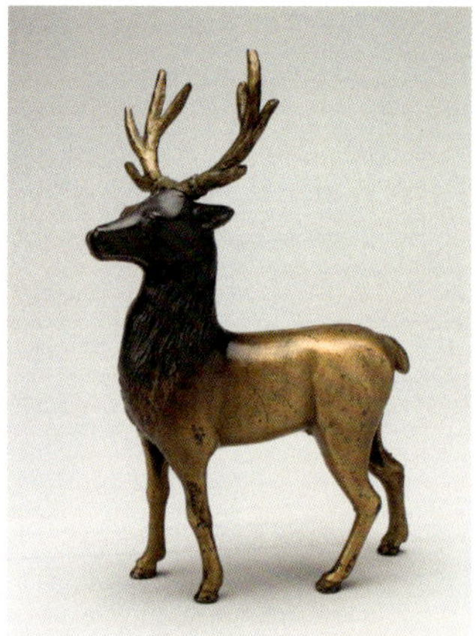

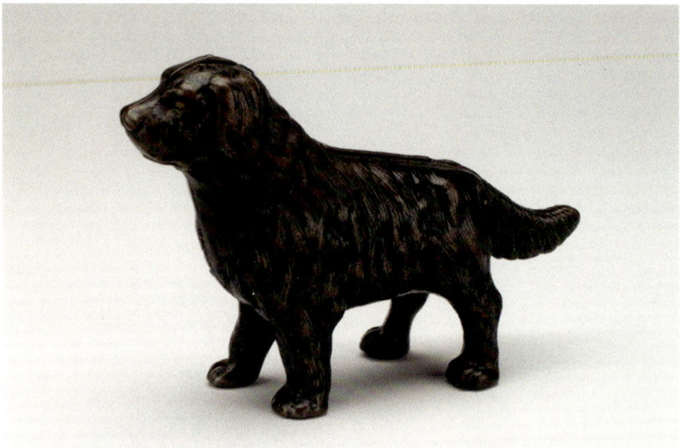

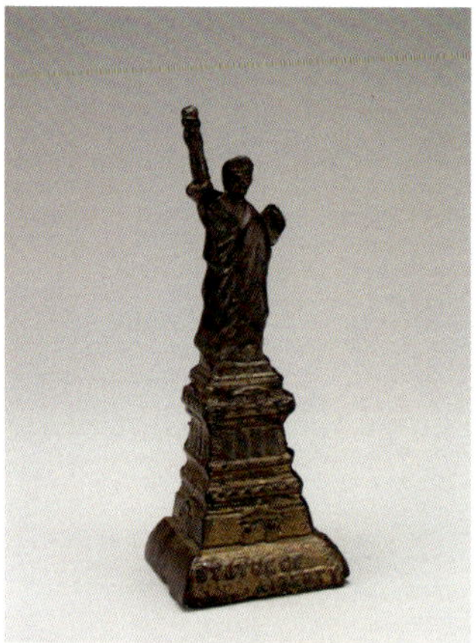

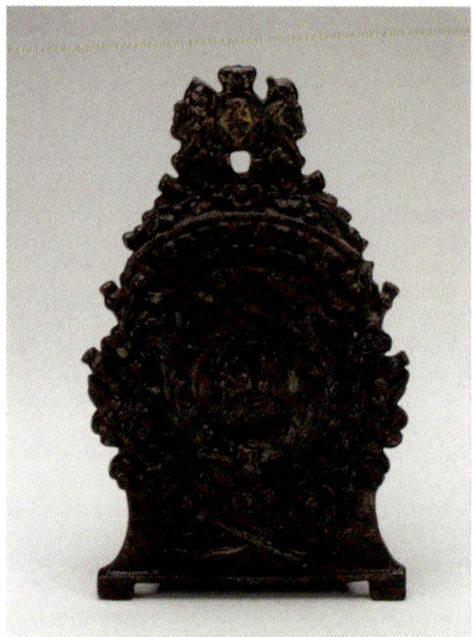

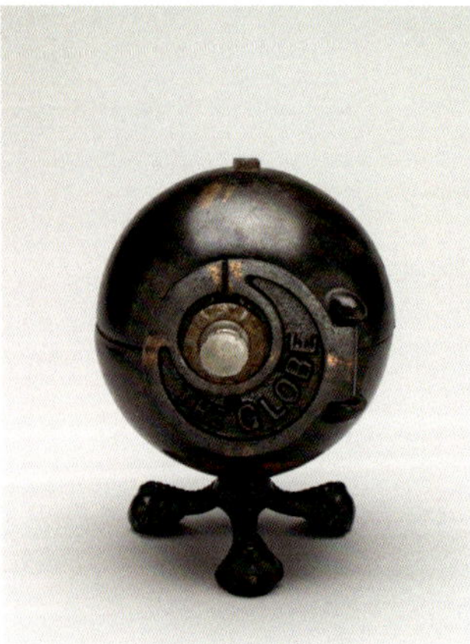

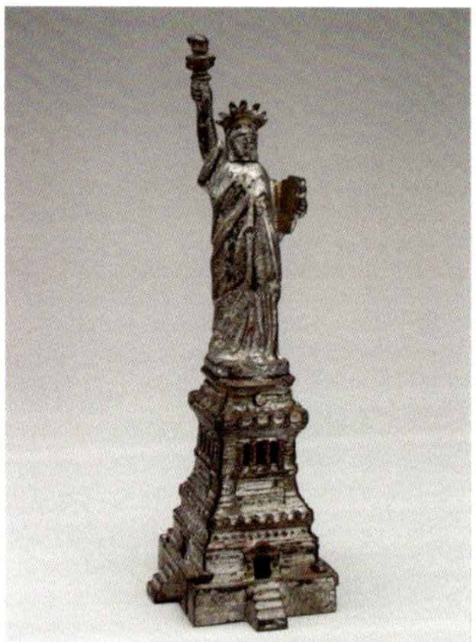

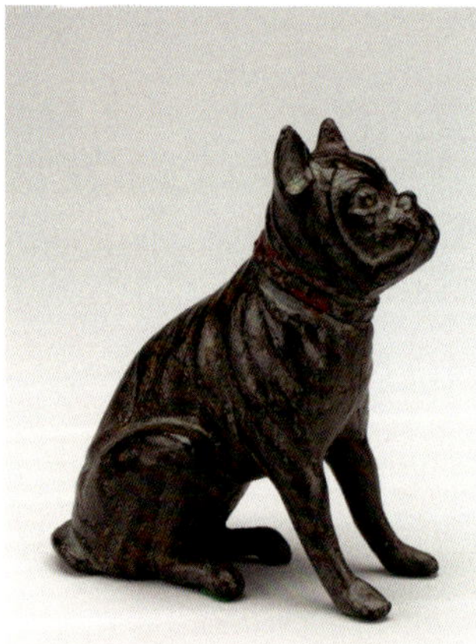

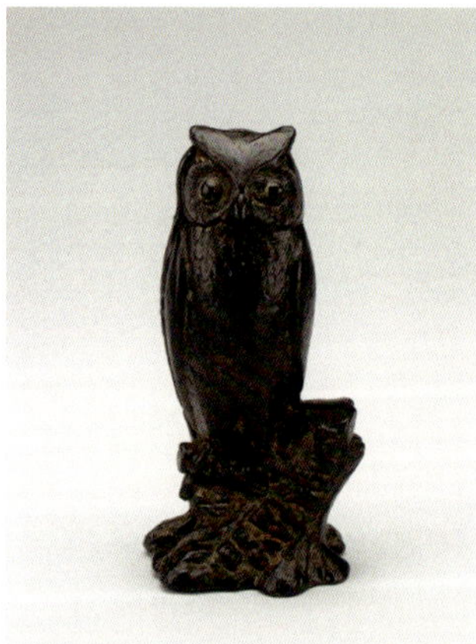

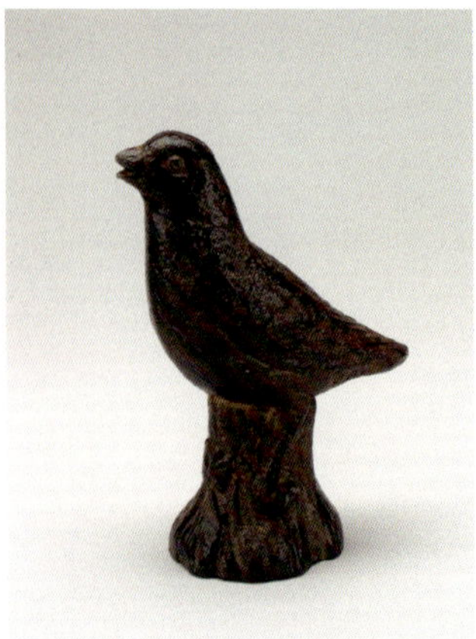

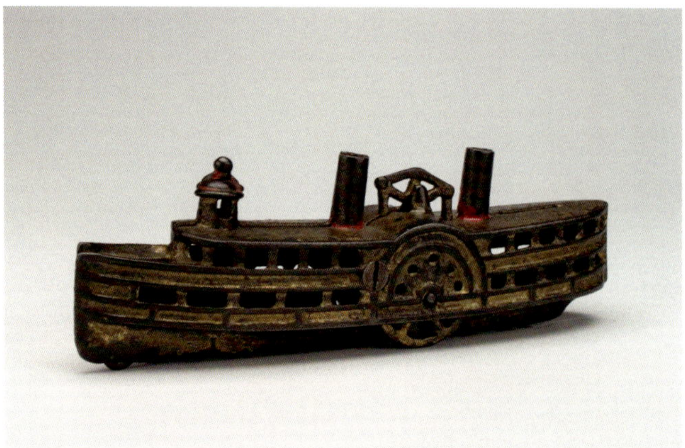

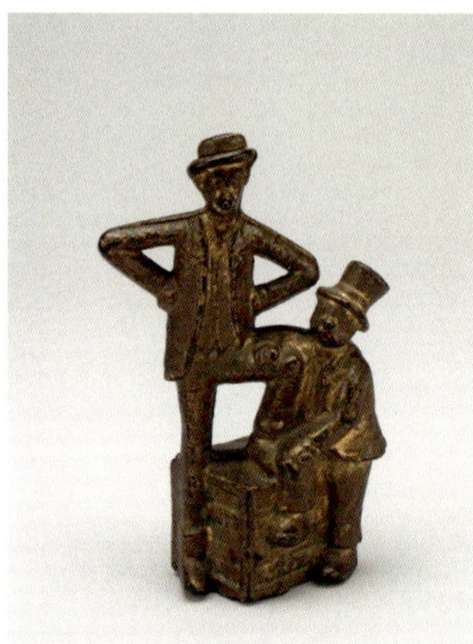

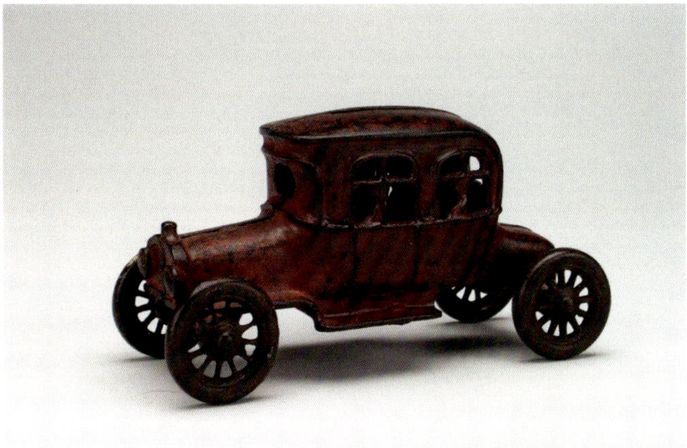
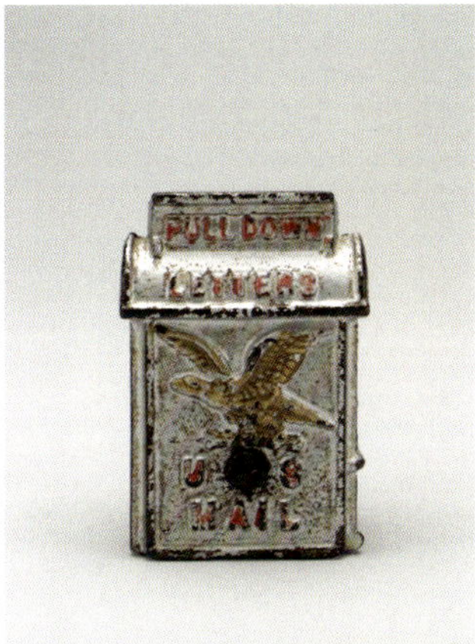
PULL DOWN
LETTERS
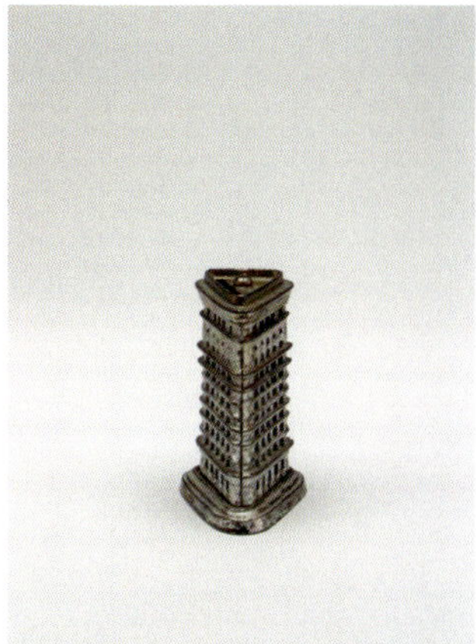
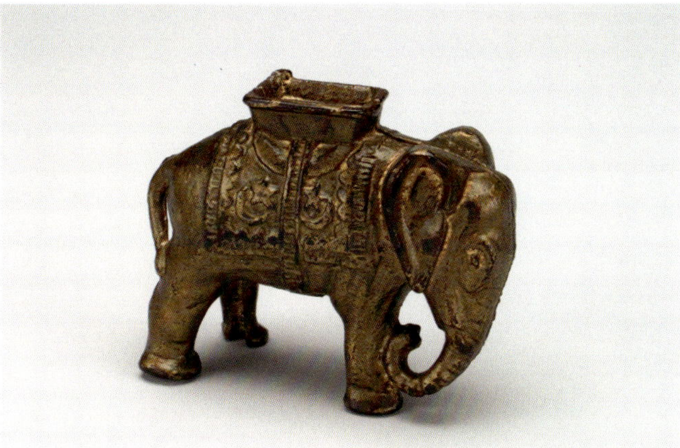
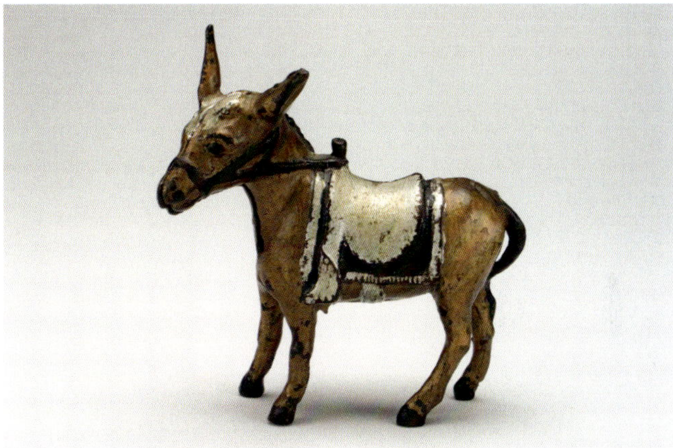
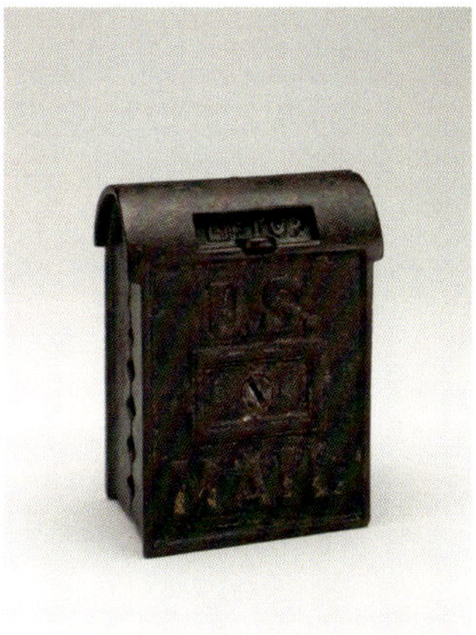
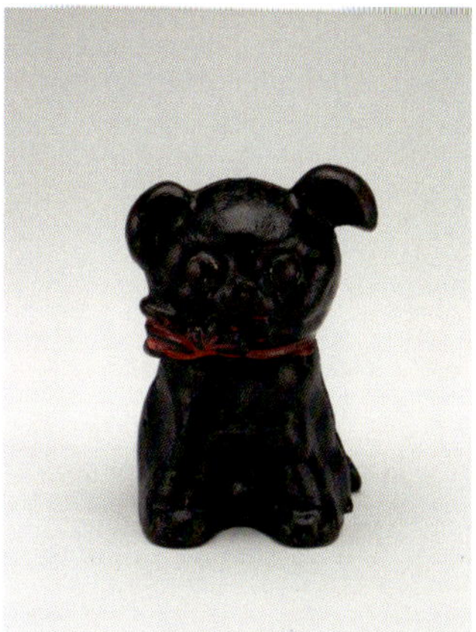
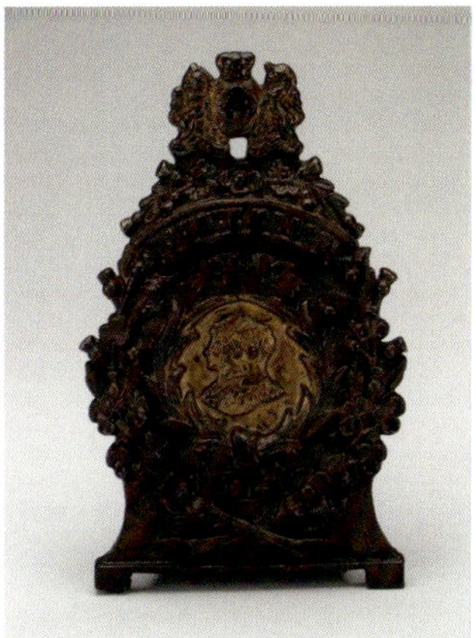
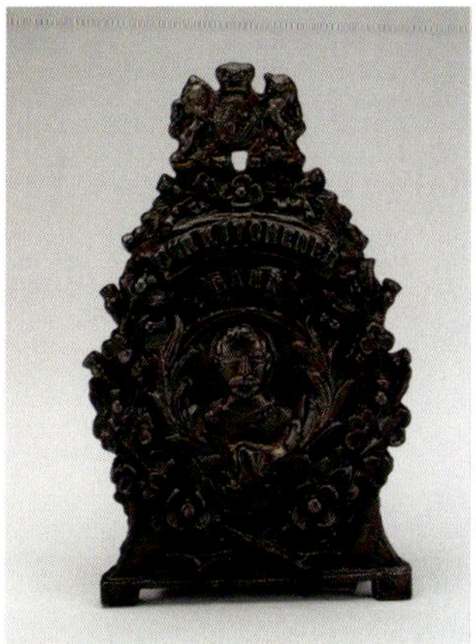
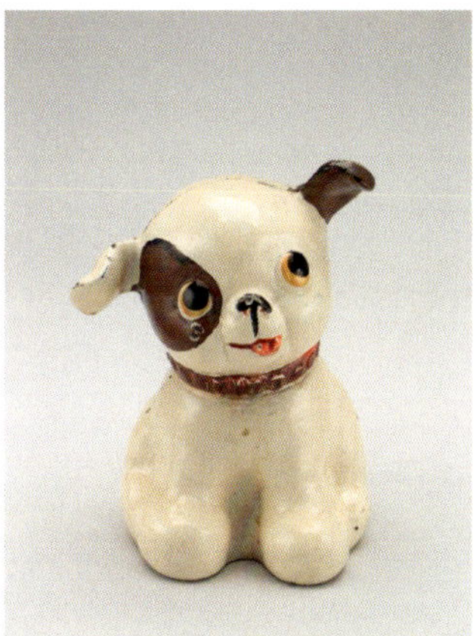
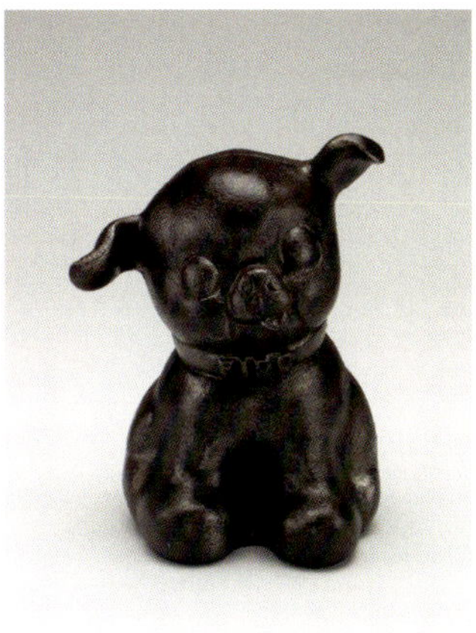
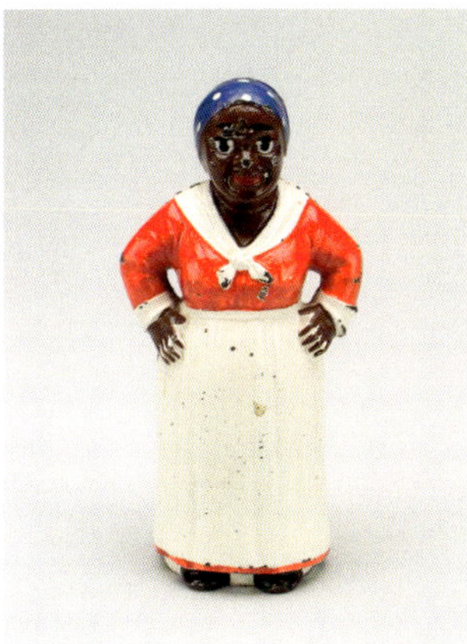
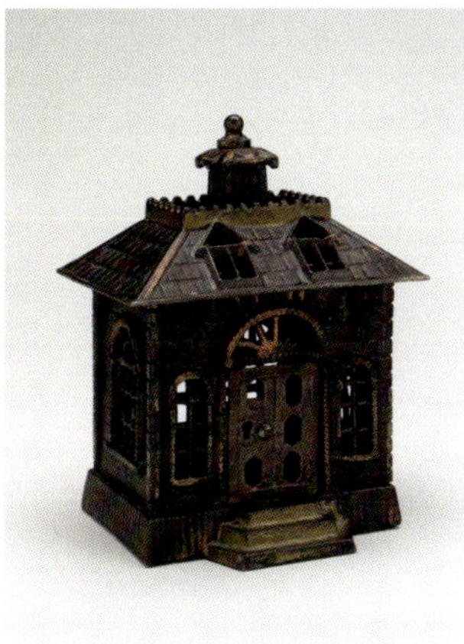

Flatiron Building Bank, Small, c. 1912 – 36
Kenton Hardware Manufacturing Company, Kenton, Ohio (1890 – 1950), manufacturer
Iron, pigment
3 5/16 x 2 3/8 x 2 in.
2003.236.145

U.S. Mail with Eagle, c. 1912 – 31
Kenton Hardware Manufacturing Company, Kenton, Ohio (1890 – 1950), manufacturer
Iron, pigment
3 3/4 x 2 3/8 x 1 7/16 in.
2003.236.1008

Auto, Four Passengers, c. 1912 – 31
A. C. Williams Company, Ravenna, Ohio (est. 1886), manufacturer
Iron, pigment
3 1/4 x 6 5/16 x 2 5/8 in.
2003.236.290

Donkey, Small, c. 1913 – 32
Arcade Manufacturing Company, Freeport, Illinois (1868 – 1946), manufacturer
Iron, pigment
4 3/4 x 4 5/8 x 1 9/16 in.
2003.236.285

Elephant with Howdah, Small, c. 1912 – 31
A. C. Williams Company, Ravenna, Ohio (est. 1886), manufacturer
Iron, pigment
3 x 4 1/8 x 1 3/4 in.
2003.236.1025

Our Kitchener, 1914
Probably Sydenham & McOustra, Walsall, England, manufacturer
Iron, pigment
6 1/2 x 4 1/2 x 1 3/4 in.
2003.236.749

Our Empire, George V and Mary, 1914
Probably Sydenham & McOustra, Walsall, England, manufacturer
England
Iron, pigment
6 1/2 x 4 1/2 x 1 3/4 in.
2003.236.748

Cutie, c. 1914
Hubley Manufacturing Company, Lancaster, Pennsylvania (est. 1894), manufacturer
Iron, pigment
3 7/8 x 2 11/16 x 2 9/16 in.
2003.236.782

U.S. Mail, 1913
Arcade Manufacturing Company, Freeport, Illinois (1868 – 1946), manufacturer
Iron, pigment
3 1/2 x 2 11/16 x 1 3/4 in.
2003.236.995

State Bank, c. 1915
Possibly Kenton Hardware Manufacturing Company, Kenton, Ohio (1890 – 1950), manufacturer
6 x 5 5/8 x 3 5/8 in.
Iron, pigment
2003.236.922

Mammy with Hands on Hips, c. 1914 – 46
Hubley Manufacturing Company, Lancaster, Pennsylvania (est. 1894), manufacturer
Iron, pigment
5 1/4 x 2 11/16 x 1 15/16 in.
2003.236.624

Fido, c. 1914 – 46
Hubley Manufacturing Company, Lancaster, Pennsylvania (est. 1894), manufacturer
Iron
5 x 4 x 4 1/8 in.
2003.236.781

Fido, c. 1914 – 46
Hubley Manufacturing Company, Lancaster, Pennsylvania (est. 1894), manufacturer
Iron, pigment
5 x 4 x 4 1/8 in.
2003.236.237

Camel, Large, c. 1917 – 20s
A. C. Williams Company, Ravenna, Ohio (est. 1886), manufacturer
Iron, pigment
$7\frac{3}{8} \times 2\frac{1}{8} \times 6\frac{1}{2}$ in.
2003.236.407

Indian with Tomahawk, c. 1915 – 30s
Hubley Manufacturing Company, Lancaster, Pennsylvania (est. 1894), manufacturer
Iron, pigment
$6 \times 3\frac{5}{8} \times 1\frac{5}{8}$ in.
2003.236.633

Woolworth Building, 1915
Kenton Hardware Manufacturing Company, Kenton, Ohio (1890 – 1950), manufacturer
Iron, pigment
$8 \times 1\frac{3}{4} \times 2\frac{1}{4}$ in.
2003.236.158

Woolworth Building, 1915
Kenton Hardware Manufacturing Company, Kenton, Ohio (1890 – 1950), manufacturer
Iron, pigment
$5\frac{7}{8} \times 1\frac{3}{16} \times 1\frac{11}{16}$ in.
2003.236.157

U.S. Tank, c. 1919
Nelson T. Hasenplug, American, designer
Iron
$1\frac{7}{8} \times 4 \times 2\frac{7}{16}$ in.
2003.236.288

Bungalow Bank (or *Cottage with Porch*), c. 1918 – 28
Grey Iron Casting Company, Mount Joy, Pennsylvania (1881 – 1969), manufacturer
Iron, pigment
$3\frac{11}{16} \times 3\frac{1}{8} \times 2\frac{7}{8}$ in.
2003.236.178

General Pershing, c. 1918
Grey Iron Casting Company, Mount Joy, Pennsylvania (1881 – 1969), manufacturer
Iron, bronze electroplate
$7\frac{3}{4} \times 3\frac{1}{2} \times 3\frac{1}{4}$ in.
2003.236.374

Domed Mosque, c. 1920
Kenton Hardware Manufacturing Company, Kenton, Ohio (1890 – 1950), manufacturer
Iron, pigment
$4\frac{3}{8} \times 4\frac{1}{4} \times 2\frac{3}{8}$ in.
2003.236.926

Cow, c. 1920
A. C. Williams Company, Ravenna, Ohio (est. 1886), manufacturer
Iron, pigment
$3\frac{9}{16} \times 5\frac{3}{8} \times 1\frac{9}{16}$ in.
2003.236.284

Teddy Roosevelt, 1919
A. C. Williams Company, Ravenna, Ohio (est. 1886), manufacturer
Iron, pigment
$5\frac{1}{4} \times 3\frac{1}{2} \times 2$ in.
2003.236.377

Buffalo, Small, c. 1920 – 25
Arcade Manufacturing Company, Freeport, Illinois (1868 – 1946), manufacturer
Iron, pigment
$3\frac{1}{8} \times 4\frac{1}{2} \times 1\frac{9}{16}$ in.
2003.236.291

Horse on Wheels (missing wheels), c. 1920
A. C. Williams Company, Ravenna, Ohio (est. 1886), manufacturer
Iron, pigment
$4\frac{3}{4} \times 3\frac{7}{8} \times 1\frac{3}{4}$ in.
2003.236.168

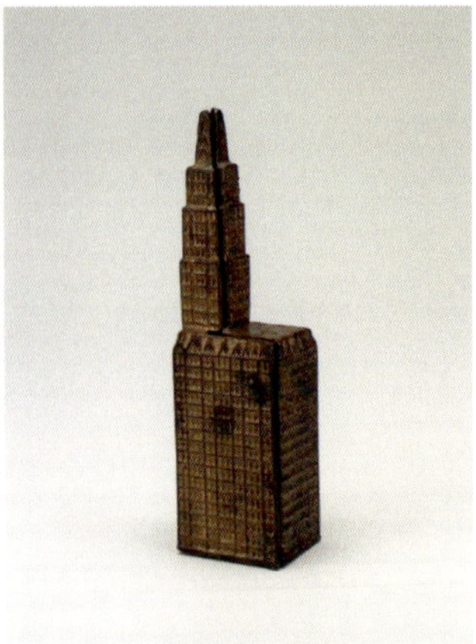

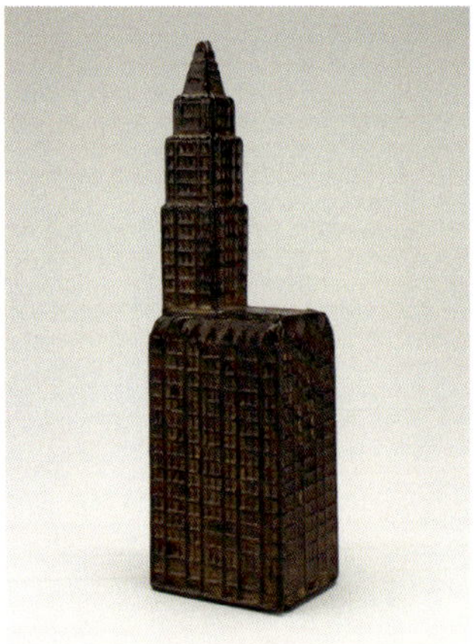

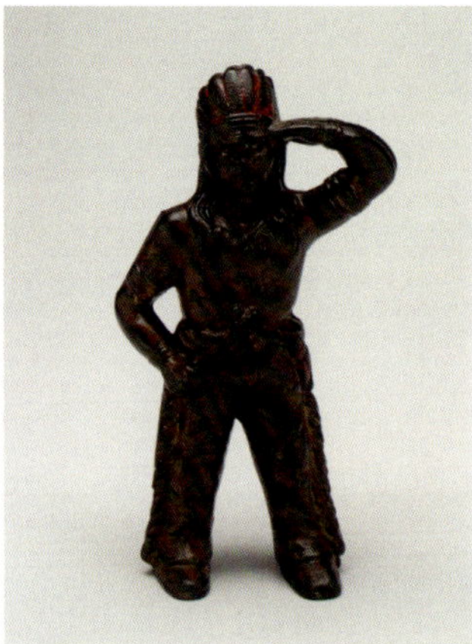

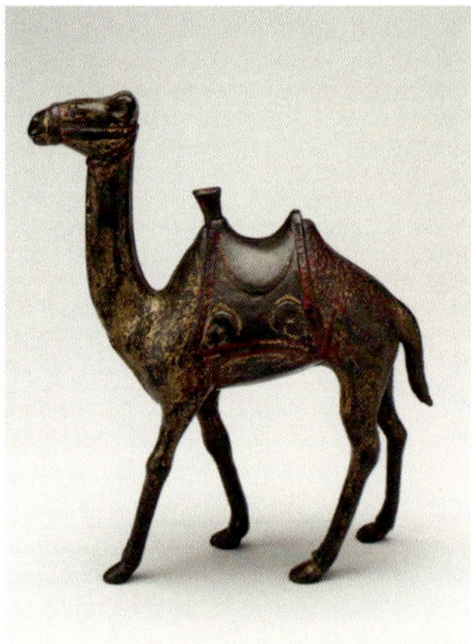

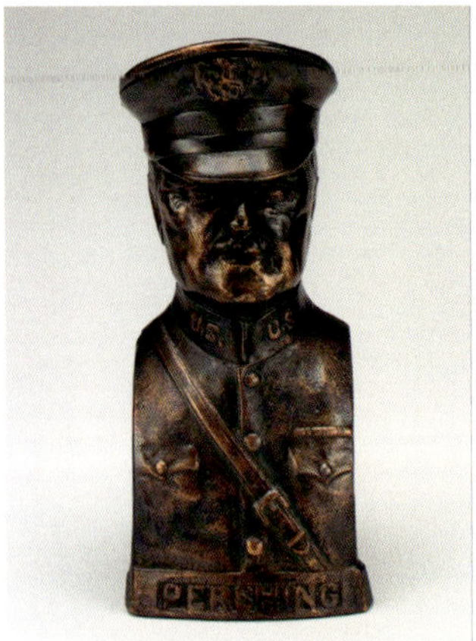
PERSHING

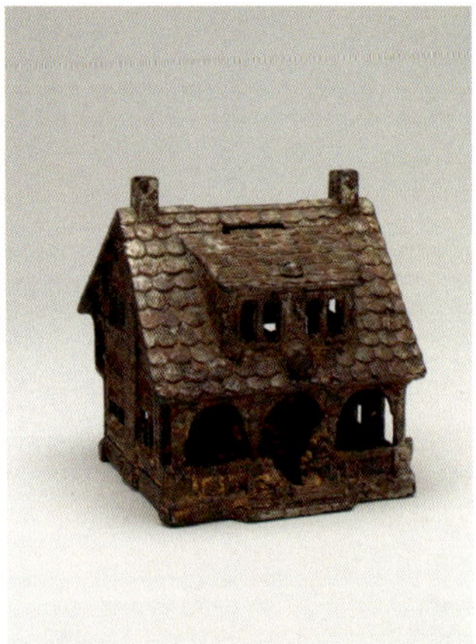

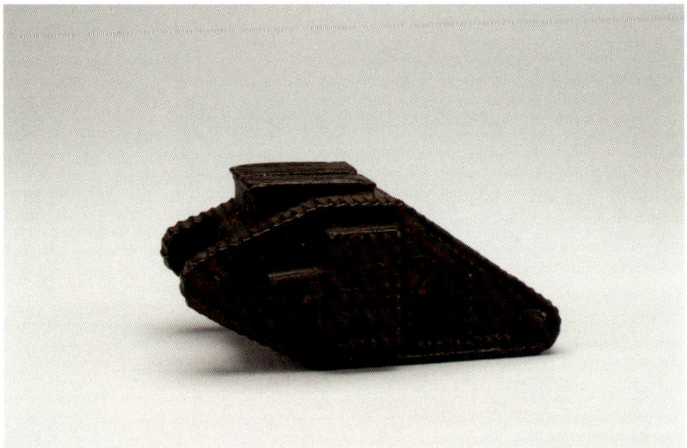

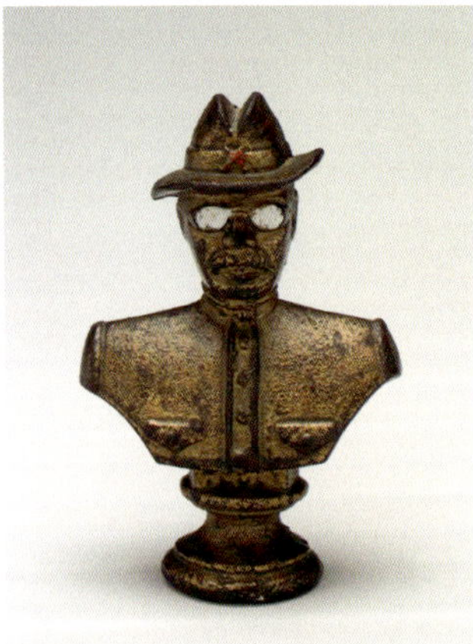

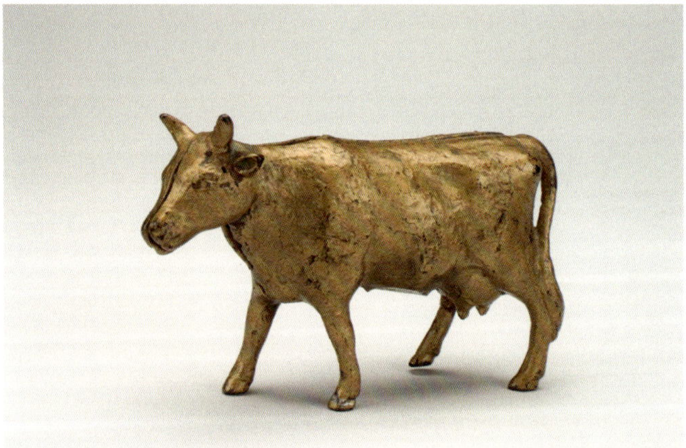

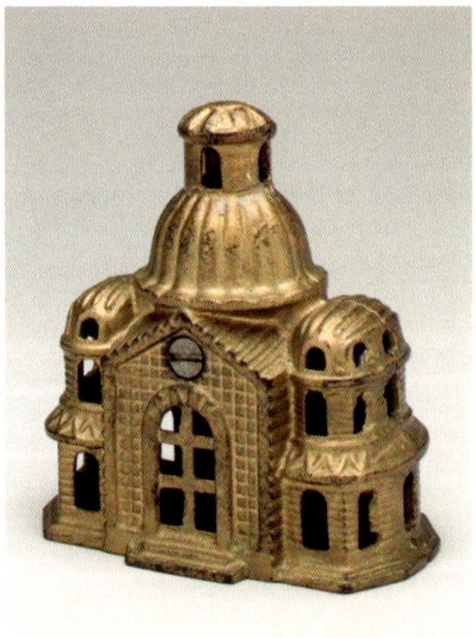

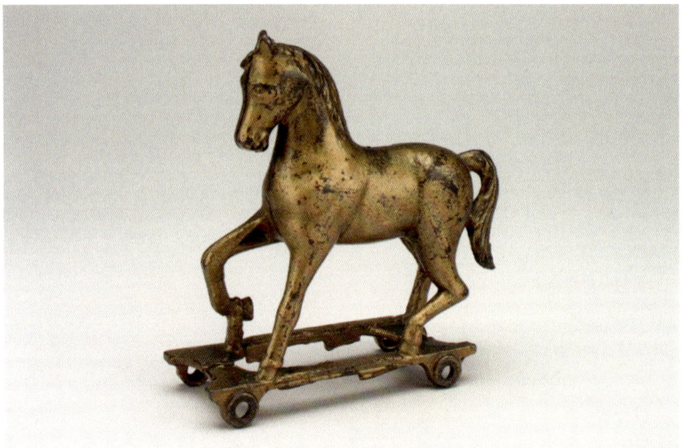

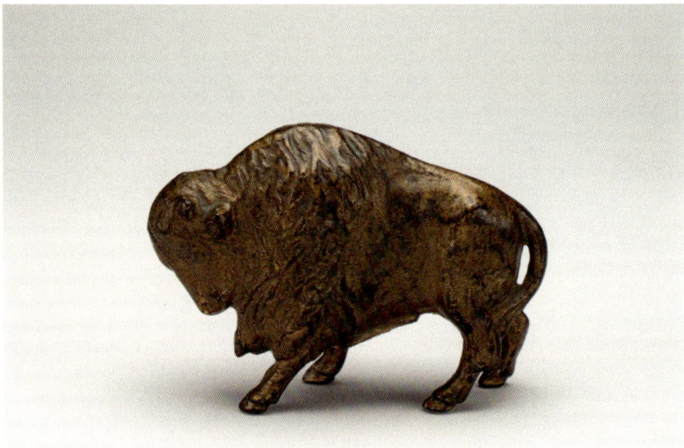

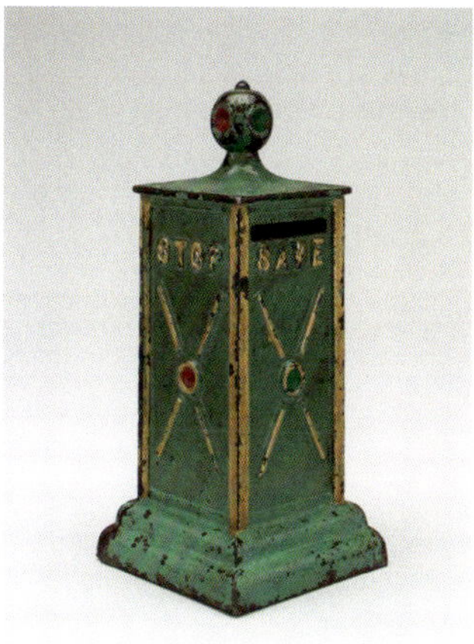
STOP
SAVE

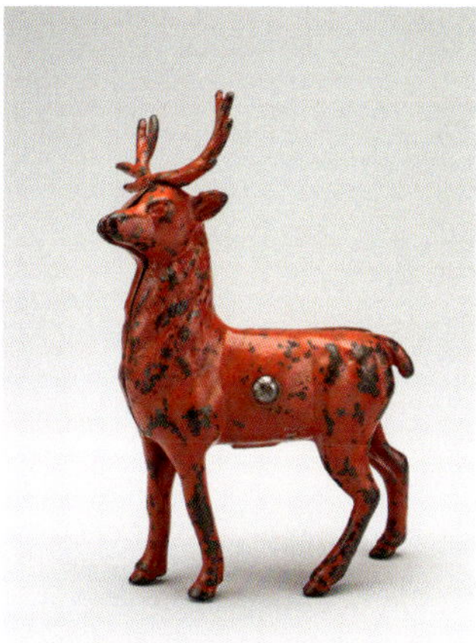

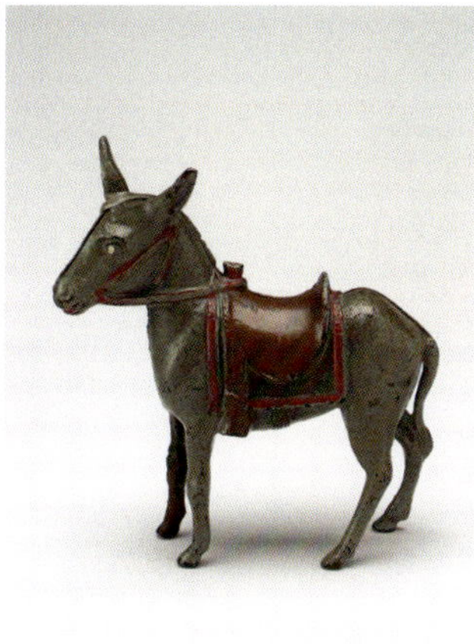

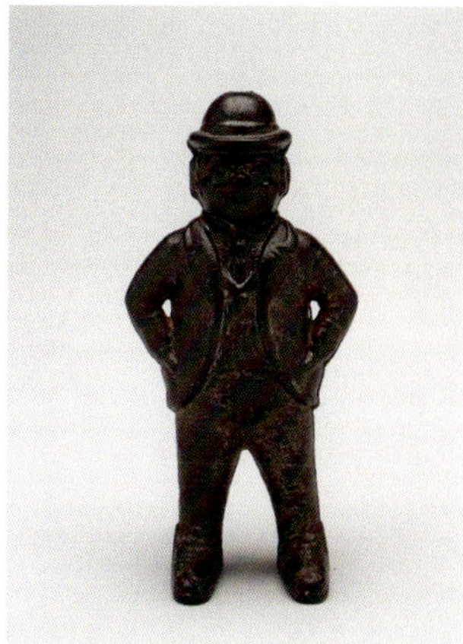

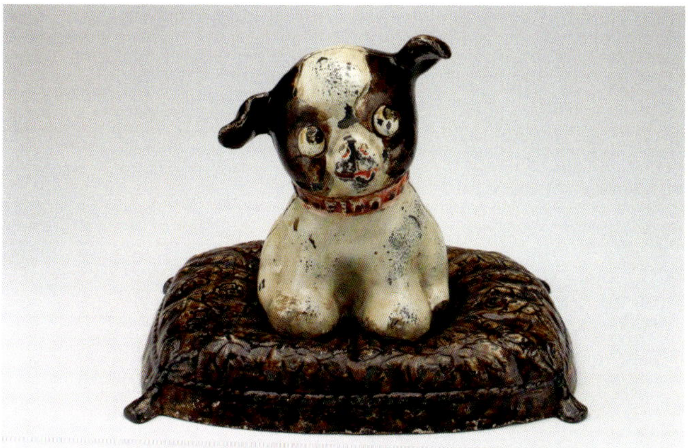

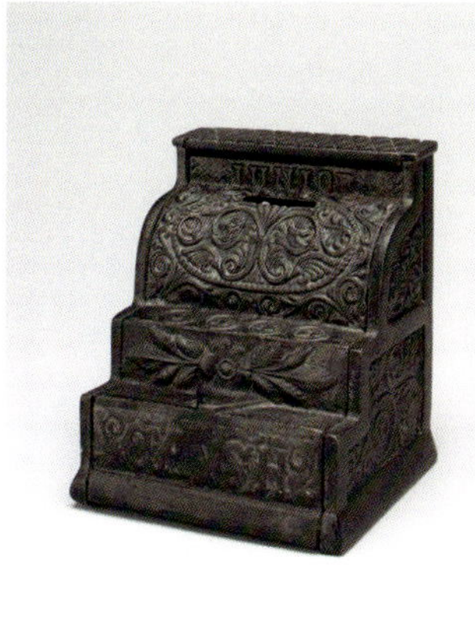

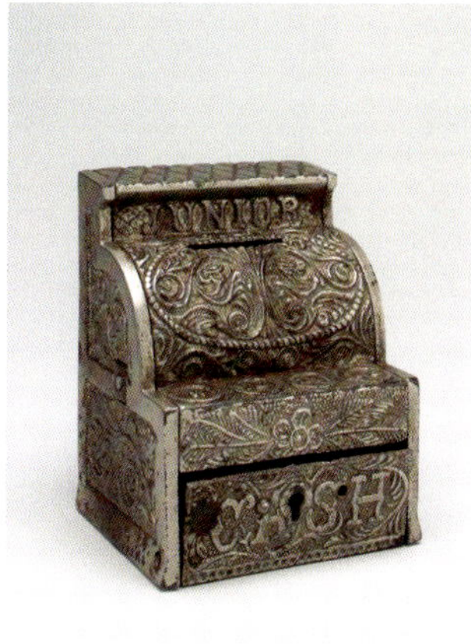
CASH

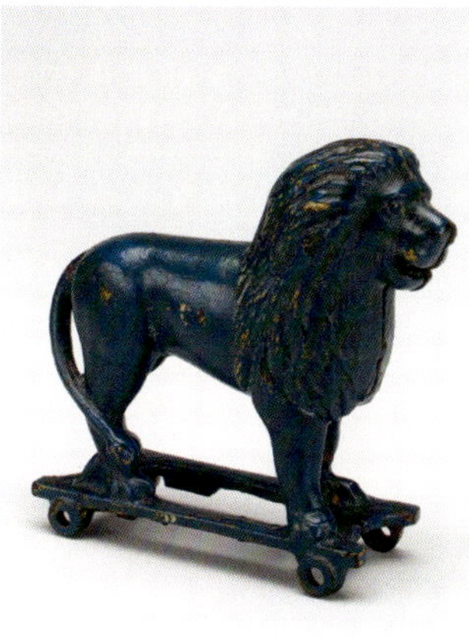

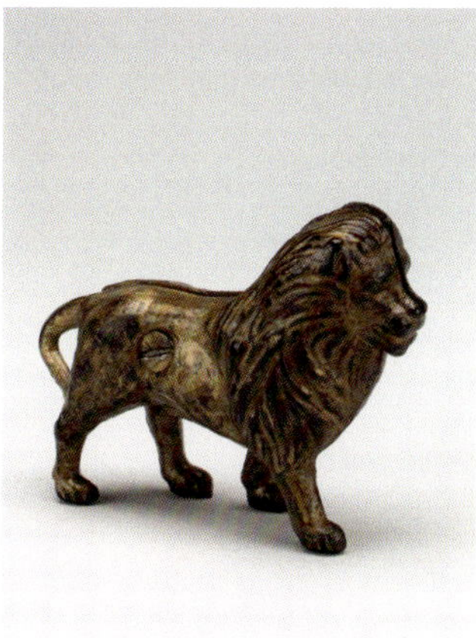

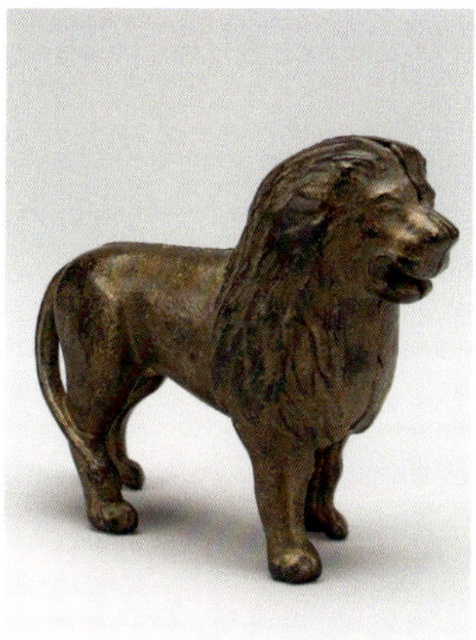

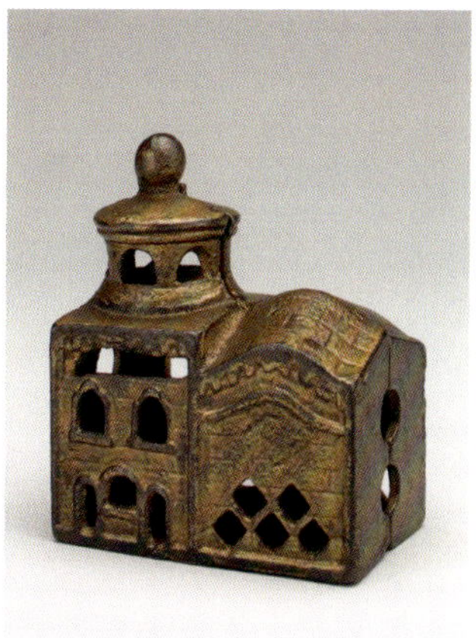

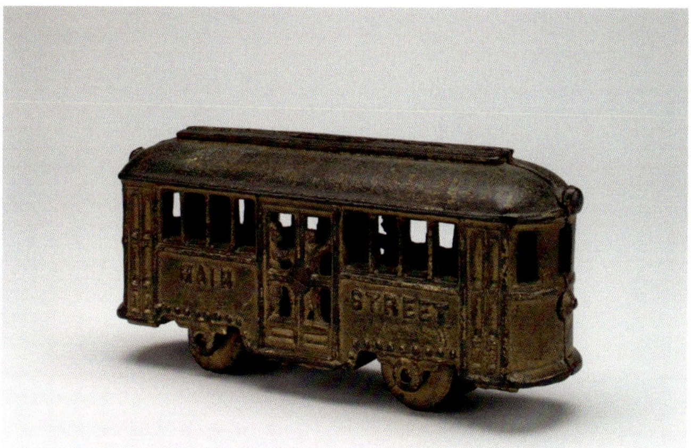
MAIN
STREET

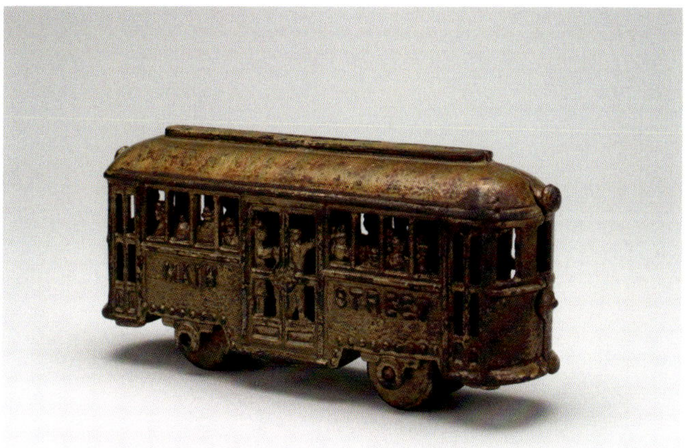
MAIN
STREET

Foxy Grandpa (or *Grandpa Bank*), c. 1920s
Hubley Manufacturing Company, Lancaster, Pennsylvania (est. 1894), manufacturer
Iron, pigment
5 1/2 x 2 11/16 x 1 1/2 in.
2003.236.636

Donkey, Large, c. 1920s
A. C. Williams Company, Ravenna, Ohio (est. 1886), manufacturer
Iron, pigment
6 7/8 x 2 1/2 x 7 3/4 in.
2003.236.405

Deer, c. 1920s
A. C. Williams Company, Ravenna, Ohio (est. 1886), manufacturer
Iron, pigment
5 7/8 x 2 1/4 x 4 1/4 in.
2003.236.404

Stop Sign, Large, 1920
Dent Hardware Company, Fullerton, Pennsylvania (1895 – 1973), manufacturer
Iron, pigment
5 3/4 x 2 1/2 x 2 1/2 in.
2003.236.955

Junior Cash Register, Small, c. 1920s
J. & E. Stevens Company, Cromwell, Connecticut (1843 – 1950s), manufacturer
Iron
4 3/16 x 3 1/2 x 3 in.
2003.236.393

Junior Cash Register, Large, c. 1920s
J. & E. Stevens Company, Cromwell, Connecticut (1843 – 1950s), manufacturer
Iron
5 1/8 x 4 5/8 x 4 3/16 in.
2003.236.460

Fido on Pillow, c. 1920s
Hubley Manufacturing Company, Lancaster, Pennsylvania (est. 1894), manufacturer
Iron, pigment
6 x 7 1/2 x 5 5/16 in.
2003.236.773

Mosque, c. 1920s
A. C. Williams Company, Ravenna, Ohio (est. 1886), manufacturer
Iron, pigment
2 13/16 x 2 7/16 x 1 5/8 in.
2003.236.660

Lion, Tail Right, c. 1920s
A. C. Williams Company, Ravenna, Ohio (est. 1886), manufacturer
Iron, pigment
3 9/16 x 4 1/2 x 1 3/8 in.
2003.236.173

Lion, Tail Left, c. 1920s
A. C. Williams Company, Ravenna, Ohio (est. 1886), manufacturer
Iron, pigment
2 1/2 x 3 5/8 x 1 in.
2003.236.174

Lion on Wheels, c. 1920s
A. C. Williams Company, Ravenna, Ohio (est. 1886), manufacturer
Iron, pigment
4 3/16 x 4 11/16 x 2 3/4 in.
2003.236.175

Main Street Trolley, with People, c. 1920s
A. C. Williams Company, Ravenna, Ohio (est. 1886), manufacturer
Iron, pigment
3 3/16 x 6 13/16 x 1 3/4 in.
2003.236.286

Main Street Trolley, No People, c. 1920s
A. C. Williams Company, Ravenna, Ohio (est. 1886), manufacturer
Iron, pigment
3 1/8 x 6 13/16 x 1 7/8 in.
2003.236.287

Pete the Pig, American Mission to Lepers, c. 1920s
A. C. Williams Company, Ravenna, Ohio (est. 1886), manufacturer
Iron, pigment
$2\frac{7}{8}$ x $2\frac{3}{16}$ x $4\frac{9}{16}$ in.
2003.236.975

My Pet Horse, c. 1920s
Arcade Manufacturing Company, Freeport, Illinois (1868 – 1946), manufacturer
Iron, pigment
$4\frac{1}{4}$ x 5 x $1\frac{1}{4}$ in.
2003.236.161

Mosque, c. 1920s
A. C. Williams Company, Ravenna, Ohio (est. 1886), manufacturer
Iron, pigment
$3\frac{5}{8}$ x $2\frac{1}{2}$ x $1\frac{5}{8}$ in.
2003.236.774

Red Goose Shoes, c. 1920s
Arcade Manufacturing Company, Freeport, Illinois (1868 – 1946), manufacturer
Iron, pigment
$4\frac{5}{8}$ x $2\frac{7}{8}$ x 2 in.
2003.236.940

Prancing Horse on Oval Base, c. 1920s
Attributed to Hubley Manufacturing Company, Lancaster, Pennsylvania (est. 1894), or A. C. Williams Company, Ravenna, Ohio (est. 1886), manufacturer
Iron, pigment
$5\frac{1}{8}$ x 5 x $1\frac{3}{4}$ in.
2003.236.999

Prancing Horse, c. 1920s
Arcade Manufacturing Company, Freeport, Illinois (1868 – 1946), manufacturer
Iron, pigment
$4\frac{1}{4}$ x $4\frac{5}{16}$ x $1\frac{1}{8}$ in.
2003.236.163

Tank Bank USA, 1918, c. 1920s
A. C. Williams Company, Ravenna, Ohio (est. 1886), manufacturer
Iron, pigment
$2\frac{1}{2}$ x 2 x $4\frac{3}{4}$ in.
2003.236.312

Red Goose Shoes, c. 1920s
Iron, pigment
$3\frac{7}{8}$ x $1\frac{1}{2}$ x 2 in.
2003.236.947

Red Goose Shoes, c. 1920s
Arcade Manufacturing Company, Freeport, Illinois (1868 – 1946), manufacturer
Iron, pigment
$3\frac{3}{4}$ x $1\frac{3}{8}$ x 2 in.
2003.236.946

Lion on Tub, Small, c. 1920 – 30s
A. C. Williams Company, Ravenna, Ohio (est. 1886), manufacturer
Iron, pigment
$4\frac{3}{8}$ x 2 x 2 in.
2003.236.838

Grandfather Clock, c. 1920 – 30s
Iron, pigment
$9\frac{1}{4}$ x $3\frac{7}{16}$ x $1\frac{5}{8}$ in.
2003.236.834

Camel, Small, c. 1920 – 30s
Hubley Manufacturing Company, Lancaster, Pennsylvania (est. 1894), or A. C. Williams Company, Ravenna, Ohio (est. 1886), manufacturer
Iron, pigment
$4\frac{5}{8}$ x $4\frac{3}{16}$ x $1\frac{5}{16}$ in.
2003.236.500

Lion, Fine-Haired Mane, c. 1920 – 30
A. C. Williams Company, Ravenna, Ohio (est. 1886), manufacturer
Iron, pigment
$3\frac{5}{16}$ x $4\frac{7}{8}$ x $1\frac{5}{16}$ in.
2003.236.171

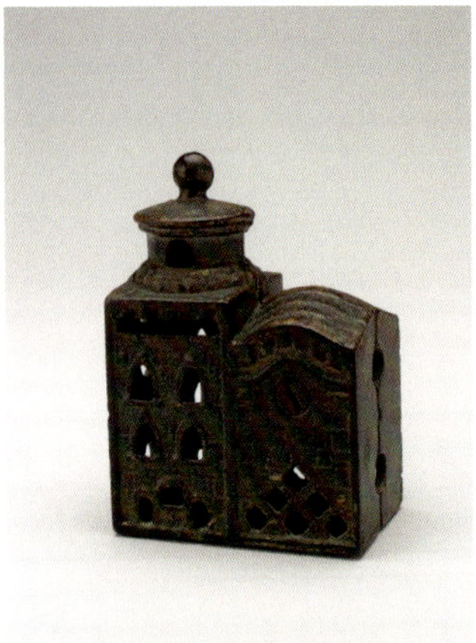

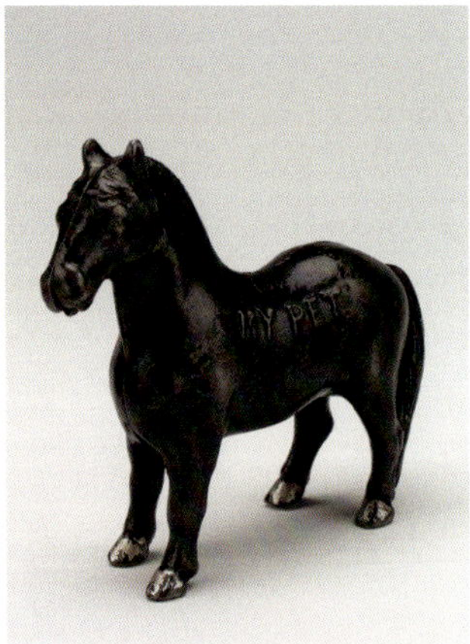
MY PET

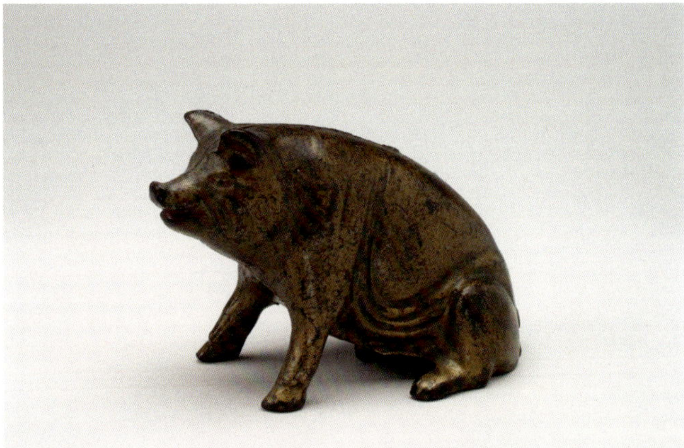

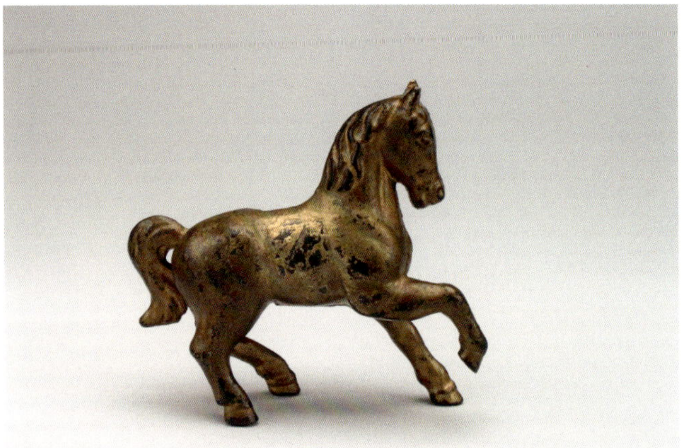

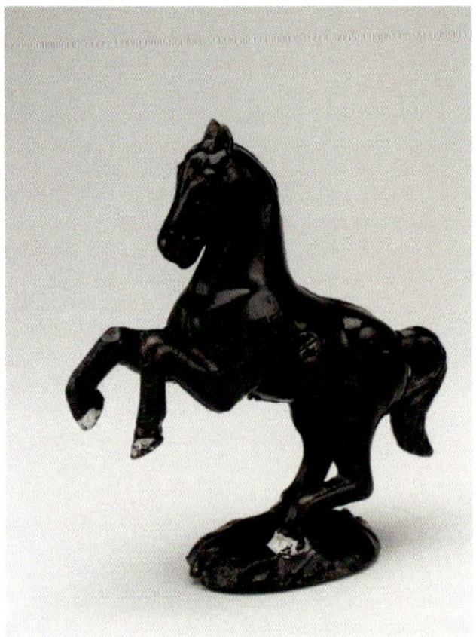

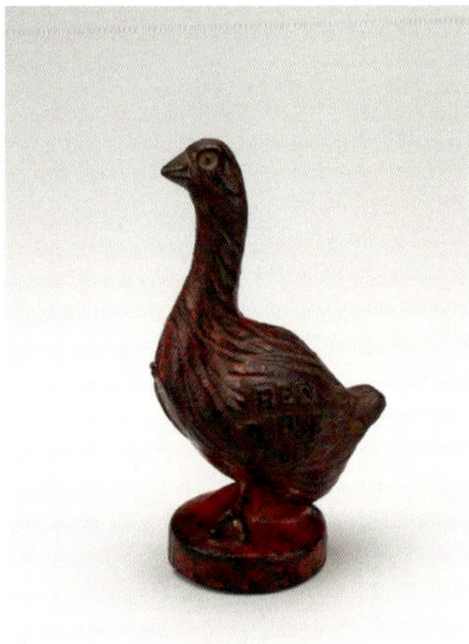

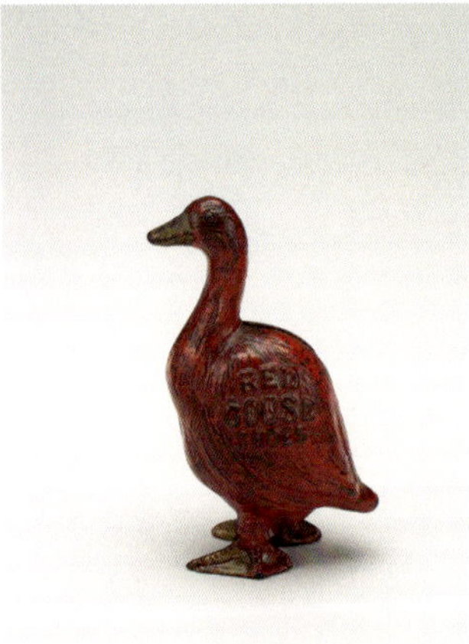

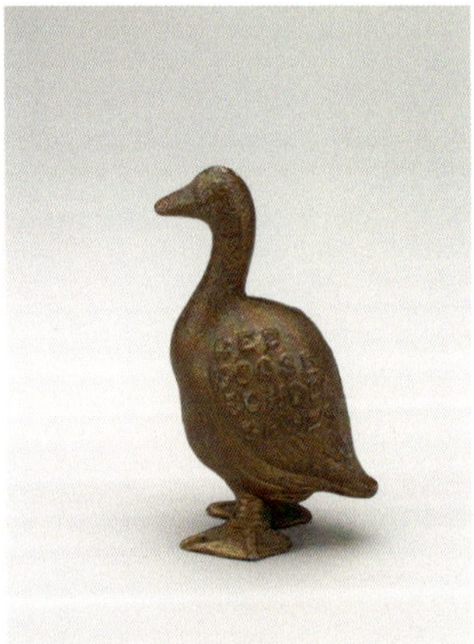

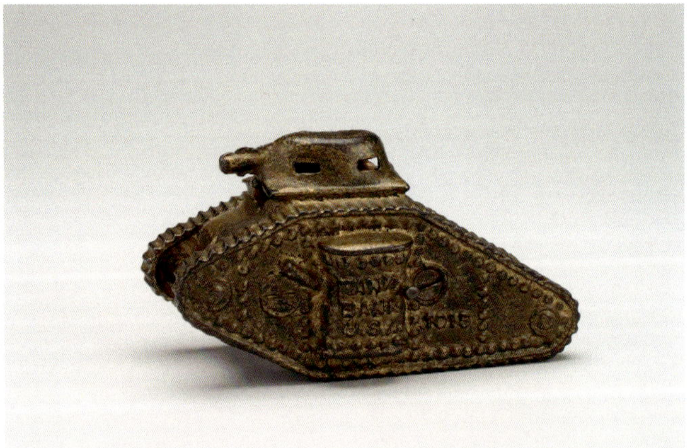

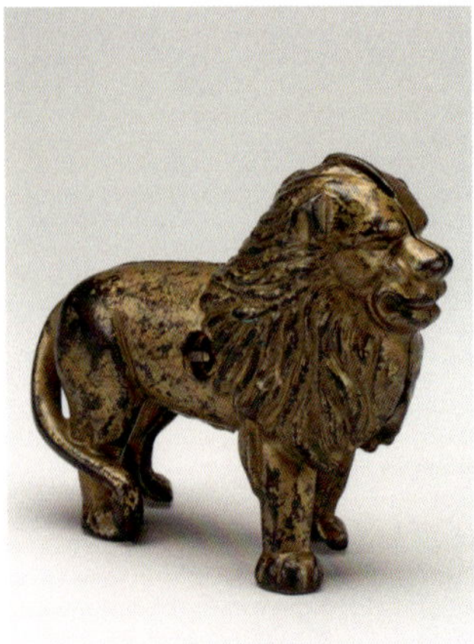

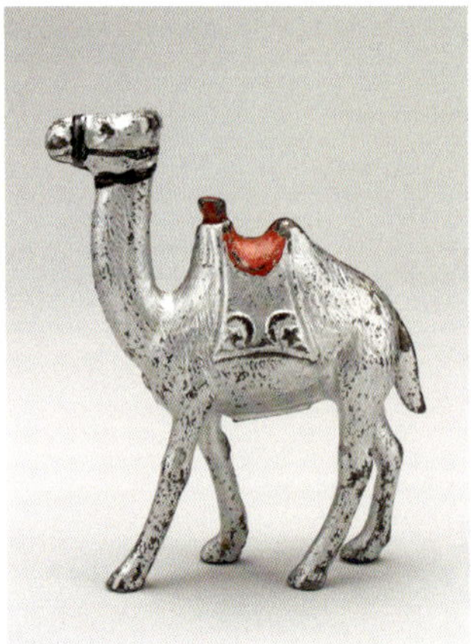

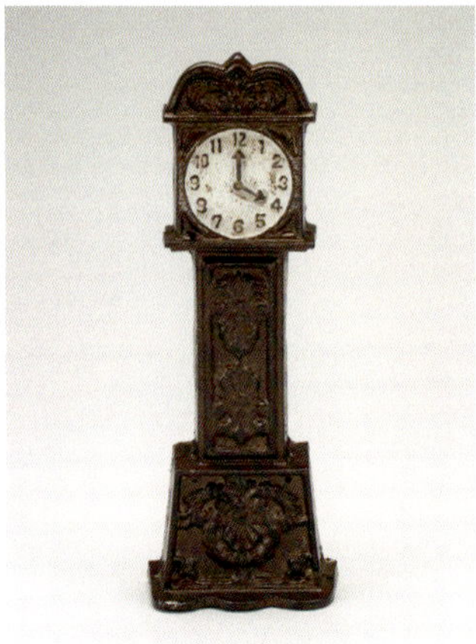

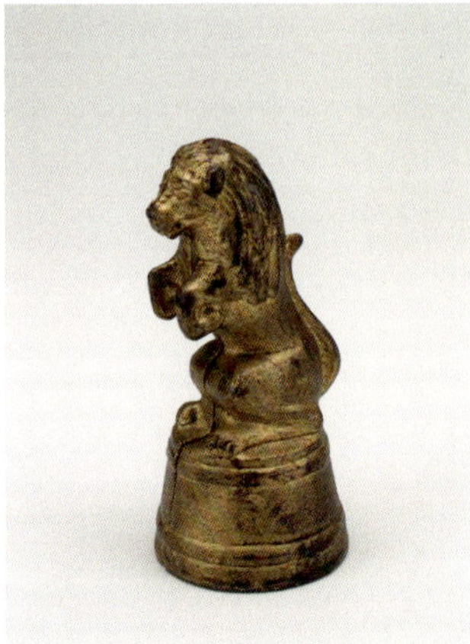

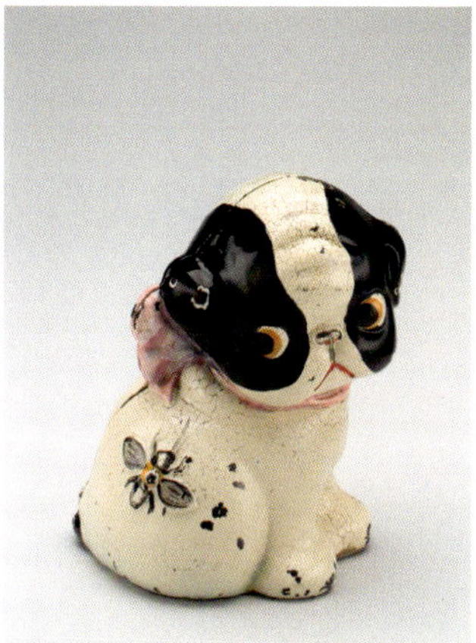

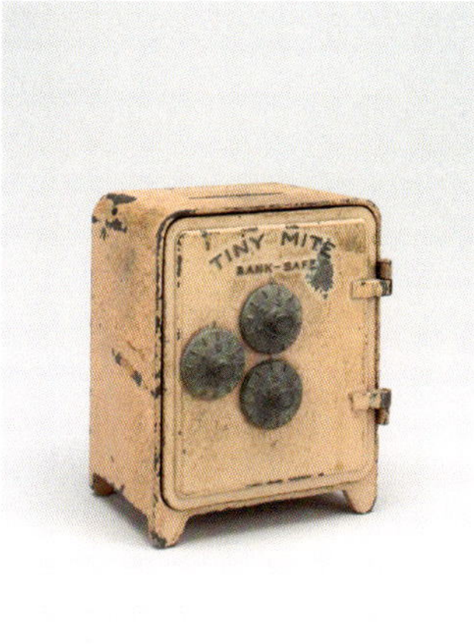
TINY MITE
BANK-SAFE

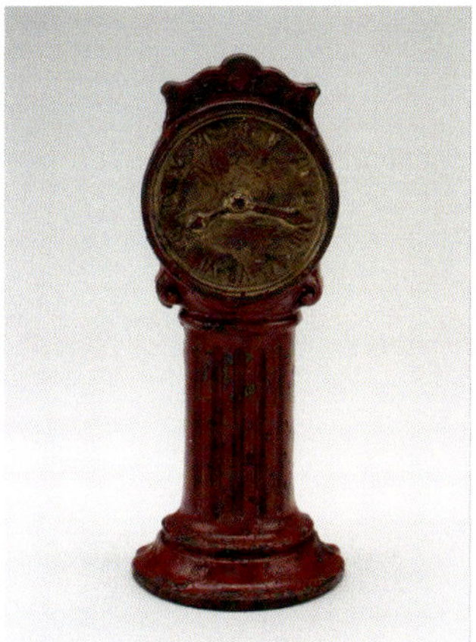

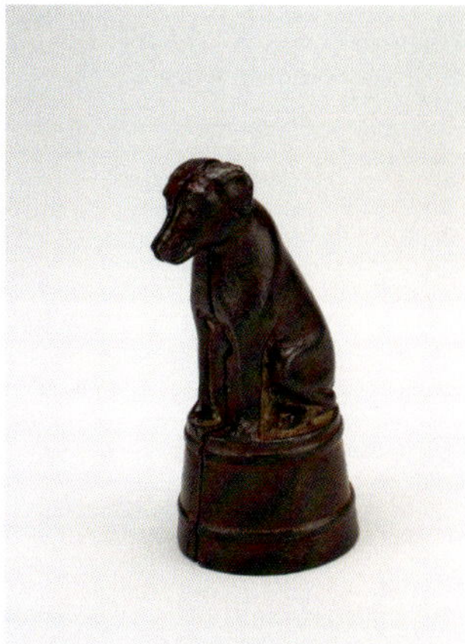

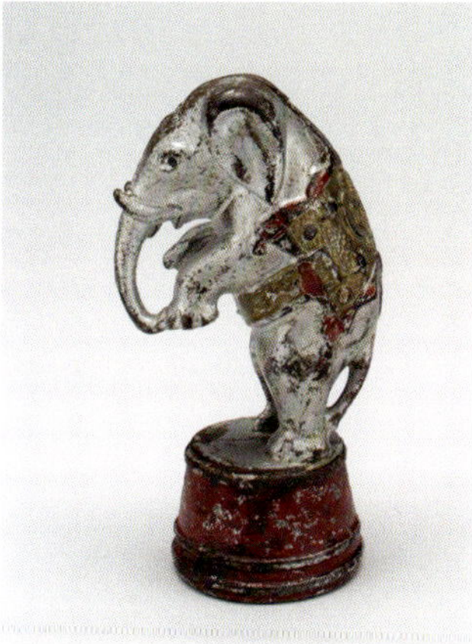

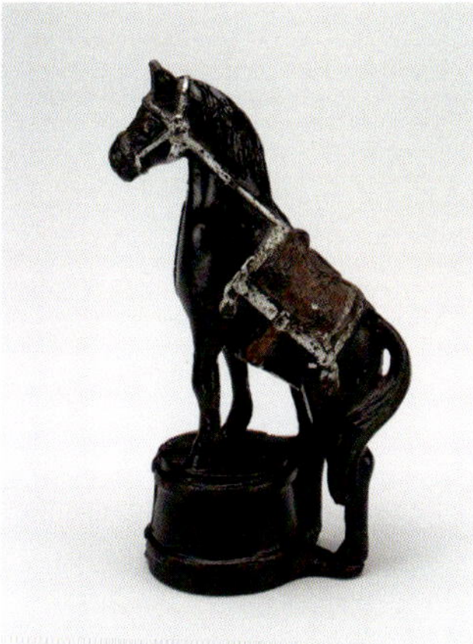

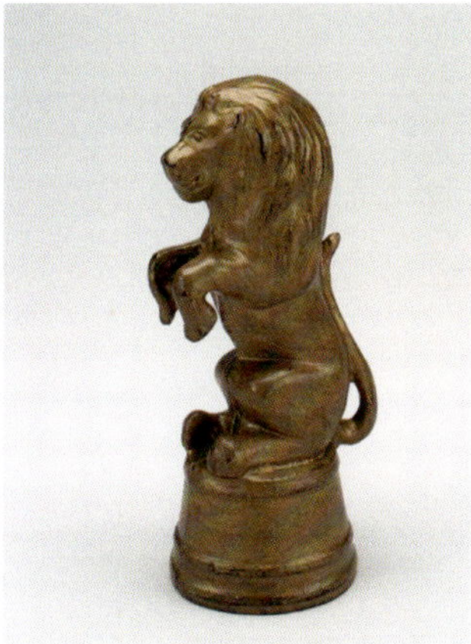

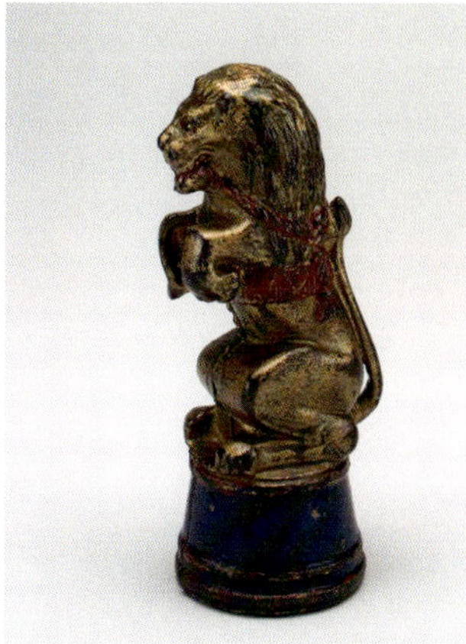

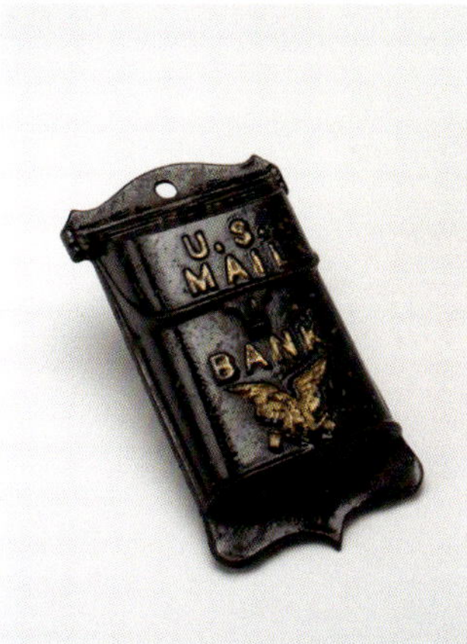
U.S.
MAIL
BANK

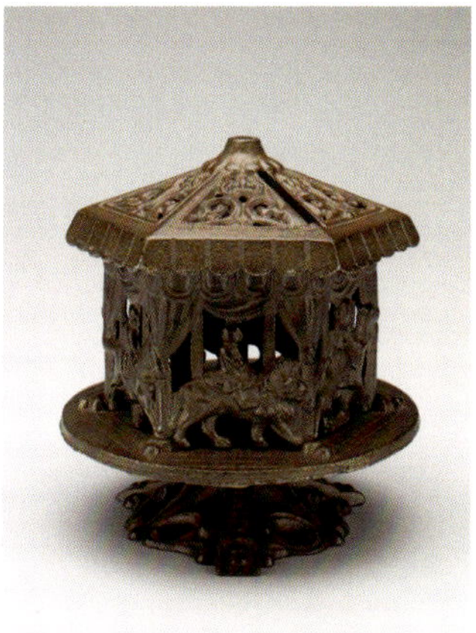

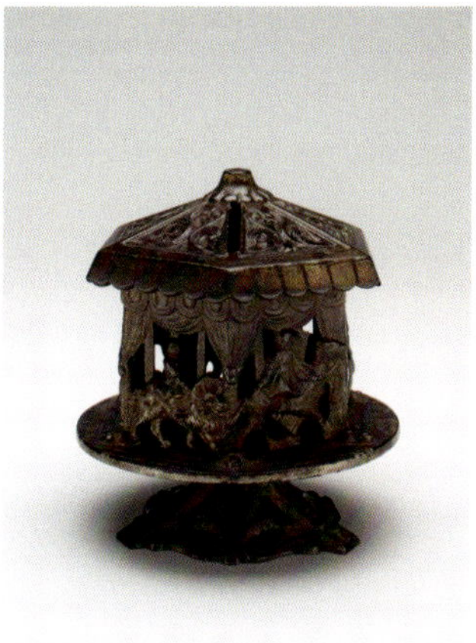

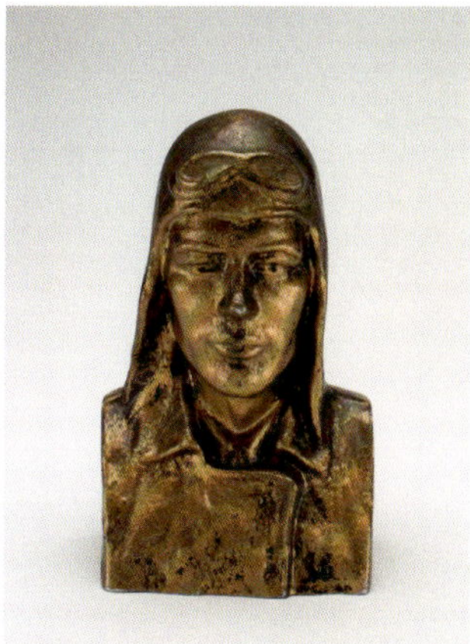

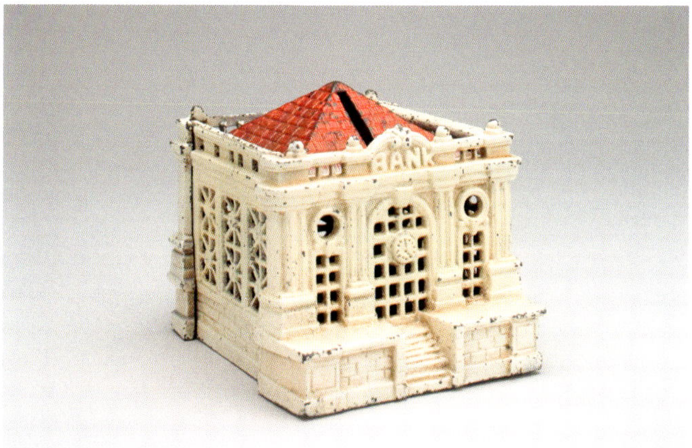
BANK

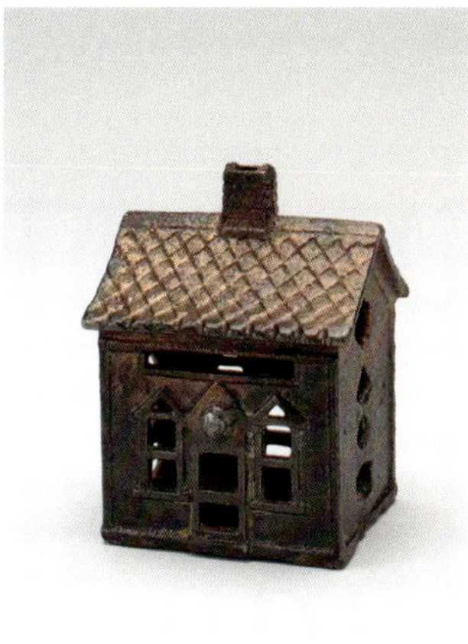

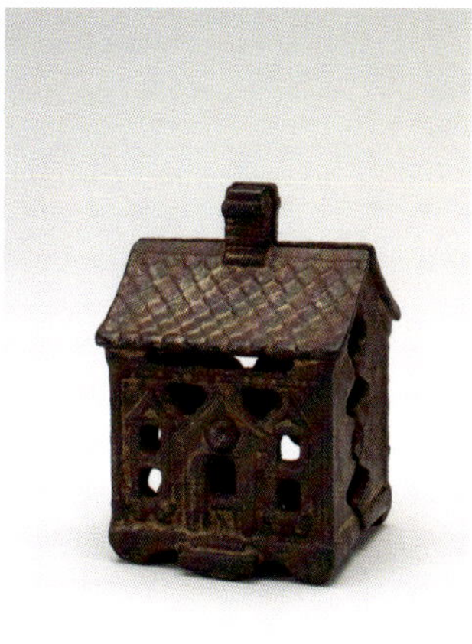

Dog on Tub, c. 1920s – 34
A. C. Williams Company, Ravenna, Ohio (est. 1886), manufacturer
Iron, pigment
4 3/16 x 1 15/16 x 2 1/16 in.
2003.236.1000

Street Clock, c. 1920 – 31
A. C. Williams Company, Ravenna, Ohio (est. 1886), manufacturer
Iron, pigment
6 1/8 x 2 5/16 x 1 13/16 in.
2003.236.950

Tiny-Mite, c. 1920 – 30s
Arrow Specialties, Los Angeles, manufacturer
Iron, pigment
3 9/16 x 2 13/16 x 1 7/8 in.
2003.236.746

Puppo, c. 1920 – 30s
Hubley Manufacturing Company, Lancaster, Pennsylvania (est. 1894), manufacturer
Iron, pigment
5 x 3 7/8 x 3 3/8 in.
2003.236.771

Lion on Tub, Decorated, c. 1920s – 34
A. C. Williams Company, Ravenna, Ohio (est. 1886), manufacturer
Iron, pigment
5 1/2 x 2 1/8 x 2 1/8 in.
2003.236.998

Lion on Tub, Small, c. 1920s – 34
A. C. Williams Company, Ravenna, Ohio (est. 1886), manufacturer
Iron, pigment
5 1/2 x 2 x 2 5/8 in.
2003.236.1027

Horse on Tub, Decorated, c. 1920s – 34
A. C. Williams Company, Ravenna, Ohio (est. 1886), manufacturer
Iron, pigment
4 5/16 x 3 3/16 x 1 5/8 in.
2003.236.1007

Elephant on Tub, Decorated, c. 1920s – 34
A. C. Williams Company, Ravenna, Ohio (est. 1886), manufacturer
Iron, pigment
5 3/8 x 2 1/16 x 2 1/4 in.
2003.236.1024

Lindy Bank, c. 1927
Grannis and Tolton, Inc., Detroit, manufacturer
Iron, pigment
6 3/8 x 3 7/8 x 2 11/16 in.
2003.236.375

Merry-Go-Round, c. 1925 – 28
Grey Iron Casting Company, Mount Joy, Pennsylvania (1881 – 1969), manufacturer
Iron, nickel
4 7/8 x 4 1/2 x 4 1/2 in.
2003.236.401

Merry-Go-Round, c. 1925 – 28
Grey Iron Casting Company, Mount Joy, Pennsylvania (1881 – 1969), manufacturer
Iron
4 7/8 x 4 1/2 x 4 1/2 in.
2003.236.400

U.S. Mail Bank, Hanging, c. 1921 – 34
A. C. Williams Company, Ravenna, Ohio (est. 1886), manufacturer
Iron, pigment
5 1/4 x 2 1/2 x 1 in.
2003.236.148

One-Story House, 1927
Kenton Hardware Manufacturing Company, Kenton, Ohio (1890 – 1950), manufacturer
Iron, pigment
3 1/8 x 2 x 1 13/16 in.
2003.236.780

One-Story House, 1927
Kenton Hardware Manufacturing Company, Kenton, Ohio (1890 – 1950), manufacturer
Iron, pigment
2 15/16 x 2 x 1 13/16 in.
2003.236.657

U.S. Treasury Bank, c. 1925 – 28
Grey Iron Casting Company, Mount Joy, Pennsylvania (1881 – 1969), manufacturer
Iron, metal, pigment
3 x 3 1/8 x 3 5/8 in.
2003.236.1053

Two-Car Garage, c. 1927 – 31
A. C. Williams Company, Ravenna, Ohio (est. 1886), manufacturer
Iron, pigment
2 1/4 x 2 13/16 x 2 1/2 in.
2003.236.656

Radio Bank, Three Dials, c. 1927 – 31
Kenton Hardware Manufacturing Company, Kenton, Ohio (1890 – 1950), manufacturer
Iron, pigment
3 x 4 3/4 x 2 7/8 in.
2003.236.997

Standing Mailbox, Small, 1928
Hubley Manufacturing Company, Lancaster, Pennsylvania (est. 1894), manufacturer
Iron, pigment
3 3/16 x 1 7/8 x 1 1/2 in.
2003.236.994

Seated Bulldog, c. 1928
Hubley Manufacturing Company, Lancaster, Pennsylvania (est. 1894), manufacturer
Iron, pigment
3 7/8 x 4 7/8 x 2 7/16 in.
2003.236.977

Coin Deposit Bank, c. 1928
Grey Iron Casting Company, Mount Joy, Pennsylvania (1881 – 1969), manufacturer
Iron, pigment
4 13/16 x 2 15/16 x 2 3/4 in.
2003.236.768

Trumpeting Elephant, c. 1930
Vanio, United States, manufacturer
Iron, pigment
5 1/4 x 3 x 3 1/2 in.
2003.236.1076

No. 40 Safe, c. 1929
J. & E. Stevens Company, Cromwell, Connecticut (1843 – 1950s), manufacturer
Iron
6 x 4 3/4 x 4 1/2 in.
2003.236.468

Saddle Horse, 1928
Grey Iron Casting Company, Mount Joy, Pennsylvania (1881 – 1969), manufacturer
Iron, pigment
4 7/16 x 5 11/16 x 1 1/8 in.
2003.236.160

Dutch Girl Holding Flowers, c. 1930s
Hubley Manufacturing Company, Lancaster, Pennsylvania (est. 1894), manufacturer
Iron, pigment
5 1/4 x 3 x 2 5/8 in.
2003.236.617

Dutch Boy on Barrel, c. 1930s
Hubley Manufacturing Company, Lancaster, Pennsylvania (est. 1894), manufacturer
Iron, pigment
5 5/8 x 2 9/16 x 3 3/16 in.
2003.236.618

Art Deco Elephant, c. 1930s
Arcade Manufacturing Company, Freeport, Illinois (1868 – 1946), manufacturer
Iron, pigment
4 1/4 x 4 1/2 x 1 5/16 in.
2003.236.1026

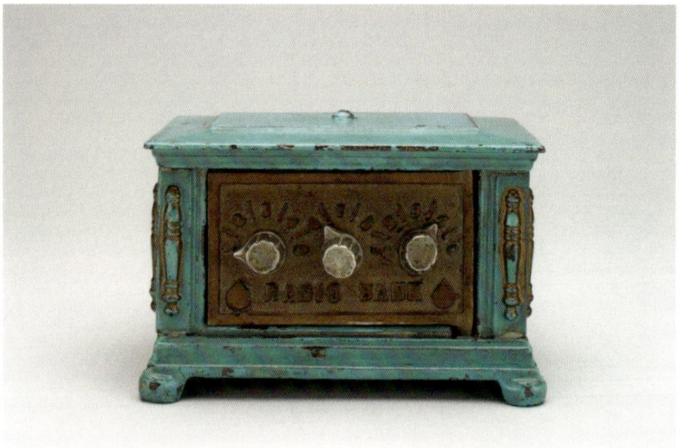

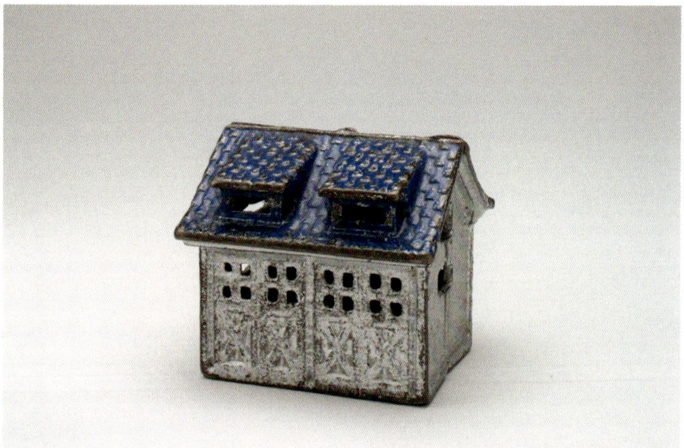

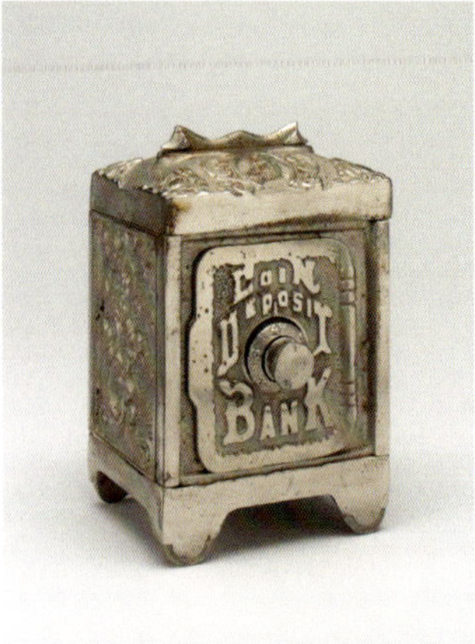
COIN
DEPOSIT
BANK

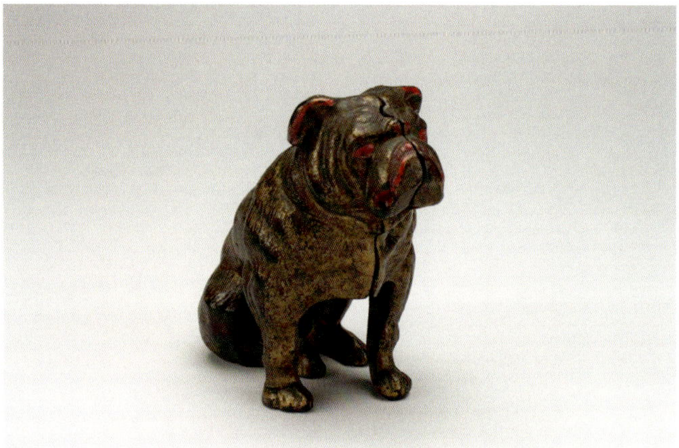

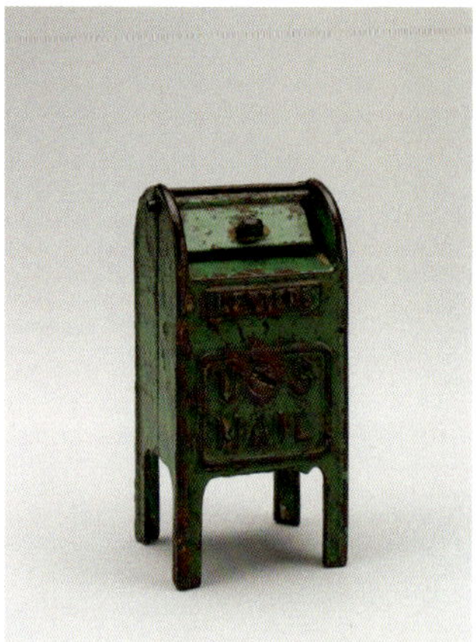

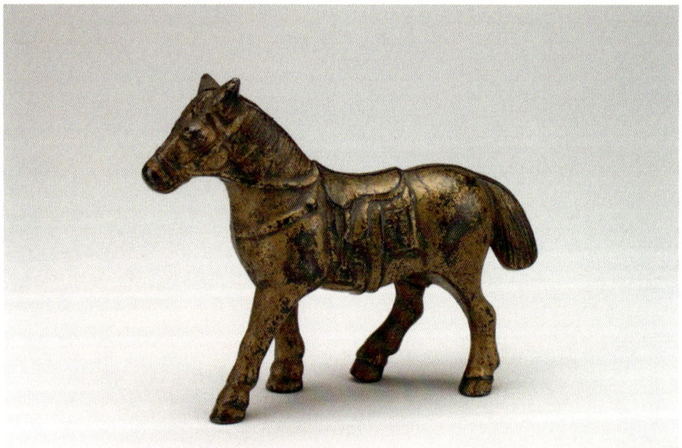

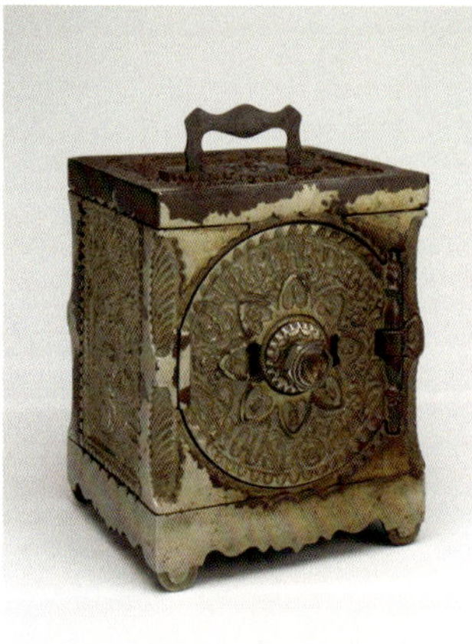

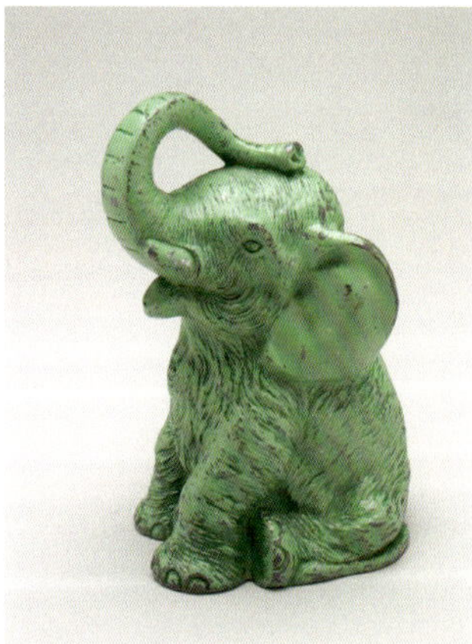

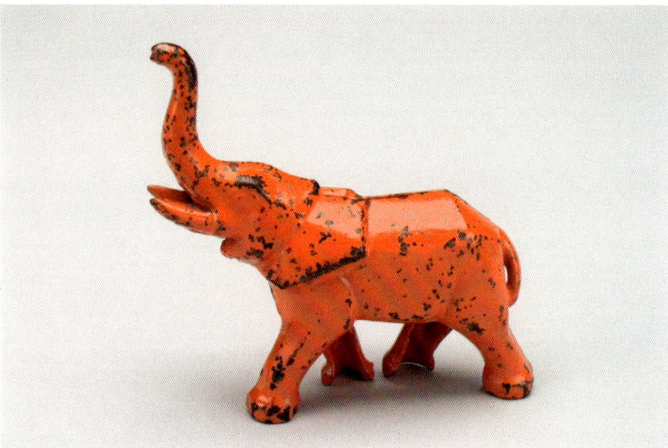

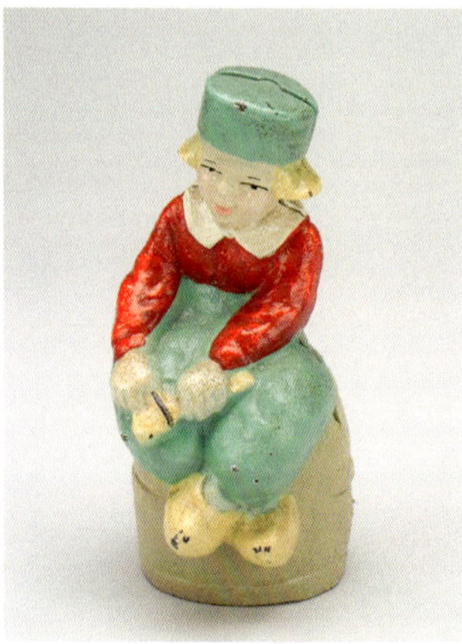

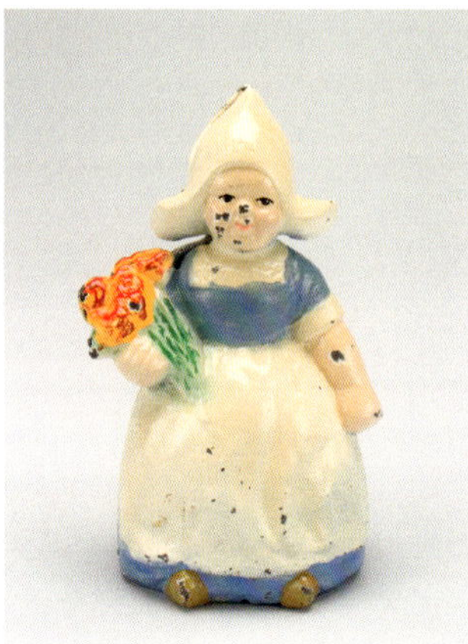

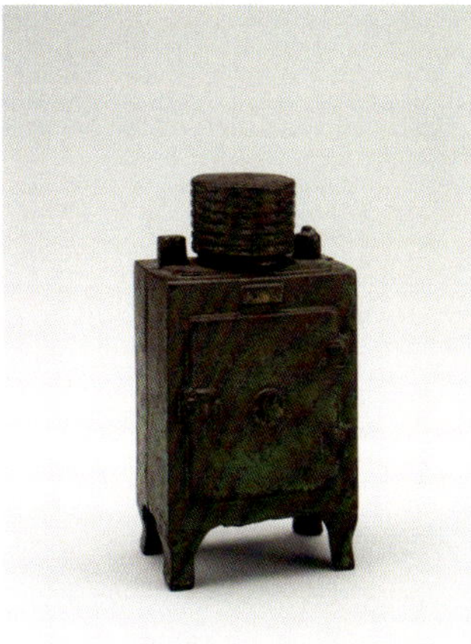

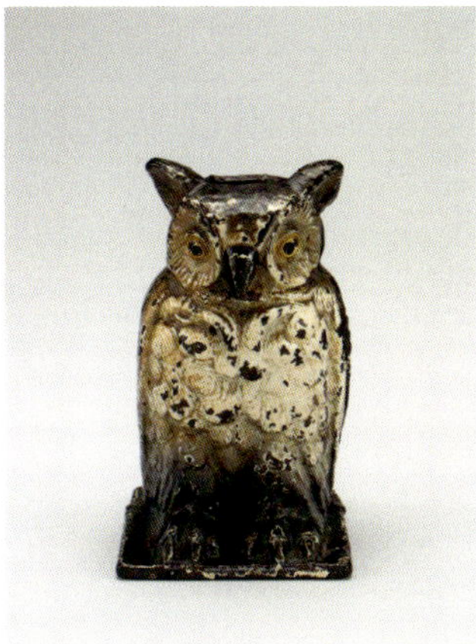

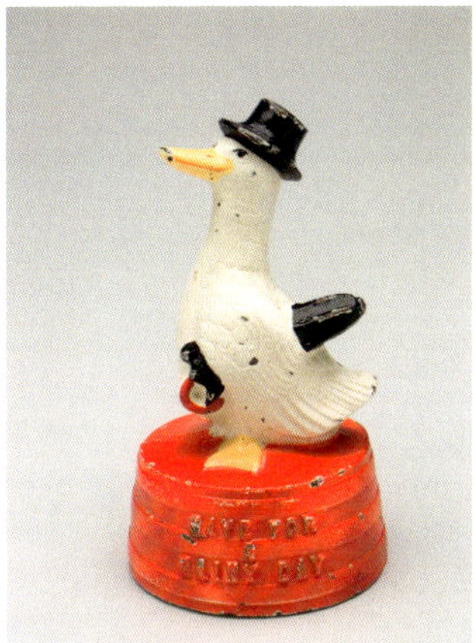
SAVE FOR A RAINY DAY

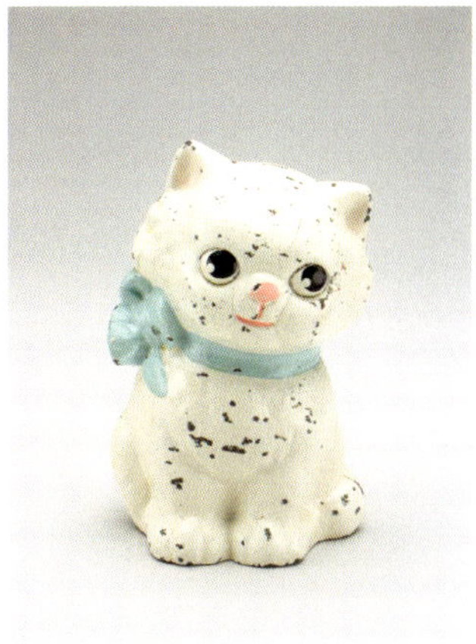

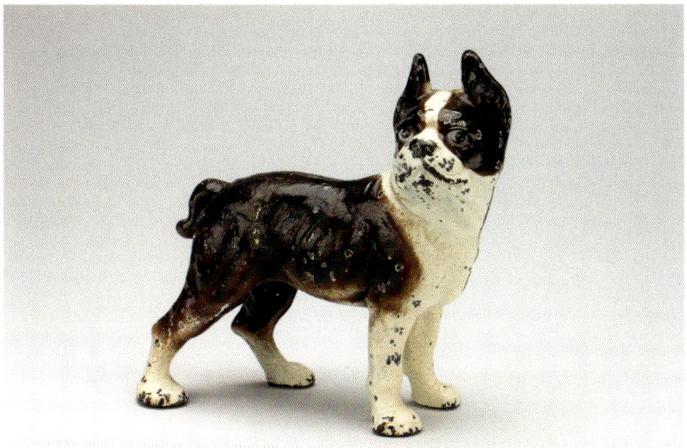

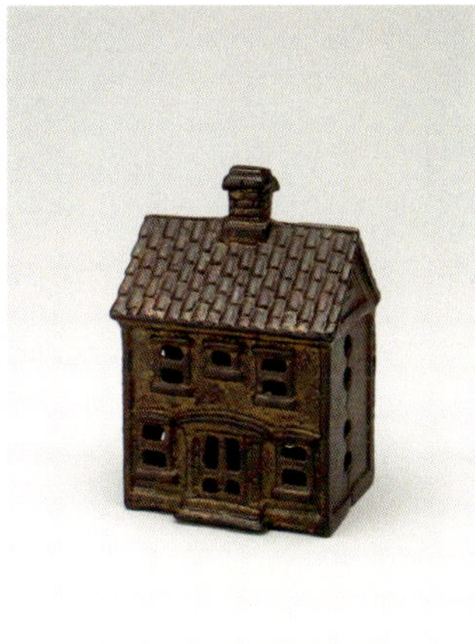

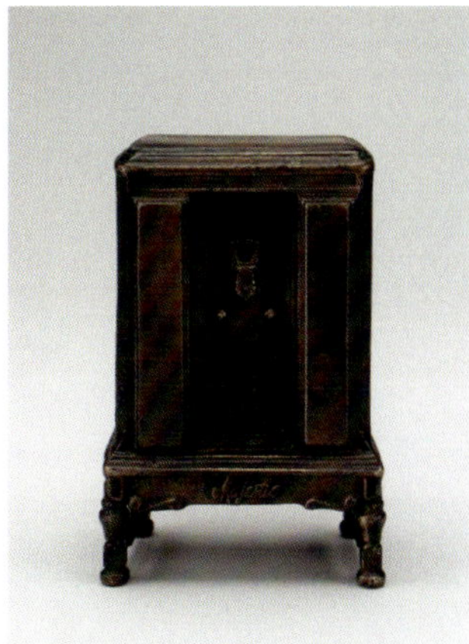

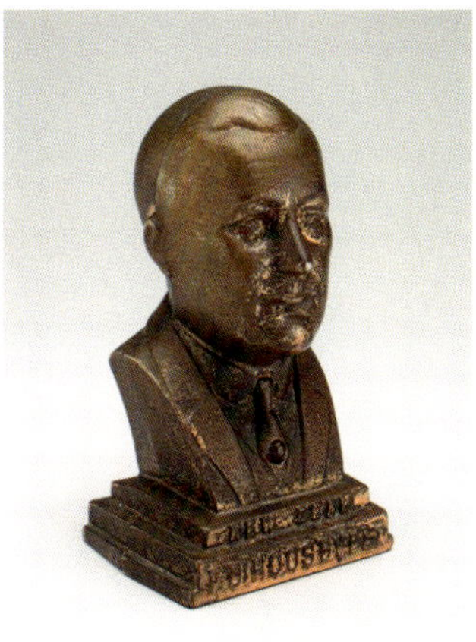

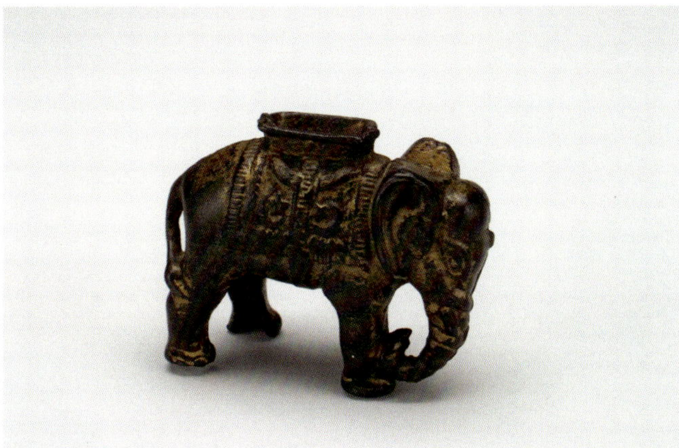

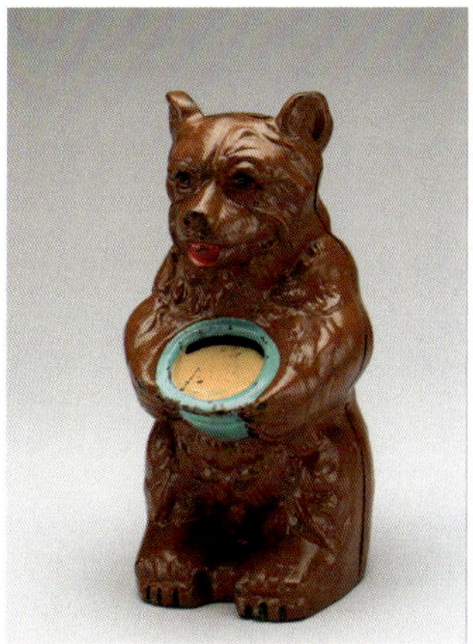

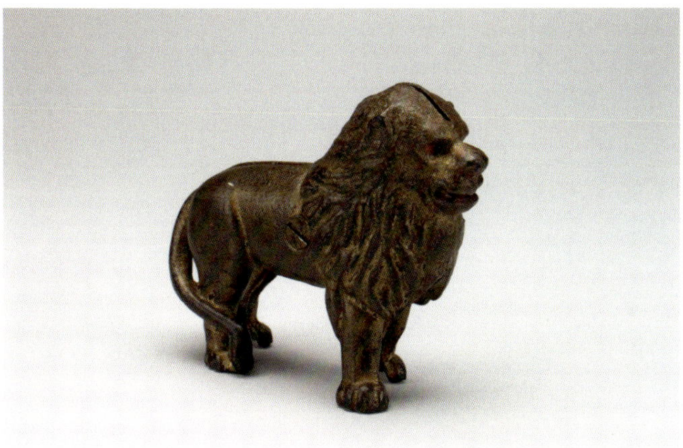

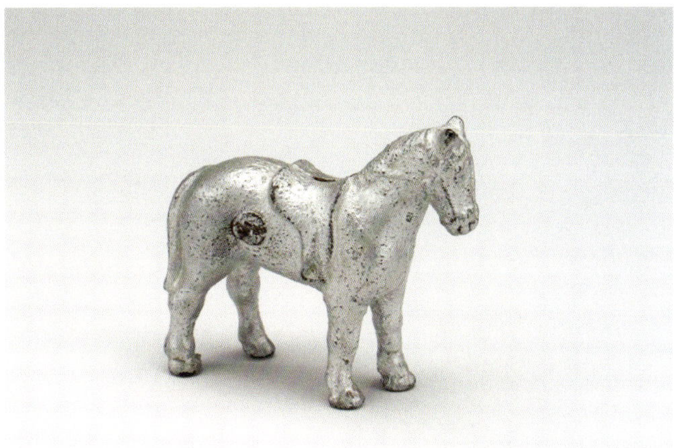

Kitty Bank, c. 1930s – 46
Hubley Manufacturing Company, Lancaster, Pennsylvania (est. 1894), manufacturer
Iron, pigment
5 x 3 1/16 x 3 1/4 in.
2003.236.772

Duck on Tub (or *Save for a Rainy Day*), c. 1930 – 36
Hubley Manufacturing Company, Lancaster, Pennsylvania (est. 1894), manufacturer
Iron, pigment
5 1/4 x 3 1/16 x 3 1/16 in.
2003.236.972

Owl, c. 1930s
National Sewing Machine Company (Vindex Toys), Belvidere, Illinois (1886 – 1954), manufacturer
Iron pigment
4 7/16 x 2 1/2 x 2 1/2 in.
2003.236.953

General Electric Refrigerator, Small, c. 1930s
Arcade Manufacturing Company, Freeport, Illinois (1868 – 1946), manufacturer
Iron, pigment
3 11/16 x 1 15/16 x 1 1/4 in.
2003.236.951

Majestic Radio, c. 1932 – 34
Arcade Manufacturing Company, Freeport, Illinois (1868 – 1946), manufacturer
Iron, pigment
4 15/16 x 2 5/8 x 1 11/16 in.
2003.236.991

Two-Story House, c. 1931 – 34
A. C. Williams Company, Ravenna, Ohio (est. 1886), manufacturer
Iron, pigment
3 1/4 x 2 1/16 x 1 7/8 in.
2003.236.655

Boston Bull Terrier, c. 1931
National Sewing Machine Company (Vindex Toys), Belvidere, Illinois (1886 – 1954), manufacturer
Iron, pigment
5 1/2 x 6 1/2 x 2 1/2 in.
2003.236.979

Bear with Honey Pot, 1936
Hubley Manufacturing Company, Lancaster, Pennsylvania (est. 1894), manufacturer
Iron, pigment
6 3/4 x 4 x 3 5/8 in.
2003.236.981

Elephant with Howdah, Tiny, 1934
A. C. Williams Company, Ravenna, Ohio (est. 1886), manufacturer
Iron, pigment
2 7/16 x 3 1/8 x 1 5/16 in.
2003.236.1005

Roosevelt, New Deal, c. 1933 – 36
Kenton Hardware Manufacturing Company, Kenton, Ohio (1890 – 1950), manufacturer
Iron
4 7/8 x 2 13/16 x 2 1/4 in.
2003.236.379

Saddle Horse, Small, 1934
A. C. Williams Company, Ravenna, Ohio (est. 1886), manufacturer
Iron, pigment
2 3/4 x 3 1/4 x 1 in.
2003.236.167

Lion, Ears Up, Turnpin, 1934
A. C. Williams Company, Ravenna, Ohio (est. 1886), manufacturer
Iron, pigment
3 3/8 x 4 1/2 x 1 1/8 in.
2003.236.172

George Washington, Mechanical Bank Collectors of America, c. 1962
Grey Iron Casting Company, Mount Joy, Pennsylvania (1881–1969), manufacturer
Iron, pigment, wood, plastic
7 3/4 x 2 3/4 x 2 1/4 in. (including base)
2003.236.217

Covered Bridge, c. 1960s
John Wright, Wrightsville, Pennsylvania (est. 1880), manufacturer
Iron, pigment
2 5/8 x 6 1/4 x 2 1/4 in.
2003.236.1091

Coronation Crown, Elizabeth II, 1953
Iron, pigment
3 5/16 x 3 1/16 x 3 1/16 in.
2003.236.956

Sunbonnet Sue (or *Dolly Dimple*), c. 1970
United States
Iron, pigment
7 15/16 x 4 1/4 x 3 1/4 in.
2003.236.673

Dry Sink, c. 1970
John Wright, Wrightsville, Pennsylvania (est. 1880), manufacturer
Iron, pigment
3 1/8 x 2 13/16 x 1 9/16 in.
2003.236.1078

Apollo, Plain, c. 1970
John Wright, Wrightsville, Pennsylvania (est. 1880), manufacturer
Iron, pigment
4 1/2 x 3 1/4 x 3 1/4 in.
2003.236.526

Indian Seated on Log, c. 1970s
A. Ouve, American, designer
Iron, pigment
3 11/16 x 2 13/16 x 2 3/8 in.
2003.236.1061

Lamb, Painted, 1970
John Wright, Wrightsville, Pennsylvania (est. 1880), manufacturer
Iron, pigment
3 3/8 x 1 1/2 x 5 1/2 in.
2003.236.315

Dot Stove, 1970
John Wright, Wrightsville, Pennsylvania (est. 1880), manufacturer
Iron, pigment
4 3/8 x 3 1/2 x 2 5/8 in.
2003.236.1094

Bull with Horns, c. 1970s
John Wright, Wrightsville, Pennsylvania (est. 1880), manufacturer
Iron, pigment
3 3/4 x 4 7/8 x 1 5/8 in.
2003.236.976

Lucky Cabin, 1970
John Wright, Wrightsville, Pennsylvania (est. 1880), manufacturer
Iron, pigment
4 1/8 x 6 x 3 1/8 in.
2003.236.1048

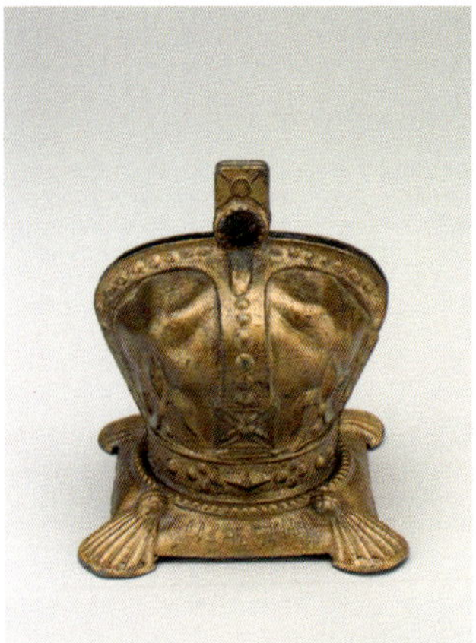

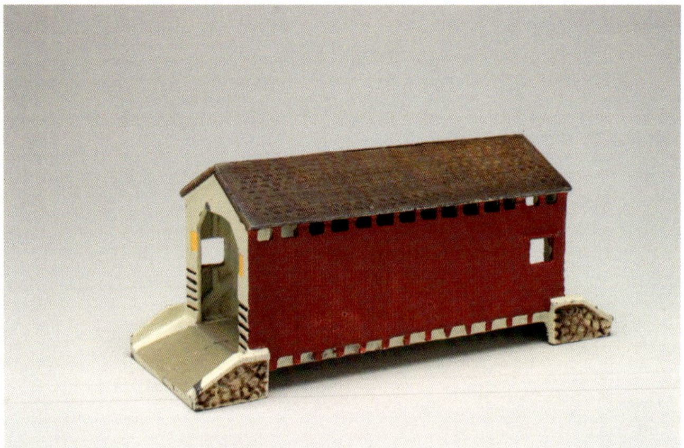

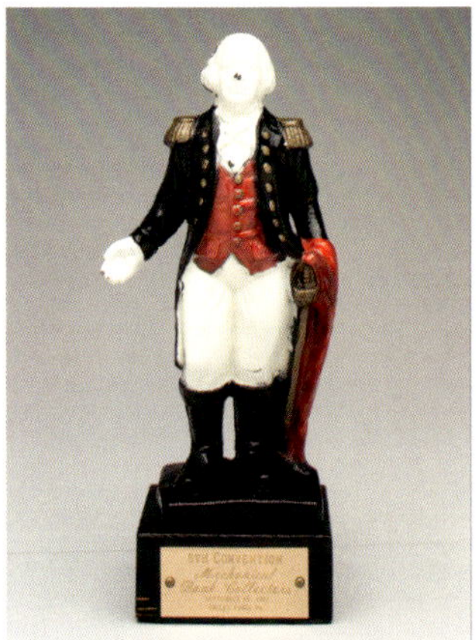

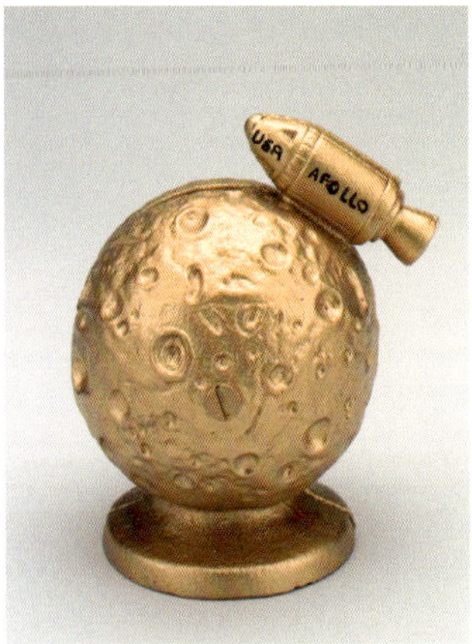
USA
APOLLO

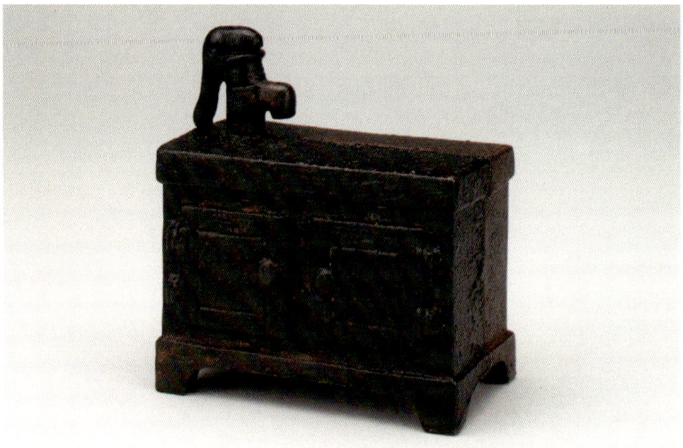

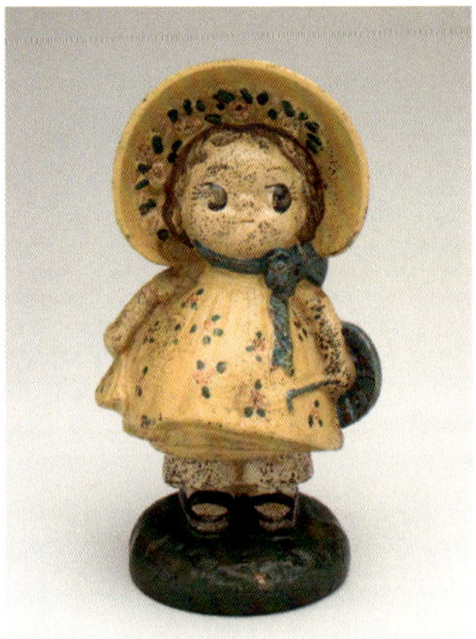

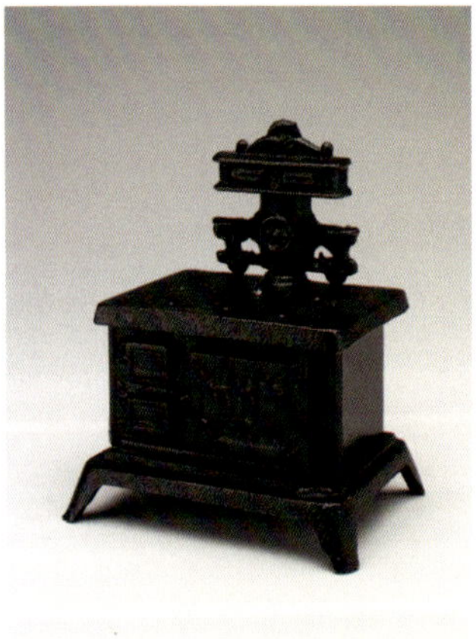

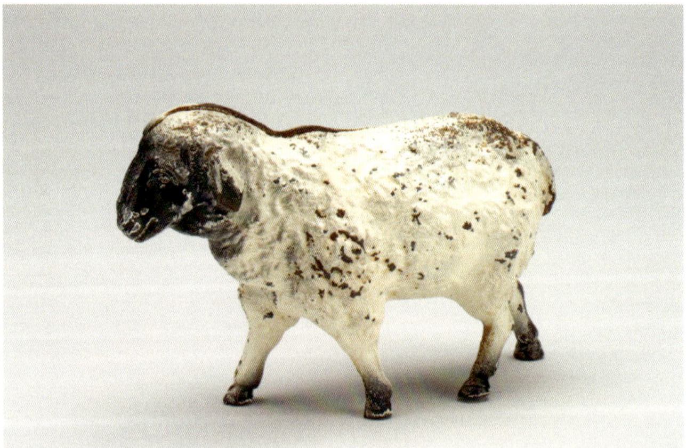

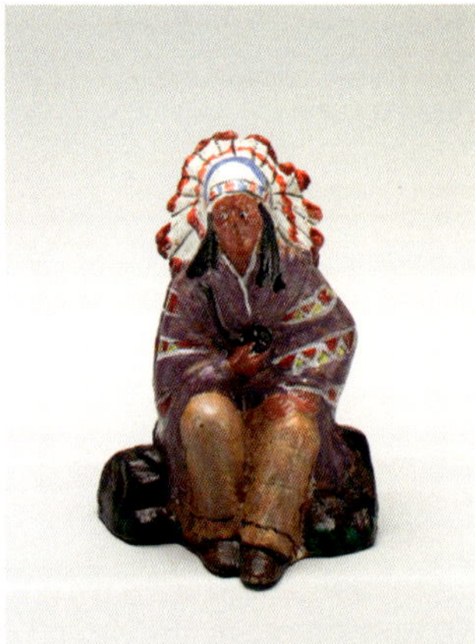

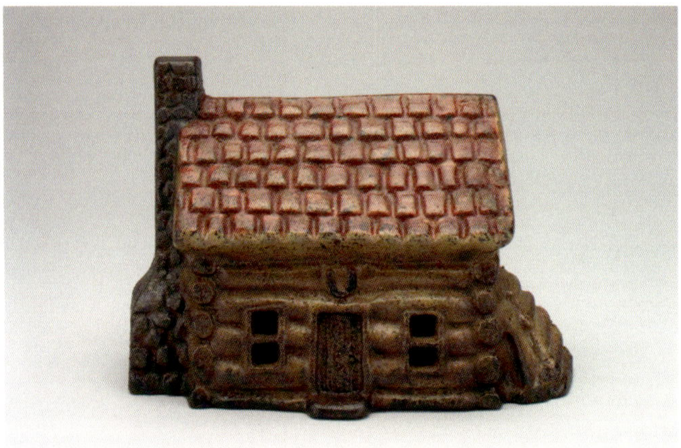

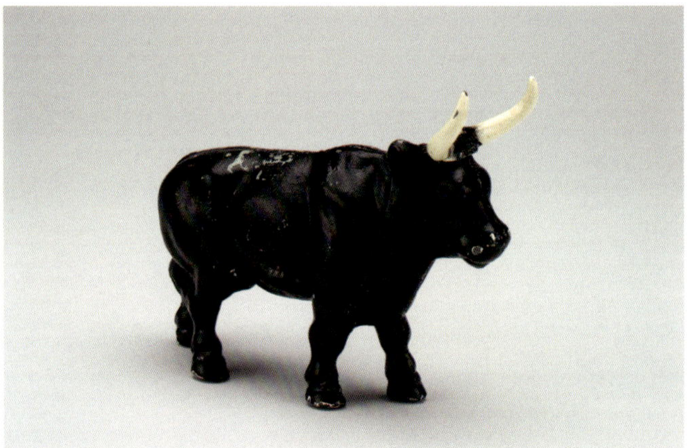

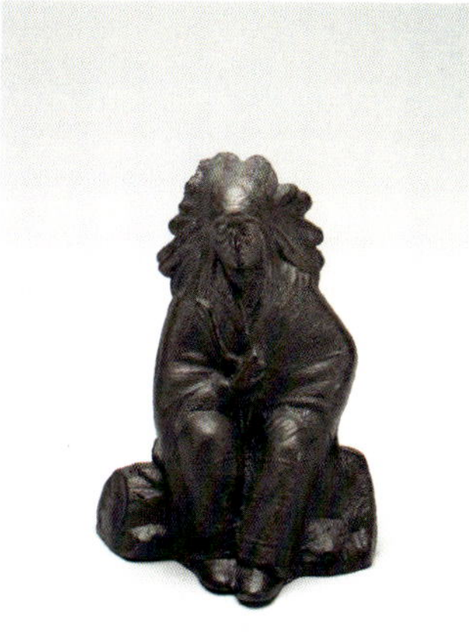

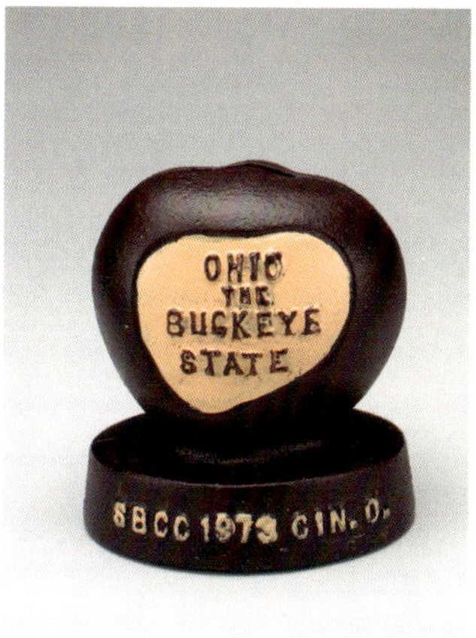
OHIO
THE
BUCKEYE
STATE
SBCC 1973 CIN. O.

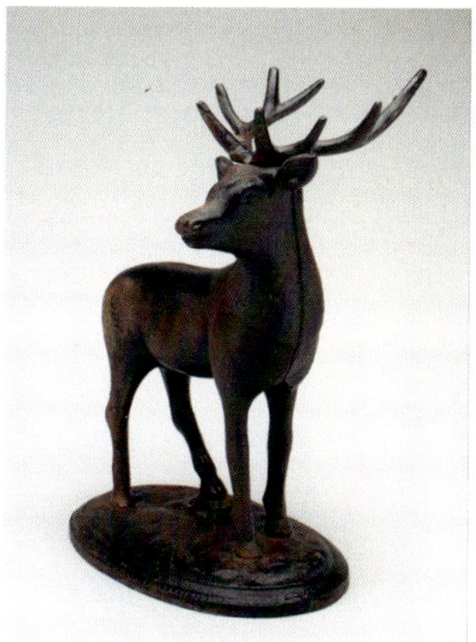

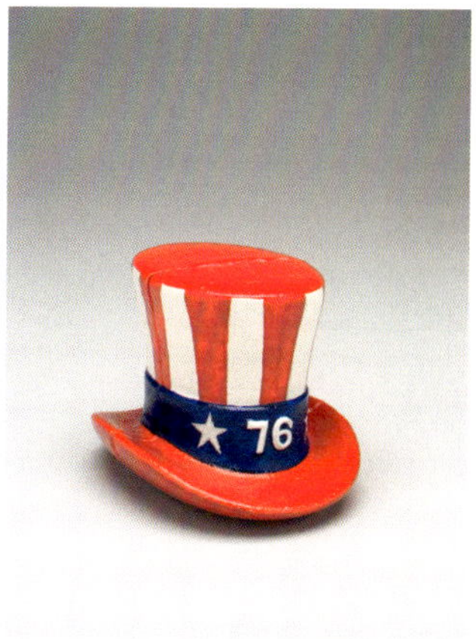
76

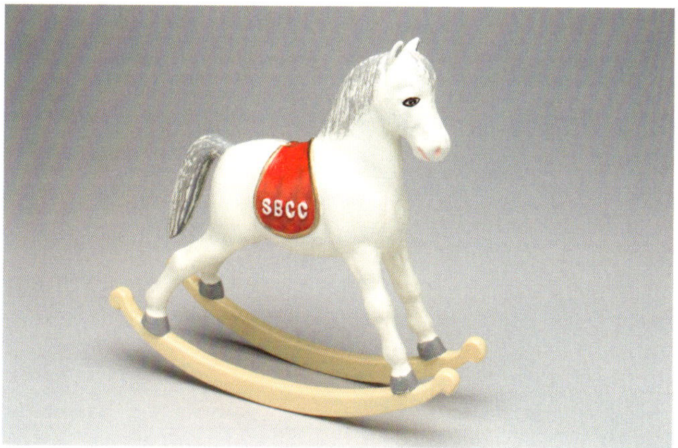
SBCC

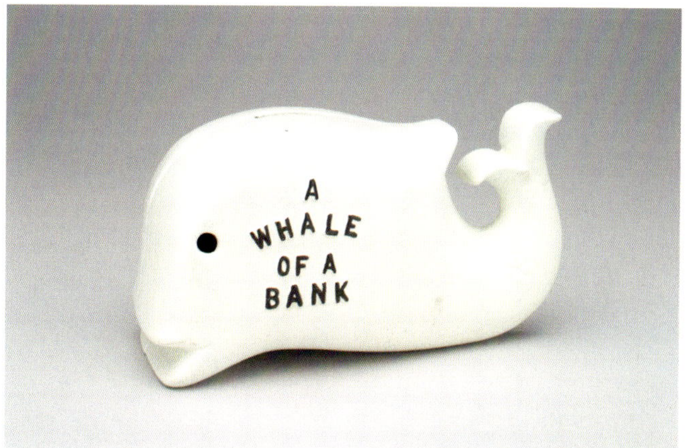
A
WHALE
OF A
BANK

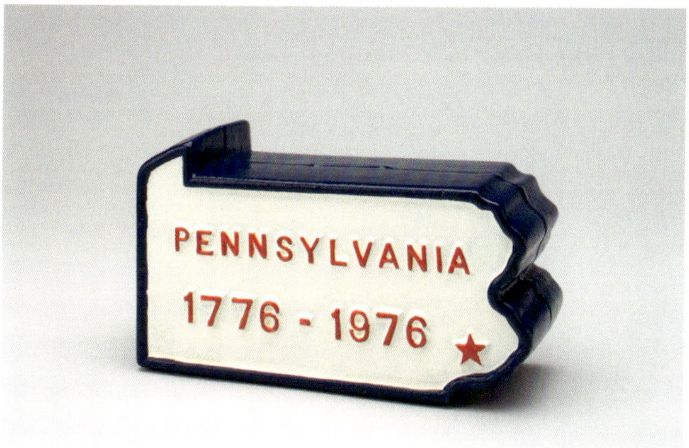
PENNSYLVANIA
1776 - 1976

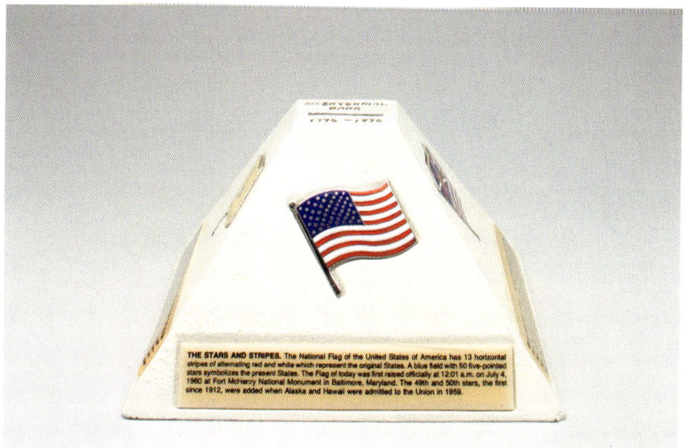
THE STARS AND STRIPES. The National Flag of the United States of America has 13 horizontal stripes of alternating red and white which represent the original States. A blue field with 50 five-pointed stars symbolizes the present States. The Flag of today was first raised officially at 12:01 a.m. on July 4, 1960 at Fort McHenry National Monument in Baltimore, Maryland. The 49th and 50th stars, the first since 1912, were added when Alaska and Hawaii were admitted to the Union in 1959.

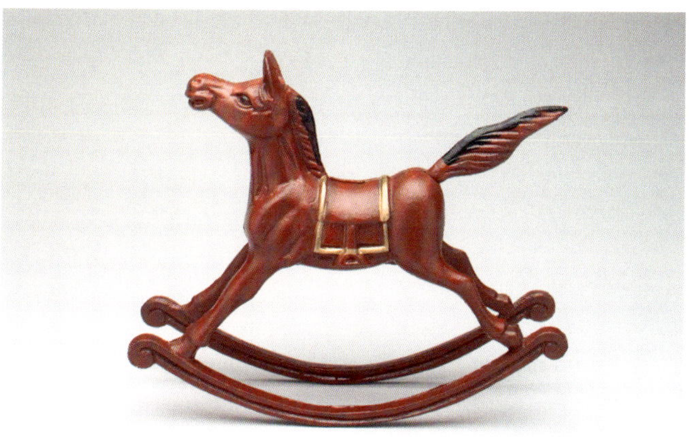

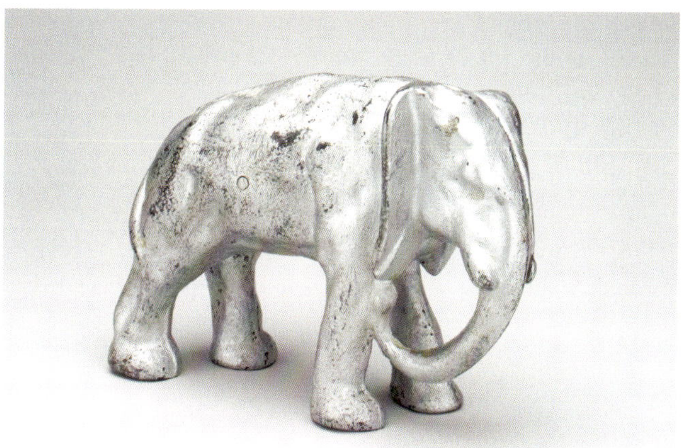

Uncle Sam Hat, c. 1976
George Knerr, American (1911–1979), designer
Williamsport Foundry Company, Williamsport, Pennsylvania (est. 1916), manufacturer
Iron, pigment
2 1/8 x 3 1/8 x 2 1/2 in.
2003.236.223

Reindeer on Base, 1973
John Wright, Wrightsville, Pennsylvania (est. 1880), manufacturer
Iron, pigment
9 1/4 x 7 5/16 x 5 3/4 in.
2003.236.808

Buckeye, Still Bank Collectors Club of America, 1973
Lou Filler, American, designer
Iron, pigment
3 1/2 x 3 1/8 x 2 1/4 in.
2003.236.896

Indian Seated on Log, c. 1970s
A. Ouve, American, designer
Iron, pigment
3 11/16 x 2 13/16 x 2 3/8 in.
2003.236.1070

A Whale of a Bank, 1975
George Knerr, American (1911–1979), designer
Iron, pigment
2 5/8 x 2 1/16 x 5 1/8 in.
2003.236.1084

Rocking Horse, Still Bank Collectors Club of America, 1975
George Knerr, American (1911–1979), designer
Williamsport Foundry Company, Williamsport, Pennsylvania (est. 1916), manufacturer
Iron, pigment
5 7/8 x 6 3/16 x 1 15/16 in.
2003.236.215

The Flags Bank, Still Bank Collectors Club of America, 1976
Littlestown Hardware & Foundry, Littlestown, Pennsylvania (1916–present), manufacturer
Iron, pigment, metal
3 5/8 x 6 x 6 in.
2003.236.220a,b

Pennsylvania, 1776–1976 (or *Bicentennial Bank*), c. 1976
George Knerr, American (1911–1979), designer
Williamsport Foundry Company, Williamsport, Pennsylvania (est. 1916), manufacturer
Iron, pigment
2 13/16 x 5 1/16 x 1 15/16 in.
2003.236.224

Elephant, c. 1981
Iron, pigment
5 1/4 x 7 1/4 x 2 5/8 in.
2003.236.676

Rocking Horse, c. 1980s
United States
Iron, pigment
8 x 2 3/8 x 9/16 in.
2003.236.591

Sailboat, Still Bank Collectors Club of America, 1988
Laverne A. Worley and Don Duer, American, designers
Iron, pigment
5 x 4 7/16 x 1 15/16 in.
2003.236.225

St. Louis Arch, Still Bank Collectors Club of America, c. 1987
Laverne A. Worley, American, designer
Iron, pigment
4 3/16 x 4 9/16 x 2 15/16 in.
2003.236.216

Book, Still Bank Collectors Club of America, c. 1986
Iron, pigment
3 5/8 x 2 11/16 x 1 3/16 in.
2003.236.219

Toy Soldier, Still Bank Collectors Club of America, 1982
Laverne A. Worley, American, designer
Iron, pigment
7 11/16 x 2 13/16 x 2 13/16 in.
2003.236.218

Boston Terrier, 20th century
Iron, pigment, leather
10 3/8 x 4 3/4 x 11 in.
2003.236.410

Train Car, Still Bank Collectors Club of America, c. 1989
Iron, pigment
2 1/16 x 6 13/16 x 1 3/8 in.
2003.236.214

Mailbox, 20th century
United States
Iron, pigment, paper
3 7/8 x 2 5/8 x 1 5/8 in.
2003.236.1098

Liberty Bell, 20th century
Iron, pigment
3 1/2 x 3 1/4 x 3 1/4 in.
2003.236.962

Church Altar, 20th century
Iron, pigment
7 3/16 x 5 x 2 in.
2003.236.818

Punch on Wheeled Base, 20th century
Xonex International, Inc., Cleveland, manufacturer
Iron, pigment
12 13/16 x 3 7/8 x 4 1/4 in.
2003.236.457

Mean Standing Bear, 20th century
United States
Iron, pigment
5 1/2 x 2 3/4 x 3 1/16 in.
2003.236.965

Lion (converted doorstop), 20th century
Iron, pigment
7 x 4 1/2 x 9 1/2 in.
2003.236.409

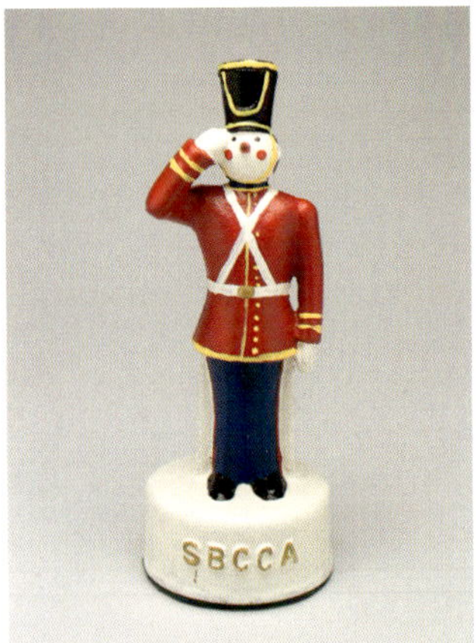
SBCCA

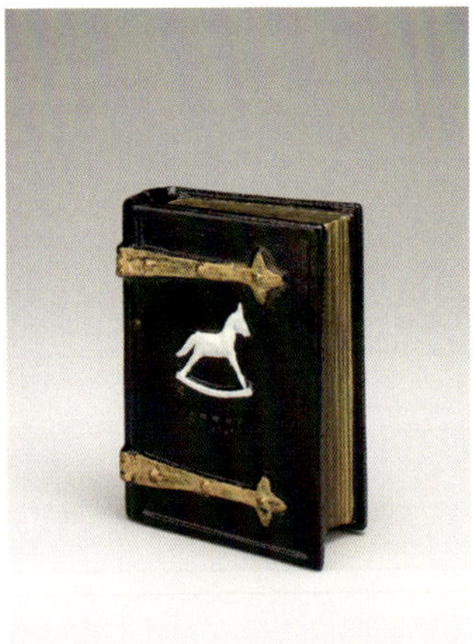

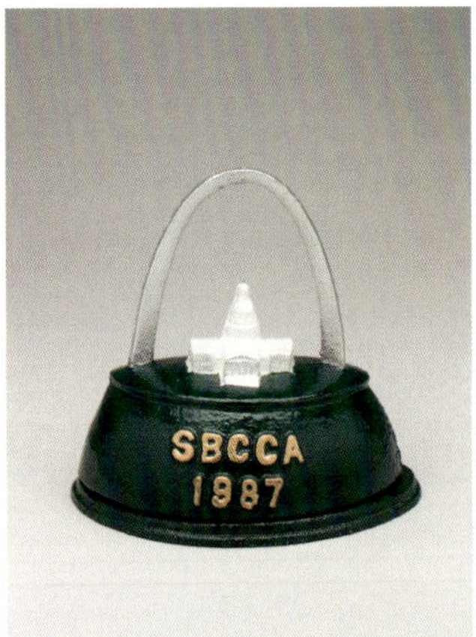
SBCCA
1987

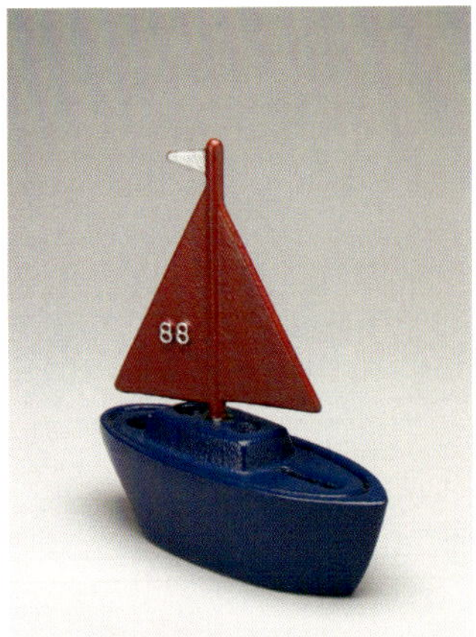
88

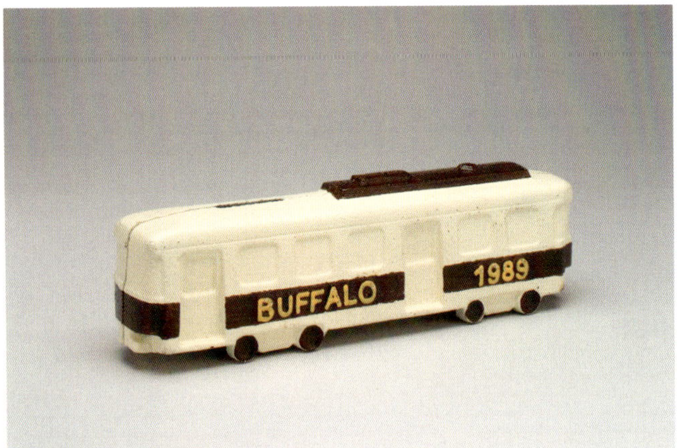
BUFFALO
1989

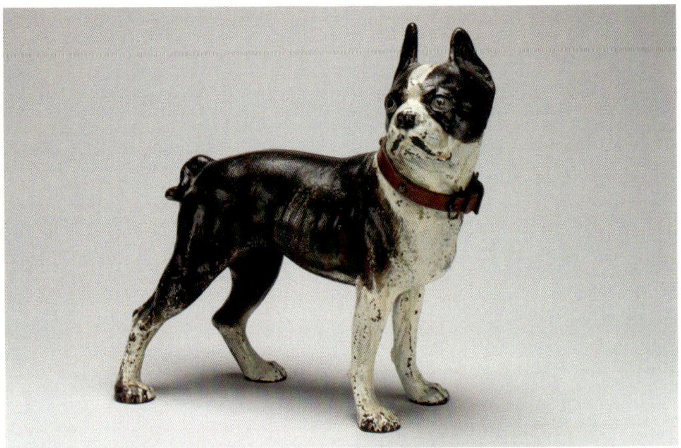

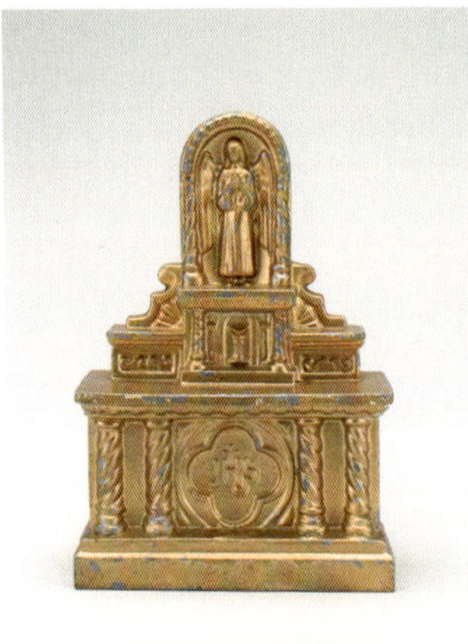

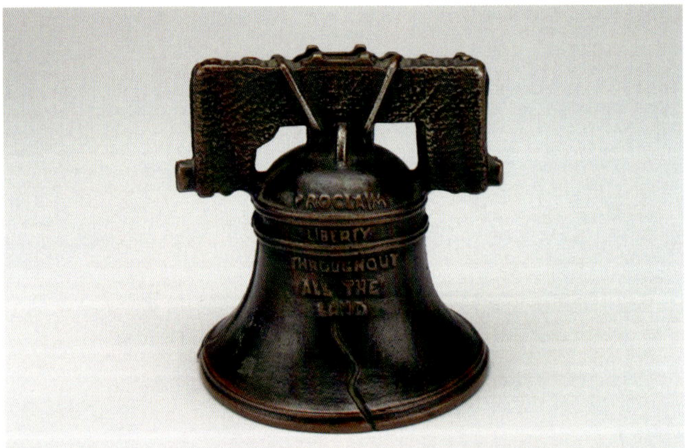

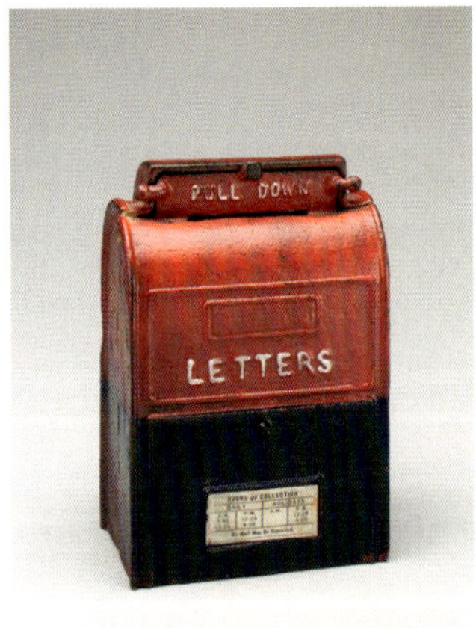
PULL DOWN
LETTERS

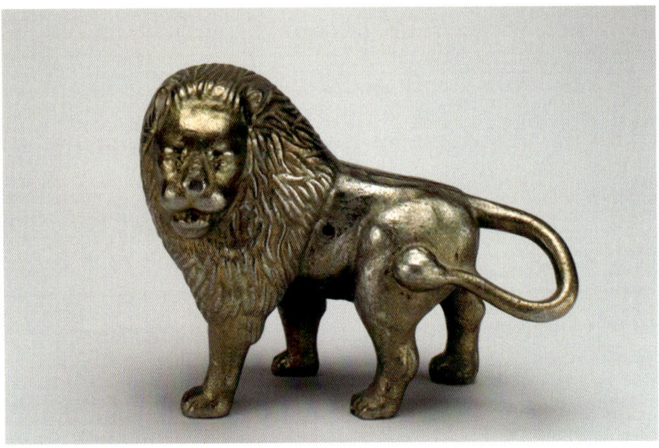

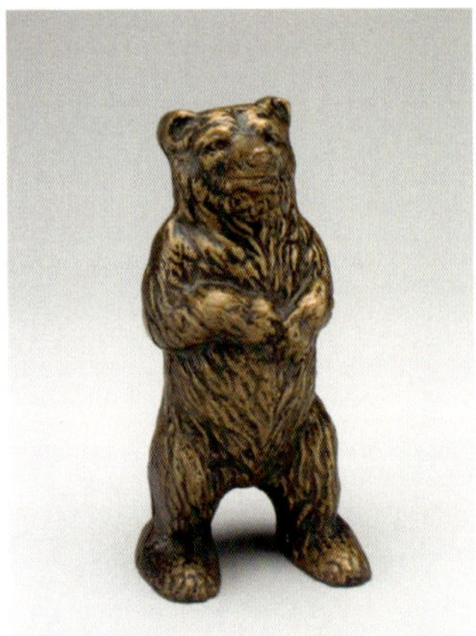

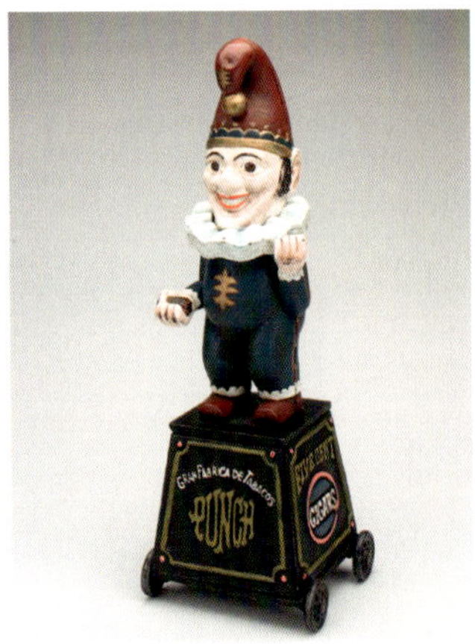
PUNCH

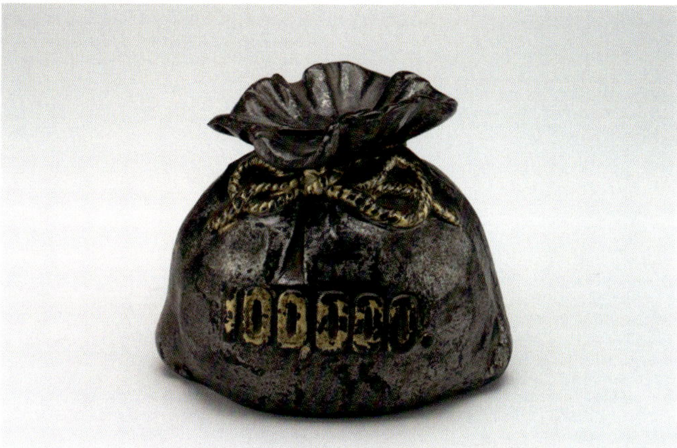

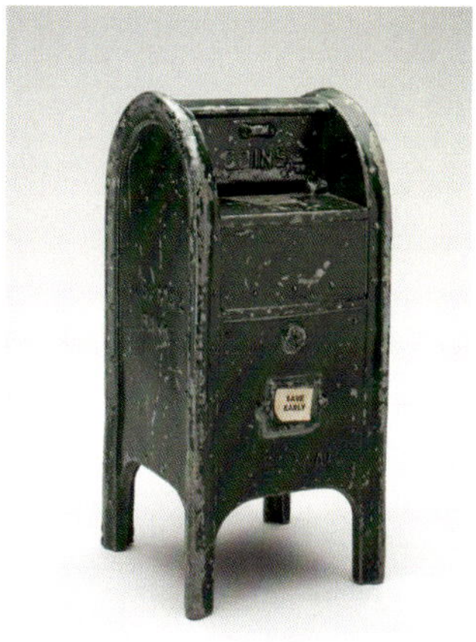

STILL BANKS: Tin

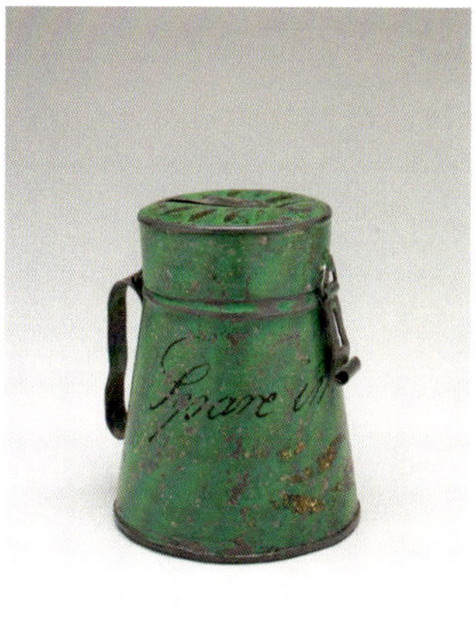

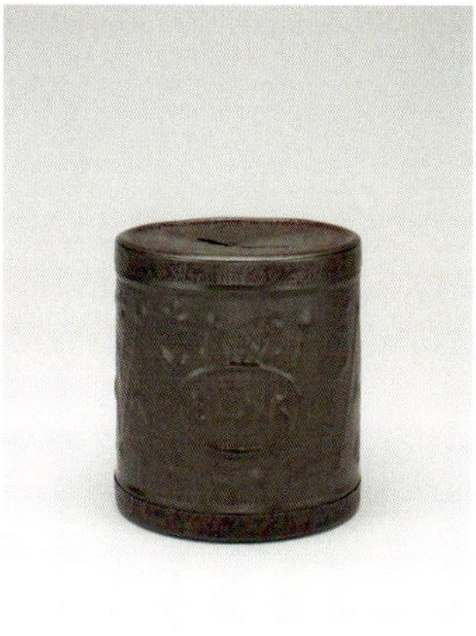

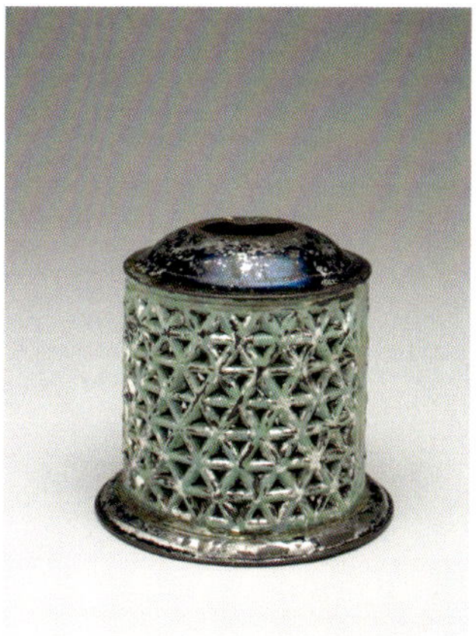

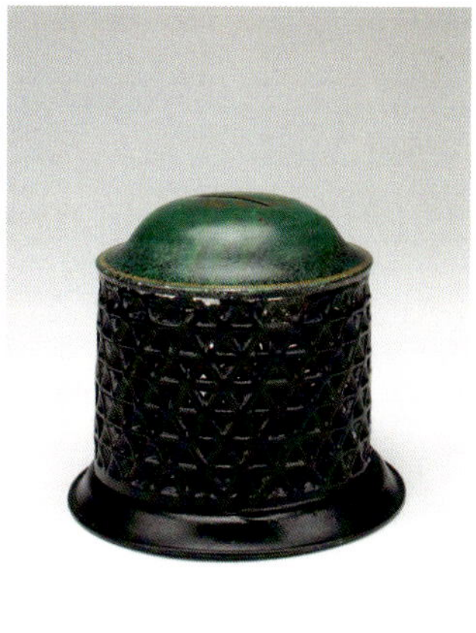

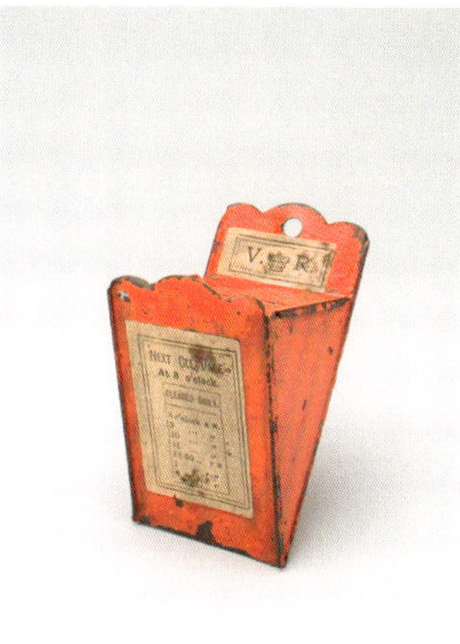

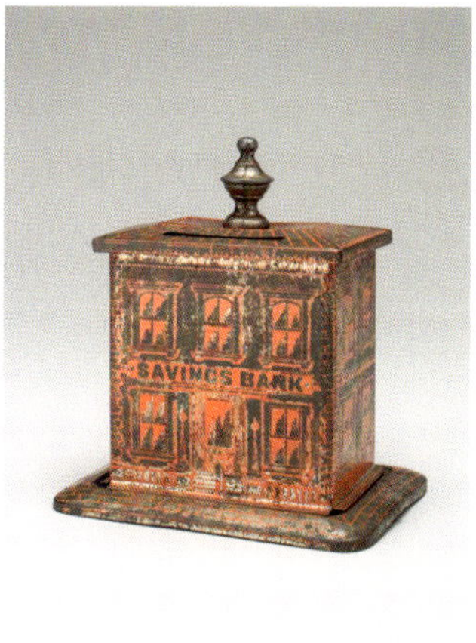

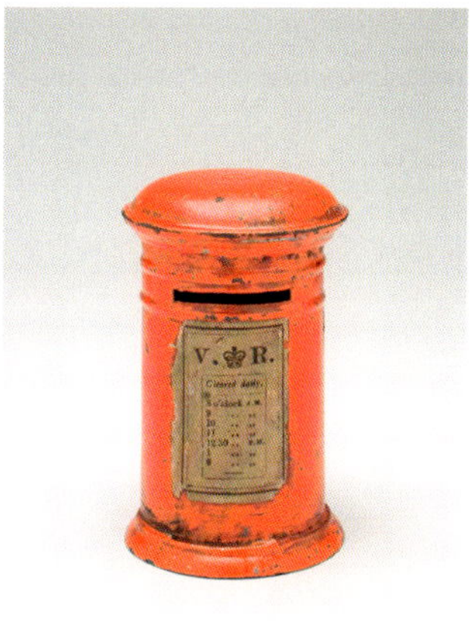

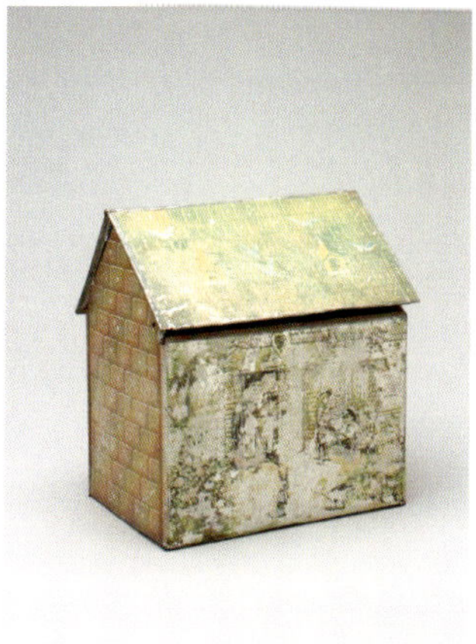

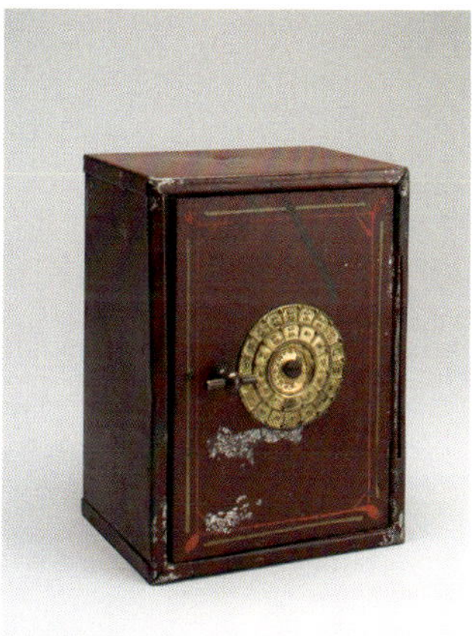

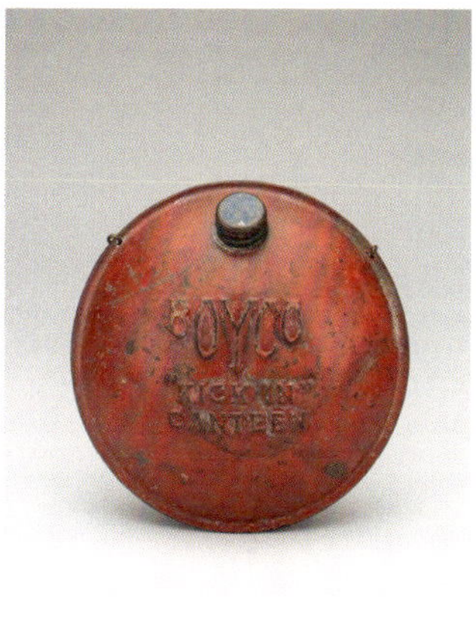

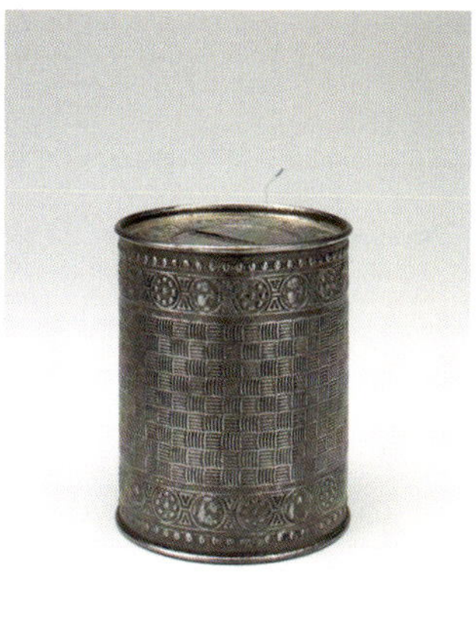

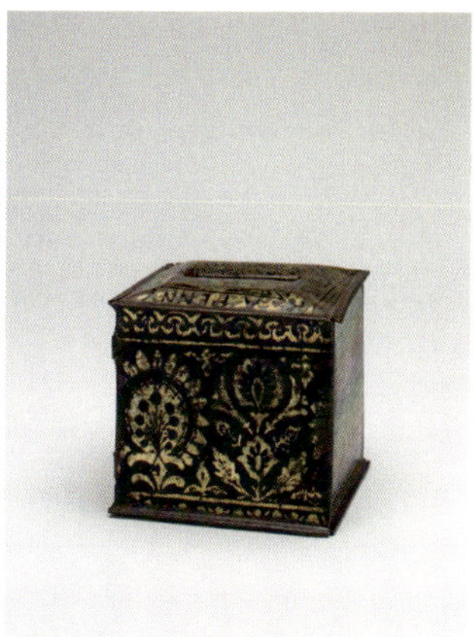

STILL BANKS: Tin

U.S. Mailbox, 20th century
Iron, pigment, paper
5 1/2 x 2 9/16 x 2 1/2 in.
2003.236.1101

$100,000, 20th century
United States
Iron, pigment
3 1/2 x 4 1/8 x 2 11/16 in.
2003.236.993

Pierced tin, c. 1870
United States
Tin, pigment
3 1/4 x 3 7/8 x 3 7/8 in.
2003.236.262

Pierced tin, c. 1870
United States
Tin, pigment
2 15/16 x 3 1/16 x 3 1/16 in.
2003.236.246

Drum, c. 1870
United States
Tin, pigment
3 1/8 x 2 15/16 x 2 15/16 in.
2003.236.241

Can, mid-to-late 19th century
Germany
Tin, pigment
2 3/4 x 2 3/16 x 2 7/16 in.
2003.236.1060

Fairy Tale House, c. 1880s
England
Tin, pigment
7 5/16 x 6 1/2 x 4 9/16 in.
2003.236.190

Savings Bank, c. 1880
United States
Tin, pigment
3 1/8 x 3 3/16 x 2 1/2 in.
2003.236.352

VR Postbox, 1875
England
Tin, pigment, paper
4 3/16 x 2 5/8 x 2 5/8 in.
2003.236.256

Postbox, 1875
England
Tin, pigment
4 1/2 x 2 1/4 x 2 1/2 in.
2003.236.185

The Child's Bank, 19th century
England
Tin, pigment
2 1/2 x 2 5/8 x 2 5/8 in.
2003.236.182

Can with pressed design, 19th century
England
Tin
3 1/4 x 2 11/16 x 2 11/16 in.
2003.236.261

Boyco "Kick In" Canteen, c. 1898
Boyle Manufacturing Company, Los Angeles, manufacturer
Tin, pigment
4 1/4 x 4 1/4 x 1 3/4 in.
2003.236.1001

Acme Safe, c. 1890
Pennsylvania
Tin, pigment
5 9/16 x 4 1/4 x 3 9/16 in.
2003.236.1041

Our 10-Cents-a-Day Plan, c. 1900
United States
Tin, pigment
7 13/16 x 5 1/8 x 7/8 in.
2003.236.533

Cupola, late 19th century
United States
Tin, pigment
4 1/4 x 3 1/8 x 2 1/2 in.
2003.236.360

Champion Cash Register, early 20th century
United States
Tin, pigment
3 1/2 x 3 1/2 x 5 in.
2003.236.599

House, c. 1900
Tin, pigment
3 1/2 x 2 5/8 x 1 3/4 in.
2003.236.257

Lucky Money Wheel,
early 20th century
England
Tin, pigment
7 13/16 x 4 3/8 x 2 3/4 in.
2003.236.878

House, early 20th century
Tin, pigment
6 5/8 x 3 15/16 x 3 1/4 in.
2003.236.186

Cylinder, early 20th century
United States
Tin, pigment
3 3/4 x 2 11/16 x 2 11/16 in.
2003.236.1020

Church steeple,
early 20th century
Probably United States
Tin, pigment
10 1/8 x 3 7/8 x 3 3/4 in.
2003.236.804

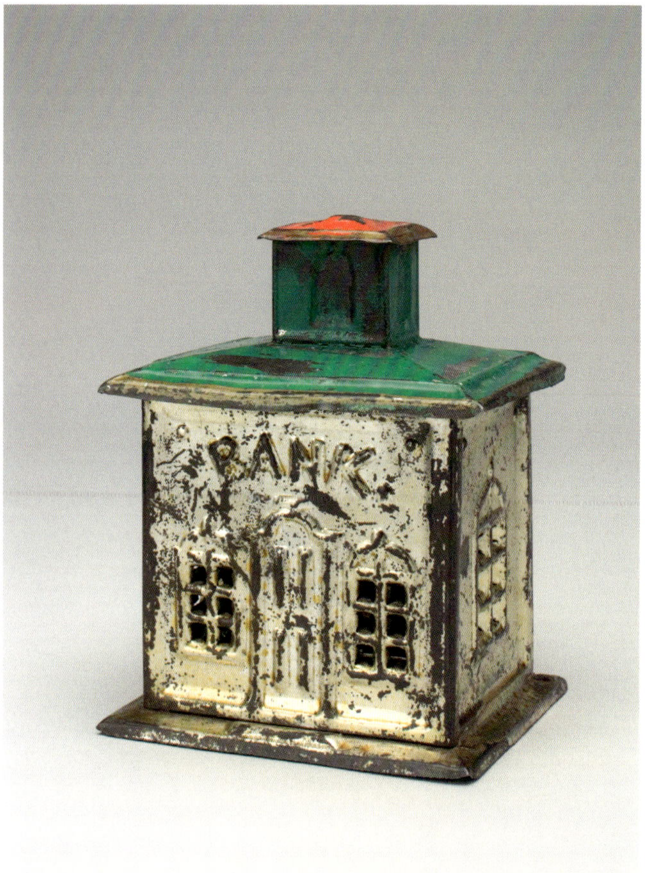
BANK

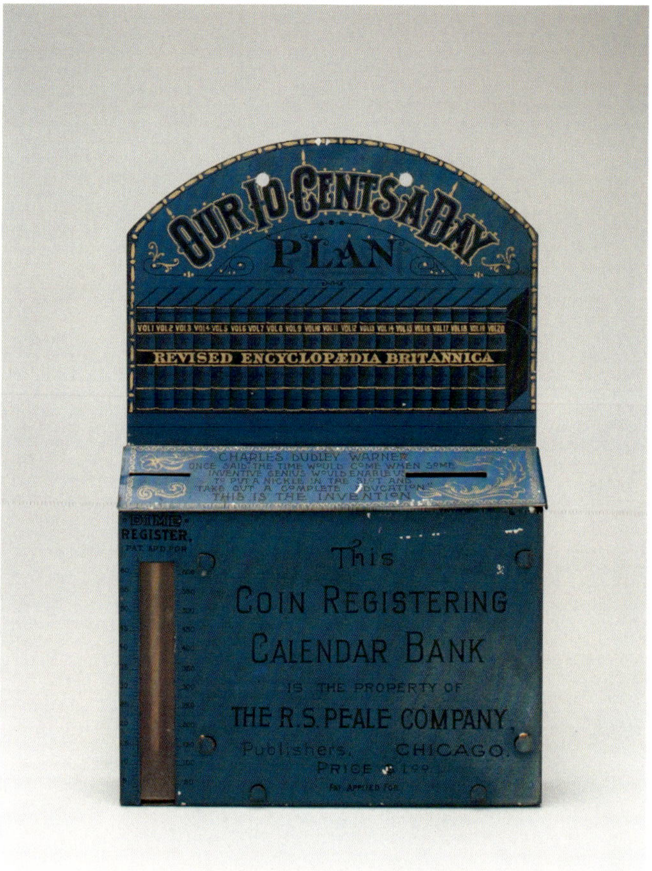
OUR 10 CENTS A DAY
PLAN
REVISED ENCYCLOPÆDIA BRITANNICA
DIME REGISTER.
This
COIN REGISTERING
CALENDAR BANK
IS THE PROPERTY OF
THE R. S. PEALE COMPANY
Publishers, CHICAGO.

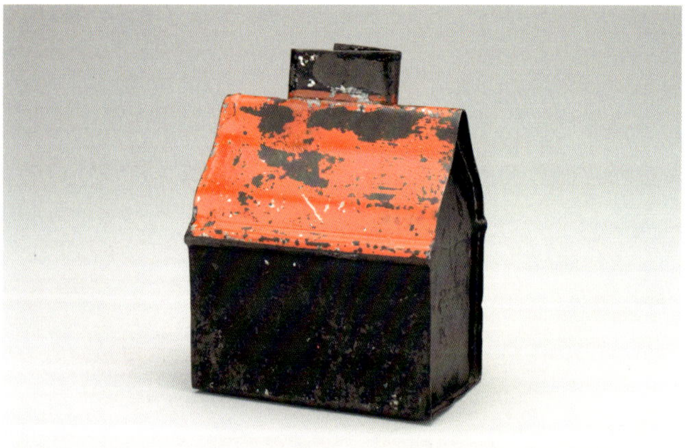

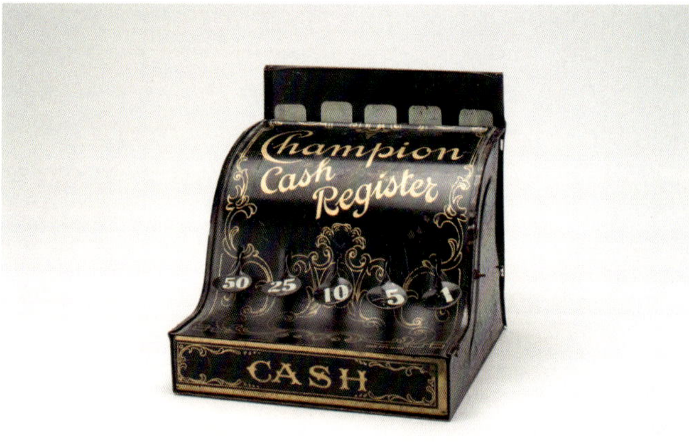
Champion
Cash Register
50 25 10 5 1
CASH

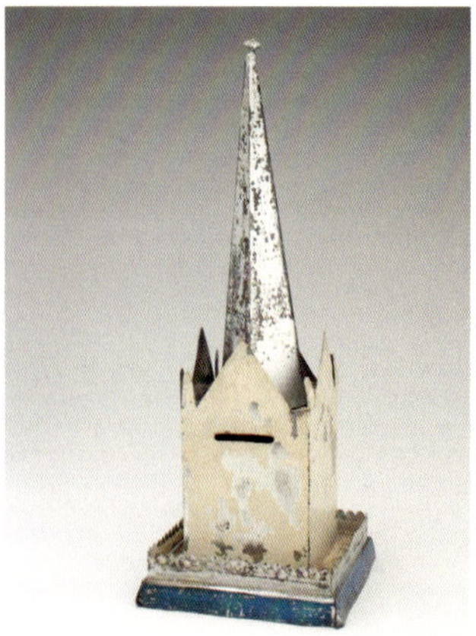

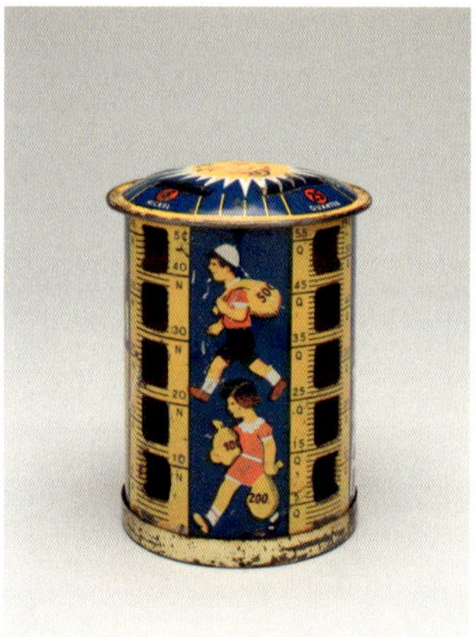

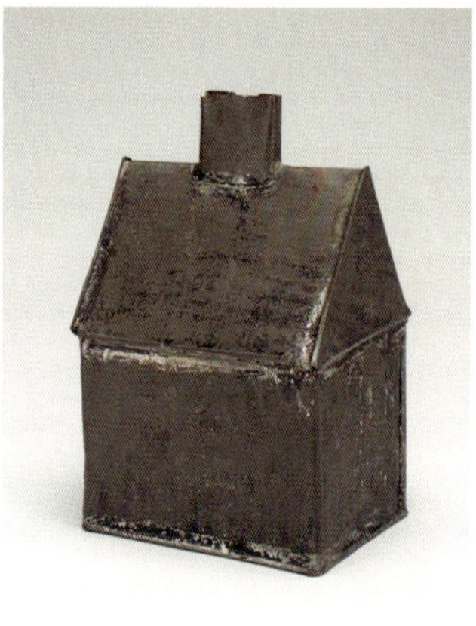

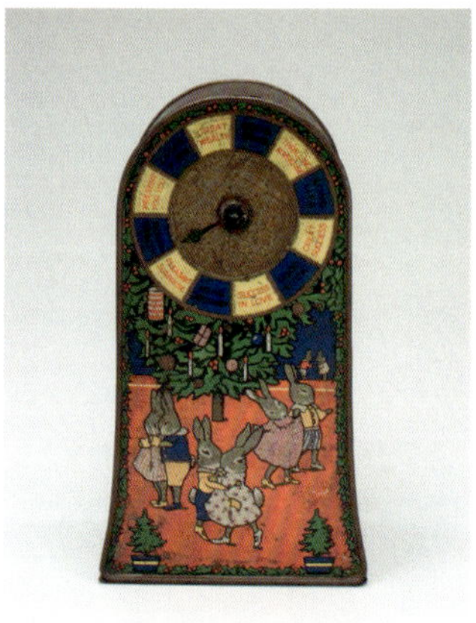

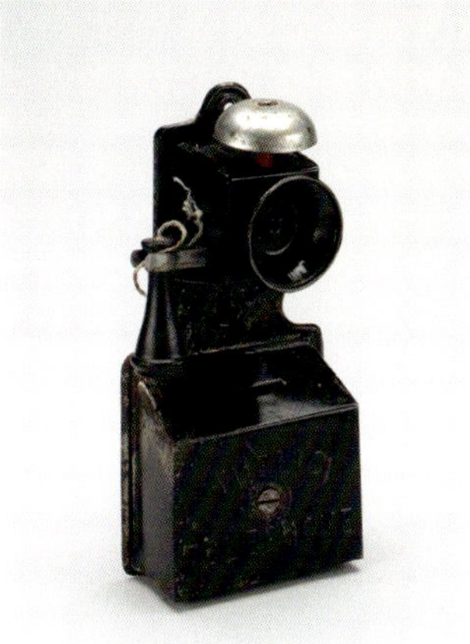

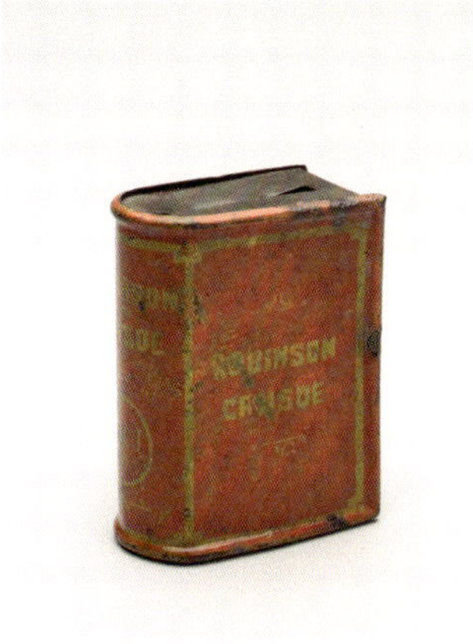
ROBINSON
CRUSOE

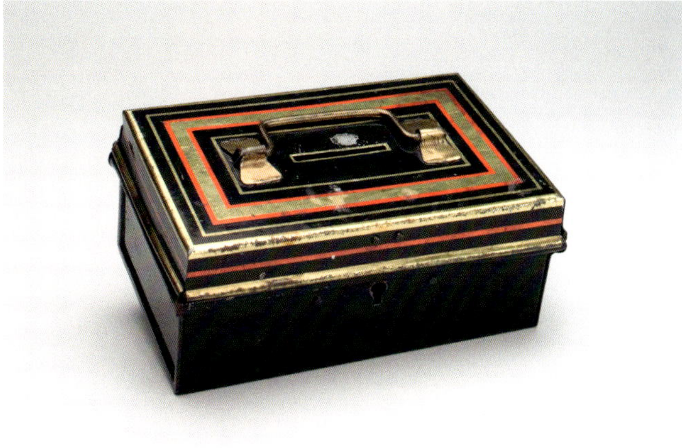

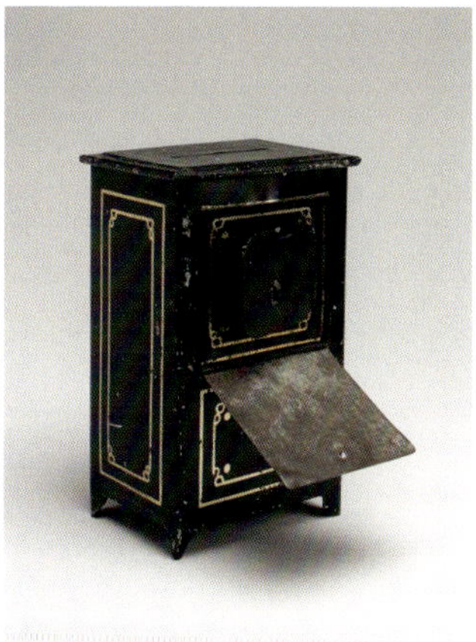

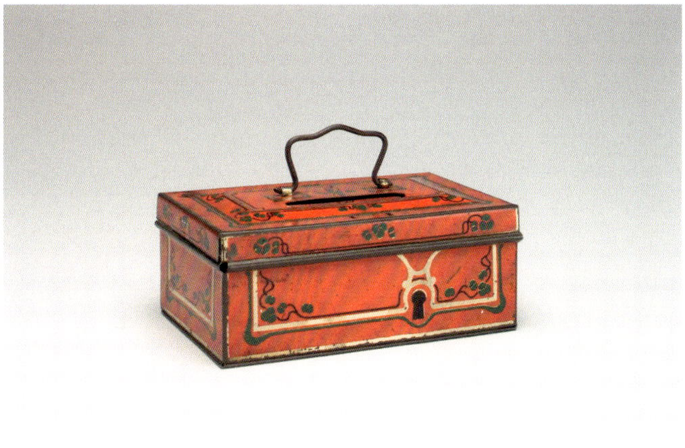

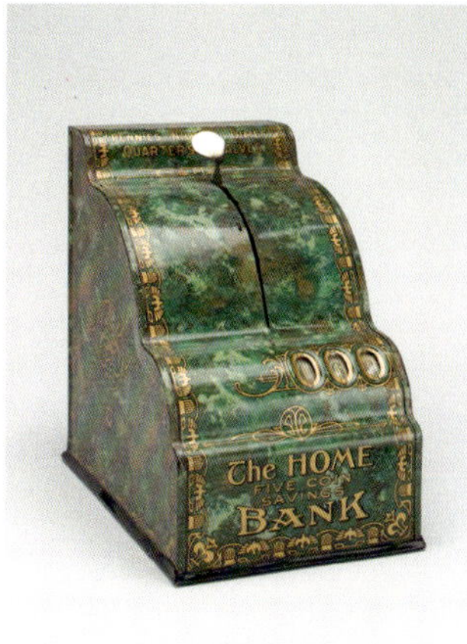
The HOME
BANK

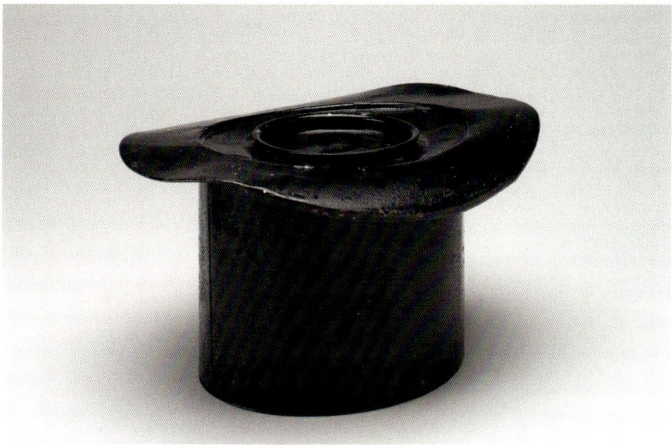

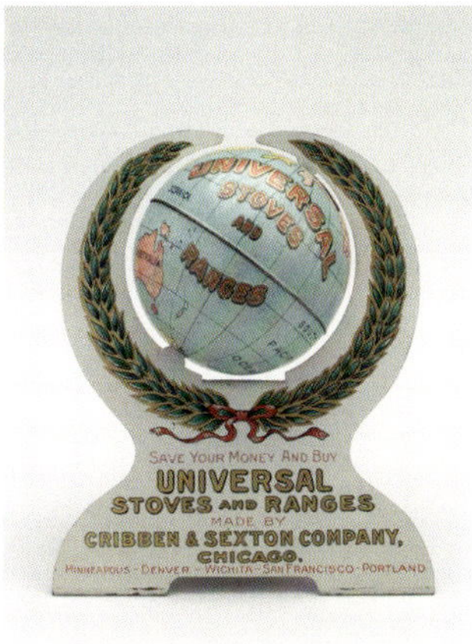
UNIVERSAL STOVES AND RANGES
SAVE YOUR MONEY AND BUY
UNIVERSAL
STOVES AND RANGES
MADE BY
CRIBBEN & SEXTON COMPANY,
CHICAGO.
MINNEAPOLIS - DENVER - WICHITA - SAN FRANCISCO - PORTLAND

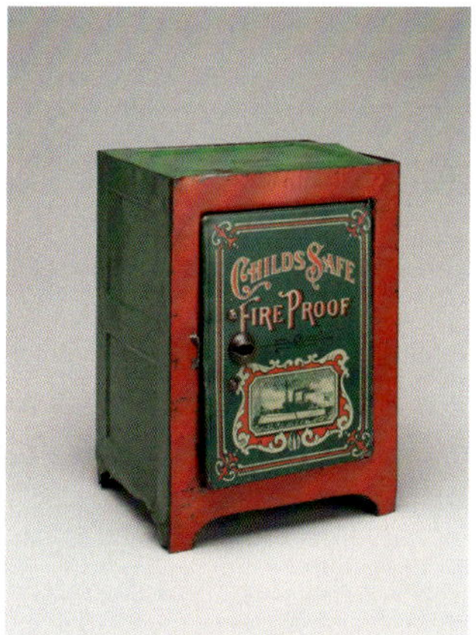
CHILDS SAFE
FIRE PROOF

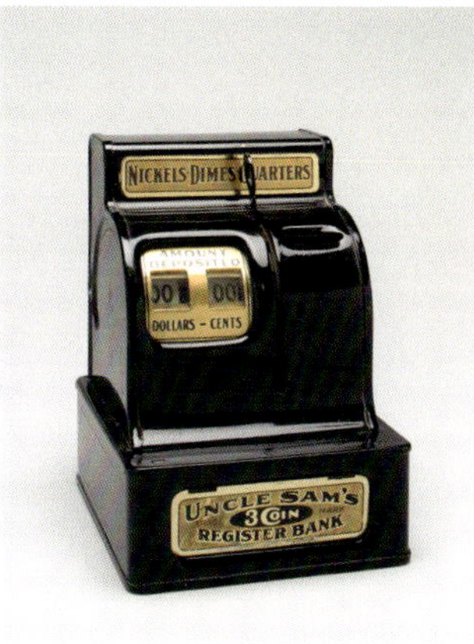
NICKELS DIMES QUARTERS
DOLLARS - CENTS
UNCLE SAM'S 3 COIN REGISTER BANK

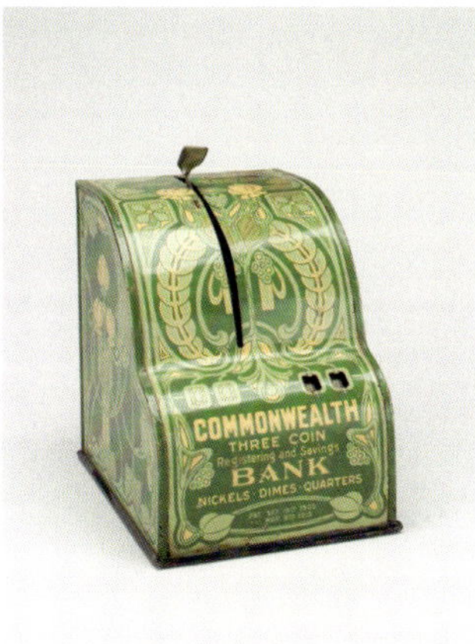
COMMONWEALTH
THREE COIN
BANK
NICKELS DIMES QUARTERS

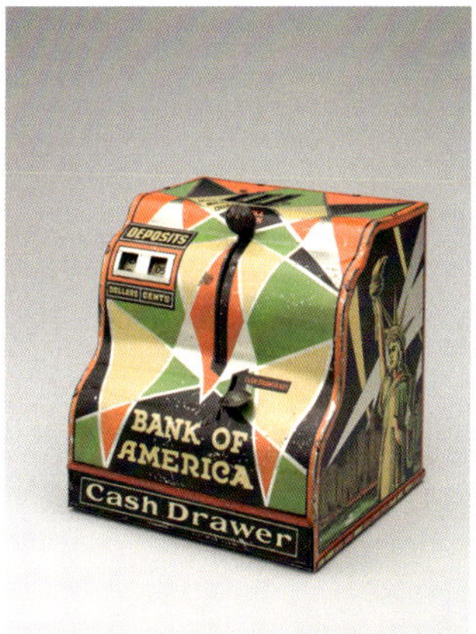
DEPOSITS
DOLLARS CENTS
BANK OF
AMERICA
Cash Drawer

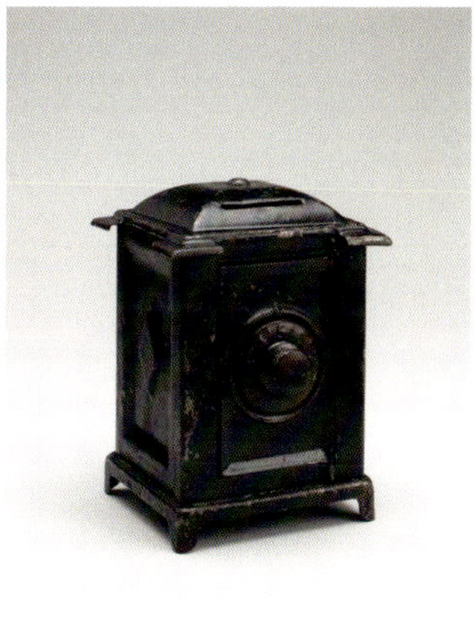

Security Box, early 20th century
England
Tin, pigment
2 1/4 x 5 1/16 x 3 1/4 in.
2003.236.258

Robinson Crusoe (book), early 20th century
Possibly England
Tin, pigment
1 7/8 x 1 7/16 x 1 3/16 in.
2003.236.534

Public Telephone, early 20th century
United States
Tin, wood, string, pigment
7 3/8 x 3 9/16 x 1 1/2 in.
2003.236.303

The Home Five-Coin Saving Bank (registering), early-to-mid-20th century
Charles M. Shonk Company, Chicago (1906 – 73), manufacturer
Tin, pigment, paper
6 7/8 x 6 7/8 x 4 3/4 in.
2003.236.504

Security Box, early 20th century
Probably England
Tin, pigment
1 1/4 x 3 1/4 x 2 in.
2003.236.536

Safe, early 20th century
Tin, pigment
4 3/8 x 2 3/4 x 2 1/16 in.
2003.236.1021

Childs Safe, Fire Proof, c. 1906
J. Chein & Company, New York (1903 – 92), manufacturer
Tin, pigment
5 7/16 x 3 15/16 x 3 1/2 in.
2003.236.1028

Universal Stoves and Ranges Globe, c. 1905
W. L. Martin & Company Lithograph, Chicago, manufacturer
Tin, pigment
3 3/4 x 3 5/16 x 2 in.
2003.236.651

Top Hat, early 20th century
Tin, pigment
Probably United States
3 3/4 x 5 5/16 x 7 3/16 in.
2003.236.1030

Safe Bank, c. 1920
Tin, pigment
United States
4 x 2 11/16 x 2 1/2 in.
2003.236.1029

Bank of America Cash Drawer (registering), c. 1920
Girard Model Works, Inc., Girard, Pennsylvania (1919 – 75), manufacturer
Tin, pigment
4 5/8 x 4 1/2 x 4 1/8 in.
2003.236.567

Commonwealth Three-Coin Registering and Savings Bank, c. 1915
Shonk Works American Can Company, Maywood, Illinois, manufacturer
Tin, pigment
5 13/16 x 4 1/8 x 5 1/2 in.
2003.236.236

Uncle Sam's Three-Coin Register Bank (registering), c. 1912 – 30s
Durable Toy and Novelty Corporation, New York and Cleveland (est. c. 1912), manufacturer
Tin, pigment, plastic
6 3/16 x 4 1/2 x 5 1/4 in.
2003.236.235

The Queen's Doll House, c. early 1920s
England
Tin, pigment
$3\frac{1}{2} \times 4\frac{1}{8} \times 2\frac{1}{2}$ in.
2003.236.361

Get Rich Quick (registering),
c. 1920 – 30
Louis Marx & Company, New York (1919 – 79), manufacturer
Tin, pigment
$3\frac{9}{16} \times 2\frac{3}{8} \times 3\frac{9}{16}$ in.
2003.236.565

Saving Elves (registering),
c. 1920
England
Tin, pigment
$4\frac{15}{16} \times 3\frac{11}{16} \times 1\frac{15}{16}$ in.
2003.236.1019

Singer Electric Sewing Machine, c. 1925
Germany
Tin, iron, pigment
$5\frac{1}{4} \times 4\frac{9}{16} \times 2\frac{3}{4}$ in.
2003.236.134

Cuba National Bank, c. 1920s
W. F. Burns and Company, Chicago, manufacturer
Tin, pigment
$3\frac{1}{4} \times 4\frac{3}{8} \times 2\frac{3}{16}$ in.
2003.236.1093a,b

Medical Donation, c. 1925
England
Tin, pigment
$6\frac{7}{16} \times 2\frac{9}{16} \times 1\frac{5}{8}$ in.
2003.236.249

Globe Glow Boy (stove),
c. 1920s – early 1930s
American Art Works, Inc., Coshocton, Ohio (1924 – 34), manufacturer
Tin, pigment
$5\frac{3}{8} \times 2\frac{3}{4} \times 2\frac{3}{4}$ in.
2003.236.1100

Goody Bank, c. 1930
United States
Tin, pigment
$\frac{7}{16} \times 2\frac{1}{16} \times 2\frac{1}{16}$ in.
2003.236.1023

Children's Stein, c. 1930
Probably Germany
Tin, cardboard, pigment
$2\frac{3}{4} \times 2\frac{1}{2} \times 2\frac{7}{16}$ in.
2003.236.354

Home Budget, c. 1929
Elmer Sas, American, designer
Tudor Metal Products, New York (est. 1929), manufacturer
Tin, pigment
$2\frac{5}{8} \times 6 \times 6\frac{5}{16}$ in.
2003.236.267

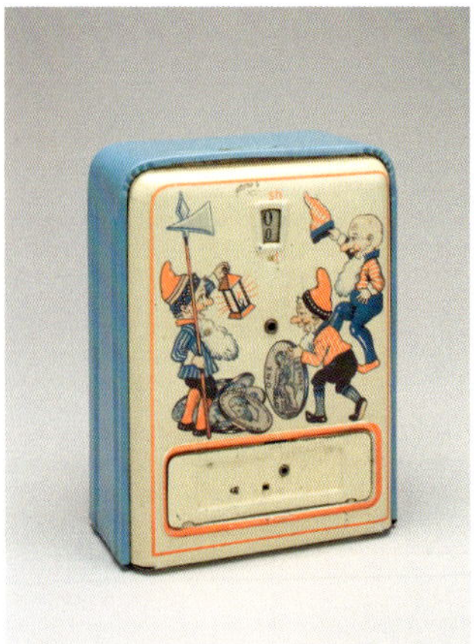

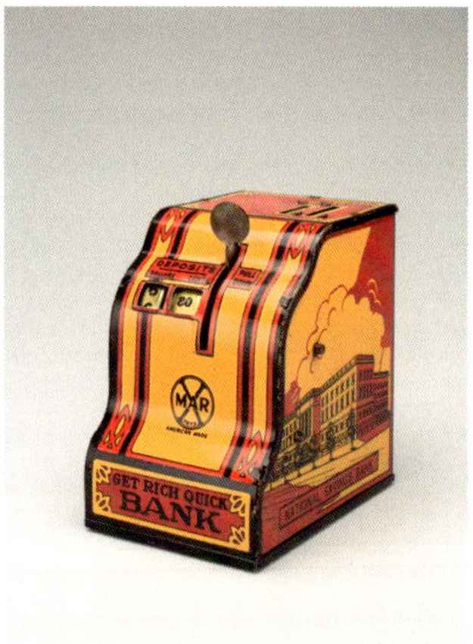
GET RICH QUICK
BANK

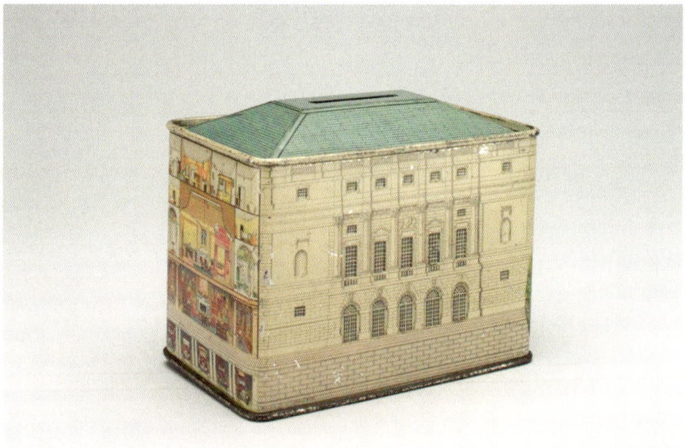

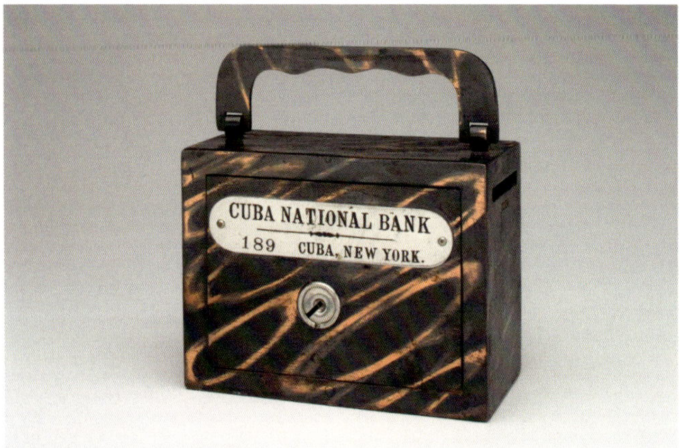
CUBA NATIONAL BANK
189 CUBA, NEW YORK.

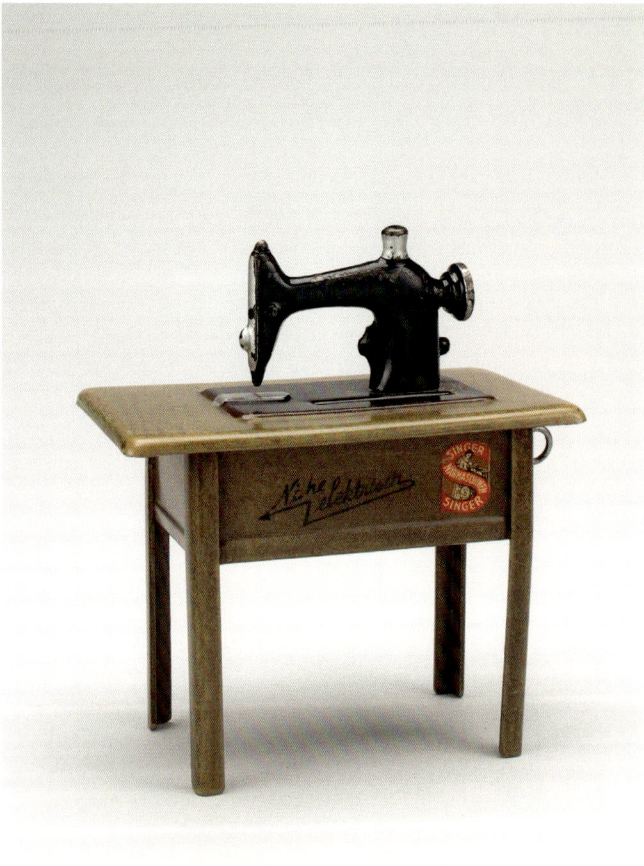
SINGER
SINGER

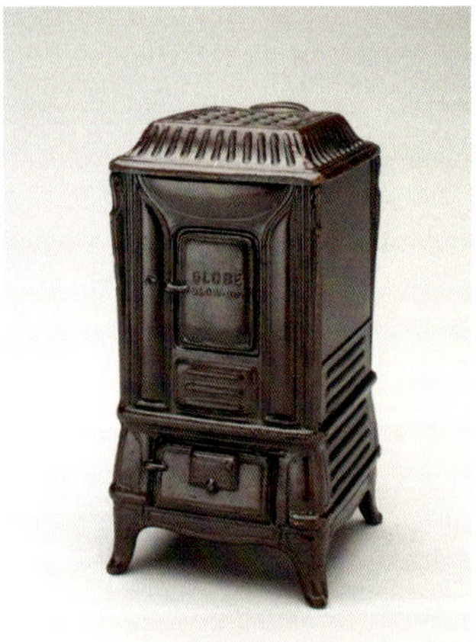

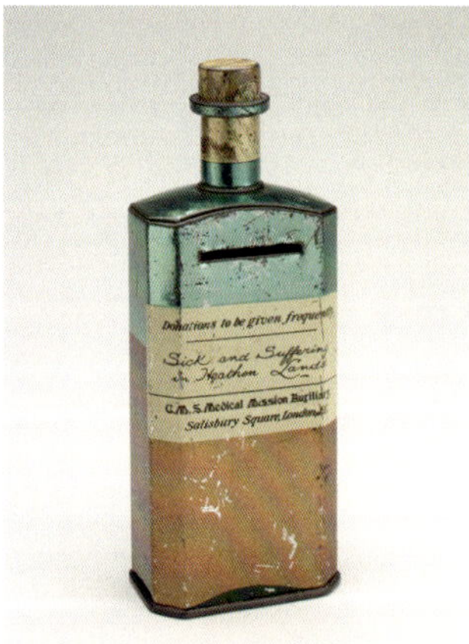
Donations to be given
Sick and
Heathen
Medical
Salisbury Square

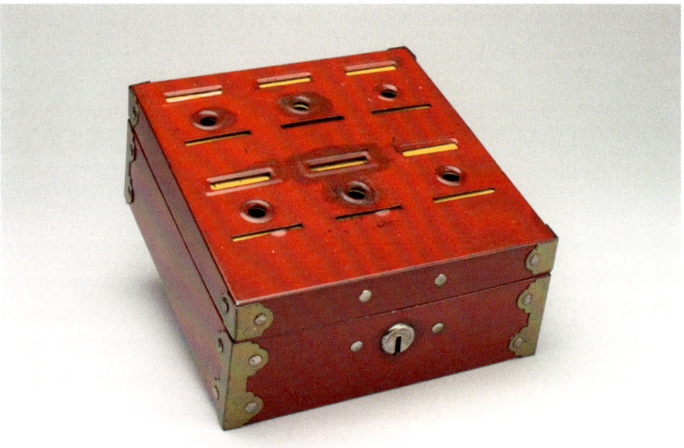

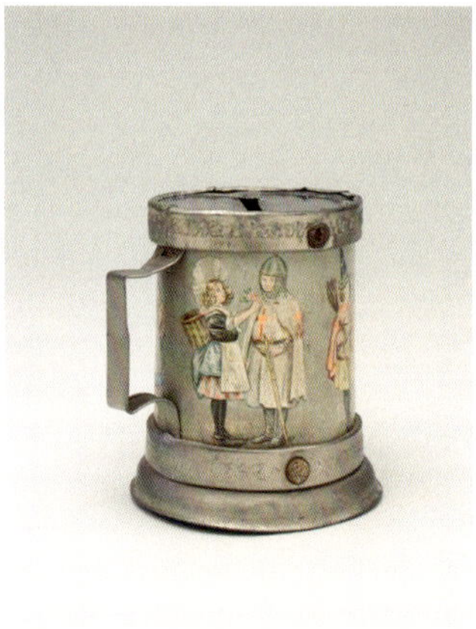

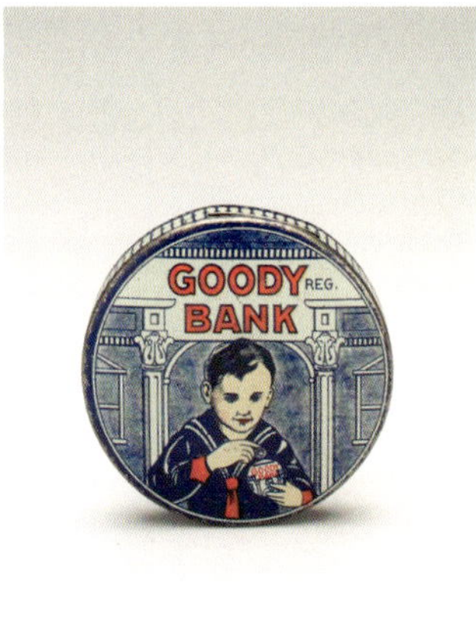
GOODY REG.
BANK

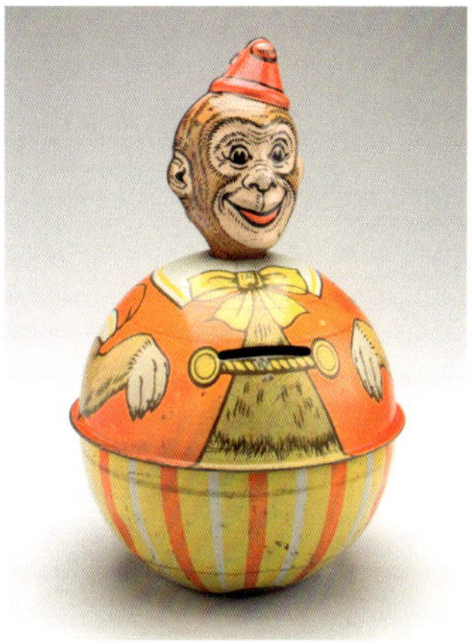

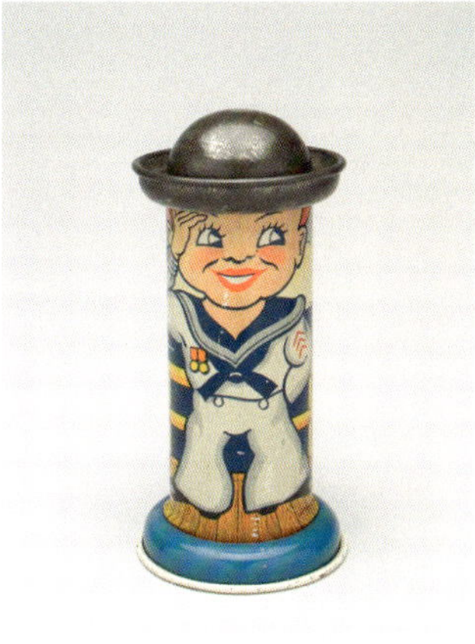

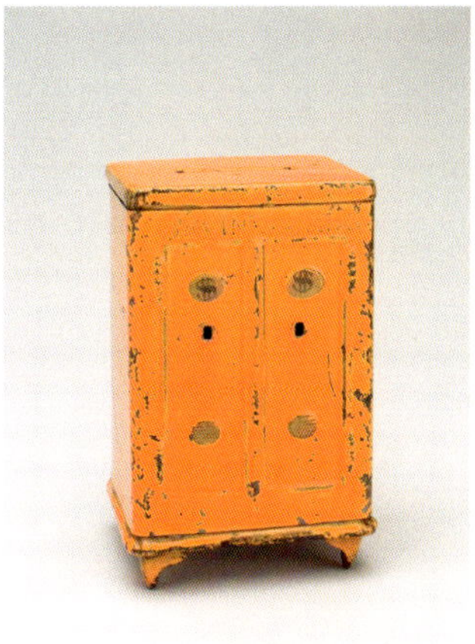

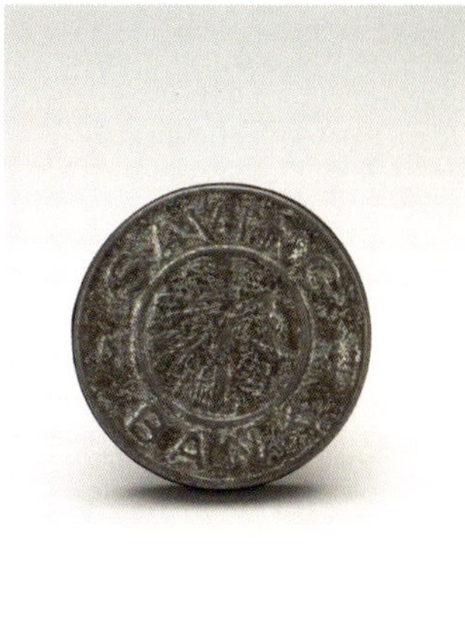

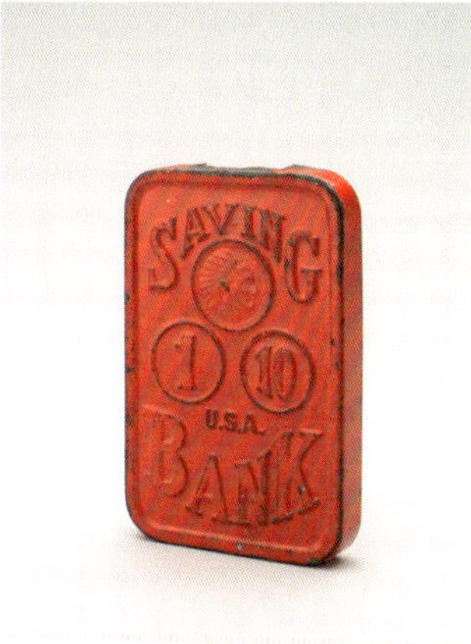
SAVING
1 10
U.S.A.
BANK

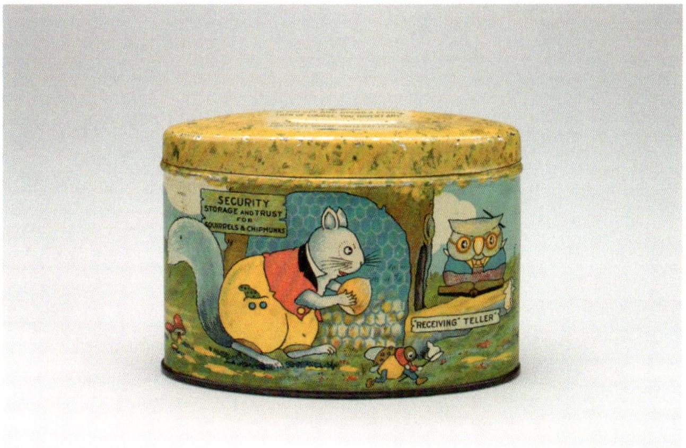
SECURITY STORAGE AND TRUST FOR SQUIRRELS & CHIPMUNKS
"RECEIVING" TELLER

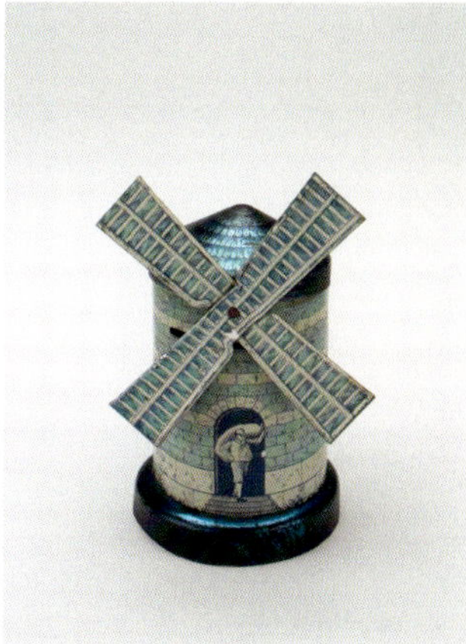

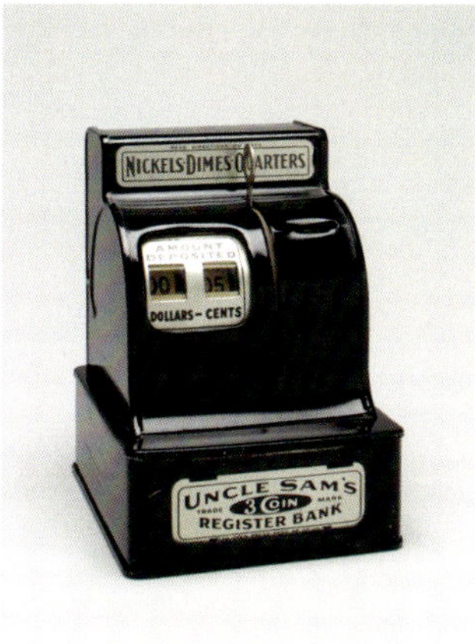
NICKELS DIMES QUARTERS
DOLLARS – CENTS
UNCLE SAM'S 3 COIN REGISTER BANK

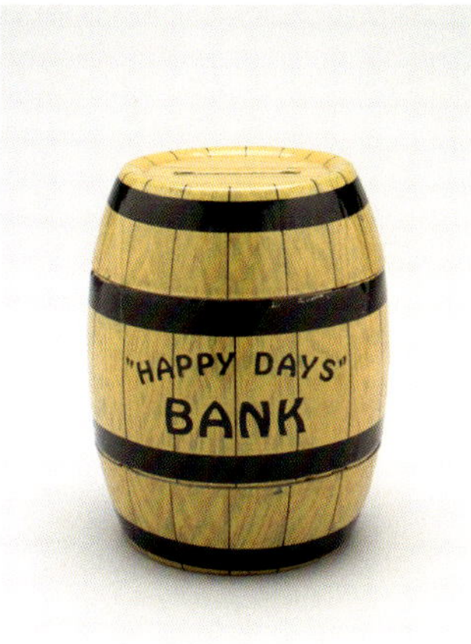
"HAPPY DAYS"
BANK

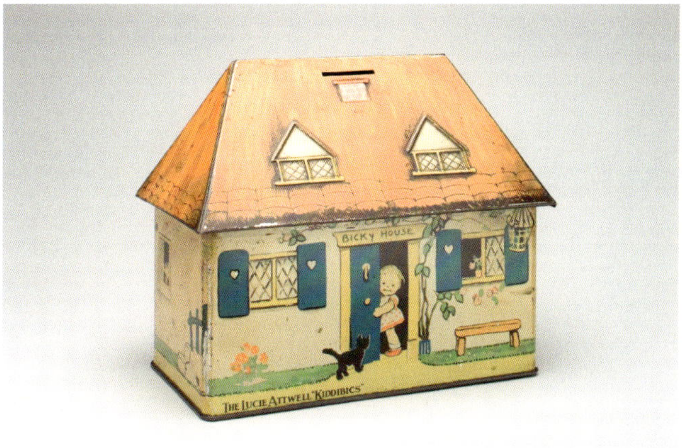
BICKY HOUSE
THE LUCIE ATTWELL "KIDDIBICS"

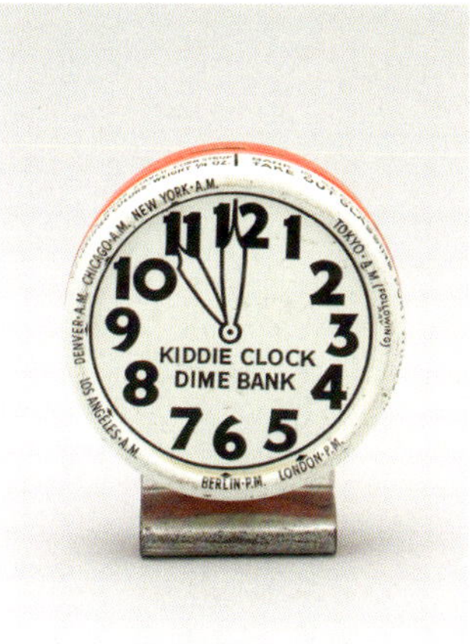
KIDDIE CLOCK
DIME BANK

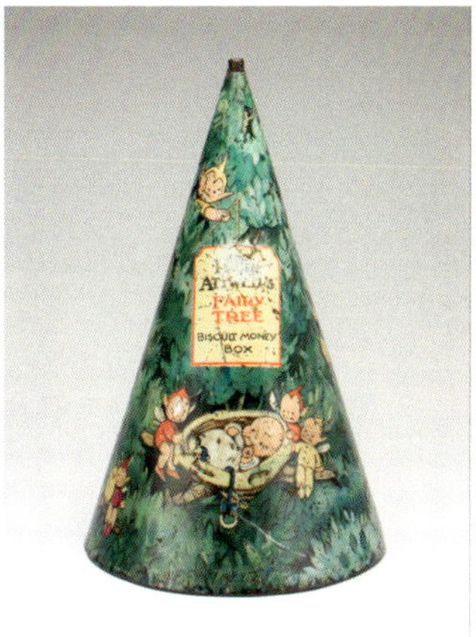
FAIRY TREE
BISCUIT MONEY BOX

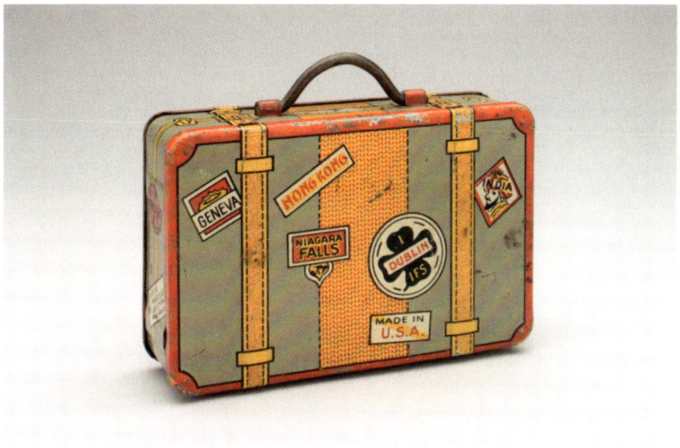
GENEVA
HONG KONG
NIAGARA FALLS
DUBLIN
INDIA
MADE IN U.S.A.

Saving Bank, c. 1930
United States
Tin
1 11/16 x 3/8 x 3/8 in.
2003.236.1017

Saving Bank, c. 1930
Japan
Tin, pigment
5 x 3 1/16 x 2 1/2 in.
2003.236.184

Sailor, c. 1930
United States
Tin, metal, pigment
4 7/8 x 2 7/16 x 2 7/16 in.
2003.236.244

Roly-Poly Monkey, c. 1930
J. Chein & Company, New York (1903 – 92), manufacturer
Tin, pigment
6 5/8 x 3 15/16 x 3 15/16 in.
2003.236.1038

Windmill, c. 1930
The Netherlands
Tin, pigment
3 1/4 x 2 1/8 x 2 1/8 in.
2003.236.12a,b

Squirrel Bank, c. 1930
United States
Tin, pigment
2 15/16 x 4 1/4 x 1 3/4 in. (oval)
2003.236.1043

Saving Bank, c. 1930
United States
Tin, pigment
3 1/4 x 2 1/8 x 5 in.
2003.236.1037

Lucie Attwell's Bicky House, c. 1930s
Mabel Lucie Attwell, English (1879 – 1964), designer
William Crawford & Sons, London, manufacturer
Tin, pigment
7 x 8 3/16 x 4 13/16 in.
2003.236.263

Happy Days Bank, c. 1930s
J. Chein & Company, New York (1903 – 92), manufacturer
Tin, pigment
3 3/4 x 2 13/16 x 2 13/16 in.
2003.236.1031

Uncle Sam's Three-Coin Register Bank (registering), c. 1930 – 60
Durable Toy and Novelty Corporation, New York and Cleveland (est. c. 1912), manufacturer
Tin, pigment, plastic
6 3/16 x 4 9/16 x 5 1/4 in.
2003.236.234

Suitcase, c. 1930s
Louis Marx & Company, New York (1919 – 79), manufacturer
Tin, pigment
4 1/16 x 2 11/16 x 1 1/16 in.
2003.236.1042

Lucie Attwell's Fairy Tree Biscuit Money Box, c. 1930s
Mabel Lucie Attwell, English (1879 – 1964), designer
England
Tin, pigment
10 1/4 x 3 x 6 3/16 in.
2003.236.806

Kiddie Clock Dime Bank, c. 1930s
J. C. Crosetti Company, Jeannette, Pennsylvania, manufacturer
Tin, pigment, glassine
2 5/16 x 1 7/8 x 5 in.
2003.236.1056

Coin Registering Bank, c. 1932
Kingsbury Manufacturing Company, Keene, New Hampshire, manufacturer
Tin, pigment, glass
$6\frac{7}{8}$ x $5\frac{1}{8}$ x $3\frac{7}{16}$ in.
2003.236.667

Wright's Thermo X Gas Fire, c. 1930s
John Wright & Company, Birmingham, England, manufacturer
Tin, pigment
$4\frac{1}{2}$ x $4\frac{3}{8}$ x $1\frac{3}{4}$ in.
2003.236.715

Telephone, c. 1930s
United States
Tin, pigment, string
$3\frac{1}{2}$ x $7\frac{1}{2}$ x $6\frac{1}{8}$ in.
2003.236.1044

George VI Coronation Souvenir Money Box, 1937
OXO, Ltd, London (est. 1914), manufacturer
Tin, pigment
3 x $2\frac{1}{2}$ x $1\frac{1}{2}$ in.
2003.236.358a,b

George VI and Queen Elizabeth Coronation Bank, 1937
England
Tin, pigment
$3\frac{5}{8}$ x $3\frac{7}{8}$ x $1\frac{11}{16}$ in.
2003.236.353a,b

Postbox, c. 1936 – 52
England
Tin, pigment
5 x $3\frac{1}{2}$ x 2 in.
2003.236.355

Globe Bank, c. 1934 – 77
J. Chein & Company, New York (1903 – 92), manufacturer
Tin, pigment
$4\frac{9}{16}$ x $3\frac{3}{8}$ x $3\frac{3}{8}$ in.
2003.236.181

Daily Dime Piggy Bank (registering), c. 1949
Kalon Manufacturing Corporation, Brooklyn, New York, manufacturer
Tin, pigment
$2\frac{5}{8}$ x $2\frac{5}{8}$ x $\frac{5}{8}$ in.
2003.236.1016

Het Apeldoornsche Bosch, c. 1940s
Bekkers Dordrecht, the Netherlands, manufacturer
Tin, pigment, fabric
$3\frac{3}{4}$ x $3\frac{1}{8}$ x $2\frac{3}{8}$ in.
2003.236.306

Capitol Dime Register Bank (registering), c. 1940 – 50
United States
Tin, pigment
$2\frac{9}{16}$ x $2\frac{9}{16}$ x $\frac{5}{8}$ in.
2003.236.1012

Snow White Dime Register (registering), c. 1938
United States
Tin, pigment
$2\frac{9}{16}$ x $2\frac{9}{16}$ x $\frac{5}{8}$ in.
2003.236.1013

Mickey Mouse Post Office, c. 1950
PACA, Liverpool, England, manufacturer
Tin, pigment
$4\frac{13}{16}$ x $2\frac{3}{8}$ x $2\frac{3}{8}$ in.
2003.236.580

Mickey Mouse and Minnie Mouse Post Office, c. 1950
England
Tin, pigment
6 x $2\frac{11}{16}$ x $2\frac{11}{16}$ in.
2003.236.250

Daily Dime Vacation Bank (registering, with attached card), c. 1949
Kalon Manufacturing Corporation, Brooklyn, New York, manufacturer
Tin, pigment, paper
$2\frac{5}{8}$ x $2\frac{5}{8}$ x $\frac{5}{8}$ in.
2003.236.1014a,b

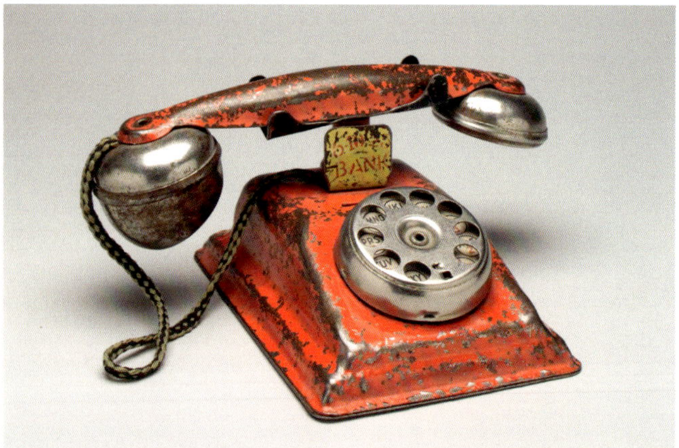
BANK

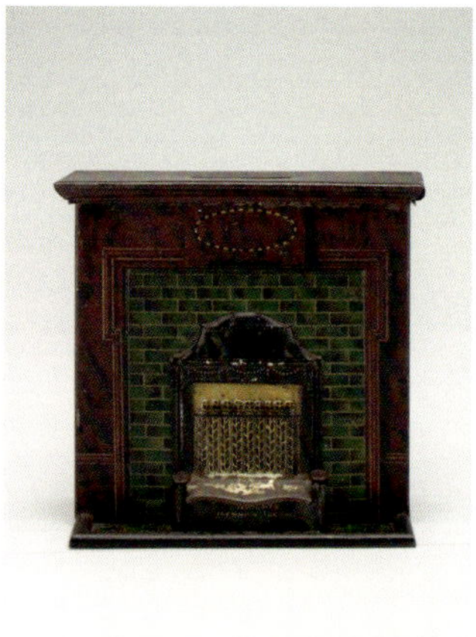

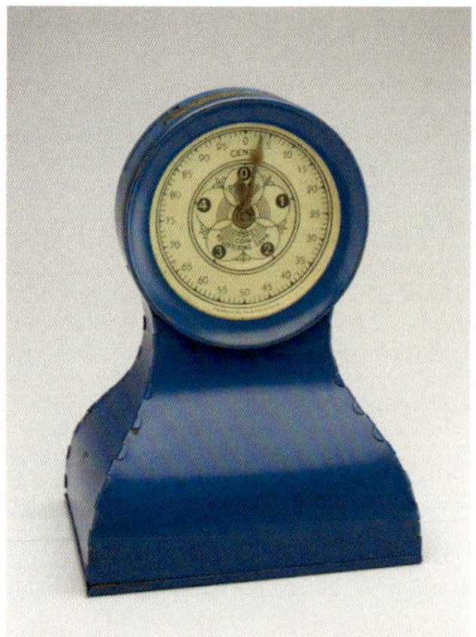

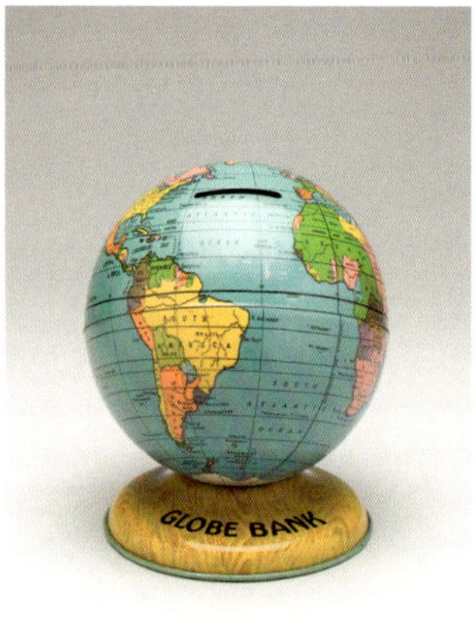
GLOBE BANK

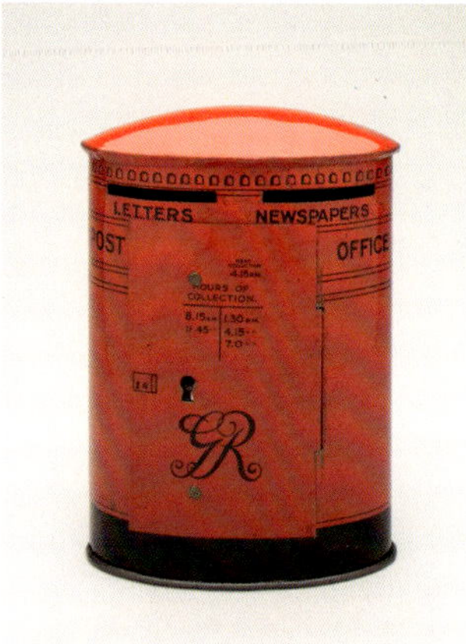
LETTERS
NEWSPAPERS
POST
OFFICE
GR

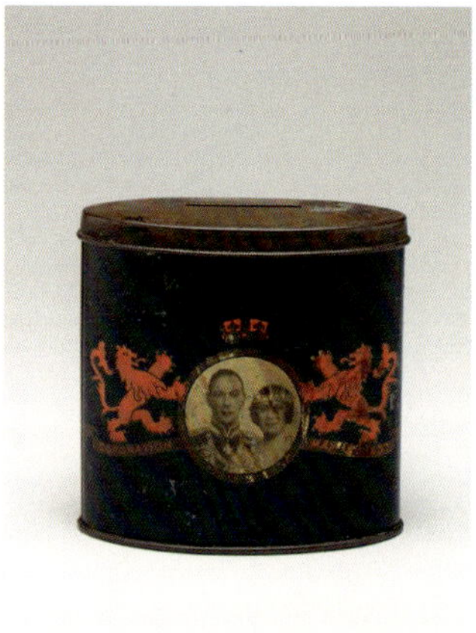

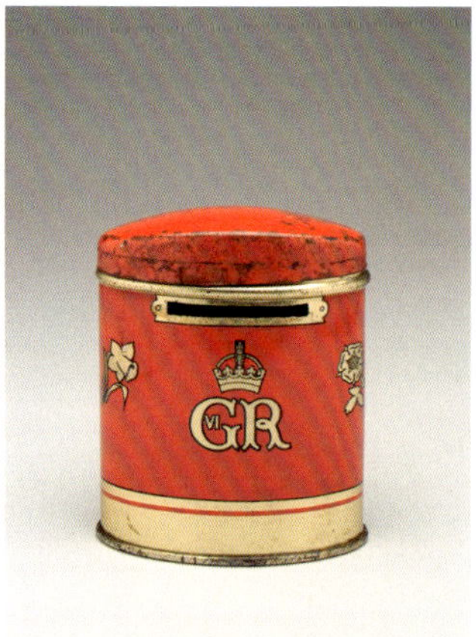
VI
GR

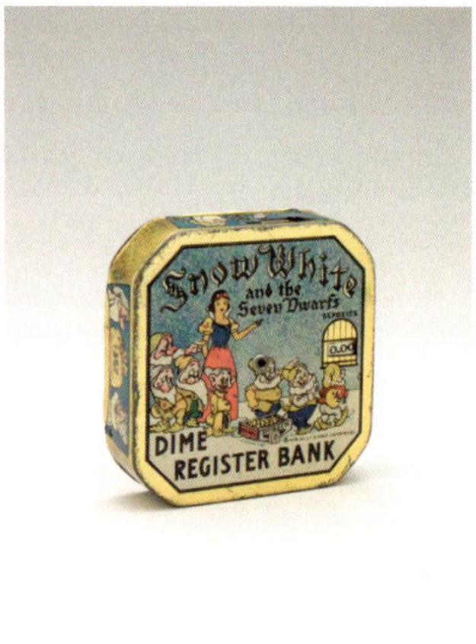
Snow White
and the
Seven Dwarfs
DIME
REGISTER BANK

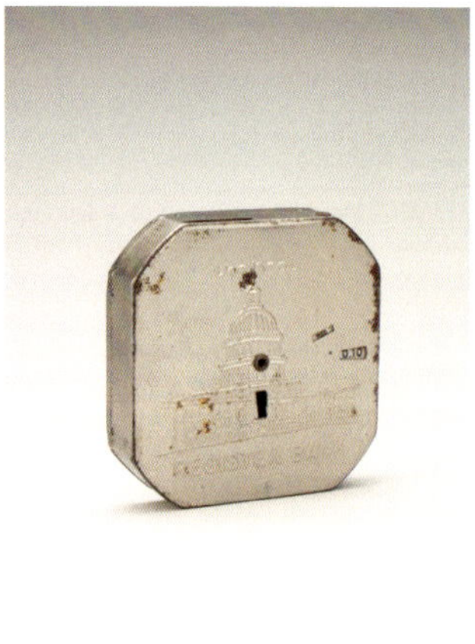

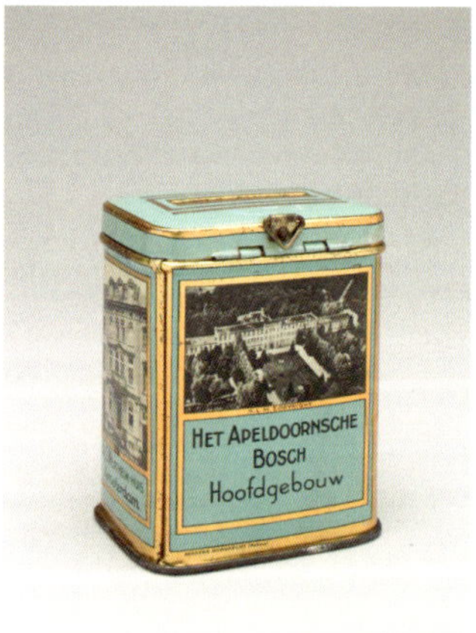
HET APELDOORNSCHE
BOSCH
Hoofdgebouw

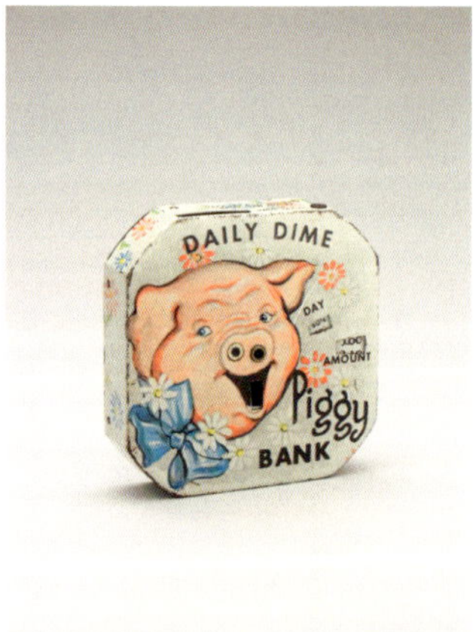
DAILY DIME
DAY
AMOUNT
Piggy
BANK

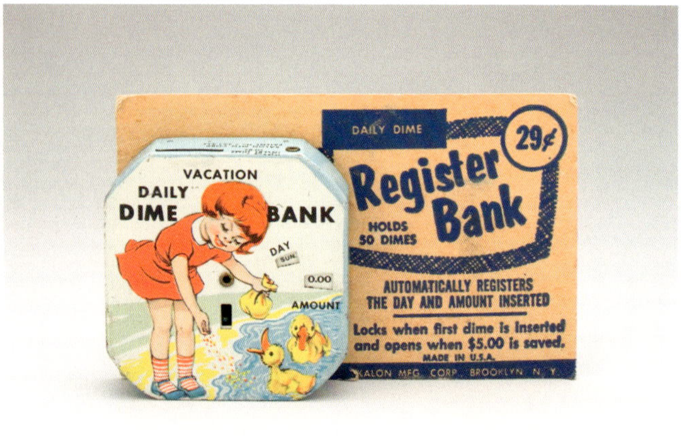
VACATION
DAILY
DIME
BANK
DAY
AMOUNT
DAILY DIME
Register
Bank
HOLDS
50 DIMES
29¢
AUTOMATICALLY REGISTERS
THE DAY AND AMOUNT INSERTED
Locks when first dime is inserted
and opens when $5.00 is saved.
MADE IN U.S.A.
KALON MFG. CORP. BROOKLYN N.Y.

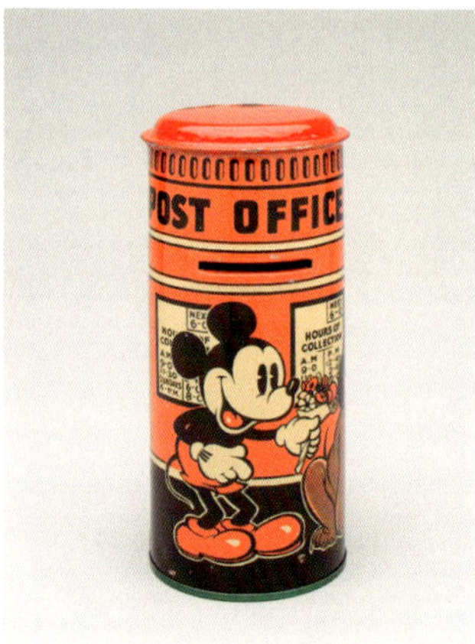
POST OFFICE

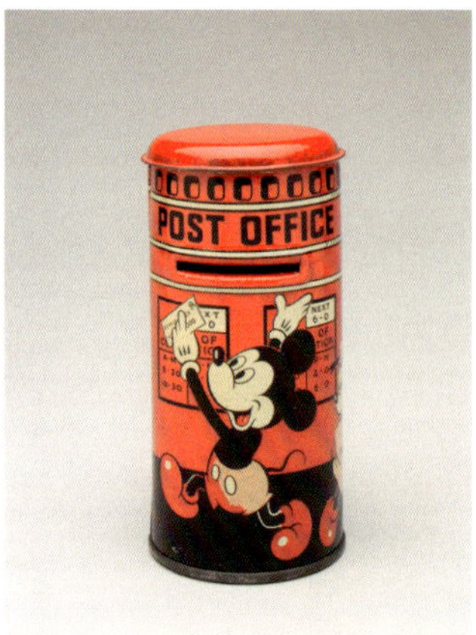
POST OFFICE

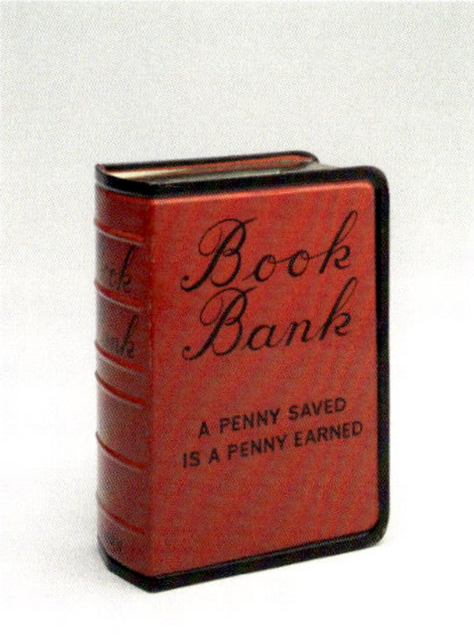
Book Bank
A PENNY SAVED
IS A PENNY EARNED

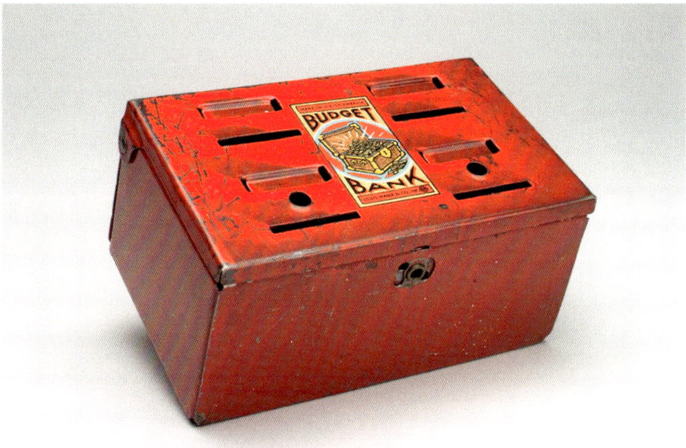
BUDGET
BANK

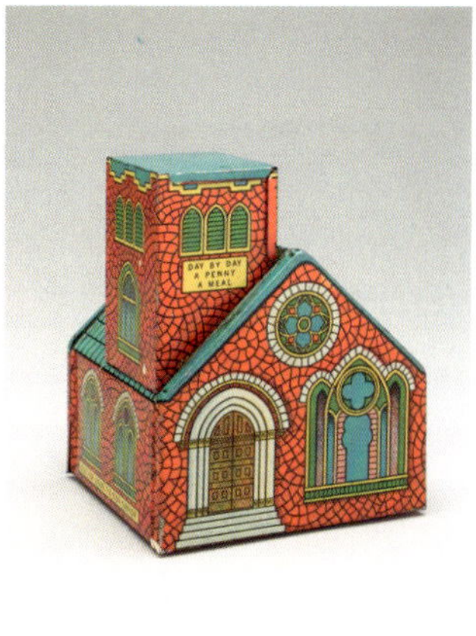
DAY BY DAY
A PENNY
A MEAL

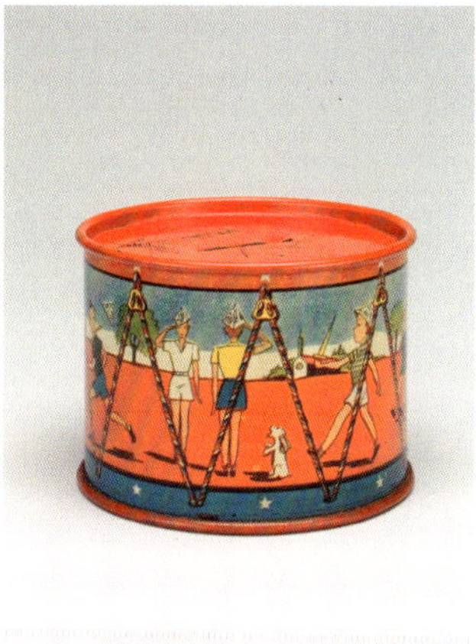

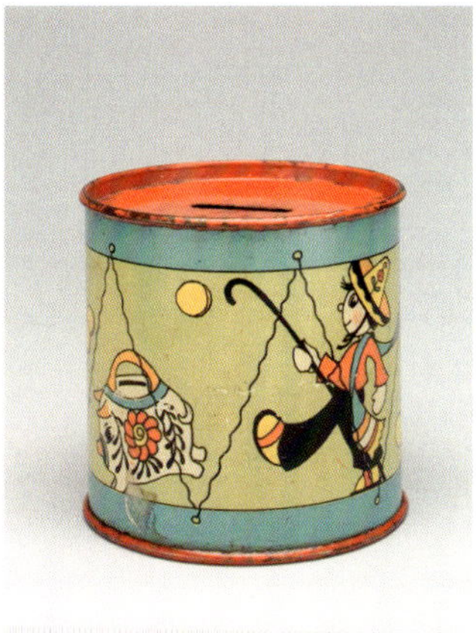

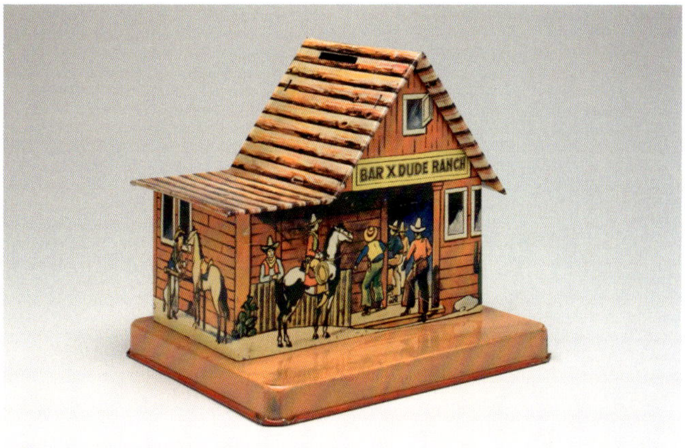
BAR X DUDE RANCH

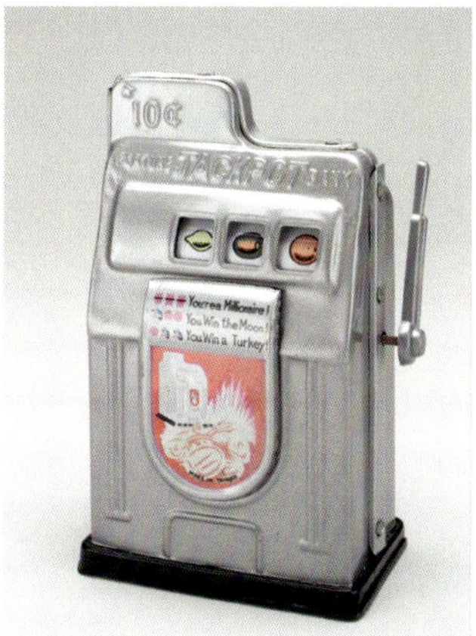
10¢

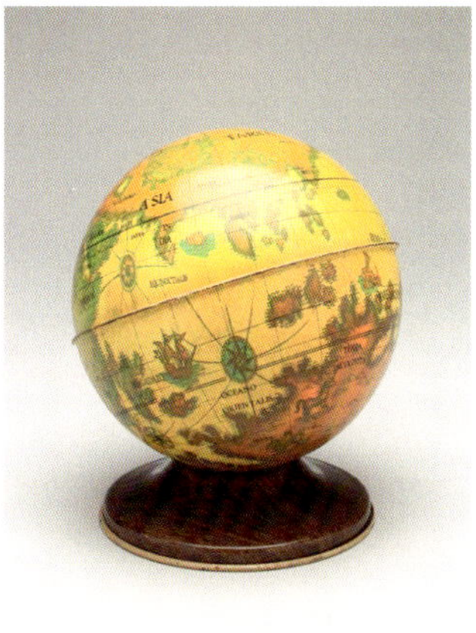

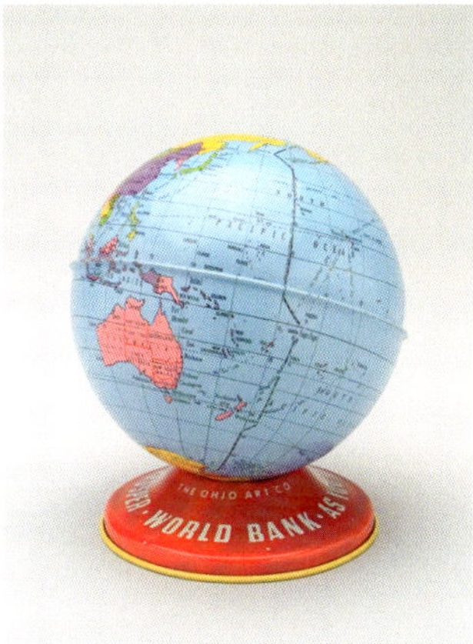
WORLD BANK

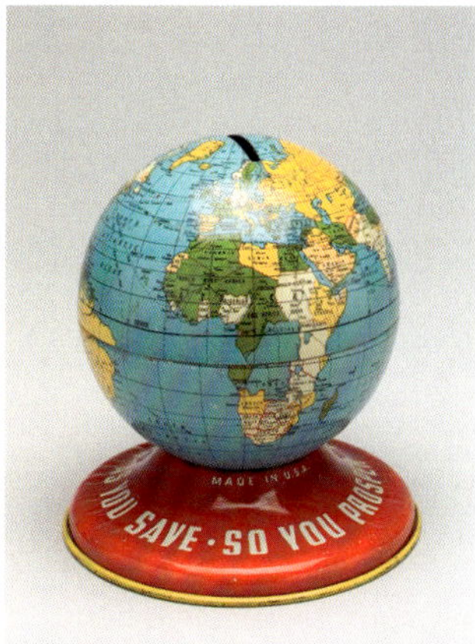
SAVE · SO YOU

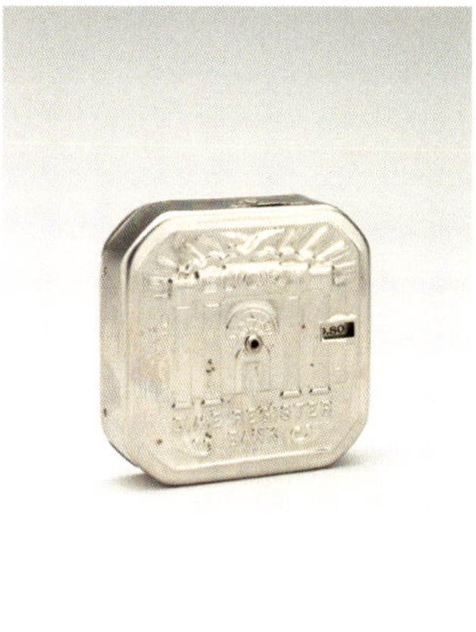

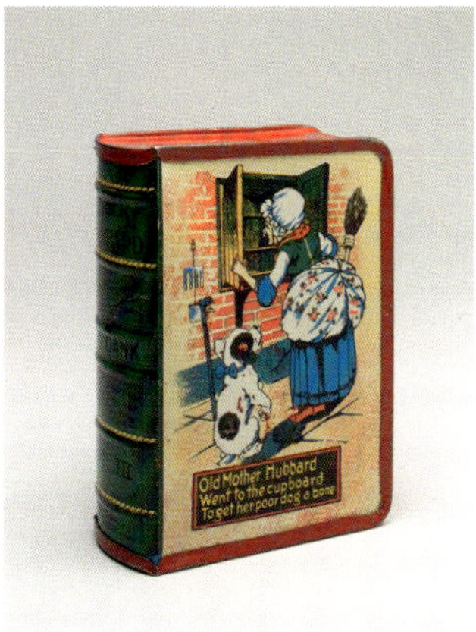
Old Mother Hubbard
Went to the cupboard
To get her poor dog a bone

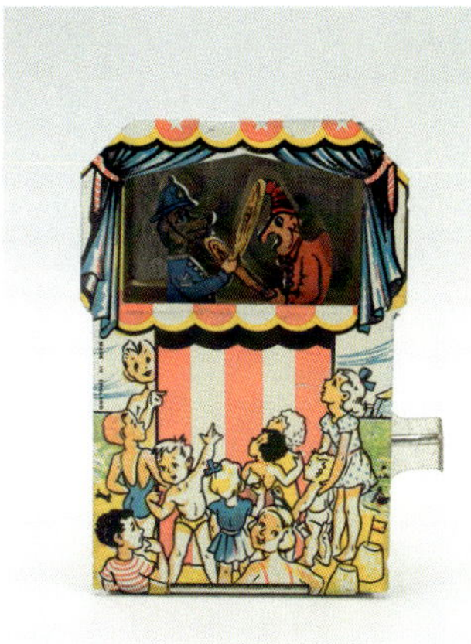

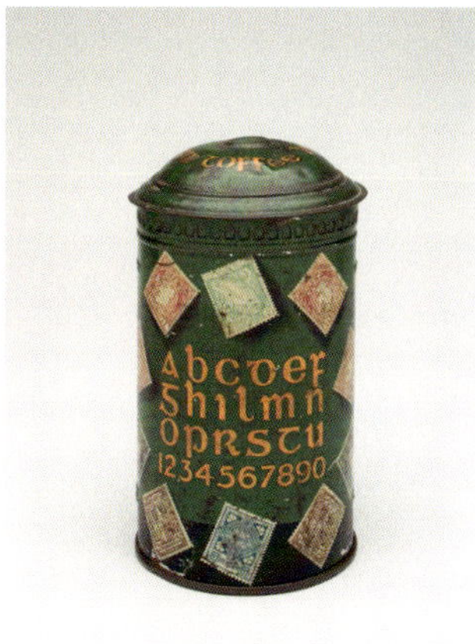
1234567890

Day by Day, a Penny a Meal, mid-20th century
J. Chein & Company, New York (1903 – 92), manufacturer
Tin, pigment
3 7/8 x 3 1/4 x 3 in.
2003.236.305

Budget Bank, mid-20th century
Louis Marx & Company, New York (1919 – 79), manufacturer
Tin, pigment
2 11/16 x 6 3/4 x 3 1/2 in.
2003.236.180

Book Bank, mid-20th century
Japan
Tin, pigment
3 11/16 x 2 11/16 x 1 1/4 in.
2003.236.1036

Bar X Dude Ranch, mid-20th century
U.S. Metal Toy Manufacturing Company, New York, manufacturer
Tin, pigment
4 5/8 x 5 13/16 x 4 1/8 in.
2003.236.359

Drum, mid 20th century
Ohio Art Company, Bryan, Ohio (est. 1908), manufacturer
Tin, pigment
3 1/16 x 3 1/4 x 3 1/4 in.
2003.236.1040

Drum, mid-20th century
Ohio Art Company, Bryan, Ohio (est. 1908), manufacturer
Tin, pigment
2 5/16 x 3 1/8 in.
2003.236.1039

Globe Bank, mid-20th century
Ohio Art Company, Bryan, Ohio (est. 1908), manufacturer
Tin, pigment
3 1/2 x 3 3/8 x 3 3/8 in.
2003.236.1071

Globe, mid-20th century
Ohio Art Company, Bryan, Ohio (est. 1908), manufacturer
Tin, pigment
4 9/16 x 4 3/16 x 4 3/16 in.
2003.236.265

Globe, mid-20th century
Ohio Art Company, Bryan, Ohio (est. 1908), manufacturer
Tin, pigment
4 9/16 x 4 1/8 x 4 1/8 in.
2003.236.264

Fortune Jackpot Bank, mid-20th century
Taiwan
Tin, plastic, pigment
5 3/4 x 3 9/16 x 2 3/8 in.
2003.236.197

N. K. M. Cream Toffee Postbox, c. 1950s
North Kerry Manufacturing Company, Dublin, Ireland, manufacturer
Tin, pigment
6 3/8 x 3 3/4 x 3 3/4 in.
2003.236.251a,b

Punch and Judy, mid-20th century
England
Tin, pigment
4 5/16 x 3 1/16 x 1 7/16 in.
2003.236.85

Mother Hubbard, mid-20th century
Kirchhof, Newark, New Jersey, manufacturer
Tin, pigment
3 15/16 x 3 x 1 5/16 in.
2003.236.1035

Lucky Dime Register Bank (registering), mid-20th century
United States
Tin, pigment
2 9/16 x 2 9/16 x 5/8 in.
2003.236.1022

Post Office, c. 1950s
England
Tin, pigment
4 3/4 x 3 9/16 x 2 9/16 in.
2003.236.255

Post Office, c. 1950s
Hong Kong
Tin, pigment
4 3/4 x 2 3/16 x 2 3/16 in.
2003.236.247a,b

School, mid-20th century
U.S. Metal Toy Manufacturing Company, New York, manufacturer
Tin, pigment
4 7/16 x 5 1/4 x 4 1/4 in.
2003.236.179

World Champions, c. 1950s
Ohio Art Company, Bryan, Ohio (est. 1908), manufacturer
Tin, pigment
3 11/16 x 3 1/2 x 3 1/2 in.
2003.236.1058

Welcome Bank Service Station, c. 1950s
United States
Tin, pigment
2 1/4 x 8 1/4 x 3 1/16 in.
2003.236.242

T.V. Bank, c. 1950s
United States
Tin, pigment
3 15/16 x 2 1/8 x 1 11/16 in.
2003.236.581

U.S. Mailbox, c. 1960
Japan
Tin, pigment
7 1/4 x 3 1/2 x 3 1/2 in.
2003.236.304a,b

Sputnik Bank, c. 1957
Japan
Tin, pigment
3 1/2 x 3 x 3 in.
2003.236.738

Popeye Daily Dime Bank (registering), c. 1956
United States
Tin, pigment
2 9/16 x 2 9/16 x 5/8 in.
2003.236.1015

Festival of Britain (registering), c. 1951
Great Britain
Tin, pigment
4 7/8 x 3 1/8 x 1 3/4 in.
2003.236.1011

Clock Bank, c. 1980
China
Tin, plastic, pigment
6 x 5 x 2 1/2 in.
2003.236.356

Rainbow Money Box, c. 1970s
Rainbow Designs, London, manufacturer
Tin, pigment
3 11/16 x 2 13/16 x 2 13/16 in.
2003.236.590a,b

Buddy L. Easy-Saver (registering), c. 1970s
Buddy L. Corporation, Hong Kong, manufacturer
Tin, plastic, pigment
6 5/16 x 4 1/2 x 5 1/4 in.
2003.236.192

My Snoopy Bank, 1960s or 1970s
United States
Tin, paper, pigment
4 7/16 x 2 15/16 x 2 15/16 in.
2003.236.245

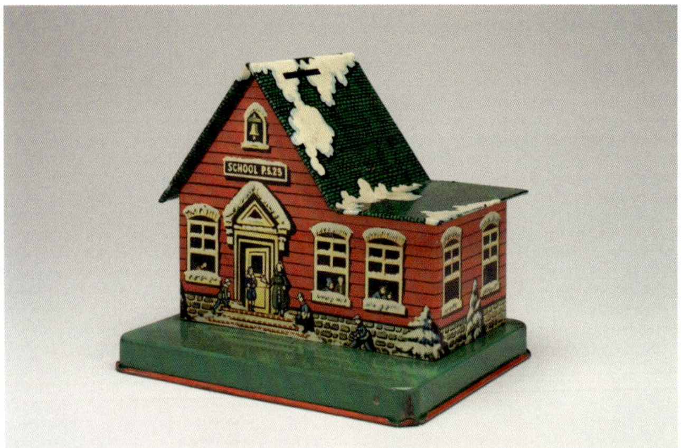
SCHOOL P.S.23

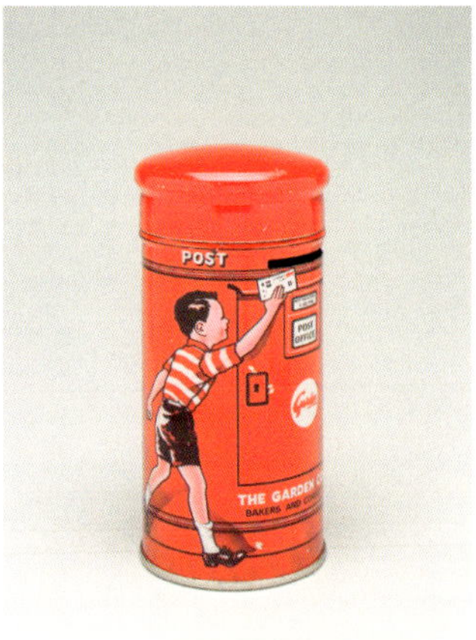
POST

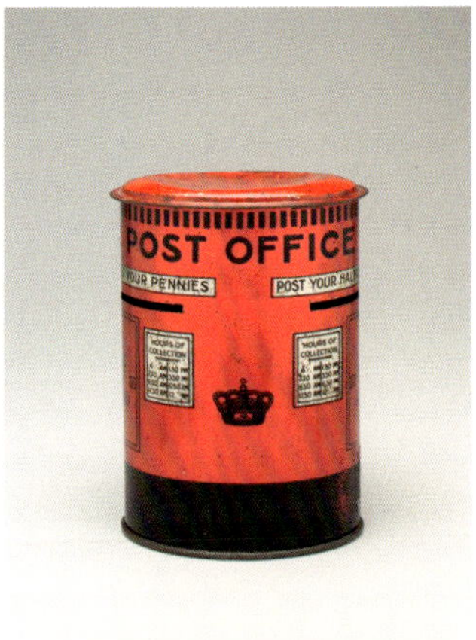
POST OFFICE

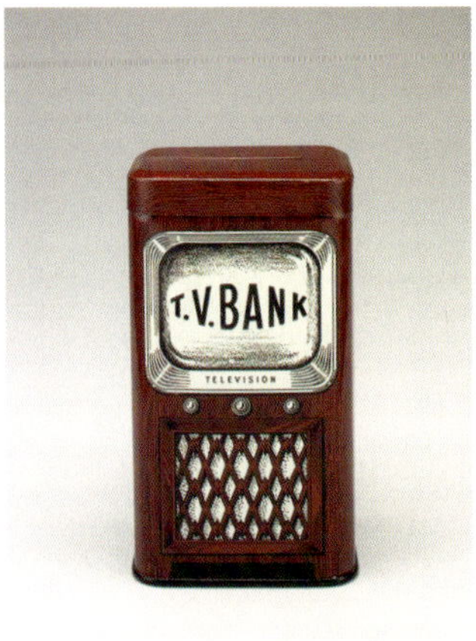
T.V. BANK
TELEVISION

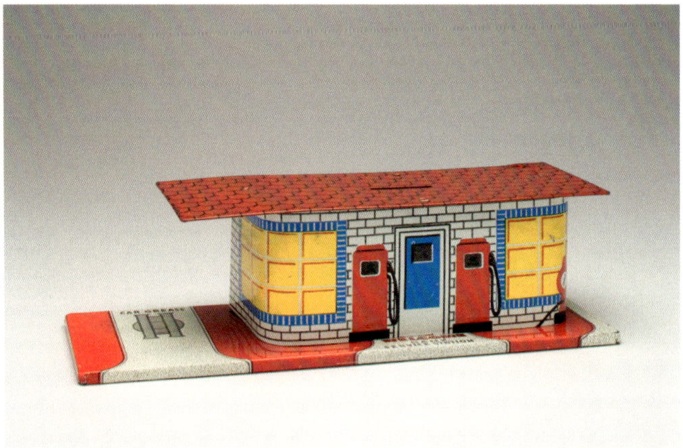

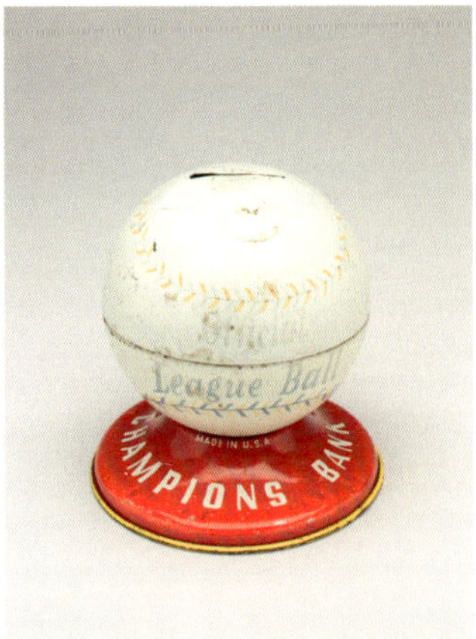
League Ball
CHAMPIONS BANK

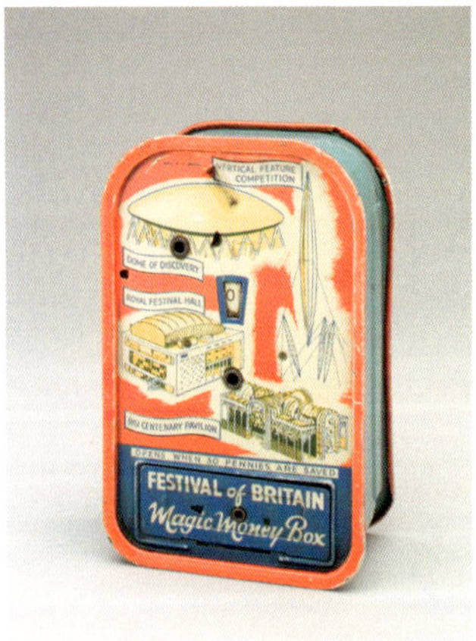
FESTIVAL of BRITAIN
Magic Money Box

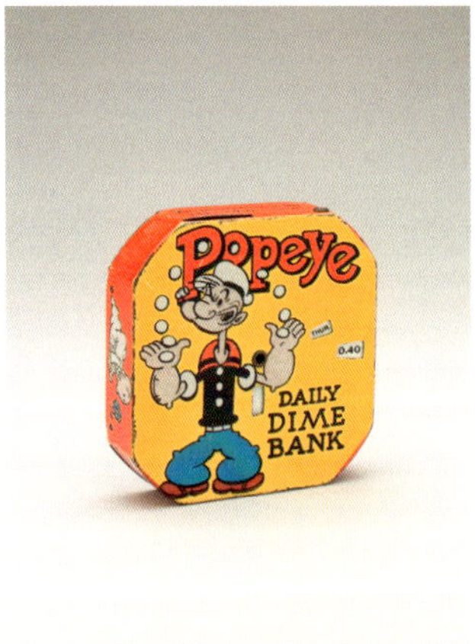
Popeye
DAILY DIME BANK

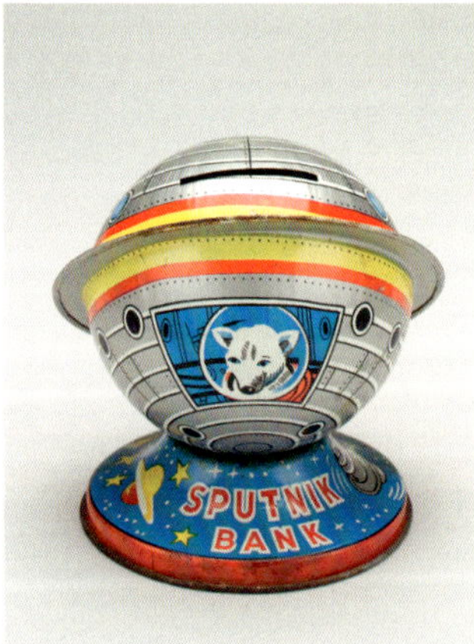
SPUTNIK BANK

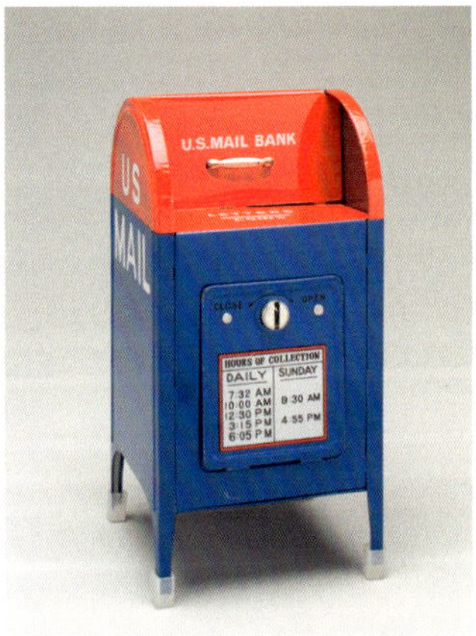
U.S. MAIL BANK
US MAIL

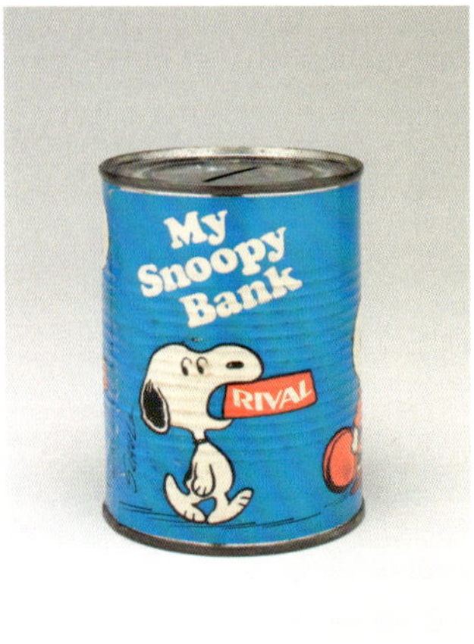
My Snoopy Bank
RIVAL

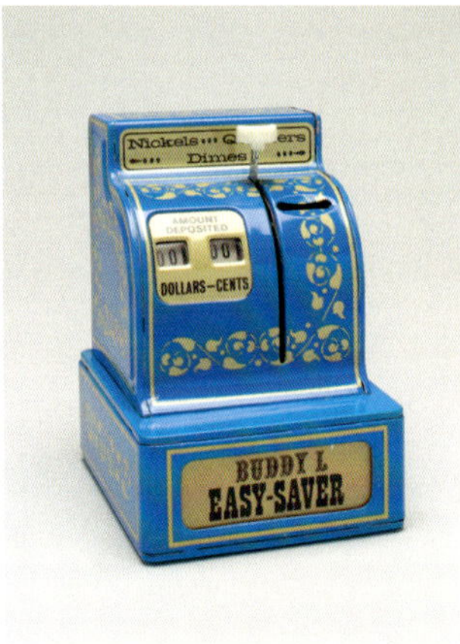
DOLLARS—CENTS
BUDDY L
EASY-SAVER

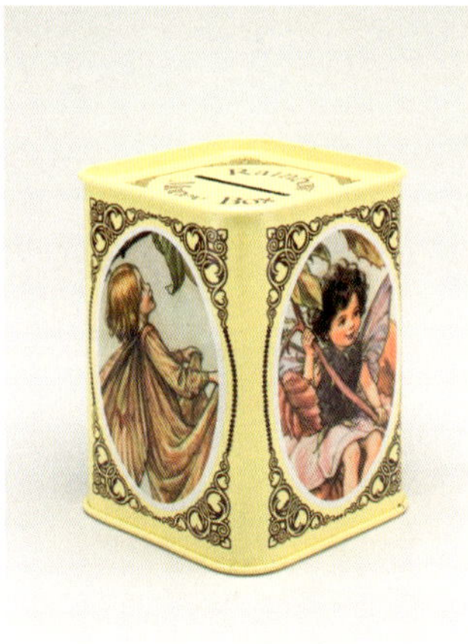

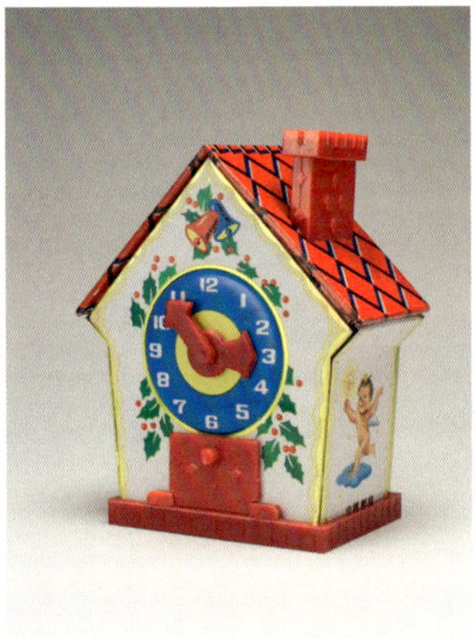

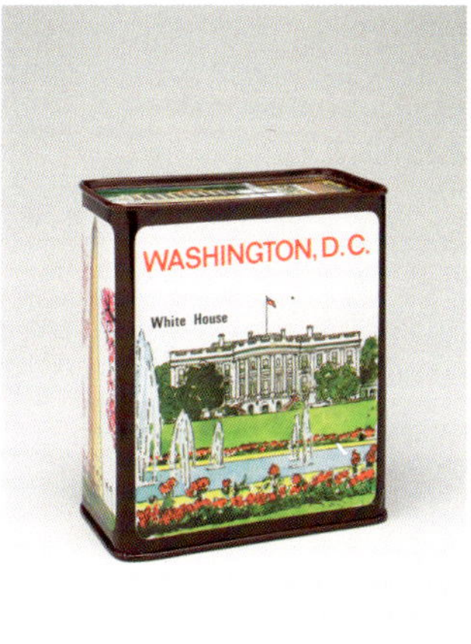
WASHINGTON, D.C.
White House

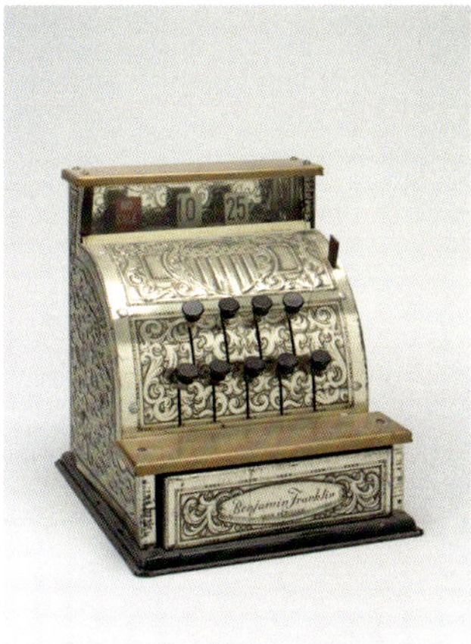

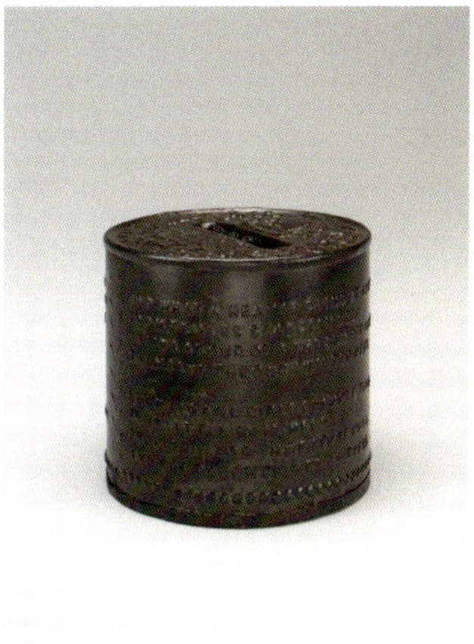

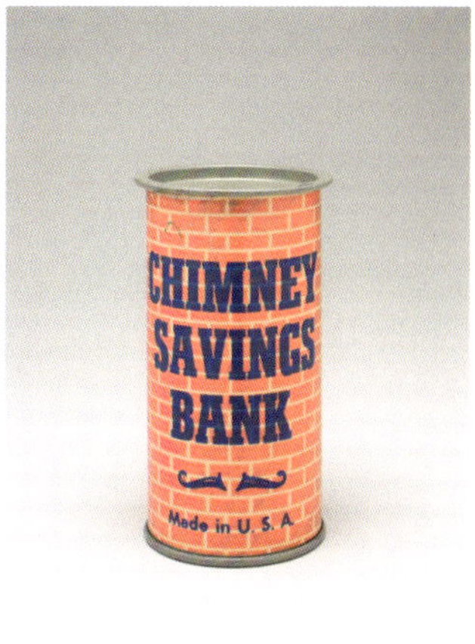
CHIMNEY
SAVINGS
BANK
Made in U.S.A.

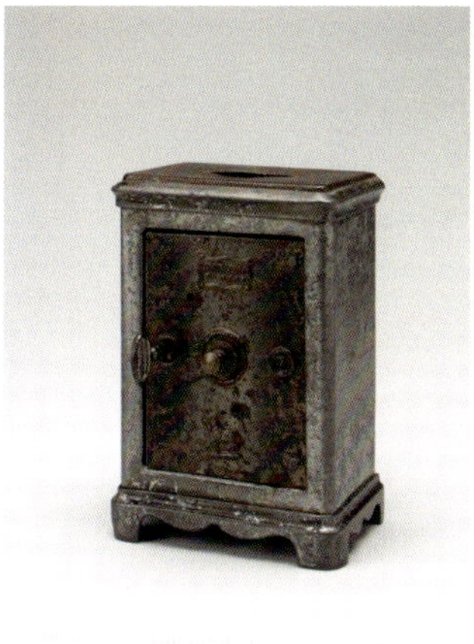

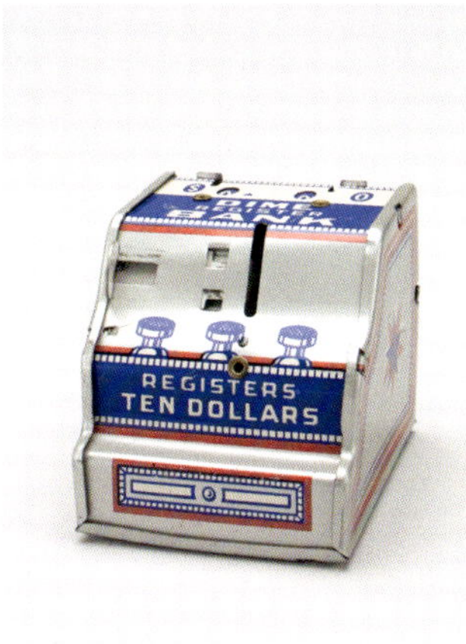
REGISTERS
TEN DOLLARS

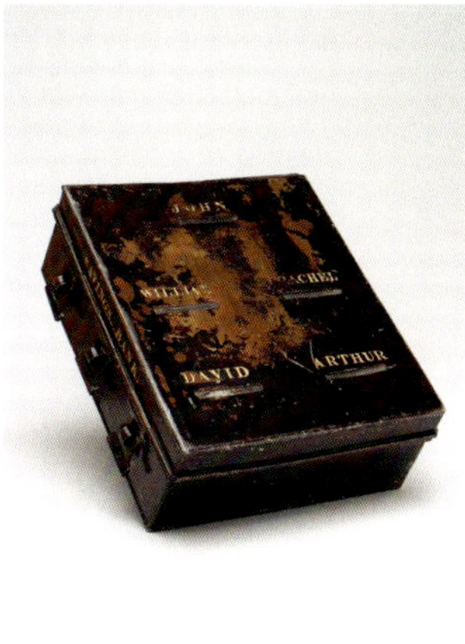
DAVID
ARTHUR

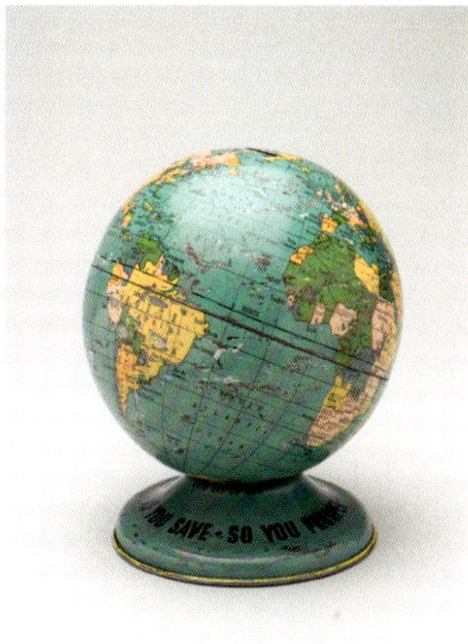

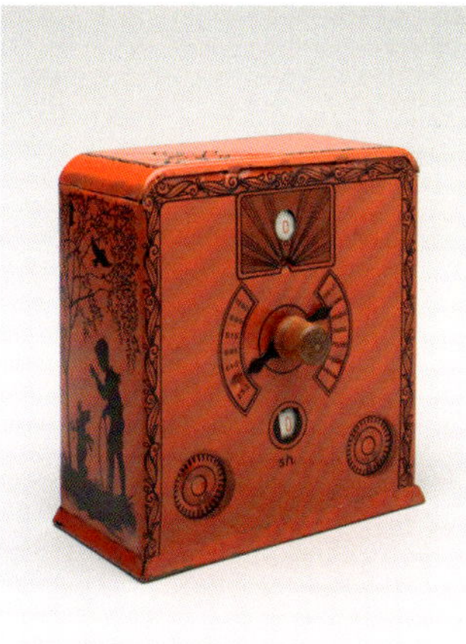

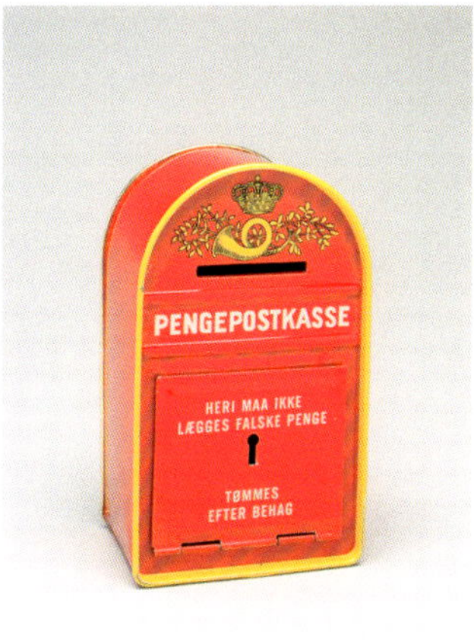
PENGEPOSTKASSE
HERI MAA IKKE
LÆGGES FALSKE PENGE
TØMMES
EFTER BEHAG

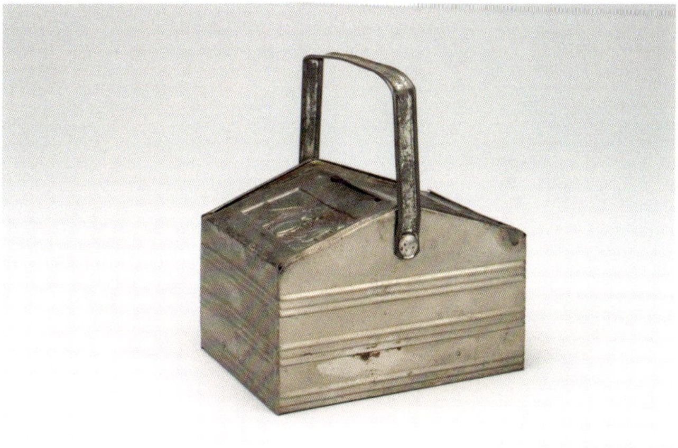

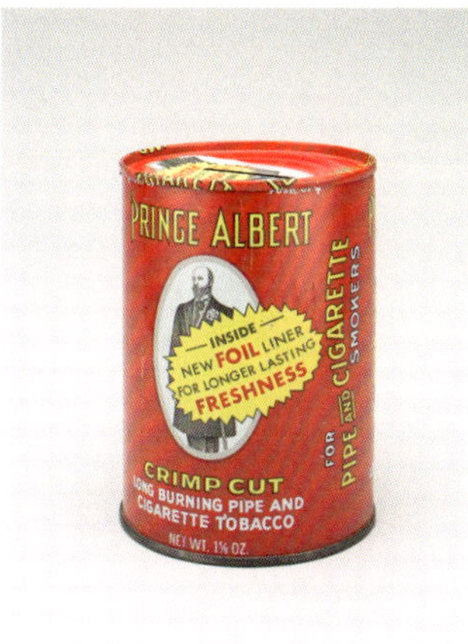
PRINCE ALBERT
INSIDE
NEW FOIL LINER
FOR LONGER LASTING
FRESHNESS
CRIMP CUT
LONG BURNING PIPE AND
CIGARETTE TOBACCO
FOR PIPE AND CIGARETTE SMOKERS

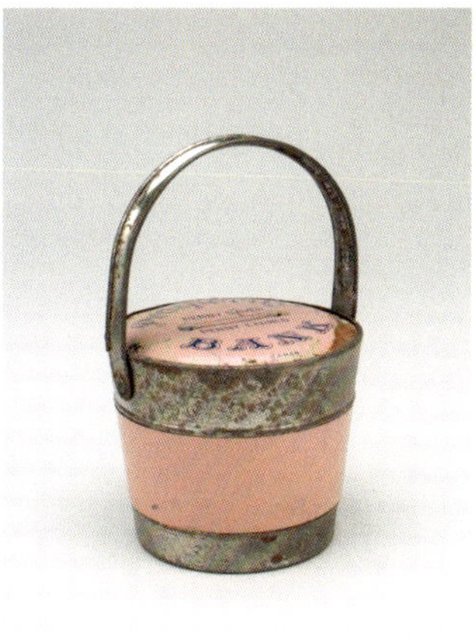

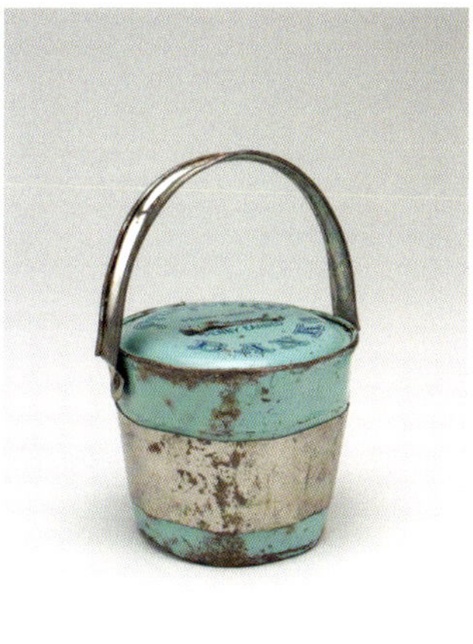

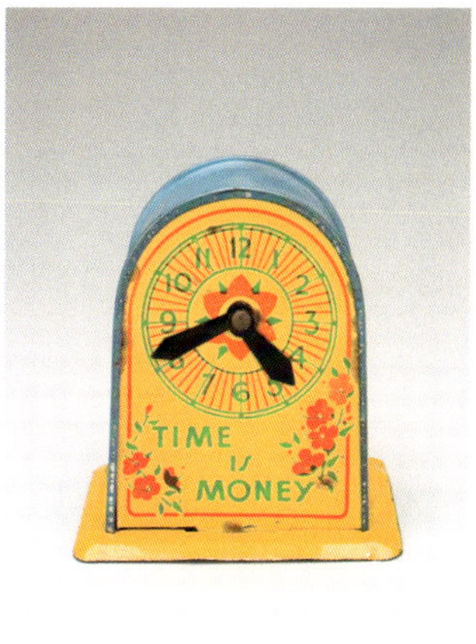
TIME
IS
MONEY

Chimney Savings Bank, 20th century
United States
Tin, paper, pigment
4 3/4 x 2 11/16 x 2 11/16 in.
2003.236.253

Busy Bee, 20th century
Probably England
Tin
2 1/2 x 2 3/4 x 2 3/4 in.
2003.236.254

Benjamin Franklin Cash Register (registering), 20th century
Kamkap, Inc., New York, manufacturer
Tin, pigment
7 3/8 x 6 3/4 x 7 1/2 in.
2003.236.194

Washington, D.C., Still Bank Collectors Club of America, 1981
Hong Kong
Tin, pigment
4 15/16 x 4 3/8 x 2 7/16 in.
2003.236.211

Globe, 20th century
Ohio Art Company, Bryan, Ohio (est. 1908), manufacturer
Tin, pigment
5 1/16 x 4 x 4 in.
2003.236.301

Family Savings Bank, 20th century
Tin, pigment, lacquer
7 1/2 x 6 9/16 x 2 1/2 in.
2003.236.187

Dime Register (registering), 20th century
J. Chein & Company, New York (1903 – 92), manufacturer
Tin, pigment
2 x 2 1/16 x 2 7/16 in.
2003.236.566

Coffreford Safe, 20th century
Tin, pigment
4 1/4 x 2 7/8 x 1 7/8 in.
2003.236.1034

Picnic Basket, 20th century
Germany
Tin
2 x 3 3/8 x 2 3/8 in.
2003.236.268

Pengepostkasse (Penny Postbox), 20th century
Denmark
Tin, pigment
4 9/16 x 2 9/16 x 1 7/8 in.
2003.236.357

Money Converter (registering), 20th century
Germany
Tin, pigment
4 1/4 x 3 15/16 x 2 1/2 in.
2003.236.664

Time Is Money, 20th century
England
Tin, paper, pigment
3 9/16 x 3 1/4 x 2 1/4 in.
2003.236.545

Prosperity Bank, 20th century
J. Chein & Company, New York (1903 – 92), manufacturer
Tin, pigment
2 1/4 x 3 x 3 in. (without handle)
2003.236.260

Prosperity Bank, 20th century
Japan
Tin, pigment
2 5/16 x 3 x 3 in. (without handle)
2003.236.259

Prince Albert (tobacco can), 20th century
R. J. Reynolds Tobacco Company, Winston-Salem, North Carolina (est. 1875), manufacturer
Tin, pigment
4 1/4 x 3 1/8 x 3 1/8 in.
2003.236.588

Time to Save, 20th century
Tin, pigment
3 11/16 x 5 7/16 x 1 7/8 in.
2003.236.183

Pyramid, 20th century
Tin, pigment
2 1/8 x 3 3/16 x 3 1/4 in.
2003.236.577

STILL BANKS: Other Metals

Tom Thumb Cash Register (registering), 20th century
Western Stamping Company, Jackson, Michigan, manufacturer
Tin, plastic, pigment
7 1/2 x 6 9/16 x 7 5/16 in.
2003.236.195

White House, 20th century
Elizabeth Greene, designer
Avon Tin, Bristol, England, manufacturer
Tin, pigment
4 x 4 3/4 x 2 15/16 in.
2003.236.362a,b

Trunk, c. 1890
Piaget, United States, manufacturer
Metal, pigment
2 5/8 x 3 5/8 x 2 1/8 in.
2003.236.275

Birth Bank, Large, c. 1860
England
Brass, steel
7 3/4 x 4 11/16 x 2 1/2 in.
2003.236.683

Birth Bank with Clock, c. 1840
England
Brass, steel, paper, glass
7 x 5 1/8 x 3 in.
2003.236.682

Churchyard, late 19th century
France
Brass
3 7/8 x 9 1/4 x 6 in.
2003.236.920

Birth Bank, 19th century
Continental Europe
Brass
7 13/16 x 6 13/16 x 8 1/2 in.
2003.236.193

Jane's Wee Bellows, 1896
Scotland
Metal
8 11/16 x 4 x 1 5/8 in.
2003.236.188

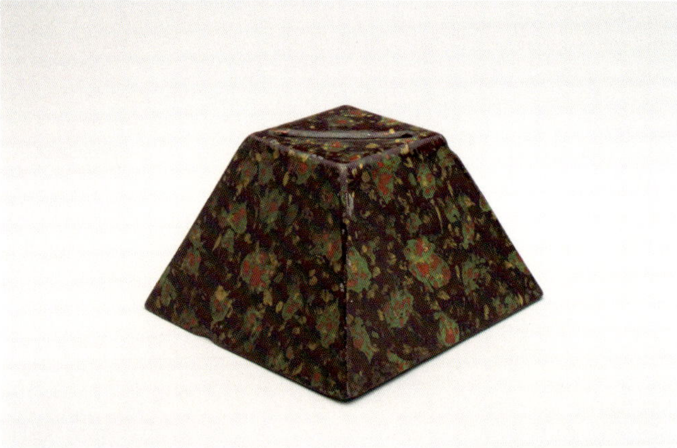

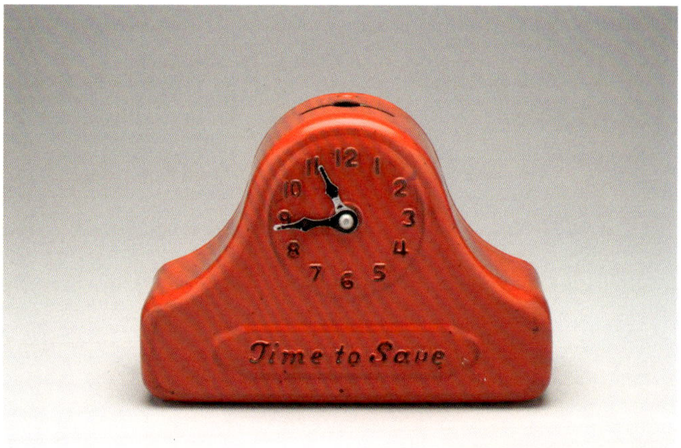

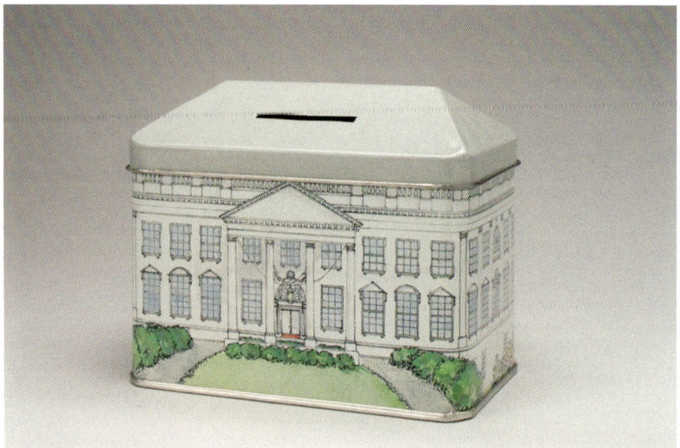

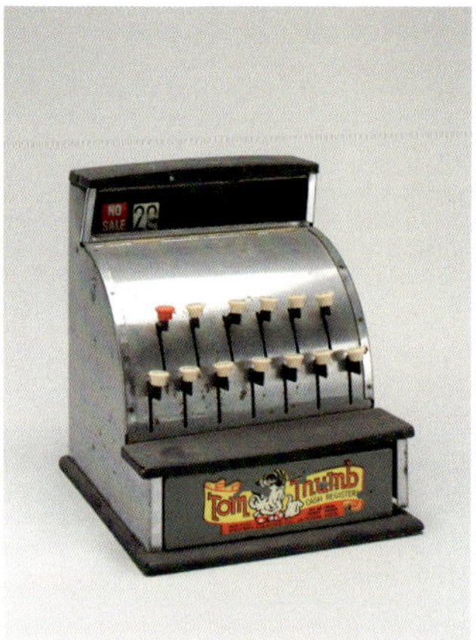

STILL BANKS: Other Metals

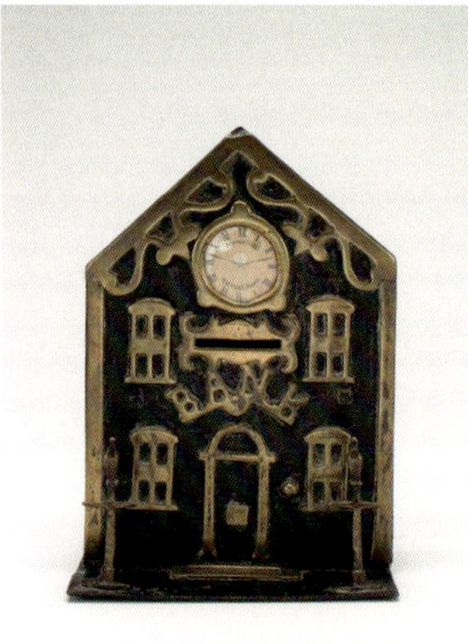

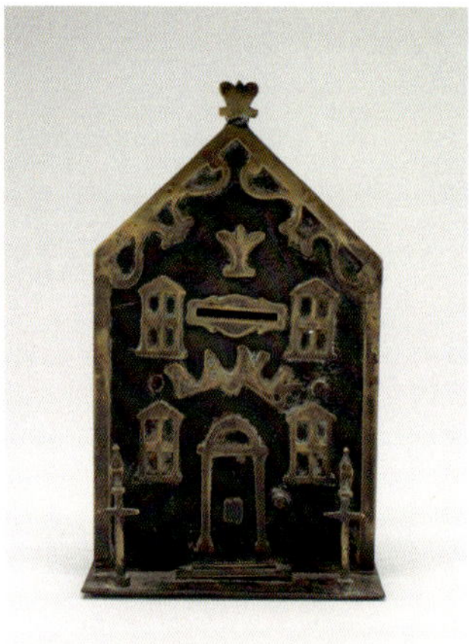

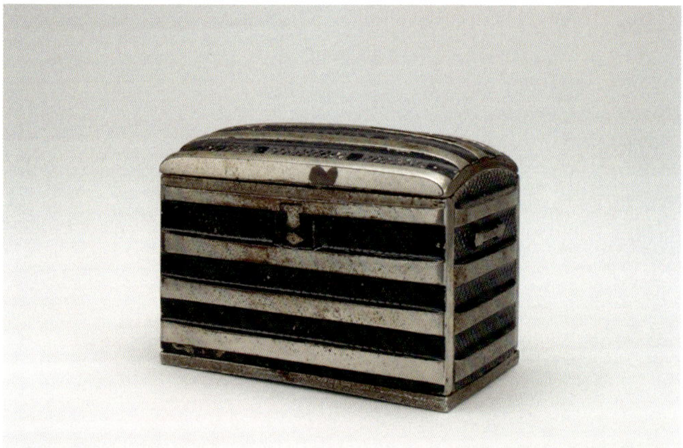

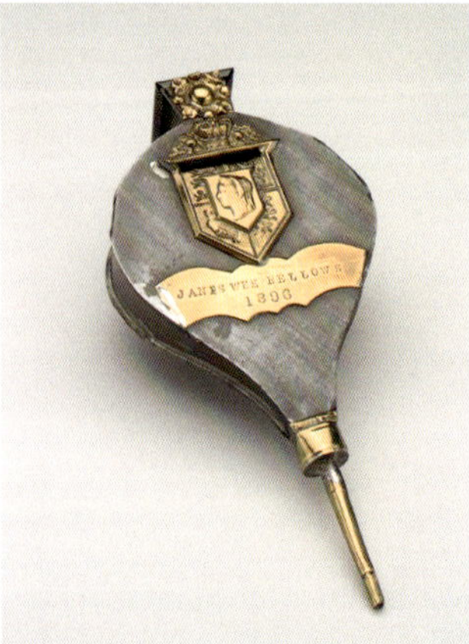

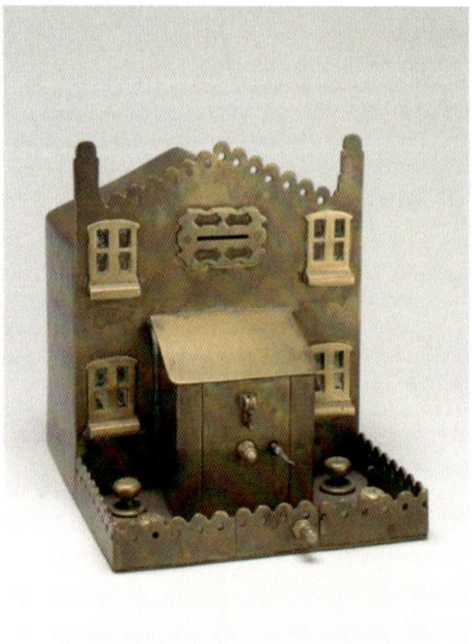

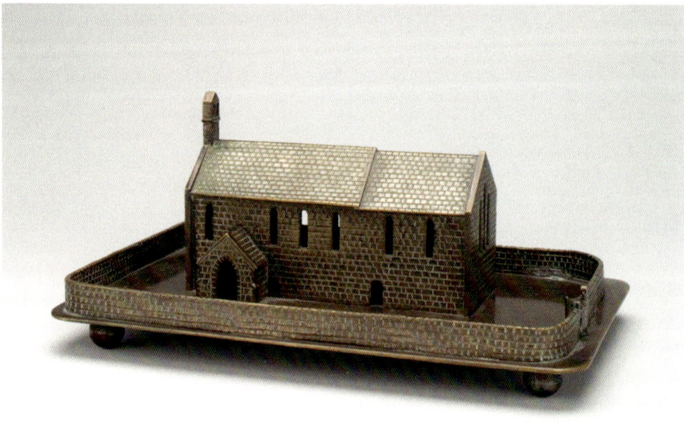

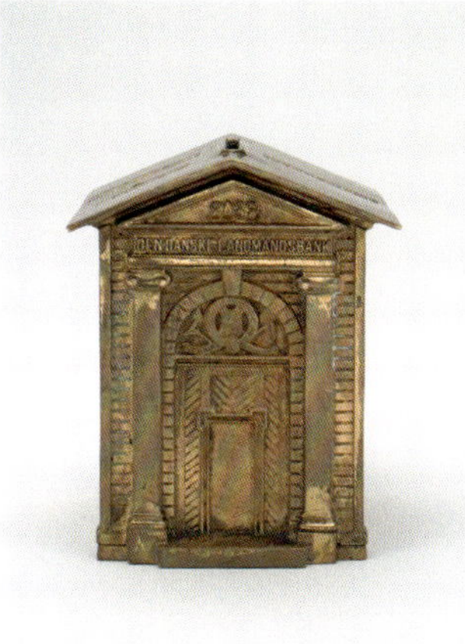

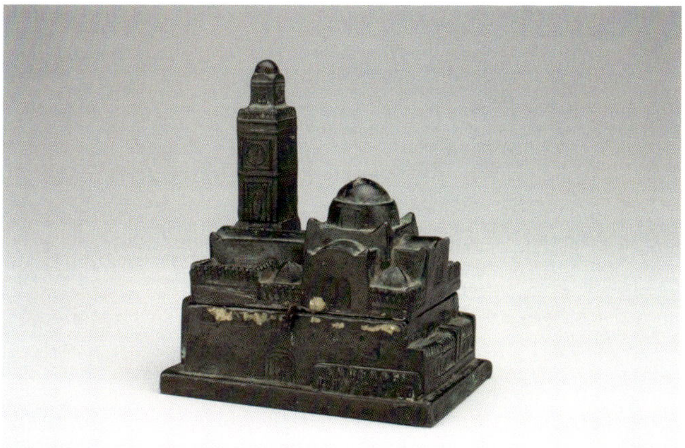

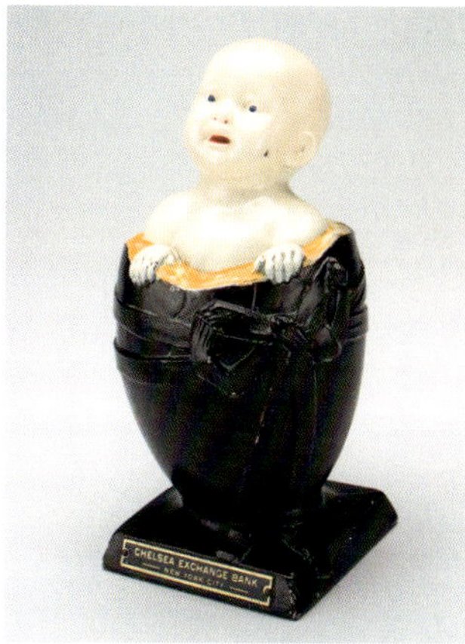
CHELSEA EXCHANGE BANK

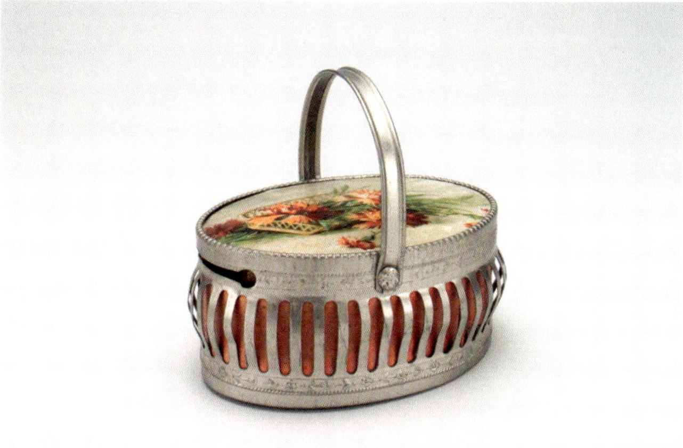

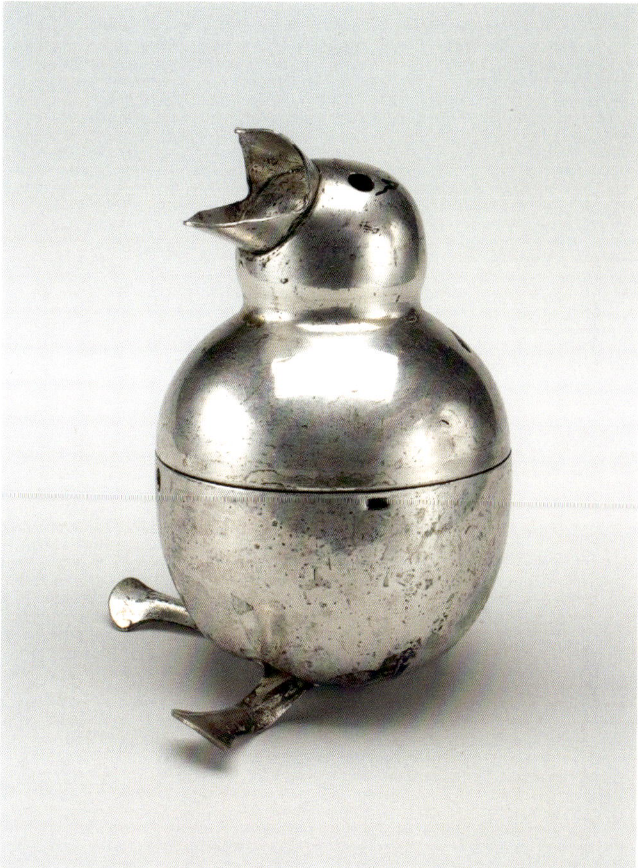

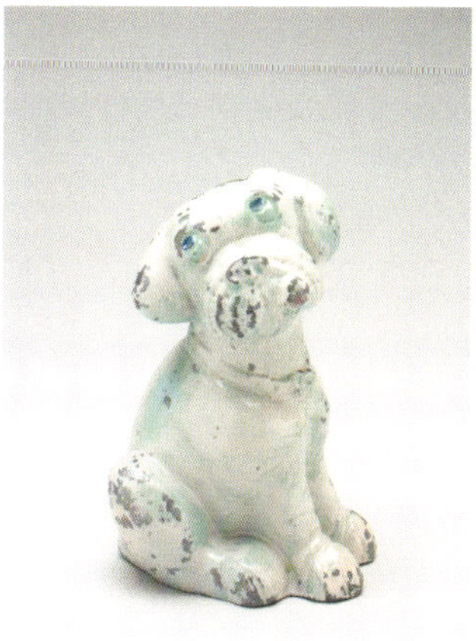

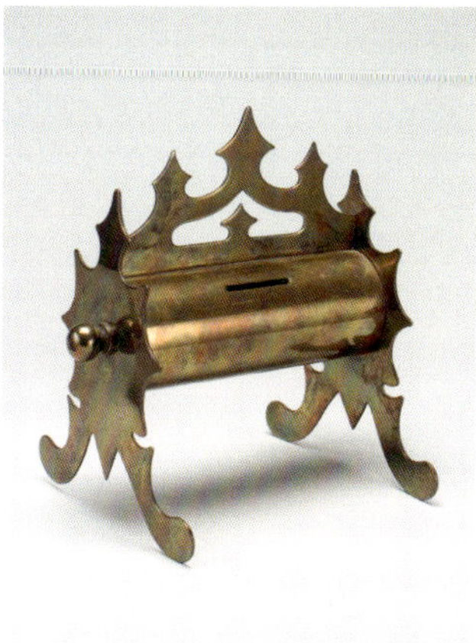

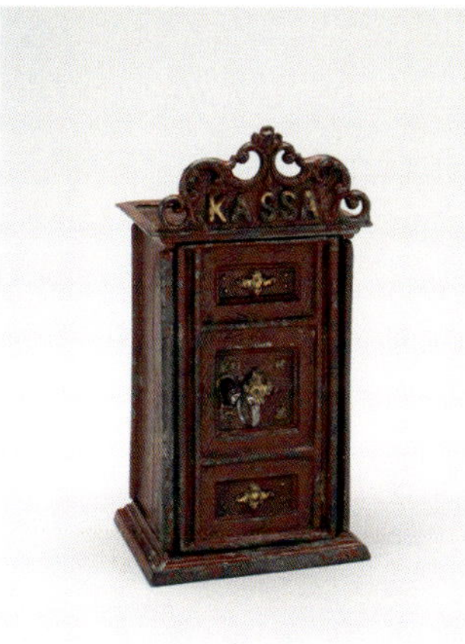
KASSA

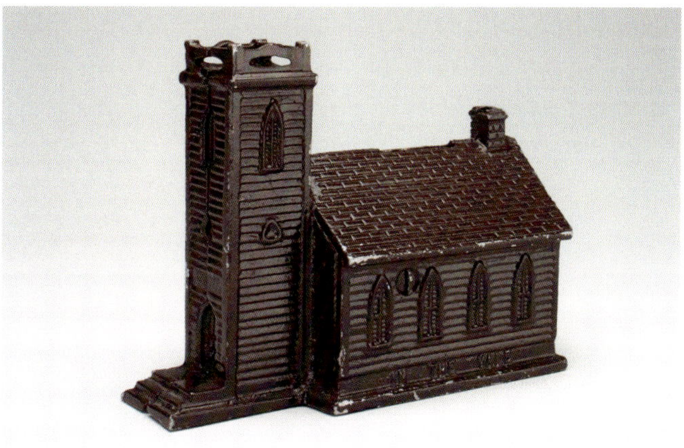

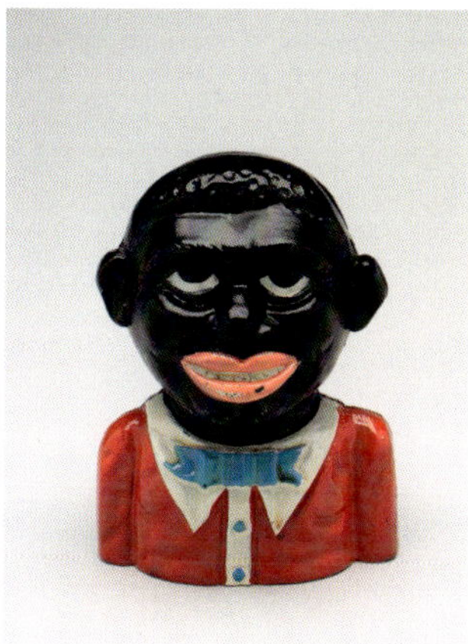

Baby in Egg, early 20th century
United States
Lead, pigment
7 1/4 x 3 1/2 x 3 1/2 in.
2003.236.813

Souvenir of Warsaw, late 19th century
Poland
Lead
3 3/4 x 3 3/8 x 2 1/4 in.
2003.236.1057

Den Danske Landmandsbank, 19th century
Kjorenhavns Dorgreb & Metalvarefrabrik, the Netherlands, manufacturer
Brass
4 9/16 x 3 13/16 x 3 1/8 in.
2003.236.226

Baby Bird, early 20th century
Napier Company, Meriden, Connecticut (est. 1875), manufacturer
Metal, silver plate
3 3/8 x 2 3/8 x 2 9/16 in.
2003.236.830

Flower Basket, early 20th century
United States
Metal, paper, pigments
3 1/2 x 3 1/2 x 2 7/16 in.
2003.236.546

Gothic cylinder, early 20th century
Probably England
Brass
7 1/16 x 6 13/16 x 5 in.
2003.236.232

Forlorn Dog, early 20th century
United States
Metal, pigment
5 x 3 x 3 3/8 in.
2003.236.1072

Young Negro, early 20th century
England
Aluminum, pigment
4 1/2 x 3 9/16 x 3 1/4 in.
2003.236.840

Little Brown Church, early 20th century
Bloom Manufacturing Company, Nashua, Iowa (est. 1904), manufacturer
Aluminum, pigment
4 x 2 3/8 x 5 3/16 in.
2003.236.1050

Kassa (Ticket Office), early 20th century
Possibly Russia
Metal, pigment
4 3/4 x 2 9/16 x 2 1/8 in.
2003.236.921

Cup and Saucer, early-to-mid-20th century
Possibly Germany
Brass
$1\frac{3}{4} \times 4\frac{1}{2} \times 4\frac{1}{2}$ in.
2003.236.582

U.S. Mail (registering), early 20th century
United States
Metal, glass, paper
$4\frac{5}{8} \times 5\frac{1}{4} \times 2\frac{1}{8}$ in.
2003.236.597

National Bank of America, early-to-mid-20th century
A. C. Rehberger Manufacturing Company,
Chicago, manufacturer
Zinc alloy
$2\frac{3}{4} \times 3 \times 4$ in.
2003.236.1052

Indian Bust with Headdress,
early-to-mid-20th century
Probably Europe
Metal, pigment
$4\frac{7}{8} \times 3 \times 2\frac{13}{16}$ in.
2003.236.1068

Dime Tube, early-to-mid-20th century
B & R Manufacturing Company,
New York, manufacturer
Metal
$2\frac{3}{4} \times \frac{11}{16} \times \frac{11}{16}$ in.
2003.236.564

Basket Bank (Smooth), c. 1902
Charles A. Braun, American, designer
Victor M. Grab & Company, Chicago, manufacturer
Steel
$2\frac{3}{4} \times 3\frac{1}{2} \times 3\frac{1}{2}$ in.
2003.236.416

Dinna Waste Your Wind, John, 1901
Scotland
Metal
$8\frac{3}{4} \times 4\frac{1}{16} \times 1\frac{9}{16}$ in.
2003.236.189

Safe, early-to-mid-20th century
Germany
Zinc alloy
$3\frac{3}{4} \times 2\frac{3}{8} \times 2$ in.
2003.236.1033

The Traveling Teller (registering), c. 1904
Automatic Recording Safe Company, Chicago, manufacturer
Metal
$2\frac{1}{16} \times 3\frac{13}{16} \times 1\frac{13}{16}$ in.
2003.236.665

I Made Chicago Famous, 1902
James M. Harper, Chicago, designer
Chicago Hardware Foundry Company, North Chicago, manufacturer
Brass
$2\frac{1}{16} \times 1\frac{1}{4} \times 3\frac{7}{8}$ in.
2003.236.992

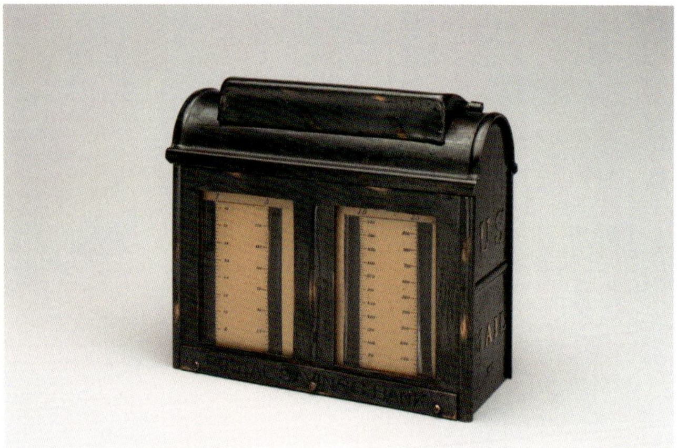

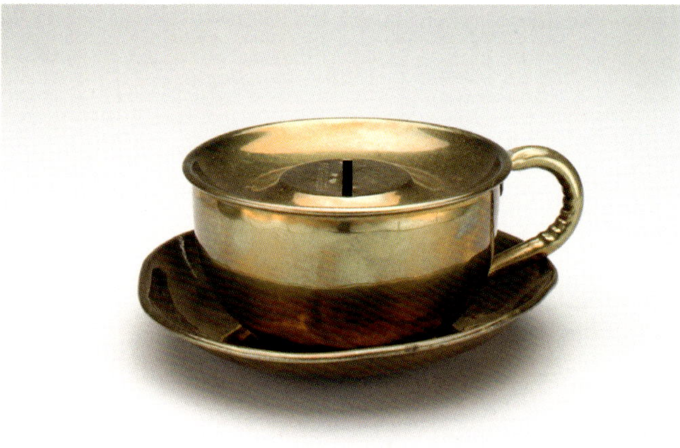

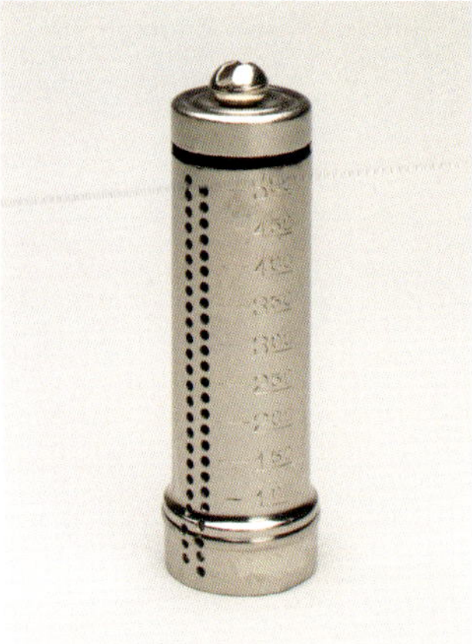

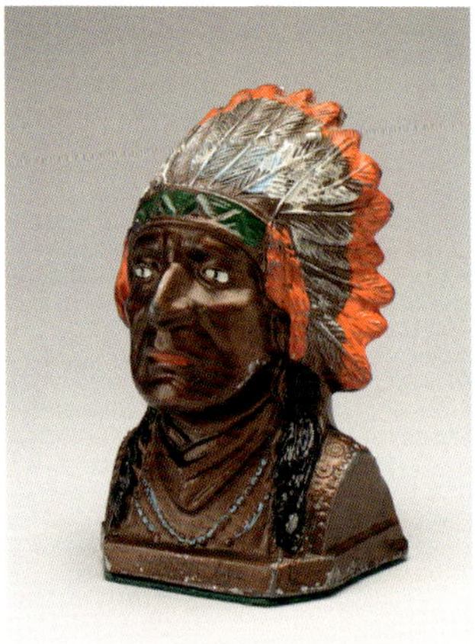

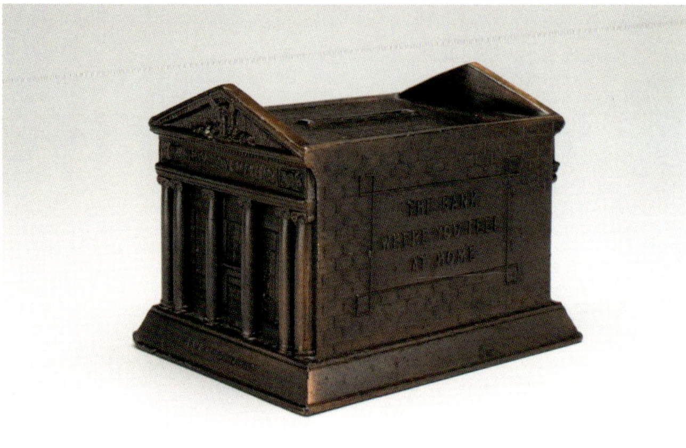

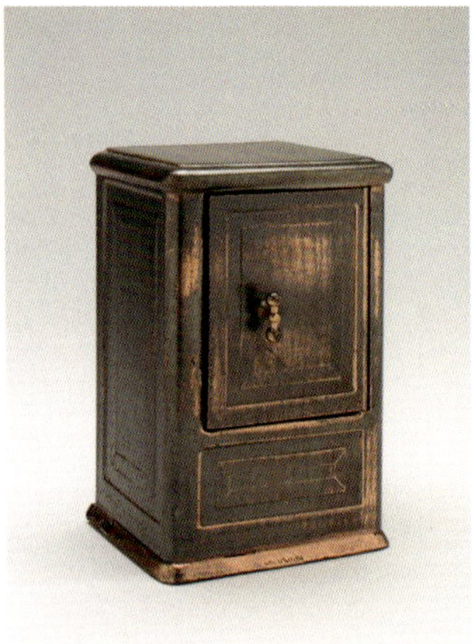

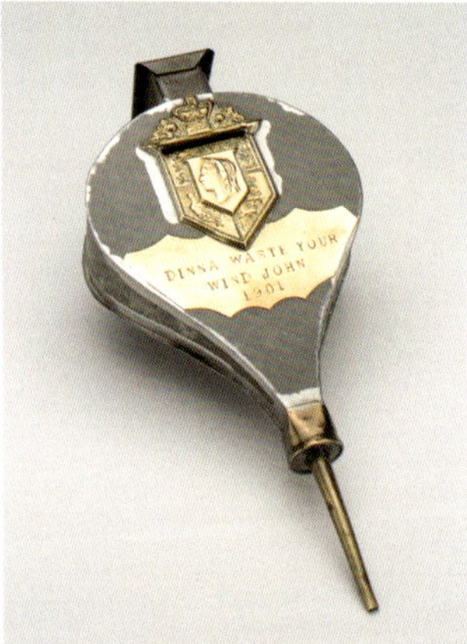
DINNA WASTE YOUR
WIND JOHN
1901

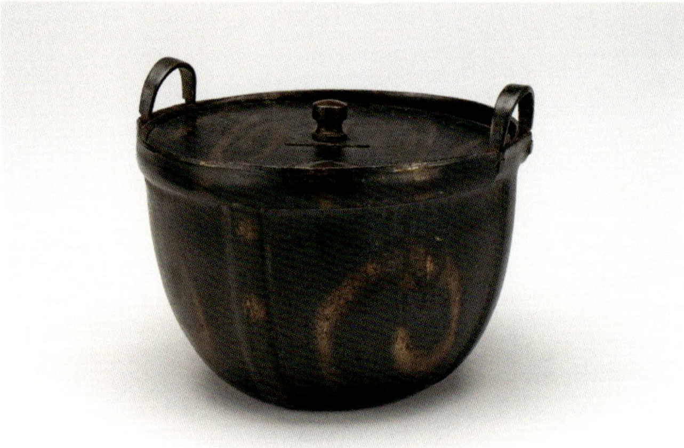

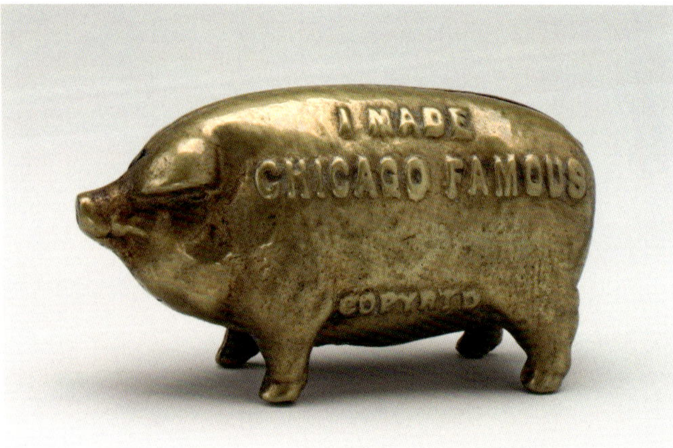
I MADE
CHICAGO FAMOUS

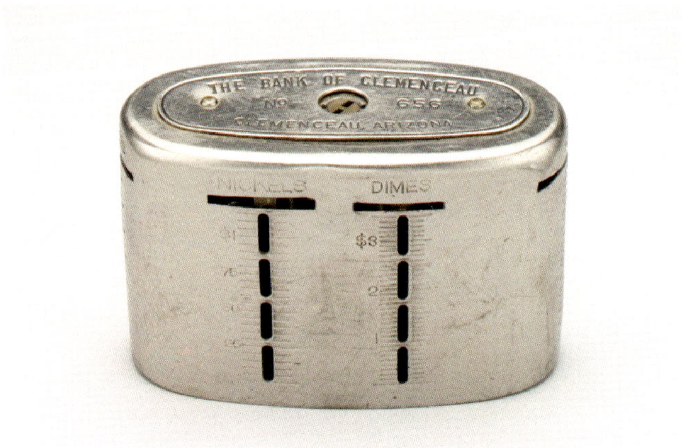
THE BANK OF CLEMENCEAU
No 656
CLEMENCEAU, ARIZONA
NICKELS
DIMES

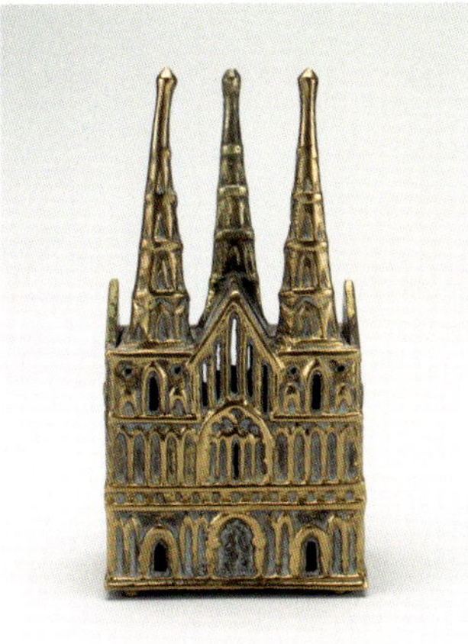
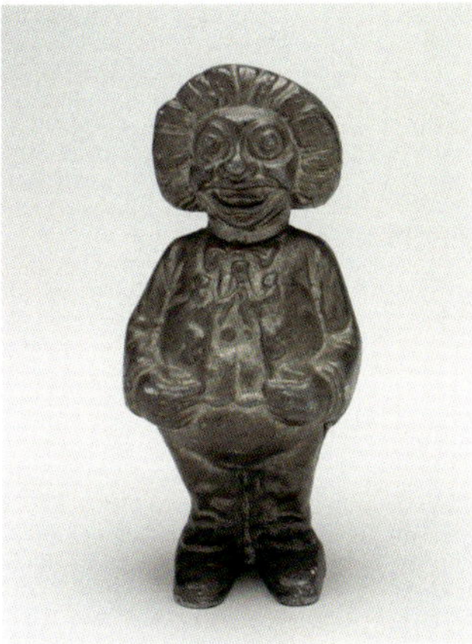
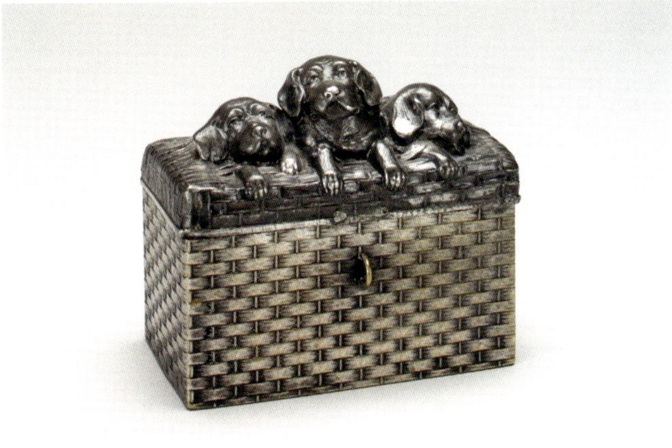
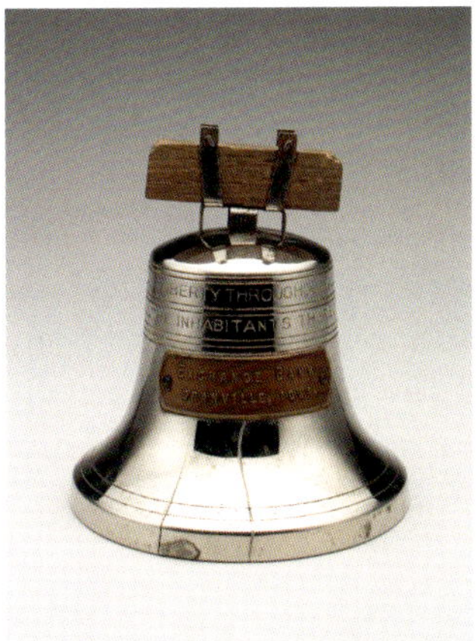
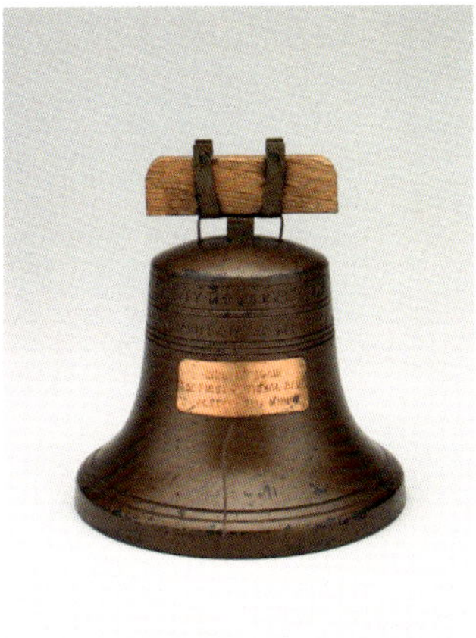
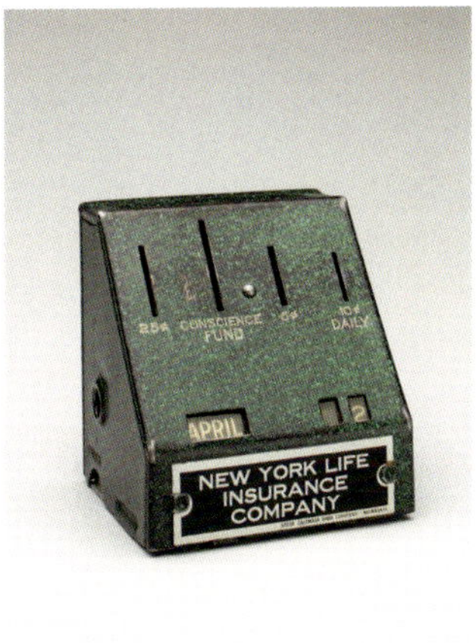
APRIL
NEW YORK LIFE
INSURANCE
COMPANY
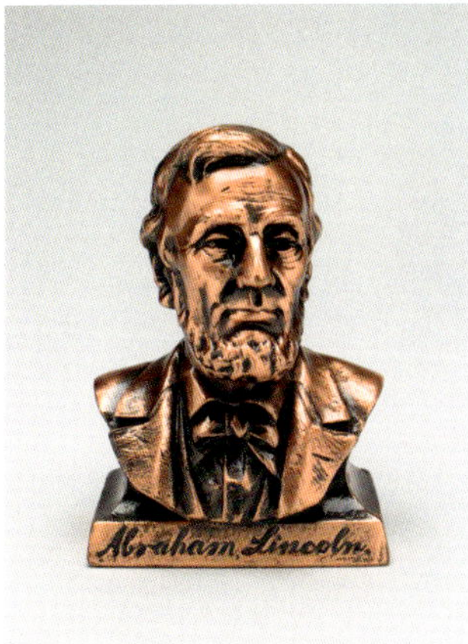
Abraham Lincoln
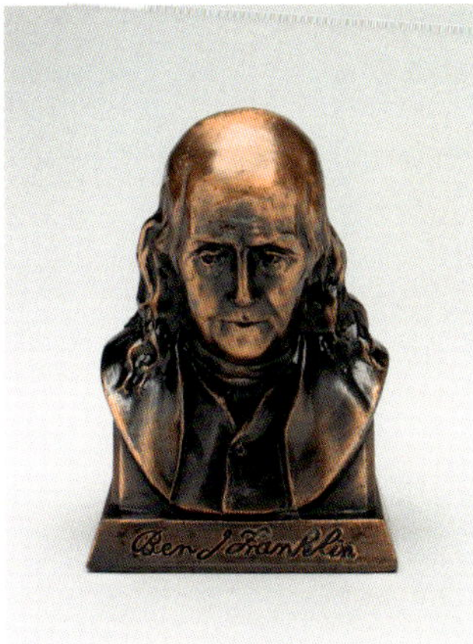
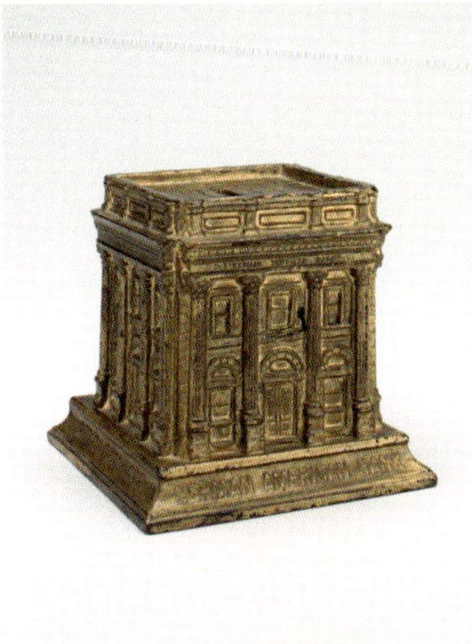
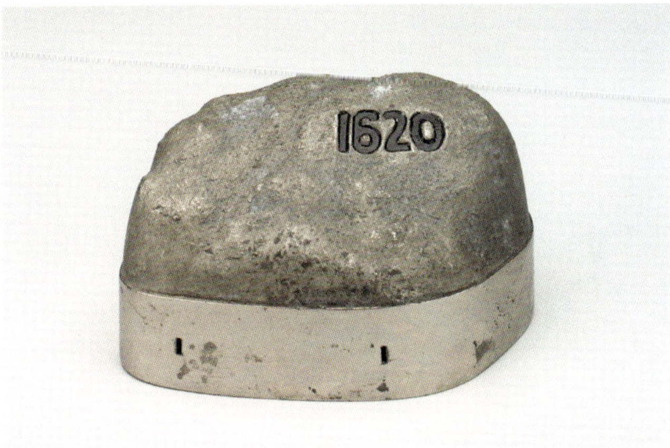
1620
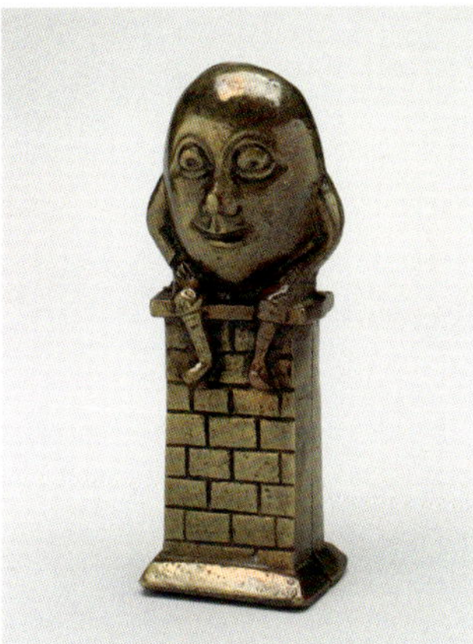
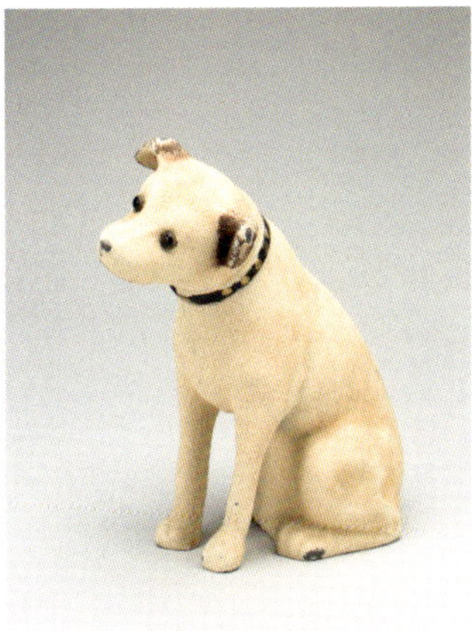
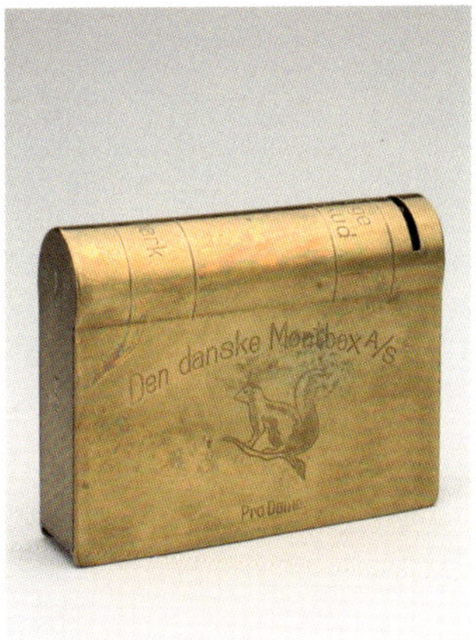
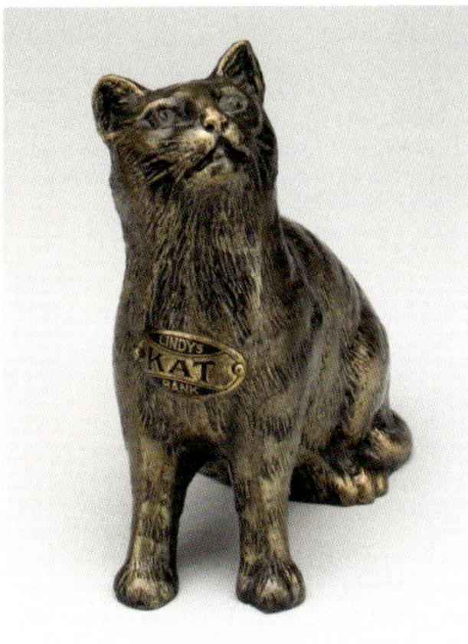

Dogs in Trunk, c. 1915
Germany
Metal, silver plate
2 1/2 x 2 7/8 x 1 7/8 in.
2003.236.1063

Golliwog, c. 1910 – 25
John Harper & Company, Ltd., Willenhall, England (1790 – 1980s), manufacturer
Aluminum
5 7/8 x 2 13/16 x 2 1/4 in.
2003.236.627

Litchfield Cathedral, c. 1908
Chamberlain & Hill, Walsall, England (est. 19th century), manufacturer
6 1/2 x 3 3/8 x 2 1/8 in.
2003.236.679

Abraham Lincoln, c. 1920s
A. C. Rehberger Manufacturing Company, Chicago, manufacturer
Lead
5 x 4 9/16 x 2 1/2 in.
2003.236.553

Conscience Fund, c. 1920
Speer Calendar Bank Company, Milwaukee, Wisconsin, manufacturer
Metal, pigment, glass
3 3/4 x 3 1/2 x 3 1/8 in.
2003.236.653

Liberty Bell, First National Bank, c. 1919
United States
Zinc alloy, wood
3 3/4 x 3 3/4 x 3 3/4 in.
2003.236.1102

Liberty Bell, Exchange Bank, c. 1919
United States
Metal, wood
3 3/4 x 3 3/4 x 3 3/4 in.
2003.236.1096

Plymouth Rock, c. 1921
International Service Company, Cleveland, manufacturer
Metal, pigment
2 x 3 7/8 x 2 3/4 in.
2003.236.957

German American Bank of Minneapolis, c. 1920s
Art Metal Works, Newark, New Jersey (1914 – 30), manufacturer
Metal, pigment
3 5/8 x 4 3/4 x 4 3/4 in.
2003.236.924

Benj. Franklin, c. 1920s
Preferred Bank Service Company, United States, manufacturer
Metal, pigment
5 1/2 x 3 13/16 x 2 5/16 in.
2003.236.199

Lindy's Kat Bank, c. 1927
Hewter Corporation, Silver Creek, New York, manufacturer
Lead, pigment
4 1/2 x 4 1/2 x 2 7/16 in.
2003.236.858

Danish Money Box, c. 1927
Denmark
Brass
3 1/16 x 2 3/8 x 13/16 in.
2003.236.1054

Nipper, Flocked (or *His Master's Voice*), c. 1920s
United States
Metal, flocking
6 1/16 x 2 3/16 x 4 in.
2003.236.886

Humpty Dumpty, c. 1920s
England
Brass, metal
5 3/4 x 2 7/16 x 1 1/2 in.
2003.236.856

Hansel and Gretel, c. 1930
Denmark
Brass, silver plate
4 1/16 x 4 1/2 x 3 7/16 in.
2003.236.825

The Wise Pig, c. 1929
Jessie McCutcheon Nelson, American, designer
Lead, pigment
6 3/16 x 2 13/16 x 2 7/8 in.
2003.236.986

Ben Franklin, c. 1928
Artvertising Corporation, Los Angeles, manufacturer
Zinc alloy
4 7/8 x 3 5/8 x 2 in.
2003.236.385

Umbrella, c. 1930
Napier Company, Meriden, Connecticut (est. 1875), manufacturer
Metal, silver plate
3 x 6 1/4 x 3 in.
2003.236.542

Mohawk and Hudson Railroad, c. 1930
Van Gytenbeek Manufacturing Company, Inc., New York, manufacturer
Metal, pigment
2 3/8 x 7 x 2 1/4 in.
2003.236.228

Remington Typewriter, 1939
National Products Corporation, Chicago, manufacturer
Metal, pigment
1 3/8 x 2 3/4 x 2 9/16 in.
2003.236.1079

Teepee, c. 1939
Vanio, Boston, manufacturer
Metal, pigment
4 5/8 x 3 1/2 x 3 1/2 in.
2003.236.1062

Liberty Bell, Iowa Women's Relief Corps, c. 1938
United States
Zinc alloy
3 1/2 x 3 3/16 x 3 3/16 in.
2003.236.1099

Bulldog with Sailor Cap, c. 1930s
Germany
Lead, pigment
4 1/2 x 3 3/8 x 3 3/8 in.
2003.236.1073

Davy Crockett with Rifle, c. 1940s – 50s
Banthrico, Inc., Chicago (1931 – 85), manufacturer
Zinc alloy
5 3/8 x 4 1/8 x 2 3/4 in.
2003.236.372

Des Moines Building-Loan and Savings, c. 1940s
Banthrico, Inc., Chicago (1931 – 85), manufacturer
Zinc alloy
4 1/4 x 3 7/16 x 2 11/16 in.
2003.236.415

Bullet Bank (Buster Brown Shoes), c. 1940s
United States
Brass, metal, pigment
4 1/4 x 1 3/4 x 1 3/4 in.
2003.236.1074

Abraham Lincoln, c. 1940
Banthrico, Inc., Chicago (1931 – 85), manufacturer
Zinc alloy
5 3/4 x 3 5/8 x 2 1/4 in.
2003.236.387

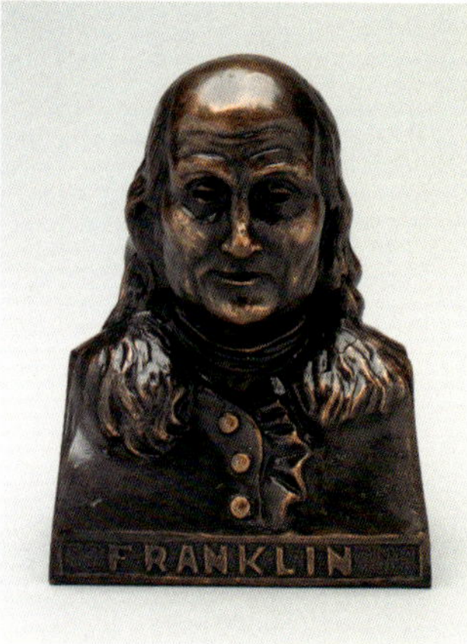
FRANKLIN

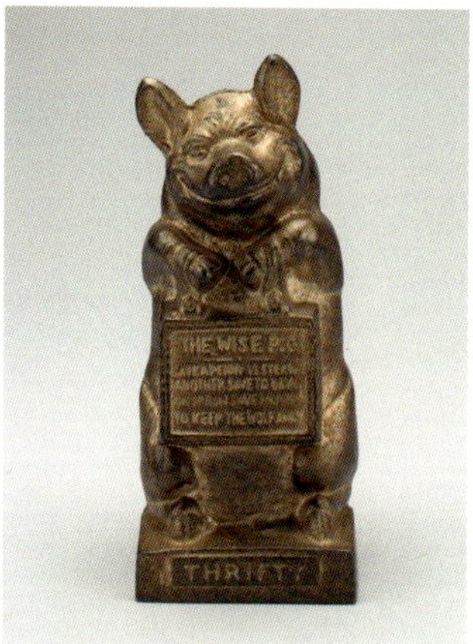
THE WISE PIG
THRIFTY

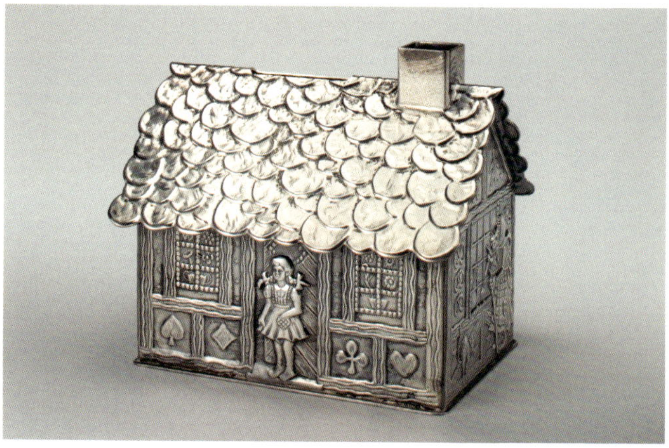

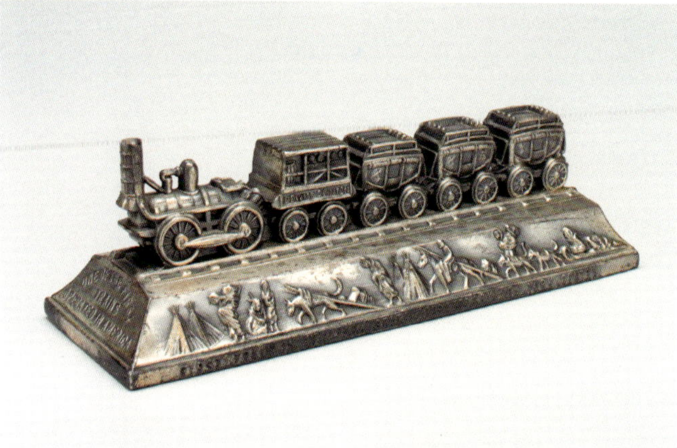

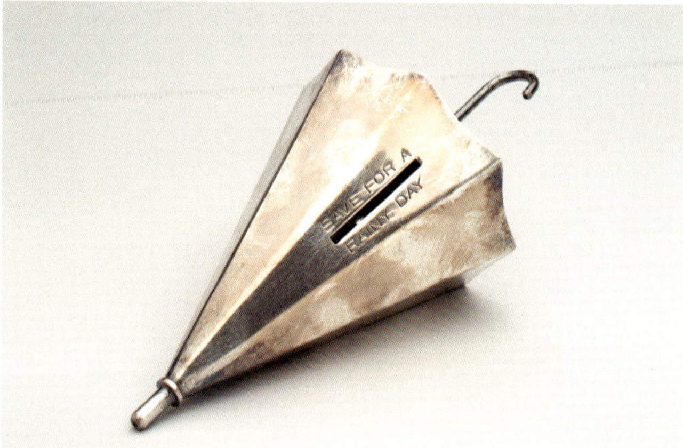
SAVE FOR A
RAINY DAY

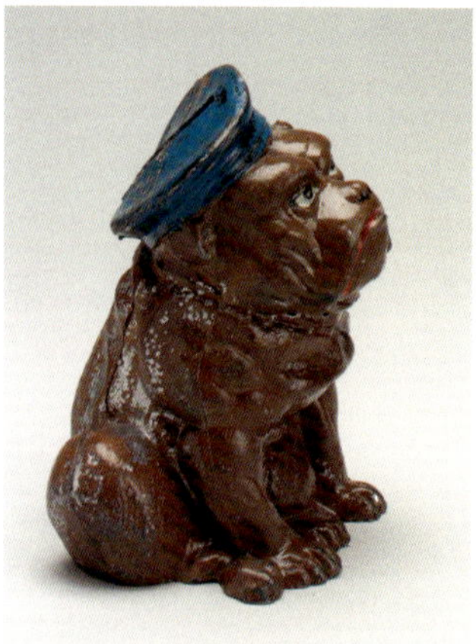

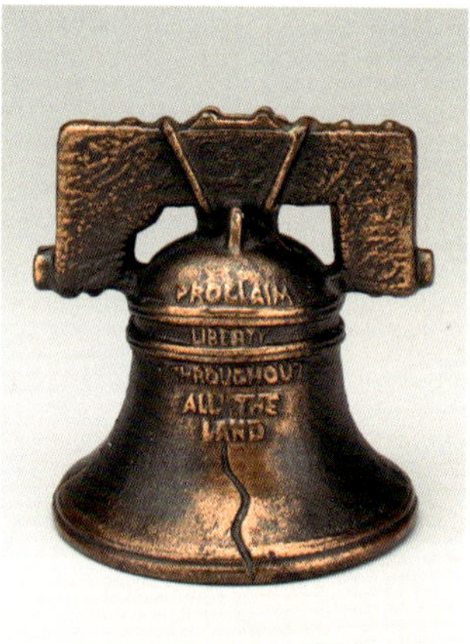
PROCLAIM
LIBERTY
THROUGHOUT
ALL THE
LAND

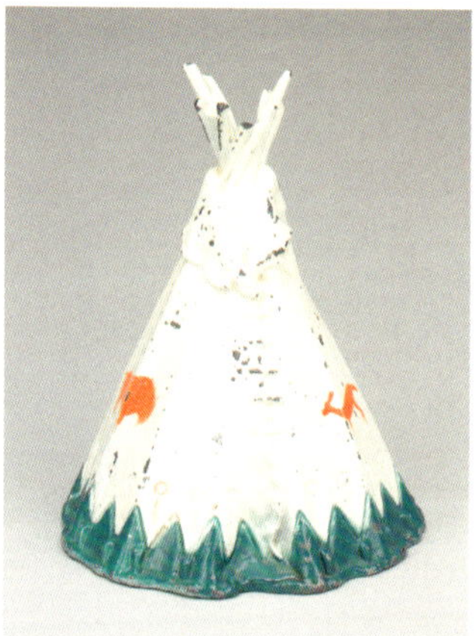

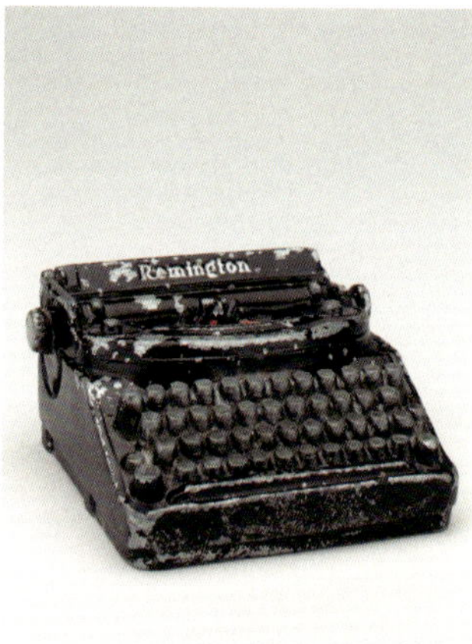
Remington

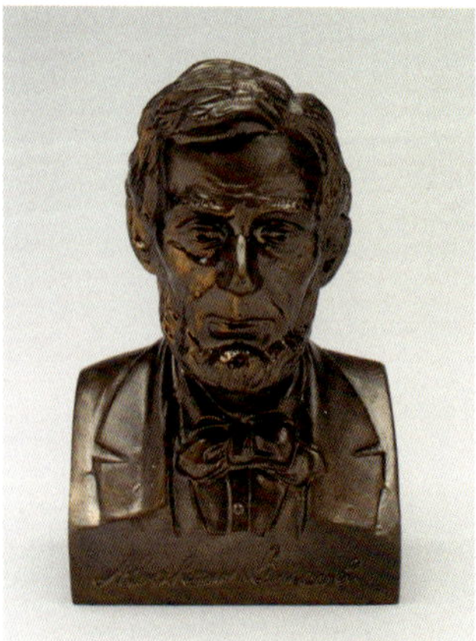

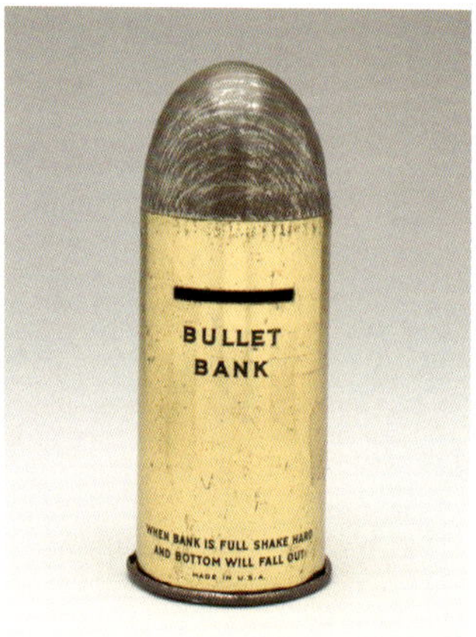
BULLET
BANK

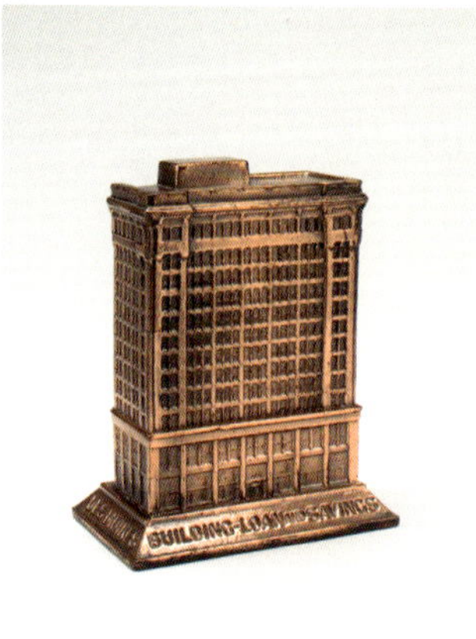

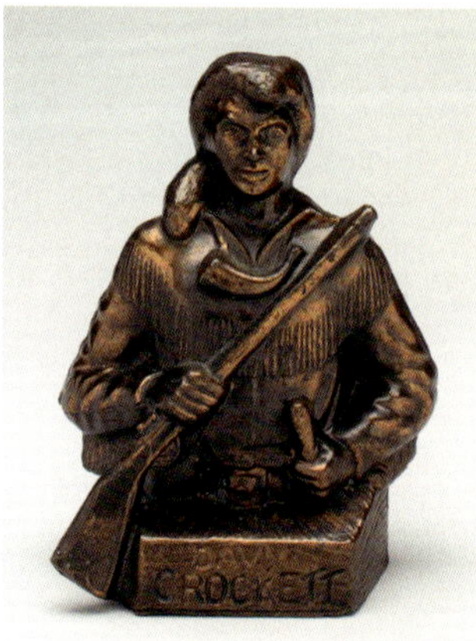
CROCKETT

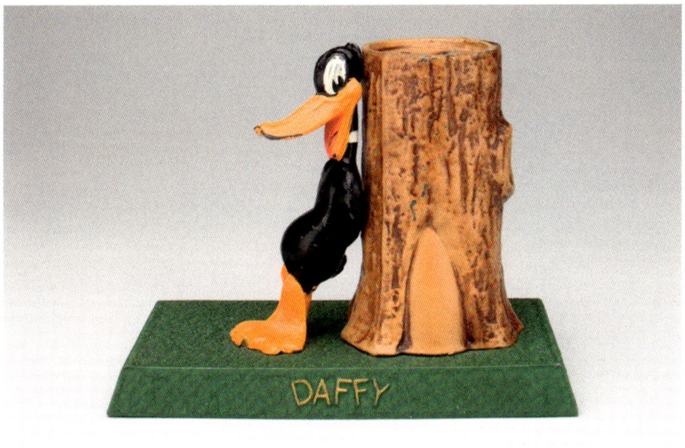
DAFFY

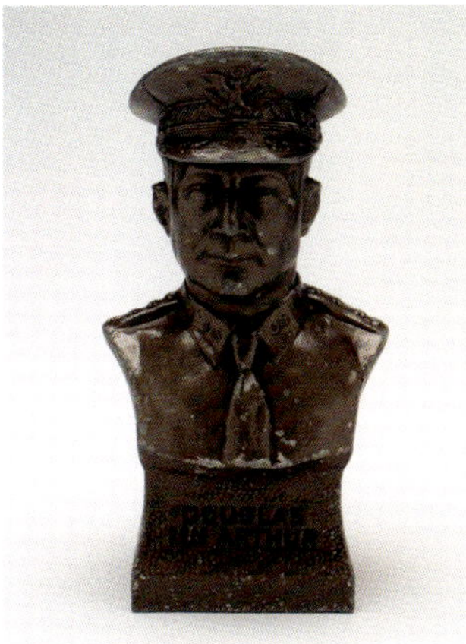

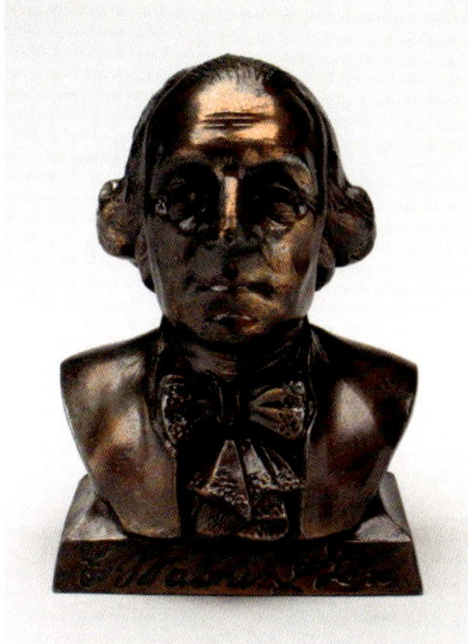

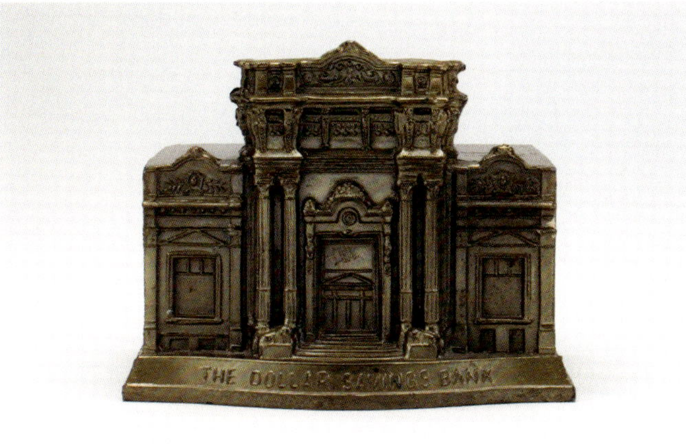
THE DOLLAR SAVINGS BANK

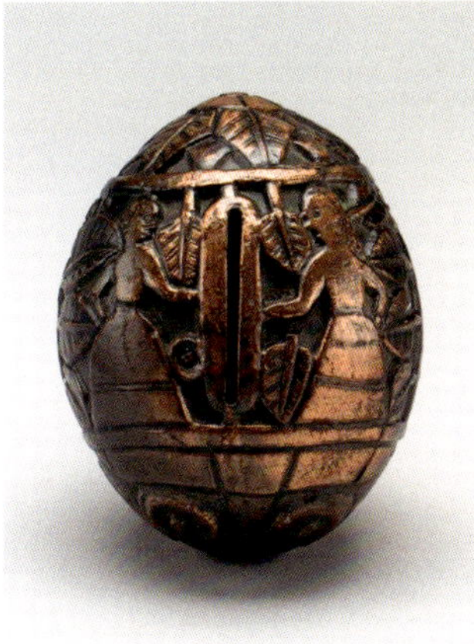

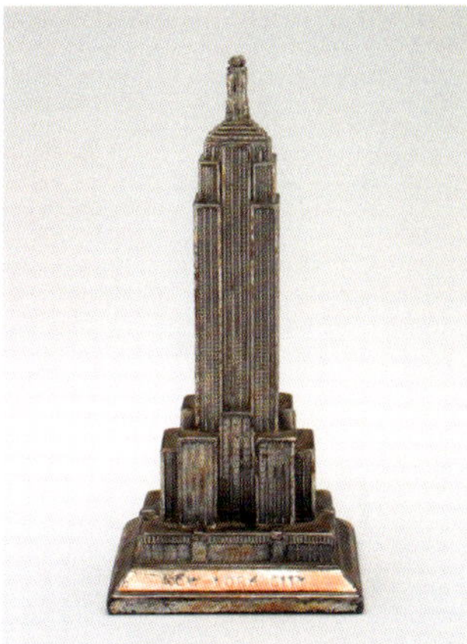

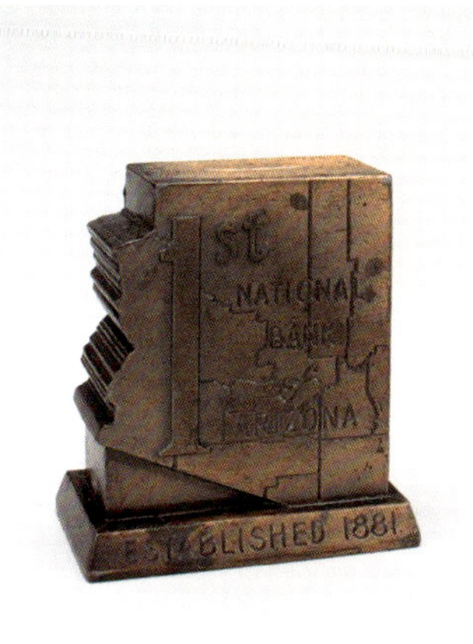
NATIONAL
BANK
ARIZONA

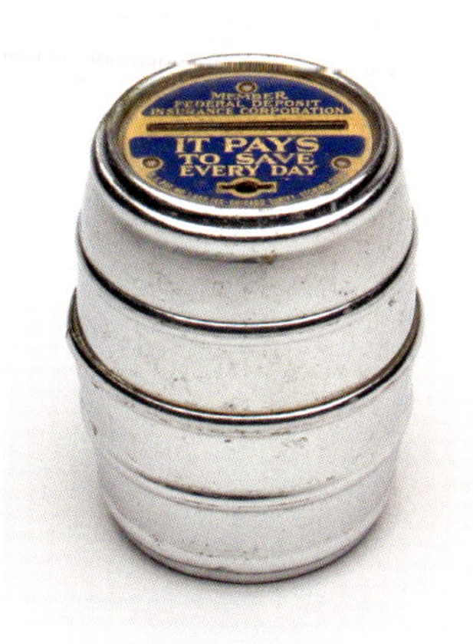
MEMBER
FEDERAL DEPOSIT
INSURANCE CORPORATION
IT PAYS
TO SAVE
EVERY DAY

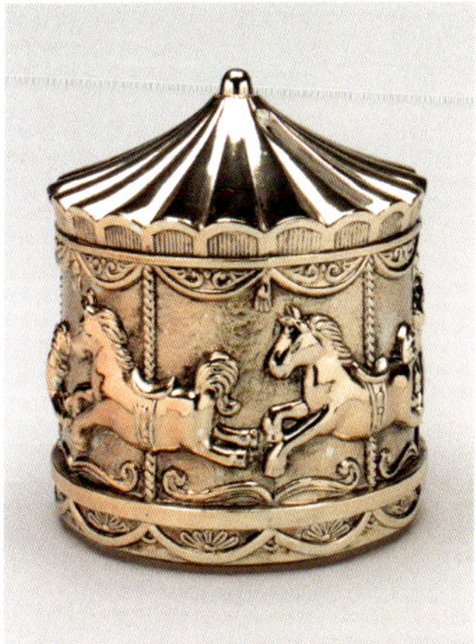

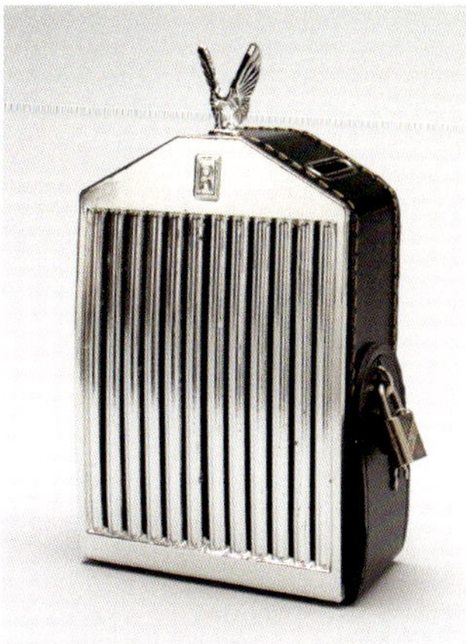

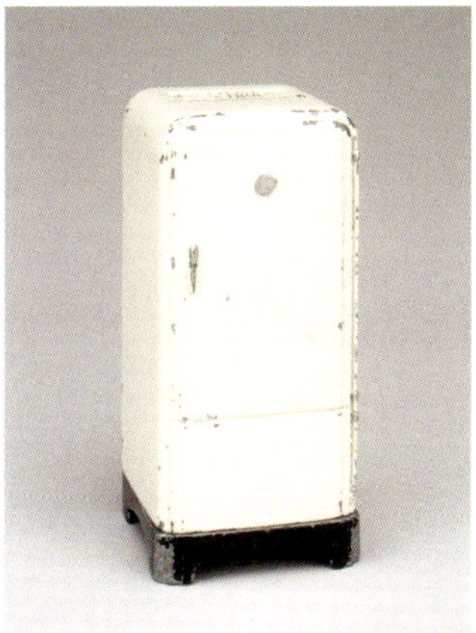

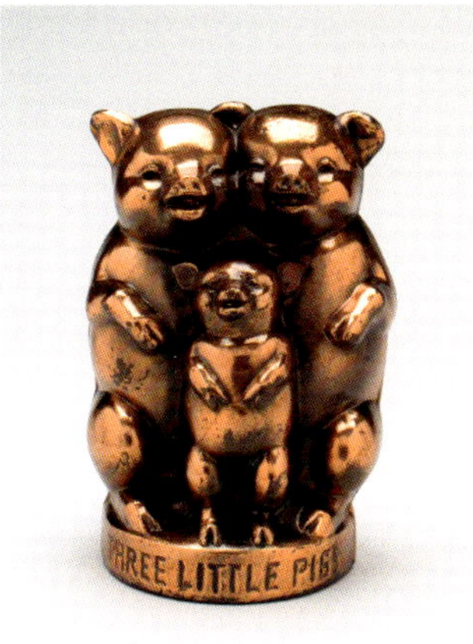
LITTLE

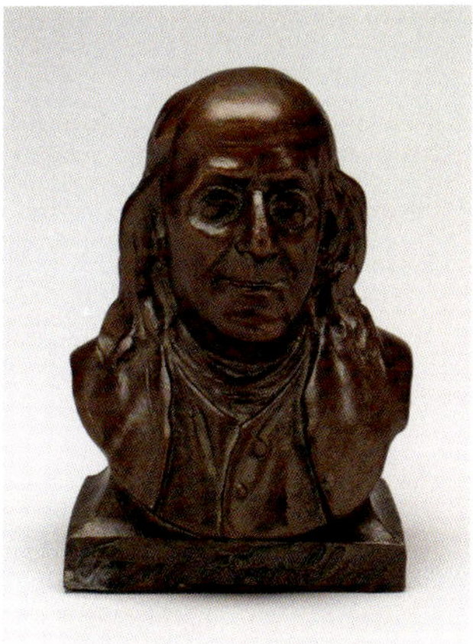

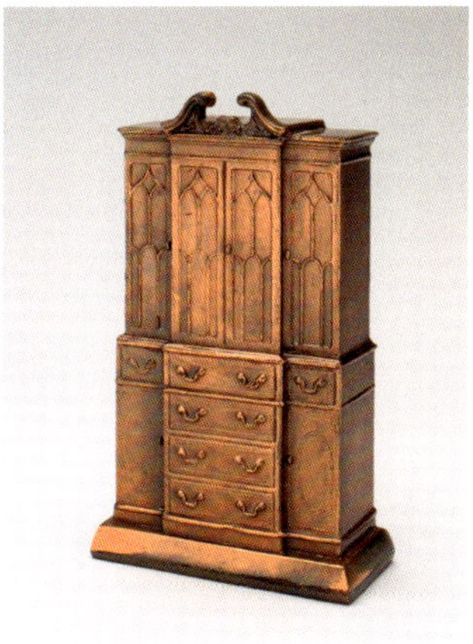

George Washington, c. 1947
Banthrico, Inc., Chicago (1931 – 85), manufacturer
Zinc alloy
5 1/8 x 3 3/4 x 3 in.
2003.236.391

Douglas MacArthur, c. 1946
Banthrico, Inc., Chicago (1931 – 85), manufacturer
Zinc alloy, pigment
6 x 3 1/8 x 2 5/8 in.
2003.236.380

Daffy Duck, c. 1945
Moss Metal Company, Chicago, manufacturer
Metal, pigment
4 3/16 x 5 3/4 x 3 1/16 in.
2003.236.1092

Empire State Building, mid-20th century
United States
Lead, silver plate
5 3/4 x 2 1/4 x 2 In.
2003.236.1055

Egg, mid-20th century
Banthrico, Inc., Chicago (1931 – 85), manufacturer
Zinc alloy
2 1/2 x 3 x 2 3/4 in.
2003.236.848

The Dollar Savings Bank of Pittsburgh, mid-20th century
Banthrico, Inc., Chicago (1931 – 85), manufacturer
Zinc alloy, lacquer
3 1/8 x 4 1/16 x 2 11/16 in.
2003.236.120

Rolls-Royce Grille, mid-20th century
Metal, vinyl, plastic
7 3/4 x 4 1/2 x 2 3/8 in.
2003.236.299

Merry-Go-Round, mid-20th century
Japan
Metal, silver plate
2 3/4 x 2 1/8 x 2 1/8 in.
2003.236.829

It Pays to Save Every Day (barrel), mid-20th century
Chicago Thrift Etching Corporation, Chicago, manufacturer
Metal, pigment
2 11/16 x 2 1/8 x 2 1/8 in.
2003.236.495

First National Bank of Arizona, mid-20th century
Banthrico, Inc., Chicago (1931 – 85), manufacturer
Zinc alloy
4 3/16 x 2 5/16 x 3 15/16 in.
2003.236.402

Furniture Cabinet, Union National, Inc., c. 1950s
Banthrico, Inc., Chicago (1931 – 85), manufacturer
Zinc alloy
5 11/16 x 3 1/2 x 1 9/16 in.
2003.236.1095

Benj. Franklin, c. 1950
Banthrico, Inc., Chicago (1931 – 85), manufacturer
Zinc alloy
5 3/8 x 3 3/4 x 2 3/4 in.
2003.236.390

Three Little Pigs, mid-20th century
United States
Zinc alloy
5 x 3 1/2 x 3 1/4 in.
2003.236.551

Servel Electrolux, mid-20th century
National Die Casting Company, Chicago, manufacturer
Metal, pigment
4 1/16 x 1 7/8 x 1 3/4 in.
2003.236.855

Covered Wagon, c. 1950s
Banthrico, Inc., Chicago (1931 – 85), manufacturer
Zinc alloy
3 7/8 x 2 9/16 x 4 5/8 in.
2003.236.831

Thunderbird Bank, mid-20th century
United States
Zinc alloy
3 1/8 x 6 1/8 x 3 5/8 in.
2003.236.824

Robert E. Lee, c. 1955
Banthrico, Inc., Chicago
(1931 – 85), manufacturer
Zinc alloy
5 1/2 x 3 7/8 x 2 3/4 in.
2003.236.386

Eisenhower, c. 1953
Banthrico, Inc., Chicago
(1931 – 85), manufacturer
Zinc alloy
5 x 3 9/16 x 2 7/16 in.
2003.236.376

Coronation Bank, Elizabeth II,
c. 1953
England
Metal, pigment
3 3/8 x 3 x 3 in.
2003.236.958

Weatherball Tower, c. 1950s
Banthrico, Inc., Chicago
(1931 – 85), manufacturer
Zinc alloy
6 7/8 x 2 3/4 x 2 in.
2003.236.1049

Syracuse Savings Bank, c. 1960s
Banthrico, Inc., Chicago
(1931 – 85), manufacturer
Zinc alloy
5 3/4 x 4 x 3 in.
2003.236.366

Thomas A. Edison, c. 1958
Banthrico, Inc., Chicago
(1931 – 85), manufacturer
Zinc alloy
5 1/4 x 3 5/8 x 2 11/16 in.
2003.236.381

Cook County Federal Savings, c. 1954
Banthrico, Inc., Chicago (1931 – 85), manufacturer
Zinc alloy
4 1/2 x 5 3/4 x 3 1/4 in.
2003.236.827

John Fitzgerald Kennedy, c. 1964
Metal, plastic
4 15/16 x 4 15/16 x 1 1/2 in.
2003.236.382

John F. Kennedy, c. 1963
Banthrico, Inc., Chicago
(1931 – 85), manufacturer
Zinc alloy
5 1/8 x 3 5/8 x 2 3/8 in.
2003.236.378

Gate City Savings, c. 1960s
Banthrico, Inc., Chicago (1931 – 85), manufacturer
Zinc alloy
4 x 2 3/4 x 4 in.
2003.236.1051

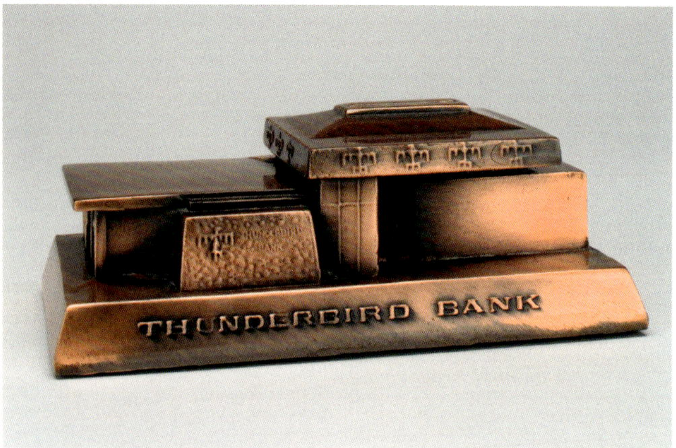
THUNDERBIRD BANK

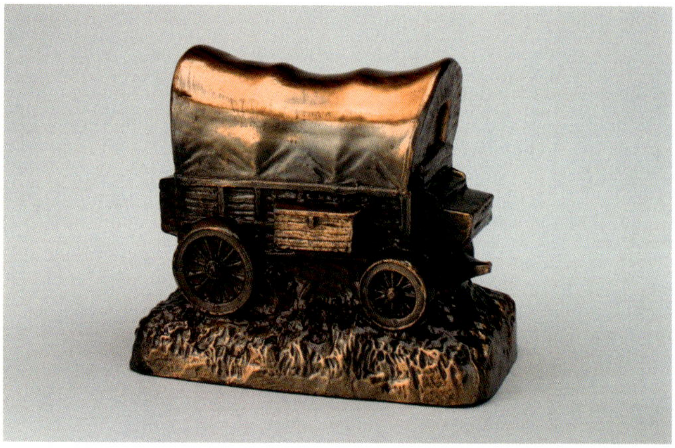

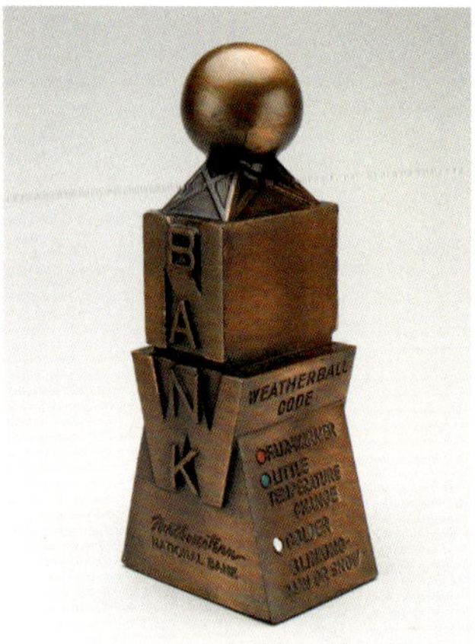
BANK
WEATHERBALL CODE

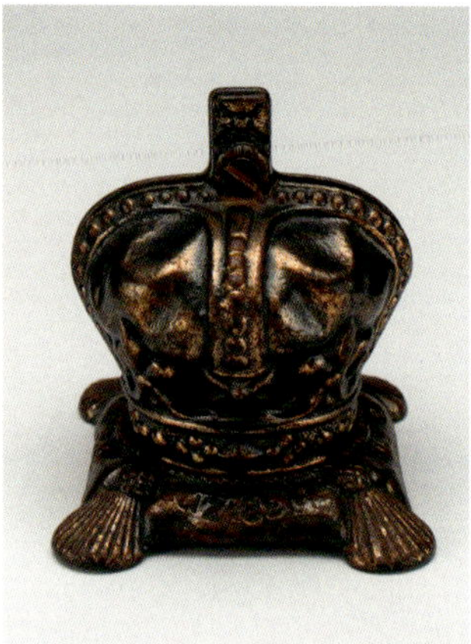

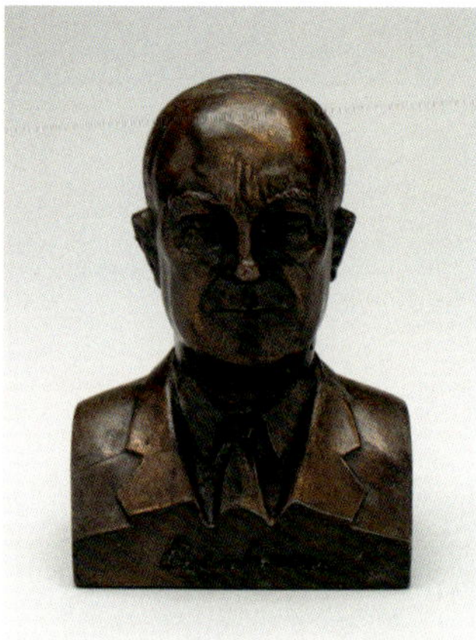

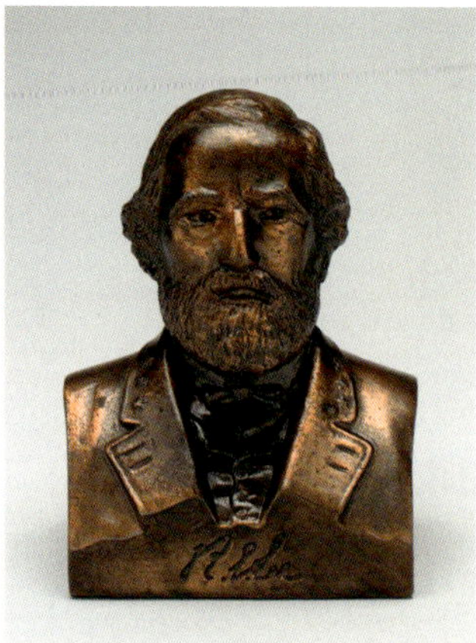

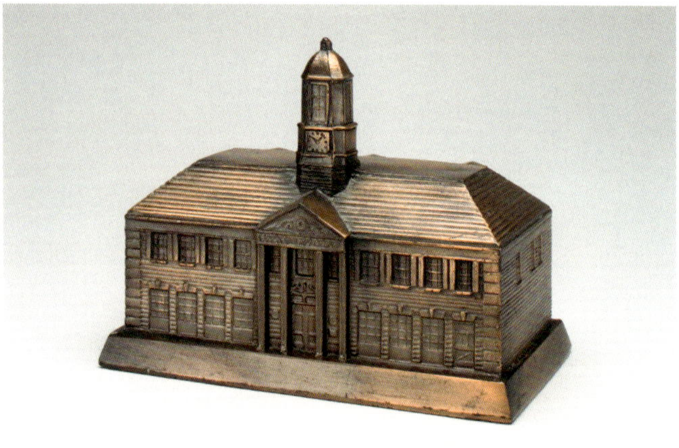

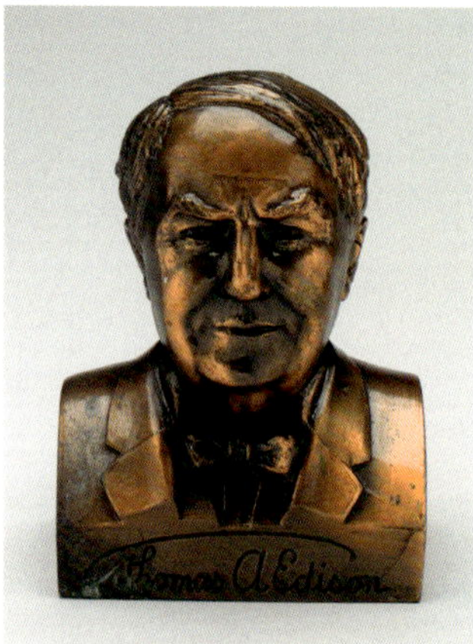
Thomas A. Edison

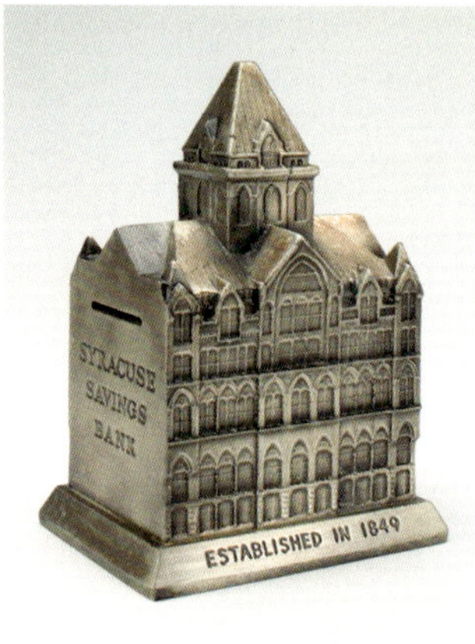
SYRACUSE SAVINGS BANK
ESTABLISHED IN 1849

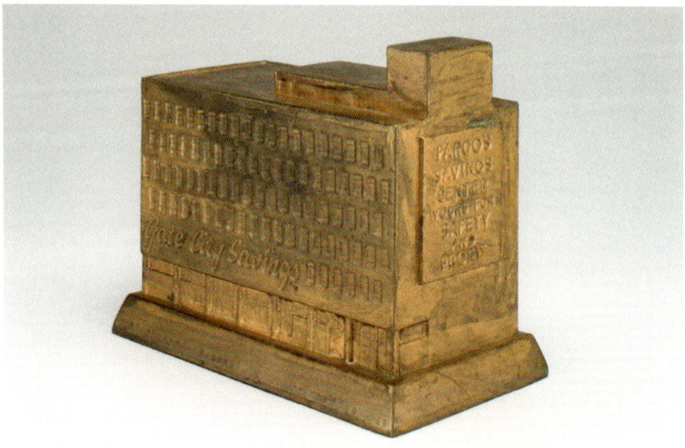
Gate City Savings

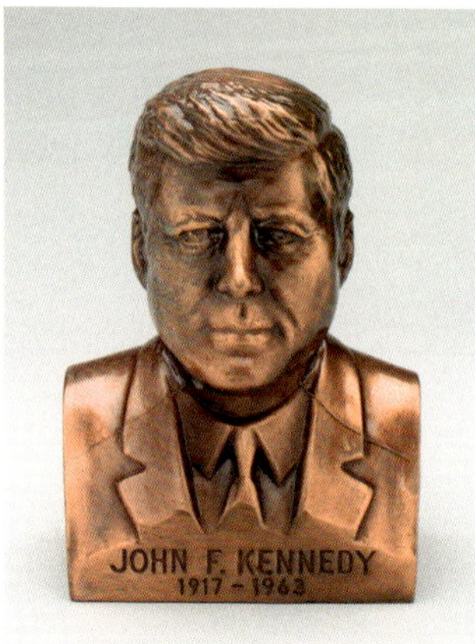
JOHN F. KENNEDY
1917 - 1963

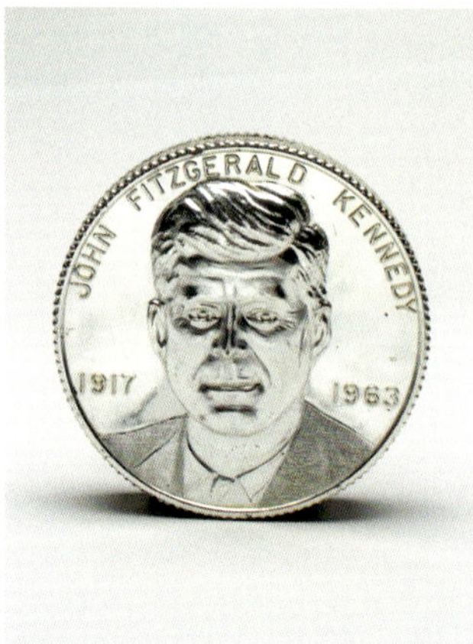
JOHN FITZGERALD KENNEDY
1917
1963

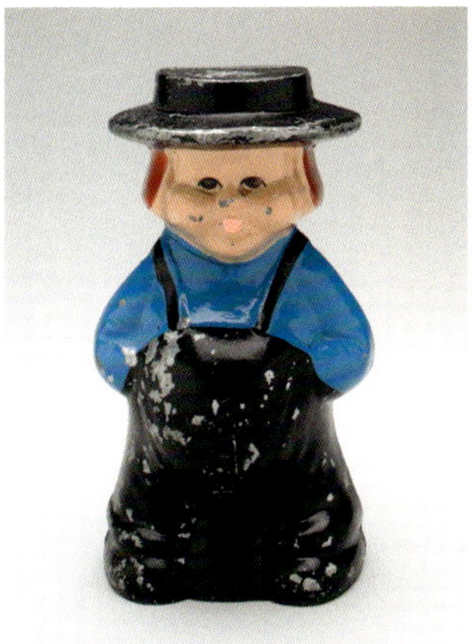
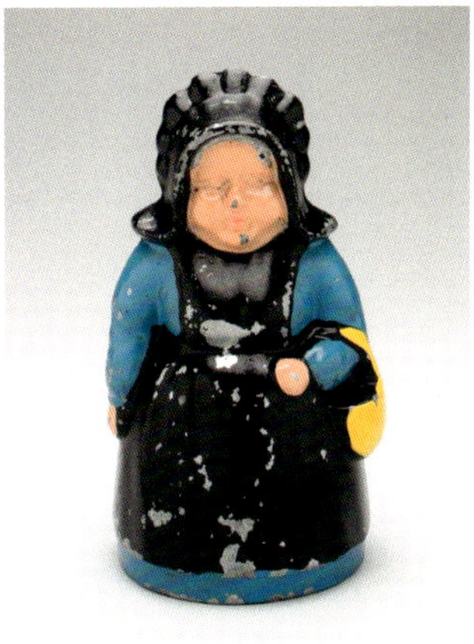
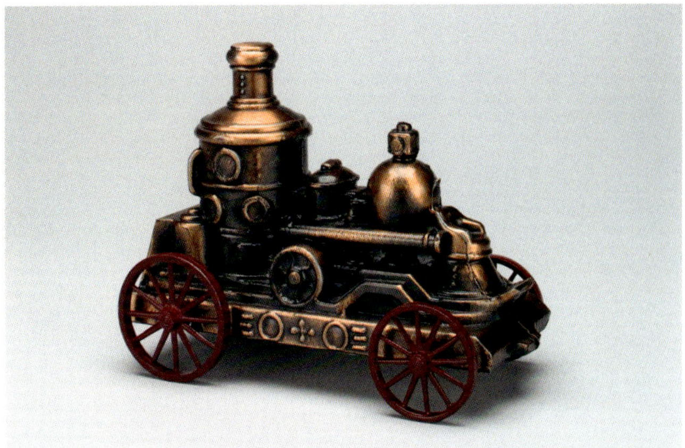
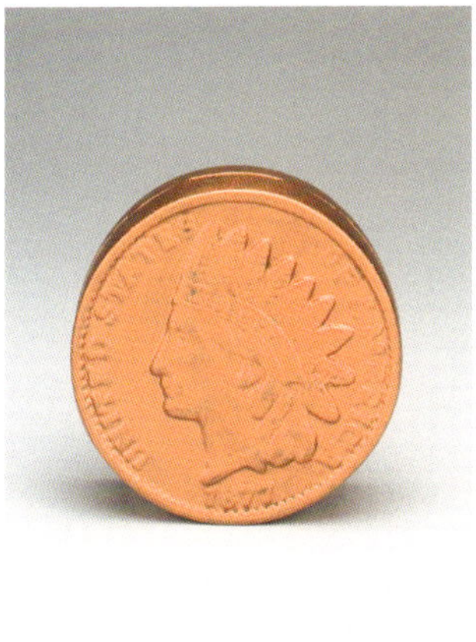
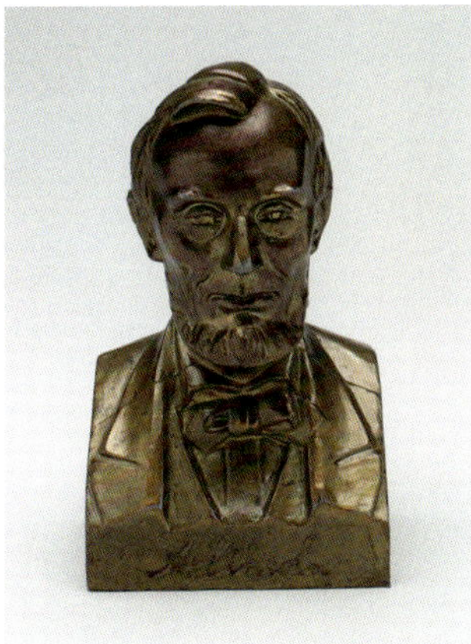
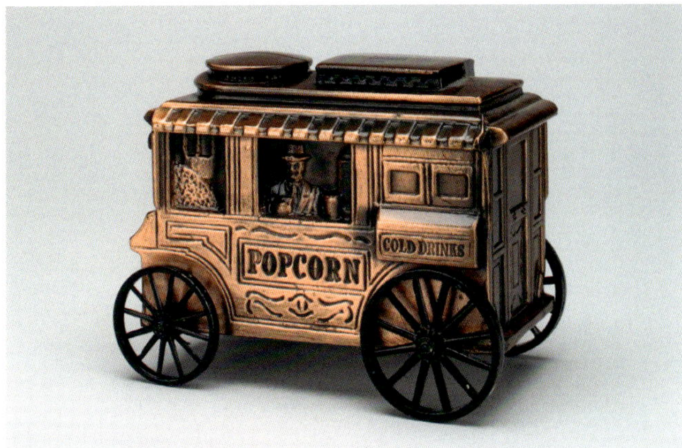
POPCORN
COLD DRINKS
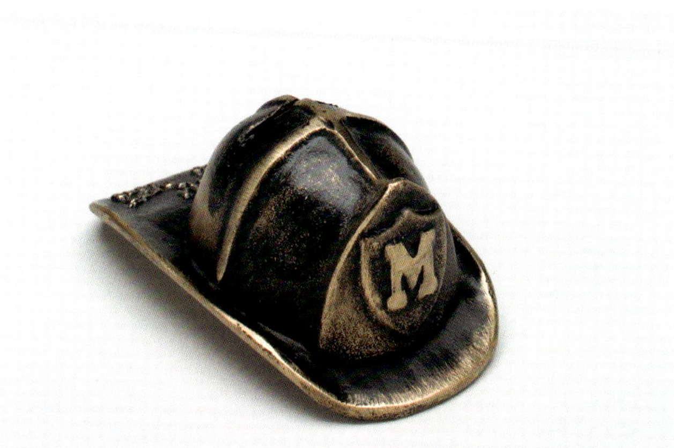
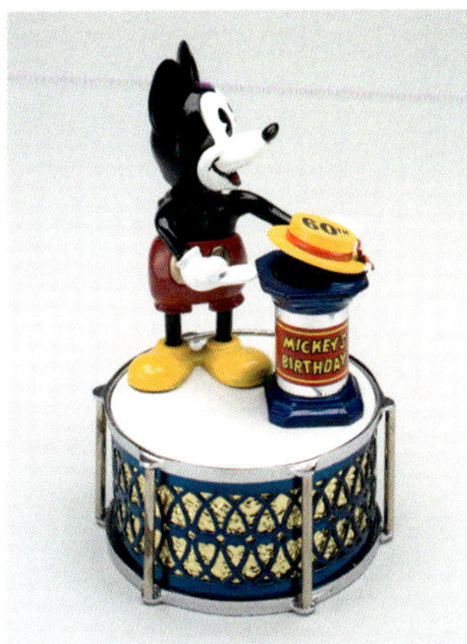
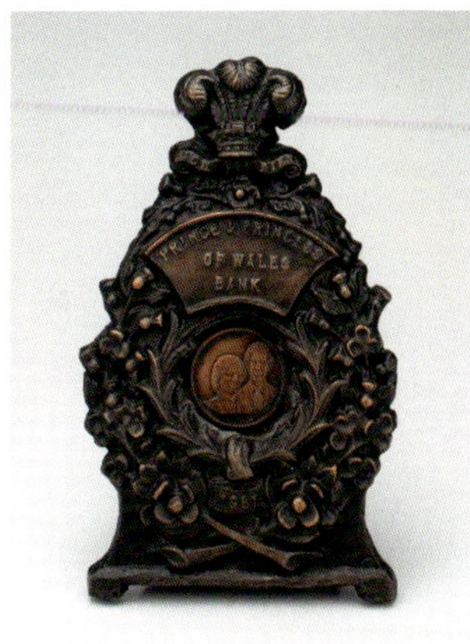
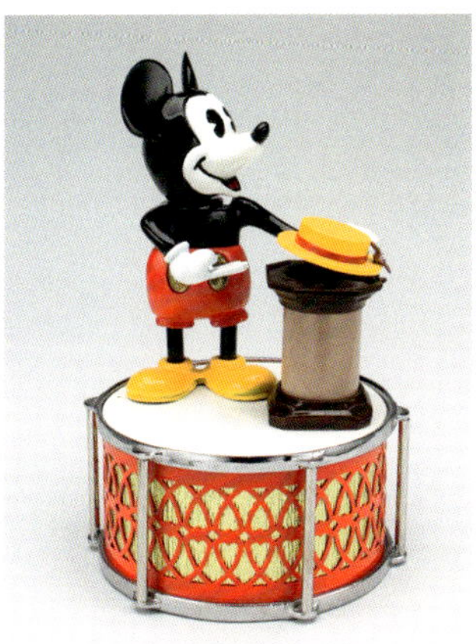
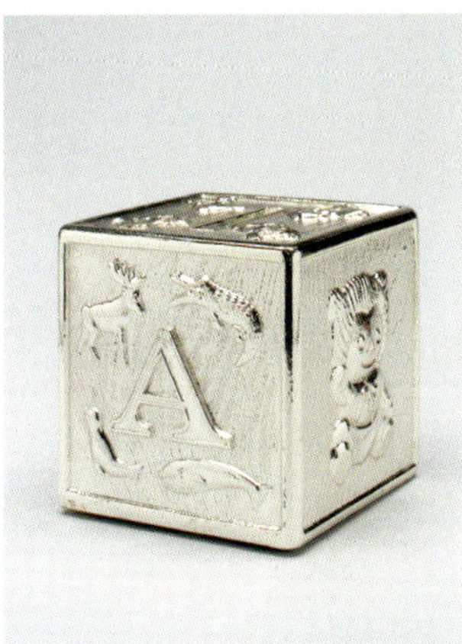
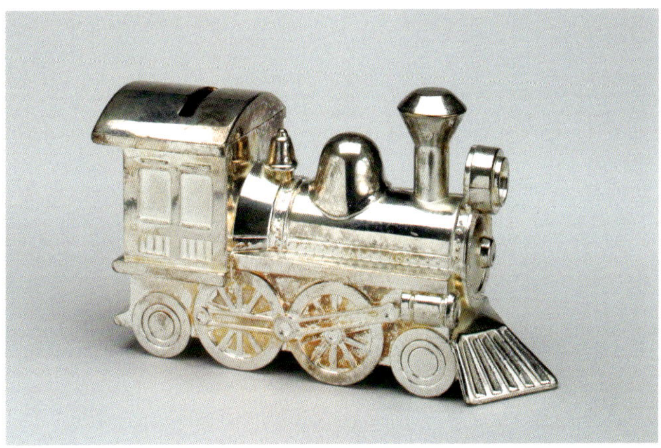

Steam Engine, c. 1970s
Banthrico, Inc., Chicago (1931 – 85), manufacturer
Zinc alloy
4 3/16 x 2 5/8 x 5 3/8 in.
2003.236.822

Amish Girl, c. 1970
John Wright, Wrightsville, Pennsylvania (est. 1880), manufacturer
Aluminum, pigment
5 1/4 x 2 9/16 x 3 1/8 in.
2003.236.1066

Amish Boy, c. 1970
John Wright, Wrightsville, Pennsylvania (est. 1880), manufacturer
Aluminum, pigment
5 1/8 x 3 1/4 x 2 7/8 in.
2003.236.1065

Popcorn Wagon, c. 1974
Banthrico, Inc., Chicago (1931 – 85), manufacturer
Zinc alloy
3 5/8 x 3 9/16 x 4 1/2 in.
2003.236.833

Abraham Lincoln, c. 1974
Banthrico, Inc., Chicago (1931 – 85), manufacturer
Zinc alloy
5 3/4 x 3 9/16 x 2 7/16 in.
2003.236.389

Indian Head Penny, 1972
George Knerr, American (1911 – 1979), designer
Metal, pigment
3 3/16 x 3 1/4 x 1 1/8 in.
2003.236.206

Prince and Princess of Wales, 1981
Robert Brown, Welsh, designer
Zinc alloy
6 11/16 x 4 5/16 x 2 in.
2003.236.1080

Mickey Mouse, c. 1980
Pride Lines, Ltd., Lindenhurst, New York, manufacturer
Metal, pigment
6 1/2 x 4 5/16 x 4 5/16 in.
2003.236.317

Fireman's Helmet, c. 1978
United States
Zinc alloy, pigment
1 9/16 x 4 3/16 x 2 11/16 in.
2003.236.119

Bradley Train Engine, c. 1998
Probably United States
Metal, silver plate
3 1/8 x 1 7/8 x 5 9/16 in.
2003.236.835

Toy block, c. 1984
Japan
Metal, silver plate
2 15/16 x 2 15/16 x 2 15/16 in.
2003.236.826

Mickey Mouse, c. 1982
Pride Lines, Ltd., Lindenhurst, New York, manufacturer
Metal, pigment
6 1/2 x 4 5/16 x 4 5/16 in.
2003.236.316

Birdhouse, 20th century
United States
Metal, glass, pigment
1 3/8 x 1 7/16 x 1 5/8 in.
2003.236.248

Bear Stealing Pig, 20th century
United States
Brass, pigment
5 5/16 x 2 9/16 x 2 1/8 in.
2003.236.278

Baby, 20th century
United States
Metal
4 7/16 x 2 15/16 x 2 15/16 in.
2003.236.252

Abraham Lincoln, 20th century
Zinc alloy
6 x 3 7/8 x 3 in.
2003.236.388

Calendar (registering), 20th century
United States
Metal, pigment, plastic
4 1/16 x 4 3/8 x 1 1/2 in.
2003.236.596

Browns Valley State Bank (hat), 20th century
Stronghart Company, Chicago, manufacturer
Metal, pigment, cord
1 7/8 x 3 1/4 x 3 1/4 in.
2003.236.277

Boxer Head, 20th century
Germany
Lead, pigment
2 5/8 x 2 3/4 x 2 9/16 in.
2003.236.1059

Donkey, Facing Left, 20th century
Germany
Lead, pigment
3 7/8 x 3 7/8 x 1 1/2 in.
2003.236.836

Building, 20th century
Metal, pigment
9 3/8 x 7 1/8 x 8 7/8 in.
2003.236.458a,b

Furnace, 20th century
Ciney, manufacturer
Metal, enameling
3 1/2 x 4 3/8 x 2 5/8 in.
2003.236.383

First National Bank, Webster City, Iowa (registering), 20th century
National Recording Safe Company, Chicago, manufacturer
Metal, pigment
2 7/16 x 3 5/8 x 3 5/8 in.
2003.236.652

Drum, 20th century
Leonard Silver Manufacturing Company, Boston (est. 1969), manufacturer
Metal, silver plate, plastic
3 1/2 x 3 1/8 x 3 1/8 in.
2003.236.857

Drum, 20th century
Gorham & Company, Providence, Rhode Island (est. 1831), manufacturer
Metal, silver plate, plastic, pigment, paper
4 x 2 3/4 x 2 3/4 in.
2003.236.853

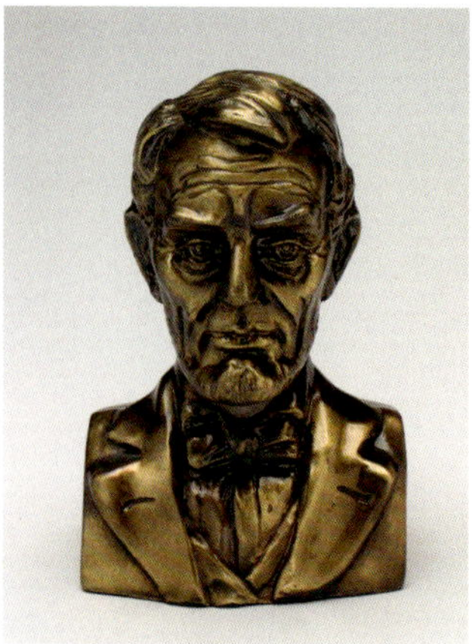

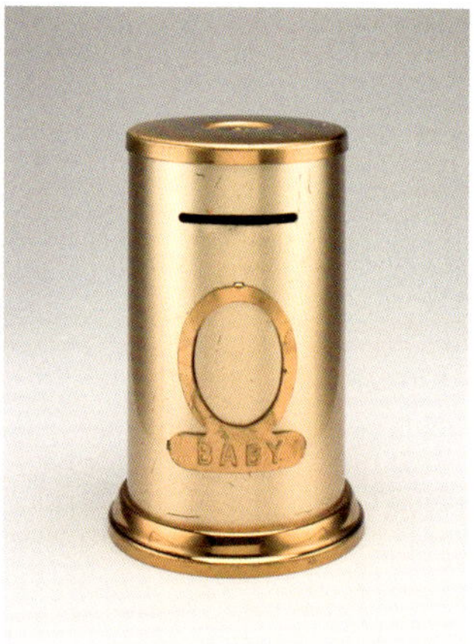
BABY

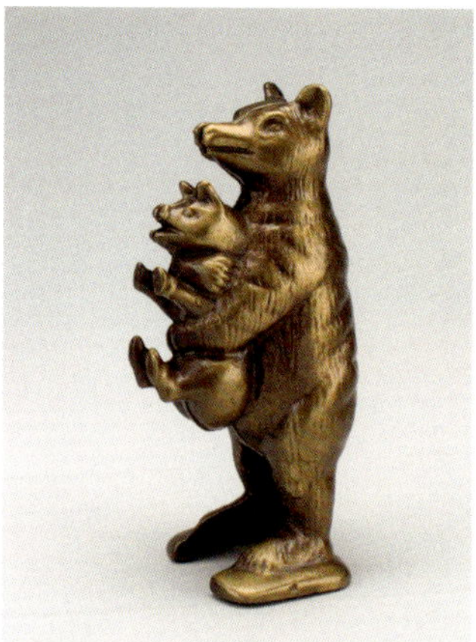

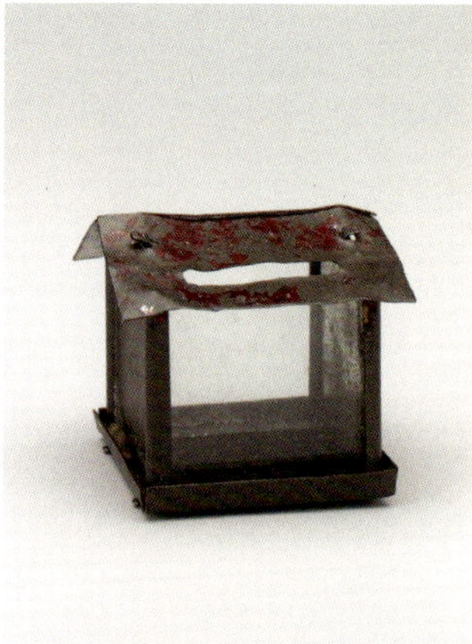

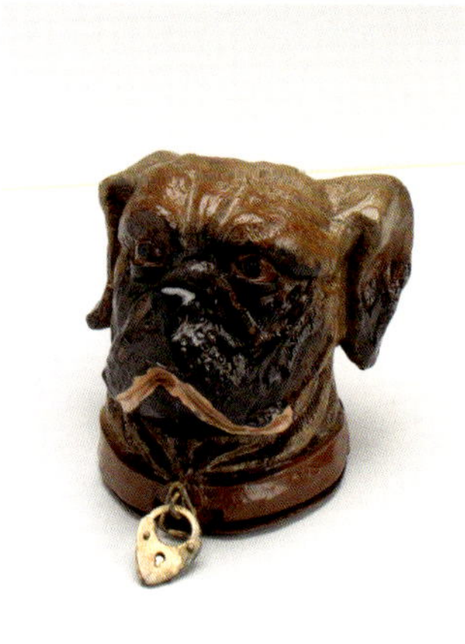

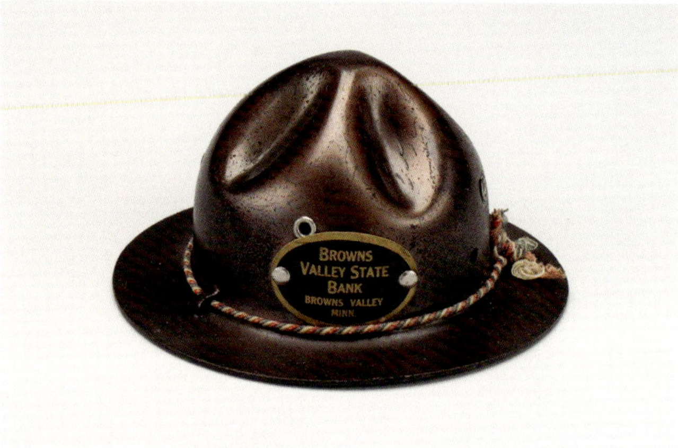
BROWNS
VALLEY STATE
BANK
BROWNS VALLEY
MINN

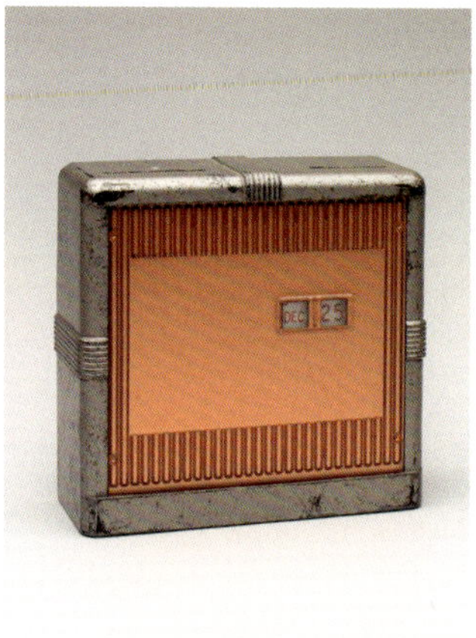

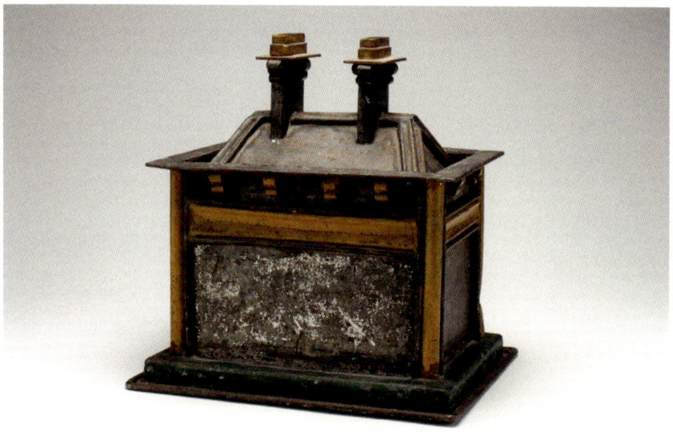

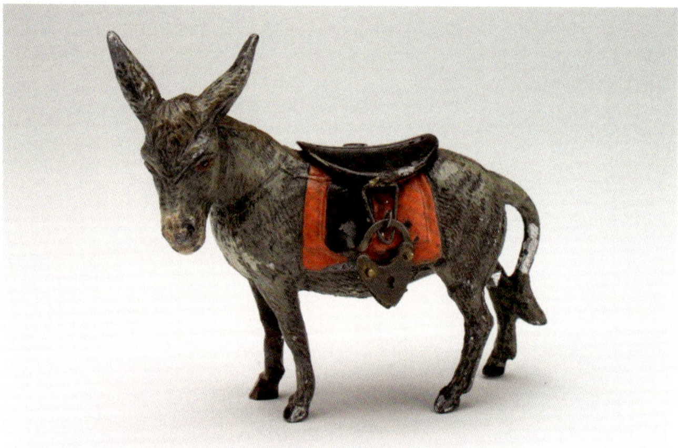

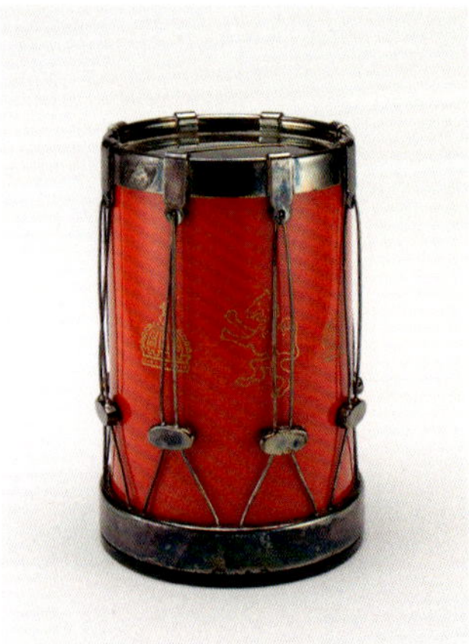

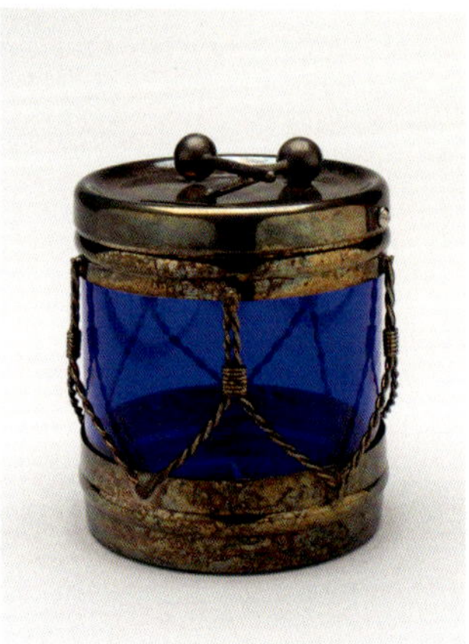

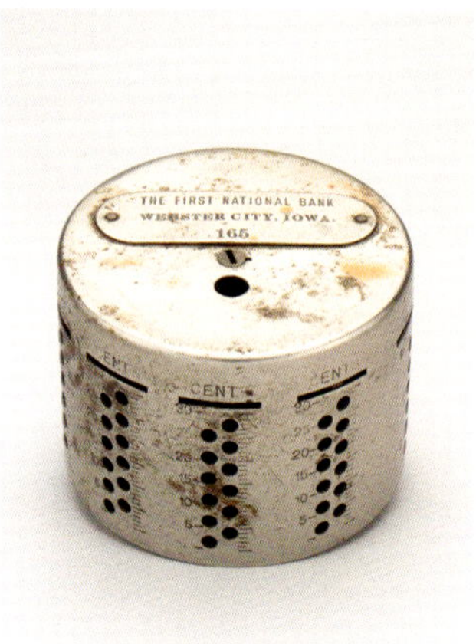
THE FIRST NATIONAL BANK
WEBSTER CITY, IOWA.
165
CENT

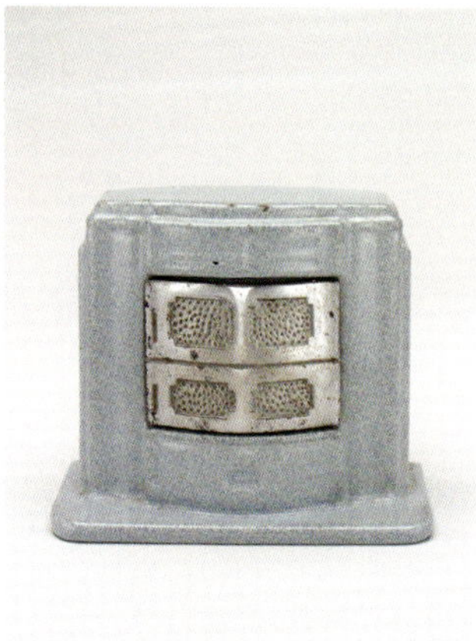

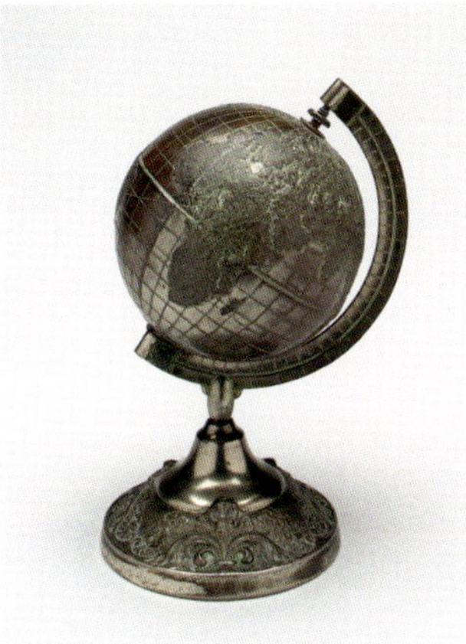

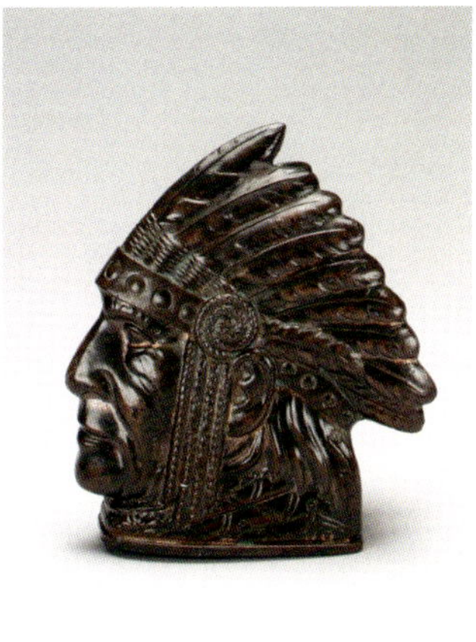

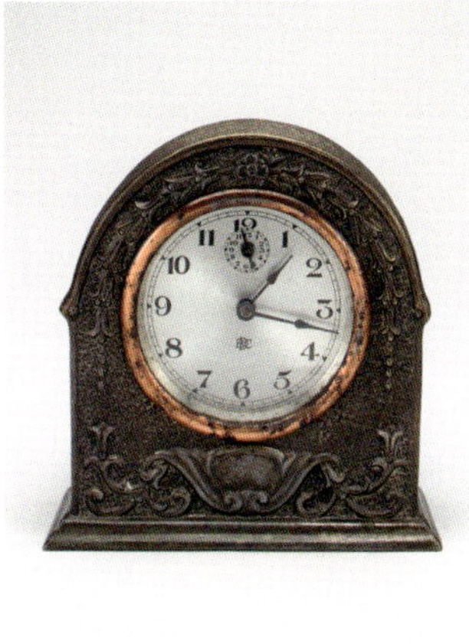

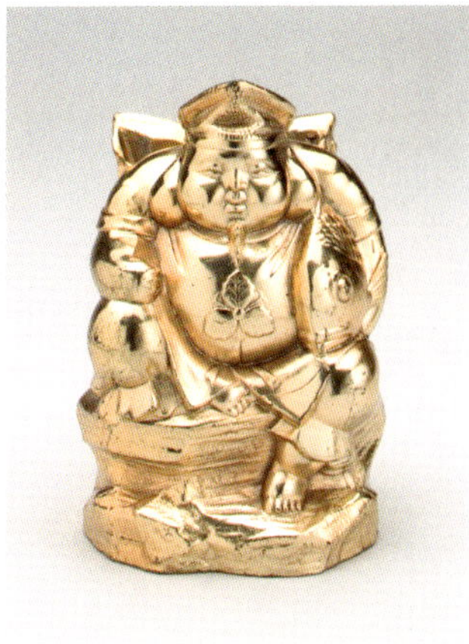

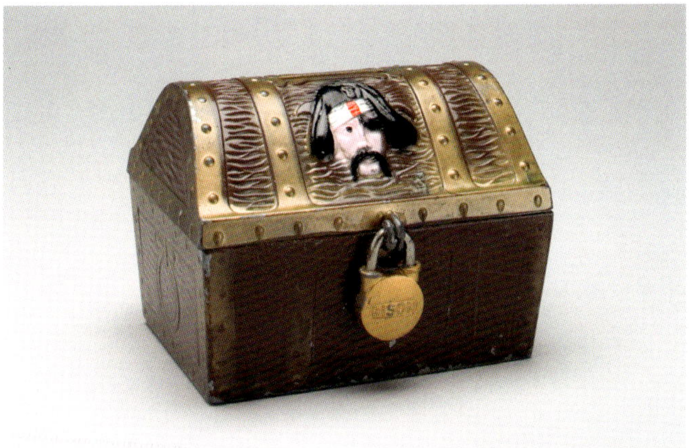

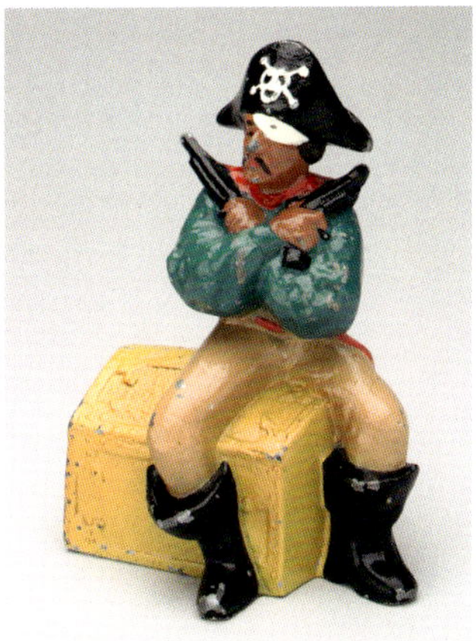

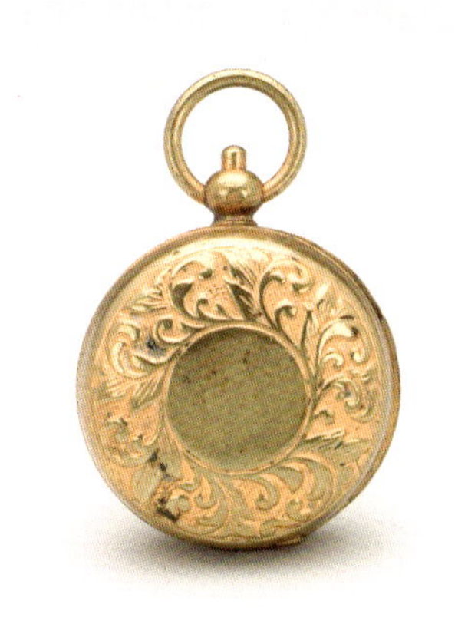

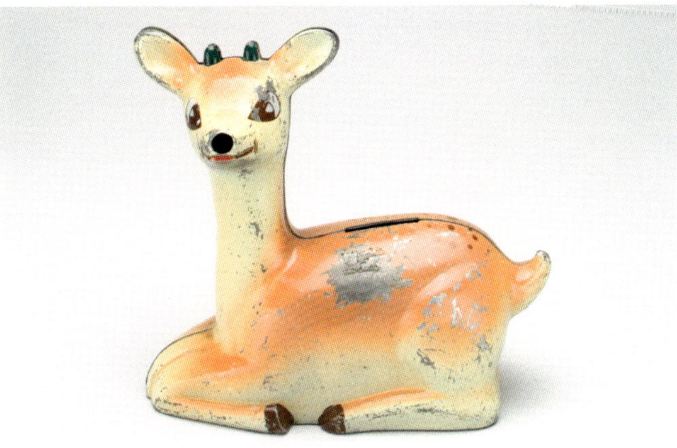

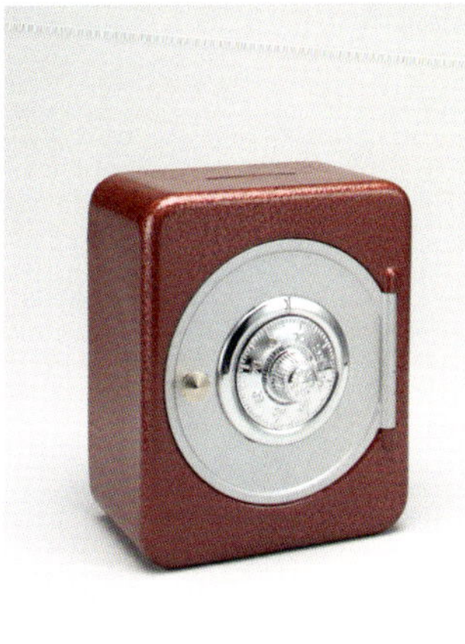

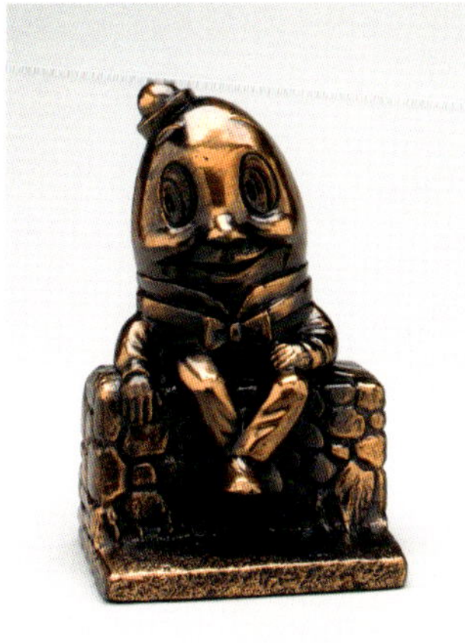

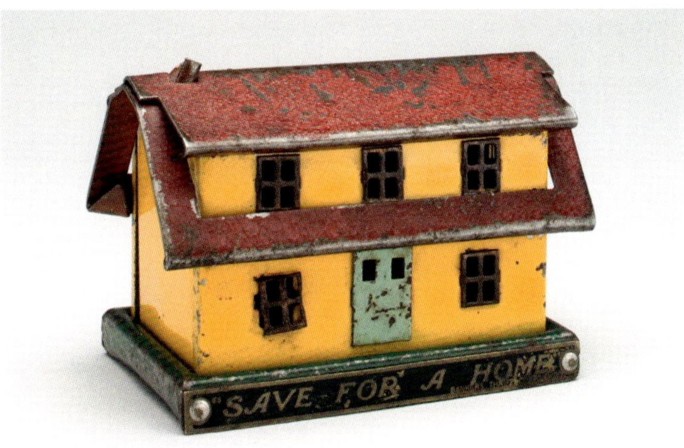
SAVE FOR A HOME

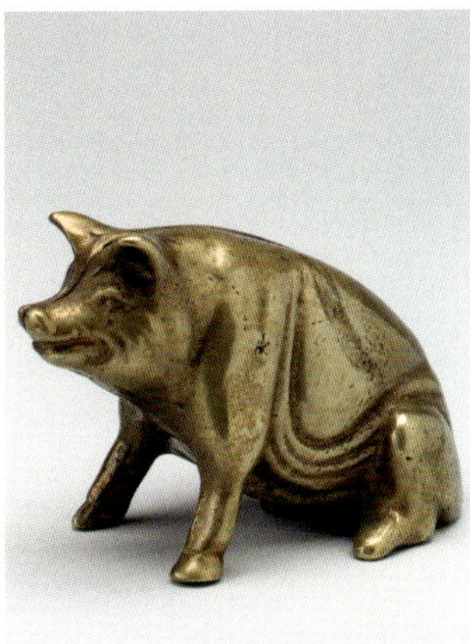

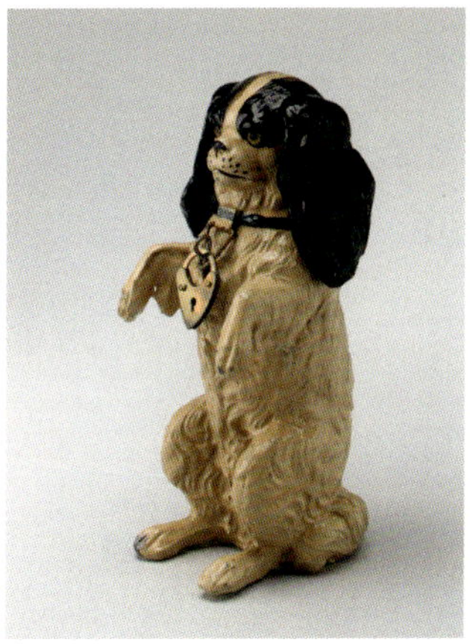

Man with fish, 20th century
Japan
Metal, pigment
3 1/4 x 2 3/16 x 2 in.
2003.236.1077

Mantle Clock, 20th century
United States
Metal, pigment, glass
5 15/16 x 5 13/16 x 3 in.
2003.236.230

Indian Bust, Profile, 20th century
Japan
Lead, pigment
4 x 1 5/8 x 3 1/2 in.
2003.236.1069

Globe on Arc, 20th century
United States
Brass
7 1/4 x 4 7/8 x 4 15/16 in.
2003.236.350

Pocket Watch, 20th century
England
Metal, pigment
5 x 1 1/8 x 1 1/4 in.
2003.236.1018

Pistol-Packing Pirate, 20th century
United States
Metal, pigment
5 13/16 x 4 1/4 x 3 3/8 in.
2003.236.1067

Pirate Chest, 20th century
E. J. Kahn Company, Chicago, manufacturer
Metal, pigment
2 7/8 x 3 13/16 x 3 1/16 in.
2003.236.1075

Seated Humpty Dumpty, 20th century
United States
Metal
5 1/2 x 3 9/16 x 2 1/2 in.
2003.236.198

Safe, 20th century
Metal, plastic, pigment
5 x 4 1/8 x 2 7/8 in.
2003.236.392

Rudolph the Red-nosed Reindeer, 20th century
Aluminum, pigment, glass
5 1/4 x 2 1/2 x 6 in.
2003.236.412

Seated Spaniel Dog, 20th century
Germany
Lead, pigment
4 3/8 x 1 7/16 x 2 in.
2003.236.1064

Seated Pig, 20th century
United States
Brass
2 5/8 x 2 1/4 x 4 3/8 in.
2003.236.983

Save for a Home, 20th century
Bankers Thrift Corporation, Chicago, manufacturer
Steel, pigment
2 1/2 x 3 3/8 x 2 3/16 in.
2003.236.363

Moravian box, c. 1756
Adamstown, Pennsylvania
Wood
3 3/4 x 5 3/4 x 3 1/2 in.
2003.236.557a,b

STILL BANKS: Wood and Other Organic Media

Toy block, 20th century
Hong Kong
Metal, silver plate
2 15/16 x 2 7/8 x 2 7/8 in.
2003.236.832

Disappearing Coin Money Box, c. 1850
Probably United States
Wood, metal
7 3/16 x 5 7/8 x 5 3/8 in.
2003.236.811

Chest of drawers, c. 1820
Probably United States
Wood, pigment
9 1/4 x 6 1/8 x 2 1/2 in.
2003.236.869

Owl, c. 1800
United States
Wood, pigment
11 7/16 x 2 1/4 x 3 1/16 in.
2003.236.816

Chest of drawers, c. 1790
Pennsylvania
Wood, pigment, metal
5 13/16 x 5 1/4 x 2 1/2 in.
2003.236.861

Trinitarian Bible Society (book), mid-to-late 19th century
England
Wood, pigment, paper
6 7/16 x 1 3/4 x 4 1/4 in.
2003.236.874

Money box, mid-to-late 19th century
Probably United States
Wood, metal
3 3/4 x 6 7/16 x 3 3/4 in.
2003.236.859

English and Foreign Bible Society (book), c. 1850
England
Wood, pigment, paper
6 1/2 x 1 3/4 x 4 1/2 in.
2003.236.873

Barrel, c. 1870
Probably Scotland
Wood (Tartanware), pigment
2 7/8 x 2 5/8 x 2 5/8 in.
2003.236.513

New Bridge, Westminster (money box), c. 1862
Probably Scotland
Wood, pigment
3 15/16 x 2 3/8 x 2 3/8 in.
2003.236.419a,b

Money box, c. 1860
Probably United States
Wood, metal
1 3/8 x 3 1/8 x 1 3/4 in.
2003.236.327

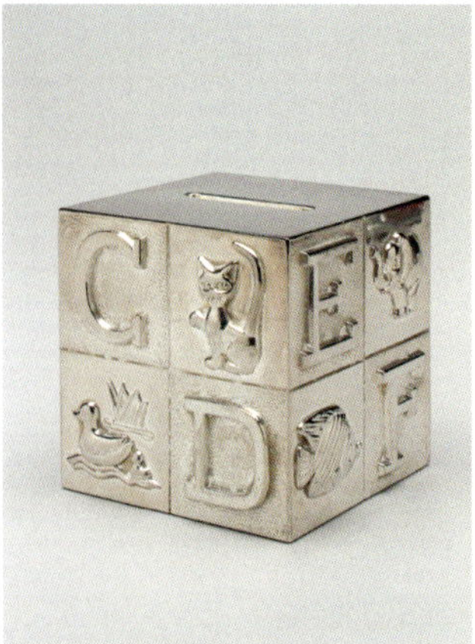

STILL BANKS: Wood and Other Organic Media

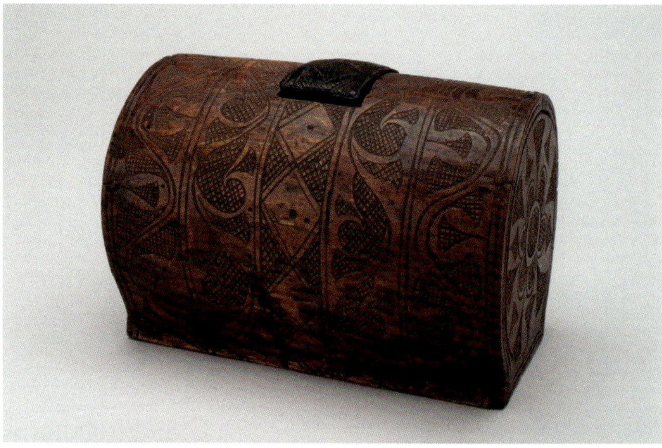

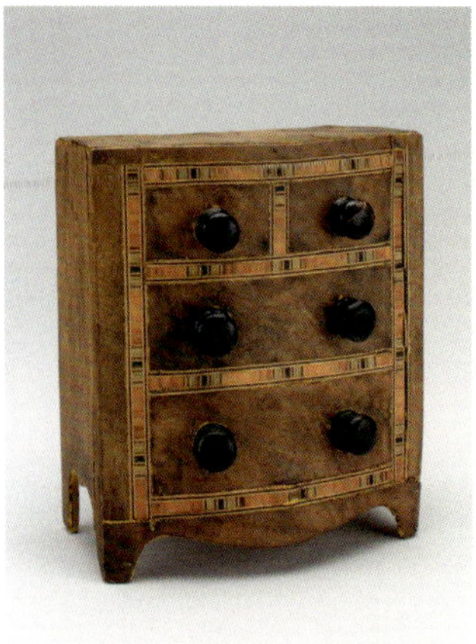

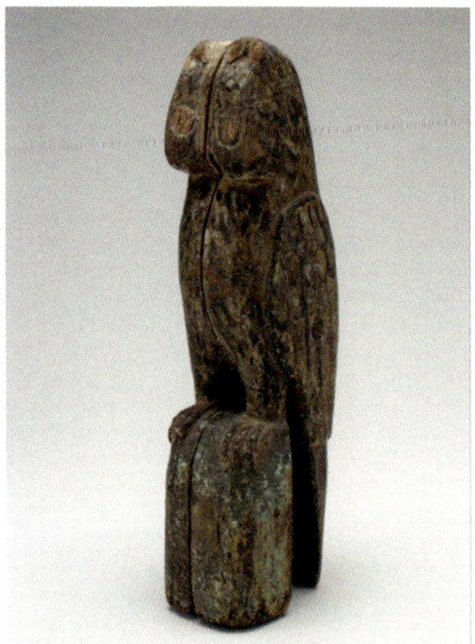

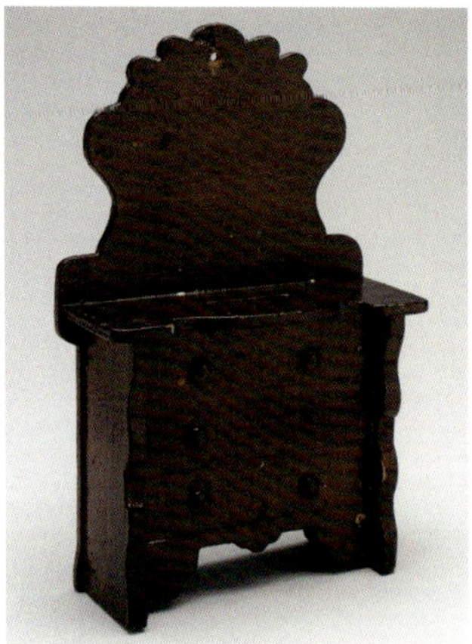

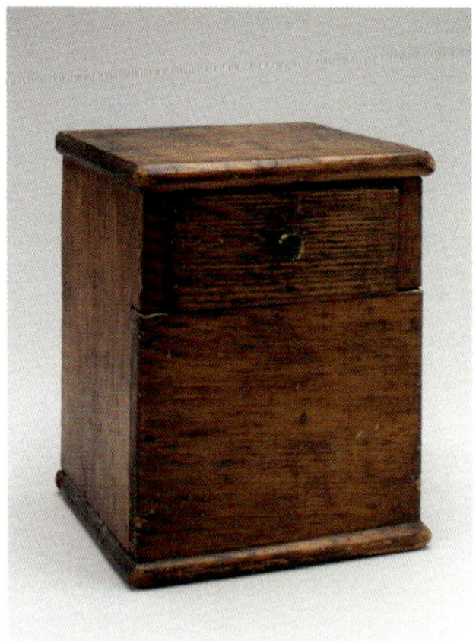

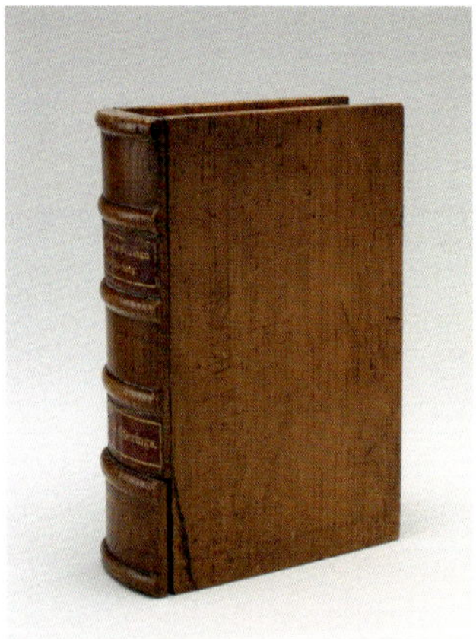

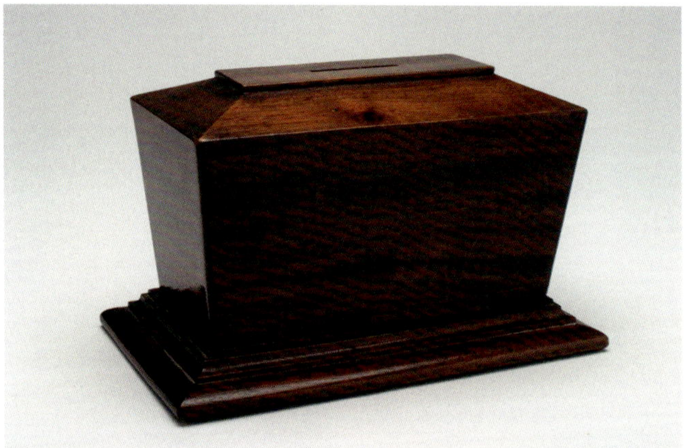

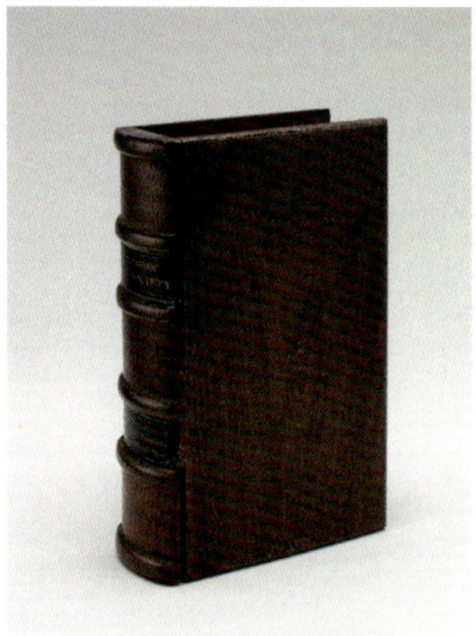

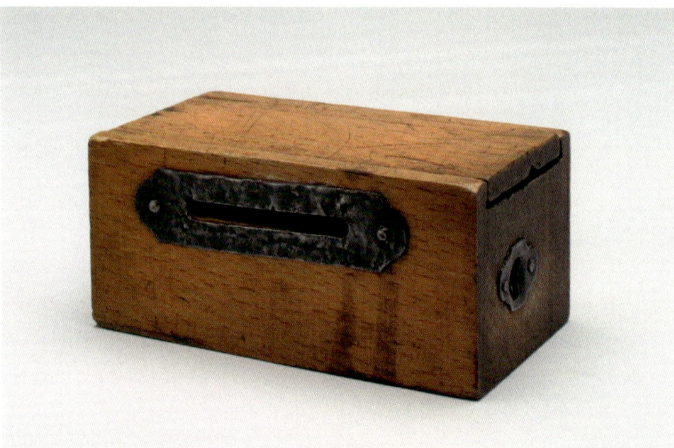

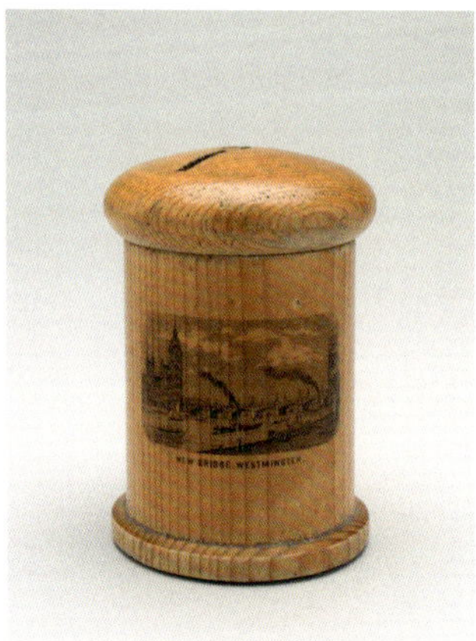

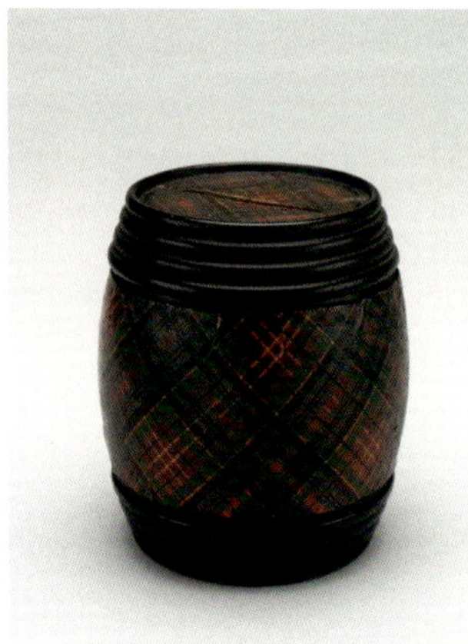

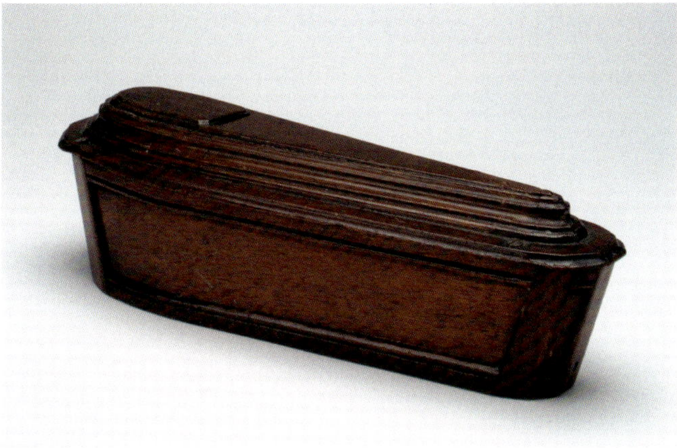

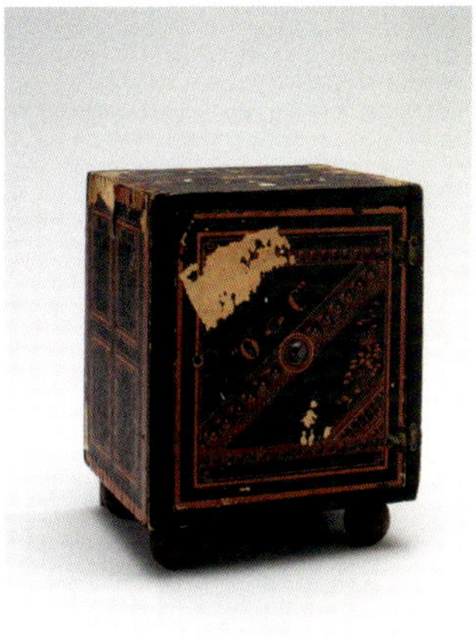

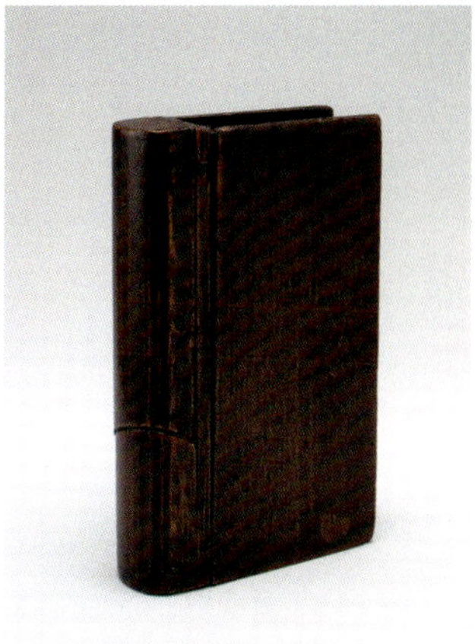

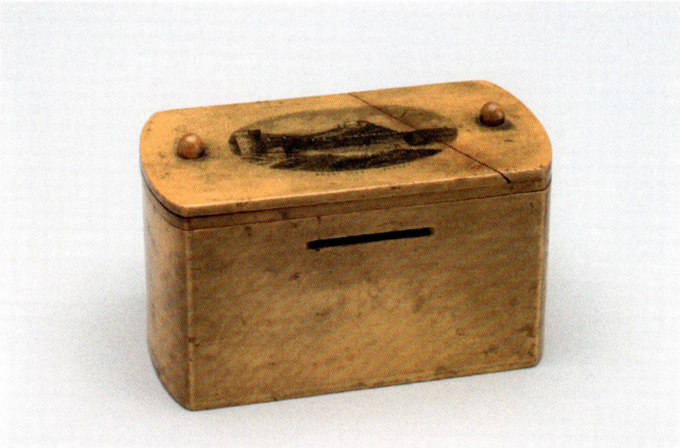

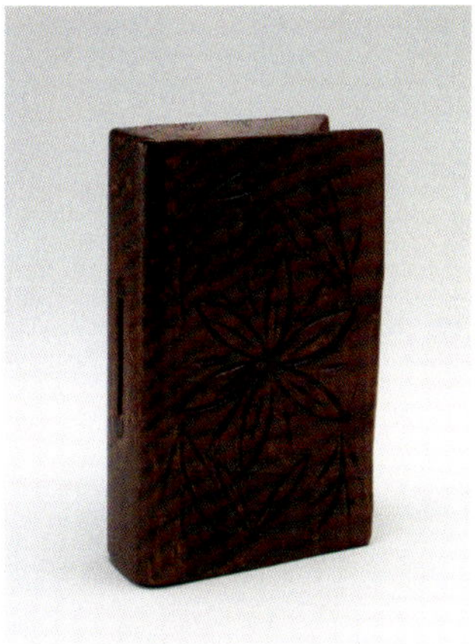

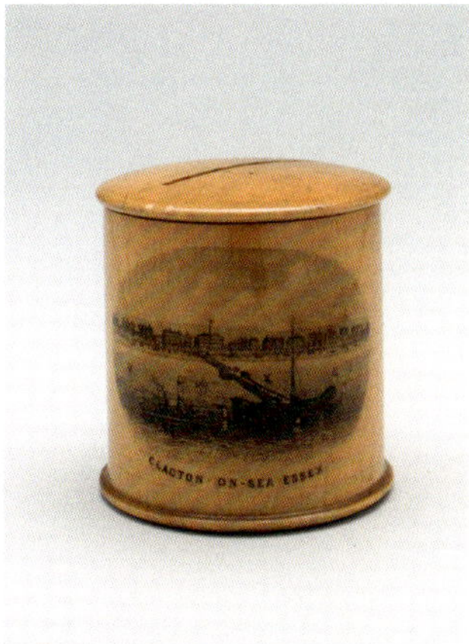
CLACTON-ON-SEA ESSEX

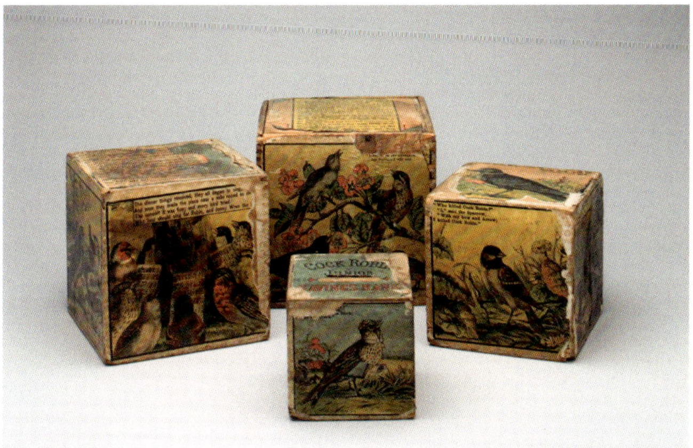

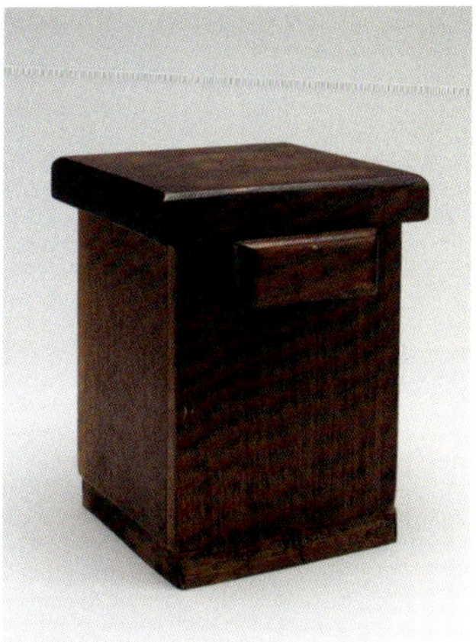

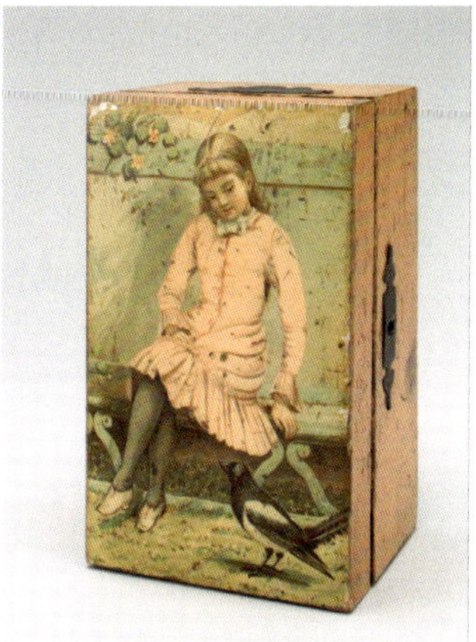

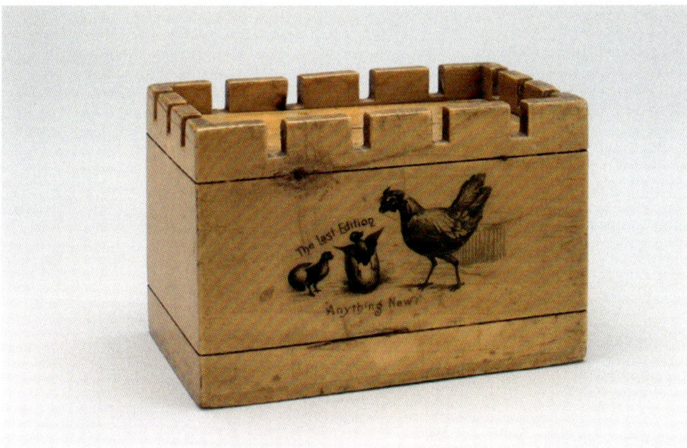
The last Edition
Anything New?

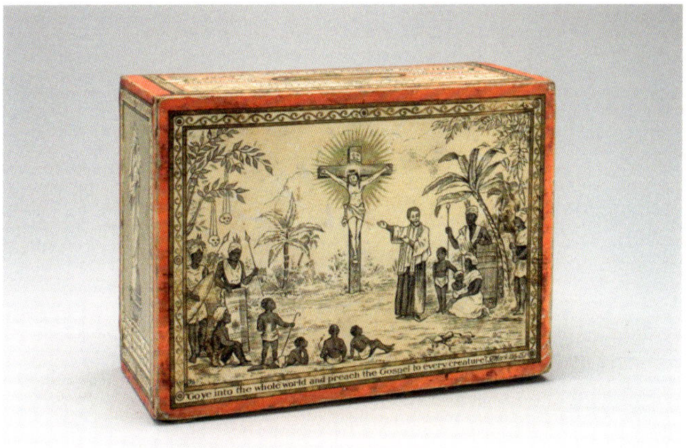
Go ye into the whole world and preach the Gospel to every creature.

Book, 19th century
Possibly England
Wood
6 1/4 x 3 7/8 x 1 1/16 in.
2003.236.875

Cabinet, c. 1890
United States
Wood, metal, pigment, paper
6 1/2 x 5 3/8 x 4 1/2 in.
2003.236.555

Coffin, c. 1870
Wilson Wettach & Company, Legh, New York, manufacturer
Wood, metal
3 1/16 x 10 7/8 x 3 7/16 in.
2003.236.423

Clacton-on-Sea, Essex (money box), 19th century
Scotland
Wood (Mauchline ware), pigment, paper
2 1/8 x 2 1/8 x 2 1/8 in.
2003.236.323

Book, 19th century
Possibly England
Wood
5 5/16 x 3 5/16 x 1 7/16 in.
2003.236.876

Mount Orgueil, Jersey (money box), c. 1895
Scotland
Wood (Mauchline ware), pigment, paper
2 1/4 x 4 5/16 x 2 5/8 in.
2003.236.326

Girl with Bird, late 19th century
England
Wood, paper, pigment, metal
2 13/16 x 5 3/4 x 3 1/2 in.
2003.236.867

Disappearing Coin Money Box, late 19th century
Probably United States
Wood, metal
5 7/16 x 4 1/2 x 4 3/4 in.
2003.236.1113

Cock Robin Junior Savings Bank, late 19th century
England
Wood, paper
5 3/8 x 5 7/16 x 5 1/2 in.
2003.236.446.1-4

St. Joseph's Society for Foreign Missions, late 19th century
England
Wood, paper
4 1/16 x 6 7/16 x 2 13/16 in.
2003.236.721

The Last Edition: Anything New? (money box), late 19th century
Probably Scotland
Wood, pigment
2 5/8 x 4 1/8 x 2 1/2 in.
2003.236.325

Eagle, late 19th or early 20th century
United States
Papier-mâché, pigment
4 3/4 x 3 5/8 x 2 5/8 in.
2003.236.760

Chest of drawers, late 19th or early 20th century
Leonard, maker
Probably United States
Wood, pigment, paper, glass
9 5/16 x 4 7/8 x 3 1/8 in.
2003.236.863

Beehive, late 19th or early 20th century
Probably England
Wood
3 9/16 x 3 9/16 x 3 9/16 in.
2003.236.332a,b

Alnwick Castle (mantle clock), late 19th or early 20th century
Scotland
Wood (Mauchline ware), pigment, paper
4 5/16 x 3 3/8 x 2 9/16 in.
2003.236.330

Lacquered box, late 19th or early 20th century
Japan
Wood, pigment, metal
1 15/16 x 4 13/16 x 2 7/8 in.
2003.236.341

Drop-leaf table, late 19th or early 20th century
Probably United States
Wood, metal, pigment
5 3/16 x 7 1/16 x 4 1/8 in.
2003.236.424

London Missionary Society, late 19th or early 20th century
England
Wood, pigment
3 1/4 x 5 1/2 x 2 1/4 in.
2003.236.511

London Bridge (money box), late 19th or early 20th century
Germany
Wood, pigment
3 1/8 x 2 5/16 x 2 5/16 in.
2003.236.328

Holyrood Palace (mantle clock), late 19th or early 20th century
Scotland
Wood (Mauchline ware), pigment, paper
5 1/2 x 3 3/4 x 2 5/8 in.
2003.236.329

Crusade of Rescue Homes for Destitute Children, early 20th century
England
Wood, paper
6 3/4 x 4 1/4 x 6 7/8 in.
2003.236.441

Urn, late 19th or early 20th century
Probably United States
Wood, pigment, ivory, brass
3 3/4 x 3 7/8 x 3 7/8 in.
2003.236.336

Rolltop desk, late 19th or early 20th century
Germany
Wood, pigment, metal
6 1/2 x 6 1/2 x 3 3/16 in.
2003.236.860

Regulator Clock, late 19th or early 20th century
United States
Wood, pigment
5 15/16 x 3 1/2 x 3/4 in.
2003.236.426

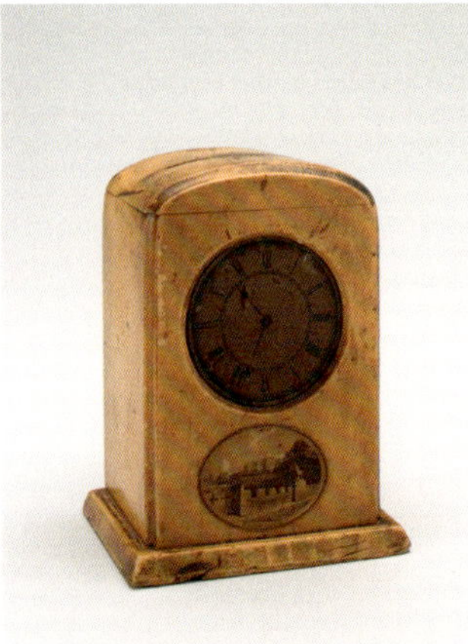
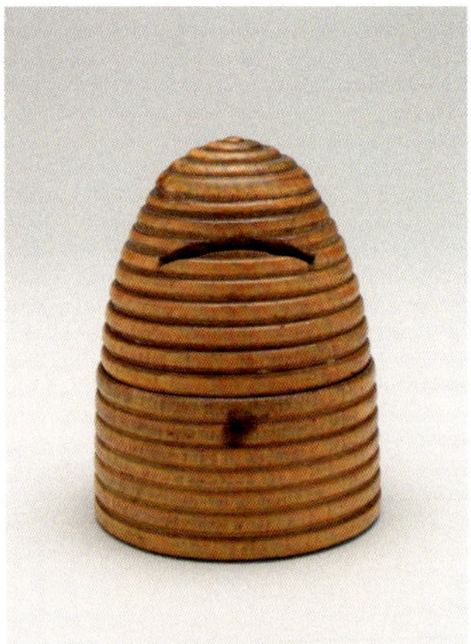
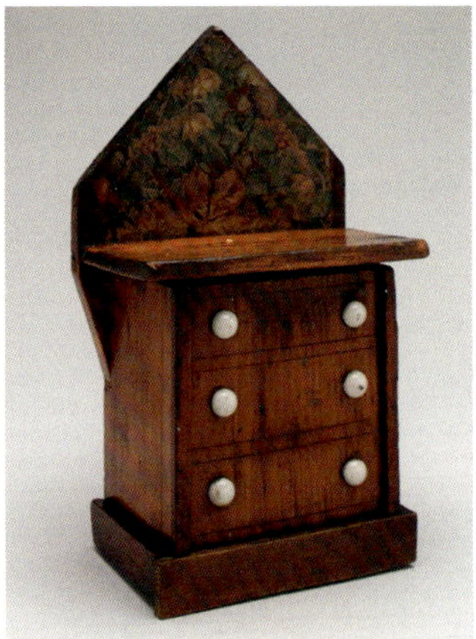
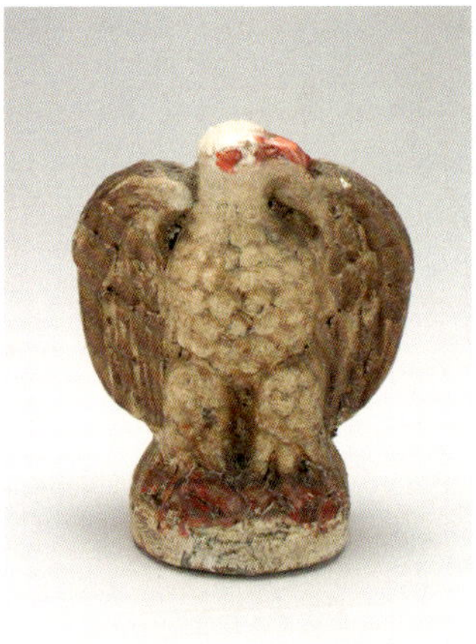
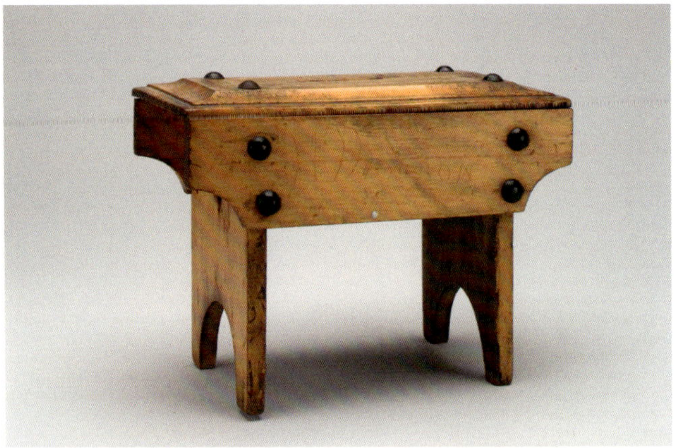
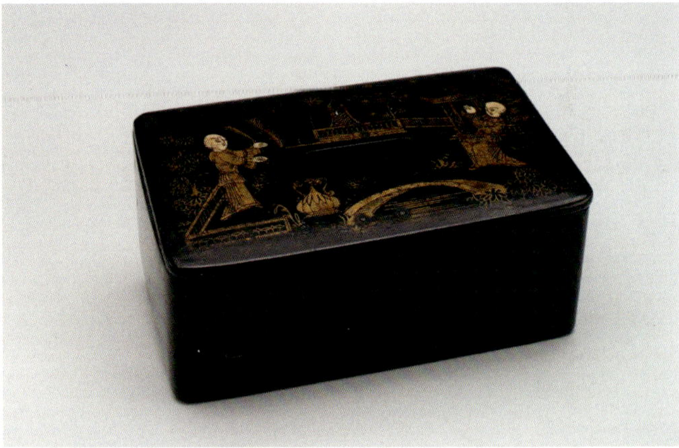
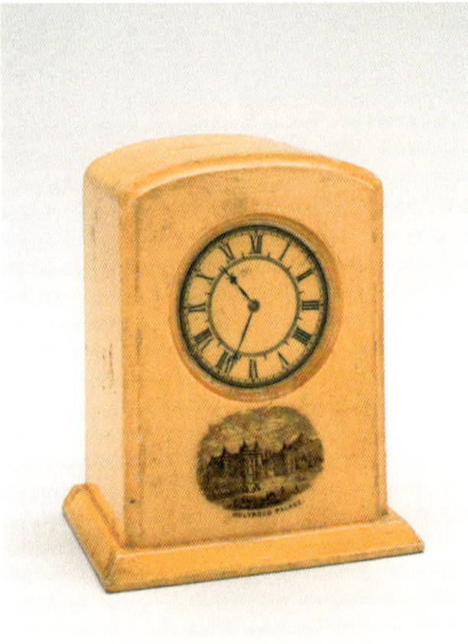
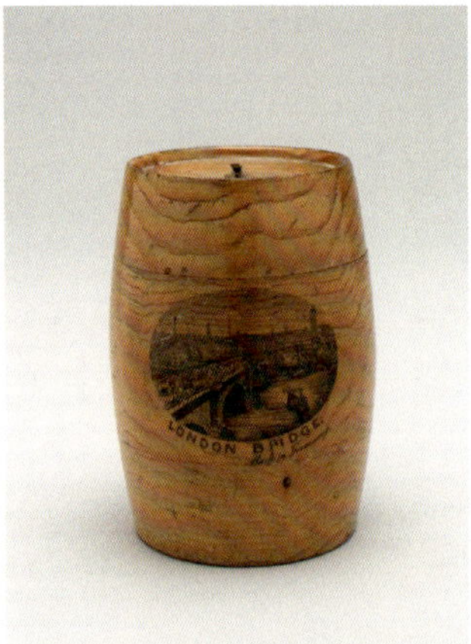
LONDON BRIDGE
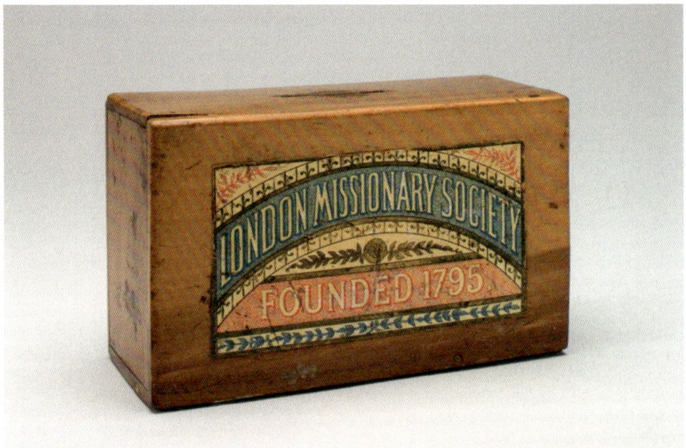
LONDON MISSIONARY SOCIETY
FOUNDED 1795
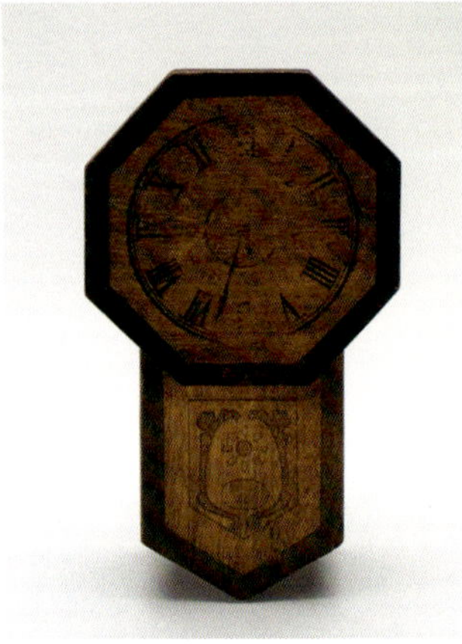
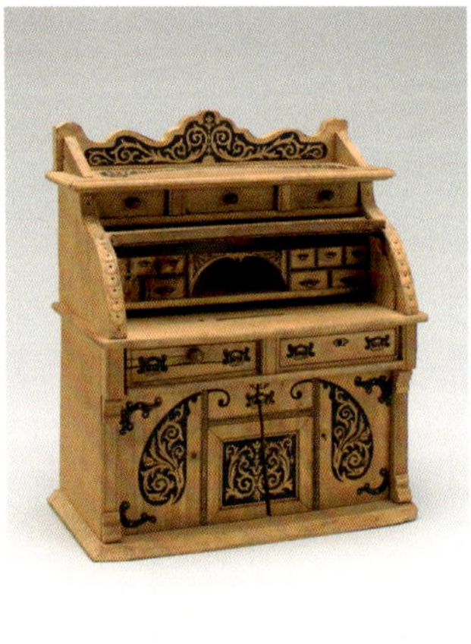
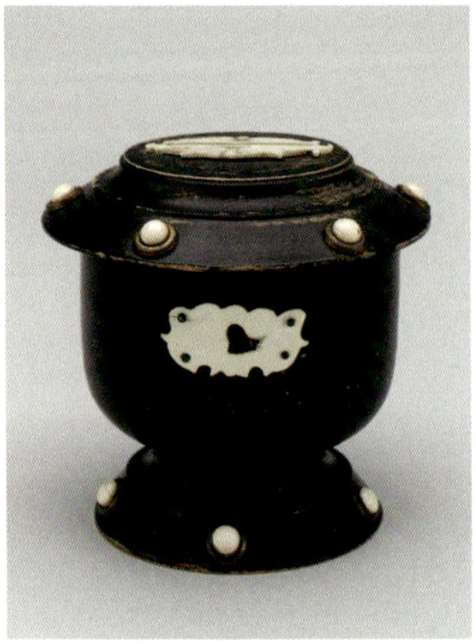
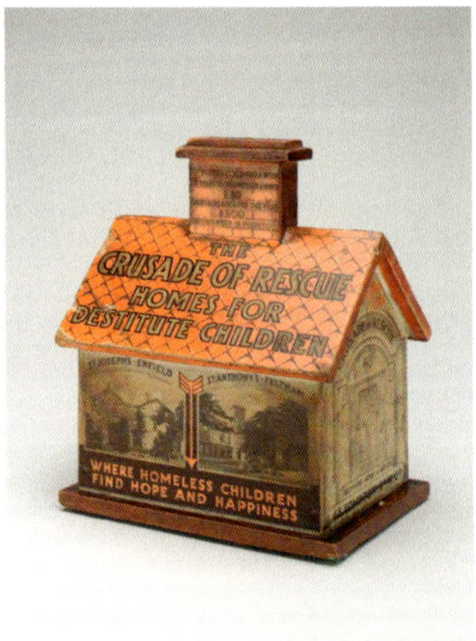
THE
CRUSADE OF RESCUE
HOMES FOR
DESTITUTE CHILDREN
WHERE HOMELESS CHILDREN
FIND HOPE AND HAPPINESS

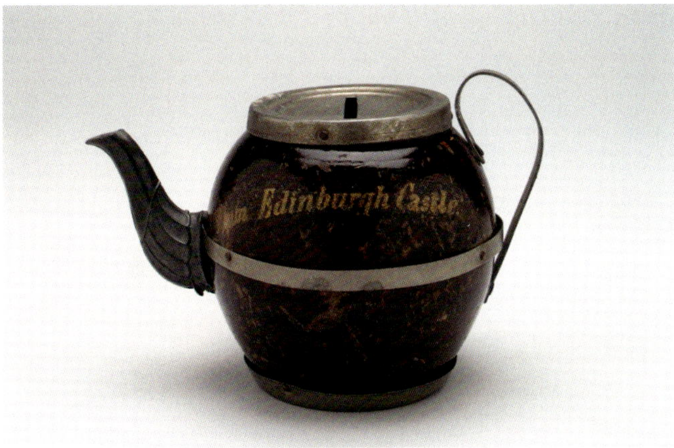
Edinburgh Castle

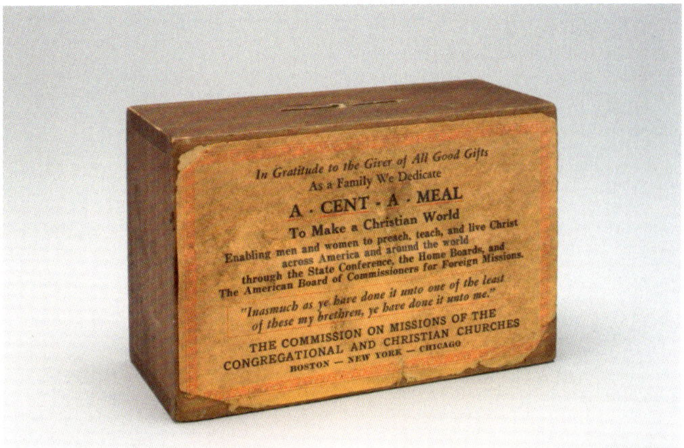
In Gratitude to the Giver of All Good Gifts
As a Family We Dedicate
A · CENT · A · MEAL
To Make a Christian World
Enabling men and women to preach, teach, and live Christ
across America and around the world
through the State Conference, the Home Boards, and
The American Board of Commissioners for Foreign Missions.
"Inasmuch as ye have done it unto one of the least
of these my brethren, ye have done it unto me."
THE COMMISSION ON MISSIONS OF THE
CONGREGATIONAL AND CHRISTIAN CHURCHES
BOSTON — NEW YORK — CHICAGO

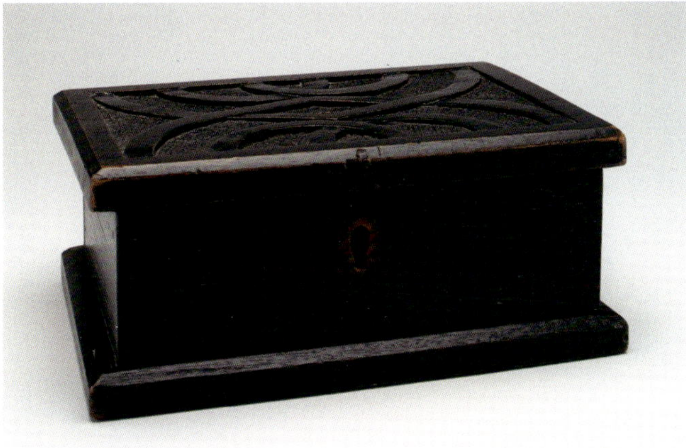

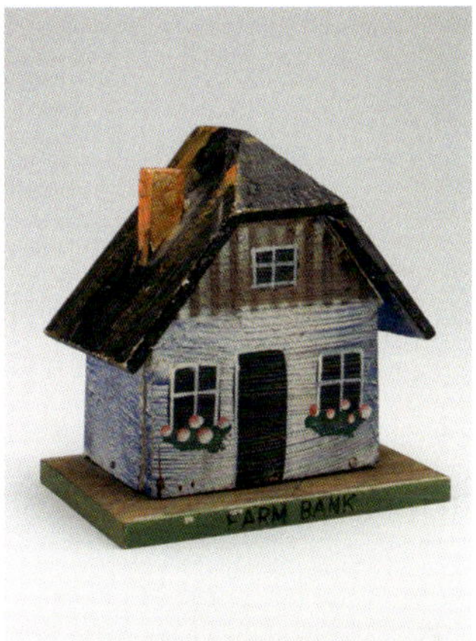
FARM BANK

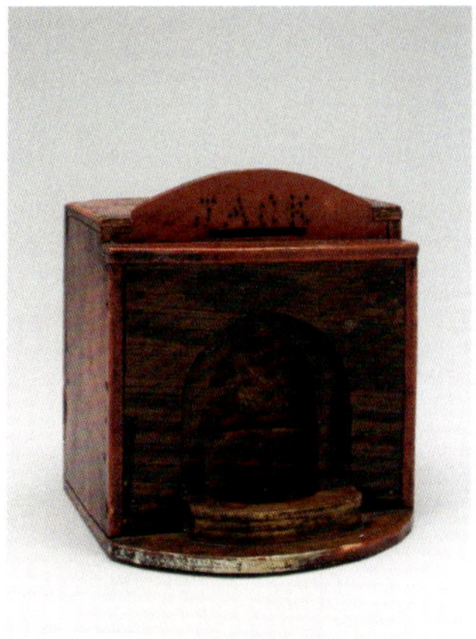

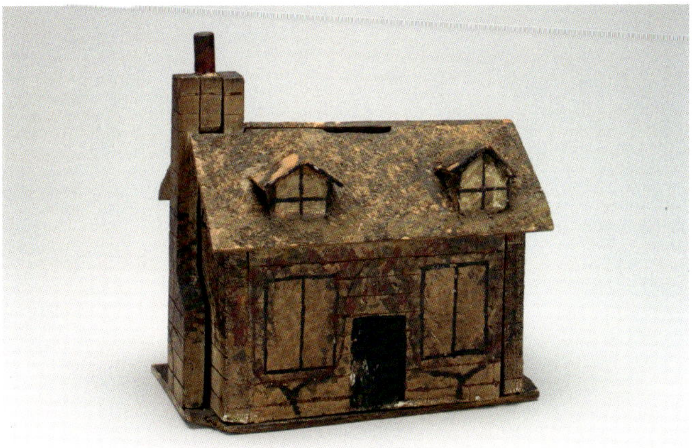

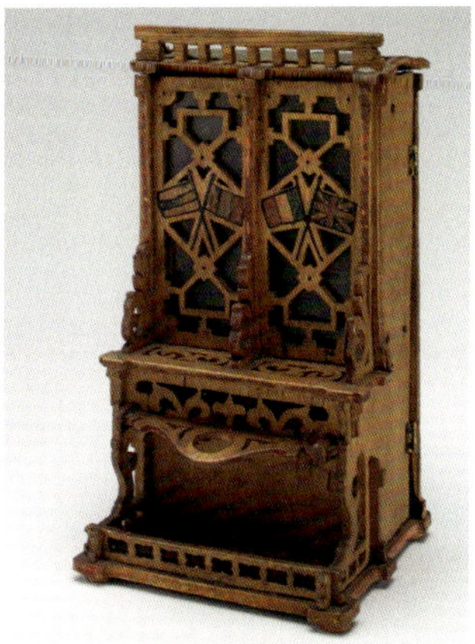

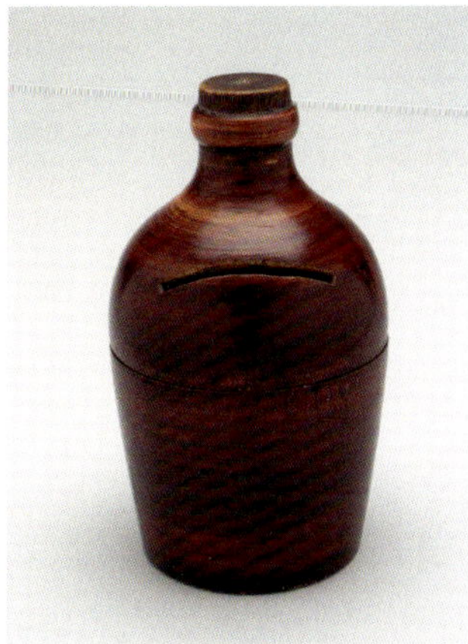

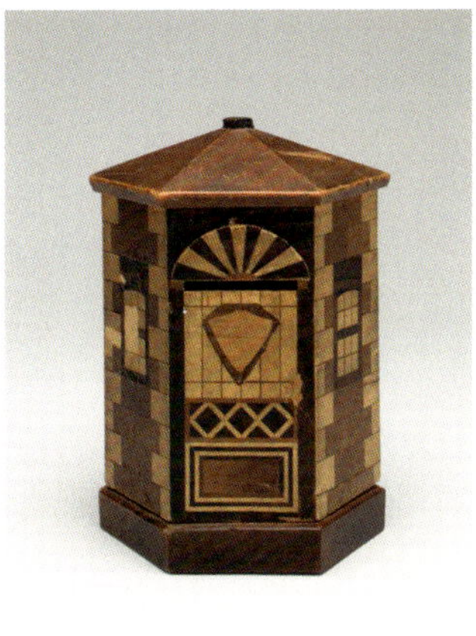

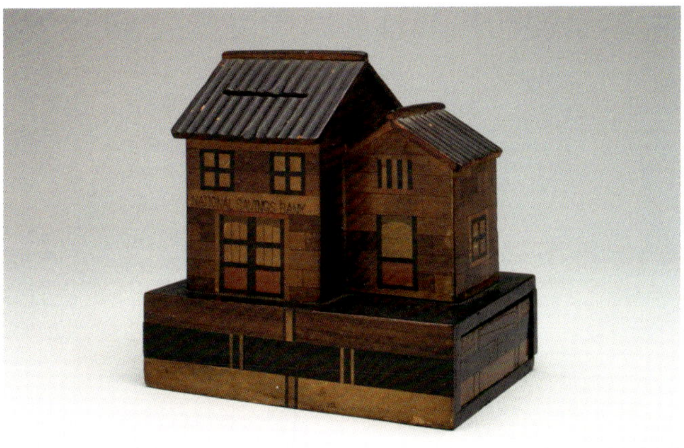

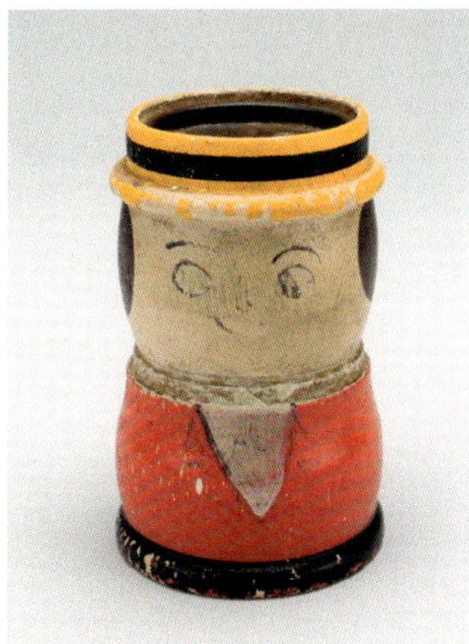

A Cent-a-Meal: American Board of Commissioners for Foreign Missions, early 20th century
United States
Wood, paper
4 7/8 x 2 13/16 x 1 7/8 in.
2003.236.713

Edinburgh Castle (teapot), c. 1900
England
Wood, metal, pigment
3 3/8 x 4 5/8 x 3 in.
2003.236.322

Fireplace, early 20th century
Probably United States
Wood, pigment
4 1/2 x 4 1/2 x 4 1/8 in.
2003.236.812

Farm Bank, early 20th century
Probably United States
Wood, pigment
4 1/16 x 4 1/16 x 2 9/16 in.
2003.236.427

Chest, early 20th century
Probably United States
Wood, metal, pigment
3 1/2 x 8 1/4 x 6 in.
2003.236.810

Jug, early 20th century
Probably United States
Wood, pigment
4 x 2 1/4 x 2 1/4 in.
2003.236.517

Hutch, early 20th century
Probably United States
Wood, metal, pigment, string
8 3/4 x 3 7/8 x 4 7/8 in.
2003.236.862

House, early 20th century
Probably United States
Wood, pigment
6 1/2 x 6 1/2 x 3 1/2 in.
2003.236.720

Standing man,
early 20th century
Probably United States
Wood, metal, pigment
3 1/2 x 2 5/16 x 2 5/16 in.
2003.236.642

National Savings Bank (house), early 20th century
United States
Wood, pigment
5 1/4 x 5 7/16 x 4 15/16 in.
2003.236.639

Marquetry box,
early 20th century
Probably United States
Wood
4 15/16 x 3 x 3 in.
2003.236.714

House, early-to-mid-20th century
Germany
Wood, pigment
4 3/4 x 4 x 3 in.
2003.236.516a,b

Church with steeple, early-to-mid-20th century
Probably United States
Wood, pigment
4 5/8 x 3 3/8 x 2 3/4 in.
2003.236.515a,b

Church with bell tower, early-to-mid-20th century
Probably United States
Wood, pigment
4 1/2 x 3 3/8 x 3 3/8 in.
2003.236.722

Teahouse, early 20th century
Wood, pigment
3 3/4 x 3 1/16 x 2 5/16 in.
2003.236.640

Barrel, c. 1920s
Bankers Thrift Corporation, Chicago, manufacturer
Wood, metal, pigment
2 15/16 x 2 3/8 x 2 3/8 in.
2003.236.456

Standing man, c. 1920
Probably United States
Wood, pigment
4 7/8 x 1 7/8 x 1 7/8 in.
2003.236.641

Fines Box, c. 1904
United States
Wood, metal
6 1/2 x 4 1/2 x 4 in.
2003.236.866

Five-dial combination box, c. 1960
United States
Wood
4 7/8 x 9 5/8 x 4 in.
2003.236.603

Male figure (one of a pair), 1959
Lund, Sweden
Wood, pigment, metal
7 x 2 13/16 x 2 13/16 in.
2003.236.447.1a,b

Six-sided building, c. 1921
Wood, pigment
5 3/4 x 4 x 1 3/4 in.
2003.236.512

Rocking Horse Tin, Still Bank Collectors Club of America, 1977
United States
Cardboard, tin, paper, pigment
3 1/8 x 2 3/8 x 2 3/8 in.
2003.236.212a,b

Korean figure, c. 1960s
Wood, pigment, metal
5 11/16 x 1 7/8 x 1 7/8 in.
2003.236.718

Frog on pedestal, c. 1960s
East Germany
Wood, pigment, metal
3 1/2 x 2 13/16 x 2 13/16 in.
2003.236.422

Female figure (one of a pair), 1960
Lund, Sweden
Wood, pigment, metal
6 3/8 x 2 7/8 x 2 7/8 in.
2003.236.447.2

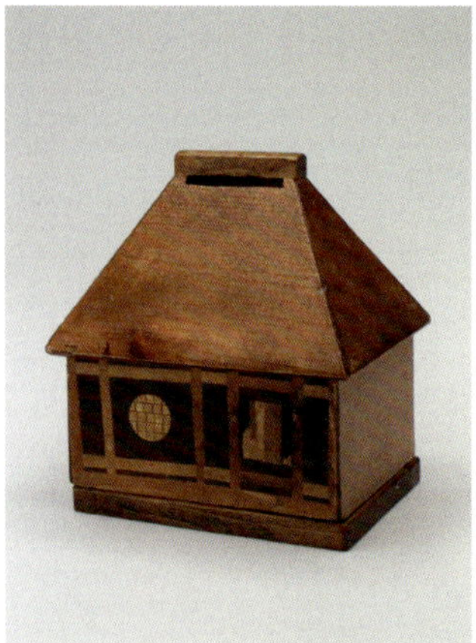

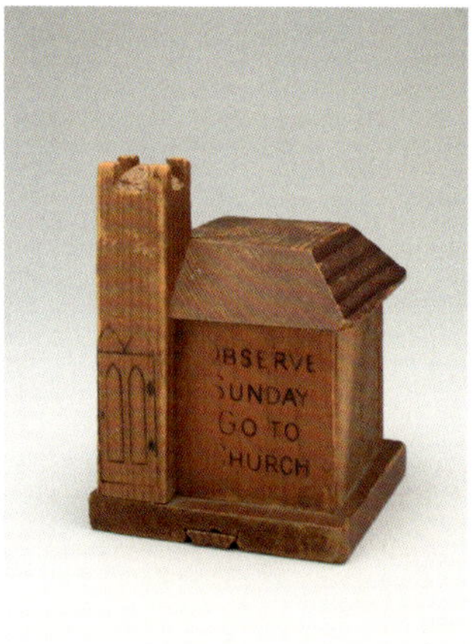
BSERVE
SUNDAY
GO TO
HURCH

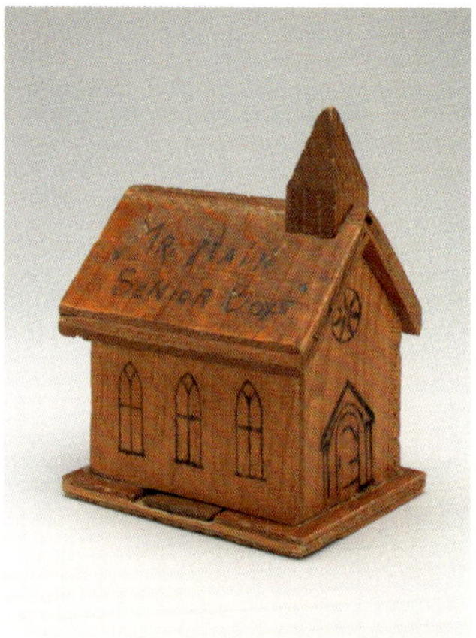

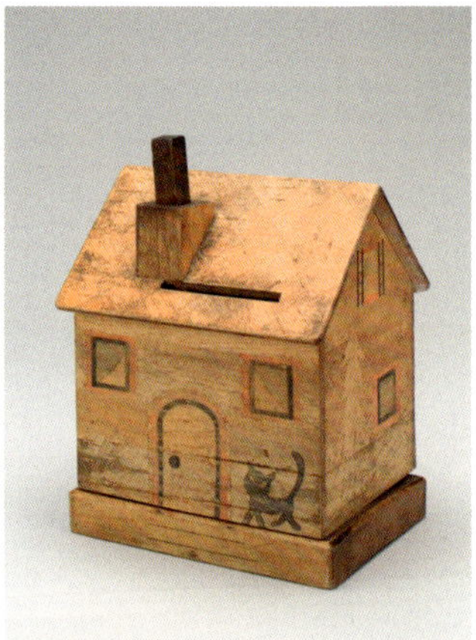

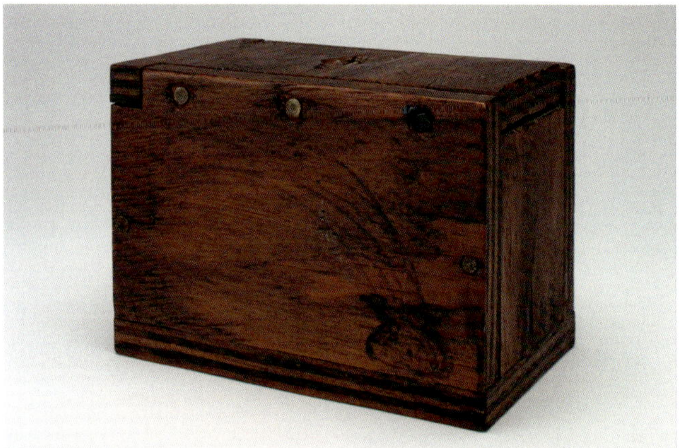

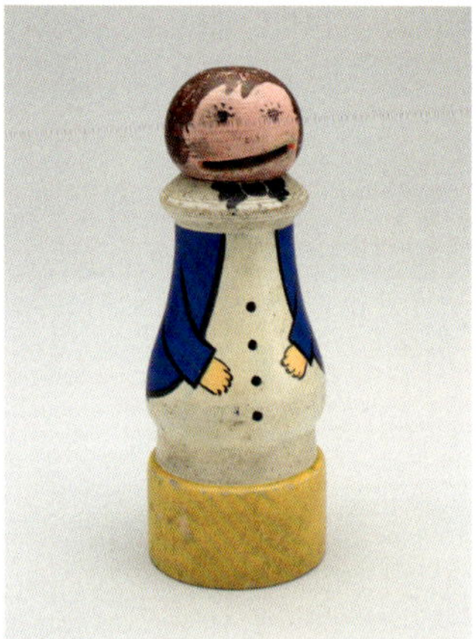

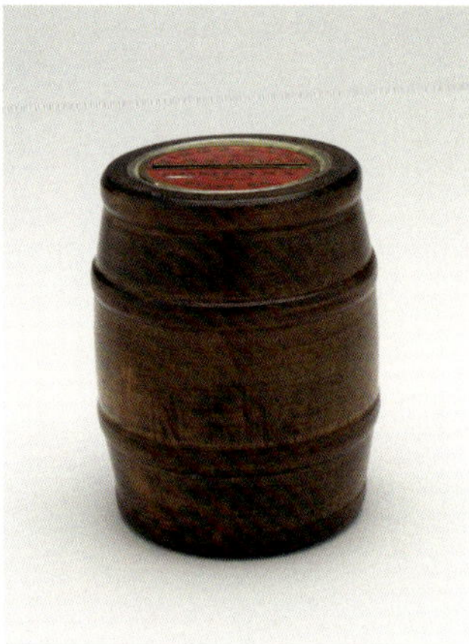

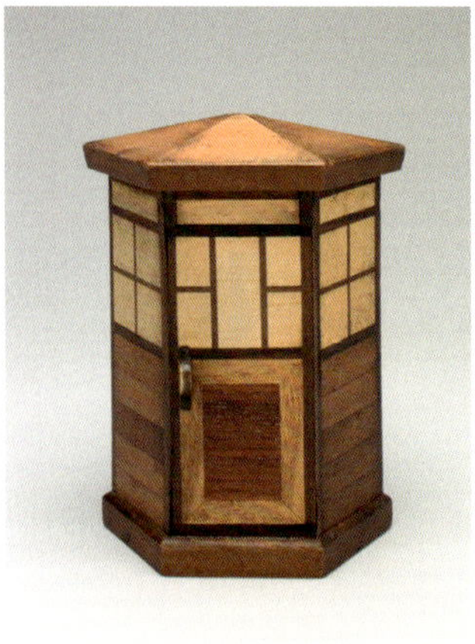

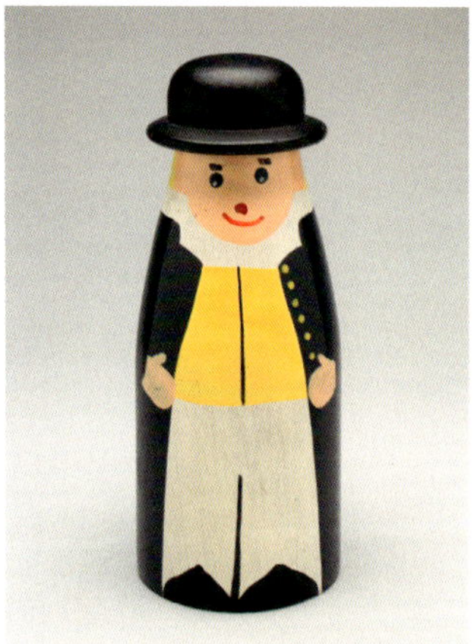

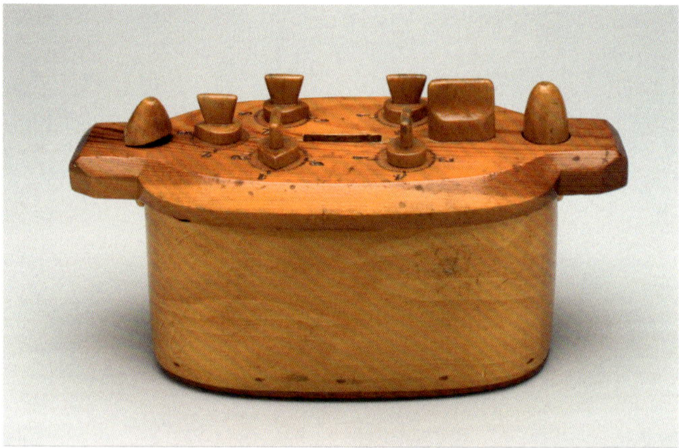

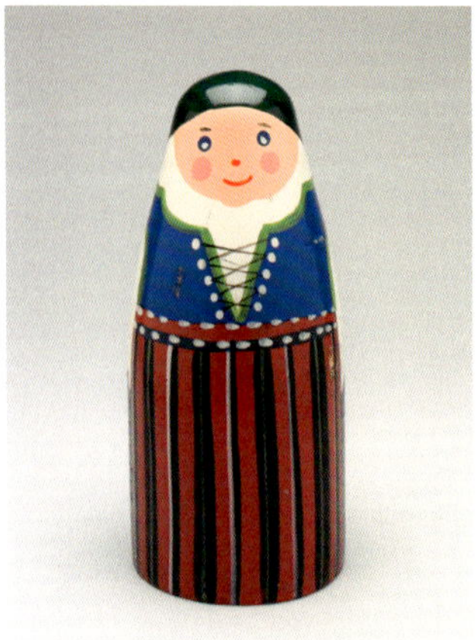

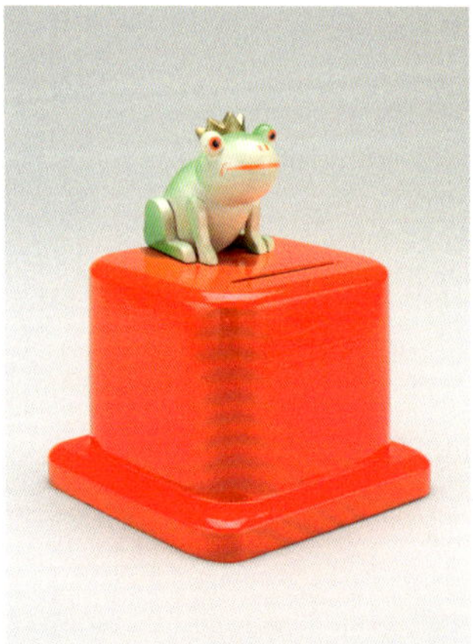

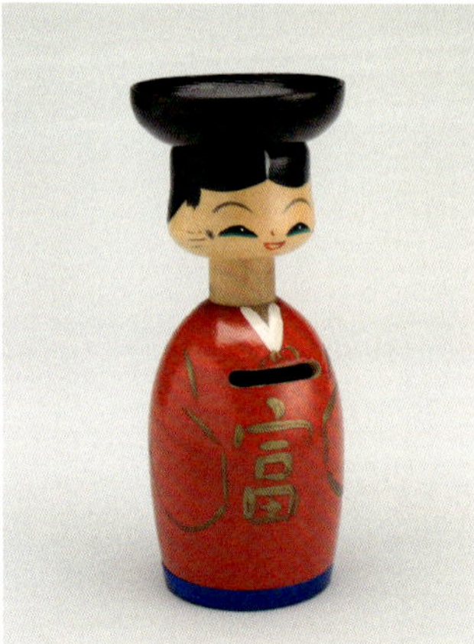

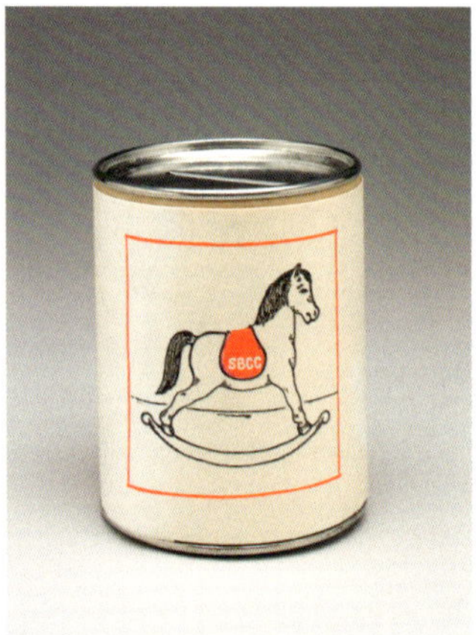
SBCC

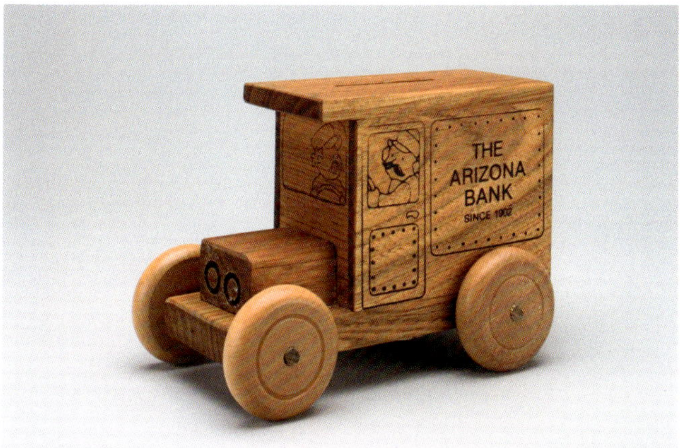
THE
ARIZONA
BANK
SINCE 1902

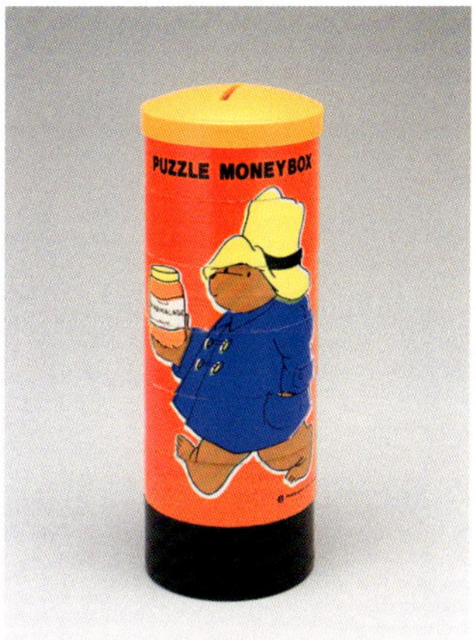
PUZZLE MONEYBOX

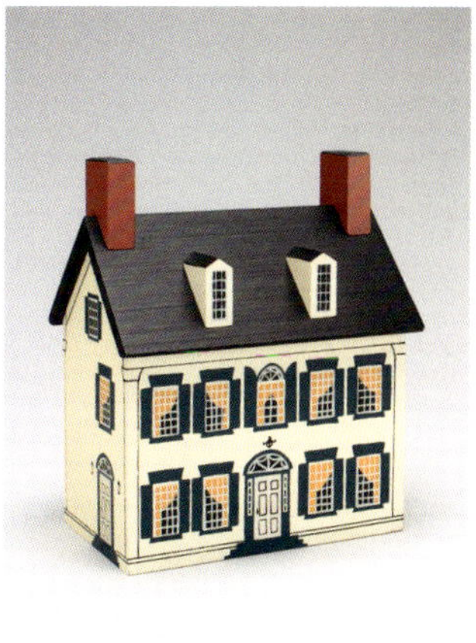

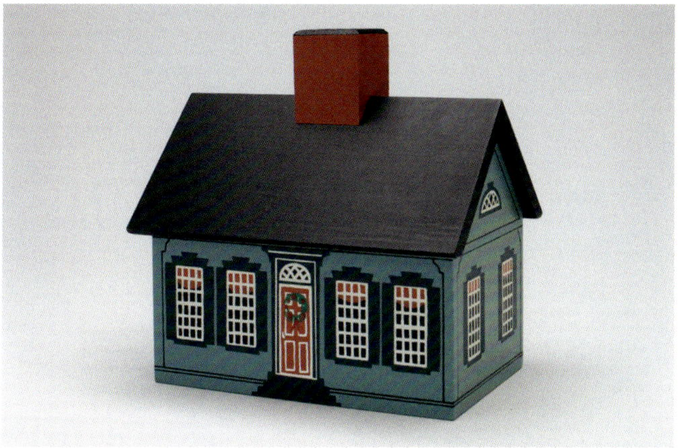

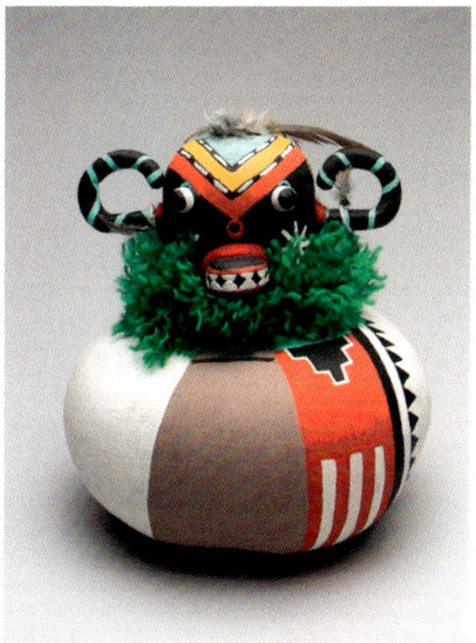

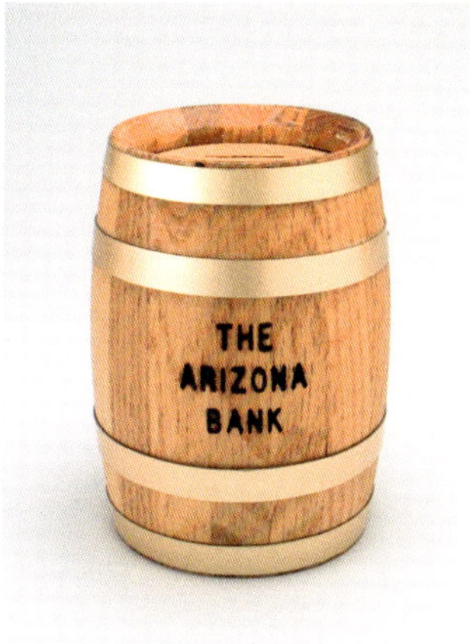
THE
ARIZONA
BANK

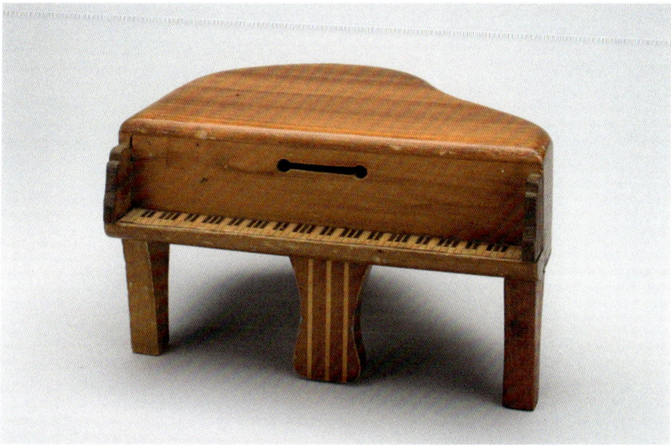

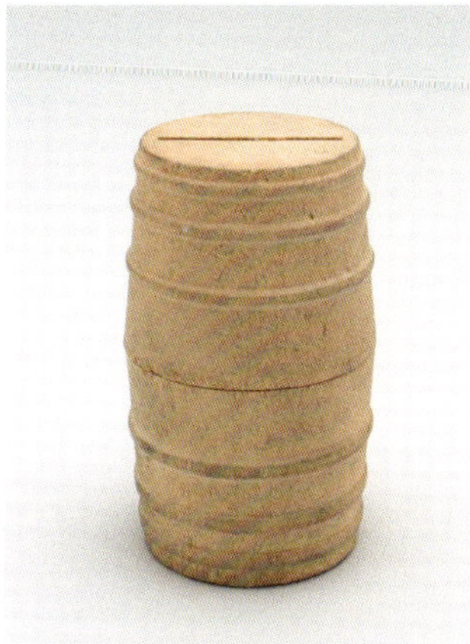

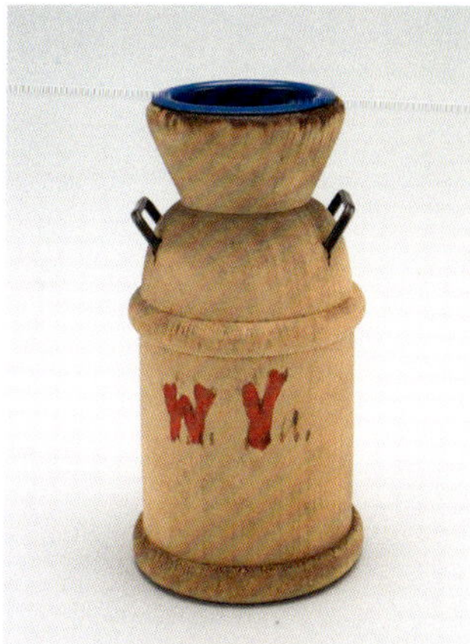
W. Y.

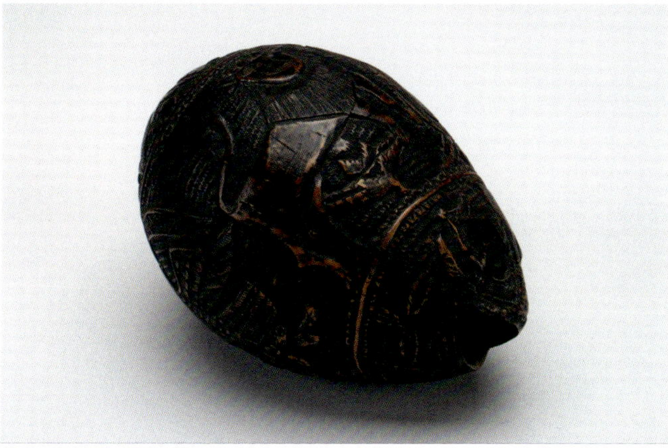

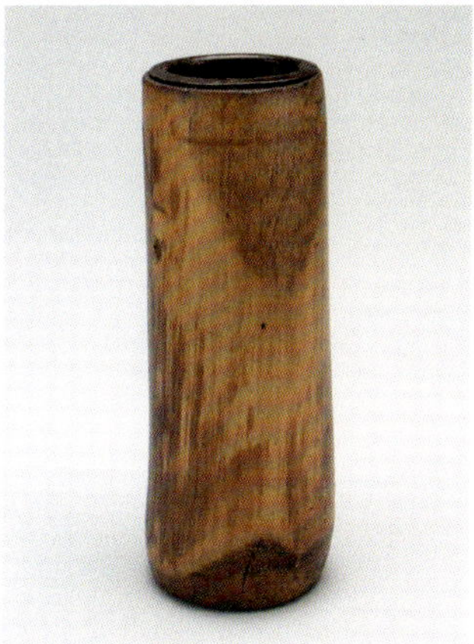

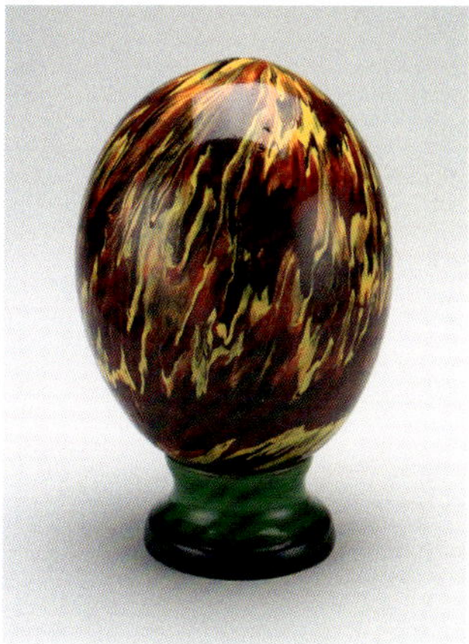

House, 1981
Henry Musser, American, designer
Windfield Designs, Inc., Glens Falls, New York, manufacturer
Wood, metal, pigment
6 1/4 x 5 3/8 x 3 in.
2003.236.510

Paddington Bear Puzzle Money Box, c. 1980
PIC Novelties, Ltd., Harrogate, England, manufacturer
Cardboard, plastic
6 5/16 x 2 3/8 x 2 3/8 in.
2003.236.471

The Arizona Bank (delivery truck), 1979
Toystalgia, Inc., Golden Valley, Minnesota, manufacturer
Wood, cork, pigment
4 3/8 x 3 1/2 x 6 1/4 in.
2003.236.421

The Arizona Bank (barrel), 20th century
United States
Wood, brass, plastic
6 1/8 x 4 x 4 in.
2003.236.319

Kachina, 1986
United States
Gourd, yarn, feathers, pigment, string
6 1/2 x 6 x 6 1/2 in.
2003.236.587

Colonial House, 1984
Henry Musser, American, designer
Wood, pigment, metal
5 1/4 x 5 x 3 1/16 in.
2003.236.339

Buckhannon, W. V. (milk can), 20th century
United States
Wood, metal, pigment
4 1/16 x 2 1/16 x 2 1/16 in.
2003.236.420a,b

Barrel, 20th century
Probably United States
Wood
2 7/8 x 1 13/16 x 1 13/16 in.
2003.236.643

Baby grand piano, 20th century
Wood, paper
4 1/8 x 7 1/16 x 5 1/2 in.
2003.236.425

Egg on base, 20th century
Wood, pigment
4 3/4 x 2 1/2 x 2 1/2 in.
2003.236.320a,b

Cylinder, 20th century
Wood, metal
4 7/8 x 1 11/16 x 1 11/16 in.
2003.236.324

Egg, 20th century
Wood
5 5/8 x 3 5/8 x 3 5/8 in.
2003.236.343

Money box, 20th century
Slate, pigment
$5\ ^{11}/_{16}$ x $5\ ^{7}/_{8}$ x $4\ ^{7}/_{8}$ in.
2003.236.745

Koko Nut [sic] *Penny Bank*, 20th century
Wood, pigment
$3\ ^{3}/_{4}$ x $3\ ^{15}/_{16}$ x $3\ ^{7}/_{8}$ in.
2003.236.868

House, 20th century
Probably United States
Wood, pigment
$4\ ^{3}/_{4}$ x $3\ ^{3}/_{4}$ x $2\ ^{3}/_{4}$ in.
2003.236.518

Money box, 20th century
Probably United States
Wood, metal
$3\ ^{3}/_{4}$ x $7\ ^{13}/_{16}$ x $5\ ^{1}/_{4}$ in.
2003.236.865

Money box, 20th century
Probably United States
Wood
$2\ ^{1}/_{2}$ x $6\ ^{1}/_{2}$ x $3\ ^{11}/_{16}$ in.
2003.236.864

Old Mother Hubbard, 20th century
Wood, pigment, metal
$5\ ^{3}/_{8}$ x $6\ ^{7}/_{8}$ x $3\ ^{7}/_{16}$ in.
2003.236.717

Newark, New Jersey (windmill), 20th century
United States
Wood, metal
4 x $2\ ^{1}/_{8}$ x $2\ ^{1}/_{8}$ in.
2003.236.716

New York Life Insurance Company (book), 20th century
Zell Products Corporation, New York, manufacturer
Leather, metal, plastic
$4\ ^{1}/_{2}$ x $3\ ^{7}/_{8}$ x $1\ ^{11}/_{16}$ in.
2003.236.496

Puzzle Box, 20th century
Probably United States
Wood
3 x 3 x 3 in.
2003.236.418

Puzzle Box, 20th century
Wood
$1\ ^{15}/_{16}$ x $3\ ^{3}/_{4}$ x $3\ ^{13}/_{16}$ in.
2003.236.321a,b

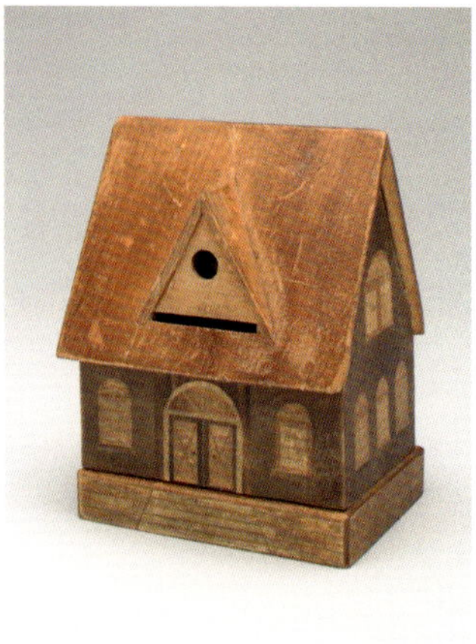
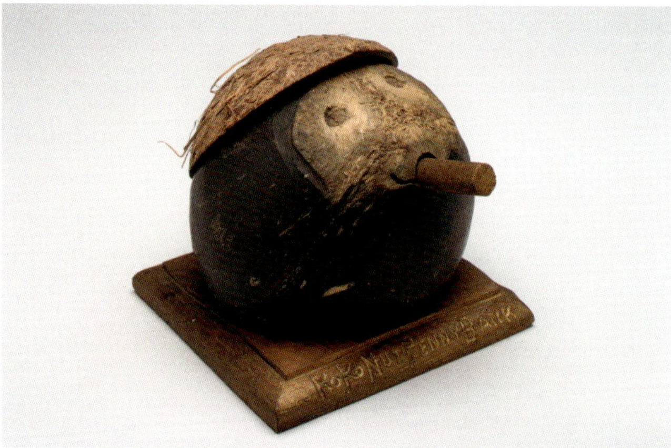
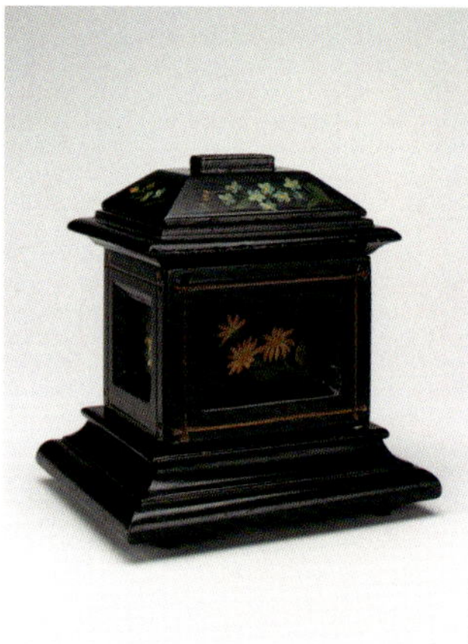
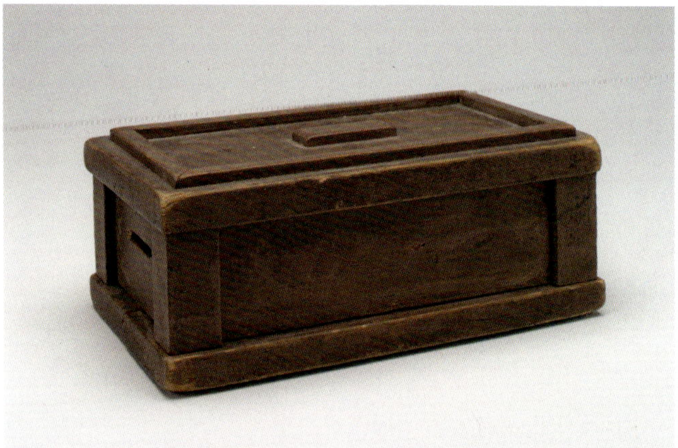
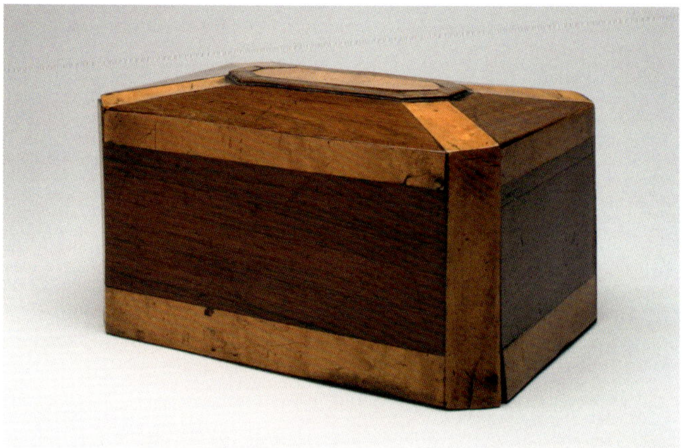
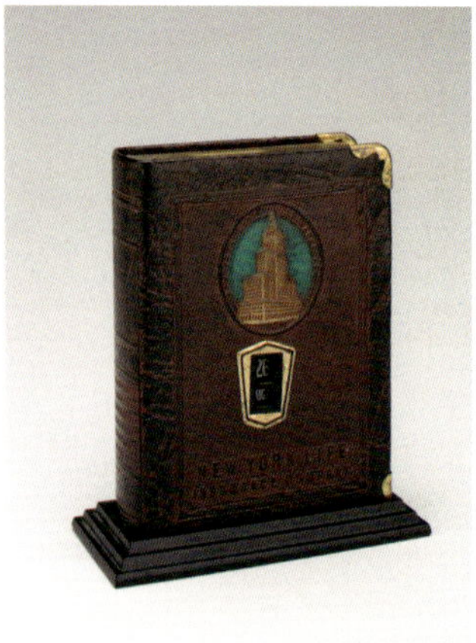
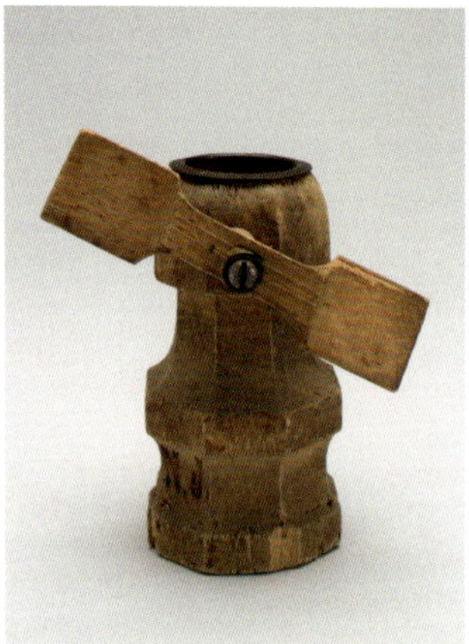
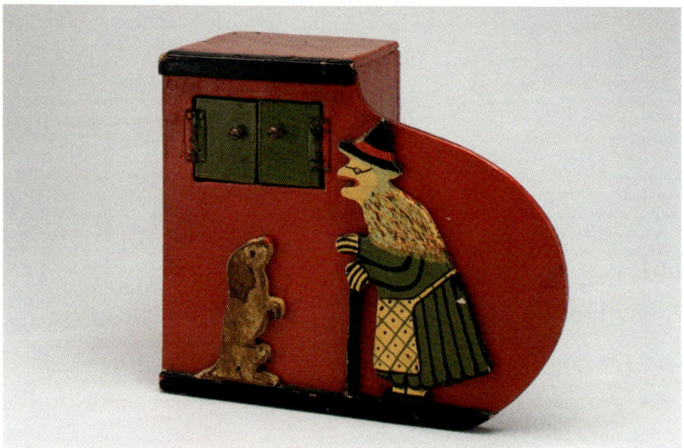
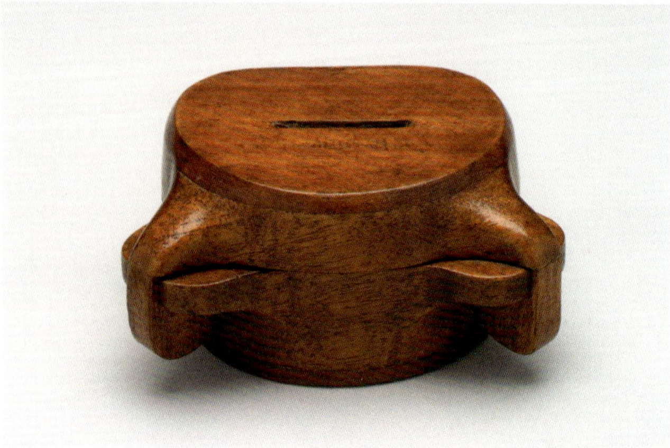
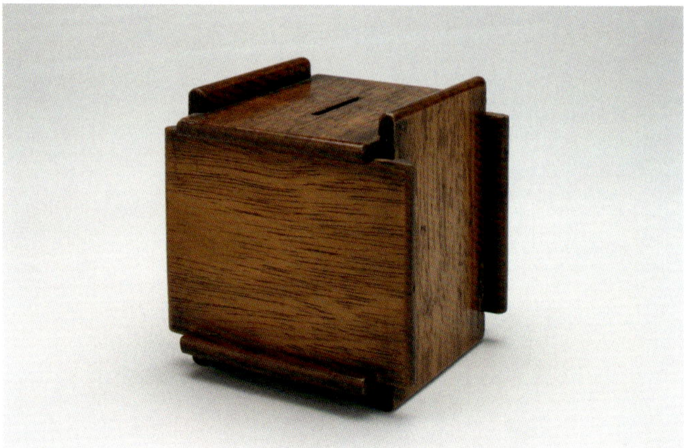

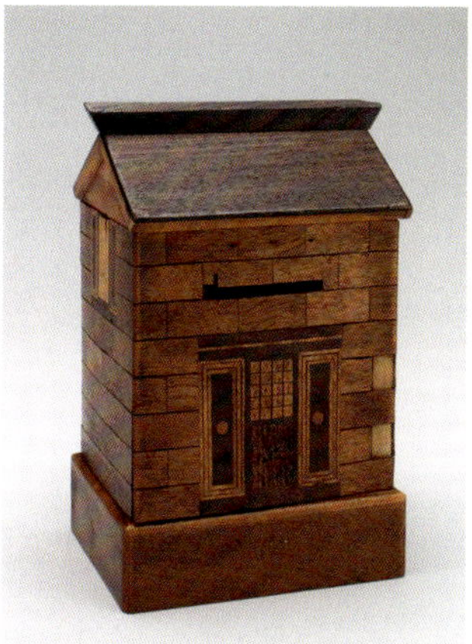

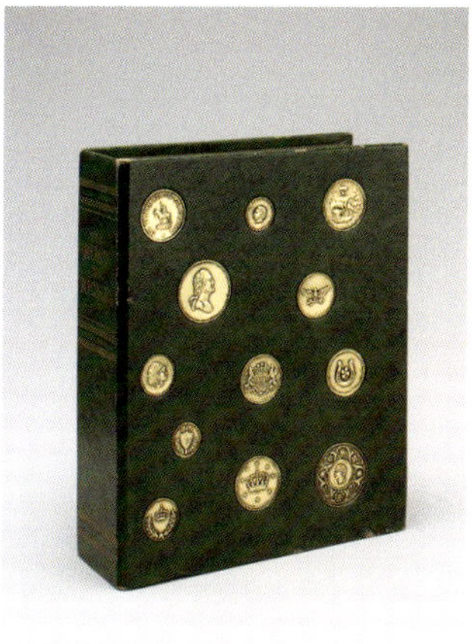

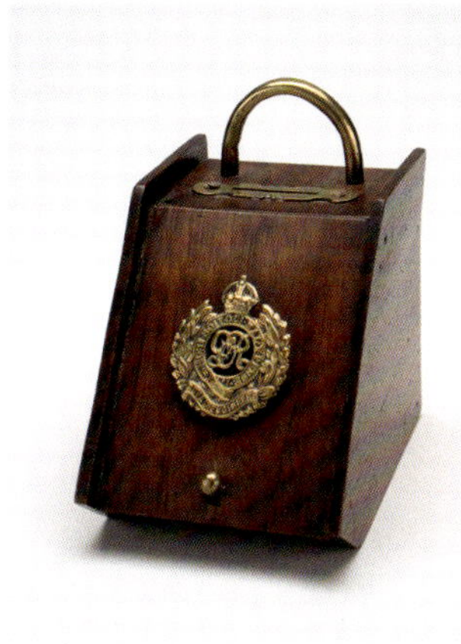

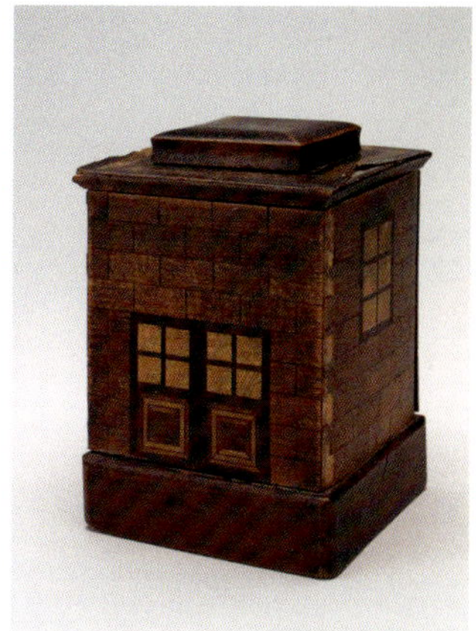

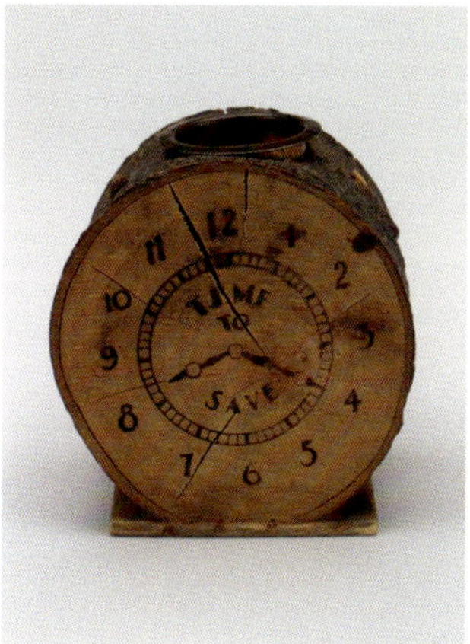

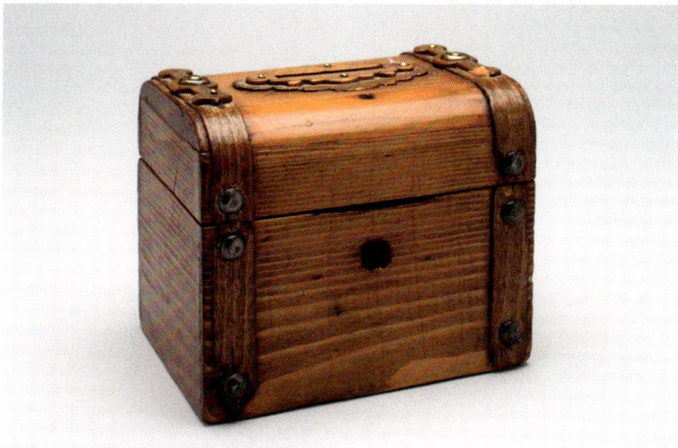

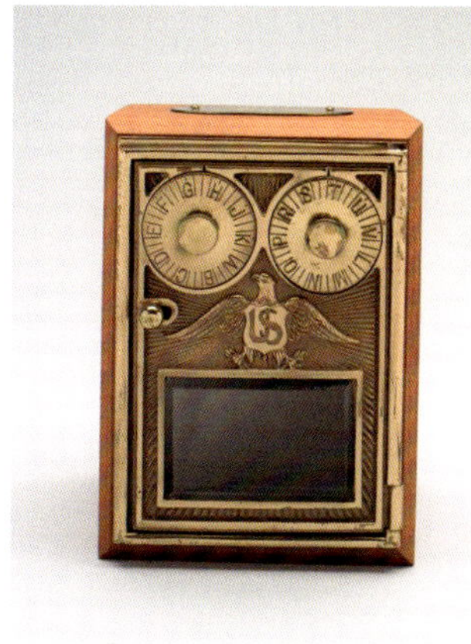

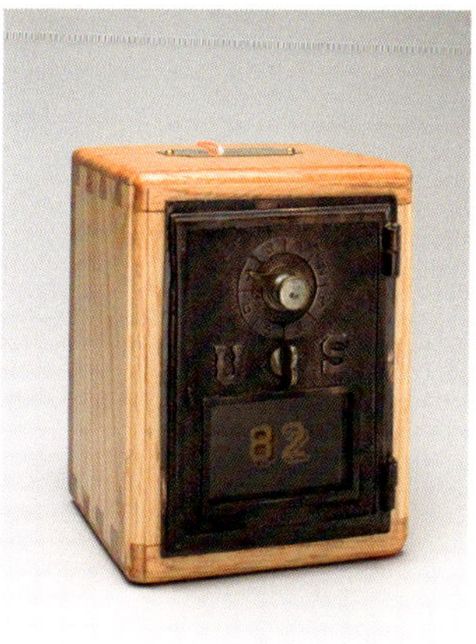

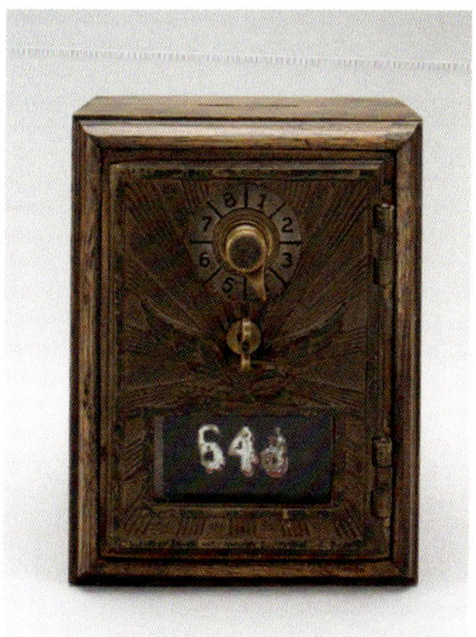

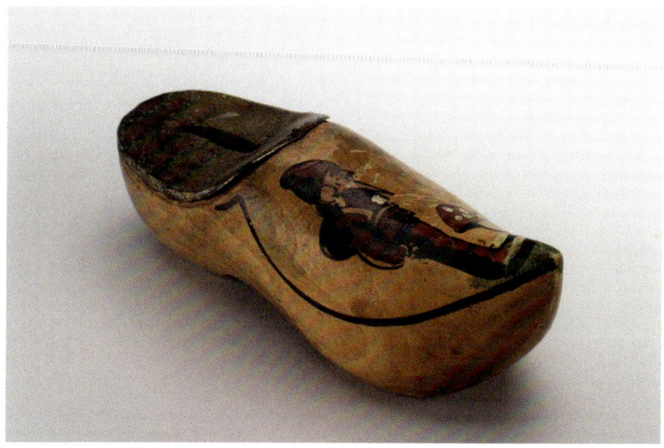

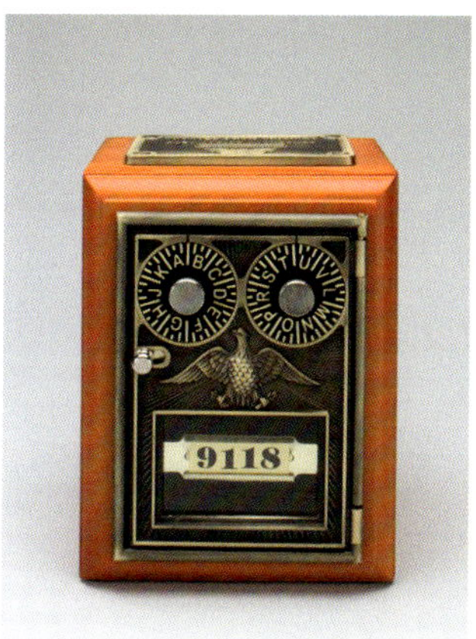

STILL BANKS: Ceramic

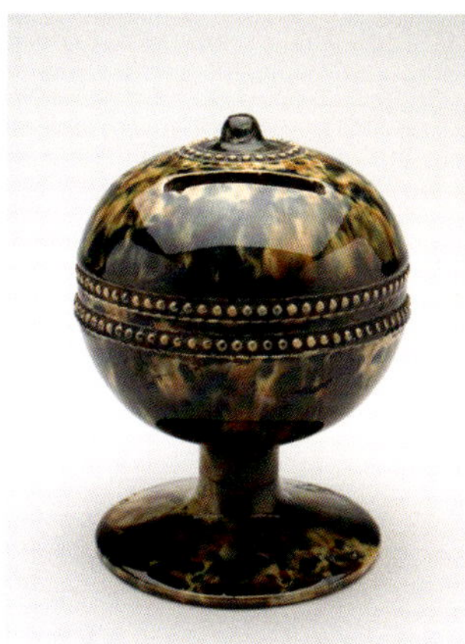

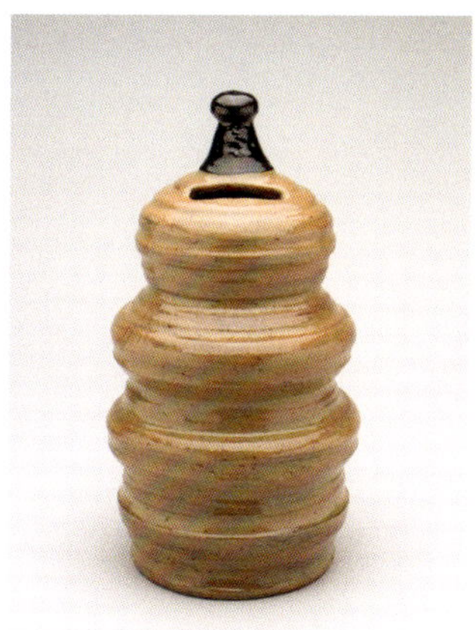

Square building with marquetry veneer, 20th century
Probably United States
Wood
4 1/2 x 2 3/8 x 2 3/8 in.
2003.236.723

Royal Engineers (coal scuttle), 20th century
England
Wood, brass
5 3/8 x 3 5/8 x 5 1/2 in.
2003.236.338

The Road to Riches (book), 20th century
Paper, pigment, metal
7 1/2 x 6 1/4 x 2 in.
2003.236.872

Puzzle Bank, 20th century
Wood, pigment
5 1/2 x 3 1/2 x 2 13/16 in.
2003.236.509

U.S. Post Office Box, 20th century
Antiqrafts, Indiana, Pennsylvania, manufacturer
Wood, brass, glass
5 9/16 x 4 1/8 x 4 1/4 in.
2003.236.556

Trunk, 20th century
Wood, metal
3 7/16 x 4 1/8 x 3 3/16 in.
2003.236.871

Time to Save (tree-stump clock), 20th century
Probably United States
Wood, copper, pigment
3 1/2 x 3 3/8 x 2 1/8 in.
2003.236.508a,b

Utrecht (wooden shoe), 20th century
Probably the Netherlands
Wood, pigment, metal
2 1/4 x 2 x 6 in.
2003.236.340

U.S. Post Office Box, 20th century
Odyssey Creations, Inc., Dallas, manufacturer
Wood, metal, glass, pigment, paper
7 1/2 x 5 1/2 x 2 1/2 in.
2003.236.870

U.S. Post Office Box, 20th century
United States
Wood, glass, metal
6 1/8 x 4 3/4 x 4 5/8 in.
2003.236.719

Albany Slip Bank, c. 1820
United States
Ceramic
7 9/16 x 4 1/8 x 4 1/8 in.
2003.236.528

Scottish Money Bank, c. 1780
Scotland
Ceramic
5 5/16 x 4 1/8 x 4 1/8 in.
2003.236.529

STILL BANKS: Ceramic

U.S. Post Office Box (reproduction), 20th century
China
Wood, metal, glass
6 x 4 5/8 x 5 1/8 in.
2003.236.650

Bust of girl, c. 1820
Ceramic
5 7/8 x 3 11/16 x 3 7/8 in.
2003.236.483

Bottle, c. 1820
United States
Ceramic
4 1/2 x 2 1/2 x 2 1/2 in.
2003.236.491

Money Box, Two Slots, c. 1810
Leeds, England
Pearlware
3 x 4 5/8 x 3 11/16 in.
2003.236.571

Bust of woman, c. 1850
Probably England
Ceramic
4 x 2 7/8 x 2 11/16 in.
2003.236.474

House, c. 1830
Staffordshire, England
Ceramic, pigment
3 3/4 x 2 1/8 x 1 3/8 in.
2003.236.905

Crimped top jar, c. 1830
Ceramic
4 3/8 x 3 13/16 x 3 13/16 in.
2003.236.498

Seated Bear, c. 1820
Ohio
Ceramic
5 1/2 x 3 1/8 x 2 9/16 in.
2003.236.724

Jar, c. 1860
United States
Ceramic
5 1/2 x 3 15/16 x 3 15/16 in.
2003.236.532

Melon, c. 1860
Pennsylvania
Ceramic
3 7/8 x 4 x 4 in.
2003.236.486

Chest, c. 1850
United States
Ceramic
2 3/4 x 3 x 2 1/4 in.
2003.236.1045

Acorn Stoves, c. 1880
Bennington, Vermont
Ceramic
3 1/8 x 3 x 3 in.
2003.236.475

Clown, c. 1850
United States
Chalkware
3 11/16 x 3 1/2 x 3 1/4 in.
2003.236.480

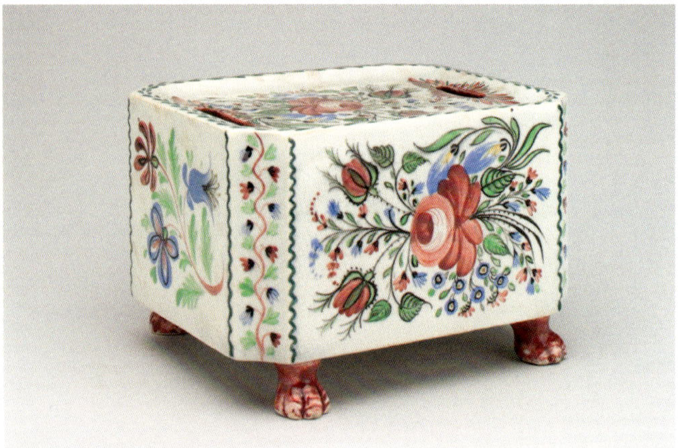
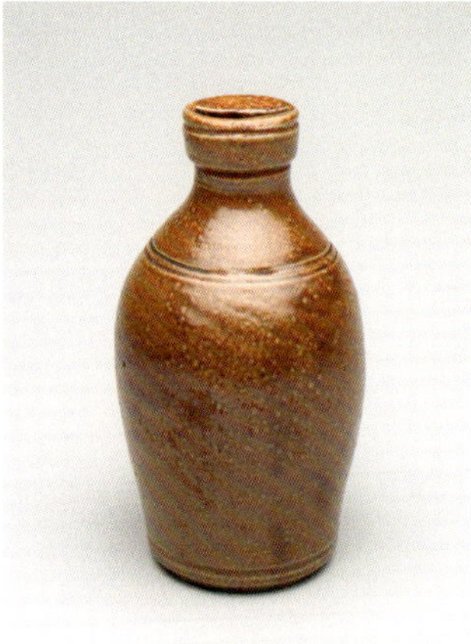
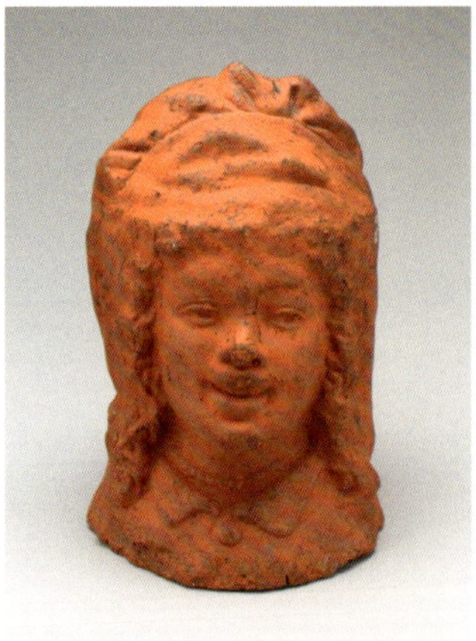
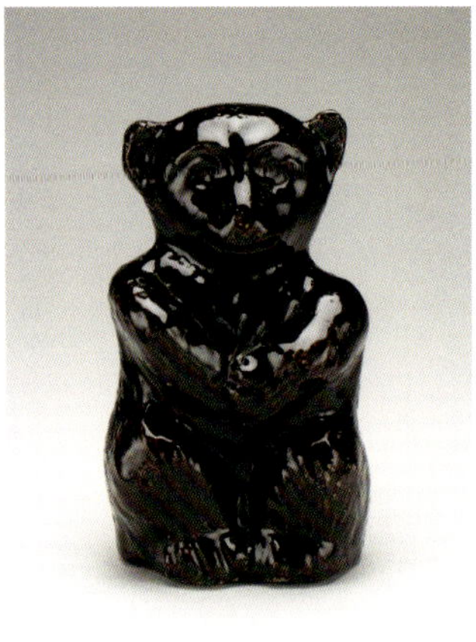
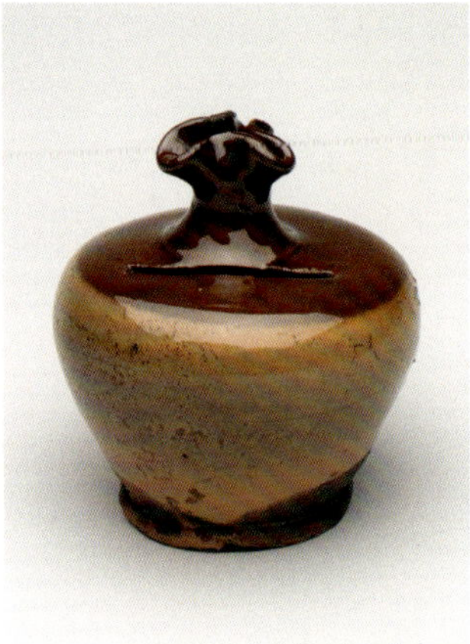
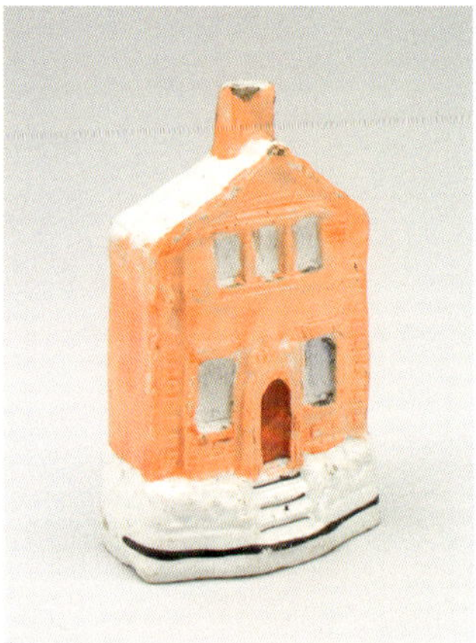
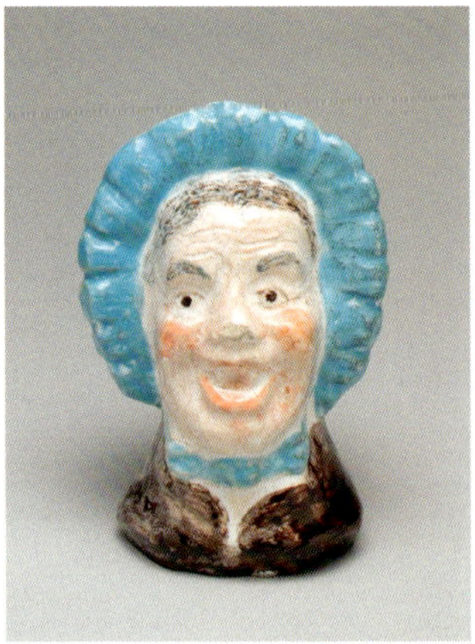
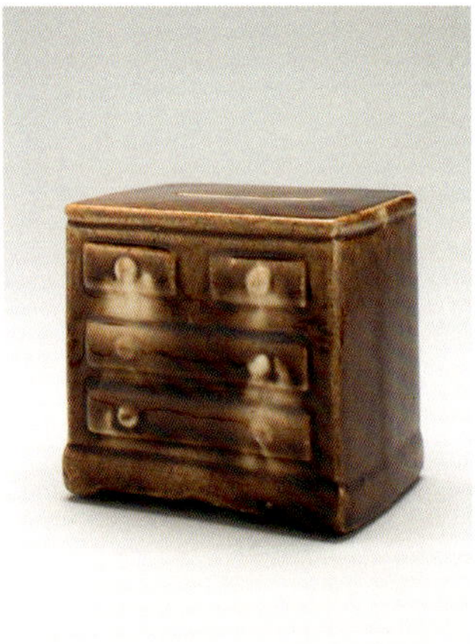
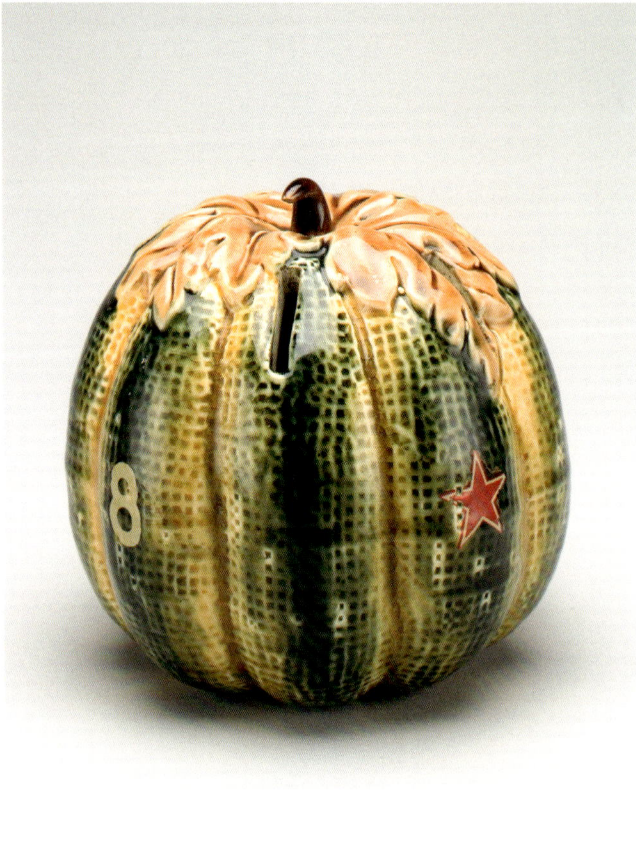
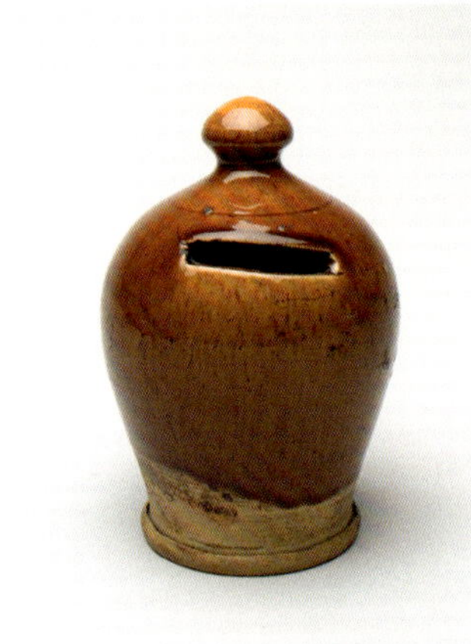
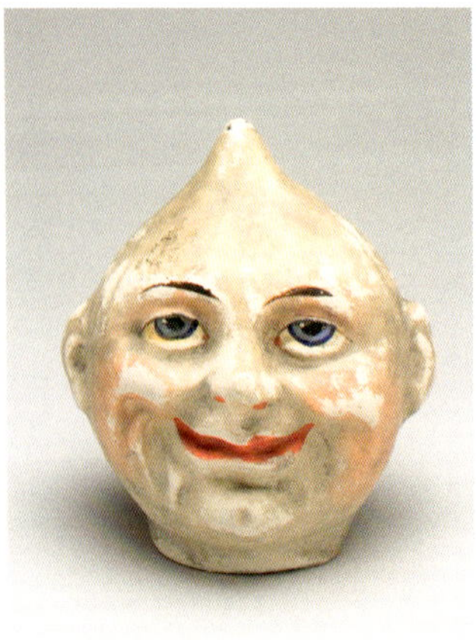
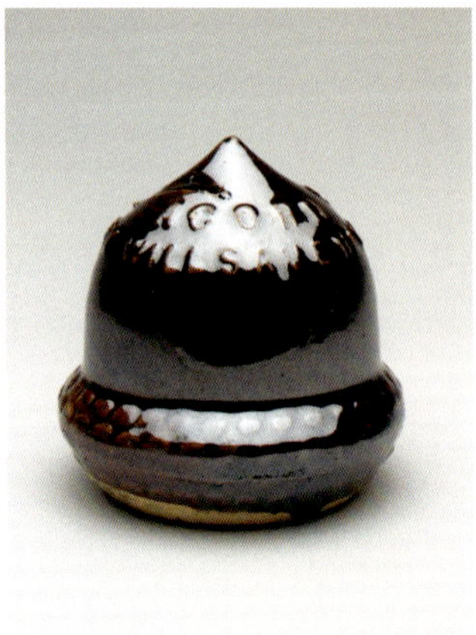

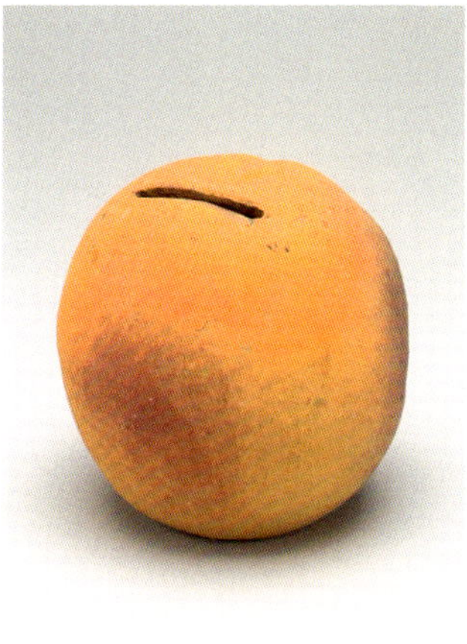
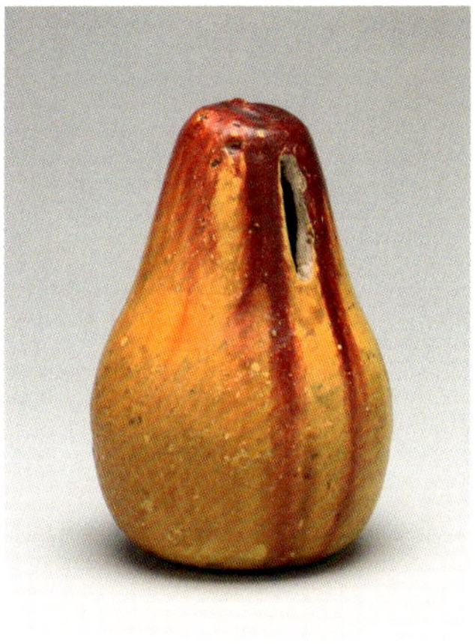
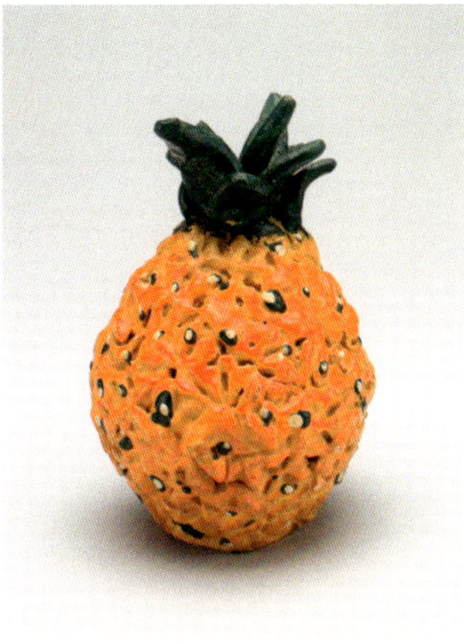
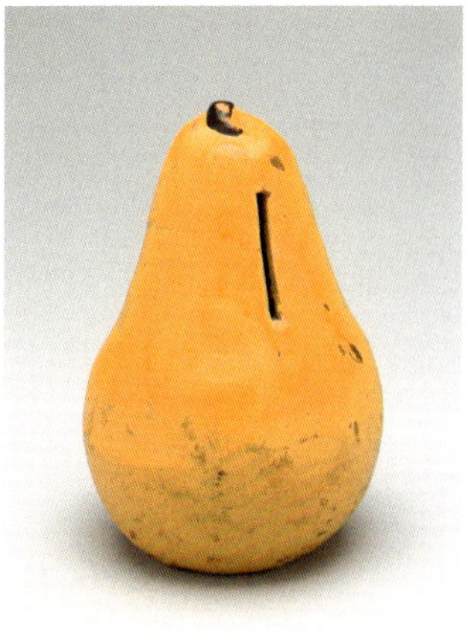
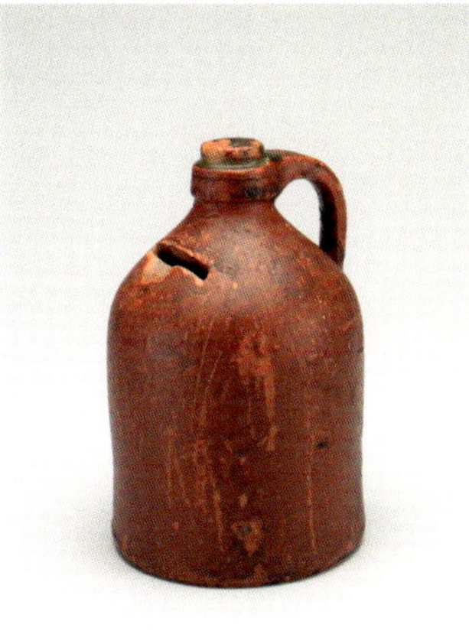
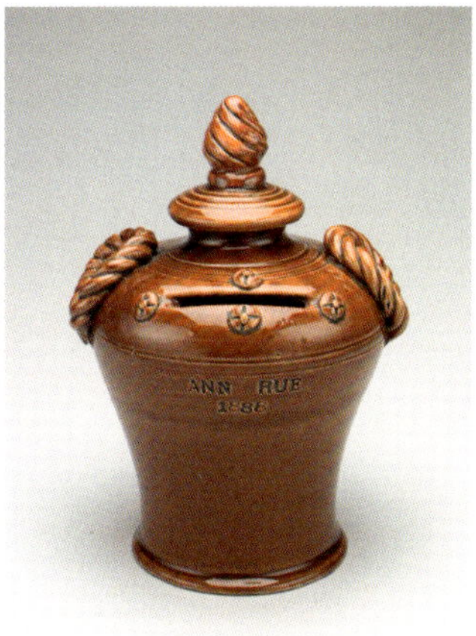
ANN RUE
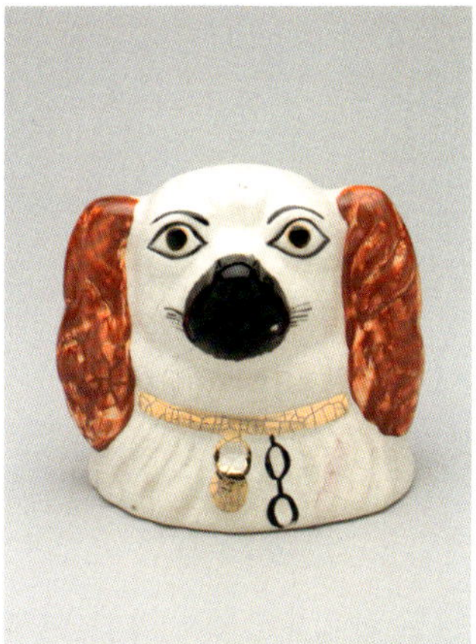
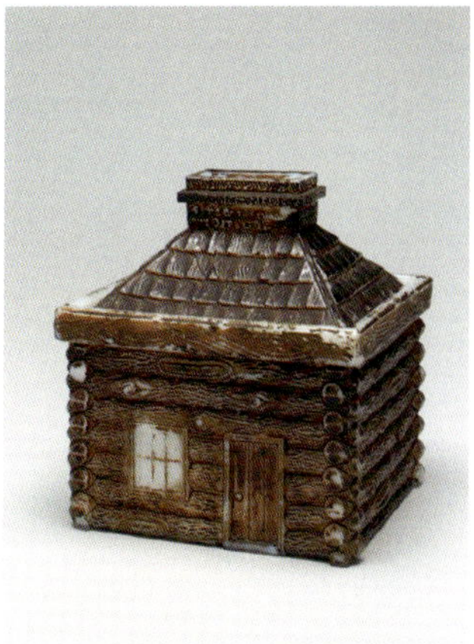
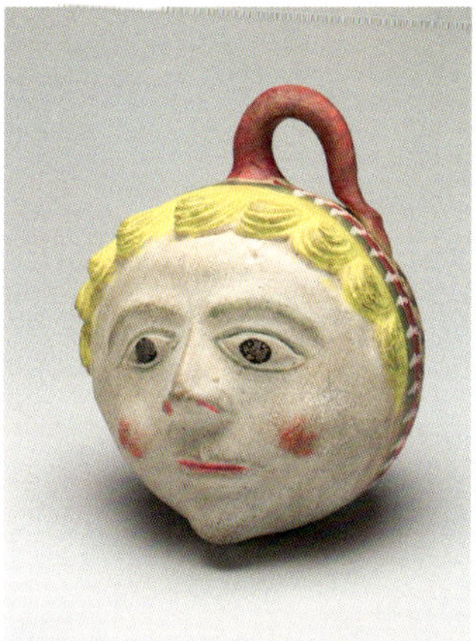
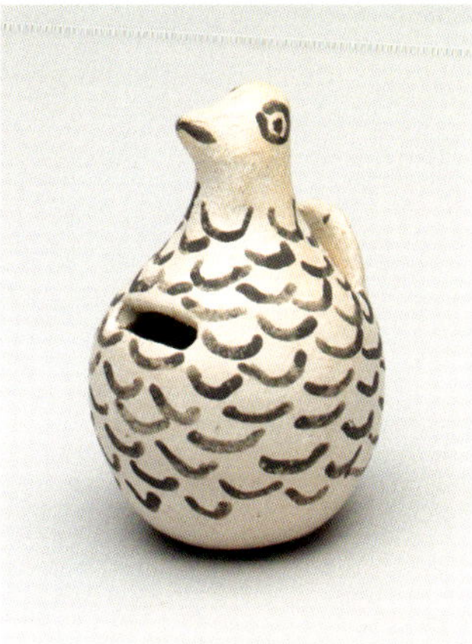
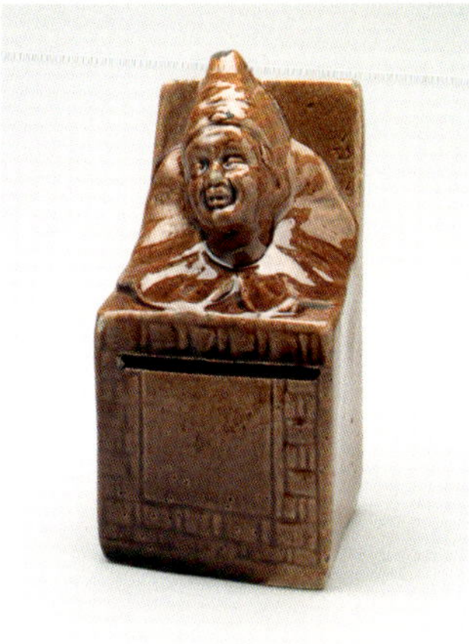
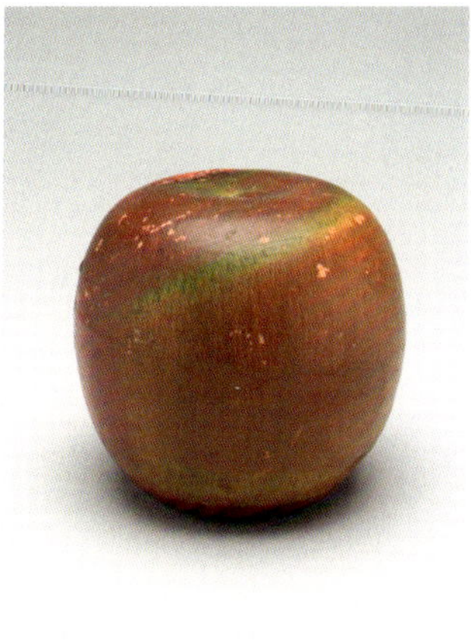
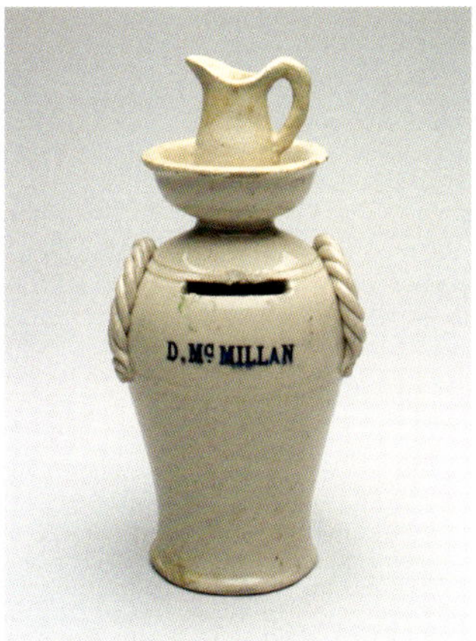
D. McMILLAN
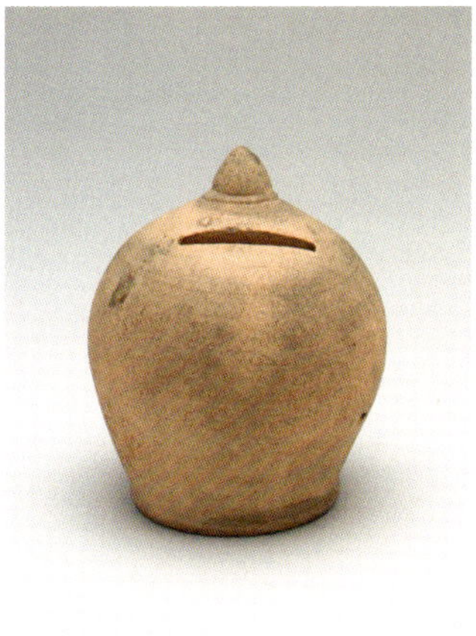
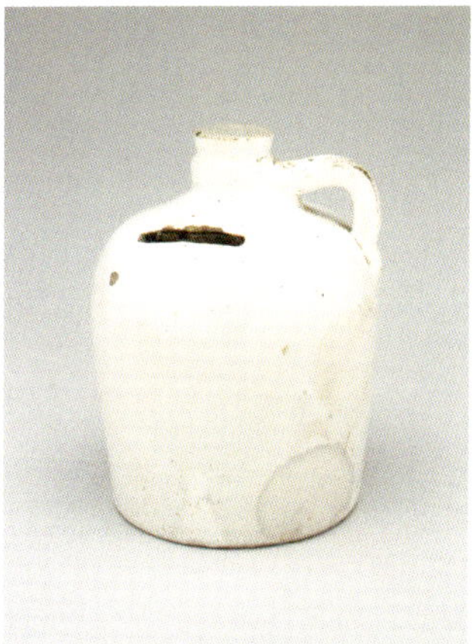
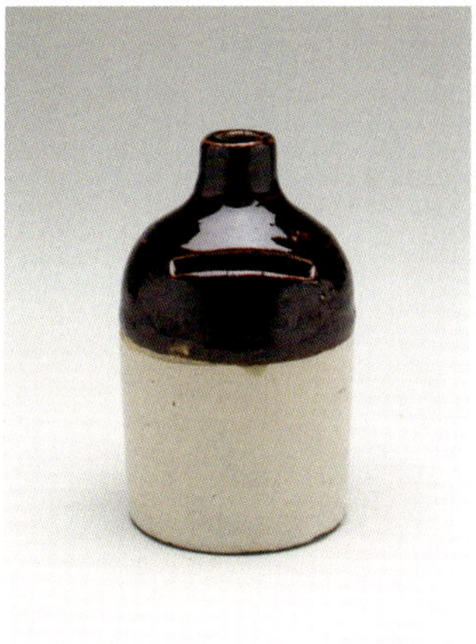

Pear, c. 1870
Ohio
Ceramic, pigment
4 1/2 x 3 x 3 in.
2003.236.1082

Pineapple, c. 1860
United States
Chalkware, pigment
4 3/8 x 3 1/16 x 3 1/16 in.
2003.236.691

Pear, c. 1860
Ohio or Pennsylvania
Ceramic
4 1/2 x 3 1/16 x 3 1/16 in.
2003.236.1047

Peach, c. 1860
Ohio or Pennsylvania
Ceramic, pigment
3 x 3 5/16 x 3 5/16 in.
2003.236.1046

Log Cabin (mustard jar), c. 1890
Westmoreland Specialty Company, Grapeville, Pennsylvania (1889–1984), manufacturer
Ceramic
2 1/2 x 3 5/8 x 3 1/4 in. (cabin);
1 7/8 x 3 1/4 x 2 11/16 in. (roof)
2003.236.538a,b

Dog's head, c. 1890
Staffordshire, England
Ceramic
4 1/8 x 4 3/4 x 3 5/8 in.
2003.236.888

Ann Rue 1888 (birth bank), c. 1888
England
Ceramic
6 x 4 1/2 x 4 1/2 in.
2003.236.530

Jug, c. 1880
Pennsylvania
Redware, pigment
4 1/8 x 2 11/16 x 2 11/16 in.
2003.236.885

Apple, 19th century
United States
Chalkware, pigment
3 1/4 x 3 5/8 x 3 5/8 in.
2003.236.1090

Jack-in-the-Box, c. 1895
United States
Ceramic
4 3/4 x 2 3/8 x 2 1/8 in.
2003.236.742

Cochiti bird, c. 1890–1900
Cochiti pueblo, New Mexico
Ceramic, pigment
2 13/16 x 1 15/16 x 1 7/8 in.
2003.236.563

Woman's head, c. 1890
Ceramic, pigment
5 1/4 x 4 1/4 x 4 3/8 in.
2003.236.744

Jug, 19th century
United States
Ceramic
3 x 1 3/4 x 1 3/4 in.
2003.236.1089

Jug, 19th century
Ohio
Ceramic
3 1/2 x 2 13/16 x 2 15/16 in.
2003.236.1081

Jar, 19th century
United States
Ceramic
3 1/8 x 2 5/8 in.
2003.236.1088

D. McMillan (birth bank), 19th century
Probably England
Ceramic
7 1/16 x 3 1/8 x 2 13/16 in.
2003.236.891

Orange, 19th century
United States
Ceramic, pigment
3 x $3\frac{3}{8}$ x $3\frac{3}{8}$ in.
2003.236.1083

Man seated on bag, 19th century
France
Porcelain
$3\frac{1}{2}$ x 2 x $1\frac{3}{4}$ in.
2003.236.912

Man in Tricorn Hat, 19th century
England
Rockingham ware, paper
$5\frac{1}{4}$ x $2\frac{1}{4}$ x $2\frac{5}{8}$ in.
2003.236.479

Log Cabin, 19th century
United States
Ceramic
$5\frac{3}{8}$ x $3\frac{3}{16}$ x $4\frac{1}{8}$ in.
2003.236.884

Pig with ridge on back (or *Fish-Pig*), 19th century
Possibly England
Ceramic
3 x $6\frac{1}{2}$ x $2\frac{1}{4}$ in.
2003.236.520

Pig with ridge on back (or *Fish-Pig*), 19th century
Possibly England
Ceramic
3 x 7 x $2\frac{1}{2}$ in.
2003.236.519

S. W. (jug with birds), 19th century
Pennsylvania
Redware
$9\frac{1}{4}$ x $5\frac{1}{2}$ x $5\frac{1}{2}$ in.
2003.236.578

Seated Spaniel, 19th century
Staffordshire, England
Ceramic, pigment
$5\frac{1}{8}$ x $3\frac{1}{8}$ x $1\frac{7}{8}$ in.
2003.236.887

Seated man with pitcher, 19th century
Possibly Bennington, Vermont
Ceramic
$4\frac{3}{8}$ x $2\frac{1}{2}$ x $2\frac{5}{8}$ in.
2003.236.478

Savings Bank (house), 19th century
England
Porcelain
$5\frac{1}{4}$ x $2\frac{7}{8}$ x $2\frac{1}{4}$ in.
2003.236.913

Apple, late 19th or early 20th century
Ceramic
$3\frac{1}{2}$ x $4\frac{1}{4}$ x $4\frac{1}{4}$ in.
2003.236.493

Covered dish, late 19th century
George Ohr, American (1857–1918), designer
Ceramic
$2\frac{3}{4}$ x 4 x 4 in.
2003.236.494

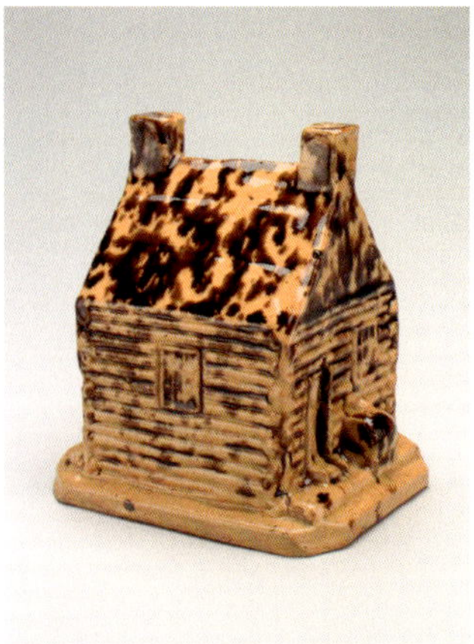

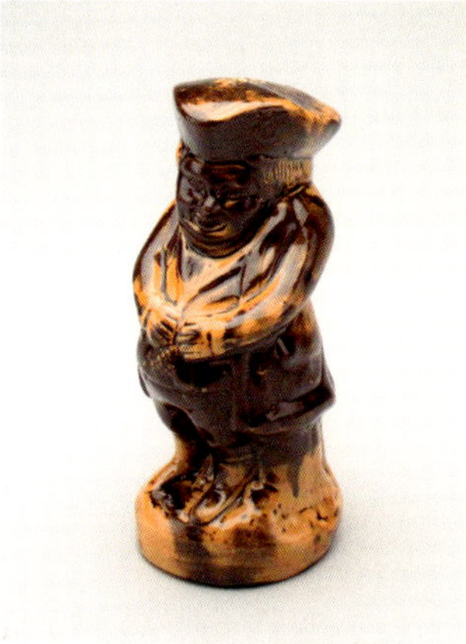

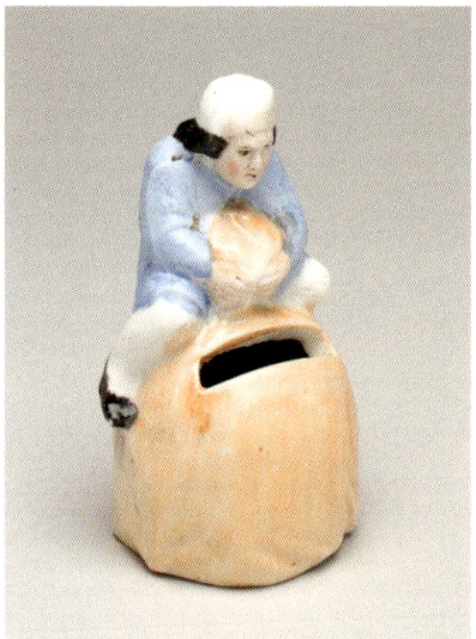

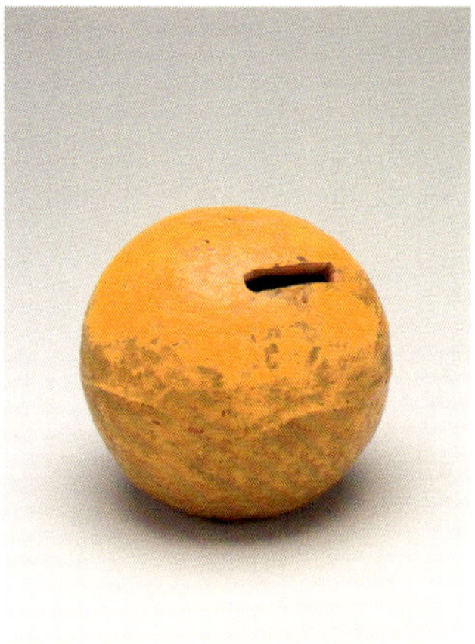

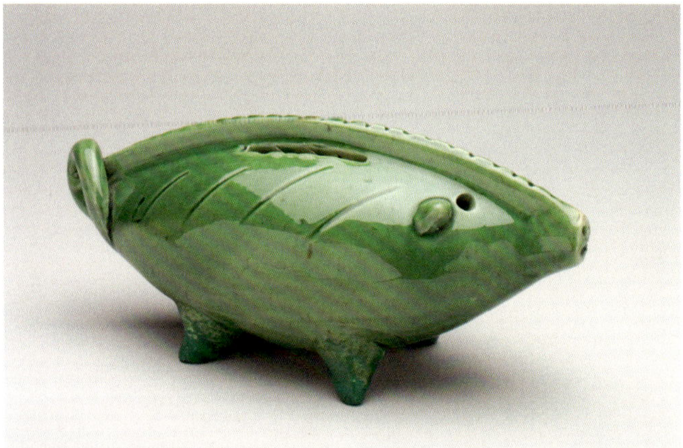

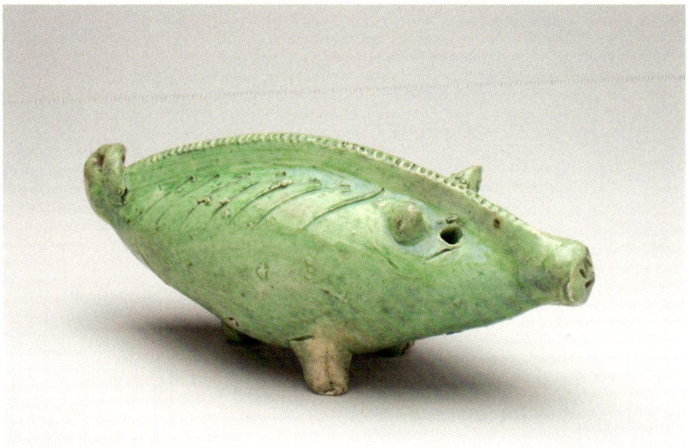

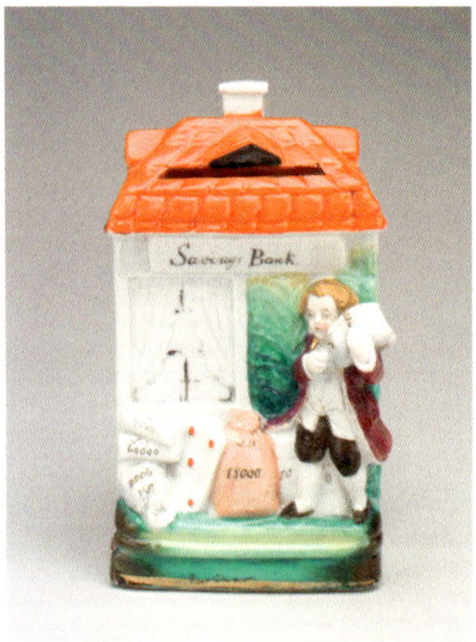
Savings Bank
£1000

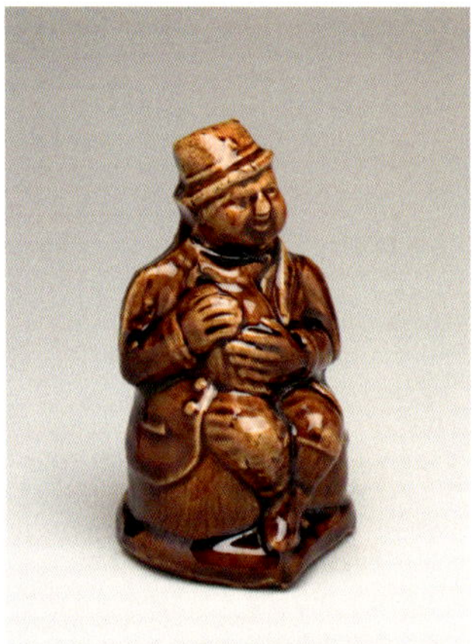

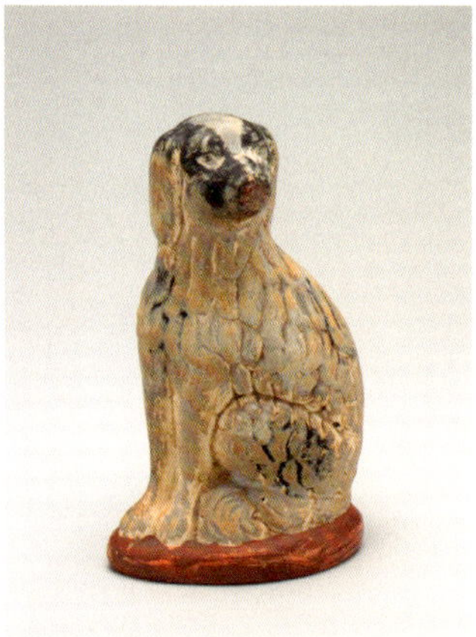

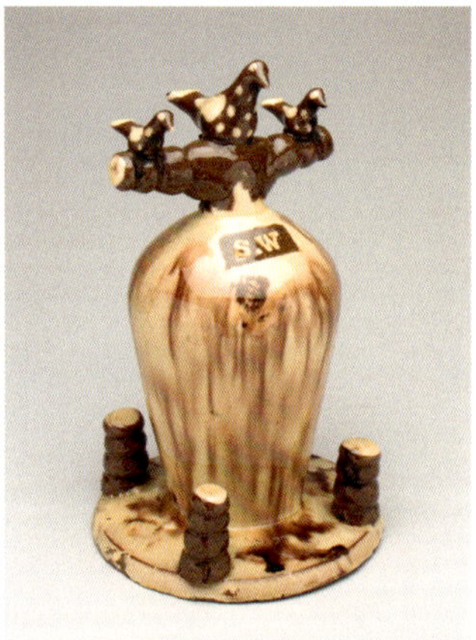
S.W

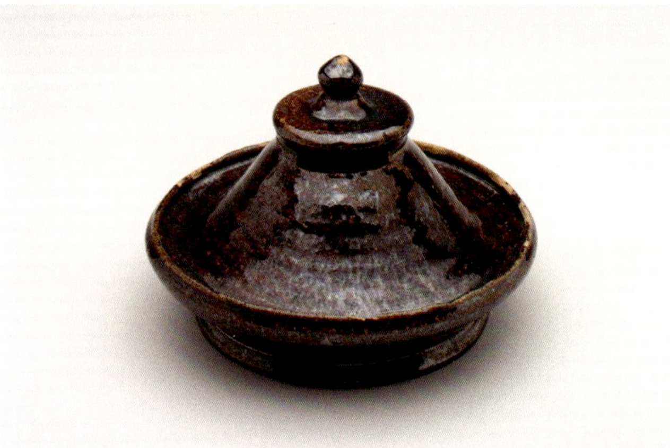

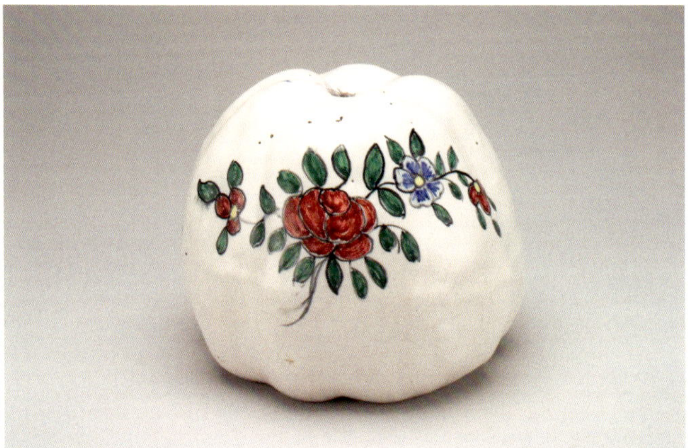

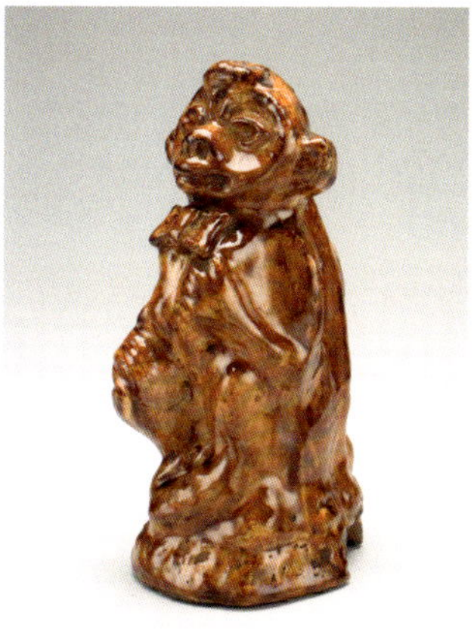
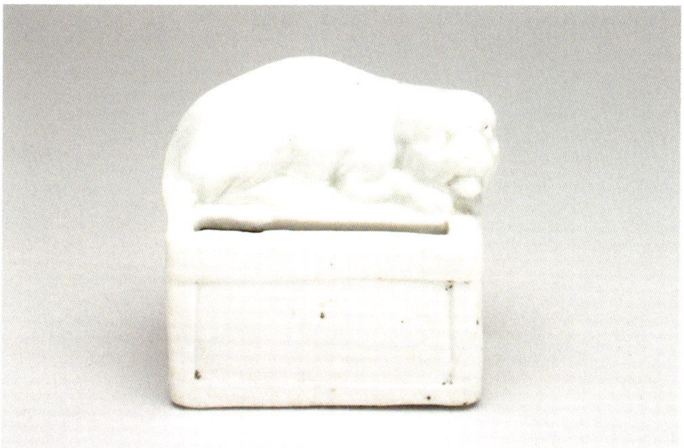
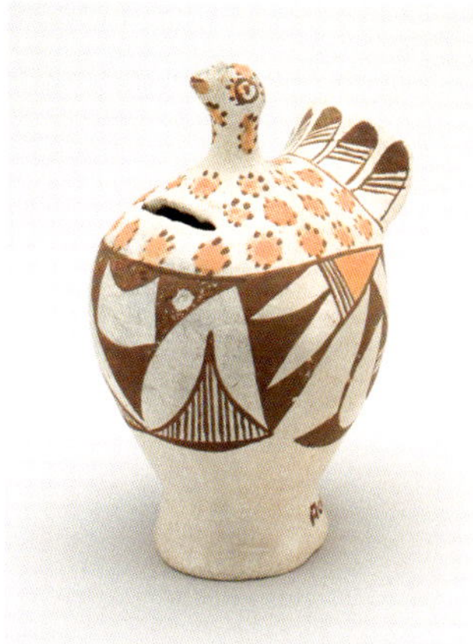
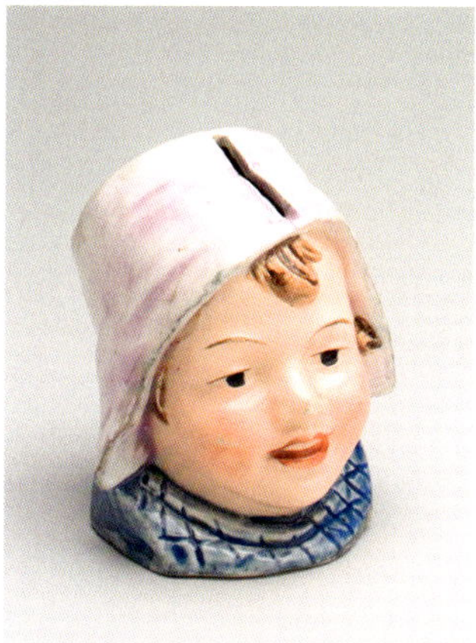
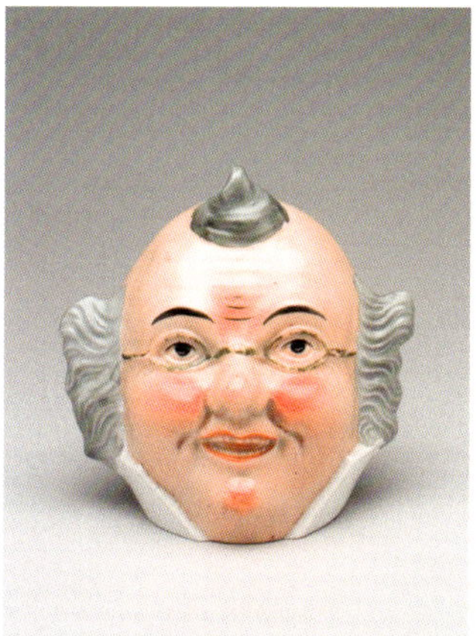
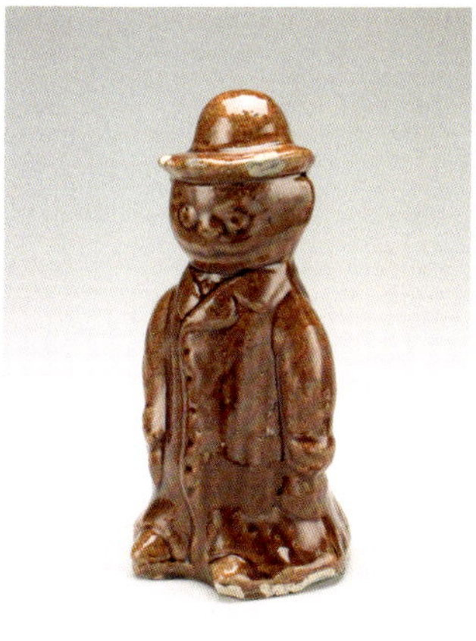
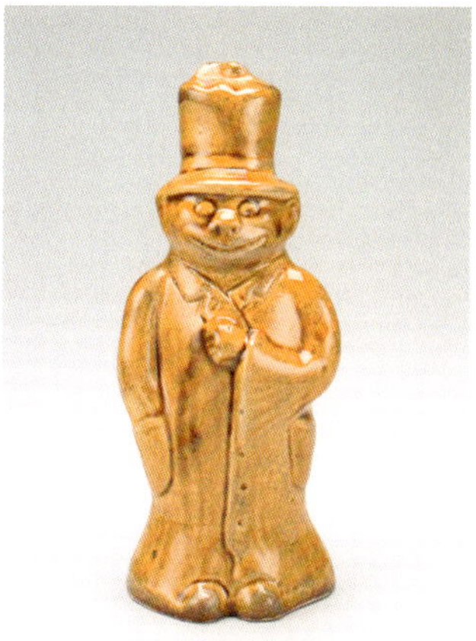
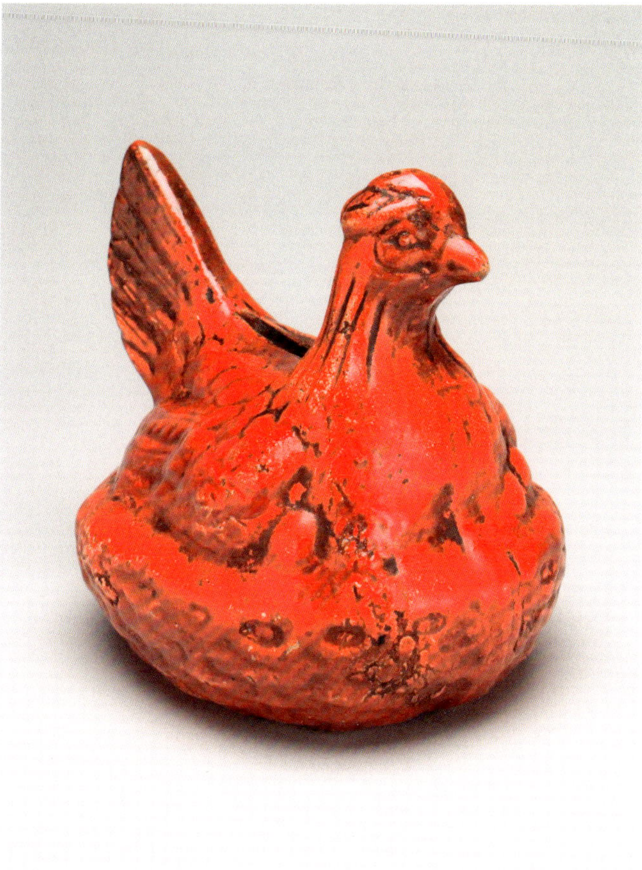
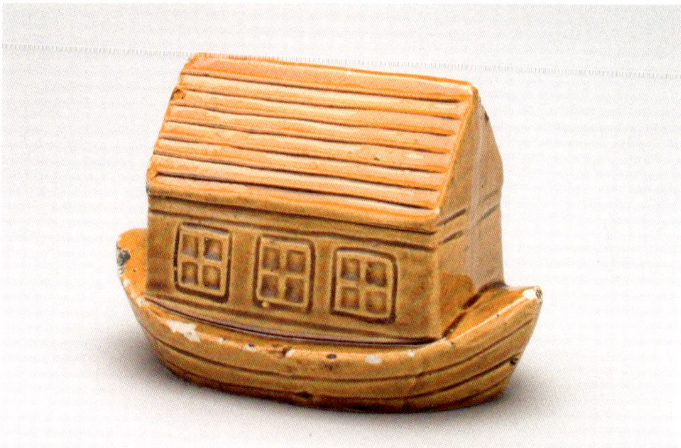
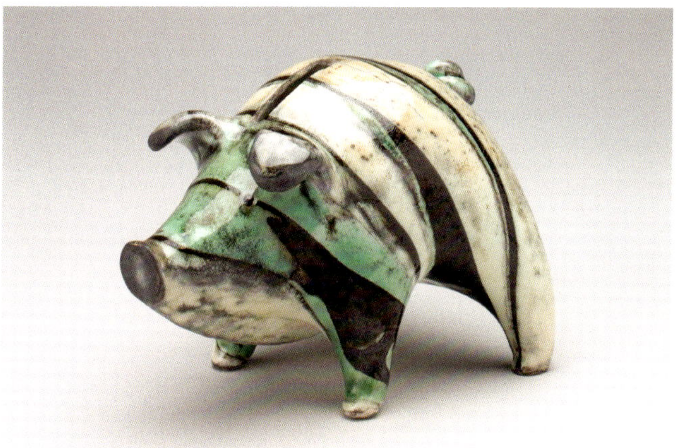

Bird, c. 1900
Acoma pueblo, New Mexico
Ceramic, pigment
5 1/2 x 3 1/8 x 3 1/2 in.
2003.236.902

Sleeping Dog, late 19th or early 20th century
Probably England
Ceramic
2 1/16 x 2 1/8 x 1 7/16 in.
2003.236.535

Monkey, late 19th century
Pennsylvania
Redware
6 1/8 x 2 1/2 x 2 1/2 in.
2003.236.726

Happy Hooligan, Standing, c. 1900
Austria
Ceramic
5 7/8 x 2 1/2 x 1 7/8 in.
2003.236.731

Grumpy Gus, c. 1900
Austria
Ceramic
5 1/2 x 2 3/4 x 2 5/8 in.
2003.236.735

Foxy Grandpa, c. 1900
United States
Chalkware, paper
3 11/16 x 3 13/16 x 3 3/16 in.
2003.236.476

Dutch Girl, c. 1900
Austria
Ceramic
3 5/8 x 2 7/8 x 3 1/16 in.
2003.236.473

Noah's Ark, c. 1900
Austria
Ceramic
3 x 2 3/16 x 4 3/4 in.
2003.236.569

Hen on Nest, c. 1900
United States
Ceramic
3 7/16 x 2 15/16 x 3 11/16 in.
2003.236.573

Pig, c. 1900
The Netherlands
Ceramic
3 9/16 x 3 3/4 x 4 9/16 in.
2003.236.736

Jug, early-to-mid-20th century
United States
Ceramic
3 11/16 x 3 1/2 x 3 1/2 in.
2003.236.1086

Jar, early-to-mid-20th century
United States
Redware
5 3/4 x 5 1/16 x 5 1/16 in.
2003.236.531

Jar, early-to-mid-20th century
United States
Ceramic
4 1/2 x 3 5/16 x 3 5/16 in.
2003.236.497

Think of Me! (beehive),
early 20th century
Ceramic
5 x 3 3/4 x 3 3/4 in.
2003.236.585

Cat Head, c. 1920
Austria
Ceramic
3 1/4 x 2 5/8 x 2 15/16 in.
2003.236.727

Victory Bank, c. 1918
England
Ceramic
6 1/2 x 3 3/16 in.
2003.236.485

Owl, c. 1915
Zuni pueblo, New Mexico
Ceramic, pigment
6 3/4 x 7 3/8 x 8 1/8 in.
2003.236.672

Beehive, c. 1904
Heinrich & Company, Selb,
Germany (est. 1904),
manufacturer
Ceramic, pigment, metal
2 7/8 x 3 1/8 x 3 1/8 in.
2003.236.472

Zuni Turkey, c. 1920s
Acoma pueblo, New Mexico
Ceramic, pigment
2 3/4 x 2 1/4 x 2 1/8 in.
2003.236.562

Nipper (RCA Victor dog),
c. 1920s
Sarsaparilla, Japan,
manufacturer
Porcelain, rubber
9 3/16 x 10 5/16 x 3 3/4 in.
2003.236.451a,b

Mojave frog, c. 1920s
B. Johnson, New Mexico, maker
Ceramic, pigment
2 x 2 3/8 x 2 7/8 in.
2003.236.561

Globe, c. 1920
Austria
Ceramic
3 1/8 x 3 5/16 x 3 5/16 in.
2003.236.725

Scottie Dog, c. 1930
Japan
Ceramic
5 1/4 x 2 5/8 x 3 3/8 in.
2003.236.892

Oriental Elephant, c. 1930
Japan
Ceramic
3 1/4 x 6 9/16 x 2 1/16 in.
2003.236.915

Little Brown Church, c. 1930
United States
Ceramic
3 9/16 x 2 7/16 x 4 1/16 in.
2003.236.909

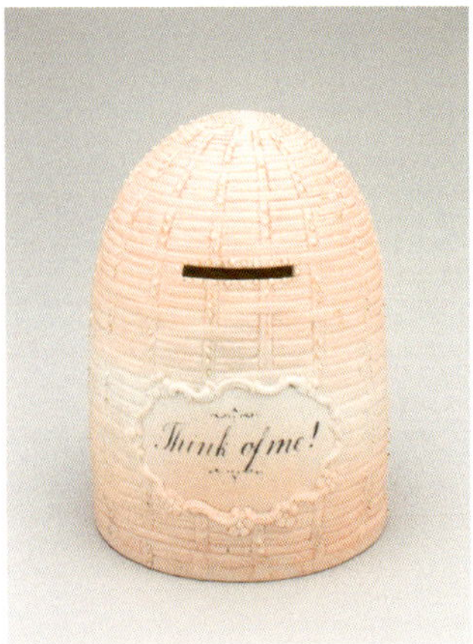
Think of me!

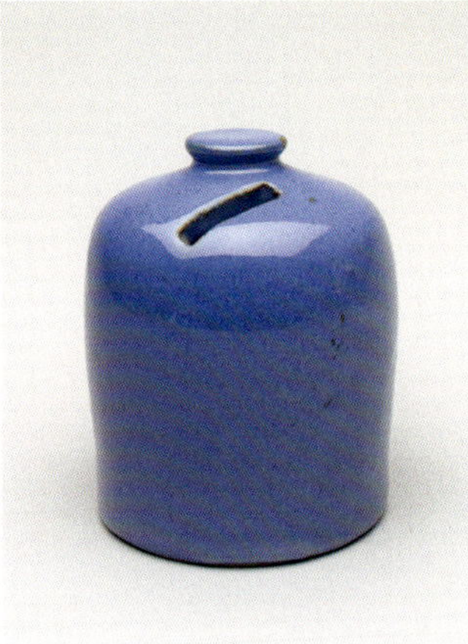

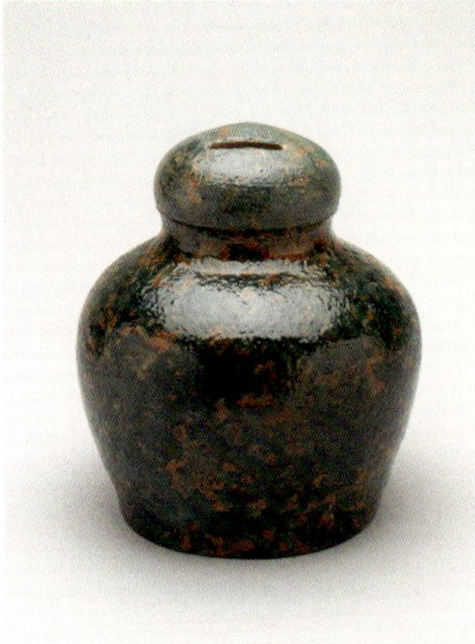

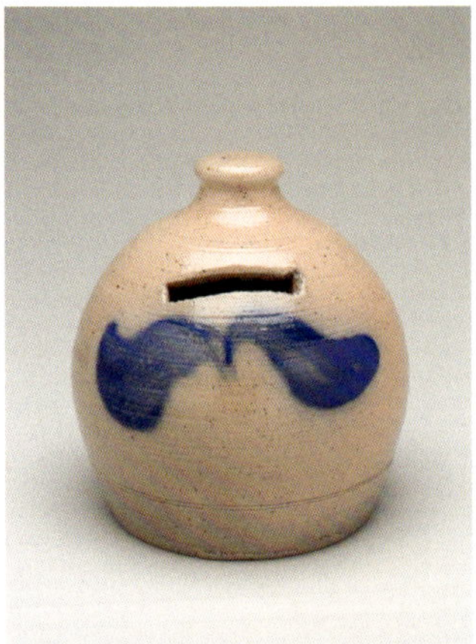

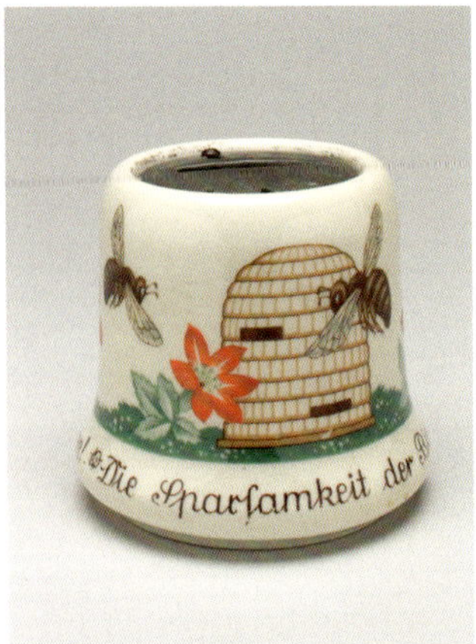
Die Sparſamkeit der

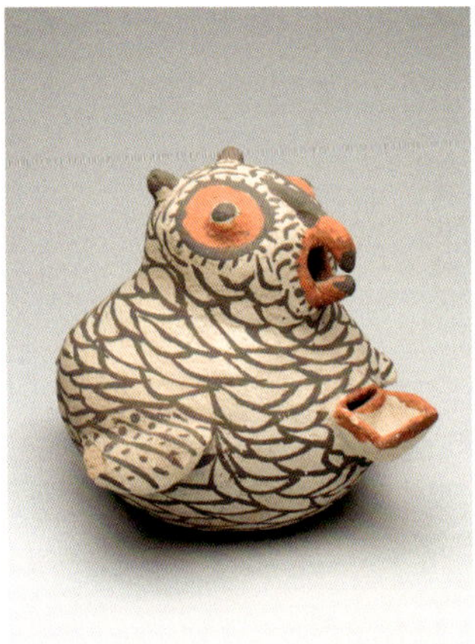

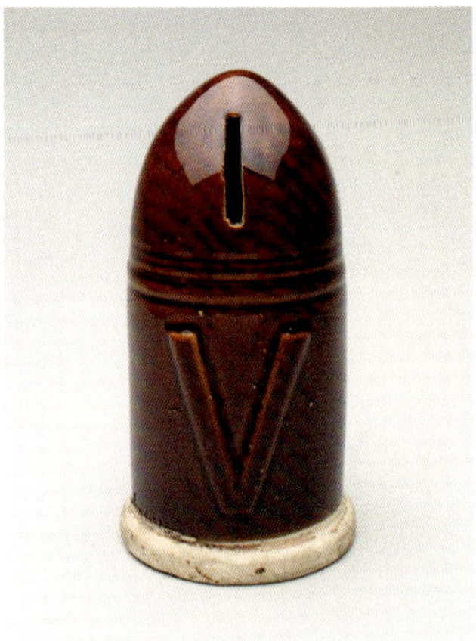

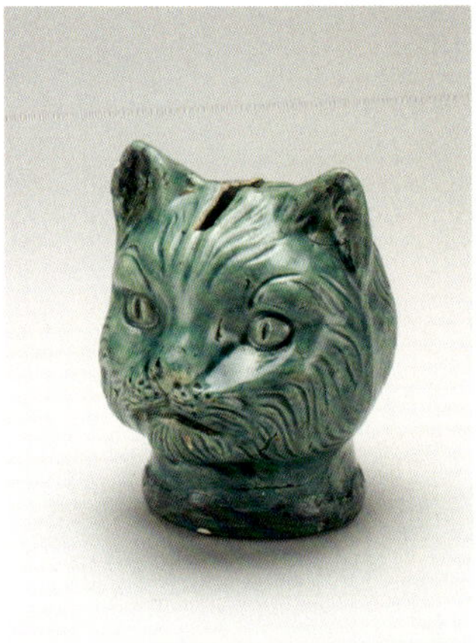

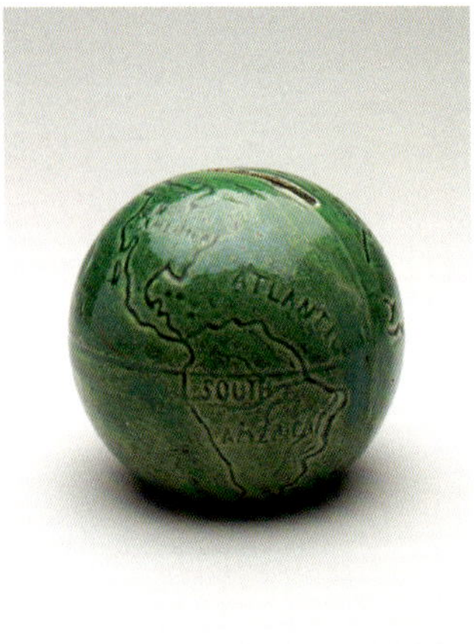
SOUTH

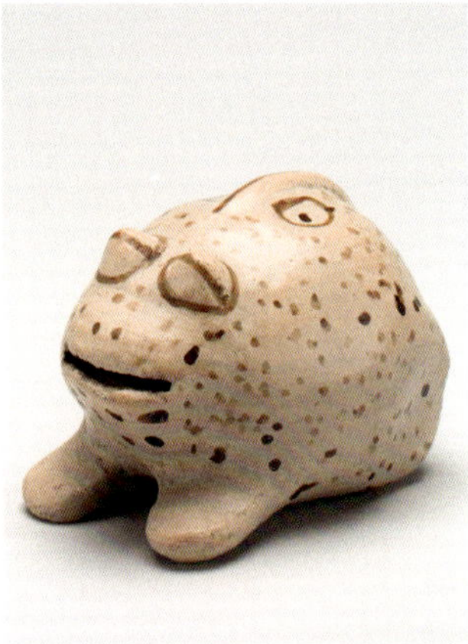

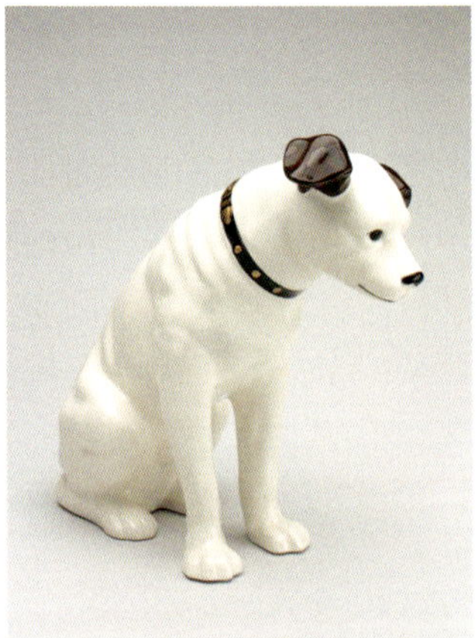

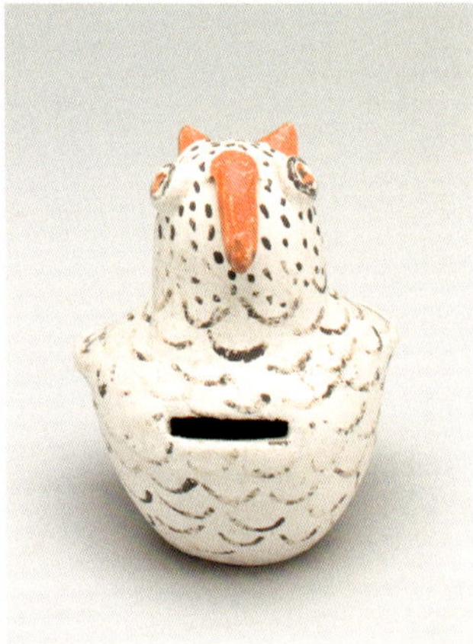

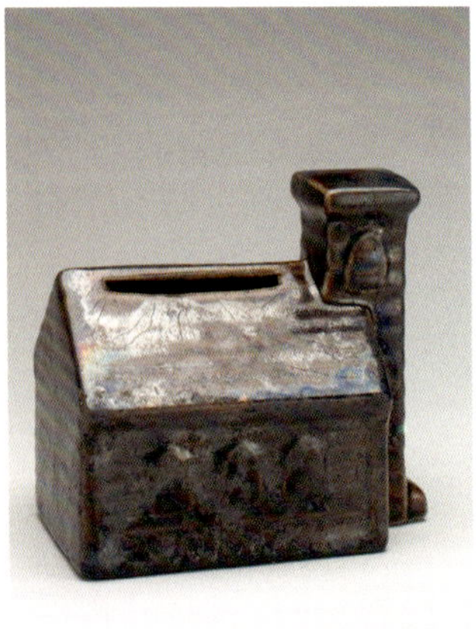

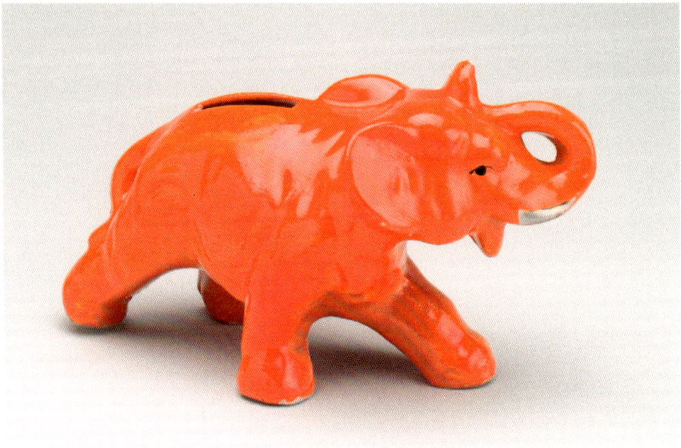

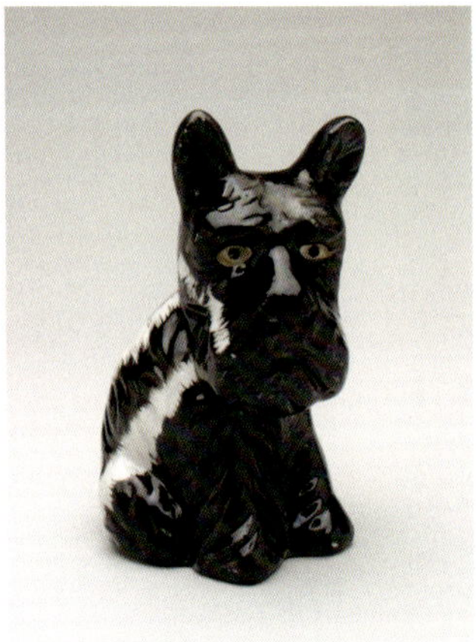

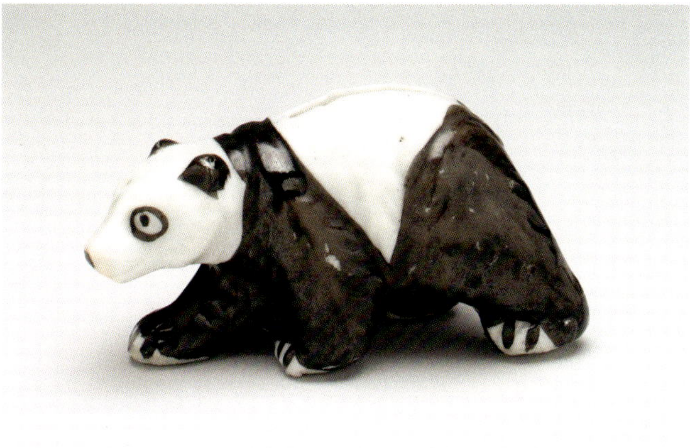

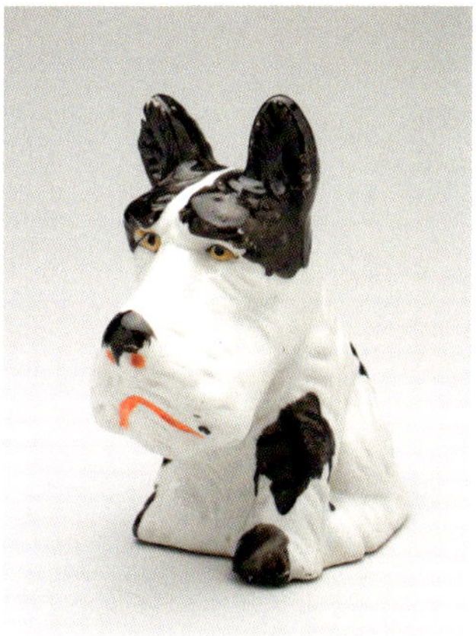

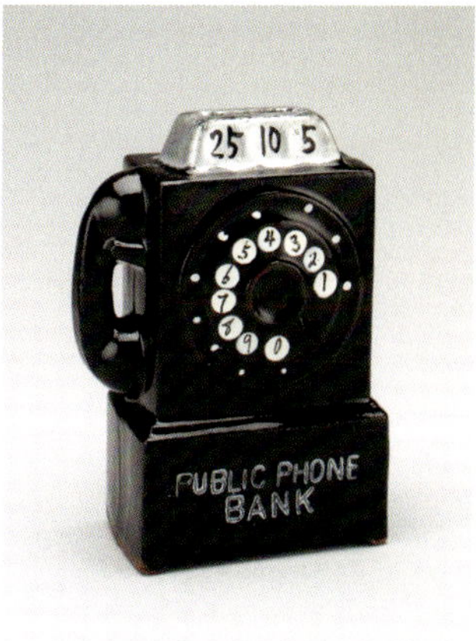
25 10 5
PUBLIC PHONE
BANK

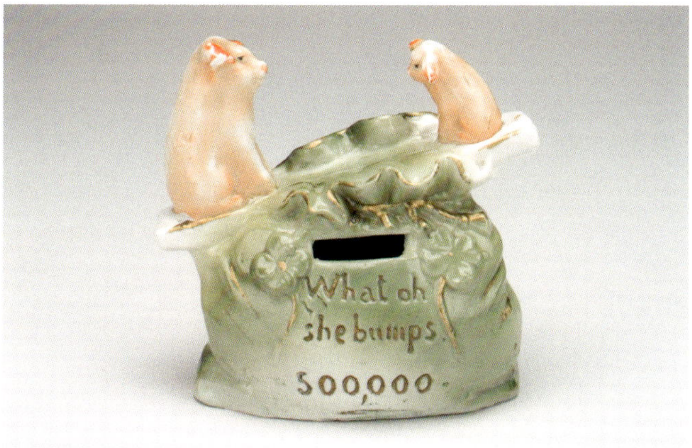
What oh
she bumps.
500,000

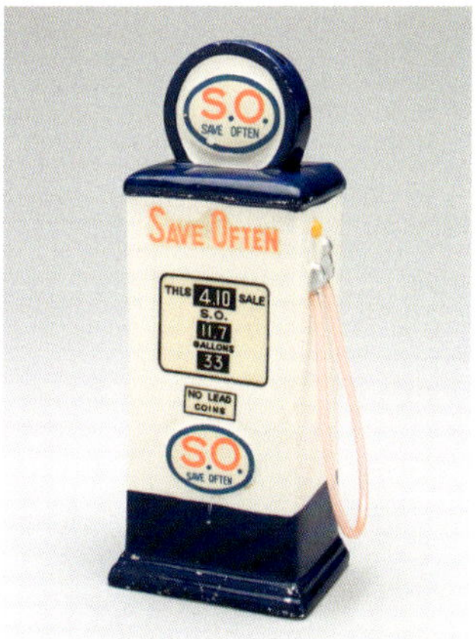
S.O.
SAVE OFTEN
S.O.

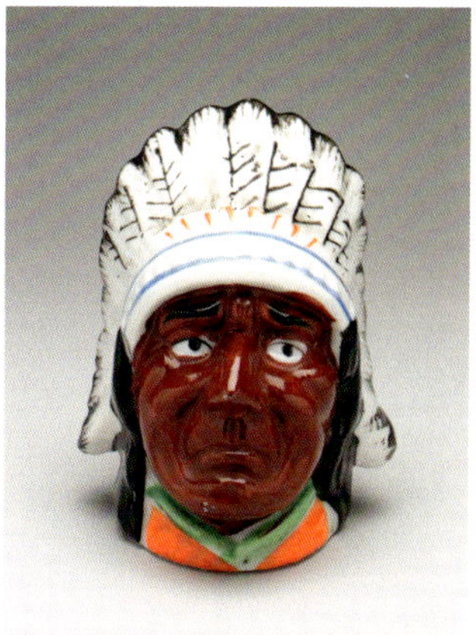

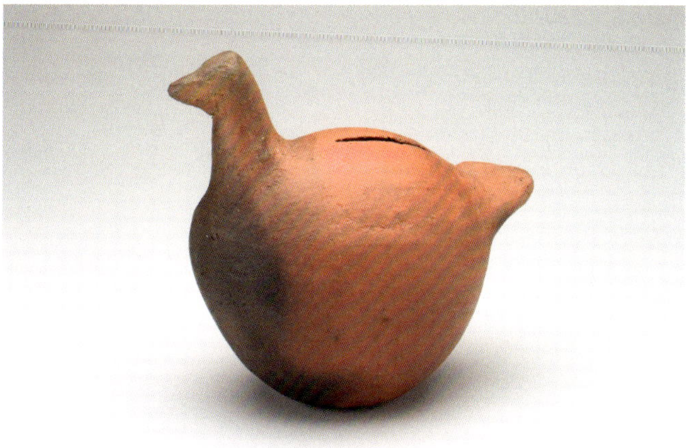

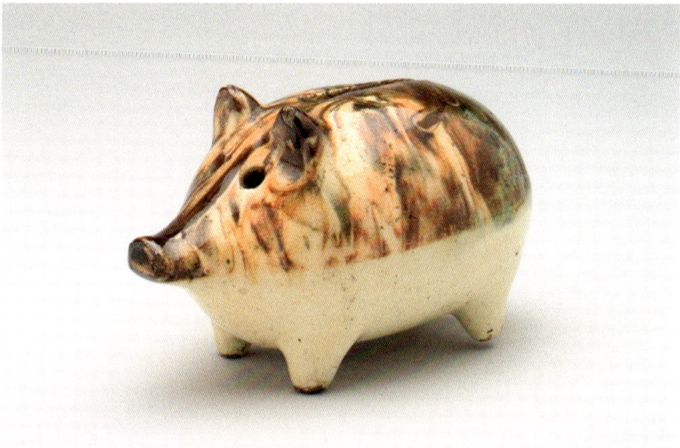

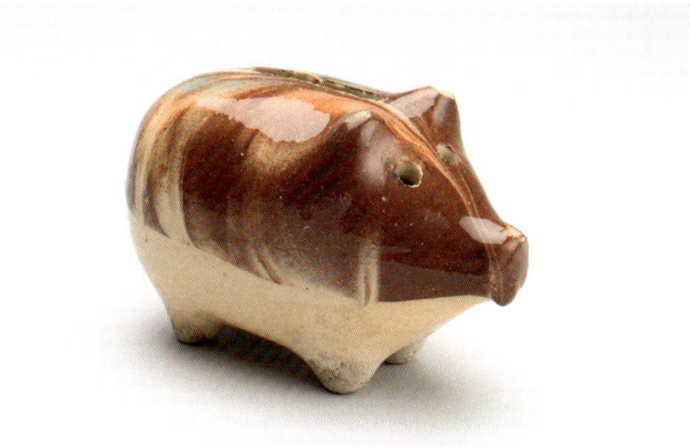

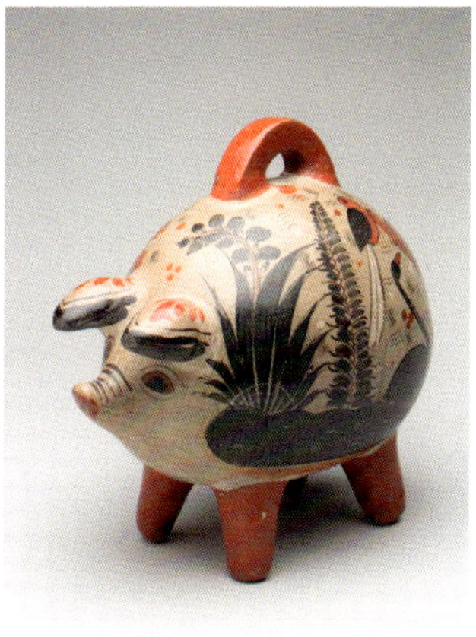

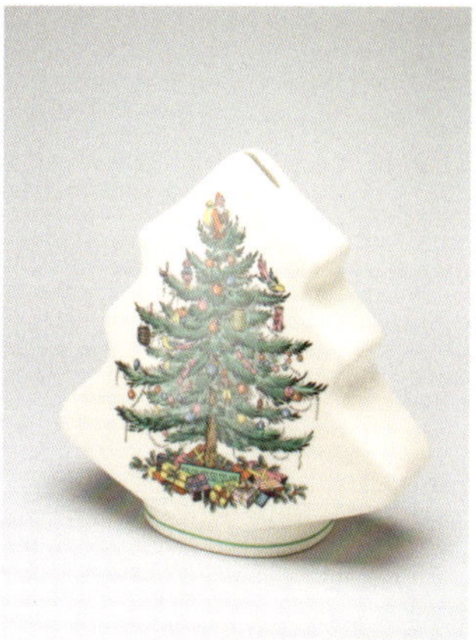

Public Phone Bank, c. 1930s
United States
Ceramic
3 3/4 x 2 3/8 x 1 3/8 in.
2003.236.488

Scottie Dog, c. 1930
Japan
Ceramic
5 1/4 x 2 11/16 x 4 3/8 in.
2003.236.893

Panda bear, c. 1930
Japan
Porcelain
3 5/8 x 1 1/2 x 2 1/8 in.
2003.236.733

Indian Bust with Headdress, mid-20th century
Japan
Porcelain, pigment
4 x 3 1/4 x 3 1/16 in.
2003.236.205

Gas Pump, c. 1950
United States
Ceramic, plastic
7 7/16 x 3 1/16 x 2 1/16 in.
2003.236.645

Two Pigs on Seesaw (or *What Oh She Bumps*), c. 1930
Germany
Ceramic
3 1/4 x 3 5/8 x 1 3/4 in.
2003.236.732

Pig, mid-20th century
United States
Ceramic
2 1/4 x 3 7/8 x 2 in.
2003.236.522

Bird, mid-20th century
United States
Ceramic
4 1/4 x 4 11/16 x 2 13/16 in.
2003.236.669

Christmas Tree, mid-to-late 20th century
Spode, Stoke-on-Trent, England (est. 1776), manufacturer
Porcelain, plastic
6 1/16 x 6 1/4 x 2 7/8 in.
2003.236.449a,b

Pig, mid-20th century
Mexico
Ceramic, pigment
8 x 7 3/4 x 5 in.
2003.236.671

Pig, mid-20th century
United States
Ceramic
2 5/8 x 4 1/4 x 2 1/4 in.
2003.236.523

Hopi Miniature Jug, c. 1950s – 60s
Rachel Nampeyo, American (1902 – 1985), maker
Ceramic, pigment
2 7/16 x 5 3/16 x 5 1/8 in.
2003.236.668

Batman, c. 1950s – 60s
Ceramic
6 15/16 x 3 3/8 x 2 5/16 in.
2003.236.482

Emmett Kelly, Jr., mid-to-late 20th century
Flambro, Taiwan, manufacturer
Ceramic
4 7/8 x 3 3/4 x 6 in.
2003.236.490

Prince of Wales Investiture Bank, c. 1969
Wedgwood & Company, Staffordshire, England (est. 1759), manufacturer
Ceramic, metal
3 3/16 x 3 5/8 x 3 5/8 in.
2003.236.527

Chubb Commemorative Safe, c. 1968
Wedgwood & Company, Staffordshire, England (est. 1759), manufacturer
Ceramic, metal
4 1/8 x 3 x 2 3/16 in.
2003.236.484

Hubert the Harris Lion, c. 1960s
Japan
Ceramic, metal
7 x 4 1/8 x 3 7/8 in.
2003.236.593a,b

Sleeping Santa (Large Chair), c. 1954
Banthrico, Inc., Chicago (1931 – 85), manufacturer
Ceramic, pigment
7 7/16 x 5 7/8 x 5 15/16 in.
2003.236.454

Chicken Feed Bag, c. 1975
George Knerr, American (1911 – 1979), designer
Ceramic, rubber
4 3/4 x 4 1/8 x 2 3/4 in.
2003.236.487

Bag, c. 1970
William Brown, designer
Ceramic, cork
2 9/16 x 2 15/16 x 3 3/16 in.
2003.236.481

Fish-Pig, c. 1969
Delft Pottery, Delft, the Netherlands, manufacturer
Ceramic
3 x 2 3/4 x 7 3/4 in.
2003.236.919

Havalina, 1976
Peter's Pottery Works, United States, manufacturer
Ceramic
6 x 5 3/8 x 6 7/8 in.
2003.236.670

Pear, c. 1976
Lester Breininger, American, designer
Breininger Pottery, Robesonia, Pennsylvania, manufacturer
Ceramic
4 5/16 x 2 3/8 x 2 3/8 in.
2003.236.889

Peach, c. 1975
Lester Breininger, American, designer
Breininger Pottery, Robesonia, Pennsylvania, manufacturer
Ceramic
3 x 4 1/4 x 3 1/4 in.
2003.236.688

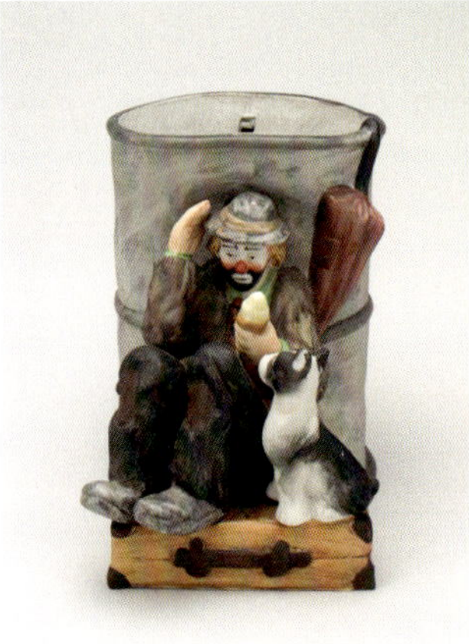

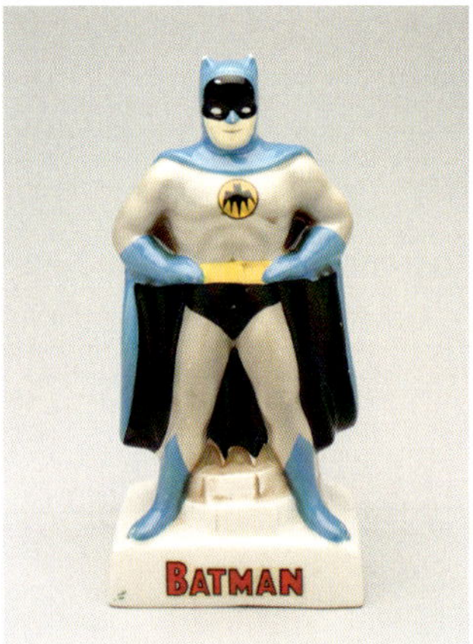
BATMAN

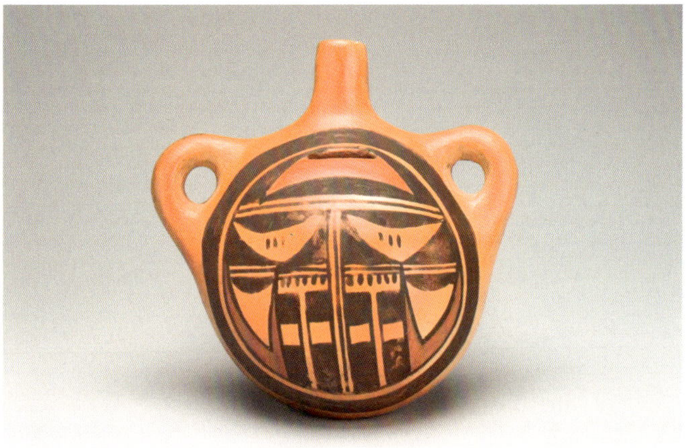

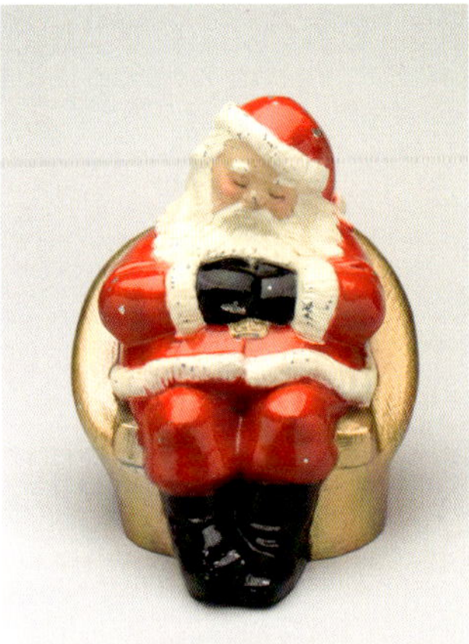

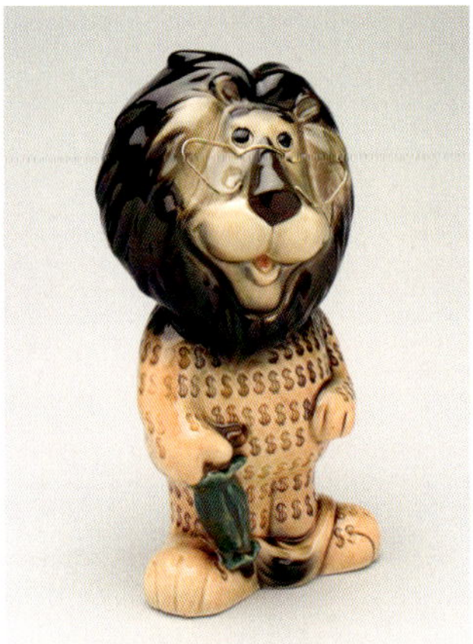

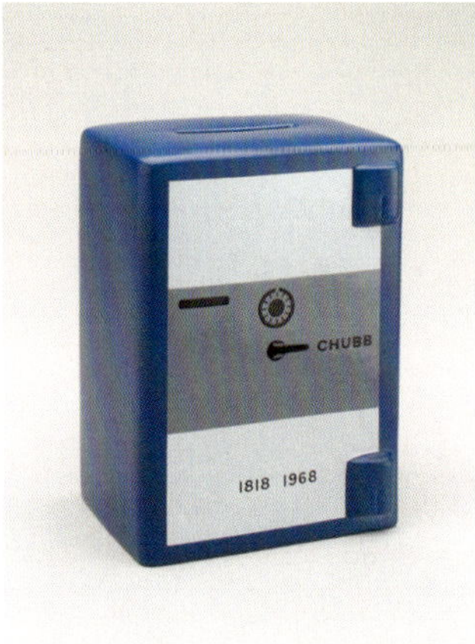
CHUBB
1818 1968

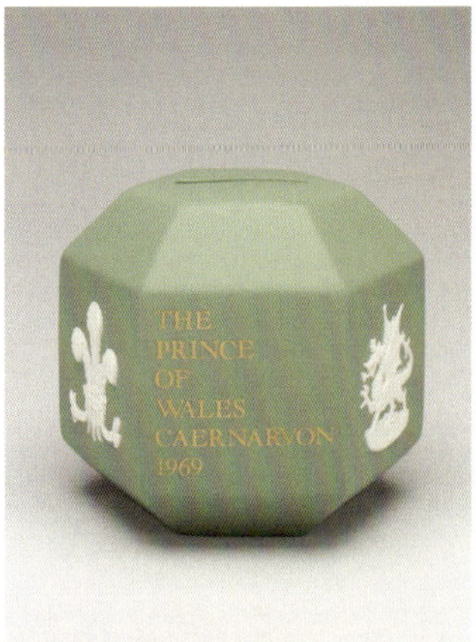
THE
PRINCE
OF
WALES
CAERNARVON
1969

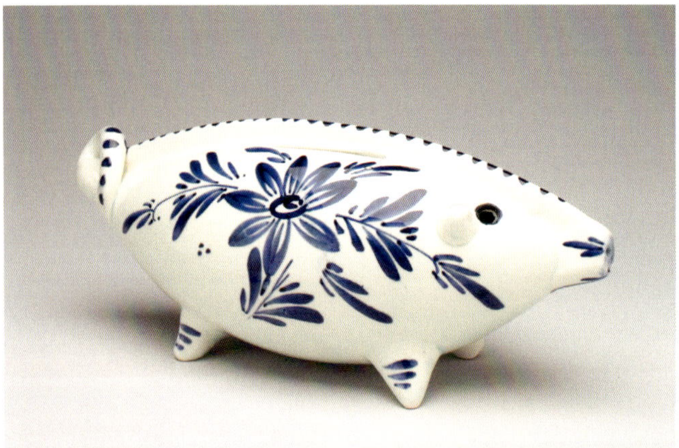

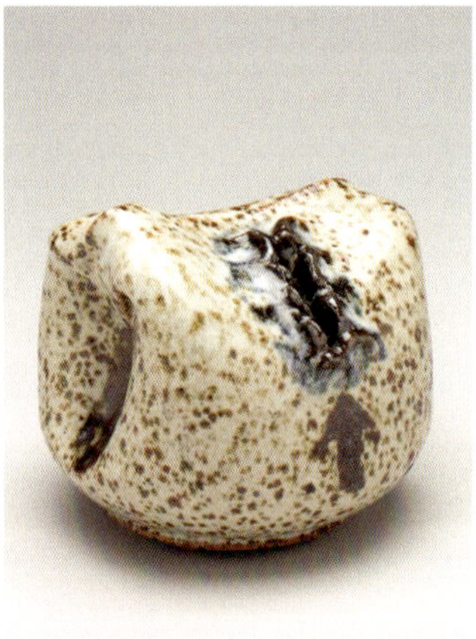

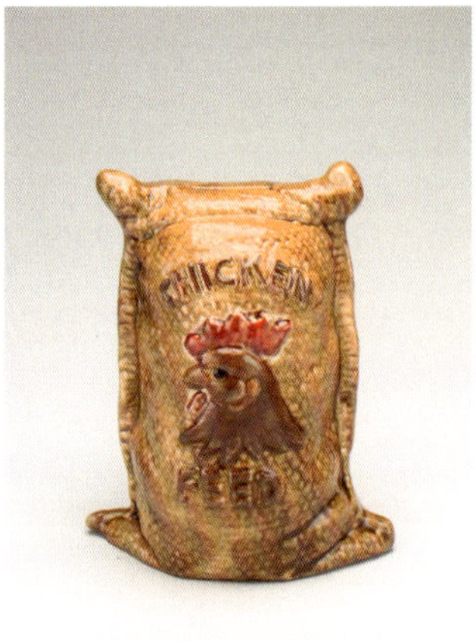
CHICKEN

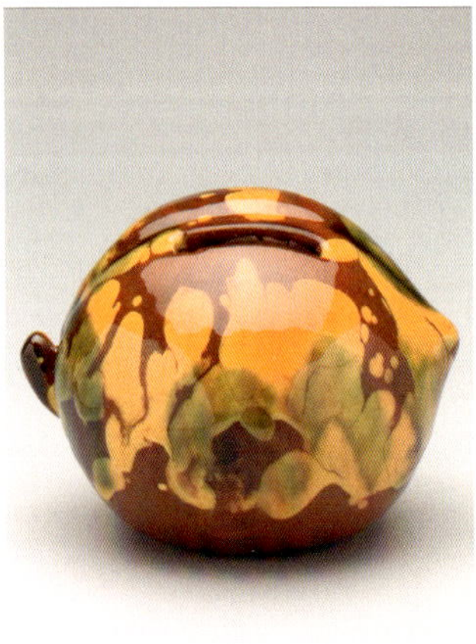

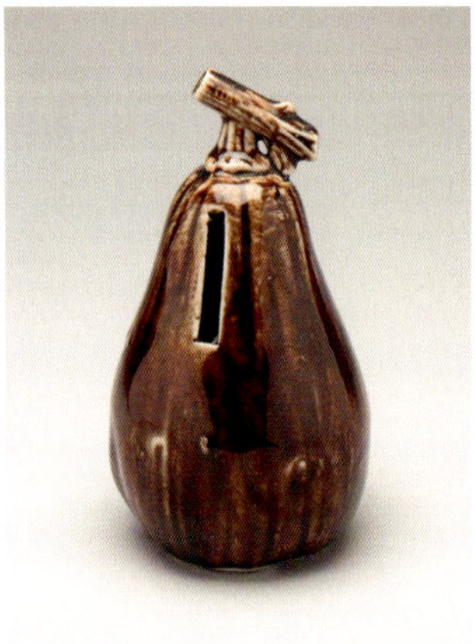

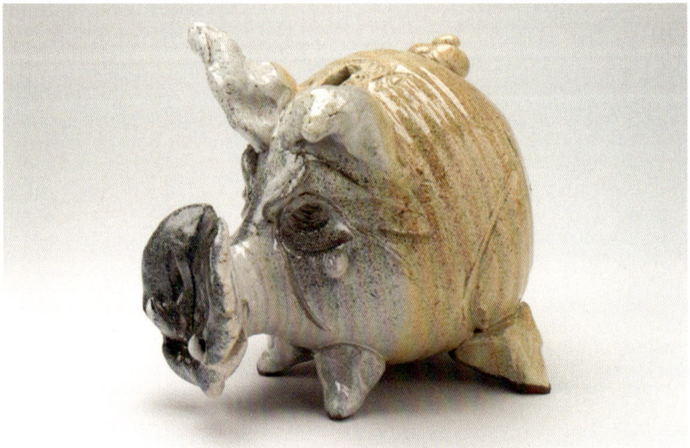

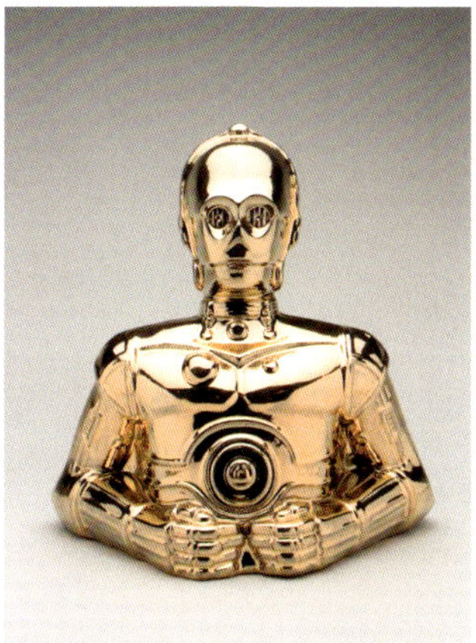

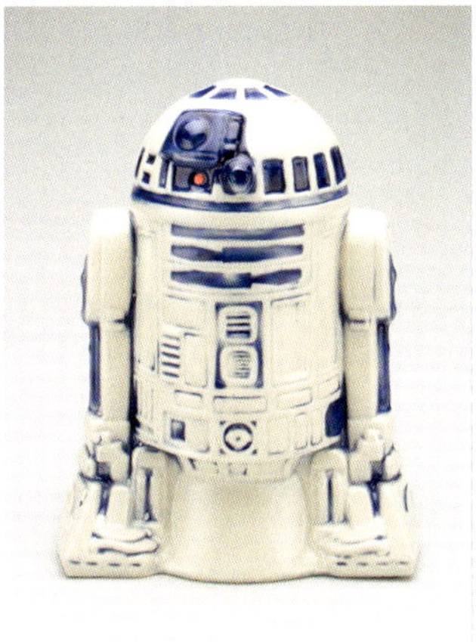

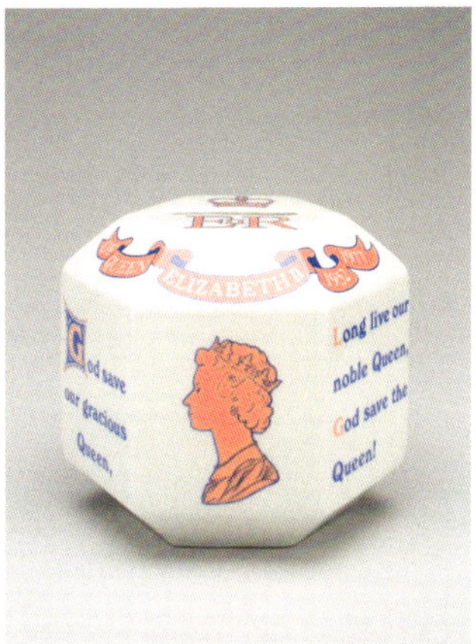
ELIZABETH
God save our gracious Queen,
Long live our noble Queen,
God save the Queen!

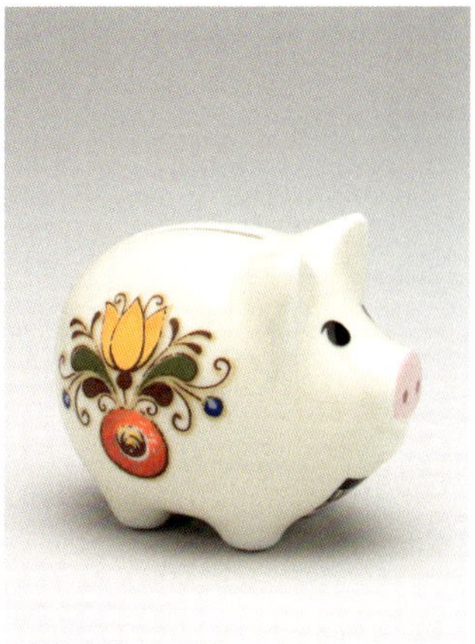

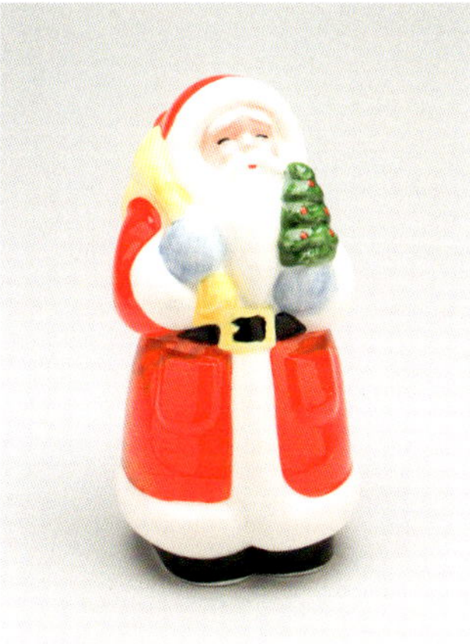

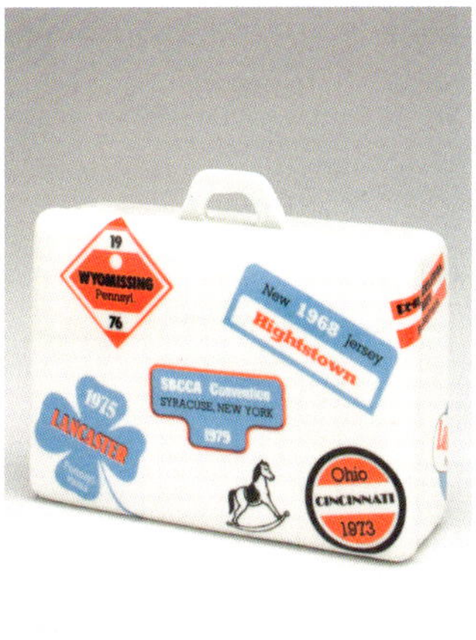
WYOMISSING
New 1968 Jersey
Highstown
SBCCA Convention
SYRACUSE, NEW YORK
1975
LANCASTER
Ohio
CINCINNATI
1973

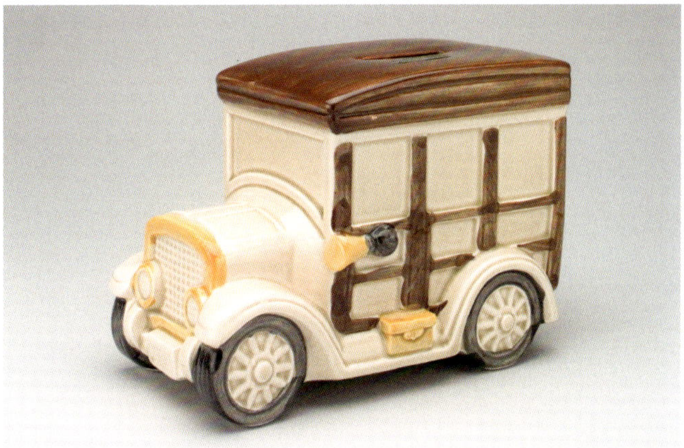

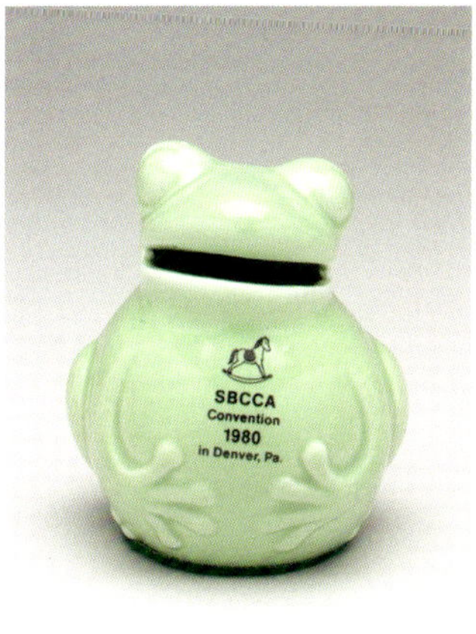
SBCCA
Convention
1980
in Denver, Pa.

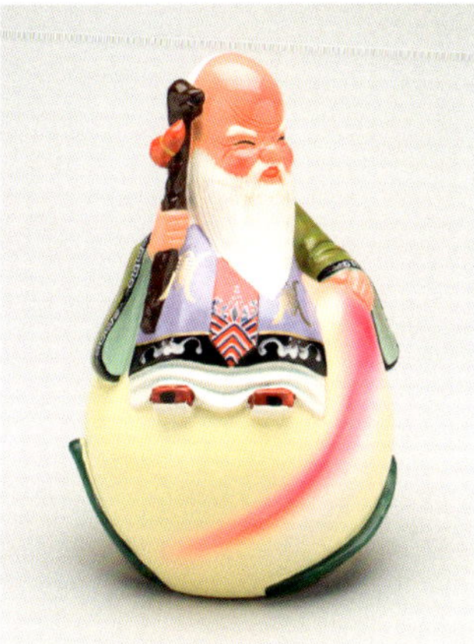

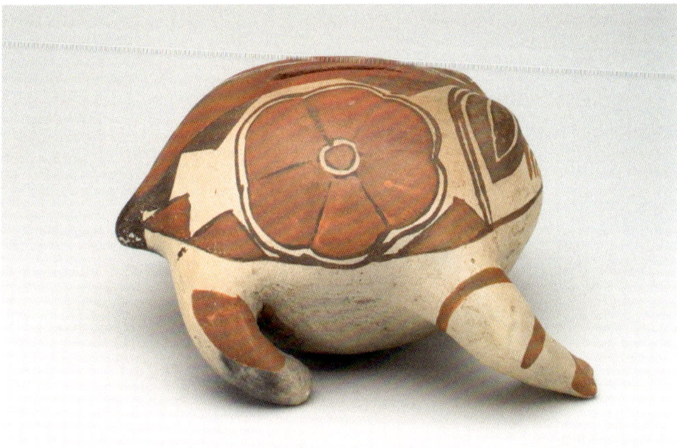

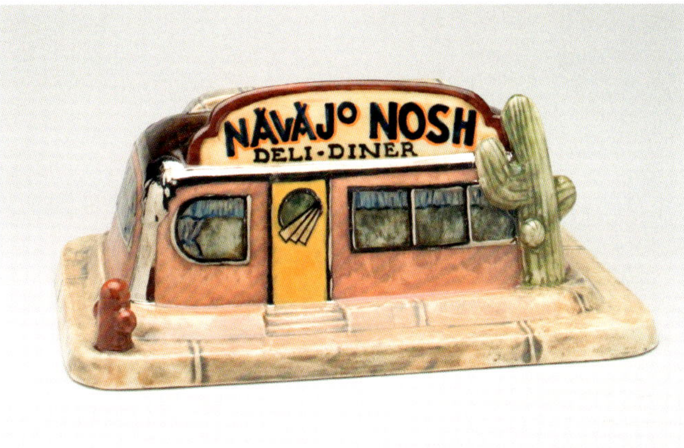
NAVAJO NOSH
DELI-DINER

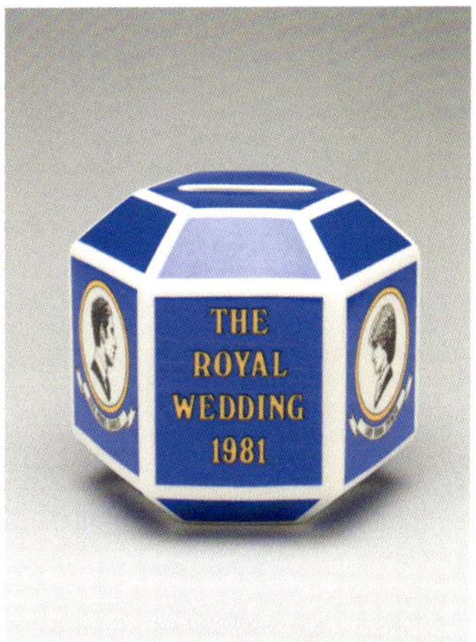
THE
ROYAL
WEDDING
1981

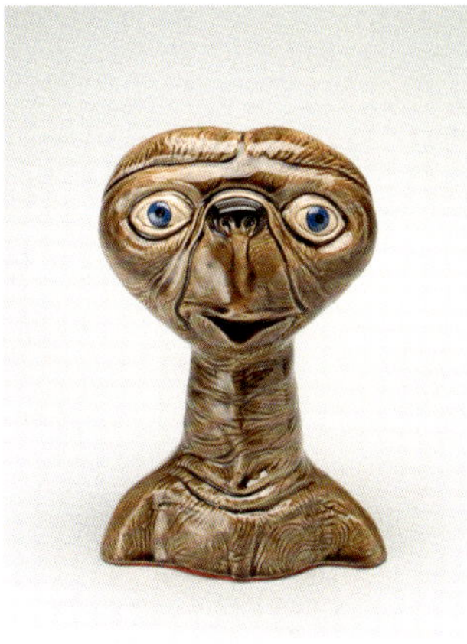

Piggy Bank, Still Bank Collectors Club of America, 1978
Tresor Verlag, Affalterback, Germany (est. 1958), manufacturer
Porcelain
1 3/4 x 2 3/8 x 1 5/8 in.
2003.236.221

Queen Elizabeth Silver Jubilee, 1977
Adams China Company, Staffordshire, England (est. 1769), manufacturer
Ceramic, metal
3 1/16 x 3 1/8 x 3 1/8 in.
2003.236.540

R2-D2, c. 1977
Roman Ceramics, Chicago, manufacturer
Ceramic
8 1/8 x 6 5/16 x 3 3/16 in.
2003.236.450a,b

C3PO, c. 1977
Roman Ceramics, Chicago, manufacturer
Ceramic, rubber
7 1/2 x 7 1/2 x 4 1/4 in.
2003.236.579

Antique Car, c. 1980
Otagiri, Japan, manufacturer
Ceramic
4 5/16 x 6 1/4 x 3 1/2 in.
2003.236.543

Suitcase, Still Bank Collectors Club of America, 1979
Tresor Verlag, Affalterback, Germany (est. 1958), manufacturer
Gerhard Reigraf, German, designer
Porcelain
3 x 3 5/8 x 1 3/16 in.
2003.236.213

Father Christmas, c. 1979
Japan
Ceramic
6 3/16 x 3 1/4 x 3 1/4 in.
2003.236.452a,b

Frog, c. 1981
New Mexico
Ceramic, pigment
3 9/16 x 6 1/4 x 6 in.
2003.236.675

Old Chinese Man, 1980
Chinese Still Clay Factory, manufacturer
Ceramic
5 3/4 x 4 x 3 1/4 in.
2003.236.560

Frog Bank, Still Bank Collectors Club of America, 1980
Tresor Verlag, Affalterback, Germany (est. 1958), manufacturer
Porcelain
2 3/4 x 2 3/8 x 2 3/8 in.
2003.236.222

E. T., c. 1982
Porcelain
6 3/4 x 4 5/8 x 3 11/16 in.
2003.236.440

The Royal Wedding, 1981
Wedgwood & Company, Staffordshire, England (est. 1759), manufacturer
Ceramic, metal
3 x 3 5/16 x 3 5/16 in.
2003.236.539

Navajo Nosh Deli-Diner, c. 1981
H. Cavanagh, designer
Ceramic, pigment, plastic
3 x 7 15/16 x 5 1/8 in.
2003.236.674

Barrel, 20th century
Ohio or Pennsylvania
Ceramic, pigment
3 5/8 x 3 3/16 x 3 3/16 in.
2003.236.1087

Barrel, 20th century
United States
Ceramic, pigment
3 5/8 x 3 1/8 x 3 1/8 in.
2003.236.1085

Barrel, 20th century
Ohio or Pennsylvania
Redware, pigment
3 7/8 x 2 3/4 x 2 3/4 in.
2003.236.589

Barrel, 20th century
Ohio or Pennsylvania
Ceramic
3 3/4 x 3 1/2 x 3 1/2 in.
2003.236.541

Bird, 20th century
Candelaria Montero, designer
Ceramic, pigment
2 5/8 x 6 x 2 in.
2003.236.910

Bell, 20th century
Ceramic
5 1/4 x 4 5/8 x 4 5/8 in.
2003.236.499

Bearded man, 20th century
Mexico
Ceramic
5 7/8 x 4 1/16 x 4 1/2 in.
2003.236.592

Elephant, 20th century
Netherlands
Ceramic, rubber
2 1/2 x 1 13/16 x 3 1/2 in.
2003.236.906

Cow, 20th century
Probably United States
Ceramic
3 3/8 x 4 7/16 x 2 3/8 in.
2003.236.730

C. D. Kenny Co. (pig),
20th century
Austria
Ceramic
2 1/8 x 3 3/4 x 2 in.
2003.236.521

Duck in basket, 20th century
Ceramic
5 1/2 x 3 1/16 x 5 3/8 in.
2003.236.741

Dog, 20th century
Mexico
Ceramic
4 1/4 x 3 1/16 x 5 1/2 in.
2003.236.583

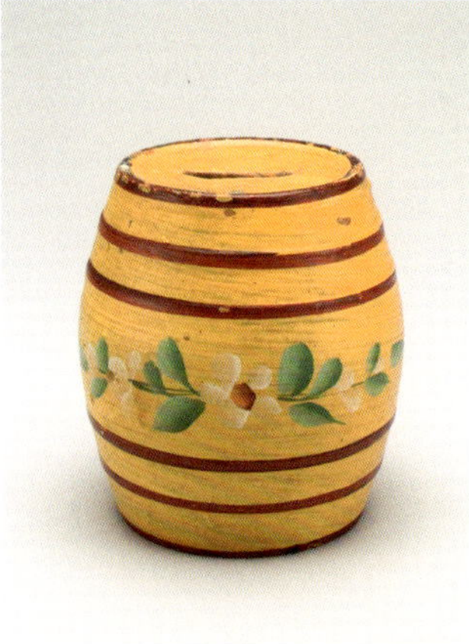

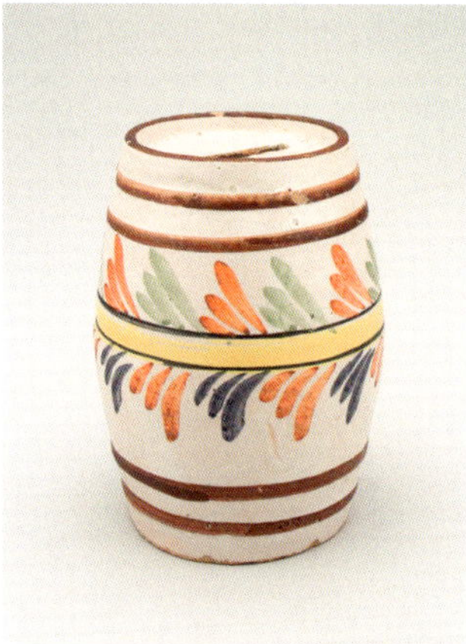

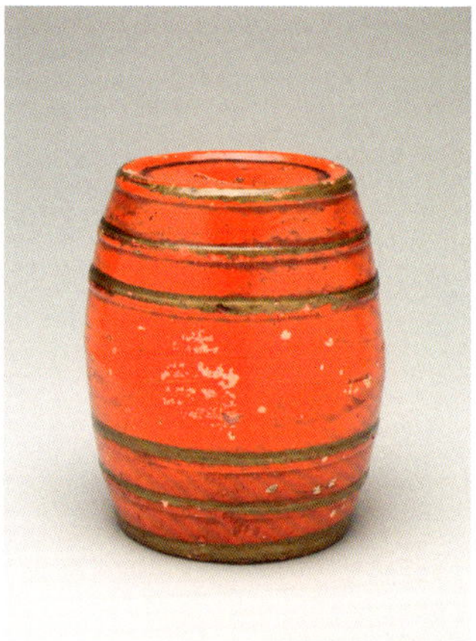

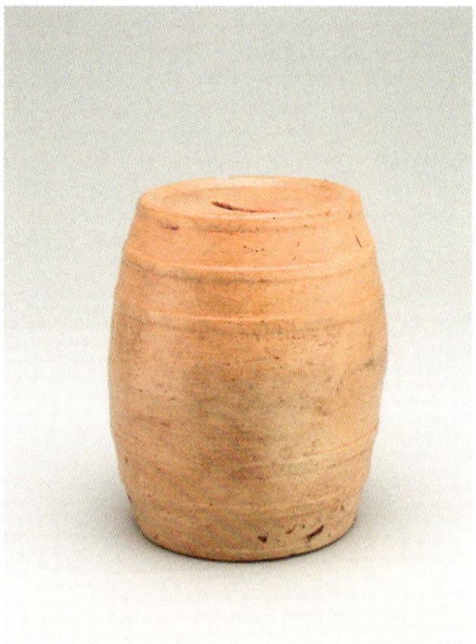

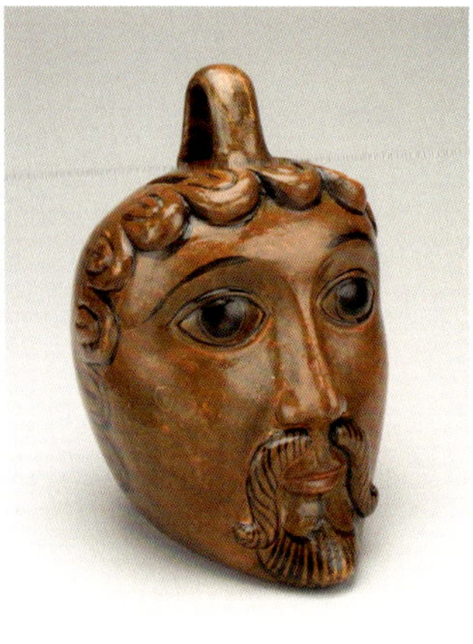

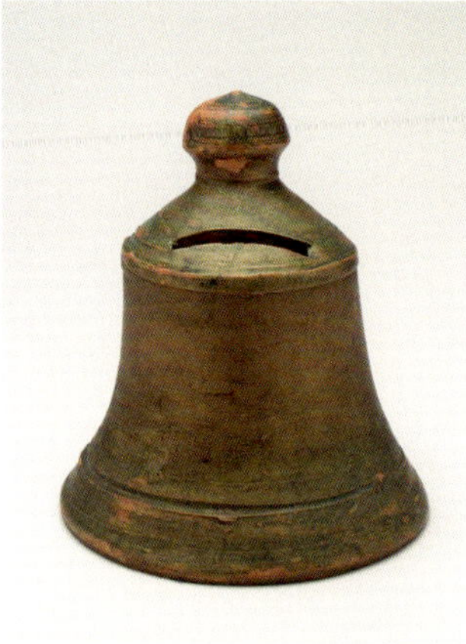

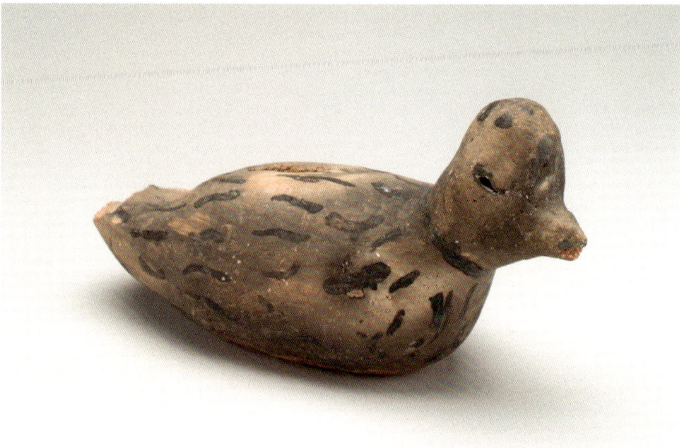

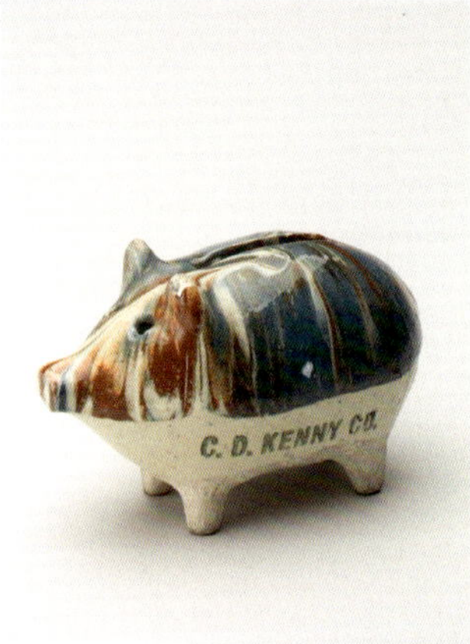
C. D. KENNY CO.

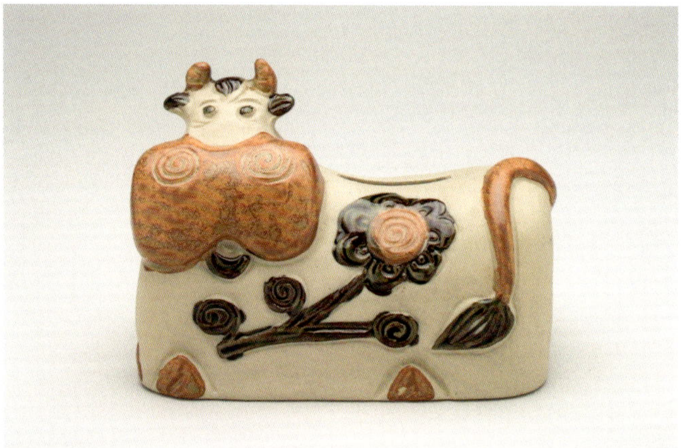

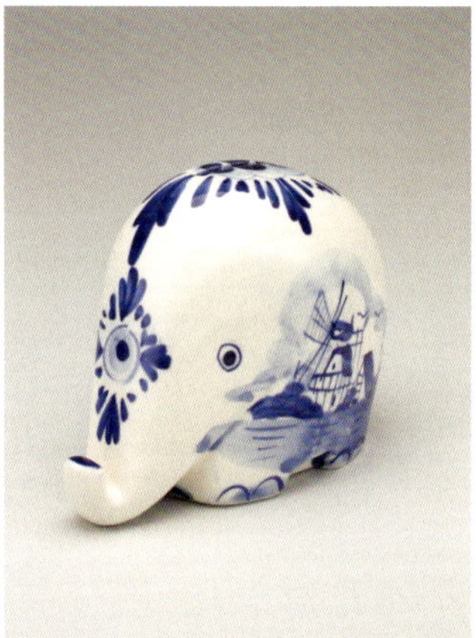

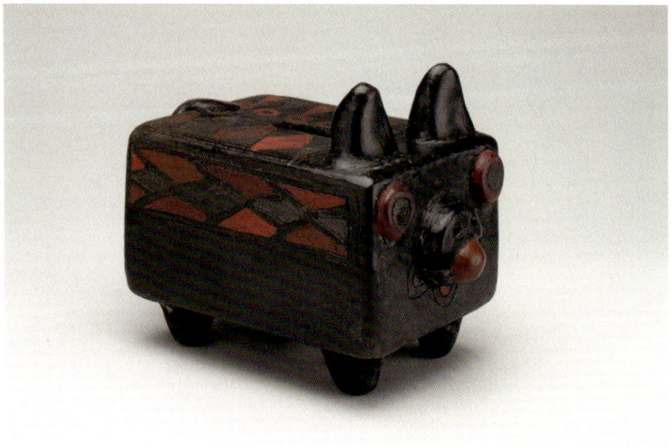

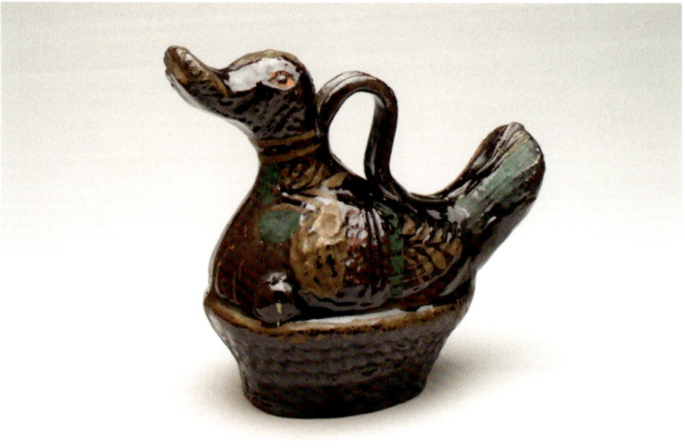

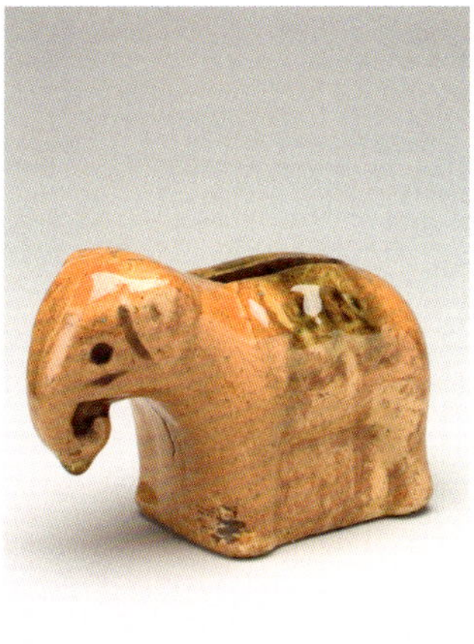

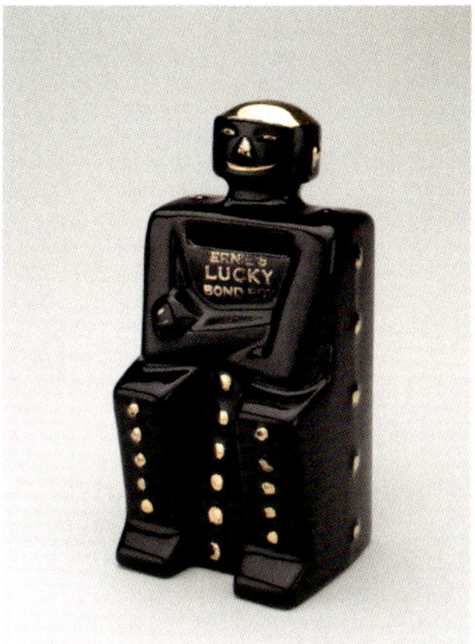
ERNIE'S
LUCKY

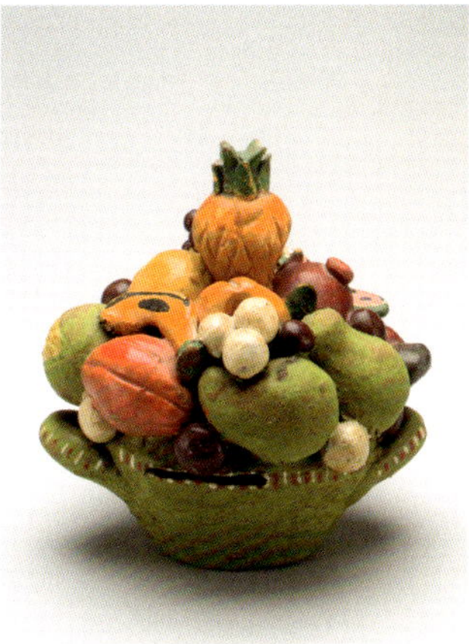

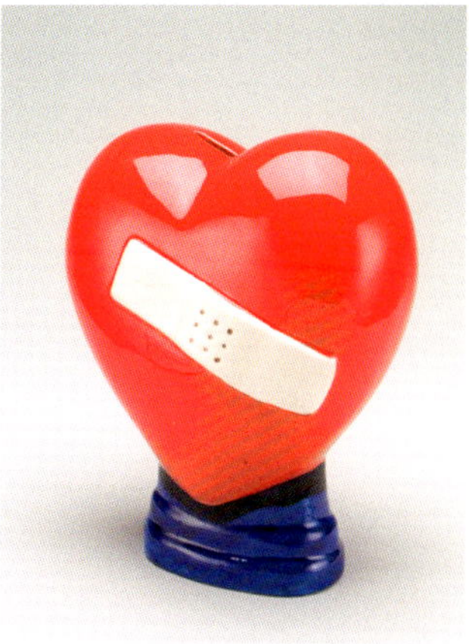

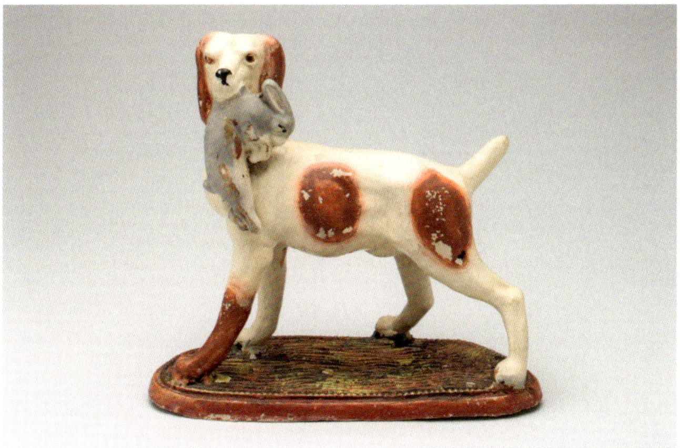

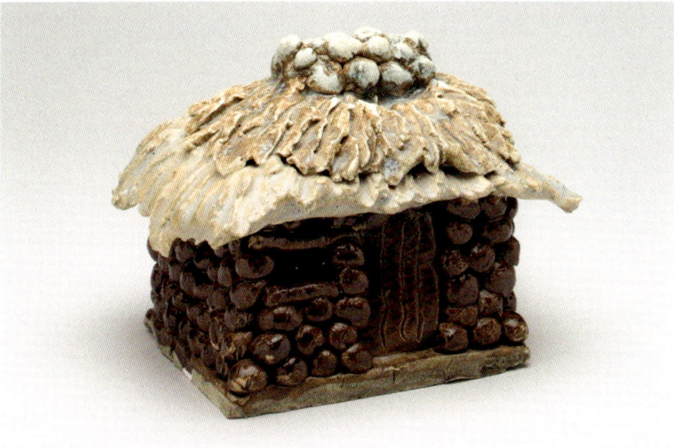

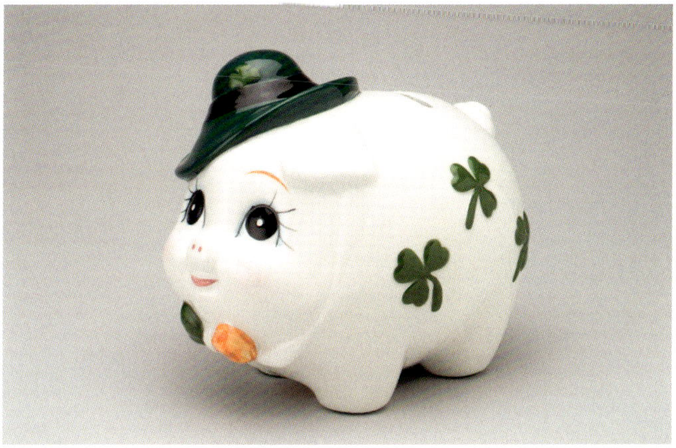

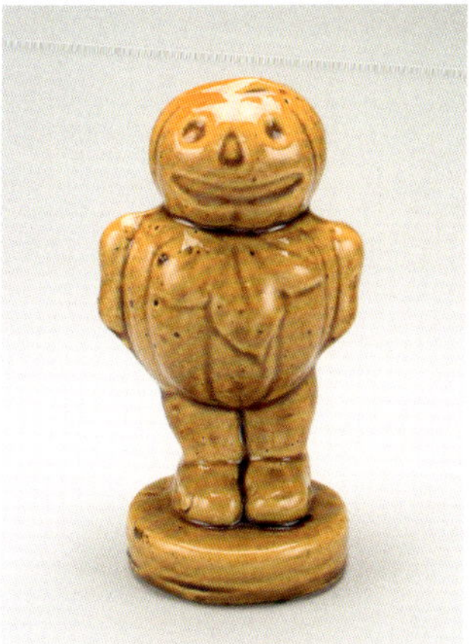

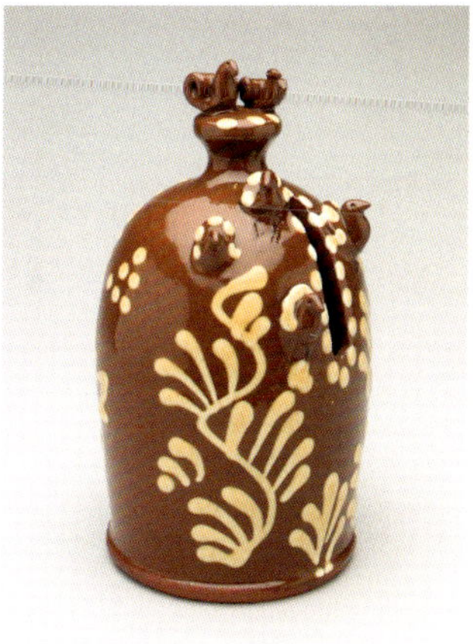

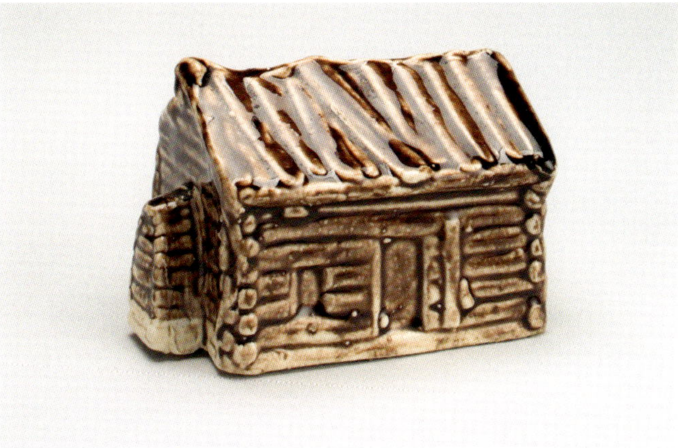

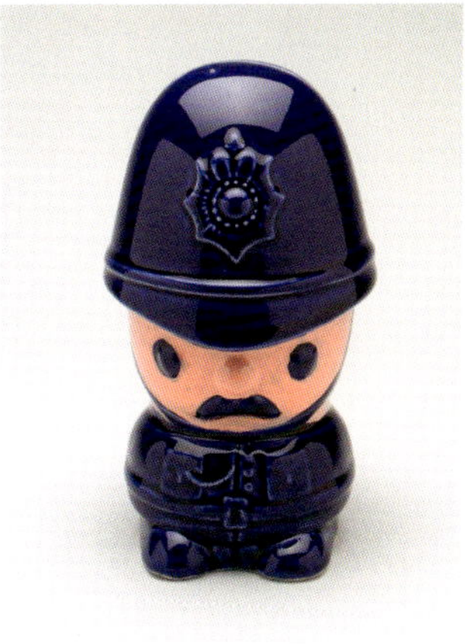

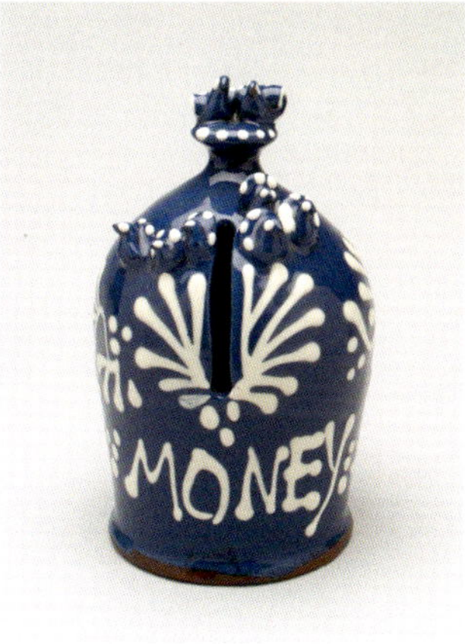
MONEY

Heart with bandage, 20th century
England
Ceramic
5 1/4 x 4 1/2 x 2 1/8 in.
2003.236.584

Fruit Basket, 20th century
United States
Redware
4 13/16 x 3 5/8 x 4 5/16 in.
2003.236.572

Ernie's Lucky Bond Box, 20th century
England
Ceramic, paper
5 11/16 x 2 11/16 x 2 3/8 in.
2003.236.477

Elephant, 20th century
Ceramic
2 5/8 x 4 x 2 in.
2003.236.916

Hut, 20th century
Ceramic
3 5/16 x 4 x 3 5/16 in.
2003.236.549

Hunting Dog with Rabbit, 20th century
Ceramic, pigment
6 3/8 x 7 x 3 1/8 in.
2003.236.895

Jug with Birds, 20th century
Wetheriggs Country Pottery, Penrith, England (est. c. 1855), manufacturer
Ceramic
6 x 3 3/8 x 3 3/8 in.
2003.236.537

Jack-o-Lantern, 20th century
United States
Ceramic
5 1/2 x 3 x 2 5/8 in.
2003.236.728

Irish Pig, 20th century
Otagiri, Japan, manufacturer
Ceramic, rubber
5 x 4 x 5 in.
2003.236.544

Money (jug), 20th century
Wetheriggs Country Pottery, Penrith, England (est. c. 1855), manufacturer
Ceramic
5 1/8 x 3 9/16 x 3 9/16 in.
2003.236.586

London Bobby, 20th century
England
Ceramic, plastic
6 x 3 1/2 x 4 in.
2003.236.570

Lincoln's Cabin, 20th century
Austria
Ceramic
2 1/2 x 3 13/16 x 2 3/8 in.
2003.236.548

Pig, 20th century
Probably United States
Ceramic
3 7/16 x 5 1/4 x 2 13/16 in.
2003.236.734

Owl, 20th century
Possibly Guatemala
Ceramic, pigment
3 1/4 x 2 3/16 x 2 in.
2003.236.904

Monkey, 20th century
Japan
Ceramic
4 1/8 x 2 3/4 x 1 15/16 in.
2003.236.729

Pig, 20th century
Ceramic
2 3/16 x 2 x 3 9/16 in.
2003.236.903

Pig, 20th century
Ceramic
2 3/4 x 4 1/8 x 2 1/4 in.
2003.236.901

Pig, 20th century
Ceramic
4 5/16 x 3 9/16 x 4 9/16 in.
2003.236.894

Queen's Guard, 20th century
England
Ceramic, plastic
6 1/2 x 3 1/2 x 3 in.
2003.236.558

Pig with handle, 20th century
Ceramic
5 3/4 x 3 1/4 x 4 3/4 in.
2003.236.743

Pig, 20th century
Japan
Ceramic
1 11/16 x 3 1/2 x 1 5/8 in.
2003.236.918

Savings Bank (house),
20th century
Probably England
Ceramic
3 11/16 x 1 3/4 x 1 7/16 in.
2003.236.908

Santa Claus, 20th century
Porcelain
6 1/2 x 4 x 5 1/2 in.
2003.236.453a,b

Rabbit, 20th century
Bremen, Germany
Ceramic, metal
4 15/16 x 4 13/16 x 2 13/16 in.
2003.236.917

Rabbit, 20th century
The Netherlands
Ceramic, rubber
3 1/2 x 3 x 4 1/2 in.
2003.236.907

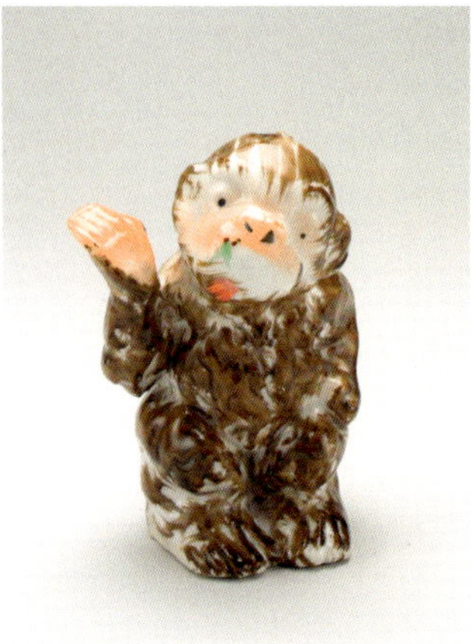
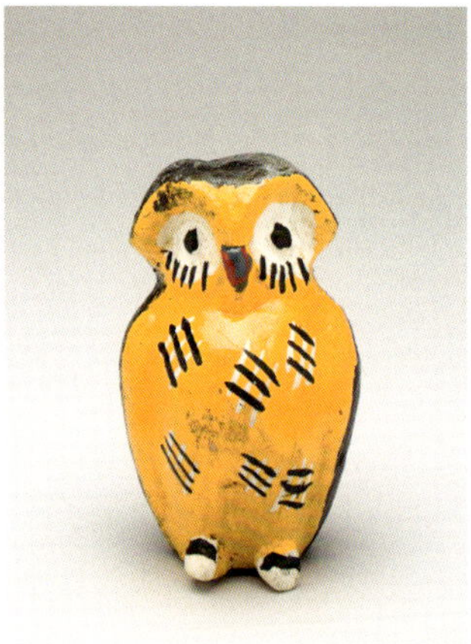
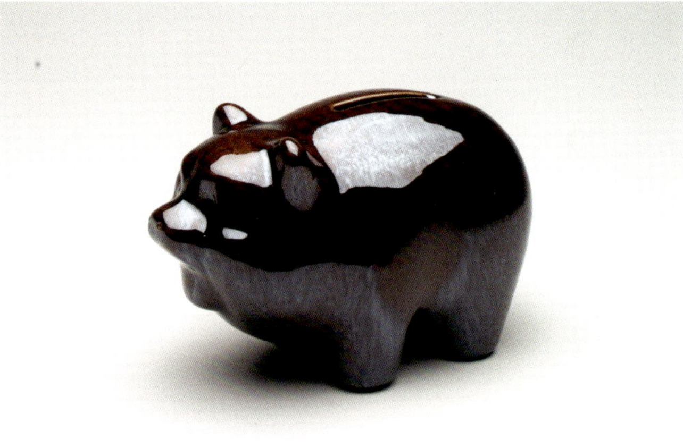
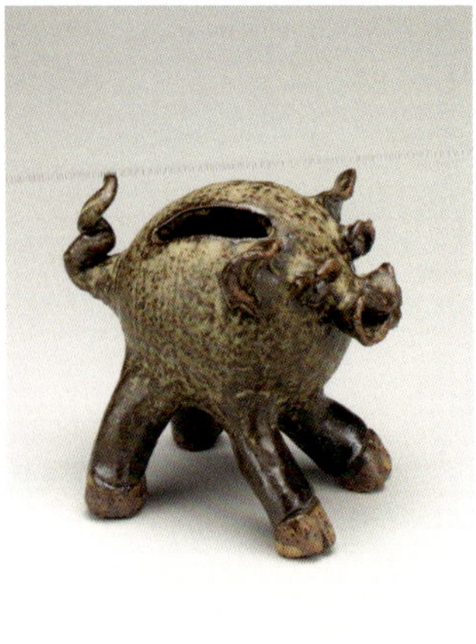
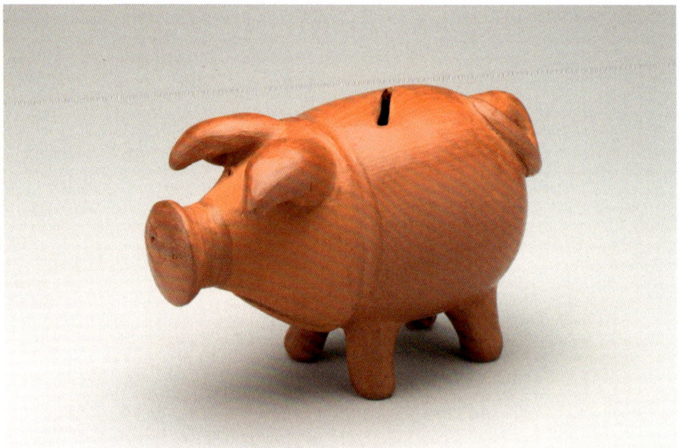
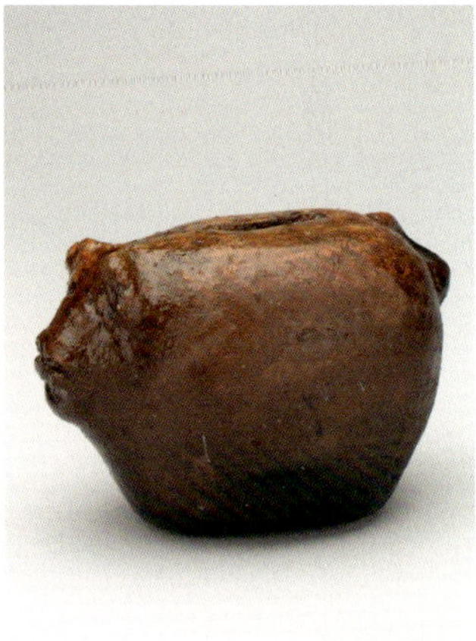
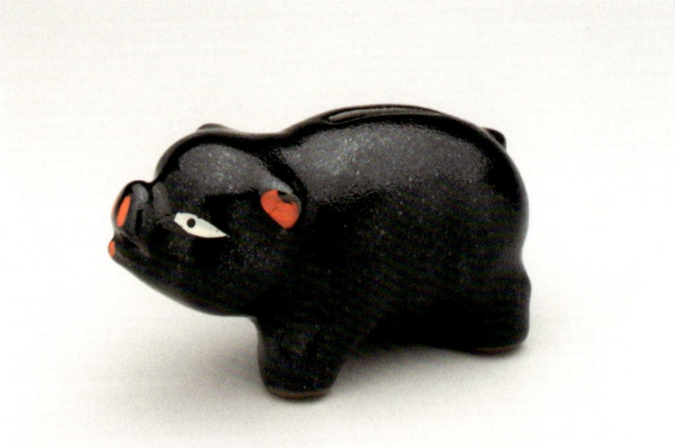
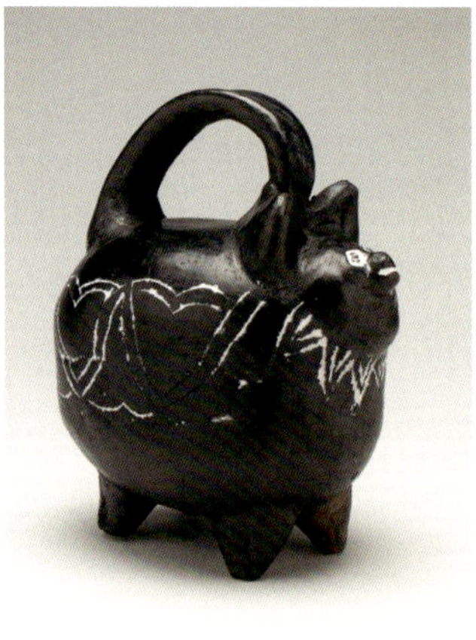
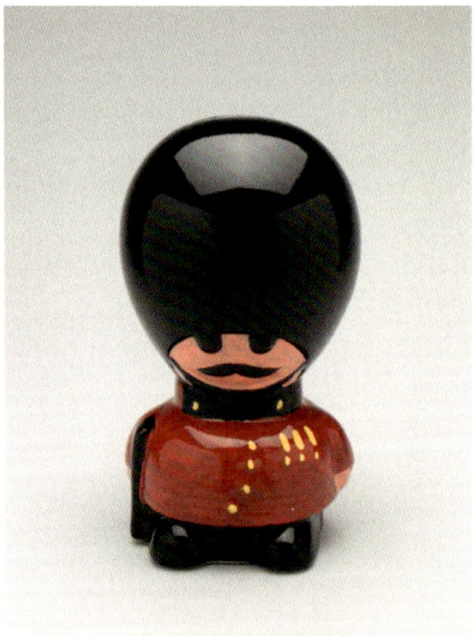
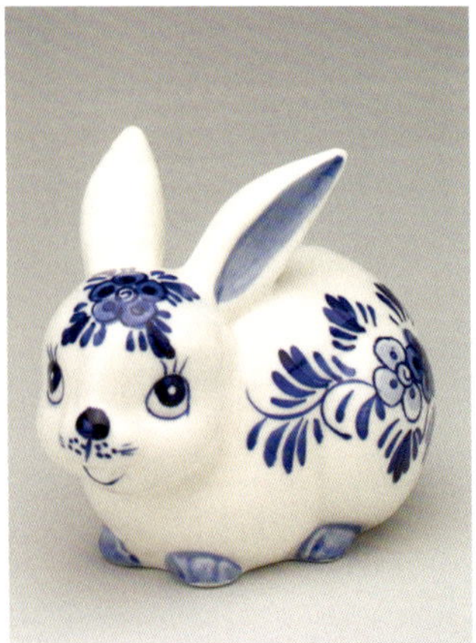
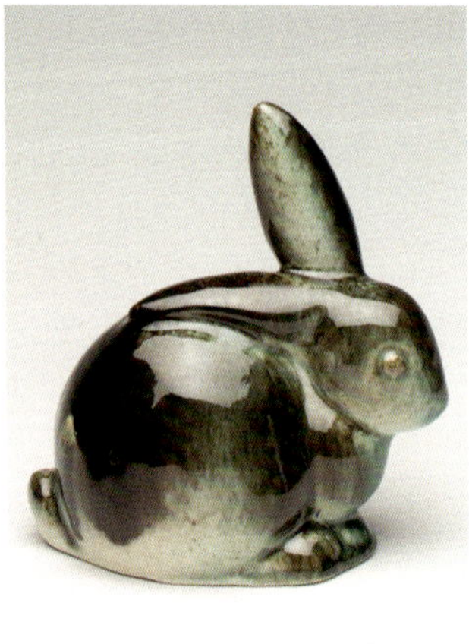
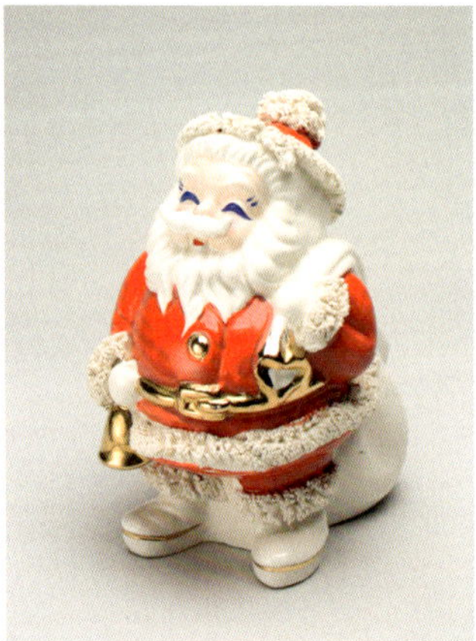
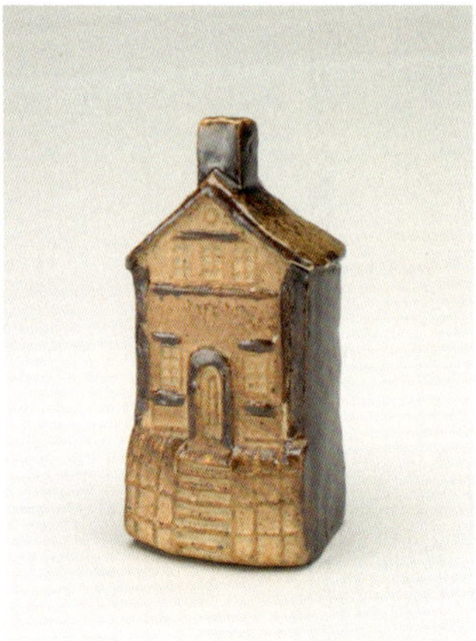

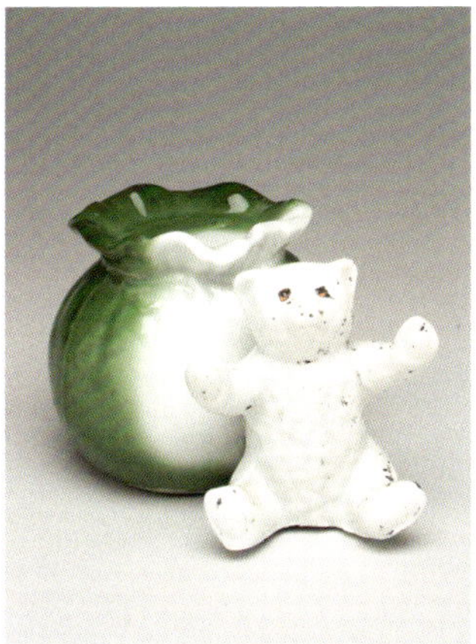

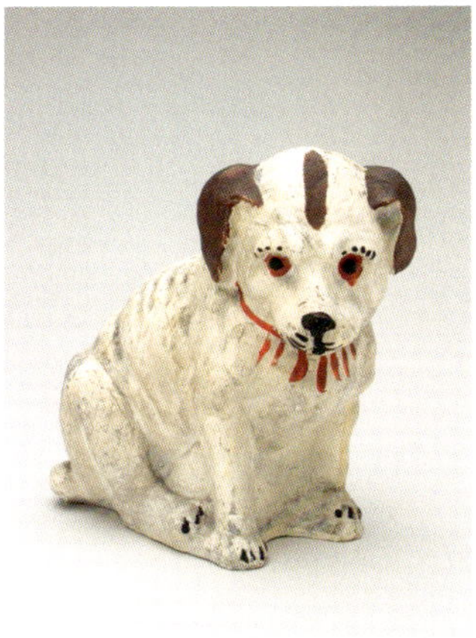

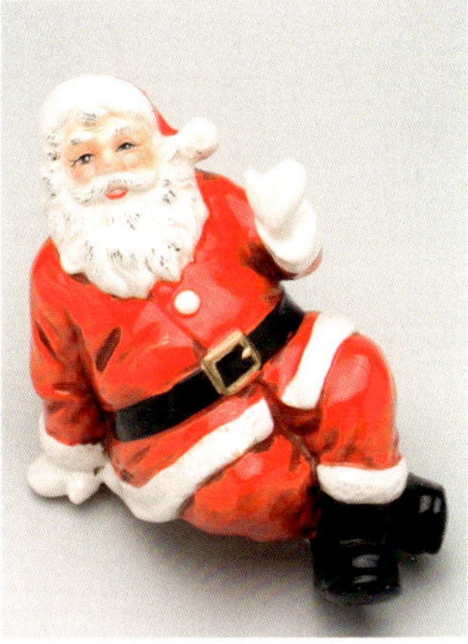

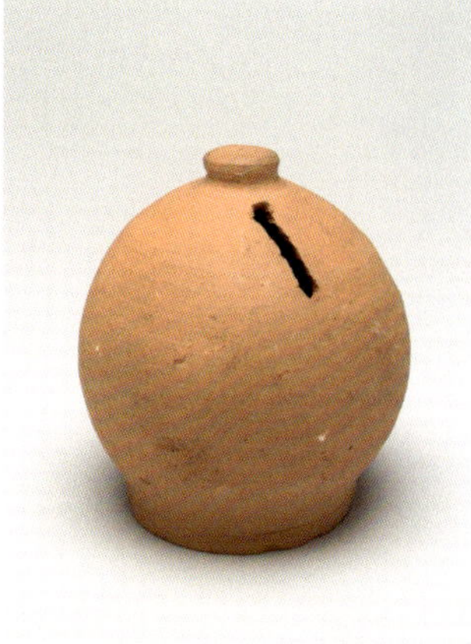

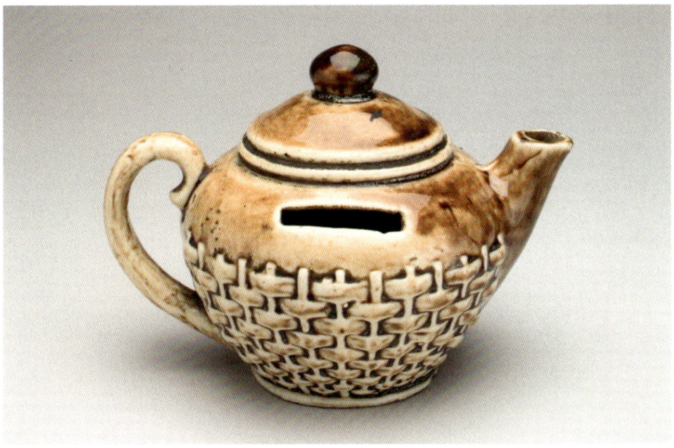

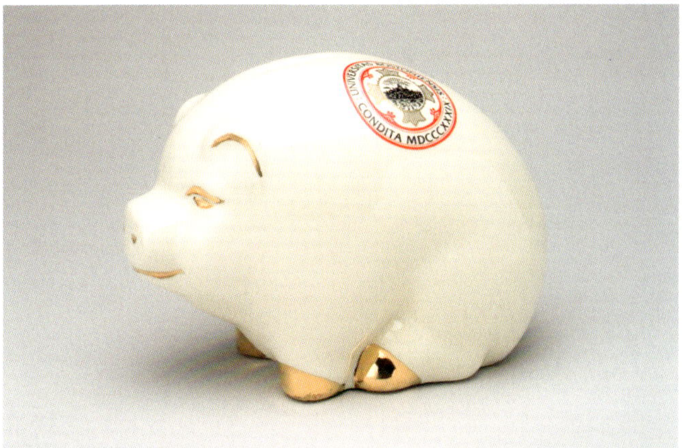

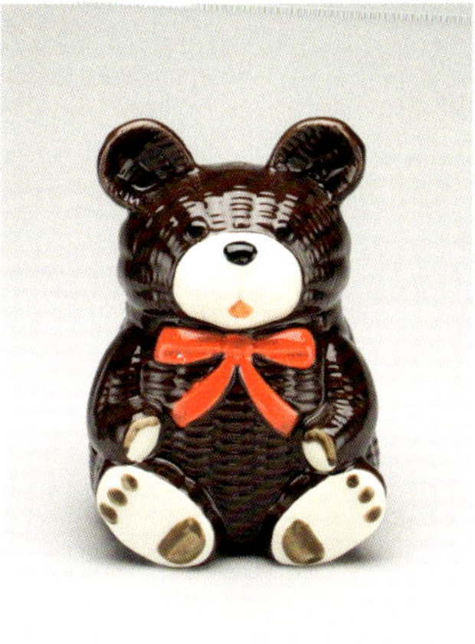

STILL BANKS: Glass

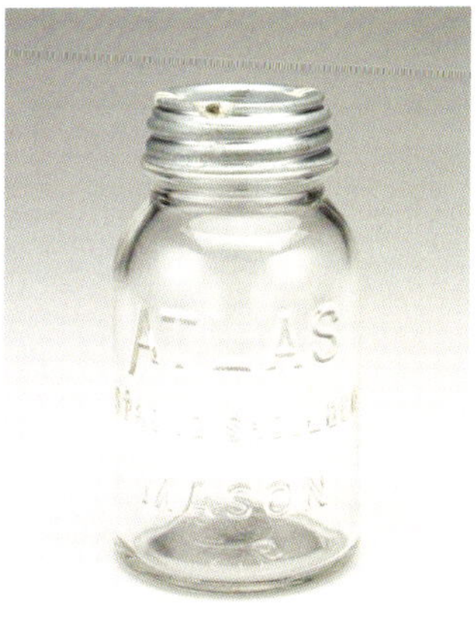

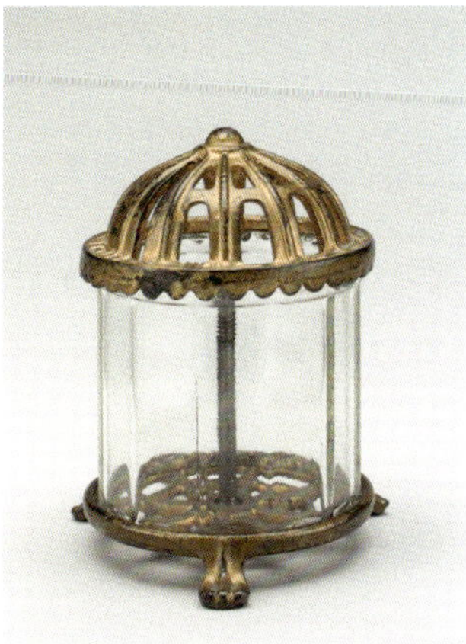

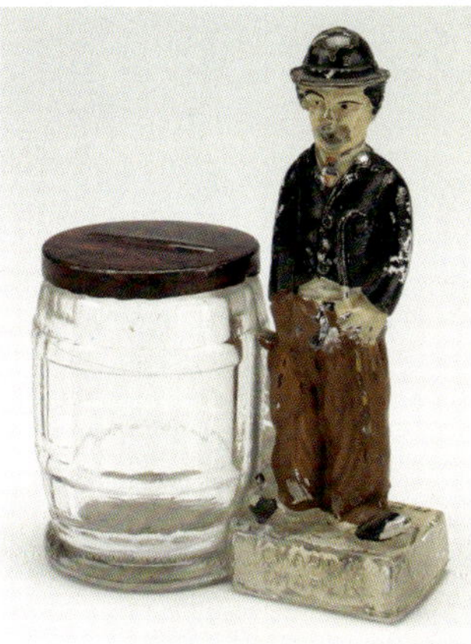

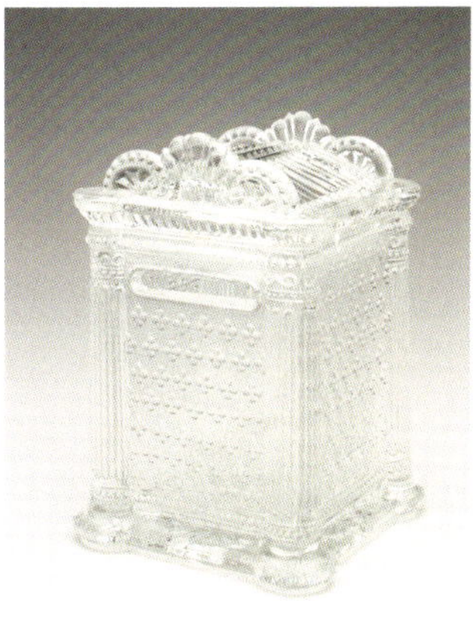

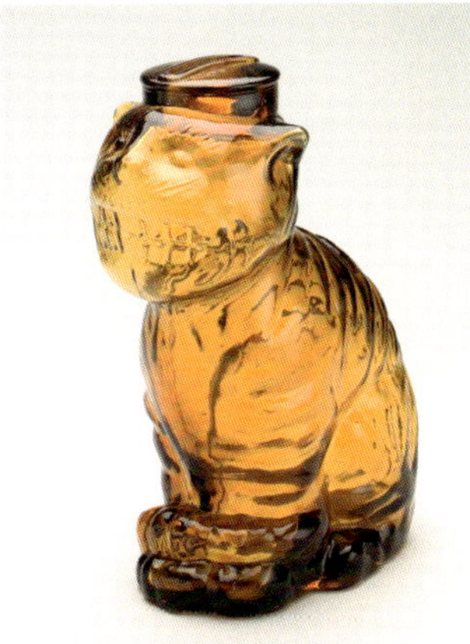

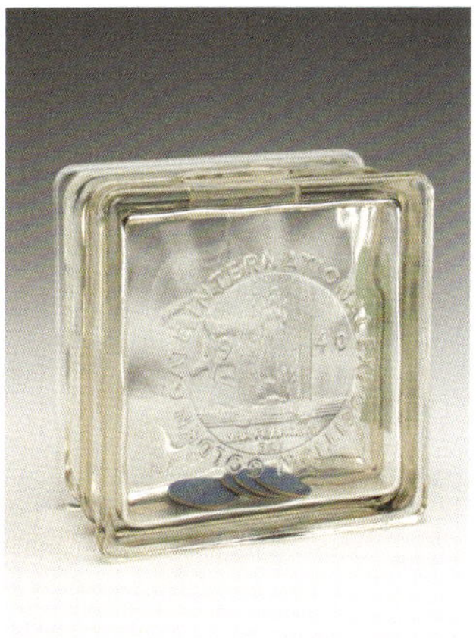

Sphere, 20th century
Ceramic
3 3/8 x 3 1/4 x 3 1/4 in.
2003.236.489

Seated Santa Claus,
20th century
Japan
Porcelain, rubber
8 7/16 x 5 3/4 x 5 1/16 in.
2003.236.455a,b

Seated dog, 20th century
Ceramic, pigment
6 x 6 15/16 x 3 7/8 in.
2003.236.890

Seated bear with sack,
20th century
Ceramic
2 x 3 3/4 x 2 3/8 in.
2003.236.914

Boston University (pig), late 20th century
Ceramic
4 1/2 x 3 9/16 x 6 1/2 in.
2003.236.547

Van Dyk Teas Teapot, 20th century
Probably England
Ceramic
3 5/16 x 4 7/8 x 3 1/2 in.
2003.236.492

Crystal Bank, c. 1910 – 25
Arcade Manufacturing
Company, Freeport, Illinois
(1868 – 1946), manufacturer
Glass, iron, pigment
4 x 3 3/16 x 3 3/16 in.
2003.236.941

Atlas Strong Shoulder Jar,
early 20th century
Hazel-Atlas Glass Company,
Wheeling, West Virginia
(1902 – 64), manufacturer
Glass, metal
3 5/8 x 2 x 2 in.
2003.236.786

STILL BANKS: Glass

Teddy Bear, 20th century
Otagiri, Japan, manufacturer
Ceramic, rubber
3 7/8 x 3 x 3 1/4 in.
2003.236.559

Golden Gate International Exposition, c. 1940
Probably United States
Glass
3 1/4 x 3 1/4 x 1 3/4 in.
2003.236.793

Cheshire Cat, c. 1930s
Probably Hazel-Atlas Glass
Company, Wheeling, West
Virginia (1902 – 64),
manufacturer
Glass
6 3/16 x 3 1/16 x 4 1/2 in.
2003.236.789

Savings Bank, c. 1930
United States
Glass
4 1/16 x 2 3/4 x 2 7/8 in.
2003.236.203

Charlie Chaplin with Ash Barrel,
c. 1920s
George Borgfeldt & Company,
New York, manufacturer
Glass, metal, pigment
3 13/16 x 3 x 1 11/16 in.
2003.236.266

Piggy Bank (large), second half of 20th century
Anchor Hocking Company, Lancaster, Ohio (est. 1880), manufacturer
Glass
$4\frac{5}{8} \times 4 \times 6\frac{3}{16}$ in.
2003.236.785

Piggy Bank (small), second half of 20th century
Anchor Hocking Company, Lancaster, Ohio (est. 1880), manufacturer
Glass
$2\frac{7}{8} \times 2\frac{3}{8} \times 4\frac{3}{8}$ in.
2003.236.699

Snoopy, 1960s–70s
Probably United States
Glass
$5\frac{3}{4} \times 3\frac{1}{2} \times 3\frac{13}{16}$ in.
2003.236.788

Mobil Oil (baseball bank), c. 1950s
Heffelfinger Publications, New York, manufacturer
Glass, plastic, pigment, metal
$3\frac{1}{2} \times 3\frac{1}{16} \times 3\frac{1}{16}$ in.
2003.236.911

Log Cabin, c. 1965
Probably United States
Glass, metal, pigment
$4\frac{5}{8} \times 4\frac{15}{16} \times 2\frac{9}{16}$ in.
2003.236.696

Bear, 20th century
Glass, plastic
$4\frac{5}{8} \times 2 \times 1\frac{7}{8}$ in.
2003.236.790

Barrel Bank, 20th century
Glass
$4\frac{5}{16} \times 2\frac{15}{16} \times 2\frac{15}{16}$ in.
2003.236.695

Half-Pint Coin Bank, 20th century
Bower Manufacturing Company, Goshen, Indiana, manufacturer
Glass, metal, paper, pigment, string
$4\frac{1}{2} \times 2\frac{5}{16} \times 2\frac{5}{16}$ in.
2003.236.787

Globe, 20th century
United States
Glass
$4\frac{1}{8} \times 3\frac{11}{16} \times 3\frac{11}{16}$ in.
2003.236.200

Elephant, 20th century
Grapette Products Company, Camden, Arkansas, manufacturer
Glass, metal, pigment
$7\frac{1}{8} \times 3\frac{1}{4} \times 2\frac{3}{4}$ in.
2003.236.796

Clown, 20th century
Grapette Products Company, Camden, Arkansas, manufacturer
Glass, metal, pigment
$7\frac{1}{8} \times 3\frac{1}{8} \times 2\frac{13}{16}$ in.
2003.236.797

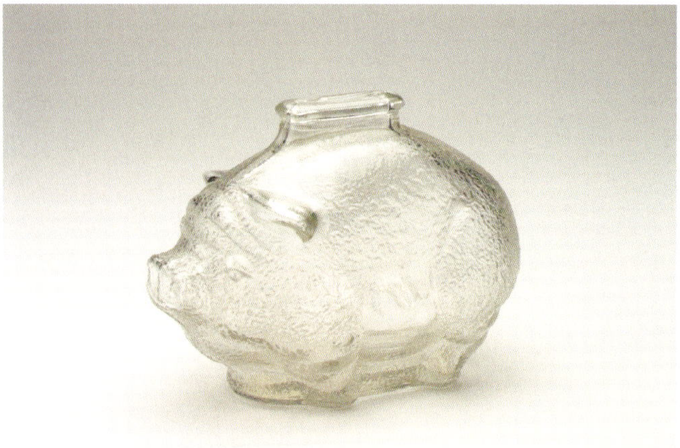

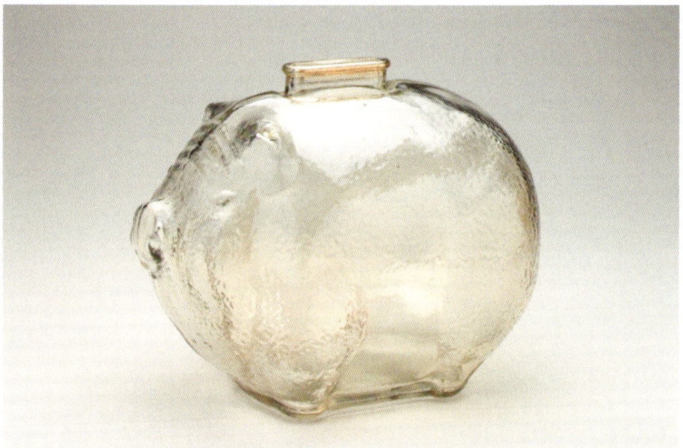

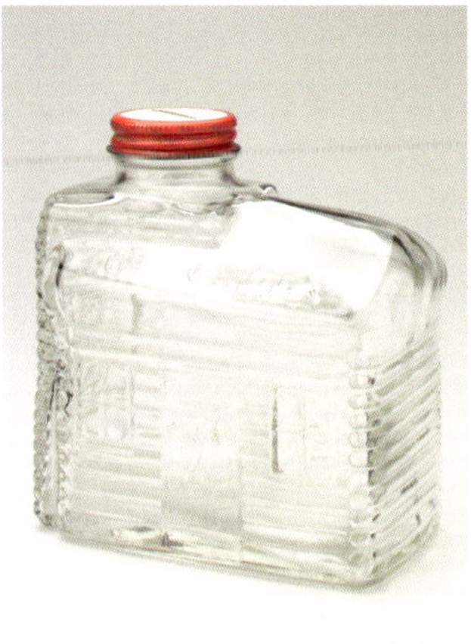

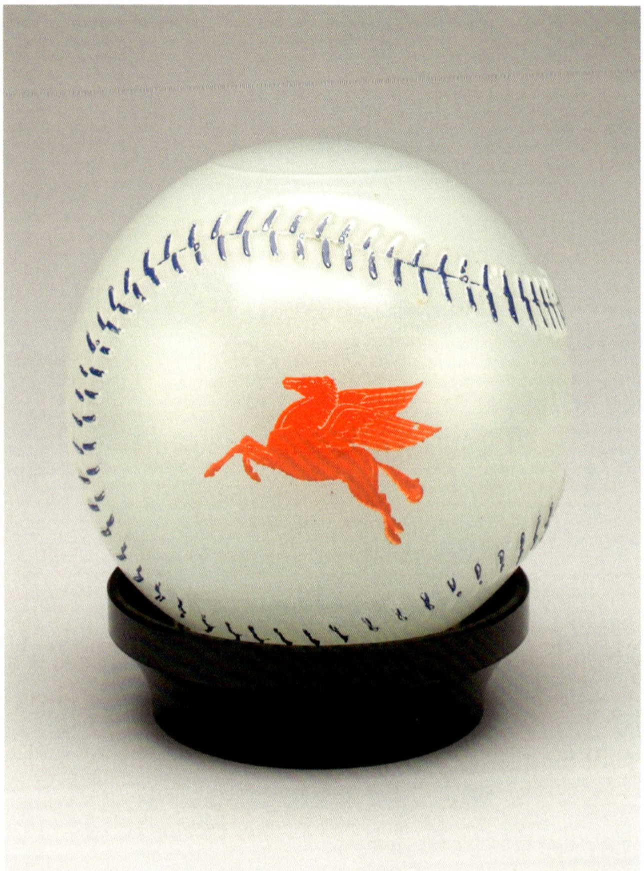

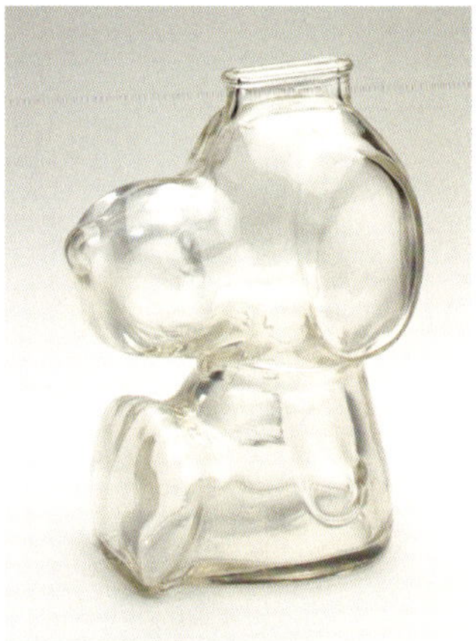

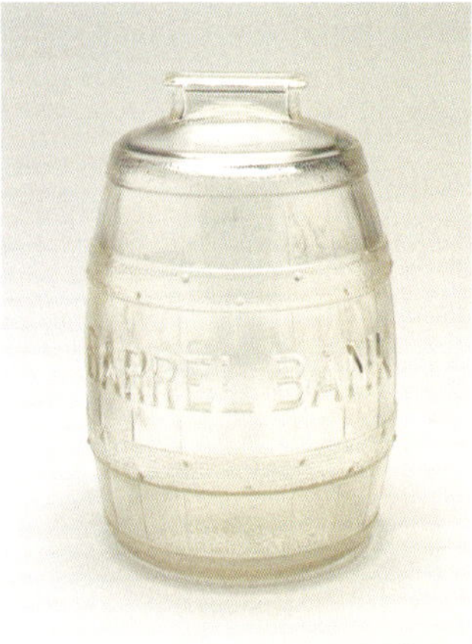
BARREL BANK

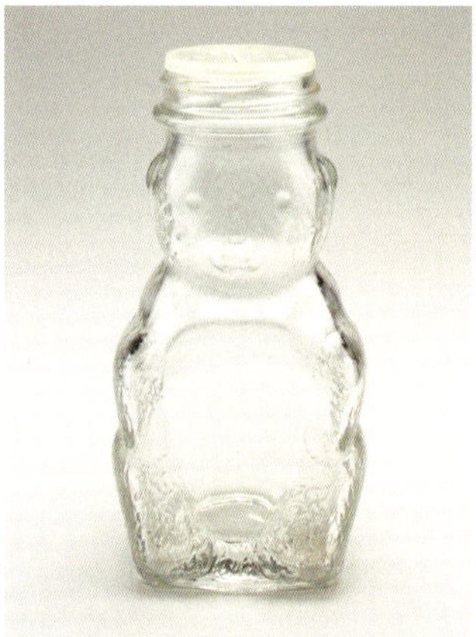

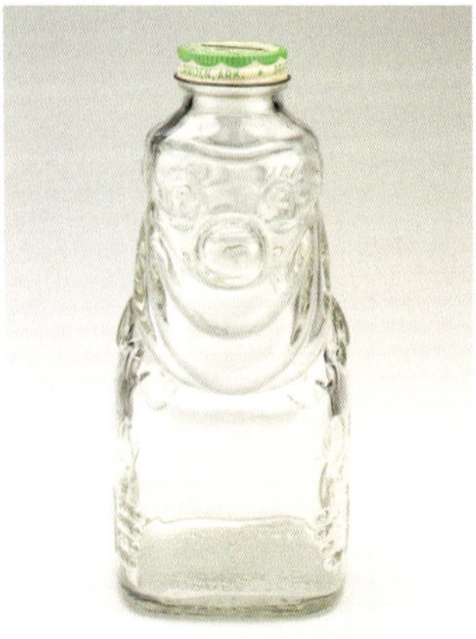

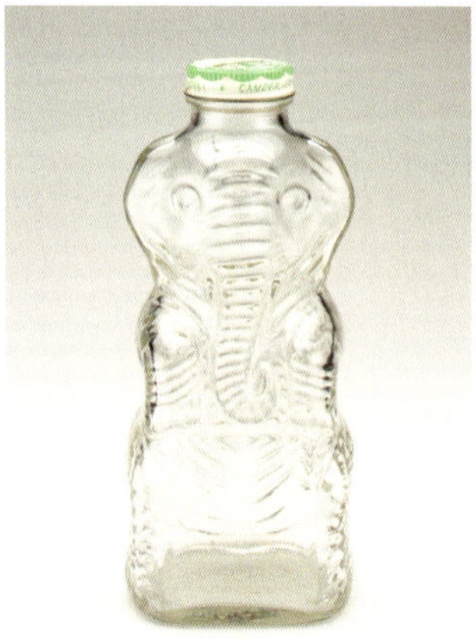

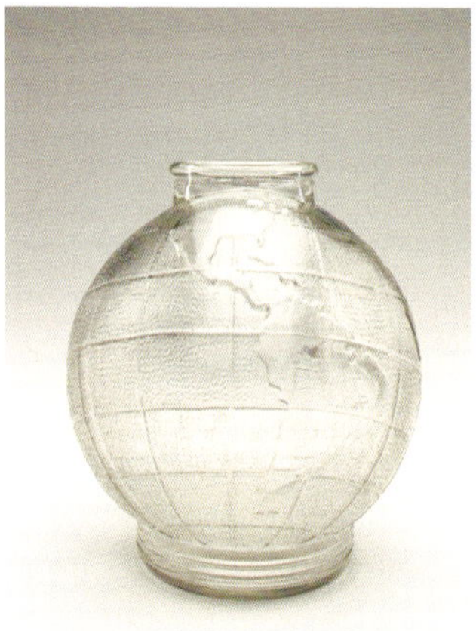

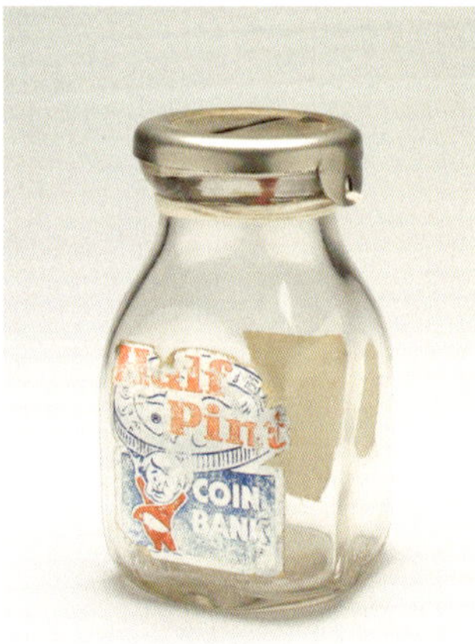
Half
Pint
COIN
BANK

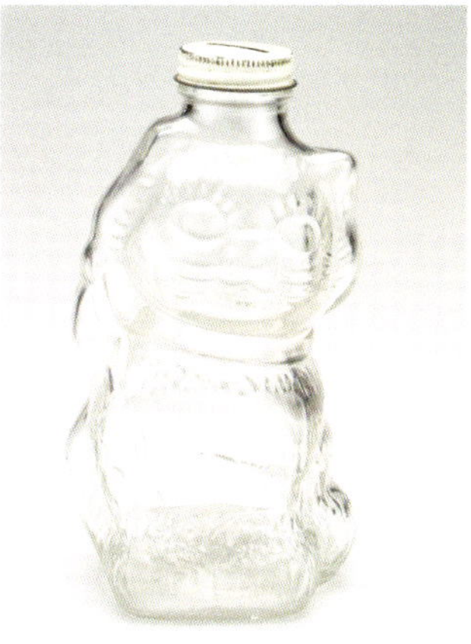

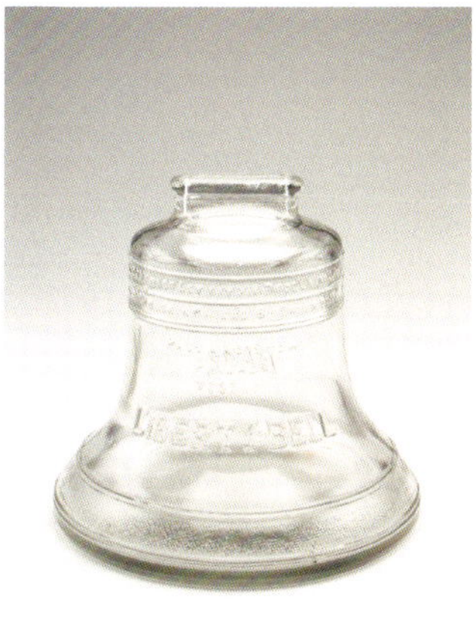

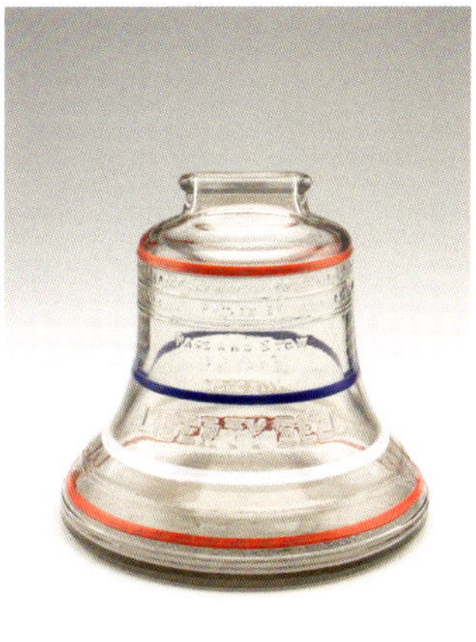

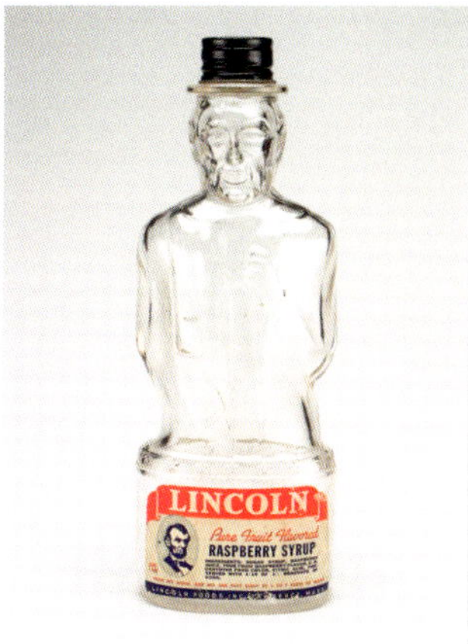
LINCOLN
Pure Fruit Flavored
RASPBERRY SYRUP

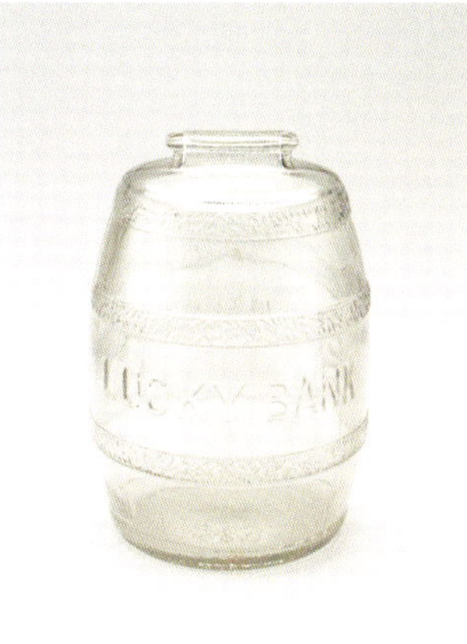

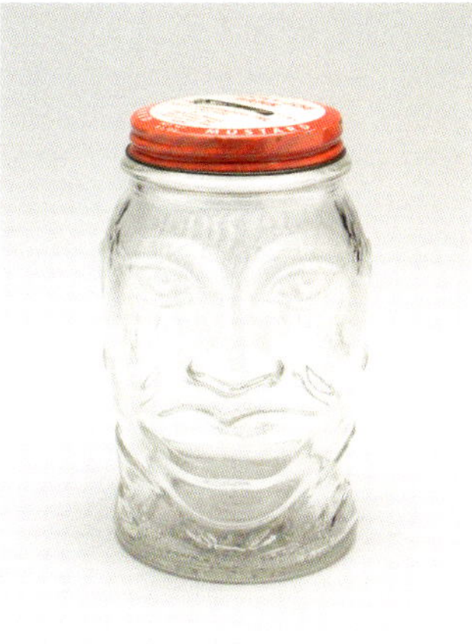

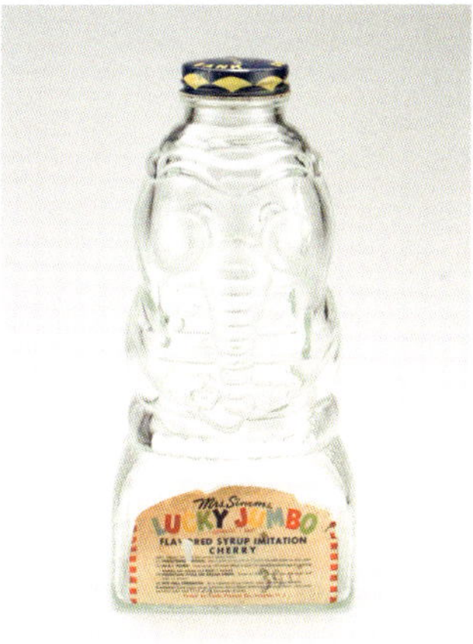
LUCKY JUMBO
CHERRY

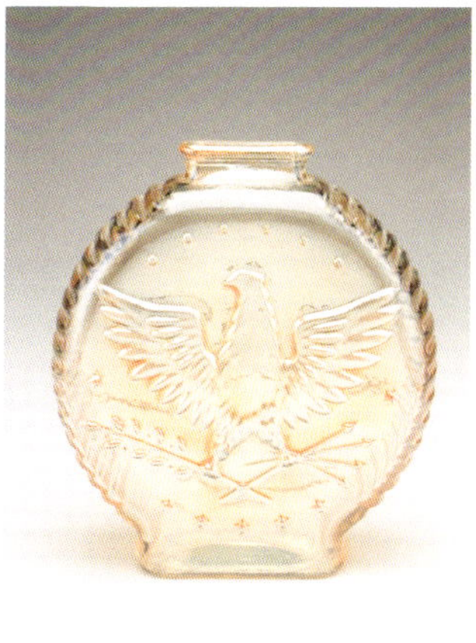

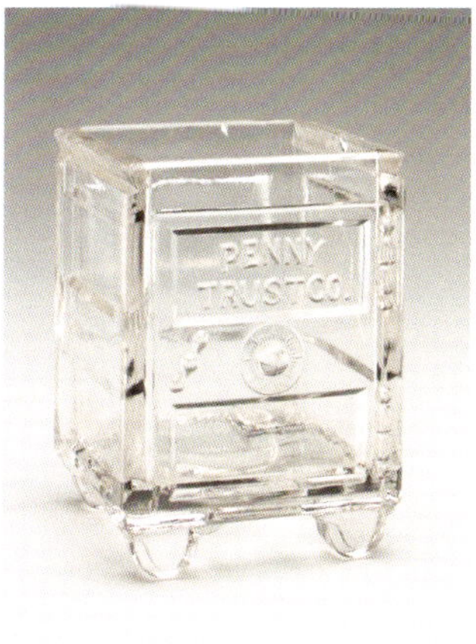
PENNY
TRUST CO.

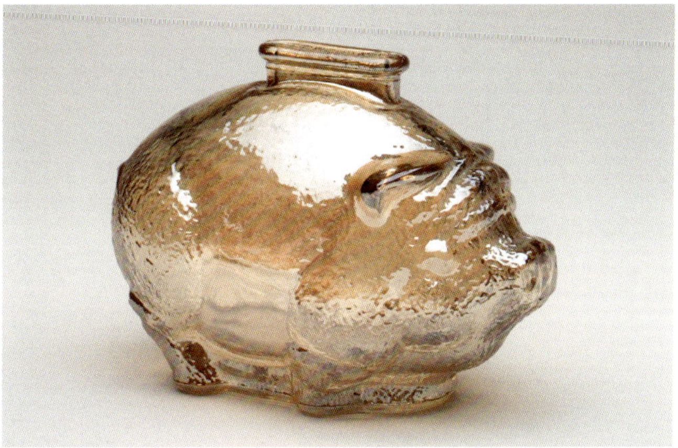

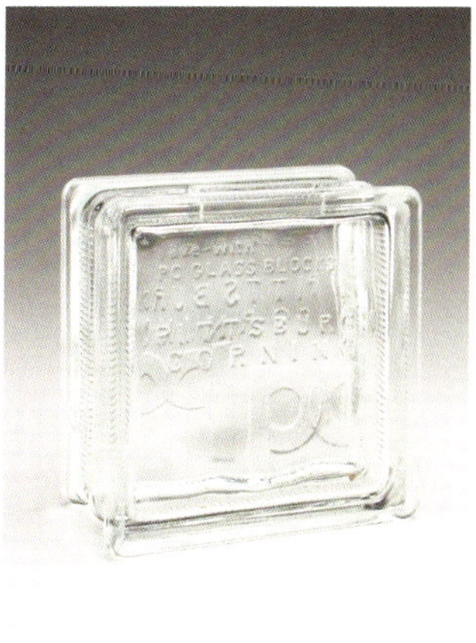

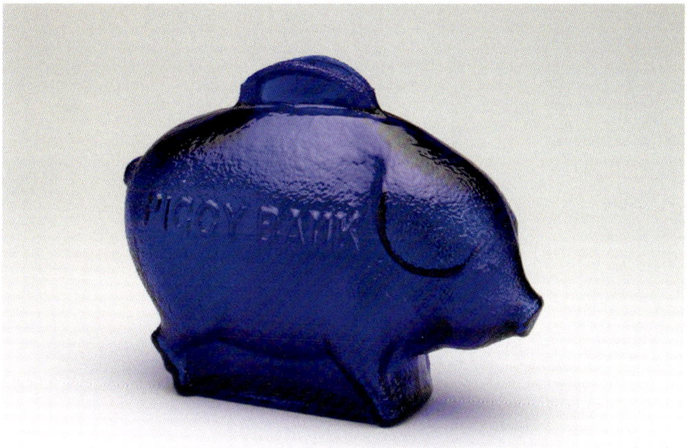

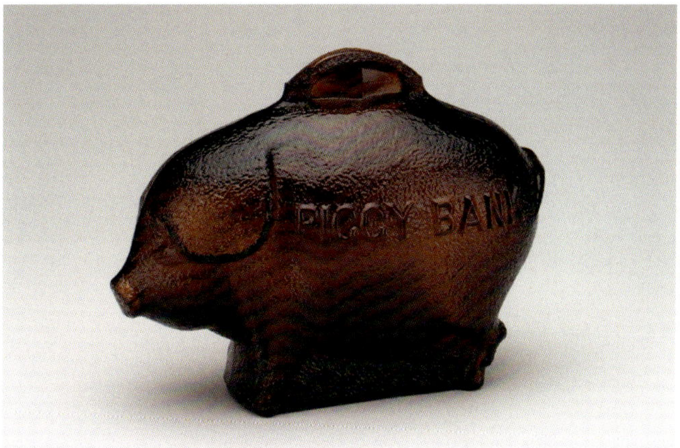

Lincoln, 20th century
Lincoln Foods, Inc., Lawrence, Massachusetts, manufacturer
Glass, metal, pigment, paper
9 5/8 x 3 1/2 x 2 1/16 in.
2003.236.795

Liberty Bell, 20th century
United States
Glass, pigment
3 3/4 x 4 1/8 x 4 1/8 in.
2003.236.208

Liberty Bell, 20th century
United States
Glass
3 3/16 x 4 1/8 x 4 1/8 in.
2003.236.207

Cat, 20th century
Grapette Products Company, Camden, Arkansas, manufacturer
Glass, metal
6 5/8 x 3 3/4 x 3 3/8 in.
2003.236.794

Patriotic Eagle, 20th century
United States
Glass
4 1/2 x 4 1/4 x 1 5/8 in.
2003.236.202

Lucky Jumbo, 20th century
Castle Products Company, Newark, New Jersey, manufacturer
Glass, metal, pigment
7 x 3 3/8 x 2 13/16 in.
2003.236.799

Lucky Joe, 20th century
Nash-Underwood, Inc., Chicago, manufacturer
Glass, metal, pigment
4 3/8 x 2 5/8 x 2 3/4 in.
2003.236.800

Lucky Bank, 20th century
Glass
4 1/8 x 2 3/4 x 2 3/4 in.
2003.236.791

Pittsburgh Corning Glass Block, 20th century
Pittsburgh Corning Glass Block, Corporation, Pittsburgh, Pennsylvania (est. 1937), manufacturer
Glass
3 1/4 x 3 1/4 x 1 1/4 in.
2003.236.693

Piggy Bank, 20th century
United States
Glass
3 x 4 3/8 x 2 1/2 in.
2003.236.201

Penny Trust Co., 20th century
Glass
2 15/16 x 2 1/8 x 2 1/8 in.
2003.236.792

Piggy Bank (amber), 20th century
Probably United States
Glass
3 11/16 x 2 1/4 x 5 3/16 in.
2003.236.698

Piggy Bank (blue), 20th century
Probably United States
Glass
3 11/16 x 2 1/4 x 5 3/16 in.
2003.236.697

Snow Crest, 20th century
Snow Crest Beverages, Inc., Salem, Massachusetts, manufacturer
Glass, metal, paper
7 1/4 x 3 13/16 x 3 1/8 in.
2003.236.1106

Radio Bank, 20th century
Probably United States
Glass
3 3/16 x 4 1/8 x 2 3/16 in.
2003.236.204

Pittsburgh Paints Glass Block, 20th century
Pittsburgh Corning Glass Block Corporation, Pittsburgh, Pennsylvania (est. 1937), manufacturer
Glass
3 1/4 x 3 1/4 x 1 3/4 in.
2003.236.694

Monkey on Box, c. 1929
Germany
Elastolin, pigment, metal
4 7/8 x 2 1/16 x 2 1/16 in.
(irregular base)
2003.236.761

Standing child, early-to-mid-20th century
Japan
Celluloid, metal
6 3/4 x 2 3/4 x 1 11/16 in.
2003.236.574

STILL BANKS: Plastic

Toy block, 20th century
Glass, metal
2 15/16 x 2 15/16 x 2 15/16 in.
2003.236.798

Cash Register (registering), mid-20th century
Hong Kong
Plastic
3 5/8 x 3 1/4 x 3 3/4 in.
2003.236.524

The Bank of Douglas, mid-20th century
Tom Thrift Enterprises, New Canaan, Connecticut, manufacturer
Plastic, pigment, metal
3 1/8 x 4 1/4 x 3 in.
2003.236.568

Hopalong Cassidy, c. 1950s
Probably United States
Plastic
4 1/4 x 2 1/2 x 2 in.
2003.236.373

Jukebox, mid-20th century
Plastic, metal, pigment
6 1/8 x 4 3/16 x 2 in.
2003.236.550

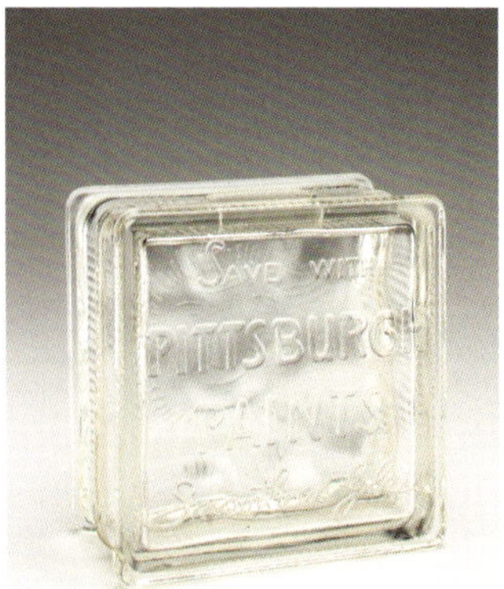

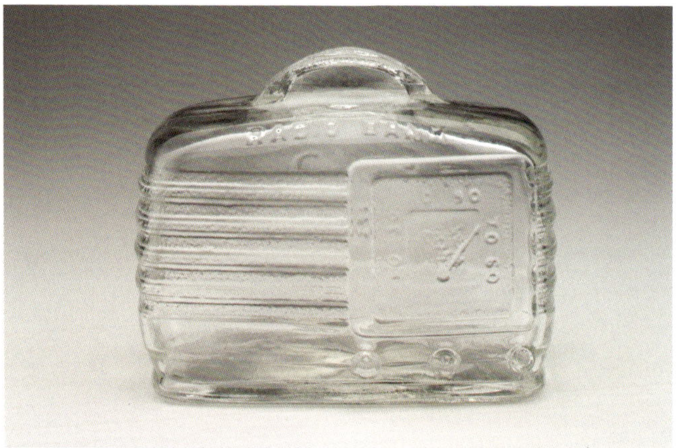

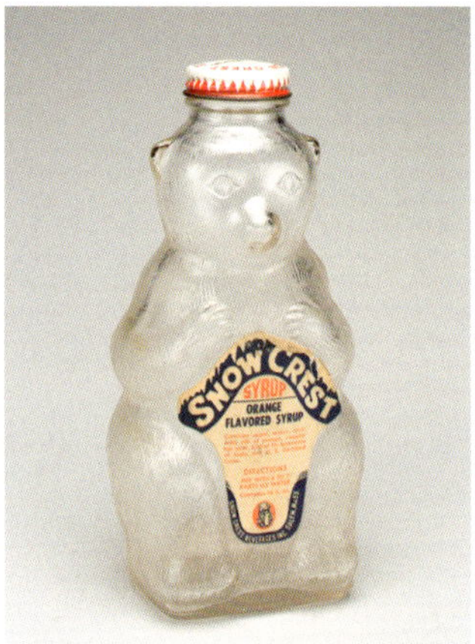

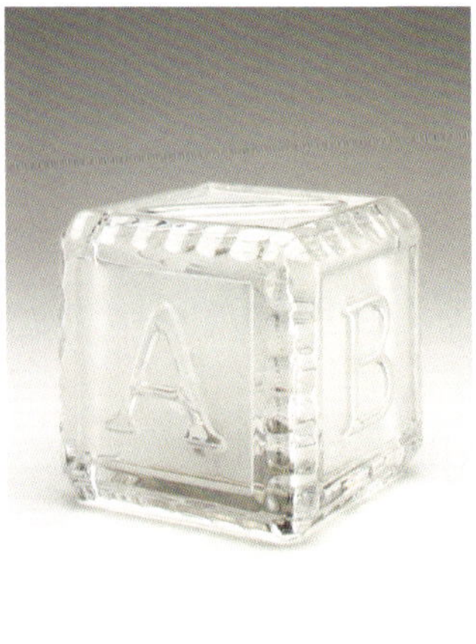

STILL BANKS: Plastic

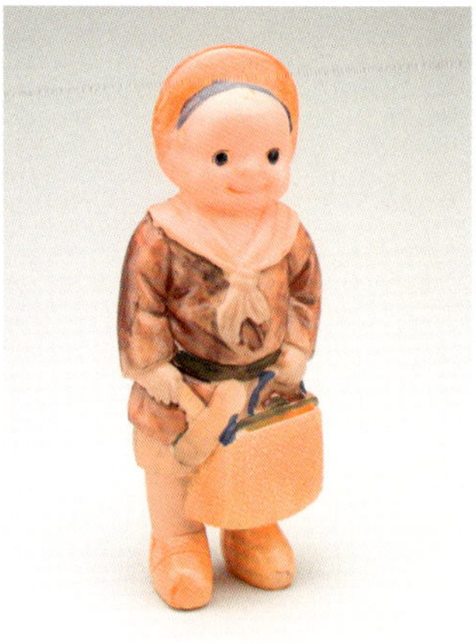

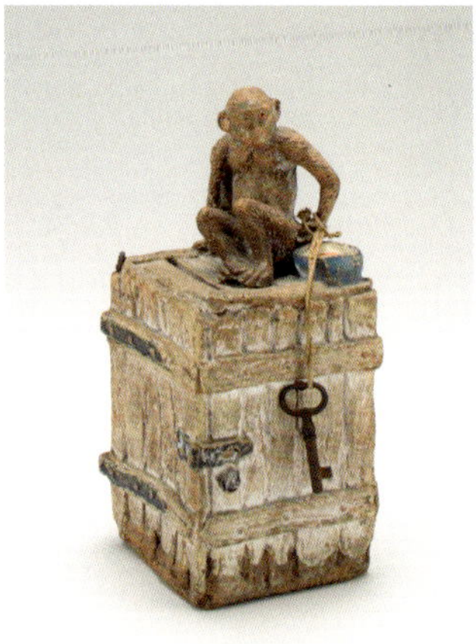

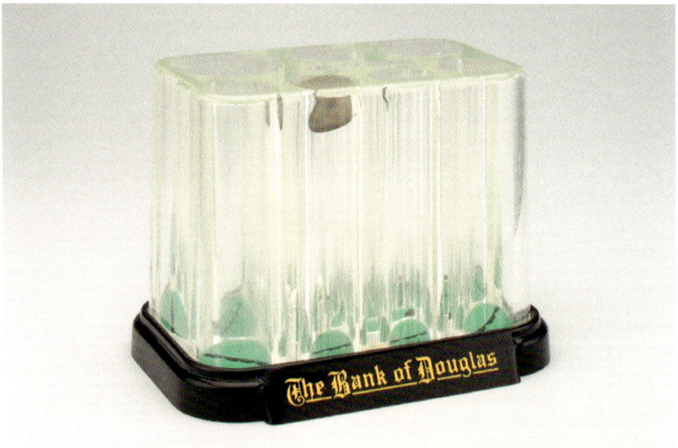

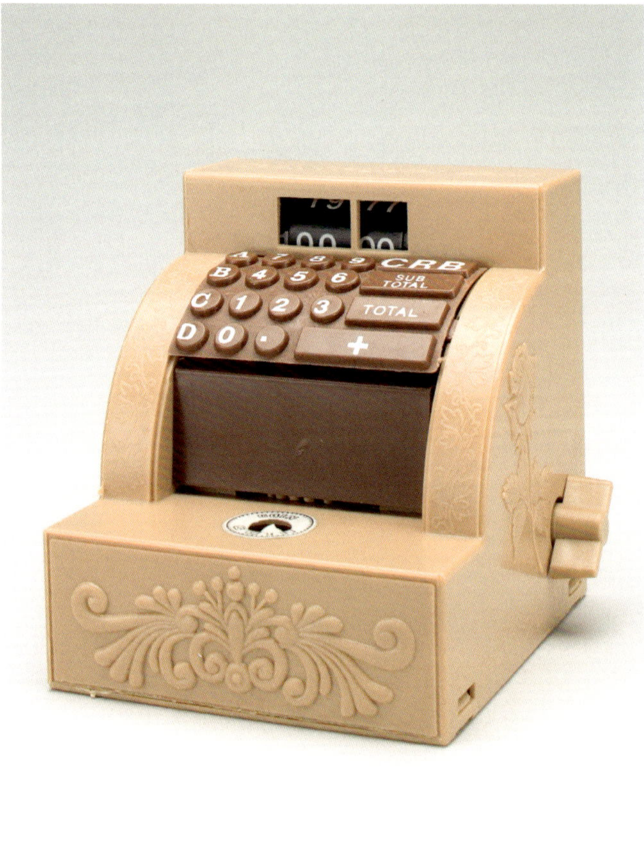

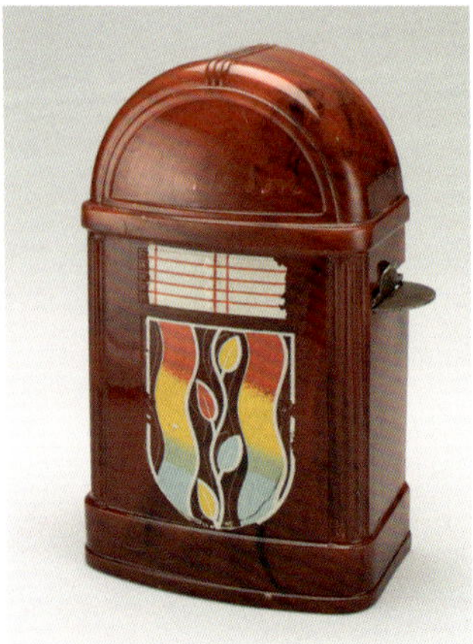

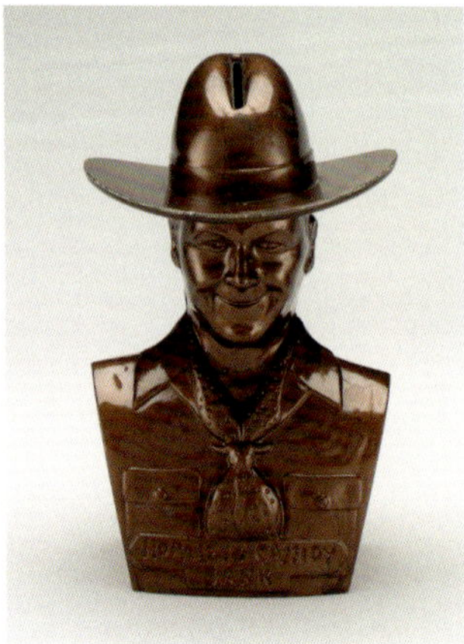

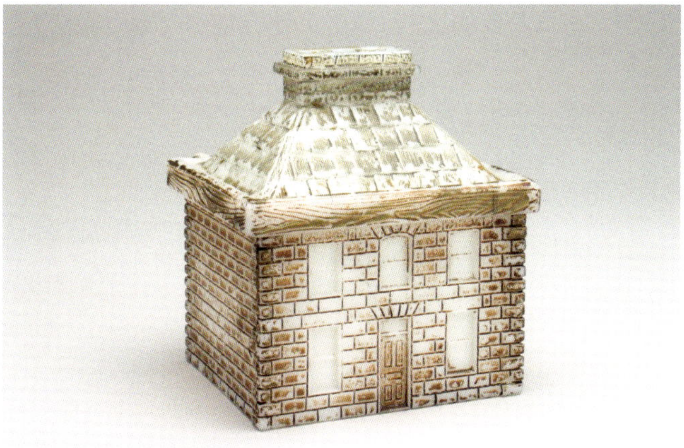

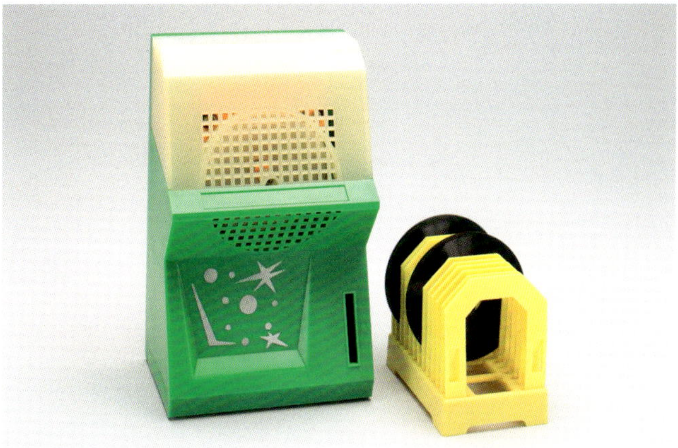

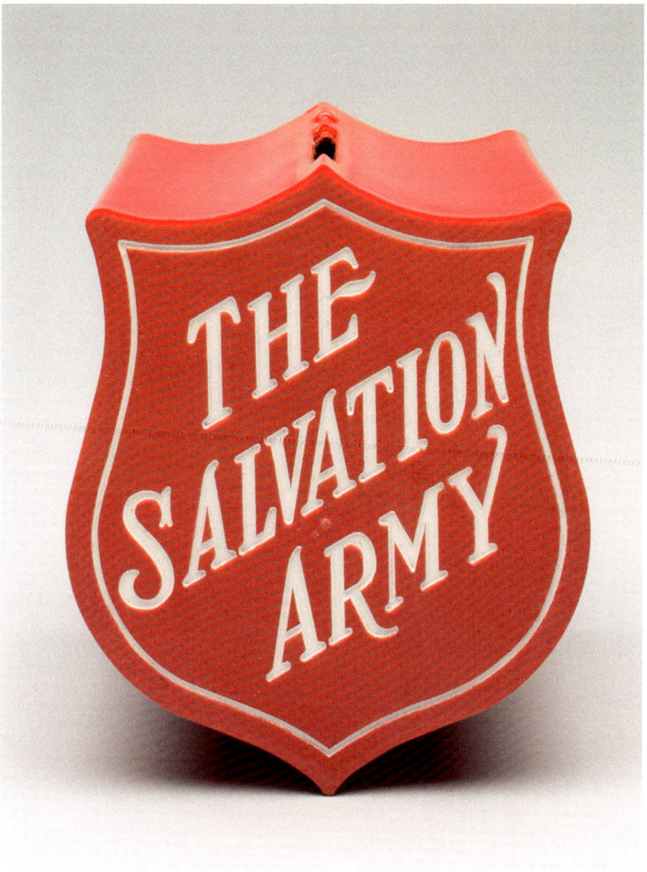
THE
SALVATION
ARMY

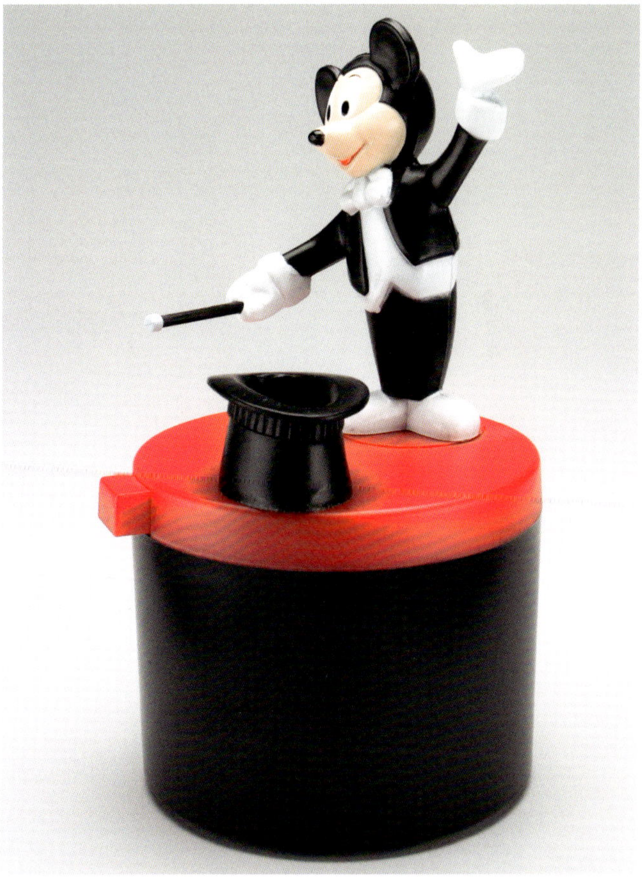

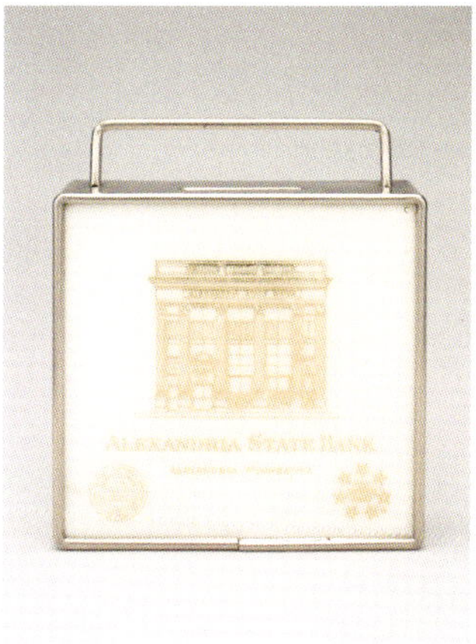

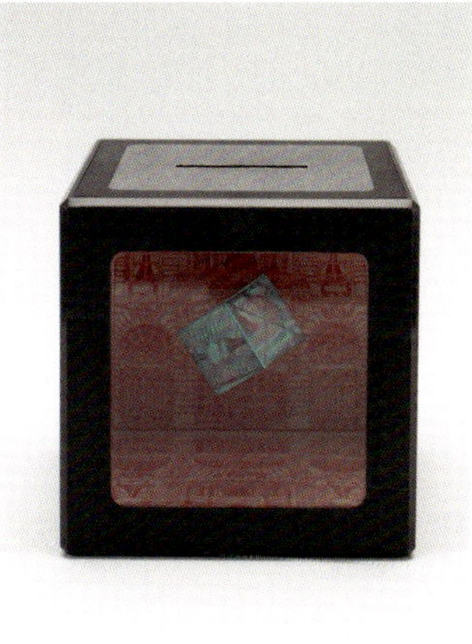

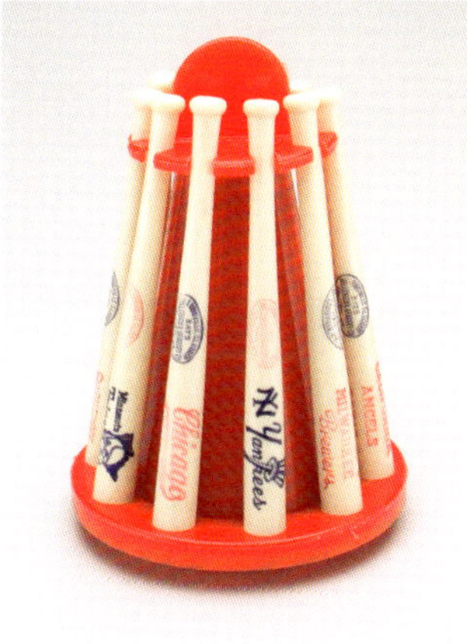

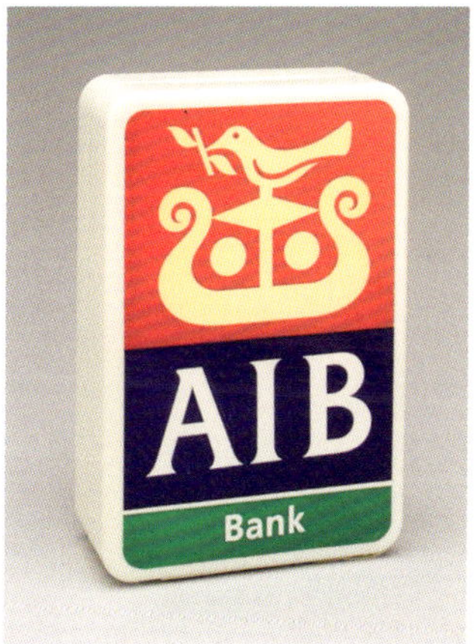
AIB
Bank

Jukebox, c. 1960s
Italy
Plastic
6 x 3 5/8 x 2 7/8 in. (jukebox)
2003.236.196a–e

Westmoreland Specialty Company Mustard, mid-20th century
Probably United States
Plastic, pigment, wax
4 x 3 3/4 x 3 1/8 in.
2003.236.938

Mickey Mouse, Magician, c. 1981
Reiss Games, Inc., New York, manufacturer
Plastic
7 x 3 3/4 x 3 3/4 in.
2003.236.318

The Salvation Army, c. 1980s
Plastic, pigment
4 9/16 x 5 3/4 x 3 3/4 in.
2003.236.575

AIB Bank (Allied Irish Banks), late 20th century
Ireland
Plastic, paper
4 7/16 x 3 1/16 x 1 7/16 in.
2003.236.470

National League Bats, 20th century
United States
Plastic, pigment
5 7/8 x 4 1/8 x 4 1/8 in.
2003.236.576a-k

Art Bank, c. 1989
Tenyo, Japan, manufacturer
Plastic
2 3/4 x 2 3/4 x 2 3/4 in.
2003.236.762

Alexandria State Bank, c. 1984
Plastic, metal, pigment
3 13/16 x 4 x 1 in.
2003.236.666

Selected Bibliography

BOOKS

Davidson, Al. *Penny Lane: A History of Antique Mechanical Toy Banks*. Mokelumne Hill, Calif.: Long's Americana, 1987.

Duer, Don. *A Penny Saved: Still and Mechanical Banks*. Atglen, Pa.: Schiffer Publishing, 1993.

________. *Penny Banks around the World*. Atglen, Pa.: Schiffer Publishing, 1997.

Griffith, F. H. *Mechanical Banks*. Pittsburgh, Pa.: F. H. Griffith, 1966.

Hertz, Louis H. "Mechanical Toy Banks." 1947. Typescript.

Majua, Margaret, and David Weingarten. *Souvenir Buildings and Miniature Monuments*. New York: Harry N. Abrams, 1996.

Moore, Andy and Susan. *The Penny Bank Book: Collecting Still Banks*. Atglen, Pa.: Schiffer Publishing, 2000.

Norman, Bill. *The Bank Book: The Encyclopedia of Mechanical Bank Collecting*. San Diego, Calif.: Accent Studios, 1984.

Redwine, James L. *Coin Banks by Banthrico*. Atglen, Pa.: Schiffer Publishing, 2001.

Rogers, Carole. *Penny Banks: A History and a Handbook*. Toronto: Clarke, Irwin, and Company, 1977.

Sommer, Bettie, and Don Duer. *The Architecture of Cast Iron Penny Banks*. n.p.: American Limited Editions, 1983.

PERIODICALS AND WEB SITES

The Mechanical Banker. Mechanical Bank Collectors of America journal, issued three times per year.

www.mechanicalbanks.org, Mechanical Bank Collectors of America Web site.

Penny Bank Post. Still Bank Collectors Club of America journal, issued three times per year.

www.stillbankclub.com, Still Bank Collectors Club of America Web site.

Index

This index includes the names of banks, designers, and manufacturers.